1975

Western Literature

II

Western Literature

II

The Middle Ages
Renaissance
Enlightenment

Edited by

Robert Hollander

PRINCETON UNIVERSITY

Under the General Editorship of

A. Bartlett Giamatti

YALE UNIVERSITY

HARCOURT BRACE JOVANOVICH, INC.

NEW YORK   CHICAGO   SAN FRANCISCO   ATLANTA

ISBN: 0-15-595277-3

Library of Congress Catalog Card Number: 75-152578

Printed in the United States of America

ACKNOWLEDGMENTS

APPLETON-CENTURY-CROFTS for selections from Voltaire's *Candide or Optimism,* edited by Norman L. Torrey. Copyright 1946. Professor Torrey's notes reproduced by permission of Appleton-Century-Crofts, Educational Division, Meredith Corporation.

ROSICA COLIN LIMITED for Boccaccio's *The Decameron,* translated by Richard Aldington, and Voltaire's *Candide,* translated by Richard Aldington. Copyright Madame Catherine Guillaume.

MRS. NICOLETE GRAY AND THE SOCIETY OF AUTHORS, on behalf of the Lawrence Binyon Estate, for Lawrence Binyon's translation of Dante's *Inferno.*

HARCOURT BRACE JOVANOVICH, INC. (1) For selections from *A Chaucer Reader* edited by Charles W. Dunn, copyright 1952, by Harcourt Brace Jovanovich, Inc. and reprinted with their permission. (2) For *Othello* from *Six Plays of Shakespeare* edited by G. B. Harrison, copyright 1948, 1949, by Harcourt Brace Jovanovich, Inc. and reprinted with their permission. (3) For selections from *Paradise Lost* from *The College Survey of English Literature* edited by Alexander M. Witherspoon, copyright 1942, 1951, by Harcourt Brace Jovanovich, Inc. and reprinted with their permission. (4) For "Ballade of the Ladies of Time Past," translation from Villon, © 1964 by Richard Wilbur. Reprinted from his volume *Walking to Sleep: New Poems and Translations* by permission of Harcourt Brace Jovanovich, Inc. (5) *The Misanthrope* by Molière translated by Richard Wilbur, copyright 1954, 1955, by Richard Wilbur. Reprinted by permission of Harcourt Brace Jovanovich, Inc.
CAUTION: Professionals and amateurs are hereby warned that this translation, being fully protected under the copyright laws of the United States of America, the British Empire, including the Dominion of Canada, and all other countries which are signatories to the Universal Copyright Convention and the International Copyright Union, is subject to royalty. All rights, including professional, amateur, motion picture, recitation, lecturing, public

reading, radio broadcasting, and television, are strictly reserved. Particular emphasis is laid on the question of readings, permission for which must be secured from the author's agent in writing. Inquiries on professional rights should be addressed to Mr. Gilbert Parker, Curtis Brown, Ltd., 60 East 56th Street, New York, N. Y. 10022. The amateur acting rights are controlled exclusively by the Dramatists Play Service, Inc., 440 Park Avenue South, New York, N. Y. 10016. No amateur performance of the play may be given without obtaining in advance the written permission of the Dramatists Play Service, Inc., and paying the requisite fee.

HERITAGE PRESS for selections from the Heritage Press edition of *Gargantua and Pantagruel,* translated by Jacques LeClercq, copyright 1936 and 1964; used by arrangement with The George Macy Companies, Inc.

NEW DIRECTIONS PUBLISHING CORPORATION for "Ballata X," by Guido Cavalcanti, translated by Ezra Pound, from *Translations.* Copyright 1954 by Ezra Pound. Reprinted by permission of New Directions Publishing Corporation.

YALE UNIVERSITY PRESS for Sonnets 3 and 364, by Petrarch, translated by T. G. Bergin from *Lyric Poetry of the Italian Renaissance* published by Yale University Press. Copyright © 1954 by L. R. Lind.

Contents

General Introduction   ix
A. BARTLETT GIAMATTI

MEDIEVAL AND RENAISSANCE LOVE LYRICS   2
Jaufré Rudel   3
  Poem

Guido Cavalcanti   5
  Ballata X

Dante Alighieri   6
  Sonnet

Francesco Petrarch   6
  Sonnet 3
  Sonnet 364

François Villon   8
  Ballade of the Ladies of Time Past

Clément Marot   9
  Poem

Sir Thomas Wyatt   10
  Who So List to Hunt

Pierre de Ronsard   10
  Sonnet

Sir Philip Sidney   11
  Sonnet

Edmund Spenser   12
  Sonnet 9

William Shakespeare   13
  Sonnet 73
  Sonnet 130

THREE POEMS OF PASSIONATE SHEPHERDS
Christopher Marlowe 14
The Passionate Shepherd to His Love
Sir Walter Raleigh 15
The Nymph's Reply to the Shepherd
John Donne 16
The Bait

John Donne 17
A Valediction: Forbidding Mourning

Andrew Marvel 18
To His Coy Mistress

DANTE ALIGHIERI 22
FROM *Inferno*

GIOVANNI BOCCACCIO 64
FROM *The Decameron*

GEOFFREY CHAUCER 92
FROM *The Canterbury Tales*
The General Prologue 95
Nun's Priest's Tale 110
Pardoner's Tale 126

FRANÇOIS RABELAIS 142
FROM *Gargantua and Pantagruel*

WILLIAM SHAKESPEARE 182
Othello

MIGUEL CERVANTES 284
FROM *Don Quixote*

MOLIÈRE (JEAN-BAPTISTE POQUELIN) 352
The Misanthrope

JOHN MILTON 408
FROM *Paradise Lost*

JONATHAN SWIFT 448
FROM *Gulliver's Travels*, BOOK FOUR

VOLTAIRE (FRANÇOIS-MARIE AROUET) 492
FROM *Candide*

General Introduction

The three volumes of *Western Literature* are intended to provide the student with a broad view of the literature of the Western world. The volume on the Ancient World contains some of the best representative examples of the Hebraic and Greco-Roman traditions and of the origins of Christian writing. The second volume, covering the Middle Ages, Renaissance, and Enlightenment, opens with a troubadour's lyric to a faraway love and ends with Voltaire's satire on complacent optimism. The third volume, devoted to the Modern World, traces the contemporary spirit from Rousseau to two current masters of the Americas.

Certain principles have guided the editors, both individually and collectively, in their selections. An effort has been made to include, wherever possible, complete works or at least substantial excerpts of large works. This has not always been possible, and in a very few cases it has meant not including an author when no representative work of manageable length could be found. The underlying assumption here is that the artistic integrity of a literary work has primary importance.

The editors have tried to include translations of continental poetry by other notable poets—for example, John Milton's translation of Horace or Ezra Pound's of Cavalcanti—in order to provide the reader not only with distinguished renderings but with instances of the critical operation of one poetic sensibility on another. The editors have also been guided by their sense of the wholeness of literature, by their conviction that literature is the expression of a fundamental human activity, the urge to order memory and desire by making a new world with the imagination. Finally, if there is one overriding principle that informs the selections in these three volumes, it is that what man has written about himself over the centuries is our best indication of where we are, and who we are.

A. B. GIAMATTI
GENERAL EDITOR

Medieval and Renaissance
Love Lyrics

THE LOVE POEM IS A LITERARY GENRE WITH ROOTS IN SUCH ancient and diverse sources as the Greek lyric poems and the Biblical Song of Solomon. During the greater part of the Christian Middle Ages, however, this genre was in eclipse, only to reappear with the troubadours in the south of Europe about 1100 A.D. These poets composed songs in praise of ladies in the various dialects of Provençal, a tongue that resembles both French and Italian. The vogue for such poems was to last through the Renaissance, although their Provençal origins, represented here by the poem of Rudel, were often forgotten.

By the thirteenth century, Italian poets had joined the school of love: Cavalcanti and Dante were two among many Italian practitioners, and Dante's prose writing contains a number of valuable historical and critical comments upon the origin of the school. Still, it was Petrarch who became recognized by later poets as the initiator of the tradition of the lyric poem in praise of the lady who gives the poet's life all its meaning. Ronsard in France and Wyatt, Sydney, and Spenser in England were all, for at least part of their careers, imitators of the great Petrarchan model. Sonnet sequences in France and England owe their birth to Petrarch, not to his precursors. It was only toward the very end of the sixteenth century that the Petrarchan tradition became an object of derision in such poems as Shakespeare's sonnet 130. In the early seventeenth century, poets like Donne and Marvell revitalized the tradition by bringing style and subject away from merely conventional expression, thus making the love poem in praise of a lady the worthy instrument of strong feeling and hard thought.

Medieval and Renaissance
Love Lyrics

Jaufré Rudel (1140?–1170?)

Rudel, a Provençal poet, wrote his love poems to a faraway lady who was said to be the countess of Tripoli. No one knows who she was, but in the process he developed the poetic myth of idealized, unconsummated love.

Now that the days are long in May
I love to hear birds sing afar,
And as I slowly move away
Then I recall my love afar;
I roam in sadness, head so bent
That neither songs nor hawthorn's scent
Can please me more than winter's blast.

No lie against the Lord I say,
Through Whom I'll see my love afar;
But 'til such favor shows the way   10
I am twice cursed—it is so far.
Ah! that I were a pilgrim sent
And on my dress of penitent
Her lovely eyes were gently cast!

Joy will become me on the day
I ask, God's love! to lodge afar;
And, if it please, near her I'll stay
Though I am from a land afar;
Then speech will be magnificent—
When far is near, and time is spent   20
In whispered joys, words unsurpassed.

3

And then I'll go, downcast and gay,
If e'er I see her, love afar;
I don't foresee that holiday—
The space between us is so far;
Many the roads, steep the ascent,
And who can foretell God's intent,
Though all is what He will, at last.

My joy of love will soon decay
Without joy of my love afar;   30
For none more lovely does array
Any land, whether near or far;
So great her worth I'd be content—
My slavery her monument—
To serve a Saracen, bound fast.

God, Who summons and sends astray,
And Who has made this love afar,
Grant me strength—for this I pray—
That I may see my love afar
Stand before me and assent,   40
Turning the room or where we went
Into our own love palace vast.

Truly he says that I display
Thickening greed for love afar,
For other joys cannot outweigh
The joy of loving from afar.
But what I beg cannot be lent;
Some lurking force holds back consent—
I am unloved; I love steadfast.

But what I love cannot be lent.   50
Curse all creatures who won't relent,
Who render me unloved, steadfast.

—TR. A. BARTLETT GIAMATTI

Guido Cavalcanti (1255?–1300)

With Dante Alighieri, Guido Cavalcanti was a leader of the Florentine poets in the late thirteenth century. The following poem is one of some dozen *ballate* Guido wrote. It celebrates, according to most scholars, Guido's lady, Giovanna.

Ballata X

Now can I tell you tidings of mine eyes,
News which such pleasure to my heart supplyeth
That Love himself° for glory of it sigheth.

This new delight which my heart drinketh in
Was drawn from nothing save a woman seen
Who hath such charm and a so courtly mien
And such fair fashion that the heart is fain
To greet her beauty, which nor base nor mean
Can know, because its hue and qualities demand
Intelligence in him who would understand.   10

I see Love grow resplendent in her eyes
With such great power and such noble thought
As hold therein all gracious ecstacies,
From them there moves a soul so subtly wrought
That all compared thereto are set at naught
And judgment of her speaks no truth save this:
'A splendor strange and unforeseen she is.'

(Envoi)°
Go, Ballatetta, forth and find my Lady,
Ask if she have it this much of mercy ready,   20
This namely, that she turn her eyes toward thee?
Ask in his name whose whole faith rests in her,
And if she gracious, this much grace accord thee,
Offer glad-voiced incense of sweet savour
Proclaiming of whom thou receiv'st such favour.

—TR. EZRA POUND

3. *Love himself:* love personified as a god, following the classical tradition. 18. *(Envoi):* A stanza in which the author speaks to his poem is called an envoy, from the French *envoi,* or "sending off."

Dante Alighieri

Dante's *Vita Nuova* ("New Life"), from which the following sonnet is taken, is a history in poetry and prose of the poet's love for the lady Beatrice. Beginning with his first vision of her when they were both children, the sequence of thirty-one lyrics culminates in the death of Beatrice and in the changes effected in Dante by her death. This sonnet describes the effect of Beatrice's beauty on all who see her. For more information on Dante, see the headnote to the *Divine Comedy* (p. 22).

Sonnet

So noble and so worthy is my lady's air
When she to others offers her salute
That every tongue is tremorous and mute
And every eye repents its urge to stare.
She goes to sound of praise for being fair,
Keeping humility against men's suit,
Her earthly being Heaven's attribute,
A miracle shown forth this world to share.

To gaze upon her does so gratify
That eyes convey her beauty to the heart—   10
This not one single novice comprehends—
Until it seems that from her lips intends
A gentle, love-full spirit to depart,
Which comes and speaks unto the soul: "Now sigh."

—TR. ROBERT HOLLANDER

Francesco Petrarch (1304–1374)

Many scholars consider Petrarch the first renaissance man of letters; he was renowned throughout Europe in his lifetime for his enormous and varied literary production. One of his most influential works was the *Canzoniere,* a collection of lyrics in honor of his lady, Laura, which established a convention of love poetry that was to last for centuries. The *Canzoniere* contains 366 poems, of which two sonnets are presented below. The first records the poet's first vision of Laura, in a church at Avignon on Good Friday, 1327; the second sonnet, written from a vantage point in the poet's late years, looks back to Laura's death during the plague of 1348.

Sonnet 3

It was the day the sun had overcast
In pity of his Maker, his bright sheen
When I fell prey to peril unforeseen,
For your eyes, lady, caught and held me fast.
I took no care to shelter 'gainst Love's blast
Wherefore, amidst the melancholy scene
Of dole and penance, my own anguish keen
Was born that has the general grief surpassed.
Through eyes that now but serve to weep my ills
Love stormed my heart as I walked unalarmed,   10
Thinking that day I might pay him no heed.
Meanwhile to you, secure and fully armed,
He did not even show his shaft° that kills—
Here's shabby glory for great Love, indeed.

—TR. T. R. BERGIN

Sonnet 364

Through twenty-one long years love held me burning
In blissful flame while hope assuaged my smart;
My lady, bearing heavenward my heart,
Left me another ten in idle yearning.
A-weary now in my life's course discerning
How wayward error with persistent art
Has smothered virtue; ere I yet depart
To Thee, All Highest, all my vows are turning.
Sad and remorseful for the years thus spent,
Years that I should have put to better use   10
In flight from care, in search of soul's content,
Lord, I do ask Thee, from this prison loose

13. *shaft*: Cupid's arrow.

My soul, withhold eternal banishment:
I know my sin and offer no excuse.

—TR. T. R. BERGIN

François Villon (1431–1463?)

As a young scholar at the University of Paris, Villon led a turbulent life in the streets, taverns, and prisons of France. In 1463, after narrowly escaping the death sentence for a charge of thievery, he disappeared from history. This *ballade* is perhaps Villon's most famous poem. It is one of a series of poems, grouped under the common title *The Testament,* which the poet composed upon his release after a prison sentence in 1461.

Ballade of the Ladies of Time Past

O tell me where, in lands or seas,
Flora,° that Roman belle, has strayed,
Thais,° or Archipiades,°
Who put each other in the shade,
Or Echo° who by bank and glade
Gave back the crying of the hound,
And whose sheer beauty could not fade.
But where shall last year's snow be found?

Where too is learned Héloïse,°
For whom shorn Abélard was made   10
A tonsured monk upon his knees?
Such tribute his devotion paid.
And where's that queen° who, having played
With Buridan,° had him bagged and bound

2. *Flora:* Roman courtesan; also, the name of the Roman goddess of flowers. 3. *Thais:* renowned Greek courtesan; *Archipiades:* probably Alcibiades, who was, in the Middle Ages, considered a woman because of references to his amorous relationships with various Athenian men. 5. *Echo:* nymph who loved Narcissus. 9. *Héloïse:* beloved of *Abélard* (l. 10), twelfth-century poet, scholastic, and philosopher, who was forced to become a monk as part of his punishment for their love affair. 13. *queen:* Joan of Navarre, who supposedly did away with her discarded lovers by having them thrown into the river Seine. 14. *Buridan:* one of Joan's intended victims who escaped.

To swim the Seine thus ill-arrayed?
But where shall last year's snow be found?

Queen Blanche° the fair, whose voice could please
As does the siren's serenade,°
Great Bertha,° Beatrice,° Alice°—these,
And Arembourg° whom Maine obeyed,   20
And Joan° whom Burgundy betrayed
And England burned, and Heaven crowned:
Where are they, Mary,° Sovereign Maid?
But where shall last year's snow be found?

Not next week, Prince, nor next decade,
Ask me these questions I propound.
I shall but say again, dismayed,
Ah, where shall last year's snow be found?

—TR. RICHARD WILBUR

Clément Marot (1496?–1544)

Known for his sonnets, pastorals, and translations of the Psalms,
the French poet Marot is represented below by one of his translations of the *Epigrams* of Martial (40?–104?).[1]

Though rich Pauline is keen on me
She is so old I fear her.
If she were one-third older yet
I'd marry her without regret,
For death would promptly set me free
And make her that much dearer.

—TR. ROBERT HOLLANDER

17. Blanche: Blanche of Castille, mother of Saint Louis, Louis IX of France
(1215–1270). *18. siren's serenade:* song of the Sirens, in ancient literature
famed for its ability to lure men to their death. *19. Bertha:* mother of Charlemagne; *Beatrice, Alice:* like Bertha, to whom they were related by marriage,
characters in an early French *chanson de geste.* *20. Arembourg:* daughter of
the Count of Maine. *21. Joan:* Joan of Arc. *23. Mary:* the Virgin Mary.

[1] "De Paula," Book X, no. 8.

Sir Thomas Wyatt (1503?–1542)

From his youth Wyatt was involved—frequently at his own cost—
in the intrigues of the court of Henry VIII. Wyatt wrote satires,
and a version of the Psalms, but he is chiefly known as one of England's great lyric poets. He is also thought to have done as much
as any other writer in the sixteenth century to make English poets
aware of their Continental precursors. Wyatt is represented here
by one of his many adaptations of Petrarch's sonnets, which are
less translations than poems in their own right. Wyatt took subjects from the Italian poet and turned them to his own purposes.
This is his version of Petrarch's "Una candida cerva sopra l'erba"
(Sonnet 190). In this poem the deer represents Laura; Wyatt's
"hind" was supposedly Anne Boleyn, the second wife of Henry
VIII.

Who so list° to hunt: I know where is an hind,
   But as for me, alas, I may no more:
   The vain travail hath wearied me so sore.
I am of them, that farthest cometh behind;
Yet may I by no means my wearied mind
   Draw from the dear; but as she fleeth afore
   Fainting I follow. I leave off therefore:
Since in a net I seek to hold the wind.
Who list her hunt I put him out of doubt
   As well as I may spend his time in vain: 10
   And, graven with diamonds, in letters plain
There is written her fair neck round about:
   "Noli me tangere° for Caesar's I am;
   And wild for to hold though I seem tame."

Pierre de Ronsard (1524?–1585)

Courtier, lyric poet, and leader of the group of seven French poets
known as the "Pléiades," Ronsard was among those most active
in developing a new French literary language and style. He, like
Petrarch, had great influence on the British sonneteers of the
sixteenth century. Near the end of his life Ronsard wrote some

1. *list:* is pleased. 13. *Noli me tangere:* Latin for "touch me not."

hundred sonnets dedicated to a young woman named Helen, of which the following sonnet is perhaps the best known.

Sonnet

When you are very old, in evening candlelight,
Moved closer to the coals and carding out your wool,
You'll sing my songs and marvel that you were such a fool:
"O Ronsard did praise me when I was young and bright."
Then you'll have no handmaid to help you pass the night,
Spinning while your gossip leads her into lull,
Until you say my name and her rousèd eyes grow full
In wonder of your glory in what Ronsard did write.

When I am in the earth, poor ghost without his bones,
A sleeper in the shade of myrtle trees and stones,   10
Then you, beside the hearth, old and crouched and gray,
Will yearn for all that's lost, repenting your disdain.
Live it well, I pray you, today won't come again:
Gather up the roses before they fall away.

—TR. ROBERT HOLLANDER

Sir Philip Sidney (1554–1586)

Sidney was one of the most brilliant courtiers of his day. His sonnet sequence, *Astrophel and Stella,* was the first to be written in English. After Sidney, the genre had a vogue of remarkable intensity but no great duration. The *Stella* of the title (many authorities identify her as the highborn lady Penelope Devereux) is Latin for "star," while *Astrophel* is derived from the Greek for "star-lover."

Sonnet

Loving in truth, and fain° in verse my love to show,
That she, dear She, might take some pleasure of my pain,—
Pleasure might cause her read, reading might make her know,
Knowledge might pity win, and pity grace obtain,—
I sought fit words to paint the blackest face of woe;

1. *fain:* desiring.

Studying inventions fine, her wits to entertain,
Oft turning others' leaves, to see if thence would flow
Some fresh and fruitful showers upon my sun-burn'd brain.
But words came halting° forth, wanting° Invention's stay;°
Invention, Nature's child, fled step-dame Study's blows;   10
And others' feet still seemed but strangers in my way.
Thus, great with child to speak, and helpless in my throes,°
Biting my truant pen, beating myself for spite;
"Fool," said my Muse to me, "look in thy heart, and write."

Edmund Spenser (1552?–1599)

Far better known for his long epic poem, *The Faerie Queene,*
Spenser also shared the renaissance poets' interest in the sonnet
sequence. The following sonnet, the ninth of the eighty-eight
that comprise his *Amoretti,* written in praise of Elizabeth Boyle,
who became his second wife, is an example of the rhetorical strict-
ness and excess that the Petrarchan convention often involved.

Sonnet 9

Long-while I sought to what I might compare
Those powerful eyes which lighten my dark spright;°
Yet find I nought on earth to which I dare
Resemble th' image of their goodly light.
Not to the sun: for they do shine by night:
Nor to the moon; for they are changèd never:
Nor to the stars; for they have purer sight:
Nor to the fire; for they consume not ever:
Nor to the lightning; for they still persever:
Nor to the diamond; for they are more tender: 10
Nor unto crystal; for nought may them sever:
Nor unto glass; such baseness mought° offend her.
Then to the Maker self° they likest be,
Whose light doth lighten all that here we see.

9. *halting:* limping; *wanting:* lacking; *stay:* support.   12. *throes:* birth pangs.
2. *spright:* spirit.   12. *mought:* might.   13. *self:* Himself.

William Shakespeare (1564–1616)

The organization of Shakespeare's sonnet sequence, as well as its "meaning," has long been problematical. Recent discussions make clear at least some of Shakespeare's intention. According to some current thought he used the traditional sequence's style and content to reach further than the genre had previously allowed. This may not be at all obvious from the first of the two poems included below unless we know that it is addressed to a man rather than to a lady. In the second sonnet, the desire to mock the conventional Petrarchan praise of the loved one's physical attributes is readily apparent. For more information on Shakespeare see the headnote to *Othello* (p. 182).

Sonnet 73

That time of year thou mayst in me behold
When yellow leaves, or none, or few, do hang
Upon those boughs which shake against the cold,
Bare ruined choirs, where late the sweet birds sang.
In me thou see'st the twilight of such day
As after sunset fadeth in the west;
Which by and by black night doth take away,
Death's second self, that seals up all in rest.
In me thou see'st the glowing of such fire,
That on the ashes of his youth doth lie,   10
As the deathbed whereon it must expire,
Consumed with that which it was nourished by.
   This thou perceiv'st, which makes thy love more strong,
   To love that well which thou must leave ere long.

Sonnet 130

My mistress' eyes are nothing like the sun;
Coral is far more red than her lips' red;
If snow be white, why then her breasts are dun;
If hairs be wires, black wires grow on her head.
I have seen roses damasked,° red and white,

5. *damasked:* pink.

But no such roses see I in her cheeks;
And in some perfumes is there more delight
Than in the breath that from my mistress reeks.
I love to hear her speak, yet well I know
That music hath a far more pleasing sound;   10
I grant I never saw a goddess go;°
My mistress, when she walks, treads on the ground.
    And yet, by heaven, I think my love as rare
    As any she belied ° with false compare.

Three Poems of "Passionate Shepherds"

You have probably already noticed that poets tend to be aware
of the work of other poets. At times this awareness may take on
the aspect of a contest or debate—sometimes in earnest, at other
times in fun. The following three poems clearly exemplify this
aspect of the poets' concern for who and what has gone before.

Christopher Marlowe (1564–1593)

The Passionate Shepherd to His Love

Come live with me and be my love,
And we will all the pleasures prove°
That hills and valleys, dales and fields,
And all the craggy mountains yields.

And we will sit upon the rocks,
Seeing the shepherds feed their flocks,
By shallow rivers to whose falls
Melodious birds sings madrigals.

And I will make thee beds of roses
And a thousand fragrant posies,   10
A cap of flowers, and a kirtle°
Embroidered all with leaves of myrtle;

11. *go:* walk.   14. *any she belied:* any woman misrepresented.   2. *prove:* try out.
11. *kirtle:* skirt.

A gown made of the finest wool
Which from our pretty lambs we pull;
Fair linèd slippers for the cold,
With buckles of the purest gold;

A belt of straw and ivy buds,
With coral clasps and amber studs:
And if these pleasures may thee move,
Come live with me and be my love.   20

The shepherd-swains° shall dance and sing
For thy delight each May morning:
If these delights thy mind may move,
Then live with me and be my love.

Sir Walter Ralegh (1552?–1618)

The Nymph's Reply to the Shepherd

If all the world and love were young,
And truth in every shepherd's tongue,
These pretty pleasures might me move
To live with thee and be thy love.

Time drives the flocks from field to fold
When rivers rage and rocks grow cold,
And Philomel° becometh dumb;
The rest complain of cares to come.

The flowers do fade, and wanton fields
To wayward winter reckoning yields;   10
A honey tongue, a heart of gall,
Is fancy's spring, but sorrow's fall.

Thy gowns, thy shoes, thy beds of roses,
Thy cap, thy kirtle, and thy posies
Soon break, soon wither, soon forgotten—
In folly ripe, in reason rotten.

21. *swains:* boys.   7. *Philomel:* the nightingale.

Thy belt of straw and ivy buds,
Thy coral clasps and amber studs,
All these in me no means can move
To come to thee and be thy love.   20

But could youth last and love still breed,
Had joys no date° nor age no need,
Then these delights my mind might move
To live with thee and be thy love.

John Donne

The Bait

Come live with me and be my love,
And we will some new pleasures prove,
Of golden sands and crystal brooks,
With silken lines and silver hooks.

There will the river whispering run,
Warmed by the eyes more than the sun.
And there the enamored fish will stay,
Begging themselves they may betray.

When thou wilt swim in that live bath,
Each fish, which every channel hath,   10
Will amorously to thee swim,
Gladder to catch thee, than thou him.

If thou, to be so seen, beest loth,
By sun or moon, thou darkenest both;
And if myself have leave to see,
I need not their light, having thee.

Let others freeze with angling reeds,°
And cut their legs with shells and weeds,
Or treacherously poor fish beset
With strangling snare, or windowy net.   20

Let coarse bold hands from slimy nest
The bedded fish in banks out-wrest,

22. *date:* end.   17. *angling reeds:* fishing rods.

Or curious traitors, sleave-silk flies,°
Bewitch poor fishes' wandering eyes.

For thee, thou needest no such deceit,
For thou thyself art thine own bait;
That fish that is not catched thereby,
Alas, is wiser far than I.

John Donne (1572–1631)

Perhaps the greatest of the English Metaphysical Poets, Donne is best known for his difficult yet passionate verse. In "The Bait" (p. 16), Donne turns the shepherd of Marlowe and Ralegh into a fisherman. "A Valediction: Forbidding Mourning" makes love into a religion. In 1615 Donne was ordained an Anglican priest. His poems and sermons from this time on leave little room for the sort of concerns present in these two poems.

A Valediction: Forbidding Mourning

As virtuous men pass mildly away,
    And whisper to their souls to go,
Whilst some of their sad friends do say,
    "The breath goes now," and some say, "No";

So let us melt, and make no noise,
    No tear-floods, nor sigh-tempests move,
'Twere profanation of our joys
    To tell the laity our love.

Moving of th' earth° brings harms and fears,
    Men reckon what it did and meant;   10
But trepidation of the spheres,
    Though greater far, is innocent.°

---

23. *sleave-silk flies:* flies made of thin filaments of silk.   9. *Moving of th' earth:* earthquake.   11–12. *trepidation . . . innocent:* Variations in the course of planets, although involving more actual movement than earthquakes, are not considered harmful.

Dull sublunary° lovers' love
    (Whose soul ° is sense) cannot admit
Absence, because it doth remove
    Those things which elemented ° it.

But we by a love so much refined
    That our selves know not what it is,
Inter-assurèd of the mind,
    Care less, eyes, lips, and hands to miss.   20

Our two souls therefore, which are one,
    Though I must go, endure not yet
A breach, but an expansion,
    Like gold to airy thinness beat.

If they be two, they are two so
    As stiff twin compasses are two;
Thy soul, the fixed foot, makes no show
    To move, but doth, if th' other do.

And though it in the center sit,
    Yet when the other far doth roam,   30
It leans and harkens after it,
    And grows erect, as that comes home.

Such wilt thou be to me, who must
    Like th' other foot, obliquely run;
Thy firmness makes my circle just,
    And makes me end where I begun.

Andrew Marvell (1621–1678)

In "To His Coy Mistress," Marvell sends two traditions of love
poetry forth to do battle. From the outset he is certain which tradition must win, since one is equipped only with extravagant
platitudes, while the other is armed with a lawyer's mind for
weaknesses in an opponent's argument and a logician's wit for
constructions of syllogistic clarity.

13. *sublunary:* beneath the moon, thus earthly, and thus subject to decay.
14. *soul:* essential nature.   16. *elemented:* composed.

To His Coy Mistress

Had we but world enough, and time,
This coyness, lady, were no crime.
We would sit down, and think which way
To walk, and pass our long love's day.
Thou by the Indian Ganges' side
Shouldst rubies find; I by the tide
Of Humber° would complain.° I would
Love you ten years before the flood,
And you should, if you please, refuse
Till the conversion of the Jews.°   10
My vegetable love should grow
Vaster than empires and more slow;
An hundred years should go to praise
Thine eyes, and on thy forehead gaze;
Two hundred to adore each breast,
But thirty thousand to the rest;
An age at least to every part,
And the last age should show your heart.
For, lady, you deserve this state,°
Nor would I love at lower rate.   20
    But at my back I always hear
Time's wingèd chariot hurrying near;
And yonder all before us lie
Deserts of vast eternity.
Thy beauty shall no more be found,
Nor, in thy marble vault, shall sound
My echoing song; then worms shall try°
That long-preserved virginity,
And your quaint honor turn to dust,
And into ashes all my lust: 30
The grave's a fine and private place,
But none, I think, do there embrace.
    Now therefore, while the youthful hue
Sits on thy skin like morning dew,
And while thy willing soul transpires°

7. *Humber:* English river near Hull; *complain:* compose sad songs of love.
10. conversion of the Jews: event not supposed to occur until immediately before the Last Judgment—in other words, for a very long time. *19. state:* pomp.
27. try: test. *35. transpires:* breathes out.

At every pore with instant fires,
Now let us sport us while we may,
And now, like amorous birds of prey,
Rather at once our time devour
Than languish in his slow-chapped° power.   40
Let us roll all our strength and all
Our sweetness up into one ball,
And tear our pleasures with rough strife
Through the iron gates of life:
Thus, though we cannot make our sun
Stand still, yet we will make him run.

40. *his slow-chapped*: time's slow-jawed.

Dante Alighieri

FROM *Inferno*

TRANSLATED BY LAURENCE BINYON

Dante Alighieri (1265–1321)

BORN INTO THE EMERGENT COMMERCIAL CLASS OF FLORENCE, Dante was marked by a passionate attachment both to learning and to Italian politics. In the last decade of the thirteenth century he became one of the leading young political figures of Florence. In 1301–1302, while he was on a mission to the Papacy in Rome, the opposition party took control of Florence, and Dante was sentenced to death by fire should he ever return to that city. He was forced to spend the rest of his life in exile, wandering across northern Italy from city to city and from patron to patron. He died at Ravenna in 1321.

The *Divine Comedy* was probably written during the last thirteen years of Dante's life. Dante was one of the most promising poets and thinkers in Italy even before he wrote his masterwork; his early writings include not only the *Vita Nuova* (see p. 6) but three other major works (the first two unfinished): a study of eloquence in the vernacular (*De Vulgari Eloquentia*), a treatise on philosophy (*Il Convivio*), and a work in political theory (*De Monarchia*). The *Divine Comedy*, however, has overshadowed everything else that he wrote—and perhaps everything else written in the thousand years before him.

The *Comedy* (the adjective *Divine* was an apt sixteenth-century addition) is so called, according to its author, because comedy "introduces some harsh complication, but brings its matter to a prosperous end." Moreover, Dante pointed out, the *Comedy* is in the "low style," being written not in Latin, the "official" literary language of Dante's day, but in Italian—"the vernacular speech, in which even women communicate."

The poem is divided into three parts, *Inferno*, *Purgatorio*, and *Paradiso*, one hundred cantos in all. These record the stages of Dante's journey-vision in the afterworld. It begins with his journey in Hell, guided by the shade of the greatest Roman poet, Virgil, and continues as Virgil leads Dante up the Mount of Purgatory, where the saved souls purge themselves of the traces of their earthly sins. At the summit of this mountain, in the Earthly Paradise, Virgil leaves the poet and Dante comes face to face with the soul of his beloved Beatrice. It is she who guides him through Paradise, bringing him finally to St. Bernard of Clairvaux, the last of his three guides, who prepares the pilgrim for his vision of God, with which the work concludes.

An Outline of Dante's Hell

(Areas encountered in the following selections appear in CAPITAL LETTERS)

(The ten circles)		CANTOS*
PROLOGUE		I & II
NEUTRALS	0	III
VIRTUOUS HEATHEN	1	IV
INCONTINENCE { LUSTFUL	2	V
Gluttonous	3	VI
Avaricious and Prodigal	4	VII
Wrathful	5	VIII
HERETICS	6	X
VIOLENCE { Violent against others		XII
Violent against self		XIII
Violent against God	7	XIV
Violent against Nature		XV–XVI
Violent against Art		XVII
FRAUD { Simple fraud, of which FALSE COUNSEL is the eighth of ten designations	8	XVIII–XXX
Treachery against kin, COUNTRY AND CAUSE, GUESTS, LORDS AND BENEFACTORS	9	XXXI–XXXIV

* Cantos IX and XI are not shown because they are transitional from one circle to another.

Inferno

Midway life's journey° I was made aware
   That I had strayed into a dark forest,
   And the right path appeared not anywhere.
Ah, tongue cannot describe how it oppressed,
   This wood, so harsh, dismal and wild, that fear
   At thought of it strikes now into my breast.
So bitter it is, death is scarce bitterer.
   But, for the good it was my hap to find,
   I speak of the other things that I saw there.
I cannot well remember in my mind   10
   How I came thither, so was I immersed
   In sleep, when the true way I left behind.
But when my footsteps had attained the first
   Slope of a hill, at the end of that drear vale
   Which with such terror had my spirit pierced,
I looked up, and beheld its shoulders pale
   Already in clothing of that planet's light°
   Which guideth men on all roads without fail.
Then had my bosom a little of respite
   From what had all the pool of my heart tost   20
   While I so piteously endured the night.
As one, whom pantings of his breath exhaust,
   Escaped from the deep water to the shore,
   Turns back and gazes on the danger crost,
So my mind, fleeing still and stricken sore,
   Turned back to gaze astonished on that pass
   Which none hath ever left alive before.

1. *Midway . . . journey:* The action of the poem begins the night before Good Friday, 1300, when Dante was thirty-five years old. (See Psalms 90:10: "The days of our years are threescore years and ten . . .") 17. *planet's light:* In the Ptolemaic system, the sun was considered a planet.

When my tired body had rested a brief space
  I trod anew the slope, desert and bare,
  With the firmer foot still in the lower place.   30
And at the ascent, as 't were on the first stair,
  Behold! a Leopard,° very swift and light
  And covered with a hide of mottled hair.
And it would not depart, but opposite
  On my path faced me, so that many a time
  I turned me to go back, because of it.
The moment was the morning's earliest prime,
  And the sun mounted up, accompanied
  By those stars that with him began to climb
When divine Love first made° through heaven to
      glide   40
  Those things of beauty, so that hope I caught
  Of that wild creature with the gaudy hide.
The hour of time and the sweet season wrought
  Thus on me; yet not so much, but when appeared
  A Lion, terror to my heart he brought.
He seemed coming against me with head reared
  Ravening with hunger, and so terrible
  That the very air seemed of his breath afeared;
And a She-Wolf, that in her famished fell°
  Looked all infuriate craving (she hath meant   50
  To many ere now that they in misery dwell)
On me with grimness of her aspect sent
  A burden that my spirit overpowered,
  So that I lost the hope of the ascent.
As one that is with lust of gain devoured,
  When comes the time that makes him lose, will rack
  His thoughts, lamenting all his hope deflowered,
To such state brought me, in dread of his attack,
  That restless beast, who by degrees perforce
  To where the Sun is silent drove me back.   60
While I was rushing on my downward course

32. *Leopard:* The significance of the three beasts, the first of which to appear
is the leopard, has been long debated. It has recently been suggested by some
scholars that the three beasts correspond to the three great areas of Hell: Leopard
—Fraud, Lion—Violence, She-Wolf—Incontinence. 40. *When . . . made:* According to one scholar, Creation was supposed to have taken place in spring,
when the sun was in the Ram (Aries), on the same date as the Incarnation and
the Crucifixion. It was the morning of Good Friday. 49. *fell:* hide, pelt.

Suddenly on my sight there seemed to start
One who appeared from a long silence hoarse.°
When I beheld him in that great desert
   "Have pity on me!" I cried out to his face,
   "Whatsoever—shade or very man—thou art."
He answered me: "Not man; man once I was.
   My parents both were of the Lombard name,
   Of Mantua by their country and by their race.
Sub Julio was I born, though late I came: 70
   In Rome the good Augustus on me shone,°
   In the time of the false Gods of lying fame.
Poet was I, and sang° of that just son
   Of old Anchises, who came out from Troy
   After the burning of proud Ilion.
But thou, why turn'st thou back to such annoy?
   Why climbest not the Mount Delectable°
   The cause and the beginning of all joy?"
"And art thou, then, that Virgil, and that well
   Which pours abroad so ample a stream of song?"   80
   I answered him abashed, with front° that fell.
"O glory and light of all the poets' throng!
   May the ardent study and great love serve me now
   Which made me to peruse thy book so long!
Thou art my Master and my Author° thou.
   Thou only art he from whom the noble style
   I took, wherein my merit men avow.
Regard yon beast from which I made recoil!
   Help me from her, renowned sage, for she
   Puts all my veins and pulses in turmoil."   90
"Needs must thou find another way to flee,"
   He answered, seeing my eyes with weeping fill,
   "If thou from this wild place wouldst get thee free;
Because this beast, at which thou criest still,
   Suffereth none to go upon her path,
   But hindereth and entangleth till she kill,

---

63. *hoarse:* "Weak" is perhaps a better translation for Dante's *fioco.* 70–71.
Sub . . . shone: "I was born so late in the reign of Julius Caesar that I became
identified with the reign of Augustus." 73. *sang:* wrote the *Aeneid.* 77.
Mount Delectable: reference to the hill of line 14. 81. *front:* forehead. 85.
Author: one of three words in the *Divine Comedy* (the other two being *scripture*
and *volume*) that are used only to denote the greatness of God and of His Book,
the Bible. Each of the words, however, is used once to refer to Virgil and his
Aeneid; this may give some sense of Dante's esteem for Virgil.

And hath a nature so perverse in wrath,
   Her craving maw never is satiated
   But after food the fiercer hunger hath.
Many are the creatures with whom she hath wed,   100
   And shall be yet more, till appear the Hound°
   By whom in pain she shall be stricken dead.
He will not batten on pelf or fruitful ground,
   But wisdom, love, and virtue shall he crave.
   'Twixt Feltro and Feltro shall his folk abound.
He that abasèd Italy shall save,
   For which Euryalus, Turnus, Nisus died,
   For which her virgin blood Camilla° gave.
And her through every city far and wide
   Back into Hell's deep dungeon shall he chase,   110
   Whence envy first let loose her ravening stride.
Wherefore I judge this fittest for thy case
   That I should lead thee, and thou follow in faith,
   To journey hence through an eternal place,
Where thou shalt hear cries of despairing breath,
   Shalt look on the ancient spirits in their pain,
   Such that each calls out for a second death.
And thou shalt see those° who in fire refrain
   From sorrow, since their hope is in the end,
   Whensoever it be, to the blessèd to attain.   120
To whom if thou desirest to ascend
   There shall be a spirit° worthier than I,
   When I depart, who shall thy steps befriend.
For that Lord Emperor who reigns on high,
   Because I was not to his law submiss,
   Wills not that I to his city come too nigh.
In every part he ruleth, and all is his,
   There is his city, there is his high seat:
   O happy, whom he chooseth for that bliss!"
And I to him: "O Poet, I entreat   130
   In the name of that God whom thou didst not know,
   So that I 'scape this ill and worse ill yet,

101–105. Hound . . . abound: possibly the single most debated passage in the *Divine Comedy.* It has been suggested by some scholars that the prophecy Dante puts in Virgil's mouth here points either to the coming of a great temporal leader or to the Second Coming of Jesus Christ. *107–108. Euryalus . . . Camilla:* four characters in the *Aeneid* who gave their lives in the struggle that resulted in the eventual founding of Rome. *118. those:* the souls in Purgatory. *122. spirit:* that of Beatrice.

Lead me where thou hast spoken of but now,
So that my eyes St. Peter's gate° may find
And those whom thou portrayest in such woe!"
Then he moved onward: and I went behind.

CANTO II

The day was going, and the darkened air
Was taking from its toil each animal
That is on the earth; I only, alone there,
Essayed to arm my spirit against all
The terror of the journey and pity's plea,
Which memory, that errs not, shall recall.
O Muses, O high Genius, strengthen me!
O Memory, that what I saw hast writ,
Here shall be made known thine integrity.
I began: "Poet, who guidest now my feet,   10
Look if the virtue in me avail to endure
The arduous pass, ere thou trust me to it.
Thou sayest the father of Silvius° went secure
In his corruptible body, and that world knew
Which Death knows not, of all his senses sure.
But if the Adversary of Sin that due°
Of favour gave him, weighing the high effect
And who, and what,° should be his great issue,
This seems not unmeet to the intellect;
For he was born to father and prepare   20
Rome and her Empire, as high Heaven's elect;
Both of which, the true history to declare,
Were the foundations of that sainted spot
Which is the seat of greatest Peter's heir.°
By this adventure, whence thy praise he got,
He learned things that for him were argument
Of victory, and the Papal Mantle wrought.
Afterwards too the Chosen Vessel° went

---

134. *St. Peter's gate:* not the gate of Heaven but that of Purgatory, where a priest stands as a vicar of St. Peter, admitting only those worthy of the journey toward Heaven.   13. *father of Silvius:* Aeneas, whose descent into the underworld is the subject of the *Aeneid,* Book VI.   16. *due:* deserved gift.   18. *who, and what:* the emperors of Rome and the Roman Imperium.   24. *heir:* the Pope. St. Peter, as founder of the Church in Rome, is thought of as being the first and greatest Pope.   28. *Chosen Vessel:* the phrase comes from Acts 9:15 and refers to St. Paul who is understood to have been taken up into Paradise (2 Cor. 12:4) and to have returned to earth.

The confirmation of that faith to bring
Which is for way of our salvation meant.   30
But I, why go? By whose commissioning?
I am not Aeneas, no, nor Paul: too weak
I, and others also, deem me for this thing.
If I resign me, then, that world to seek,
I fear the quest for folly be aspersed.
Thou art wise and canst divine more than I speak."
And like one who unwills what he willed first
And new thoughts change the intention that he had,
So that his resolution is reversed,
So on that dim slope did my purpose fade   40
For I with thinking had dulled down the zest
That at the outset sprang so prompt and glad.
"If rightly I read the trouble in thy breast,"
The shade of the Magnanimous replied,
"With cowardice thy spirit is oppressed,
Which oftentimes a man hath mortified,
So that it turns him back from noble deed,
As with false seeing a beast will start aside.
Now, that thy heart may from this fear be freed,
Hear why I came and what I heard, and where,   50
When first I felt the pity of thy need.
I was with those who are in suspense:° and there
A Lady° of so great beauty and blessedness,
I craved for her command, called me to her.
Her eyes so shone, the Morning Star shines less.
And she began to speak, gentle and low,
In the angel voice that did her soul express:
'O courteous Mantuan spirit, whom men fame so
That thy renown yet lasts, and till Time end
The motion of his hours, shall greater grow,   60
He that is my friend, but not fortune's friend,
Halts on the lonely moor, by fear deterred,
So that the path he dareth not ascend.
Already I fear he may so sore have erred
That I have risen to succour him too late,
From what of him in Heaven I have heard.
Go now, and with thy poet's speech ornate
And what means else may rescue courage weak
Help him, and me deliver of this care's weight.

52. *in suspense:* in Limbo.   53. *Lady:* Beatrice.

I am Beatrice who send thee, him to seek.   70
   I come from that place for which now I sigh.
   It was love moved me and made my lips to speak.
Often to thy praise will I testify
   When I am come into my Lord's presence.'
   She then was silent; and I made reply:
'O Lady, who art the only virtue whence
   Mankind may overpass what is contained
   Within the heaven of least circumference,°
So welcome is the bidding thou hast deigned,
   That were it now done, it were done too slow.   80
   It needs but that thy wish should be explained:
But tell me why into this core of woe
   Thou shun'st not to descend, turning thy face
   From the ample air, whither thou yearn'st to go?'
'Since thou,' she answered, 'so much of this case
   Desirest knowledge, briefly shalt thou hear
   Why I shrink not to come into this place.
Those things that have the power to wound and sear,
   To them alone should due of dread be paid;
   To the others not, they are not things to fear.   90
I am by God so, in his mercy, made,
   That misery of yours touches me not,
   Nor in the scorch of this fire am I frayed.
A Lady° in heaven is to such pity wrought
   By the hard pass, whereto I bid thee haste,
   That the strict law's remission she hath sought.
She called to her Lucy,° and made request,
   Saying, Now thy faithful one hath need of thee:
   I entrust him to thee; and do thou the rest.
Lucy, the enemy of all cruelty,   100
   Arose and came and stood within my gaze
   There, where the ancient Rachel° sat by me.
She spoke and said: Beatrice, God's true praise,
   Why helpest thou not him, who loved thee so
   That for thy sake he left the vile crowd's ways?
Hearest thou not the plaining of his woe?
   Seëst thou not what death would him undo
   By that wild flood the sea may not o'ercrow?°

---

78. *heaven . . . circumference*: that of the moon, and thus of the earth, where
all things are corruptible. *94. Lady*: the Virgin Mary. *97. Lucy*: probably
St. Lucia, as representative of Illuminating Grace. *102. Rachel*: To medieval
Biblical commentators, she represented the contemplative life. *108. o'ercrow*:
feel power over.

None in the world was ever swift to ensue
  His good, or fly his hurt, as these my feet   110
  At once, after those words were uttered few,
Hasted to come down from my blessèd seat,
  Confiding in thy spech, so nobly graced,
  It honours both thee and those hearing it.'
Having said this, her footsteps she retraced,
  Turning from me her eyes that wept and shone;
  At sight of which she made me more to haste.
Thus I came to thee, as she desired, and won
  Thee from that ravening beast which would withhold
  The short way to the Beauteous Mount begun.   120
What is it, then, keeps thee? Why, why haltest cold?
  Why in thy heart nourishest fear so base?
  Why art thou not delivered, eager, bold,
When three such blessed Ladies of their grace
  Care in the court of Heaven for thy plight,
  And my words promise thee such good to embrace?"
As little flowers, that by the chill of night
  Are closed, prick up their stems drooping and bent,
  And to the early ray re-open white,
So was it with my courage fallen and spent;   130
  And I began, as one from bondage freed,
  So good a warmth about my body went:
"O most compassionate She, who helps my need!
  O courteous thou, who to that uttered word
  Didst listen, and to its truth so swift give heed!
Thou makest me so eager in accord
  With what thou say'st, and quickenest so my heart,
  That to my first resolve I am restored.
Now it is one will moves us both; thou art
  Guide, master, lord!" These words to him I said,   140
  And then, perceiving that he made to start,
Began the desolate, arduous path to tread.

CANTO III

THROUGH ME THE WAY IS TO THE CITY OF WOE:
  THROUGH ME THE WAY INTO THE ETERNAL PAIN;
  THROUGH ME THE WAY AMONG THE LOST BELOW.
RIGHTEOUSNESS DID MY MAKER ON HIGH CONSTRAIN.
  ME DID DIVINE AUTHORITY UPREAR;

ME SUPREME WISDOM AND PRIMAL LOVE° SUSTAIN.
BEFORE I WAS, NO THINGS CREATED WERE
   SAVE THE ETERNAL, AND I ETERNAL ABIDE.
   RELINQUISH ALL HOPE, YE WHO ENTER HERE.
These words, of a dim colour, I espied   10
   Written above the lintel of a door.
   Whereat: "Master, the sense is hard," I cried.
And he, as one experienced in that lore:
   "Here all misgiving must thy mind reject.
   Here cowardice must die and be no more.
We are come to the place I told thee to expect,
   Where thou shouldst see the people whom pain stings
   And who have lost the good of the intellect." °
His hand on mine, to uphold my falterings,
   With looks of cheer that bade me comfort keep,   20
   He led me on into the secret things.
Here lamentation, groans, and wailings deep
   Reverberated through the starless air,
   So that it made me at the beginning weep.
Uncouth tongues, horrible chatterings of despair,
   Shrill and faint cries, words of grief, tones of rage,
   And, with it all, smiting of hands, were there,
Making a tumult, nothing could assuage,
   To swirl in the air that knows not day or night,
   Like sand within the whirlwind's eddying cage.   30
And I, whose mind failed to discern aright,
   Said: "Master, what is it that my ear affrays?
   Who are these that seem so crushed beneath their
      plight?"
And he to me: "These miserable ways
   The forlorn spirits endure of those who spent
   Life without infamy and without praise.
They are mingled with that caitiff° rabblement
   Of the angels, who rebelled not, yet avowed
   To God no loyalty, on themselves intent.
Heaven chased them forth, lest, being there, they cloud   40
   Its beauty, and the deep Hell refuses them,
   For, beside these, the wicked might be proud." °

5-6. *Authority . . . Wisdom . . . Love:* Authority (or Power), Wisdom, and
Love are the attributes of the triune God, corresponding, respectively, to the
Father, Son, and Holy Spirit. *18. good . . . intellect:* knowledge of God.
37. caitiff: cowardly. *42. proud:* Those who were neutral, although in the
"highest" circle of Hell, are even more hideous than any of the sinful souls contained in Hell itself (see l. 48).

And I: "Master, what is the grief extreme
  Which makes them so their fortune execrate?"
  He answered: "Brief words best their case beseem.
They have no hope of death: and their estate
  Is so abased in the blind life they own
  That they are envious of all others' fate.
Report of them the world permitteth none.
  Mercy and Justice have them in disdain.   50
  Let us not talk of them. Look, and pass on."
I, who looked, beheld a banner all a-strain,
  Which moved, and, as it moved, so quickly spun
  That never a respite it appeared to deign.
And after it I saw so many run,
  I had not believed, they seemed so numberless,
  That Death so great a legion had undone.
When I had marked some few among the press,
  I chanced the shade of him to recognize
  Who made the great refusal,° in cowardice.   60
Forthwith I was assured, and knew mine eyes
  Looked of a truth on the abject crew that were
  Odious to God and to his enemies.
These paltry, who never were alive, were bare
  As to the body, and all about were stung
  By stings of the wasps and hornets that were there.
Because of these, blood, from their faces sprung,
  Was mingled with their tears and flowed to feast
  The loathly worms about their feet that clung.
Then as my peering eyes made further quest,   70
  I saw folk on the shore of a great stream.
  "Master," I said, "make to me manifest
Who these are and what law constraineth them
  Willingly to pass over and be gone,
  If rightly I can discern by the faint gleam."
And he to me: "The things shall all be known
  To thy understanding when our steps are stayed
  Upon the mournful shores of Acheron." °
Casting abashed eyes downward, and afraid
  Lest that my words should some offence have
      wrought,   80

60. *Who . . . refusal:* Scholars believe this refers to Celestine V, a pious hermit, who after a long vacancy of the papal office, was elected Pope in July, 1294, but abdicated five months later, feeling himself physically and mentally unfit. Through his renunciation Boniface VIII, Dante's chief enemy, became Pope. 78. *Acheron:* classical river of death.

I ceased from speech until the stream we made.
And toward us lo! arriving in a boat
  An Ancient,° white with hair upon him old,
  Crying, "Woe to you, ye spirits misbegot!
Hope not that heaven ye ever shall behold.
  I come to carry you to yon shore, and lead
  Into the eternal darkness, heat and cold.
And thou who art there, a living spirit, with speed
  Get hence, nor with these who are dead delay"—
  But when he noted that I took no heed,   90
He said: "By another ferry, another way
  Of entrance must thou seek to pass, not here.
  Needs must a lighter vessel° thee convey."
My Guide to him: "Charon, thy frowns forbear.
  Thus is this thing willed there, where what is willed
  Can be accomplished. Further questions spare."
Then were the shaggy cheeks from trouble stilled
  Of that old steersman on the livid fen
  Around whose eyes flames in a circle wheeled.
But those forlorn and naked spirits of men   100
  Changed colour, chattering with their teeth, all numb,
  Soon as the harsh words sounded in their ken.
They blasphemed God, blasphemed their mother's
            womb,
  The human kind, the place, the time, the seed
  Of their engendering, and their birth and doom;
Then weeping all together in their sad need
  Betook themselves to the accursed shore
  Which awaits each who of God takes no need.
Charon, the demon, beckoning before,
  With eyes of glowing coal, assembles all: 110
  Whoever lags, he beats him with his oar.
And as the late leaves of November fall
  To earth, one after another, ever fewer,
  Till the bough sees its spoil gone past recall,
So by that river Adam's seed impure
  Cast themselves from the wharf, one after one,
  At signals, as the bird goes to the lure.°
Thus are they borne across the water dun;
  And ere they disembark on the far strand

83. *Ancient:* Charon, who in classical literature ferries the souls of the dead across Acheron.   93. *a lighter vessel:* ship that carries the saved souls of repentant Christians to Purgatory.   117. *lure:* bait.

On this another gathering is begun. 120
"Son," said the courteous Master, "understand
   That all those who have died in the anger of God
   Congregate hither out of every land.
And they are prompt to pass over the flood,
   For Divine Justice pricketh in them so
   That fear is changed to longing in their blood.
By this way no good spirit is seen to go.
   Therefore if Charon doth of thee complain,
   What his words mean thou easily may'st know."
When he had ended, the whole shadowy plain 130
   Shuddered so strongly, that the terror past
   Still at the memory bathes me in sweat again.
Out of the tear-drenched earth came forth a blast
   That made a crimson light before me leap
   And numbness over all my senses cast.
And I fell, like to one seized with a sleep.

CANTO IV

Rumble of thunder upon my brain deep-drowsed
   So shook the sleep that at the heavy sound
   I started, like a man by force aroused.
And my now rested eyes casting around
   I rose upright, with peering gaze intent
   To know the place wherein myself I found.
True it is, I stood on the edge of the descent
   Where the hollow of the gulf out of despair
   Amasses thunder of infinite lament.
Sombre, profound, and brimmed with vaporous air 10
   It was, so that I, seeking to pierce through
   To the very bottom, could se nothing there.
"Let us go down to the blind world below,"
   Began the Poet, on a sudden pale.
   "I shall be first, and thou behind me go."
And I, who had marked his colour so to quail,
   Said: "How shall I come where thou losest cheer
   Who art wont over my falterings to prevail?"
And he to me: "The misery that is here,
   Down among this folk, maketh my face wan 20
   With pity, which thine eyes mistake for fear.
Descend we: the long way constrains us on."

So he entered, and he made me enter too,
    On the first circle that the abyss doth zone.
Here was no sound that the ear could catch of rue,
    Save only of sighs, that still as they complain
    Make the eternal air tremble anew.
And this rose from the sorrow, unracked by pain,
    That was in the great multitude below
    Of children and of women and of men.   30
The good Master to me: "Wouldst thou not know
    What spirits are these thou seest and hearest grieve?
    I'd have thee learn before thou farther go,
These sinned not: ° but the merit that they achieve
    Helps not, since baptism was not theirs, the gate
    Of that faith, which was given thee to believe.
And if ere Christ they came, untimely in date,
    They worshipped not with right experience;
    And I myself am numbered in their state.
For such defect and for no other offence   40
    We are lost, and only in so far amerced°
    That without hope we languish in suspense."
I, when I heard this, to the heart was pierced,
    Because I knew men to much virtue bred
    Whose spirits in that Limbo were athirst.
"Tell me, my Master, tell me, Sir!" I said,
    Seized with a longing wholly to be assured
    Of that faith wherein error cannot tread,
"Did ever any of those herein immured
    By his own or other's merit to bliss get free?"   50
    And he, aware what meant my covert word, °
Answered: "I was yet new in this degree
    When I saw one° in power crowned appear
    On whom the signs of victory were to see.
He took from us the shade of our first sire;°
    Of his son Abel, and Noah of that same seed;

---

34. *These sinned not:* Here in Limbo are the virtuous pagans, who lived without
positive sin, but who failed to believe in Christ. It was the hard doctrine of the
age that those who lived before Christ and those born after Him, but who lived
outside the geographical limits of Christendom, should have known Him through
faith; having failed to do so, they must spend eternity in Limbo.   41. *amerced:*
punished.   51. *what . . . word:* Dante wants to know whether Virgil saw
Christ descend into Hell to take up with Him to Heaven the souls of those
Hebrews of the Old Testament who had (according to Christian tradition) believed in Christ.   53. *one:* Jesus Christ, never named in Hell, and always, like
Mary and God the Father, referred to by circumlocution.   55. *sire:* Adam.

Moses, the obedient and the law-giver;
The patriarch, Abraham, and the King, David;
    Israel with his father and with his sons;
    Rachel also, to win whom so much he did;   60
And many another; and made them blessed ones;
    And I would have thee know that, before these,
    There has been no human soul that he atones."
We ceased not to go on by slow degrees,
    Though he spoke still, and past the wood had come,
    The wood I mean of spirits thick like trees,
And, since my slumber, had not advanced therefrom
    Far, when a radiant glow beyond us shone
    Which overcame a hemisphere of gloom.
A little distance from us it lay on,   70
    Yet not so much but that I saw in part
    What honourable folk that place had won.
"O thou that honourest Science and Art,
    Who are these that have such honour and acclaim
    That it removes them from the rest apart?"
And he to me: "The glory of the name
    Which sounds of them above in the earthly sphere
    Gains favour of Heaven which thus promoteth them."
Meanwhile a voice was sounding in my ear:
    "Honour ye all the great Poet: his shade   80
    That had departed, now again is here."
After the voice had paused and silent stayed,
    I saw four great shades come with one accord.
    They had an aspect neither gay nor sad.
The good Master began to speak his word:
    "On him who bears the sword° thine eyes now cast,
    Who comes before the others, as their lord.
He is Homer, who all poets hath surpassed.
    The next who comes is Horace, satirist,
    Ovid the third, and Lucan° is the last.   90
Because each nature doth with mine consist
    Through that name which the one voice glorifies
    They do me honour, and themselves not least."
Thus came that noble school before mine eyes

---

86. *him . . . sword:* Homer wears a sword because he sang of war in the *Iliad.*
Dante had never read Homer, since he knew no Greek. Greek letters were almost entirely absent from European civilization between the sixth and the late
fourteenth centuries. *89–90. Horace . . . Ovid . . . Lucan:* three Roman poets.

Assembling round the lord of loftiest style
Who over the others like an eagle flies.
After they had talked together a little while,
    They turned to me and welcoming signs displayed:
    At which salute I saw my Master smile.°
And yet more honour unto me they paid,   100
    For me into their band did they invite,
    So that I a sixth amid such wisdom made.
Thus we went moving onwards toward the light
    Speaking such things as here were better mute,
    Though there to speak them was both meet and right.°
Now came we to a Noble Castle's foot,
    With lofty walls seven times engirdled round,
    And a fair rivulet moated it about.
This we passed over as it had been dry ground.
    Through seven gates entering with those sages, lo!   110
    A meadow of fresh verdure there I found.
On it were people with grave eyes and slow,
    And great authority was in their mien.
    They spoke seldom, with mild voices and low.
Thus we retired on one side that demesne°
    Into an open, luminous, high place,
    So that they stood where they could all be seen.
There on the green enamel, face to face,
    Were shown me the great spirits, so that I
    Exalt myself to have enjoyed such grace.   120
I saw Electra° in a great company
    Among whom Hector and Aeneas were,
    And armèd Caesar with the falcon eye.
I saw Camilla and Penthesilea there
    Over against them, and the Latian King;
    Lavinia his daughter sitting near;
That Brutus who drove out the proud Tarquin;
    Lucrece, Cornelia, Julia, Marcia, four
    Together, and by himself the Saladin.
When I had raised my eyes a little more,   130
    I saw the Master of those who know:° he sate

99. *smile:* only smile to be found in Hell.   104–105. *Speaking . . . right:* It
has been suggested that they were discussing the secrets of poetic inspiration and
craft.   115. *demesne:* region.   121. *Electra:* mother of Dardanus, founder of
Troy. In this first group of fourteen figures (ll. 21–29) we see the heroes and
ladies involved in the founding and development of Rome.   131. *Master . . .
know:* Aristotle. The twenty others in this group are all comtemplatives as opposed to those actively involved in the political and social affairs of their time.

Amid the sons Philosophy to him bore.
All do him honour, all eyes on him wait.
   Here I beheld Plato and Socrates
   Who of all are nearest to his high estate.
Democritus, whose world blind Chance decrees;
   Diogenes, Thales, Anaxagoras;
   Zeno, Heraclitus, and Empedocles:
Him who was skilled the virtue of plants to class,
   Dioscorides, I saw; and Orpheus' shade;   140
   Tully's and Linus'; moral Seneca's;
Euclid, and Ptolemy, who the stars surveyed;
   Hippocrates, Avicenna, and Galen,
   Averroes also, who the Comment made.
I may not portray all in the full scene,
   Being hurried on so by the long theme's care,
   That oft the word comes short of the thing seen.
The band of six to two hath dwindled, where
   By another road the sage Escort inclines
   Out of the quiet into the trembling air.   150
I come to a place where there is naught that shines.

CANTO V

From the first circle I thus descended down
   Into the second, which less space admits,
   And so much more pain that it stings to groan.
There Minos,° hideously grinning, sits,
   Inspects the offences at the entering in,
   Judges and, as he girds himself, commits.
I mean, that when the ill-born spirit comes in
   Before his presence, it confesses all;
   Thereon that scrutinizer of each sin
Sees what place Hell holds for its fittest stall;   10
   Round him as many times his tail doth throw
   As the degrees he wills that it should fall.
Always before him stand they, row on row;
   To sentence comes each of the wretched train:
   They tell, and hear; and straight are whirled below.
"O thou, who comest to the home of pain,"
   Said Minos to me, when my face he spied,
   Leaving his business of the great Arraign,

4. *Minos:* judge of the dead in classical mythology.

"Beware in whom thou, entering, dost confide.
   Let not the broad approach thy feet ensnare."   20
   "Why criest thou out?" answered to him my Guide:
"Hinder thou not his destined steps. Forbear!
   Thus is the thing willed there, where what is willed
   Can be accomplished. Further question spare."
Now begin notes of wailing never stilled
   To pierce into my ear; now am I come
   Where thronging lamentations hold me thrilled.
I came into a place of all light dumb
   That bellows like a storm in the sea-deep
   When the thwart winds that strike it roar and hum.   30
The abysmal tempest that can never sleep
   Snatches the spirits and headlong hurries them,
   Beats and besets them with its whirling sweep.
When they arrive before the ruin, stream
   The cries up; there the wail is and the moan,
   There the divine omnipotence they blaspheme.
I learnt that in such restless violence blown
   This punishment the carnal sinners share
   Whose reason by desire was overthrown.
And as their beating wings the starlings bear   40
   At the cold season, in broad flocking flight,
   So those corrupted spirits were rapt in air
To and fro, down, up, driven in helpless plight,
   Comforted by no hope ever to lie
   At rest, nor even to bear a pain more light.
And as the cranes in long line streak the sky
   And in procession chant their mournful call,
   So I saw come with sound of wailing by
The shadows fluttering in the tempest's brawl.
   Whereat, "O Master, who are these," I said,   50
   "On whom the black winds with their scourges fall?"
"The first of those concerning whom thou has prayed
   To know," he answered, "had dominion
   Of many tongues, which she as empress swayed.
With vice of luxury was she so undone,
   That she made lust a law by her decree,
   To obliterate the shame that she had won.
This is Semiramis:° we read that she
   Came after Ninus, and had been his bride.

58. *Semiramis:* queen of Assyria and wife of Ninus, mythical founder of the empire of Nineveh, whom she succeeded to power.

She ruled the land the Soldan holds in fee.   60
That other is she° who by her own hand died
   For Love's sake, to Sichaeus' urn untrue;
   Voluptuous Cleopatra comes beside.
See Helen,° for whose sake the long years drew
   Ill after ill; see great Achilles° there,
   Who fought with love in the end, and whom love slew.
See Paris,° Tristram!"° More than a thousand pair
   He with his finger pointing at shades of fame
   Showed me, whom love had power from life to tear.
After that I had heard my Teacher name   70
   Each lady of old, with her enamoured knight,
   My thoughts were mazed, such pity upon me came.
I began: "Poet, I fain would, if I might,
   Speak with those two° that hand in hand appear
   And, as they move, seem to the wind so light."
And he to me: "When they approach more near,
   Thou shalt see. By the love which is their guide
   Do thou entreat them then, and they will hear."
Soon as the wind's whirl made them nearer glide,
   I raised my voice up: "O tired spirits, come   80
   And speak with us, if that be not denied."
Eagerly as a pair of pigeons, whom
   Desire calls, and their will bears, as they fly
   On wide unfaltering wings to their sweet home,
So swerved those spirits from out the company
   Where Dido is, flying toward us underneath
   The fell mirk; such a power had my fond cry.
"O kind and gracious creature that hast breath
   And comest journeying through the black air
   To us who made the earth bloody with our death,   90
Were but the world's King friend to us, a prayer
   Should from us both implore Him for thy peace
   Because thou hast taken pity on our despair.
Whether to speak or listen better please,

---

61. *she:* Dido, who betrayed her vows of chastity to the memory of her dead husband, Sichaeus, when she fell in love with Aeneas. 64. *Helen:* Helen of Troy. 65. *Achilles:* In medieval tradition Achilles met his death at the hands of Paris because of his love for Polyxena, sister of Paris and one of the daughters of Priam and Hecuba. 67. *Paris:* lover of Helen of Troy; *Tristram:* hero of an old French romance, which recounts his love and death for Yseult. 74. *two:* Francesca da Rimini was betrothed by her family to Gianciotto Malatesta for political reasons; she fell in love with his younger brother Paolo. Gianciotto discovered them together and killed them.

We will speak with you, and hear and understand,
   Now while the lull'd wind spares a little ease.
The place° where I was born sits on the strand
   Where Po descends to his peace, and with him takes
   All the other streams that follow him down the land.
Love, that in gentle heart so quickly wakes,   100
   Took him with this fair body, which from me
   Was torn: the way of it still hurts and aches.
Love, that to no loved one remits his fee,
   Took me with joy of him, so deep in-wrought,
   Even now it hath not left me, as thou dost see.
Love led us both to one death. He° that sought
   And split our life—Cain's hell awaits him now."
   These words to us upon the wind were brought.
When I had heard those wounded spirits, my brow
   Sank downward, and I held it where it was,   110
   Until the Poet spoke: "What musest thou?"
And when I answered, I began: "Alas!
   How many sweet thoughts and what longings fain
   Led them into the lamentable pass!"
I turned, and I began to speak again:
   "Francesca, the tears come into mine eyes
   For sorrow, and for pity of thy pain.
But tell me: in the time of the sweet sighs
   How did Love vouchsafe proof of what he is,
   And of the obscure yearnings make you wise?"   120
And she to me: "No grief surpasses this
   (And that thy Teacher° understands full well)—
   In the midst of misery to remember bliss.
But if thou so desire to know how fell
   The seed whose first root in our bosoms fed,
   I'll tell, as one who can but weep and tell.
One day together, for pastime, we read
   Of Launcelot,° and how Love held him in thrall.
   We were alone, and without any dread.
Sometimes our eyes, at the word's secret call,   130
   Met, and our cheeks a changing colour wore.
   But it was one page only that did all.

97. *The place:* Ravenna.   106. *He:* Gianciotto, said by Francesca to occupy the
area of Hell set aside for those who have killed their own kin.   122. *Teacher:*
Virgil; These lines are borrowed from *Aeneid* II, 3f.   128. *Launcelot:* hero of
Arthurian romances, who had an illicit love affair with Guinevere, King Arthur's
queen.

When we read how that smile, so thirsted for,
  Was kissed by such a lover, he that may
  Never from me be separated more
All trembling kissed my mouth. The book I say
  Was a Galahalt° to us, and he beside
  That wrote the book. We read no more that day."
While the one spirit spoke thus, the other cried
  So lamentably, that the whole life fled   140
  For pity out of me, as if I died;
And I fell, like a body falling dead.

C A N T O   X

Now journeying along a secret track
  Between the ramparts and the sufferers
  My Master goes, and I behind his back.
"O sovran Virtue, who down the circling tiers
  Of the impious leadest me where thou dost bid,
  Satisfy," I said, "the wish that in me stirs.
The people who in these sepulchres are hid,
  May they be seen? None watches; none keeps guard.
  And see! already raised is every lid."
And he to me: "All shall be fast and barred   10
  When from Jehosophat° they shall hither hie
  Each with the body he left under the sward.
This is the quarter wherein buried lie
  Epicurus° and all those his doctrine swayed,
  Who with the body make the soul to die.
Therefore unto the question thou hast made
  Here within soon shalt thou an answer find
  And also to the wish thou hast not betrayed."
And I: "I keep not from thee, Escort kind,
  My thought, save that, as thou too didst require   20
  Ere now, I speak but in few words my mind."
"Tuscan,° who goest through the city of fire
  Alive, with comely speech upon thy tongue,

137. Galahalt: Gallehault, the character in the French romance of King Arthur who acted as go-between, arranging the first meeting between Launcelot and Guinevere. *11. Jehosophat:* valley where the Last Judgment is supposed to take place; from there all souls, having recovered their bodies, will be sent to remain in Heaven or Hell. *14. Epicurus:* Dante's chief (and only) charge against Epicurus is that he did not believe in the immortality of the soul. *22. Tuscan:* inhabitant of Tuscany, region in central Italy including Florence.

Halt here, if thou wilt tarry at my desire.
The speech thou usest manifests thee sprung
    From that famed country which, it may be, I tried
    Which I perhaps with too much trouble wrung."
Suddenly in my ear this sound was cried
    From out one of those coffers; and I drew,
    In fear, a little closer to my Guide.   30
And he to me spoke: "Turn! What dost thou do?
    See Farinata,° raising himself amain!
    From the waist all of him shall rise in view."
My gaze from him I could not now have ta'en:
    And he rose up to front me, face and breast,
    As if of Hell he had a great disdain.
With prompt, inspiriting hands my Guide then prest
    Me towards him, past the other sepulchres,
    Counselling: "Use the words thou findest best."
When I was where his tomb its front uprears,   40
    He looked at me a little, and with a kind
    Of scorn he questioned: "Who were thy forbears?"
I, who had it to obey him in my mind,
    Concealed nothing from him, but told all out,
    At which his brows upward a little inclined:
Then he said: "Fiercely did they use to flout
    Me and my forefathers; and since they spurned
    My party, twice I scattered them in rout."
"If they were chased, on all sides they returned,
    Both times," I answered, "from adversities;   50
    But yours that art have not so rightly learned."
Beside him then a shadow° by degrees
    Emerged, and was discovered to the chin:
    I think he had raised himself upon his knees.
He looked around as if he had thought to win
    Sight of some other who might be with me;
    And when that hope was wholly quenched within,
Cried weeping: "If through this blind prison, free,
    Thou goest by virtue of thy nature's height,

32. *Farinata:* This famous heretic died in 1264, a year before Dante's birth. In 1260 he had taken part in the battle of Montaperti, where the rulers of Florence suffered a terrible defeat. After this rout the neighboring towns and barons held a council at Empoli, and all but Farinata were in favor of destroying Florence; he, however, opposed the project so stoutly that it was abandoned. 52. *shadow:* shade of Cavalcante Cavalcanti, the father of Dante's fellow poet, Guido Cavalcanti; Farinata and Cavalcante Cavalcanti were related by marriage: Guido was married to Farinata's daughter.

Where is my son? Why is he not here with thee?"   60
And I to him: " 'Tis not by my own right
   I come; he that waits yonder leads me here,
   Of whom perhaps thy Guido had despite." °
His words, and manner of penance, made appear
   His name, as if I had read it on his brow,
   Therefore my answer had I made thus clear.
Suddenly erect, he cried: "What saidest thou?
   He *had?* Lives he not, then, in the sweet air?
   Does the sun's light not strike upon him now?"
When of a certain pause he was aware   70
   Ere I replied, where he had risen to stand
   Down he fell backward, and so vanished there.
But, haughty of spirit, that other, at whose demand
   I had halted, changed not aspect, nor his head
   Moved, nor his side bent, no, nor stirred a hand.
"And if," continuing his own words, he said,
   "To learn that art they have so little wit,
   It tortureth me more than doth this bed.
But fifty times shall not afresh be lit
   The countenance of the Lady° who reigns here   80
   Ere thou shalt know the cost of learning it.
And, so thou would'st return back to the dear
   Earth, tell me why in each of its decrees
   That people against my people is so severe?"
Then I: "The havoc and the butcheries
   That made the Arbia° dyed all red to run
   Hath filled our temple with such litanies."
He sighed, shaking his head; and then spoke on:
   "In that I was not single; nor, I swear,
   Would I in ill cause with the rest have gone.   90
But single I was in that place yonder,° where
   All on the ruin of Florence had agreed.
   I only with open face defended her."
"Ah, so may peace come also to thy seed,

---

63. *whom . . . despite:* Though most commentators believe it is Virgil whom
Guido did not respect enough (for reasons that are not entirely clear), some
believe it is Beatrice (also for reasons not entirely clear), since the gender of the
pronoun is not determinable in the Italian. 80. *Lady:* Proserpine, Queen of
Hell. Fifty months after this (1304), an attempt to reconcile and bring home
the Florentine exiles, Dante among them, was unsuccessful. 86. *Arbia:* river
beside the site of the battle of Montaperti (see note to l. 32). 91. *in . . .
yonder:* at the council of Empoli.

Resolve me," I prayed him, "this hard knot that ties
   My judgment in it, and the riddle read.
It seemeth, if I hear aright, your eyes
   Perceive beforehand what Time brings with him,
   But with the present ye use otherwise."
"We see like those for whom the light is dim,"   100
   He answered me, "the things that are remote;
   So much still shines for us the Lord Supreme.
When they come near, or are, then avails not
   Our understanding, and we know no more,
   Save what is told us, of your human lot.
Easily may'st thou understand, therefore,
   That all we have of knowledge shall be dead
   From that time when the Future shuts its door." °
Then pricked in conscience for my fault,° I said,
   "Will you not now acquaint that fallen one   110
   His child is not yet from the living fled?
And if before to his answer I made none
   Tell him it was my thought that was not free,
   Being in that knot which now you have undone."
And now my Master was recalling me.
   Therefore more earnestly the spirit I prest
   To tell me who were those with him. And he:
"With more than a thousand I lie here opprest.
   Yonder the Second Frederic° is inurned,
   The Cardinal° also: I speak not of the rest."   120
With that he hid himself. My steps I turned
   Back toward the ancient Poet, pondering
   That saying wherein some menace I discerned.
He moved, and as we went: "What is this thing,"
   He said to me, "which teases so thy mind?"
   I satisfied him in his questioning.
"Keep in thy memory what thine ears divined
   To be against thee," warned the Sage. "Attend
   Now," and with finger lifted he enjoined:
"When thou before the radiance shalt bend   130

108. *when . . . door:* after the Last Judgment has taken place. 109. *fault:* for
using the past definite tense, which made Cavalcante think that his son was
already dead. *119. Second Frederic:* Frederick II (1194–1250), who became
King of Sicily and Naples in 1197 and Emperor in 1212. Villani says of him
that "he was addicted to all sensual delights, and led an Epicurean life, taking
no account of any other." 120. *Cardinal:* Cardinal Ottaviano degli Ubaldini,
active member of the Ghibelline party.

Of that Lady,° whose beauteous eyes see all,
　　Thou shalt learn thy life's journey unto its end."
Then to the left he turned his steps; the wall
　　We quitted, toward the middle advancing by
　　A path that strikes into a valley's fall,
Wherefrom the fume rose noisome even thus high.

CANTO XXVI

Florence, exult that thou hast grown so great
　　That thy wings beat, the seas and lands around,
　　And wide thy name is spread within Hell's gate!
Among the Thieves° five of such note I found
　　Thy citizens, whence shame comes to my cheek,
　　Nor to thine honour doth it much redound.
But if the truth in dream of morning° speak,
　　Thou shalt in short time feel what upon thee
　　Prato, and others also, thirst to wreak.
If it were now, not too soon would it be!　　　　10
　　Since come it must, I would that come it were,
　　For, with each year, heavier it is for me.
Thence we departed; and by that same stair
　　Which served for our descent, of ledges frayed,
　　My Guide climbed back, and me with him up-bare.
And as our solitary way we made
　　Among the juts and splinters of the scarp,
　　The foot sped not without the hand to aid.
Then did I grieve, and grief returneth sharp,
　　Seeing what I saw in memory, and I rein　　　　20
　　More than of wont my genius, lest it warp
And run where Virtue is not to constrain,
　　So that if good star or aught better still
　　Enrich me, I may not grudge myself the gain.
Like fire-flies that the peasant on the hill,
　　Reposing in that season, when he who shines
　　To light our world his face doth least conceal,
At that hour when the fly to gnat resigns,
　　Sees glimmering down along the valley broad,
　　There, where perhaps he ploughs or tends the vines,—　　30

131. *lady:* Beatrice.　4. *Thieves:* in the preceding canto.　7. *truth . . . morning:* Morning dreams were considered prophetic.

So numerous the flames in the Eighth Chasm glowed
   Down all its depth, laid open to mine eyes
   Soon as I came to where the bottom showed.
As he who avenged him by the bears saw rise
   The fiery chariot that Elijah° bore
   With horses mounting straight into the skies,
For follow it with his eyes he could not more
   Than to behold only the flame serene
   Like to a little cloud above him soar;
Thus moved along the throat of that ravine   40
   Each flame, for what it stole it doth not show,
   And within each a sinner is, unseen.
I stood upon the bridge, rising tip-toe:
   Had I not caught a rock and on it leant
   I should have fallen, without thrust or blow.
The Guide, who saw me gazing thus attent,
   Said: "Within these fires are the spirits confined,
   Burned by the shroud within which they are pent."
"Master," I answered, "this had I divined
   Myself already, which thou makest plain.   50
   And ev'n now was the question in my mind:
Who is in that fire which comes so torn in twain
   As if it rose above the pyre that bare
   Eteocles° beside his brother slain?"
He answered me: "Ulysses suffers there,
   And Diomed;° as they braved Heaven's wrath before
   Together, now its vengeance must they share.
Within their flame tormented, they deplore
   The Horse and its deceiving ambuscade
   Which opened for Rome's gentle seed the door.   60
And they lament the guile, whereby the shade
   Of Deidamia° for Achilles rues;
   And for Palladium° stolen are they paid."
"If they within those sparks a voice can use,

---

35. *Elijah:* The ascent of Elijah's fiery chariot to Heaven was witnessed by Elisha, who was then mocked by children for his testimony. The children were in turn eaten by bears. (See 2 Kings 2:23–24.) 54. *Eteocles:* Eteocles and his brother Polynices, sons of Oedipus, quarrelled over the kingship of Thebes and killed one another. 56. *Ulysses . . . Diomed:* In Dante's tradition, the two Greeks primarily responsible for the ruse of the Wooden Horse, which was the proximate cause of the downfall of Troy. 62. *Deidamia:* princess who loved Achilles. 63. *Palladium:* statue of Athena held sacred by the Trojans and stolen by the Greeks.

Master," I said, "I pray thee of thy grace—
A prayer that strongly as a thousand sues—
Forbid me not to tarry in this place
　　Until the hornéd flame blow hitherward:
　　See, toward it how the longing bends my face."
And he to me: "The thing thou hast implored　　　　70
　　Deserveth praise: and for that cause thy need
　　Is answered: yet refrain thy tongue from word.
Leave me to speak, for well thy wish I read.
　　But they, since they were Greeks, might turn aside,
　　It may be, and thy voice disdain to heed."
After the fire had come, where to my Guide
　　Time and the place seemed fit, I heard him frame
　　His speech upon this manner, as he cried:
"O ye who are two within a single flame,
　　If while I lived, merit of you I won,　　　　　　80
　　If merit, much or little, had by name,
When the great verse I made beneath the sun,
　　Move not, but let the one of you be heard
　　Tell where he went to perish, being undone."
The greater horn of the ancient flame was stirred
　　To shudder and make a murmur, like a fire
　　When in the wind it struggles and is blurred,
Then tossed upon a flickering crest yet higher,
　　As it had been a tongue that spoke, it cast
　　A voice forth from the strength of its desire,　　90
Saying: "When I from Circe° broke at last,
　　Who more than a year by Gaeta (before
　　Aeneas had so named it) held me fast,
Not sweet son, nor revered old father, nor
　　The long-due love which was to have made glad
　　Penelope° for all the pain she bore,
Could conquer the inward hunger that I had
　　To master earth's experience, and to attain
　　Knowledge of man's mind, both the good and bad.
But I put out on the deep, open main　　　　　　100
　　With one ship only, and with that little band
　　Which chose not to desert me; far as Spain,
Far as Morocco, either shore I scanned.
　　Sardinia's isle I coasted, steering true,
　　And the isles of which that water bathes the strand.
I and my crew were old and stiff of thew

91. *Circe:* sorceress who turned men to swine. 96. *Penelope:* wife of Ulysses.

When, at the narrow strait, we could discern
   The boundaries Hercules° set far in view
That none should dare beyond, or further learn.
   Already I had Sevilla on the right,   110
   And on the larboard Ceuta lay astern.
'Brothers,' I said, 'who manfully, despite
   Ten thousand perils, have attained the West,
   In the brief vigil that remains of light
To feel in, stoop not to renounce the quest
   Of what may in the sun's path be essayed,
   The world that never mankind hath possessed.
Think on the seed ye spring from! Ye were made
   Not to live life of brute beasts of the field
   But follow virtue and knowledge unafraid.'   120
With such few words their spirit so I steel'd,
   That I thereafter scarce could have contained
   My comrades from the voyage, had I willed.
And, our poop° turned to where the Morning reigned,
   We made, for the mad flight, wings of our oars,
   And on the left continually we gained.
By now the Night beheld within her course
   All stars of the other pole, and ours so low,
   It was not lifted from the ocean-floors.
Five times the light had been re-kindled slow   130
   Beneath the moon and quenched as oft, since we
   Broached the high venture we were plighted to,
When there arose a mountain° in the sea,
   Dimm'd by the distance: loftier than aught
   That ever I beheld, it seemed to be.
Then we rejoiced; but soon to grief were brought.
   A storm came out of the strange land, and found
   The ship, and violently the forepart caught.
Three times it made her to spin round and round
   With all the waves; and, as Another chose,   140
   The fourth time,° heaved the poop up, the prow drowned,
Till over us we heard the waters close."

108. *Hercules:* The Strait of Gibraltar was known as the Pillars of Hercules and
was the western boundary of the known world. 124. *poop:* stern of the ship.
127–129. *By . . . ocean-floors:* That is, once having crossed the equator, Ulysses
could see the stars of the southern hemisphere. 133. *mountain:* Mount of Purgatory. 139–141. *Three . . . time:* See *Aeneid* I, 116f. for a similar description of
a shipwreck.

CANTO XXVII

Quieted now, the flame rose all upright,
   Having no more to speak, and with the accord
   Of the sweet poet was moving from our sight
When another, that came on behind it, toward
   Its summit caused us to direct our eyes
   Because of the wild sound that from it roared.
As the Sicilian bull,° that with the cries
   Of him (and it was justice) bellowed first
   Who with his file had shaped it in that guise,
Kept bellowing as the sufferer's voice outburst,   10
   So that although it was of brass compact
   The metal seemed with agony transpierced;
Thus from the fire at first, since a way lacked
   For issue, the despairing words up-cast
   Were changed into its language by the tract;
But after they had found their road at last
   Up to the tip, imparting to the flame
   The trembling the tongue gave them as they passed,
We heard it say: "O thou at whom I aim
   My voice,° who used'st speech of Lombardy   20
   Saying, 'Now go, no more of thee I claim,'
Though over-tardy I have come, maybe,
   Speak with me, so it not irk thee and if thou wilt:
   Thou seest, although I burn, it irks not me.
If into this blind world thou art but now spilt
   From that sweet Latin country whence I bore
   Hither the entire burden of my guilt,
Tell me if Romagna now have peace or war;
   For I was of the mountains there, between
   Urbino and where the springs of Tiber pour."   30
Still all attentive downward did I lean,

---

7. *Sicilian bull*: Perillus, who invented the brazen bull in which the tyrant of Agrigentum (c. 570–554 B.C.) is said to have roasted alive the victims of his cruelty, was the first to die in his own invention. The contrivance caused the shrieks of those inside it to sound like the bellowing of a bull.   20–30. *My voice*: voice of Guido da Montefeltro, one of the great Ghibellines of Romagna. Pope Boniface VIII, whom Dante hated, invited Guido to serve as advisor in the papal dispute with the Colonna family. Guido urged the pope to violate the truce he had with the Colonna and to destroy Palestrina, the stronghold in which they had taken refuge.

When soft my Leader touched me on the side
Saying, "Speak thou; a Latin this has been."
To him without ado then I replied,
    Having no need my answer° to prepare:
    "O spirit that there enshrouded dost abide,
Not now is thy Romagna, and was not e'er,
    Without war in her tyrants' hearts; but blood
    Of battle in open field I left not there.
Ravenna stands as long years it hath stood,   40
    Where covering Cervia with vans outspread
    Polenta's Eagle over it doth brood.
The city that of the French made slaughter red
    And ere that proved its fortitude so long,
    Under the Green Paws hides once more its head.
The old mastiff of Verrucchio and the young,
    Who brought Montagna into such evil state,
    After their wont still tear where they have clung.
Guideth Lamone's and Santerno's fate
    The young Lion of the white lair, changing side   50
    Winter and summer, with the seasons' date.
And that city the Savio flows beside,
    Even as it lies between the hill and plain,
    Tyranny and freedom do its life divide.
Now who thou art declare to us, nor refrain
    In harness more than others have been hard,
    So may thy name on earth its front maintain."
When for awhile the flame had shrilled and roared
    After its manner, the sharp tip it swayed
    This way and that, and then this breath outpoured: 60
"If I believed that my reply were made°
    To one who could revisit earth, this flame
    Would be at rest, and its commotion laid.
But seeing that alive none ever came
    Back from this pit, if it be truth I hear,
    I answer without dread of injured fame.
I was a man of arms, then Cordelier,°
    Hoping, so girdled, in my ways to amend;
    And certainly that hope had come entire

35–51. *my answer:* Dante's response refers to various battles and personages in Romagna's bloody history. 61–66. *made:* The first six lines of Guido's second speech were used by T. S. Eliot as the epigraph for "The Love Song of J. Alfred Prufrock." 67. *Cordelier:* a Franciscan friar.

But for the Great Priest,° whom may ill attend,   70
   Who brought me back into my sins of old,
   And how and why I'll have thee comprehend.
Whilst I was bones and pulp and in the mould
   My mother made for me, my deeds were those
   Of the sly fox, not of the lion bold.
All cunning stratagems and words that gloze
   I knew, and mastered the uses of deceit
   So that to earth's end rumour of it goes.
When at the age which counselleth retreat
   I saw me arrived, the which should all constrain   80
   To strike the sail and gather in the sheet,
That which before had pleased me now was pain,
   And from the world a penitent I withdrew.
   Ah, miserable! it should have been my gain.
The prince of the new Pharisees, who knew
   How to wage war beside the Lateran
   And not with Saracen and not with Jew,
For each one of his foes was Christian,
   And none to conquer Acre's fort had gone
   Nor trafficked in the land of the Soldán,°   90
Regarding neither the office of his throne
   Nor the Holy Orders, nor in me that cord
   Which used to make lean those that girt it on,
As on Soracte Constantine implored
   Sylvester's art his leprosy° to heal,
   So for my mastery me this man conjured
To cure his prideful fever, and made appeal
   To me for counsel: and I kept me mute,
   For like a drunkard seemed his words to reel.
And then he spoke: 'Let not thy heart misdoubt;   100
   Here I absolve thee. Now instruct me how I
   May Palestrina from the earth uproot.
Heaven, as thou knowest, I have authority
   To unlock and lock: for double is the key,°
   Which he who came before° me prized not high.'

70. *Great Priest:* Pope Boniface VIII.   90. *Soldán:* Guido's point is that Boniface was fighting for his own political aims in Italy, while Acre, the last Christian stronghold in Palestine, was falling to the Saracens.   95. *leprosy:* Legend
has it that Pope Sylvester (Pope from 314 to 335) left his hiding place on Mount
Soracte to convert the Emperor Constantine to Christianity, while also curing his
leprosy.   104. *key:* The Popes are thought of as inheritors of St. Peter's keys of
the Kingdom (see Matt. 16:19).   105. *he . . . before:* Celestine V, pope who
abdicated in favor of Boniface (see Canto III, 60).

Then that strong argument enforcing me
  To think silence the worst counsel of all,
  I said, 'Since, Father, I am cleansed by thee
Of that guilt into which I now must fall,
  Wouldst thou in the high seat hold triumphant head,   110
  Make large thy promise, its fulfilment small.'
Francis came afterwards, when I was dead,
  To take me; and one of the Black Cherubim°
  Denied him: 'Thou wilt do me wrong,' he said.
'Among my minions must I carry him
  Because he gave the treacherous advice,
  Since when by the hair I have held him, every limb.
For the unrepentant unabsolvèd dies,
  Nor can a soul repent and will the sin
  At once; in this a contradiction lies.'   120
O wretched me! How startled was I then,
  When seizing me he said: 'Thou thoughtest not,
  May be, that I had a logician been!'
To Minos then he bore me; he straightway got
  His tail eight times around his horny side
  And biting on it then with anger hot,
'To the thievish fire this sinner goes,' he cried.
  Therefore I, where thou seëst me, am borne
  Lost in this swathing, and in grief abide."
When he had ended thus his words forlorn,   130
  The flame departed sorrowing, all frayed
  With struggle and tossing upward its sharp horn.
I and my Guide with me passed on, and made
  Along the cliff to the other arch up-built
  Over the fosse° in which their fee is paid
To those who, sowing discord, harvest guilt.

CANTO XXXIII

That sinner° raised up from the brute repast
  His mouth, wiping it on the hairs left few
  About the head he had all behind made waste.
Then he began: "Thou willest that I renew
  Desperate grief, that wrings my very heart

---

113. *Black Cherubim*: fallen angels. This wicked spirit knows Guido's sinful soul well enough to deny even St. Francis' own appeal for Guido's salvation. 135. *fosse*: ditch. 1. *That sinner*: In the concluding lines of the last canto Dante had encountered Count Ugolino gnawing upon the head of his enemy, the Archbishop Ruggieri.

Even at the thought, before I tell it you.
But if my words prove seed for fruit to start
  Of infamy for the traitor I gnaw now
  Thou shalt hear words that hot with weeping smart.
Albeit I know not who thou art, nor how   10
  Thou hast descended hither, Florentine,
  Unless thy speech deceive me, seemest thou.
Know then that I was the Count Ugolin,°
  And this man Roger, the Archbishop: why
  I neighbour him so close, shall now be seen.
That by the malice of his plotting I,
  Trusting in him, was seized by treachery,
  Needs not to tell, nor that I came to die.
But what hath not yet been reported thee,
  How cruel was that dying, hear, and then   20
  Judge with what injury he hath injured me.
The narrow slit within the prison-pen
  That has from me the name of Famine's Tower
  (And it must yet imprison other men)
Had shown me through its chink the beam of more
  Than one moon, when the dream of evil taste
  For me the curtain of the future tore.
This man appeared as master and lord who chased
  The wolf, and the wolf-cubs, over the mount
  That lets not Pisan eyes on Lucca rest.   30
Hounds, trained and lean and eager, led the hunt
  Where with Gualandi and Sismondi went
  Lanfranchi;° these he had posted in the front.
Full soon it seemed both sire and sons were spent;
  And in my vision the strained flanks grew red
  Where by the tearing teeth the flesh was rent.
When I awoke before the dawn, in dread,
  I heard my children crying in their sleep,
  Them who were with me, and they cried for bread.
Cruel art thou if thou from tears canst keep   40
  To think of what my heart misgave in fear.
  If thou weep not, at what then canst thou weep?
By now they were awake, and the hour drew near
  When food should be set by us on the floor.
  Still in the trouble of our dreams we were:

13. *Count Ugolin:* Count Ugolino, head of the Guelph party in Pisa, who
treacherously intrigued with the Ghibellines of that city and was betrayed by
their leader, Ruggieri degli Ubaldini, Archbishop of Pisa.   32–33. *Gualandi*
. . . *Lanfranchi:* three Ghibelline allies of the archbishop.

And down in the horrible tower I heard the door
   Nailed up. Without a word I looked anew
   Into my sons' faces, all the four.
I wept not, so to stone within I grew.
   They wept; and one, my little Anselm, cried: 50
   'You look so, Father, what has come on you?'
But I shed not a tear, neither replied
   All that day nor the next night, until dawn
   Of a new day over the world rose wide.
A little of light crept in upon the stone
   Of that dungeon of woe; and I saw there
   On those four faces the aspect of my own.
I bit upon both hands in my despair;
   And they supposing it was in the access
   Of hunger, rose up with a sudden prayer,   60
And said: 'O Father, it will hurt much less
   If you of us eat: take what once you gave
   To clothe us, this flesh of our wretchedness.'
Then, not to make them sadder, I made me brave.
   That day and the one after we were dumb.
   Hard earth, couldst thou not open for our grave?
But when to the fourth morning we were come,
   Gaddo at my feet stretched himself with a cry:
   'Father, why won't you help me?' and lay numb
And there died. Ev'n as thou seest me, saw I,   70
   One after the other, the three fall: they drew,
   Between the fifth and sixth day, their last sigh.
I, blind now, groping arms about them threw,
   And still called on them that were two days gone.
   Then fasting° did what anguish could not do."
He ceased, and twisting round his eyes, thereon
   Seized again on the lamentable skull
   With teeth strong as a dog's upon the bone.
Ah, Pisa! thou offence to the whole people
   Of the fair land where sound is heard of Sì,°   80
   Since vengeance in thy neighbours' hands is dull,
Caprara and Gorgona shifted be°

---

75. *fasting . . . do:* There is no contemporary evidence, only some morbid inclination among nineteenth-century critics, to suggest that Ugolino ate his own children. 80. *Sì:* The various tongues of Europe were designated by the word used in each for "yes." 82. *Caprara . . . be:* That is, let these two islands move back toward land, thus clogging up the river Arno's mouth and drowning all the inhabitants of Pisa.

Into Arno's mouth, and Arno back be rolled,
   That every living soul be drowned in thee!
For if Count Ugolin by treachery sold
   Thy forts, it was not cause thou shouldst torment
   His little sons, whatever of him was told.
Their youth, O thou new Thebes, made innocent
   Uguiccione and Brigata, and those
   Two others named already in that lament.   90
We passed on, where the frost imprisons close
   Another crew, stark in a rugged heap,
   Not bent down, but reversed all where they froze.
The very weeping there forbids to weep;
   And the grief, finding in the eyes a stop,
   Turns inward, to make anguish bite more deep.
For their first tears collect in one great drop,
   And like a vizor of crystal, in the space
   Beneath the brows, fill all the hollow up.
And now although, as with a callous place   100
   Upon the skin, because the cold stung so,
   All feeling had departed from my face,
It seemed as if I felt some wind to blow.
   Wherefore I: "Master, who is it moves this air?
   Is not all heat extinguished here below?"
Whereto he answered: "Soon shalt thou be where,
   Seeing the cause which poureth down the gust,
   Thine eye to this the answer shall declare."
And one sad shadow amid the icy crust
   Cried to us: "O ye souls, so cruel found,   110
   That into the last dungeon ye are thrust,
Raise the stiff veils wherein my face is bound,
   So that the grief which chokes my heart have vent
   A little, ere the weeping harden round."
Wherefore I: "Tell me, if I to this consent,
   Who thou art; if I do not succour thee,
   May I to the bottom of the ice be sent."
"I am Friar Alberic," ° then he answered me;
   "He of the fruits out of the bad garden,
   Who, dates for figs, receive here my full fee."   120

---

118. *Friar Alberic:* Friar Alberigo. Because his younger brother hit him during an argument, Alberigo invited him and his son to a banquet a year later, where he had them both poisoned when he gave the command, "Bring the fruit." This gives at least an overtone to the proverb he cites in line 120.

"Oh," replied I to him, "thou art dead, then,
   Already?" He answered, "I have no knowledge
   How stands my body in the world of men.
This Ptolomea° hath such privilege
   That often a soul falls down into this place
   Ere Atropos° the fated thread abridge.
And that thou may'st more willingly the glaze
   Of tears wipe from my cheek-bones' nakedness,
   Know that, on the instant when the soul betrays,
As I did, comes a demon to possess   130
   Its body, and thenceforth ruleth over it
   Until the timed hour come for its decease.
The soul falls headlong to this cistern-pit:
   The body of him who winters there behind
   Perhaps among men still appears to sit.
Thou must, if newly come, call it to mind;
   It is Ser Branca d' Oria.° Years enough
   Have passed since he was to his prison assigned."
"I think," I said, "that thou dost lie; whereof
   Proof is, that Branca d' Oria never died,   140
   And eats, drinks, sleeps, and puts clothes on and off."
"Up there with the Evil Talons," he replied,
   "Where sticky pitch is boiling in its bed,
   Not yet had Michel Zanche come to bide,
When this man left a devil in his stead
   In his own body, and in one of his house
   Who with him played the traitor and did the deed.
But stretch thy hand out hither and unclose
   My eyes for me." And I unclosed them not;
   And to be rude to him was courteous.   150
Ah, Genoese, who have utterly forgot
   All honesty, and in corruption abound,
   Why from the earth will none your people blot?
For with Romagna's evillest spirit I found
   One of you, who, for deeds he did contrive
   Even now in soul is in Cocytus° drowned
And still in body appears on earth alive.

---

124. *Ptolomea*: name of this division of Hell. 126. *Atropos*: one of the three
Fates. The sinners of Ptolomea, betrayers of guests, die spiritually at once, their
souls coming here while their bodies continue to live on the earth. 137. *Branca
d'Oria*: He poisoned his father-in-law, Michel Zanche, at a banquet. 156.
Cocytus: frozen lake, nethermost of Hell's rivers, in which the action of these
last cantos of *Inferno* occurs.

CANTO XXXIV

The banners of the King of Hell proceed
    Toward us," my Guide said. "If thine eyes avail
    To espy him, forward gaze and give good heed."
As when the thick autumnal mists exhale,
    Or when night draws down on our hemisphere,
    A mill shows far away with turning sail,
Such structure to my eyes seemed now to appear;
    And, for the wind that blew, I shrank behind
    My Master, because else no rock was near.
Now was I (verse for them I fear to find)   10
    There where the frozen spirits as in glass
    Were covered wholly, and there like straw they shined.
Some prostrate lie, some standing in their place,
    This on its head, that on its soles upright,
    Another like a bow bends feet to face.
When we had gone so far as appeared right
    For the good Master's purpose to reveal
    To me the creature that was once so bright,°
He turned about and stayed me upon my heel,
    Saying: "Behold Dis, and the place behold   20
    Where thou thy soul with fortitude must steel."
How faint I then became, how frozen cold,
    Ask me not, Reader; for I write it not,
    Because all speech would fail, whate'er it told.
I died not, yet of life remained no jot.
    Think thou then, if of wit thou hast any share,
    What I became, deprived of either lot.
The Emperor of the kingdom of despair
    From the mid-breast emerged out of the ice;
    And I may with a giant more compare   30
Than giants with those monstrous arms of his:
    Consider now how huge must be the whole
    Proportioned to the part of such a size.
If he was once fair as he now is foul,
    And 'gainst his Maker dared his brows to raise,
    Fitly from him all streams of sorrow roll.
O what a marvel smote me with amaze
    When I beheld three faces on his head!

18. *bright:* Satan is also called Lucifer, the shining one; *Dis* (l. 20); and *Beelze-bub* (l. 128).

The one in front showed crimson° to my gaze;
Thereunto were the other faces wed   40
    Over the middle of either shoulder's height,
    And where the crest would be, their union made.
The right was coloured between yellow and white,
    The left was such to look upon as those
    Who come from where Nile flows out of the night.
Two mighty wings from under each arose
    Commeasurable with so great a bird:
    Never did sails at sea such form disclose.
Feathers they had not, but like bats appeared
    The fashion of them, and with these he flapped   50
    So that three winds were from their motion stirred.
Thence all Cocytus was in frost enwrapt.
    He wept with six eyes, and the tears beneath
    Over three chins with bloody slaver dropt.
At each mouth he was tearing with his teeth
    A sinner, as is flax by heckle frayed;
    Each of the three of them so suffereth.
The one in front naught of the biting made
    Beside the clawing, which at whiles so wrought
    That on the back the skin remained all flayed.   60
"That soul up there to the worst penance brought
    Is Judas the Iscariot," spoke my Lord.
    "His head within, he plies his legs without.
Of the other two, hanging with head downward,
    Brutus it is whom the black mouth doth maul.
    See how he writhes and utters not a word!
Cassius the other who seems so large to sprawl
    But night° again is rising; time is now
    That we depart from hence. We have seen all."
I clung about his neck, he showed me how,   70
    And choosing well the time and place to trust,
    When the great wings were opened wide enow,
He clutched him to the shaggy-sided bust,
    And climbed from tuft to tuft down, slipping by
    Between the matted hair and icy crust.
When we were come to that part where the thigh
    Turns on the thickness of the haunches' swell,

39. *crimson:* The colors of Satan's three heads would seem to correspond to a perverse image of the three attributes of the Godhead, thus yielding hatred, impotence, and ignorance. 68. *night:* Twenty-four hours have passed; it is the evening before Easter Sunday.

My Guide with effort and with difficulty
Turned his head where his feet had been; the fell
   He grappled then as one who is mounting, so   80
   That I conceived turning back to Hell.
"Hold fast by me, for needs must that we go,"
   Said my Guide, panting like a man quite spent,
   "By such a ladder from the core of woe."
And issuing through the rock where it was rent
   He made me sit upon the rock's edge there;
   Then toward me moved, eye upon step intent.
I lifted up my eyes, and Lucifer
   Thought to have seen as I had left him last;
   And saw him with legs uppermost appear.
And if into perplexity I was cast
   Let them be judge who are so gross of wit
   They see not what the point is I had passed.
"Rise up now," said the Master, "upon thy feet.
   The way is long, and arduous the road.
   The sun in mid-tierce° now repairs his heat."
No palace-chamber was it that now showed
   Its flinty floor, but natural dungeon this,
   Which but a starving° of the light allowed.
"Master, before I pluck me from the abyss,"   100
   Said I, when I had risen erect, "speak on
   A little, so my error to dismiss.
Where is the ice? And how is he, head prone,
   Thus fixt? And how so soon is it possible
   The sun from evening has to morning run?"
And he: "Thou dost imagine thyself still
   On the other side of the centre, where I gript
   The hair of the Worm that thrids° the earth with ill.
There wast thou while with thee I downward slipt;
   But when I turned round, from that point we fled   110
   Whereonto weight from every part is heaped.
Now thou art under the hemisphere's deep bed
   Opposite that where spreads the continent
   Of land, 'neath whose meridian perishèd
The Man who sinless came and sinless went.
   Thou hast thy feet upon a little sphere,
   Whose surface is Giudecca's complement;
When it is evening there, 'tis morning here.

96. *mid-tierce:* about 7:30 A.M.   99. *starving . . . allowed:* kept out all but a little light. 108. *thrids:* pierces.

And he whose hair for us a ladder made
  Is still fixed as before and doth not stir.   120
He fell from Heaven on this side and there stayed.
  And all the land which ere that stood forth dry,
  Covered itself with sea, by him dismayed,
And came to our hemisphere; and, him to fly
  Perhaps, what on this side is seen around
  Left its place here void and shot up on high."
There is a cave that stretches underground
  Far from Beelzebub as his tomb extends,
  Known not by sight, but only by the sound
Of a stream flowing, that therein descends   130
  Along the hollow of rock that it has gnawed,
  Nor falleth steeply down, but winds and bends.
The Guide and I, entering that secret road,
  Toiled to return into the world of light,
  Nor thought on any resting-place bestowed.
We climbed, he first, I following, till to sight
  Appeared those things of beauty that heaven wears
  Glimpsed through a rounded opening, faintly bright,
Thence issuing, we beheld again the stars.°

139. stars: Each of the three parts of the *Divine Comedy* ends with this word, reminding the reader of the beauty of God's creation, which, like Dante's poem itself, is beautiful only to draw attention to the truth of God.

Giovanni Boccaccio

FROM *The Decameron*

TRANSLATED BY RICHARD ALDINGTON

Giovanni Boccaccio (1313–1375)

The ITALIAN FOURTEENTH CENTURY WAS A PERIOD OF EX-traordinary literary activity. It served all of Europe by providing the greatest single "medieval" work—Dante's *Divine Comedy*—as well as providing later vernacular works like Petrarch's poems to Laura and Boccaccio's *Decameron,* which became models for Renaissance forms throughout Europe.

Boccaccio was born in Paris, the son of a Florentine businessman, and was brought to Italy while still a child. Although his father wanted him to go into business, Boccaccio soon abandoned this career, which he found dull, and turned to canon law and literature. Boccaccio's early works are frequently concerned with love. Written in the vernacular, rather than in Latin, they often celebrate the lady he called Fiammetta. After 1351, however, Boccaccio came under the sway of Petrarch, who had officially turned his back on vernacular love poetry. Petrarch's stern Humanism, which took the form of reverence for the Latin ancients, especially Cicero, made Boccaccio a disciple of weightier subjects. The several Latin works—a genealogy of the pagan gods in fifteen books was perhaps the most influential—which Boccaccio produced in this vein were of major importance to his lettered contemporaries but are largely unread today. His last work was a commentary on Dante's *Inferno,* delivered in Florence in public lectures that were cut short by Boccaccio's final illness. Such devotion to another poet's work is a rare event in the history of literary activity; rarely, if ever, has a man who was one of the greatest writers of his own time been content to play the role of handmaid to the work of another.

The *Decameron* marks the beginning of major vernacular prose fiction in modern times. It is hard to imagine the excitement with which it was received by Boccaccio's contemporaries, for prose fiction, though existent, was not considered a form worthy of serious men of letters. Boccaccio's one hundred tales (the number draws attention to the author's reverence for Dante's *Comedy,* with its one hundred cantos) take their pretext and their situation from the terrible Black Plague of 1348, in which sixty percent of the population of Florence died.

The Decameron

The First Day

HERE BEGINS THE FIRST DAY OF THE DECAMERON, WHEREIN, AFTER THE AUTHOR HAS SHOWED THE REASONS WHY CERTAIN PERSONS GATHERED TO TELL TALES, THEY TREAT OF ANY SUBJECT PLEASING TO THEM. . . .

Most gracious ladies, knowing that you are all by nature pitiful,[1] I know that in your judgment this work will seem to have a painful and sad origin. For it brings to mind the unhappy recollection of that late dreadful plague, so pernicious to all who saw or heard of it. But I would not have this frighten you from reading further, as though you were to pass through nothing but sighs and tears in your reading. This dreary opening will be like climbing a steep mountain side to a most beautiful and delightful valley, which appears the more pleasant in proportion to the difficulty of the ascent. The end of happiness is pain, and in like manner misery ends in unexpected happiness.

This brief fatigue (I say brief, because it occupies only a few words) is quickly followed by pleasantness and delight, as I promised you above; which, if I had not promised, you would not expect perhaps from this opening. Indeed, if I could have taken you by any other way than this, which I know to be rough, I would gladly have done so; but since I cannot otherwise tell you how the tales you are about to read came to be told, I am forced by necessity to write in this manner.

In the year 1348 after the fruitful incarnation of the Son of God, that most beautiful of Italian cities, noble Florence, was attacked by deadly plague. It started in the East either through the influence of the heavenly bodies or because God's just anger with our wicked deeds sent it as a punishment to mortal men; and in a few years killed an innumerable quantity of people. Ceaselessly passing from place to place, it extended its miserable length over the West. Against this plague all human wisdom and foresight were vain. Orders had been given to cleanse the city of filth, the

---

[1] full of pity.

entry of any sick person was forbidden, much advice was given for keeping healthy; at the same time humble supplications were made to God by pious persons in processions and otherwise. And yet, in the beginning of the spring of the year mentioned, its horrible results began to appear, and in a miraculous manner. The symptoms were not the same as in the East, where a gush of blood from the nose was the plain sign of inevitable death; but it began both in men and women with certain swellings in the groin or under the armpit. They grew to the size of a small apple or an egg, more or less, and were vulgarly called tumours. In a short space of time these tumours spread from the two parts named all over the body. Soon after this the symptoms changed and black and purple spots appeared on the arms or thighs or any other part of the body, sometimes a few large ones, sometimes many little ones. These spots were a certain sign of death, just as the original tumour had been and still remained.

No doctor's advice, no medicine could overcome or alleviate this disease. An enormous number of ignorant men and women set up as doctors in addition to those who were trained. Either the disease was such that no treatment was possible or the doctors were so ignorant that they did not know what caused it, and consequently could not administer the proper remedy. In any case very few recovered; most people died within about three days of the appearance of the tumours described above, most of them without any fever or other symptoms.

The violence of this disease was such that the sick communicated it to the healthy who came near them, just as a fire catches anything dry or oily near it. And it even went further. To speak to or go near the sick brought infection and a common death to the living; and moreover, to touch the clothes or anything else the sick had touched or worn gave the disease to the person touching.

What I am about to tell now is a marvelous thing to hear; and if I and others had not seen it with our own eyes I would not dare to write it, however much I was willing to believe and whatever the good faith of the person from whom I heard it. So violent was the malignancy of this plague that it was communicated, not only from one man to another, but from the garments of a sick or dead man to animals of another species, which caught the disease in that way and very quickly died of it. One day among other occasions I saw with my own eyes (as I said just now) the rags left lying in the street of a poor man who had died of the plague; two pigs came along and, as their habit is, turned the clothes over with their snouts and then munched at them, with the result that they both fell dead almost at once on the rags, as if they had been poisoned.

From these and similar or greater occurrences, such fear and fanciful notions took possession of the living that almost all of them adopted the same cruel policy, which was entirely to avoid the sick and everything belonging to them. By so doing, each one thought he would secure his own safety.

Some thought that moderate living and the avoidance of all superfluity would preserve them from the epidemic. They formed small communities, living entirely separate from everybody else. They shut themselves up in houses where there were no sick, eating the finest food and drinking the best wine very temperately, avoiding all excess, allowing no news or discussion of death and sickness, and passing the time in music and suchlike pleasures. Others thought just the opposite. They thought the sure cure for the plague was to drink and be merry, to go about singing and amusing themselves, satisfying every appetite they could, laughing and jesting at what happened. They put their words into practice, spent day and night going from tavern to tavern, drinking immoderately, or went into other people's houses, doing only those things which pleased them. This they could easily do because everyone felt doomed and had abandoned his property, so that most houses became common property and any stranger who went in made use of them as if he had owned them. And with all this bestial behaviour, they avoided the sick as much as possible.

In this suffering and misery of our city, the authority of human and divine laws almost disappeared, for, like other men, the ministers and the executors of the laws were all dead or sick or shut up with their families, so that no duties were carried out. Every man was therefore able to do as he pleased.

Many others adopted a course of life midway between the two just described. They did not restrict their victuals so much as the former, nor allow themselves to be drunken and dissolute like the latter, but satisfied their appetites moderately. They did not shut themselves up, but went about, carrying flowers or scented herbs or perfumes in their hands, in the belief that it was an excellent thing to comfort the brain with such odours; for the whole air was infected with the smell of dead bodies, of sick persons and medicines.

Others again held a still more cruel opinion, which they thought would keep them safe. They said that the only medicine against the plaguestricken was to go right away from them. Men and women, convinced of this and caring about nothing but themselves, abandoned their own city, their own houses, their dwellings, their relatives, their property, and went abroad or at least to the country round Florence, as if God's wrath in punishing men's wickedness with this plague would not follow them but strike only those who remained within the walls of the city, or as if they thought nobody in the city would remain alive and that its last hour had come.

Not everyone who adopted any of these various opinions died, nor did all escape. Some when they were still healthy had set the example of avoiding the sick, and, falling ill themselves, died untended.

One citizen avoided another, hardly any neighbour troubled about others, relatives never or hardly ever visited each other. Moreover, such terror was struck into the hearts of men and women by this calamity, that brother abandoned brother, and the uncle his nephew, and the sister her brother, and very often the wife her husband. What is even worse and nearly incredible is that fathers and mothers refused to see and tend their children, as if they had not been theirs.

Thus, a multitude of sick men and women were left without any care except from the charity of friends (but these were few), or the greed of servants, though not many of these could be had even for high wages. Moreover, most of them were coarse-minded men and women, who did little more than bring the sick what they asked for or watched over them when they were dying. And very often these servants lost their lives and their earnings. Since the sick were thus abandoned by neighbours, relatives and friends, while servants were scarce, a habit sprang up which had never been heard of before. Beautiful and noble women, when they fell sick, did not scruple to take a young or old manservant, whoever he might be, and with no sort of shame, expose every part of their bodies to these men as if they had been women, for they were compelled by the necessity of their sickness to do so. This, perhaps, was a cause of looser morals in those women who survived.

In this way many people died who might have been saved if they had been looked after. Owing to the lack of attendants for the sick and the violence of the plague, such a multitude of people in the city died day and night that it was stupefying to hear of, let alone to see. From sheer necessity, then, several ancient customs were quite altered among the survivors.

The custom had been (as we still see it today), that women relatives and neighbours should gather at the house of the deceased, and there lament with the family. At the same time the men would gather at the door with the male neighbours and other citizens. Then came the clergy, few or many according to the dead person's rank; the coffin was placed on the shoulders of his friends and carried with funeral pomp of lighted candles and dirges to the church which the deceased had chosen before dying. But as the fury of the plague increased, this custom wholly or nearly disappeared, and new customs arose. Thus, people died, not only without having a number of women near them, but without a single witness. Very few indeed were honoured with the piteous laments and bitter tears of their relatives, who, on the contrary, spent their time in mirth, feasting and jesting. Even the women abandoned womanly pity and adopted this custom for their own safety. Few were they whose bodies were accompanied to church by more than ten or a dozen neighbours. Nor were these grave and honourable citizens but grave-diggers from the lowest of the people who got themselves called sextons, and performed the task for money. They took up the bier and hurried it off, not to the church chosen by the deceased but to the church nearest, preceded by four or six of the clergy with few candles and often none at all. With the aid of the grave-diggers, the clergy huddled the bodies away in any grave they could find, without giving themselves the trouble of a long or solemn burial service.

The plight of the lower and most of the middle classes was even more pitiful to behold. Most of them remained in their houses, either through poverty or in hopes of safety, and fell sick by thousands. Since they received no care and attention, almost all of them died. Many ended their lives in the streets both at night and during the day; and many others who died in their houses were only known to be dead because the neighbours smelled their decaying bodies. Dead bodies filled every corner. Most of them were treated in the same manner by the survivors, who were more concerned to get rid of their rotting bodies than moved by charity towards the dead. With the aid of porters, if they could get them, they carried the bodies out of the houses and laid them at the doors, where every morning quantities of the dead might be seen. They then were laid on biers, or, as these were often lacking, on tables.

Often a single bier carried two or three bodies, and it happened frequently that a husband and wife, two or three brothers, or father and son were taken off on the same bier. It frequently happened that two priests, each carrying a cross, would go out followed by three or four biers carried by porters; and where the priests thought there was one person to bury, there would be six or eight, and often, even more. Nor were these dead honoured by tears and lighted candles and mourners, for things had reached such a pass that people cared no more for dead men than we care for dead goats. Thus it plainly appeared that what the wise had not learned to endure with patience through the few calamities of ordinary life became a matter of indifference even to the most ignorant people through the greatness of this misfortune.

Such was the multitude of corpses brought to the churches every day and almost every hour that there was not enough consecrated ground to give them burial, especially since they wanted to bury each person in the family grave, according to the old custom. Although the cemeteries were full they were forced to dig huge trenches, where they buried the bodies by hundreds. Here they stowed them away like bales in the hold of a ship and covered them with a little earth, until the whole trench was full.

Not to pry any further into all the details of the miseries which afflicted our city, I shall add that the surrounding country was spared nothing of what befell Florence. The villages on a smaller scale were like the city; in the fields and isolated farms the poor wretched peasants and their families were without doctors and any assistance, and perished in the highways, in their fields and houses, night and day, more like beasts than men. Just as the townsmen became dissolute and indifferent to their work and property, so the peasants, when they saw that death was upon them, entirely neglected the future fruits of their past labours both from the earth and from cattle, and thought only of enjoying what they had. Thus it happened that cows, asses, sheep, goats, pigs, fowls and even dogs, those faithful companions of man, left the farms and wandered at their will through the fields, where the wheat crops stood abandoned, unreaped and ungarnered. Many of these animals seemed endowed with reason, for, after they had pastured all day, they returned to the farms for the night of their own free will, without being driven.

Returning from the country to the city, it may be said that such was the cruelty of Heaven, and perhaps in part of men, that between March and July more than one hundred thousand persons died within the walls of Florence, what between the violence of the plague and the abandonment in which the sick were left by the cowardice of the healthy. And before the plague it was not thought that the whole city held so many people.

Oh, what great palaces, how many fair houses and noble dwellings, once filled with attendants and nobles and ladies, were emptied to the meanest servant! How many famous names and vast possessions and renowned estates were left without an heir! How many gallant men and fair ladies and handsome youths, whom Galen, Hippocrates and Æsculapius[2] themselves would have said were in perfect health, at noon dined with their relatives and friends, and at night supped with their ancestors in the next world!

But it fills me with sorrow to go over so many miseries. Therefore, since I want to pass over all I can leave out, I shall go on to say that when our city was in this condition and almost emptied of inhabitants, one Tuesday morning the venerable church of Santa Maria Novella had scarcely any congregation for divine service except (as I have heard from a person worthy of belief) seven young women in the mourning garments suitable to the times, who were all related by ties of blood, friendship or neighbourship. None of them was older than twenty-eight or younger than eighteen; all were educated and of noble blood, fair to look upon, well-mannered and of graceful modesty. . . .

The seven young women discuss the plight of the city and decide to leave Florence for the country. Three young gentlemen come into the church and are invited to join in the expedition, which they agree to do. All ten leave the next morning and establish themselves in the country estate of one of the ladies. To pass the hottest time of the day as pleasantly as possible, they resolve that each of them will tell one tale every afternoon. The hundred tales of the Decameron *are the result.*

[2] medical authorities of Greek antiquity.

The Fourth Day

Second Tale

FRATE ALBERTO PERSUADES A LADY THAT THE ANGEL GABRIEL IS IN
LOVE WITH HER AND THUS MANAGES TO LIE WITH HER SEVERAL TIMES.
FROM FEAR OF HER RELATIVES HE FLIES FROM HER HOUSE AND TAKES
REFUGE IN THE HOUSE OF A POOR MAN, WHO NEXT DAY TAKES HIM TO
THE PIAZZA AS A WILD MAN OF THE WOODS. HE IS RECOGNISED, AR-
RESTED AND IMPRISONED

. . . They say commonly in proverbial style: A wicked man who is
thought to be good can do evil and yet not have it believed. This gives me ample material to speak on the subject proposed,[3] and at the same time to show
the hypocrisy of the monks. Their gowns are long and wide, their faces artificially pale, their voices humble and pleading when they ask something, loud
and rude when they denounce their own vices in others, and when they declare how they obtain salvation of themselves and others by their gift. Not
as men who seek Paradise, like ourselves, but as if they were its owners and
lords, they allot a more or less eminent place there to everyone who dies,
in accordance with the amount of money he leaves them; and thereby they
first deceive themselves—if they really believe it—and then deceive those
who put faith in their words. If I were permitted to do so, I could soon
show many simple minded persons what is hidden in their ample gowns.
Would to God that all their lies had the same fate as befell a minor friar,
who was no paltry fellow, but was considered one of the best casuists of
Venice. It gives me the greatest pleasure to tell this tale, so that perhaps I
may divert your minds with laughter and amusement from the pity you feel
for Ghismonda's fate.[4]

In Imola, most worthy ladies, there lived a man of wicked and corrupt
life, named Berto della Massa. His evil deeds were so well known to many
people of Imola that no one in Imola would believe him when he spoke
truth, let alone when he lied. Seeing, then, that his tricks were useless there,
he moved in despair to Venice, that welcomer of all wickedness, thinking
that in that town he might make a different use of his vices than he had
done before. As if conscience-stricken for his wicked deeds, he gave signs
of the greatest humility. He became not only the most Catholic of men, but
made himself a minor friar, and took the name of Friar Alberto da Imola.
In this guise he began to pretend to a severe life, praising penitence and

[3] The subject chosen for the tales of the fourth day is the lover whose love has an
unhappy ending. [4] reference to a character in the preceding tale.

abstinence, and never eating flesh or drinking wine when he could not get them good enough for him.

Never before had a thief, a ruffian, a forger, a murderer turned into a great preacher without having abandoned those vices, even when he had practised them secretly. And after he had become a priest, whenever he was celebrating Mass at the altar in the presence of a large congregation, he always wept over the Saviour's Passion, for he was a man who could shed tears whenever he pleased. In short, what with his sermons and his tears, he so beguiled the Venetians that he was trustee and guardian of nearly everyone's will, the keeper of many people's money, the confessor and adviser of most men and women. Thus, from wolf he became shepherd, and in those parts the fame of his sanctity was greater than San Francesco's ever was at Assisi.

Now, it happened that a silly stupid young woman, named Madonna Lisetta da ca Quirino, the wife of a merchant who was away in Flanders with the galleys, went with other women to confess to this holy friar. As she knelt at his feet like the Venetian she was—and they are all fools—he asked her half way through her confession if she had a lover. And she tartly replied:

"Why, messer friar, have you no eyes in your head? Do you think my beauties are no more than these other women's? I could have as many lovers as I wanted. But my beauty is not to be yielded to the love of anybody. How many beauties do you see like mine, for I should be beautiful in Paradise?"

And she went on to say so many things about her beauties that it was tedious to listen to her. Friar Alberto at once saw her weakness, and, feeling that she was ready made to his hand, he fell in love with her. But, reserving his flatteries for another time, he put on his saintly air and began to reprove her, and to say this was vain-glory and other things of the kind. So the lady told him he was a fool, and did not know how to distinguish one beauty from another. And Friar Alberto, not wanting to anger her too much, finished off the confession and let her go with the others.

A few days later he went with a trusted friend to Madonna Lisetta's house and took her aside into a room where they could not be seen. There he fell on his knees before her, and said:

"Madonna, I beseech you for God's sake to forgive me for what I said to you on Sunday when you spoke of your beauty, because I was so severely punished that night I have not been able to get up until today."

Then said Madonna Pot-stick: "And who punished you?"

"I will tell you," said Friar Alberto. "While I was praying that night, as I always do, I suddenly saw a bright light in my cell. Before I could turn to see what it was, I beheld a most beautiful young man with a large stick in his hand, who took me by the cowl, dragged me to my feet and beat me as if to break my bones. I asked him why he did this, and he replied: 'Because you presumed today to reprove the heavenly beauty of Madonna Lisetta whom I love more than anything except God himself.' And I asked: 'Who are you?' And he said he was the Angel Gabriel. 'O my lord,' said I, 'I beg you will pardon me.' And he said: 'I will pardon you on condition that you go to her as soon as you can and obtain her forgiveness. And if she does not forgive you I shall return here, and so deal with you that you will be miserable for the rest of your days.' What he afterwards said to me I dare not tell you until you have pardoned me."

Donna Windy-noddle, who was as sweet as salt, was enchanted at these words, and thought them all true.

"I told you, Friar Alberto," said she, "that mine were heavenly beauties. But, so help me God, I am sorry for you, and to spare you any further trouble I forgive you, if only you will tell me truly what the Angel then said."

"Madonna," replied Friar Alberto, "since you have pardoned me, I will tell you willingly. But, you must not repeat a word of what I tell you to anyone in the world, if you do not want to destroy your happiness, you who are the luckiest woman in the world.

"The Angel Gabriel told me to tell you that he loves you so much he would often have come to spend the night with you, but for his fear of terrifying you. He now sends you a message through me to say that he wants to come to you one night and to spend part of it with you. But he is an Angel, and if he came to you in the form of an Angel you could not touch him; and so he says that for your delight he will come in a man's shape and bids you tell him when you want him to come and in whose shape, and he will come. And so you ought to think yourself more blessed than any other woman living."

Madonna Silly then said she was very glad to have the Angel Gabriel in love with her, because she loved him and always put up a fourpenny candle to him wherever she saw him painted. Whenever he liked to come to her he would be welcome and he would find her alone in her room, on one condition, which was that he would not abandon her for the Virgin Mary whom he was said to be very fond of; and she was inclined to believe this since whenever she saw his picture he was kneeling before the Virgin. In addition, she said that the Angel should come in any shape he pleased— she would not be afraid.

Then said Friar Alberto:

"Madonna, you speak wisely, and I will arrange with him as you say. But you can do me a great favour, which will cost you nothing. The favour is that you will allow him to come in my body. This will be a very great favour because he will take the soul from my body and put it in Heaven, and he will enter into me, and my soul will be in Paradise as long as he remains with you."

Then said Madonna Littlewit:

"I am content. I want you to have this consolation for the stripes you received on my account."

Said Friar Alberto:

"Tonight leave the door of your house open, so that he can come in. Since he is coming in a human body, he can only enter by the door."

The lady replied that this should be done. Friar Alberto departed, and she remained in such a state of delight that her chemise did not touch her backside, and the time she had to wait for the Angel Gabriel seemed like a thousand years.

Friar Alberto thought it better to be a good horseman than an Angel that night, so he fortified himself with all sorts of good cheer, in order not to be unhorsed too easily. He obtained permission to be out that night, and went with his trusted friend to the house of a woman friend, which he had made his starting point more than once before when he was going to ride the mare. From there he went in disguise to the lady's house, and having transformed himself into an Angel with the fripperies he had brought with him, he went upstairs into the lady's bedroom. When she saw something white come in, she kneeled down. The Angel gave her his benediction, raised her to her feet, and signed to her to get into bed. She did so immediately in her willingness to obey, and the Angel got into bed with his devotee.

Friar Alberto was a robust and handsome man and in excellent health. Donna Lisetta was fresh and pretty and found him a very different person from her husband to lie with. That night he flew many times with her without wings, which made her call herself blessed; and in addition he told her a great many things about heavenly glory. Just before dawn, he collected his trappings and returned to his friend, who had kept friendly company with the other woman so that she should not feel afraid by sleeping alone.

After the lady had dined, she went with a woman friend to see Friar Alberto, and gave him news of the Angel Gabriel, telling him how the Angel looked and what he had said about the glory of eternal life, to which she added all sorts of marvellous fables.

"Madonna," said Friar Alberto, "I know not how you were with him, all I know is that last night he came to me, and when I had delivered him your message, he suddenly took my soul to a place where there were more flowers and roses than ever I saw, one of the most delicious places that ever existed, where my soul remained until dawn this morning. But what happened to my body I do not know."

"Didn't I tell you?" said the lady. "Your body lay all night in my arms with the Angel Gabriel. And if you don't believe me, look under your left breast, where I gave the Angel such a kiss that the mark will remain for several days."

Then said Friar Alberto:

"I will do something today which I have not done for a very long time. I shall undress myself to see if what you say is true."

After a lot more chatter, the lady returned home. And Friar Alberto thereafter visited her many times in the guise of an Angel, without the slightest difficulty. But one day Madonna Lisetta was with one of her gossips, and as they were discussing their beauties, she said like the empty-pated fool she was, in order to show off:

"If you knew who was in love with my beauty you would not speak of anyone else's."

The gossip was anxious to hear about it, and knowing Lisetta well, said:

"Madonna, you may be right, but as I do not know whom you mean I shall not change my opinion so easily."

The lady, who had very little sense, then said:

"Gossip, he does not want it talked about, but the person I mean is the Angel Gabriel, who loves me more than himself, so he says, because I am the most beautiful person in the world or the Maremma." [5]

The gossip felt like laughing outright, but restrained herself to keep the conversation going, and said:

"God's faith, Madonna, if you mean the Angel Gabriel and say so, it must be true, but I did not think the angels did such things."

"Gossip," said the lady, "you are wrong. By God's favour, he does it better than my husband, and he tells me they do it up above. But, because he thinks me more beautiful than anyone in Heaven, he has fallen in love with me, and often spends a night with me. So you see!"

As soon as the gossip had left Madonna Lisetta, it seemed like a thousand years to her before she had got into a company where she could laugh at all this. She went to a gathering of women, and told them the whole tale. These women told their husbands and other women, and they told others, and so in less than two days the story was all over Venice. Among others who heard it were the lady's cousins, and, without saying anything to her, they made up their minds to find this Angel and see whether he could fly. So they watched for him every night.

Some rumours of all this came to the ears of Friar Alberto, who went to the lady one night to scold her for it. He was scarcely undressed when her cousins, who had seen him come in, were at the door. Friar Alberto heard them, and guessed what they were. He jumped up, and, having no other means of escape, opened a window overlooking the Grand Canal, from which he threw himself into the water.

The water there was deep; he was a good swimmer, and so did himself no harm. He swam to the other side of the canal and immediately entered

[5] marshy district in western Italy, known for its pestilential climate.

an open house there, begging the goodman for the love of God to save his life, and told him all sorts of lies to explain why he was there naked at that hour of night.

The goodman, who was just setting off on his business, pitied Friar Alberto and put him into bed, telling him to stop there until he came back. He then locked the friar in, and went about his business.

When the lady's cousins entered her room, they found the Angel Gabriel had left his wings behind and flown away. They abused the lady indignantly, and, leaving her very disconsolate, returned home with the Angel's trappings.

Meanwhile, soon after dawn, the goodman was on the Rialto and heard how the Angel Gabriel had gone to lie with Madonna Lisetta the night before, how he had been discovered by her relatives and had thrown himself into the canal, and how nobody knew what had become of him. So he immediately realised that this was the man in his own house. He went home and after much discussion arranged that the Friar should pay him fifty ducats not to hand him over to the cousins; and this was done. Friar Alberto then wanted to leave, but the goodman said:

"There is only one way of doing this. There is a festival today where one man leads another dressed like a bear or a wild man of the woods or one thing or another, and then there is a hunt in the Piazza di San Marco, and when that is over the festival ends. Then everyone goes off where he pleases with the person he has brought in disguise. Now, you may be spied out here, and so, if you like, I will lead you along in some disguise and can take you wherever you like. Otherwise I don't see how you can leave here without being recognised. The lady's relatives know you must be in some house in the neighbourhood, and have posted guards everywhere to catch you."

Friar Alberto did not at all like the idea, but he was so much afraid of the lady's relatives that he agreed to it, and told the man where he wanted to go, and how he should be led along. The goodman smeared him all over with honey and then covered him with feathers, put a chain round his neck and a mask on his face. In one hand he gave him a large stick and in the other two great dogs which he had brought from the butcher; and then he sent someone to the Rialto who announced that everyone who wanted to see the Angel Gabriel should go to the Piazza di San Marco. That was true Venetian good faith!

Having done this, he took the Friar out, and, walking before him, led him along on a chain; and everybody came round saying: "What's this? What's this?" And thus he took the Friar to the Piazza, where there was a great crowd of people, made up of those who had followed them and those who had come from the Rialto on hearing the announcement. He then led his wild man of the woods to a column in a conspicuous and elevated place, pretending that he was waiting for the hunt. The poor Friar was greatly plagued by flies and gad-flies, because he was smeared all over with honey. And when the goodman saw that the Piazza was full of people, he pretended that he was going to unchain his wild man; but instead he took off Friar Alberto's mask, and shouted:

"Gentlemen, since the pig has not come to the hunt and since the hunt is off, I don't want you to have gathered here for nothing, and so I want you to see the Angel Gabriel who came down from Heaven to earth last night to console the ladies of Venice."

As soon as the mask was off, Friar Alberto was recognized by everybody, and there went up a great shout against him, everybody saying the most insulting things that ever were said to any scoundrel. And first one and then another threw all sorts of filth in his face. There he was kept a long time until the news reached the other friars of his convent. Six of them came down to the Piazza, threw a gown on his back and bound him, and then in the midst of a great tumult took him back to the monastery, where he was imprisoned. And it is believed that he soon died there after a life of misery.

Thus a man who was thought to be good and acted evilly without being suspected tried to be the Angel Gabriel and was turned into a wild man of the woods; and, in the long run, was insulted as he deserved and came to weep in vain for the sins he had committed. Please God that this may happen to all like him.

The Fifth Day

Ninth Tale

FEDERIGO DEGLI ALBERIGHI LOVES, BUT IS NOT BELOVED. HE SPENDS ALL HIS MONEY IN COURTSHIP AND HAS NOTHING LEFT BUT A FALCON, AND THIS HE GIVES HIS LADY TO EAT WHEN SHE COMES TO VISIT HIM BECAUSE THERE IS NOTHING ELSE TO GIVE HER. SHE LEARNS OF THIS, CHANGES HER MIND, TAKES HIM AS HER HUSBAND, AND MAKES HIM A RICH MAN

Filomena had ceased speaking, and the queen,[6] seeing that nobody was left to speak except Dioneo (who had his privilege)[7] and herself, began cheerfully as follows:

[6] queen of that day's tales, Fiammetta.   [7] Dioneo has been given the privilege of telling the last story of the day. The topic of the fifth day concerns lovers who experience happiness after first suffering misfortune.

It is now my turn to speak, dearest ladies, and I shall gladly do so with a tale similar in part to the one before, not only that you may know the power of your beauty over the gentle heart, but because you may learn yourselves to be givers of rewards when fitting, without allowing Fortune always to dispense them, since Fortune most often bestows them, not discreetly but lavishly.

You must know then that Coppo di Borghese Domenichi, who was and perhaps still is one of our fellow citizens, a man of great and revered authority in our days both from his manners and his virtues (far more than from nobility of blood), a most excellent person worthy of eternal fame, and in the fullness of his years delighted often to speak of past matters with his neighbours and other men. And this he could do better and more orderly and with a better memory and more ornate speech than anyone else.

Among other excellent things, he was wont to say that in the past there was in Florence a young man named Federigo, the son of Messer Filippo Alberighi, renowned above all other young gentlemen of Tuscany for his prowess in arms and his courtesy. Now, as most often happens to gentlemen, he fell in love with a lady named Monna Giovanna, in her time held to be one of the gayest and most beautiful women ever known in Florence. To win her love, he went to jousts and tourneys, made and gave feasts, and spent his money without stint. But she, no less chaste than beautiful, cared nothing for the things he did for her nor for him who did them.

Now as Federigo was spending far beyond his means and getting nothing in, as easily happens, his wealth failed and he remained poor with nothing but a little farm, on whose produce he lived very penuriously, and one falcon which was among the best in the world. More in love than ever, but thinking he would never be able to live in the town any more as he desired, he went to Campi where his farm was. There he spent his time hawking, asked nothing of anybody, and patiently endured his poverty.

Now while Federigo was in this extremity it happened one day that Monna Giovanna's husband fell ill, and seeing death come upon him, made his will. He was a very rich man and left his estate to a son who was already growing up. And then, since he had greatly loved Monna Giovanna, he made her his heir in case his son should die without legitimate children; and so died.

Monna Giovanna was now a widow, and as is customary with our women, she went with her son to spend the year in a country house she had near Federigo's farm. Now the boy happened to strike up a friendship with Federigo, and delighted in dogs and hawks. He often saw Federigo's falcon fly, and took such great delight in it that he very much wanted to have it, but did not dare ask for it, since he saw how much Federigo prized it.

While matters were in this state, the boy fell ill. His mother was very much grieved, as he was her only child and she loved him extremely. She spent the day beside him, trying to help him, and often asked him if there was anything he wanted, begging him to say so, for if it were possible to have it, she would try to get it for him. After she had many times made this offer, the boy said:

"Mother, if you can get me Federigo's falcon, I think I should soon be better."

The lady paused a little at this, and began to think what she should do. She knew that Federigo had loved her for a long time, and yet had never had one glance from her, and she said to herself:

"How can I send or go and ask for this falcon, which is, from what I hear, the best that ever flew, and moreover his support in life? How can I be so thoughtless as to take this away from a gentleman who has no other pleasure left in life?"

Although she knew she was certain to have the bird for the asking, she remained in embarrassed thought, not knowing what to say, and did not answer her son. But at length love for her child got the upper hand and she determined that to please him in whatever it might be, she would not send, but go herself for it and bring it back to him. So she replied:

"Be comforted, my child, and try to get better somehow. I promise you that tomorrow morning I will go for it, and bring it to you."

The child was so delighted that he became a little better that same day. And on the morrow the lady took another woman to accompany her, and as if walking for exercise went to Federigo's cottage, and asked for him. Since it was not the weather for it, he had not been hawking for some days, and was in his garden employed in certain work there. When he heard that Monna Giovanna was asking for him at the door, he was greatly astonished, and ran there happily. When she saw him coming, she got up to greet him with womanly charm, and when Federigo had courteously saluted her, she said:

"How do you do, Federigo? I have come here to make amends for the damage you have suffered through me by loving me more than was needed. And in token of this, I intend to dine today familiarly with you and my companion here."

"Madonna," replied Federigo humbly, "I do not remember ever to have suffered any damage through you, but received so much good that if I was ever worth anything it was owing to your worth and the love I bore it. Your generous visit to me is so precious to me that I could spend again all that I have spent; but you have come to a poor host."

So saying, he modestly took her into his house, and from there to his garden. Since there was nobody else to remain in her company, he said:

"Madonna, since there is nobody else, this good woman, the wife of this workman, will keep you company, while I go to set the table."

Now, although his poverty was extreme, he had never before realised what necessity he had fallen into by his foolish extravagance in spending his wealth. But he repented of it that morning when he could find nothing with which to do honour to the lady, for love of whom he had entertained vast numbers of men in the past. In his anguish he cursed himself and his fortune and ran up and down like a man out of his senses, unable to find money or anything to pawn. The hour was late and his desire to honour the lady extreme, yet he would not apply to anyone else, even to his own workman; when suddenly his eye fell upon his falcon, perched on a bar in the sitting room. Having no one to whom he could appeal, he took the bird, and finding it plump, decided it would be food worthy of such a lady. So, without further thought, he wrung its neck, made his little maid servant quickly pluck and prepare it, and put it on a spit to roast. He spread the table with the whitest napery, of which he had some left, and returned to the lady in the garden with a cheerful face, saying that the meal he had been able to prepare for her was ready.

The lady and her companion arose and went to table, and there together with Federigo, who served it with the greatest devotion, they ate the good falcon, not knowing what it was. They left the table and spent some time in cheerful conversation, and the lady, thinking the time had now come to say what she had come for, spoke fairly to Federigo as follows:

"Federigo, when you remember your former life and my chastity, which no doubt you considered harshness and cruelty, I have no doubt that you will be surprised at my presumption when you hear what I have come here for chiefly. But if you had children, through whom you could know the power of parental love, I am certain that you would to some extent excuse me.

"But, as you have no child, I have one, and I cannot escape the common laws of mothers. Compelled by their power, I have come to ask you— against my will, and against all good manners and duty—for a gift, which I know is something especially dear to you, and reasonably so, because I know your straitened fortune has left you no other pleasure, no other rec- reation, no other consolation. This gift is your falcon, which has so fasci- nated my child that if I do not take it to him, I am afraid his present illness will grow so much worse that I may lose him. Therefore I beg you, not by the love you bear me (which holds you to nothing), but by your own nobleness, which has shown itself so much greater in all courteous usage than is wont in other men, that you will be pleased to give it me, so that through this gift I may be able to say that I have saved my child's life, and thus be ever under an obligation to you."

When Federigo heard the lady's request and knew that he could not serve her, because he had given her the bird to eat, he began to weep in her presence, for he could not speak a word. The lady at first thought that his grief came from having to part with his good falcon, rather than from anything else, and she was almost on the point of retraction. But she remained firm and waited for Federigo's reply after his lamentation. And he said:

"Madonna, ever since it has pleased God that I should set my love upon you, I have felt that Fortune has been contrary to me in many things, and have grieved for it. But they are all light in comparison with what she has done to me now, and I shall never be at peace with her again when I reflect that you came to my poor house, which you never deigned to visit when it was rich, and asked me for a little gift, and Fortune has so acted that I cannot give it to you. Why this cannot be, I will briefly tell you.

"When I heard that you in your graciousness desired to dine with me and I thought of your excellence and your worthiness, I thought it right and fitting to honour you with the best food I could obtain; so, remembering the falcon you ask me for and its value, I thought it a meal worthy of you, and today you had it roasted on the dish and set forth as best I could. But now I see that you wanted the bird in another form, it is such a grief to me that I cannot serve you that I think I shall never be at peace again."

And after saying this, he showed her the feathers and the feet and the beak of the bird in proof. When the lady heard and saw all this, she first blamed him for having killed such a falcon to make a meal for a woman; and then she inwardly commended his greatness of soul which no poverty could or would be able to abate. But, having lost all hope of obtaining the falcon, and thus perhaps the health of her son, she departed sadly and returned to the child. Now, either from disappointment at not having the falcon or because his sickness must inevitably have led to it, the child died not many days later, to the mother's extreme grief.

Although she spent some time in tears and bitterness, yet, since she had been left very rich and was still young, her brothers often urged her to marry again. She did not want to do so, but as they kept on pressing her, she remembered the worthiness of Federigo and his last act of generosity, in killing such a falcon to do her honour.

"I will gladly submit to marriage when you please," she said to her brothers, "but if you want me to take a husband, I will take no man but Federigo degli Alberighi."

At this her brothers laughed at her, saying:

"Why, what are you talking about, you fool? Why do you want a man who hasn't a penny in the world?"

But she replied:

"Brothers, I know it is as you say, but I would rather have a man who needs money than money which needs a man."

Seeing her determination, the brothers, who knew Federigo's good qualities, did as she wanted, and gave her with all her wealth to him, in spite of his poverty. Federigo, finding that he had such a woman, whom he loved so much, with all her wealth to boot, as his wife, was more prudent with his money in the future, and ended his days happily with her.

The Tenth Day

Tenth Tale

THE MARQUESS OF SALUZZO IS URGED BY HIS SUBJECTS TO TAKE A WIFE AND, TO CHOOSE IN HIS OWN WAY, TAKES THE DAUGHTER OF A PEASANT. HE HAS TWO CHILDREN BY HER AND PRETENDS TO HER THAT HE HAS KILLED THEM. HE THEN PRETENDS THAT HE IS TIRED OF HER AND THAT HE HAS TAKEN ANOTHER WIFE AND SO BRINGS THEIR OWN DAUGHTER TO THE HOUSE AS IF SHE WERE HIS NEW WIFE, AFTER DRIVING HER AWAY IN HER SHIFT. SHE ENDURES IT ALL PATIENTLY. HE BRINGS HER BACK HOME, MORE BELOVED BY HIM THAN EVER, SHOWS HER THEIR GROWN CHILDREN, HONOURS HER AND MAKES OTHERS HONOUR HER AS MARCHIONESS

. . . Gracious ladies, as far as I can see, today has been given up to Kings, Sultans and such like persons; so, not to wander away too far from you, I shall tell you about a Marquess, but not of his munificence.[8] It will be about his silly brutality, although good came of it in the end. I do not advise anyone to imitate him, for it was a great pity that good did come to him.

A long time ago the eldest son of the Marquess of Saluzzo was a young man named Gualtieri. He was wifeless and childless, spent his time hunting and hawking, and never thought about marrying or having children, wherein he was probably very wise. This displeased his subjects, who several times begged him to take a wife, so that he might not die without an heir and leave them without a ruler, offering to find him a wife born of such a father and mother as would give him good hopes of her and content him. To which Gualtieri replied:

"My friends, you urge me to do something I was determined never to do, seeing how hard it is to find a woman of suitable character, and how many of the opposite sort there are, and how wretched is the life of a man who takes a wife unsuitable to him. It is foolishness of you to think you can judge a girl by the characters of her father and mother (from which

[8] The subject for the tenth day is liberality of conduct.

you argue that you can find me one to please me), for I do not see how you can really know the fathers' or the mothers' secrets. And even if you did know them, daughters are often quite different from their fathers and mothers.

"But you want me to take these chains, and I am content to do so. If it turns out badly I want to have no one to complain of but myself, and so I shall choose for myself. And I tell you that if you do not honour the wife I choose as your lady you will find out to your cost how serious a thing it is to have compelled me by your entreaties to take a wife against my will."

They replied that they were content, if only he would take a wife.

For some time Gualtieri had been pleased by the character of a poor girl in a hamlet near his house. He thought her beautiful, and that he might live comfortably enough with her. So he decided that he would marry her without seeking any further, and, having sent for her father, who was a very poor man, he arranged to marry her. Having done this, Gualtieri called together all his friends from the surrounding country, and said:

"My friends, it has pleased you to desire that I should marry, and I am ready to do so, more to please you than from any desire I have of taking a wife. You know you promised me that you would honour anyone I chose as your lady. The time has now come for me to keep my promise to you and you to keep yours to me. I have found a girl after my heart quite near here; I intend to marry her and to bring her home in a few days. So take thought to make a handsome marriage feast and how you can honourably receive her, so that I may consider myself content with your promise as you may be with mine."

The good men cheerfully replied that they were glad of it, and that they would consider her their lady and honour her as their lady in all things. After which, they all set about preparing a great and handsome wedding feast, and so did Gualtieri. He prepared a great and fine banquet, and invited many friends and relatives and noblemen and others. Moreover, he had rich and beautiful dresses cut out and fitted on a girl, who seemed to him about the same build as the girl he proposed to marry. And he also purchased girdles and rings and a rich and beautiful crown, and everything necessary to a bride.

When the day appointed for the wedding arrived, Gualtieri about the middle of Terce[9] mounted his horse, and so did those who had come to honour him. Everything being arranged, he said:

"Gentlemen, it is time to go for the bride."

Setting out with all his company he came to the hamlet and the house of the girl's father, where he found her drawing water in great haste, so that

[9] about 9 A.M.

she could go with the other women to see Gualtieri's bride. And when
Gualtieri saw her, he called her by her name, Griselda, and asked where
her father was. She blushed and said:

"He is in the house, my lord."

Gualtieri dismounted, told everyone to wait for him, entered the poor
little house where he found the girl's father (who was named Giannucole),
and said to him:

"I have come to marry Griselda, but first I want to ask her a few things
in your presence."

He then asked her whether, if he married her, she would try to please
him, and never be angry at anything he said or did, and if she would be
obedient, and several other things, to all of which she said "Yes." Gualtieri
then took her by the hand and led her forth. In the presence of all his
company he had her stripped naked, and then the clothes he had prepared
were brought, and she was immediately dressed and shod, and he had a
crown put on her hair, all unkempt as it was. Everyone marvelled at this,
and he said:

"Gentlemen, I intend to take this girl as my wife, if she will take me as
her husband."

He then turned to her, as she stood blushing and irresolute, and said:

"Griselda, will you take me as you husband?"

"Yes, my lord," she replied.

"And I will take you as my wife," said he.

Then in the presence of them all he pledged his faith to her; and they
set her on a palfrey and honourably conducted her to his house. The wedding feast was great and handsome, and the rejoicing no less than if he
had married the daughter of the King of France.

The girl seemed to have changed her soul and manners with her clothes.
As I said, she was beautiful of face and body, and she became so agreeable,
so pleasant, so well-behaved that she seemed like the daughter of a
nobleman, and not Giannucole's child and a cattle herder; which surprised
everyone who had known her before. Moreover, she was so obedient and so
ready to serve her husband that he felt himself to be the happiest and best
matched man in the world. And she was so gracious and kindly to her husband's subjects that there was not one of them but loved her and gladly
honoured her, while all prayed for her good and her prosperity and advancement. Whereas they had said that Gualtieri had showed little wisdom in
marrying her, they now said that he was the wisest and shrewdest man in
the world, because no one else would have known the lofty virtue hidden
under her poor clothes and village garb.

In short, before long she acted so well that not only in the marquisate
but everywhere people were talking of her virtues and good actions; and
whatever had been said against her husband for having married her was

now turned to the opposite. She had not long been with Gualtieri when she became pregnant, and in due time gave birth to a daughter, at which Gualtieri rejoiced greatly.

Soon after this the idea came to him to test her patience with a long trial and intolerable things. He said unkind things to her, seemed to be angry, and said that his subjects were most discontented with her on account of her low birth, and especially when they saw that she bore children. He said they were very angry at the birth of a daughter and did nothing but murmur. When the lady heard these words, she did not change countenance or cheerfulness, but said to him:

"My lord, you may do with me what you think most to your honour and satisfaction. I shall be content, for I know that I am less than they and unworthy of the honour to which you have raised me by your courtesy."

Gualtieri liked this reply and saw that no pride had risen up in her from the honour done her by him and others.

Soon after, he informed his wife in general terms that his subjects could not endure the daughter she had borne. He then gave orders to one of his servants whom he sent to her. The man, with a dolorous visage, said:

"Madonna, if I am to avoid death I must do what my lord bids me. He tells me I am to take your daughter and . . ."

He said no more, but the lady, hearing these words and seeing the servant's face, and remembering what had been said to her, guessed that he had been ordered to kill the child. She went straight to the cradle, kissed and blessed the child, and although she felt great anguish in her heart, put the child in the servant's arms without changing her countenance, and said:

"Do what my lord and yours has ordered you to do. But do not leave her for the birds and animals to devour her body, unless you were ordered to do so."

The servant took the child and told Gualtieri what the lady had said. He marvelled at her constancy, and sent the servant with the child to a relative at Bologna, begging her to bring her up and educate her carefully, but without ever saying whose daughter she was.

After this the lady again became pregnant, and in due time brought forth a male child, which delighted Gualtieri. But what he had already done was not enough for him. He pierced the lady with a worse wound, and one day said to her in pretended anger:

"Since you have borne this male child, I cannot live at peace with my subjects, who complain bitterly that a grandson of Giannucole must be their lord after me. If I am not to be driven out, I fear I must do now as I did before, and in the end abandon you and take another wife."

The lady listened to him patiently, and her only reply was:

"My lord, content yourself and do what is pleasing to you. Do not think about me, for nothing pleases me except as it pleases you."

Not many days afterwards Gualtieri sent for his son in the same way that he had sent for his daughter, and while pretending in the same way to kill the child, sent it to be brought up in Bologna, as he had sent the girl. And his wife said no more and looked no worse than she had done about the daughter. Gualtieri marvelled at this and said to himself that no other woman could have done what she did; and if he had not seen that she loved her children while she had them, he would have thought she did it to get rid of them whereas he saw it was from obedience to him.

His subjects thought he had killed his children, blamed him severely and thought him a cruel man, while they felt great pity for his wife. And when the women condoled with her on the death of her children, she never said anything except that it was not her wish but the wish of him who begot them.

Several years after his daughter's birth, Gualtieri thought the time had come for the last test of his wife's patience. He kept saying that he could no longer endure to have Griselda as his wife, that he knew he had acted childishly and wrongly when he married her, that he therefore meant to solicit the Pope for a dispensation to marry another woman and abandon Griselda; for all of which he was reproved by many good men. But his only reply was that it was fitting this should be done.

Hearing of these things, the lady felt she must expect to return to her father's house and perhaps watch cattle as she had done in the past, and see another woman take the man she loved; at which she grieved deeply. But she prepared herself to endure this with a firm countenance, as she had endured the other wrongs of Fortune.

Not long afterwards Gualtieri received forged letters from Rome, which he showed to his subjects, pretending that the Pope by these letters gave him a dispensation to take another wife and leave Griselda. So, calling her before him, he said to her in the presence of many of his subjects:

"Wife, the Pope has granted me a dispensation to leave you and to take another wife. Now, since my ancestors were great gentlemen and lords of this country while yours were always labourers, I intend that you shall no longer be my wife, but return to Giannucole's house with the dowry you brought me, while I shall bring home another wife I have found more suitable for me."

At these words the lady could only restrain her tears by a great effort, beyond that of women's nature, and replied:

"My lord, I always knew that my lowly rank was in no wise suitable to your nobility; and the rank I have had with you I always recognised as coming from God and you, and never looked upon it as given to me, but only lent. You are pleased to take it back, and it must and does please me to return it to you. Here is the ring with which you wedded me; take it. You tell me to take the dowry I brought you; to do this there is no need for you to pay anything nor shall I need a purse or a sumpter horse[10] for I have not forgotten that I came to you naked. If you think it right that the body which has borne your children should be seen by everyone, I will go away naked. But in exchange for my virginity, which I brought here and cannot carry away, I beg you will at least be pleased to let me take away one shift over and above my dowry."

Gualtieri, who was nearer to tears than anyone else present, managed to keep his countenance stern, and said:

"You shall have a shift."

Those who were present urged him to give her a dress, so that she who had been his wife for thirteen years should not be seen to leave his house so poorly and insultingly as it would be for her to leave it in a shift. But their entreaties were vain. So the lady, clad only in her shift, unshod and with nothing on her head, commended him to God, left his house, and returned to her father accompanied by the tears and lamentation of all who saw her.

Giannucole (who had never believed it was true that Gualtieri would keep his daughter as a wife and had always expected this event), had kept the clothes she had taken off on the morning when Gualtieri married her. So she took them and put them on, and devoted herself to drudgery in her father's house, enduring the assaults of hostile Fortune with a brave spirit.

After Gualtieri had done this, he told his subjects that he was to marry the daughter of one of the Counts of Panago. He therefore made great preparations for the wedding, and sent for Griselda to come to him; and when she came, he said:

"I am bringing home the lady I have just married, and I intend to do her honour at her arrival. You know there is not a woman in the house who can prepare the rooms and do many other things needed for such a feast. You know everything connected with the house better than anyone, so you must arrange everything that is to be done, and invite all the women you think fit and receive them as if you were mistress of the house. Then, when the marriage feast is over, you can return home."

These words were a dagger in Griselda's heart, for she had not been able to dispense with the love she felt for him as she had her good fortune, but she said:

"My lord, I am ready."

So, in her coarse peasant dress, she entered the house she had left a little

[10] pack horse.

before in her shift, and had the rooms cleaned and arranged, put out hangings and carpets in the halls, looked to the kitchen, and set her hand to everything as if she had been a scullery wench of the house. And she never paused until everything was ready and properly arranged.

After this she invited all the ladies of the surrounding country in Gualtieri's name, and then awaited the feast. On the wedding day, dressed in her poor clothes, she received all the ladies with a cheerful visage and a womanly manner.

Gualtieri had had his children carefully brought up in Bologna by his relative, who was married into the family of the Counts of Panago. The daughter was now twelve years old, the most beautiful thing ever seen, and the boy was seven. He sent to her and asked her to come to Saluzzo with his son and daughter, to bring an honourable company with her, and to tell everyone that she was bringing the girl as his wife, and never to let anyone know that the girl was anything else. Her husband did what the Marquess asked, and set out. In a few days he reached Saluzzo about dinner time, with the girl and boy and his noble company; and all the peasants of the country were there to see Gualtieri's new wife.

The girl was received by the ladies and taken to the hall where the tables were spread, and Griselda went cheerfully to meet her, saying:

"Lady, you are welcome."

The ladies had begged Gualtieri, but in vain, to allow Griselda to stay in her room or to lend her one of her own dresses, so that she might not have to meet strangers in such a guise. They all sat down to table and began the meal. Every man looked at the girl and said that Gualtieri had made a good exchange, and Griselda above all praised her and her little brother.

Gualtieri now felt that he had tested his wife's patience as far as he desired. He saw that the strangeness of all this did not alter her and he was certain it was not the result of stupidity, for he knew her to be an intelligent woman. He thought it now time to take her from the bitterness which he felt she must be hiding behind a smiling face. So he called her to him, and in everyone's presence said to her smilingly:

"What do you think of my new wife?"

"My lord," replied Griselda, "I see nothing but good in her. If she is as virtuous as she is beautiful, as I well believe, I have no doubt that you will live with her the happiest lord in the world. But I beg you as earnestly as I can not to give her the wounds you gave the other woman who was your wife. I think she could hardly endure them, because she is younger and because she has been brought up delicately, whereas the other laboured continually from her childhood."

Gualtieri saw that she really believed he was to marry the other, and yet spoke nothing but good of her. He made her sit down beside him, and said:

"Griselda, it is now time that you should reap the reward of your long patience, and that those who have thought me cruel and wicked and brutal should know that what I have done was directed towards a pre-determined end, which was to teach you to be a wife, then how to choose and keep a wife, and to procure me perpetual peace so long as I live with you. When I came and took you to wife, I greatly feared that this would not happen to me; and so, to test you, I have given you the trials and sufferings you know. I have never perceived that you thwarted my wishes by word or deed, and I think that in you I have the comfort I desire. I mean to give you back now what I deprived you of for a long time, and to heal the wounds I gave you with the greatest delight. Therefore, with a glad spirit, take her whom you think to be my wife and her brother as your children and mine. They are the children whom you and others have long thought that I had cruelly murdered. And I am your husband, who loves you above all things, believing I can boast that no man exists who can so rejoice in his wife as I in you."

He then embraced and kissed her. She was weeping with happiness. They both arose and went to where their daughter was sitting, quite stupefied by what she had heard, and tenderly embraced her and her brother, thus undeceiving them and many of those present.

The ladies arose merrily from table and went with Griselda to her room. With better hopes they took off her old clothes and dressed her in one of her noble robes, and brought her back to the hall a lady, which she had looked even in her rags.

They rejoiced over their children, and everyone was glad at what had happened. The feasting and merrymaking were prolonged for several days, and Gualtieri was held to be a wise man, although they thought the testing of his wife harsh and intolerable. But above all they esteemed the virtue of Griselda.

The Count of Panago soon afterwards returned to Bologna. Gualtieri took Giannucole away from his labour and installed him as his father-in-law, so that he ended his days honourably and in great content. He afterwards married off his daughter to a nobleman of great wealth and distinction, and lived long and happily with Griselda, always honouring her as much as he could.

What more is to be said, save that divine souls are sometimes rained down from Heaven into poor houses, while in royal palaces are born those who are better fitted to herd swine than to rule over men? Who but Griselda could have endured with a face not only tearless but cheerful, the stern and unheard-of tests imposed on her by Gualtieri? It would perhaps not have been such a bad thing if he had chosen one of those women who, if she had been driven out of her home in a shift, would have let another man so shake her fur that a new dress would have come from it.

Dioneo's tale was over, and the ladies talked about it, taking first one part and then another, blaming some things and praising others. The king[11] looked up at the sky and saw that the sun was already sinking towards the hour of Vespers, and so, without rising, he spoke thus:

"Beautiful ladies, as I think you know, human wisdom does not wholly consist in remembering past things and knowing the present; but grave men esteem it the highest wisdom to be able to foresee the future from a knowledge of both.

"As you know, it will be a fortnight tomorrow since we left Florence to find some amusement to support our health and vitality, and to escape the melancholy, agony and woes which have continued in our city since the beginning of the plague. In my opinion we have virtuously performed this. We have told merry tales, which perhaps might incline to concupiscence; we have eaten and drunk well, played and sung music, all of which things incite weak minds to things less than virtuous; but so far as I have seen there has not been one word or one act on your part or on ours which could be blamed. I have noticed only continual virtue, concord and fraternal familiarity; which is certainly most pleasing to me in your honour and in mine. Now, through too long a habit something might arise which would turn to annoyance, and if we stay away too long an opportunity for scandal might occur; and moreover each of us has now for one day exercised the honour which now dwells in me. I therefore think, if you agree, that it would be well for us to return to the place from which we set out. And, if you consider the matter, our being together is already known round about, and so our company might be increased in such a way as to destroy our pleasure. If you approve my advice, I shall retain the crown until we leave, which I think should be tomorrow. If you decide otherwise, I am quite ready to crown someone for tomorrow."

The discussion between the ladies and young men was long, but at last the king's advice was adopted as wise and virtuous, and they determined to do as he had said. So, having called the steward, he discussed with him what should be done next morning, and then, standing up, gave the company their freedom until supper time. . . .

[11] that is, the king of that day's tales.

Geoffrey Chaucer

FROM *The Canterbury Tales*

NOTES, INCLUDING
"A NOTE ON CHAUCERIAN PRONUNCIATION,"
BY CHARLES W. DUNN

Geoffrey Chaucer (1340?–1400)

I<small>T WAS BECOMING POSSIBLE FOR A MAN BORN IN RELATIVELY LOW</small> estate in Chaucer's England to rise by virtue of his own abilities to a position of some respect and worth. Born into a family of wine merchants, Chaucer enjoyed the patronage that resulted from service to his king. Sent periodically on diplomatic missions to France and Italy in the 1370's, he returned to England with a keen appreciation of Continental poetry. Thus he knew, and knew well, the major literature of his own time, as well as that of the ancients. His *Canterbury Tales*, the work that occupied the last dozen years of his life, are highly "literary" in their constant allusions to many literary sources. Yet Chaucer's eye and ear for striking detail often leave the reader convinced that he has spent some few hours with the most amusing and least bookish of men. That Chaucer intended his tales to be taken as moral instruction may surprise us, but only because it is a fairly recent belief that instruction cannot be amusing.

The *Tales* have as their setting the annual pilgrimage to the shrine of St. Thomas à Becket, a twelfth-century martyr to the cause of the Catholic Church (Chaucer himself made this pilgrimage in 1388). Chaucer used this journey to present his vision of medieval English society. The richness of literary devices he employs reflects the variety of human strengths and weaknesses he portrays. From the introductory frame, the General Prologue, we have excised some 300 lines. From the tales we have chosen two of the most popular, one showing the light and one the dark side of Chaucer's subject. Each calls for the reader's careful attention to the author's indirect and ironic treatment of his poetic fictions.

A Note on Chaucerian Pronunciation

1. Pronounce all written consonants as we do those in modern English. However, *gh* as in *night*, though now silent, was pronounced like the *ch* in the Scottish pronunciation of *loch* or in the German pronunciation of *Bach*.

2. Pronounce all the syllables in a word, even those which are represented only by a final *–e* and are no longer pronounced in modern English. Thus, pronounce Chaucer's *damė* with two syllables as *dah-meh,* and his *damės* as *dah-mess.* This final unstressed vowel probably had the same sound as the final unstressed vowel, when unemphatic, in modern English *Stella* or *raven.*

It is most important for our understanding of Chaucer's meters to note that, as in classical French poetry, all final syllables were pronounced, including those ending in *–e, –ed, –en, –es, –eth.* In this Introduction and the Appendix these have been marked with a dot over the *e.*

3. Pronounce all written vowels according to their so-called "Continental" values, that is, according to the sounds which they represent in modern French or Italian, or in our modern pronunciation of Latin.

Thus, pronounce the vowel spelled *a* in Chaucer's *damė* as the *ah* sound of modern French *dame* (or modern English *father*), not as the *ay* sound of modern English *dame.* Other instances are Chaucer's *barė, carė, famė, gamė, hatė, lamė, makė, namė, pagė, ragė, savė, takė, wakė.*

Pronounce the vowel spelled *e* or *ee* in Chaucer's *regioun* as *ay* sound of modern French *région* (or modern English *able*), not as the *ee* sound of modern English *region.* Other instances are Chaucer's *be, me, thee.* There are a large number of exceptions in this case, but the important fact to remember is that Chaucer's *e* is never pronounced as the *ee* sound of modern English *region, be,* and so on.

Pronounce the vowel spelled *i* or *y* in Chaucer's *finė* as the *ee* sound in modern French *fine* (or modern English *machine*), not as the *eye* sound in modern English *fine.* Other instances are *bitė, glidė, kyndė* (modern English *kind*), *minė, primė, ridė, strivė, thinė, wyn* (modern English *wine*).

Pronounce the vowel spelled *ou* or *ow* in Chaucer's *doute* as the *ou* sound in modern French *doute* (or modern English *soup*), not as the *ow* sound in modern English *doubt*. Instances are *bour* (modern English *bower*), *doute* (modern English *doubt*), *foul, hous, mous, tour* (modern English *tower*), *out*.

The vowels represented by *o, u,* and diphthongs diverge less notably from modern usage and need not be described here.

The Canterbury Tales

The General Prologue*

Whan that° Aprill with his shoures soote°	When sweet
The droghte of March hath perced to the roote	
And bathed every veyne in swich licour°	such liquid
Of which vertu° engendred is the flour,	By power of which
Whan Zephirus eek° with his sweete breeth	also
Inspired hath in every holt° and heeth°	wood heath
The tendre croppes,° and the yonge sonne	shoots
Hath in the Ram his half cours y-ronne,¹	
And smale foweles maken° melodye	birds make
That slepen al the nyght with open eye, 10	
So priketh hem° Nature in hir corages,°	stirs them their hearts
Than longen° folk to goon° on pilgrymages,	Then long go
And palmeres° for to seken° straunge strondes,°	pilgrims seek strands
To ferne halwes kouthe° in sondry londes.	distant shrines known
And specially, from every shires ende	
Of Engelond, to Caunterbury they wende,	
The holy, blisful martir² for to seke	
That hem hath holpen° whan that they were seeke.°	helped sick
Bifel° that in that sesoun on a day	It befell
In Southwerk at the Tabard, as I lay 20	
Redy to wenden on my pilgrymage	
To Caunterbury with ful devout corage,°	heart
At nyght was come into that hostelrye	

* Lines 309–623 and 857–58 have been deleted from this version of "The General Prologue" and the remaining lines have been renumbered consecutively.
¹ Has run his half-course in the Ram. At the time Chaucer was writing, the "young sun" of spring moved through the *first* half-course (approximately) of the Ram (Aries, the first of the twelve signs into which the zodiac is divided) during the period between March 12 to March 31, and the *second* half-course between April 1 and April 11, and then entered the Bull (Taurus). The reference here is to the sun's completion of its second half-course on April 11.
² Thomas à Becket, archbishop of Canterbury. . . .

Wel nyne-and-twenty in a compaignye
Of sondry folk by aventure y-falle°   chance fallen
In felaweshipe, and pilgrymes were they alle
That toward Caunterbury wolden° ryde.   intended to
The chambres and the stables weren wyde,°   spacious
And wel we weren esed atte beste;°   entertained at the best
And shortly, whan the sonne was to reste,   30
So haddle I spoken with hem everichon°   every one
That I was of hir° felaweshipe anon;   their
And made forward ° erly for to ryse   (we) made agreement
To take oure wey ther-as° I yow devyse.°   where tell
    But, nathelees,° whil I have tyme and space,   nevertheless
Er that° I ferther in this tale pace,°   Before pass
Me thynketh it° acordant to resoun   It seems to me
To telle yow al the condicioun
Of ech of hem° so as it semed me,   them
And whiche they weren, and of what degree,   40
And eek° in what array that they were inne;   also
And at a knyght than wol I first bigynne.
    A KNYGHT ther was, and that a worthy man,
That, fro the tyme that he first bigan
To riden° out, he loved chivalrye,   ride (in expeditions)
Trouthe and honour, fredom and curteisye.
Ful worthy was he in his lordes werre,°   war
And ther-to hadde he riden, no man ferre,°   farther
As wel in Cristendom as in hethenesse,°   heathendom
And evere honoured for his worthynesse.³   50
    At Alisaundre° he was whan it was wonne.   Alexandria (Egypt)
Ful ofte tyme he hadde the bord bigonne°   table headed
Aboven alle nacions in Pruce.°   Prussia
In Lettow° hadde he reysed,° and in Ruce,°   Lithuania served Russia
No Cristen man so ofte of his degree.
In Gernade° at the seege eek° hadde he be°   Granada (Spain) also been
Of Algezir,° and riden in Belmarye.°   Algeciras Benmarin (Morocco)
At Lyeys° was he and at Satalye°   Ayas (Armenia) Adalia (Turkey)
Whan they were wonne; and in the Grete° See   Mediterranean

³ The historical allusions indicate that the Knight was a veteran of more than forty years' service. In accordance with his feudal duty to his over-lord, the king, he had fought in "his lord's war," a term presumably referring to the campaigns of the Hundred Years' War between England and France. . . . The Knight had also enlisted voluntarily against the Mohammedans both in the Moorish realms of the western Mediterranean and in the Turkish realms of the eastern, and against the pagan hordes of northeastern Europe.

At many a noble armee° hadde he be.   60   armada
At mortal batailles hadde he been fiftene,
And foghten for oure feith at Tramyssene°   Tlemçen (Algeria)
In lystes° thries, and ay° slayn his foo.   tournaments   always
This ilke° worthy Knyght hadde been also   same
Som tyme with the lord of Palatye°   Balat (Turkey)
Agayn° another hethen in Turkye.   Against
    And evere moore° he hadde a sovereyn prys,°   always   reputation
And, though that he were worthy, he was wys
And of his port° as meke as is a mayde.   deportment
He nevere yet no vileynye° ne sayde   70   anything boorish
In al his lyf unto no maner wight.°   any kind of person
He was a verray,° parfit, gentil knyght.   true
    But for to tellen yow of his array,
Hise hors° were goode, but he was nat gay.   horses
Of fustian° he wered a gypoun°   rough cotton   blouse
Al bismotered ° with his habergeoun,°   stained   coat of mail
For he was late y-come from his viage°   journey
And wente for to doon his pilgrymage.
    With hym ther was his sone, a yong SQUYER,
A lovere and a lusty bacheler,[4]   80
With lokkes crulle as° they were leyd in presse.°   curled as if   curlers
Of twenty yeer of age he was, I gesse.
    Of his stature he was of evene° lengthe,   medium
And wonderly delyvere,° and of greet strengthe;   agile
And he hadde been som tyme in chivachye°   on a raid
In Flaundres, in Artoys, and Picardye,[5]
And born° hym wel, as of so litel space,°   conducted   time
In hope to stonden° in his lady° grace.   stand   lady's
    Embrouded ° was he as it were a meede°   Embroidered   meadow
Al ful of fresshe floures white and reede.   90
Syngynge he was or floytynge° al the day.   fluting
He was as fressh as is the monthe of May.
Short was his gowne with sleves longe and wyde.

---

[4] In obedience to the customs of the aristocracy, the Squire as a "bachelor" or candidate for knighthood had dedicated himself not merely to military training but also to courtly love, and he therefore undertook as a "lover" to win the approval of a lady by valor in war and devotion in love.   [5] Under the pretext of aiding the pope at Rome against the rival pope supported by the French at Avignon, an English raiding party plundered Flanders, Artois, and Picardy in 1383. If this is the expedition alluded to, it would have provided suitable experience to the Squire without any hazard more serious than he might meet while jousting in practice tournaments.

Wel koude he sitte on hors and faire° ryde.   gracefully
He koude songes make and wel endite,°   compose words
Juste,° and eek° daunce, and wel purtreye,° and   Joust   also   draw
    write.
So hoote he lovede that by nyghtertale°   nighttime
He slepte namoore than dooth a nyghtyngale.
    Curteys he was, lowely, and servysable,
And carf ° biforn his fader at the table.   100   carved
    A YEMAN ° hadde he° and servantz namo°   yeoman   he (the knight)
                                                                     no more
At that tyme, for hym liste° ryde so,   he liked to
And he was clad in coote and hood of grene.
A sheef of pecok arwes° bright and kene   arrows
Under his belt he bar° ful thriftily.°   carried   neatly
Wel koude he dresse° his takel ° yemanly;   prepare   equipment
His arwes drouped noght with fetheres lowe.
And in his hand he bar a myghty bowe.
A not° heed hadde he, with a broun visage.   close-cropped
Of wodecraft wel koude° he al the usage.   110   knew
Upon his arm he bar a gay bracer,°   archer's guard
And by his syde a swerd ° and a bokeler,°   sword   buckler
And on that° oother syde a gay daggere,   the
Harneysed ° wel, and sharp as poynt of spere,   Mounted
A Cristofre° on his brest of silver shene.°   St. Christopher medal
                                                                     bright
An horn he bar, the bawdryk° was of grene.   carrying-belt
A forster° was he soothly,° as I gesse.   forester   truly
    Ther was also a nonne, a PRIORESSE,
That of hir smylyng was ful symple° and coy.°   unpretentious   quiet
Hir gretteste ooth was but by Seint Loy;[6]   120
And she was cleped ° Madame Eglentyne.   called
    Ful wel she soong° the servyce dyvyne,   sang
Entuned ° in hir nose ful semely,°   Intoned   properly
And Frenssh she spak ful faire and fetisly°   elegantly
After the scole of Stratford atte Bowe,[7]
For Frenssh of Parys was to hire unknowe.°   unknown
    At mete wel y-taught was she with alle;

---

[6] The talented goldsmith St. Loy (or Eligius) served as treasurer in the luxurious French court of King Dagobert in the seventh century and was appointed bishop by the king. [7] The allusion would suggest either that the Prioress had been educated at the Benedictine nunnery of St. Leonard's or that she was in charge of it. It was situated beside Stratford at the Bow on the outskirts of London and served as a finishing school for the daughters of London's middle class. Appropriately, we learn from what follows that she was preoccupied with matters of etiquette.

She leet° no morsel from hir lippes falle,   let
Ne wette hir fyngres in hir sauce depe;
Wel koude she carie a morsel, and wel kepe°   130   take care
That no drope ne fille° upon hir brest.   fell
In curteisie was set ful muchel ° hir lest.°   much   concern
Hir over lippe wyped she so clene
That in hir coppe ther was no ferthyng° sene   particle
Of grece whan she dronken hadde hir draughte.
Ful semely after hir mete she raughte,°   reached
And sikerly° she was of greet desport,°   certainly   fun
And ful plesaunt and amyable of port,°   deportment
And peyned hire° to countrefete cheere°   strove   imitate appearance
Of court, and to been estalich° of manere,   140   stately
And to been holden digne° of reverence.   considered worthy
    But for to speken of hir conscience,
She was so charitable and so pitous,°   sympathetic
She wolde wepe if that she sawe a mous
Caught in a trappe, if it were deed or bledde.
Of smale houndes⁸ hadde she that she fedde
With rosted flessh, or mylk and wastel ° breed;   white wheat
But soore wepte she if oon of hem were deed,
Or if men° smoot it with a yerde smerte.°   someone   stick severely
And al was conscience and tendre herte.   150
    Ful semely° hir wympel ° pynched ° was,   gracefully   headdress
                                                         fluted
Hir nose tretys,° hir eyen° greye as glas,   shapely   eyes
Hir mouth ful smal, and ther-to softe and reed,
But sikerly° she hadde a fair forheed;   certainly
It was almoost a spanne brood, I trowe,°   believe
For hardily° she was nat undergrowe.   undeniably
Ful fetys° was hir cloke, as I was war;°   graceful   aware
Of smal coral aboute hir arm she bar°   carried
A peyre of bedes, gauded al with grene,⁹
And ther-on heng a brooch of gold ful shene,°   160   bright
On which ther was first writen a crowned A,
And after *Amor vincit omnia.*°   Love conquers all.
    Another NONNE with hire hadde she,
That was hir chapeleyne, and preestes thre.
    A MONK ther was, a fair for the maistrye,°   an extremely fine (one)

⁸ It was contrary to religious discipline for a nun to have a pet dog, but evidently
the Prioress kept lap dogs and pampered them indulgently with meat and milk
and the second-best grade of bread, even at a time when food was scarce.   ⁹ A
set of beads (a rosary), with every *guad* (large bead among smaller beads)
colored green.

An outridere° that lovede venerye,°   supervisor hunting
A manly man, to been an abbot able.
Ful many a deyntee° hors hadde he in stable,   valuable
And whanne he rood, men myghte° his brydel heere   could
Gynglen° in a whistlynge wynd as cleere   170   Jingle
And eek° as loude as dooth the chapel belle   also
Ther-as° this lord was kepere of the celle.°   Where group
     The reule of Seint Maure or of Seint Beneit,[10]
By cause that it was old and somdel streit,°   somewhat strict
This ilke° Monk leet olde thynges pace   same
And heeld after the newe world, the space.°   for the meanwhile
He yaf ° nat of that text a pulled ° hen   gave plucked
That seith that hunters been° nat holy men,   are
Ne that a monk, whan he is recchelees,°   without a care
Is likned til ° a fissh that is waterlees,   180   like to
This is to seyn,° a monk out of his cloystre.   say
But thilke° text heeld he nat worth an oystre;   that same
And I seyde his opinioun was good.
What° sholde he studie and make hymselven wood °   Why himself insane
Upon a book in cloystre alwey to poure,°   pore
Or swynken° with his handes and laboure   work
As Austyn bit? ° How shal the world be served? [11]   commands (*biddeth*)
Lat Austyn have his swynk° to hym reserved.   work
Therefore he was a prikasour° aright.   fast rider
Grehoundes he hadde as swift as fowel ° in   bird
     flight.   190
Of prikyng° and of huntyng for the hare   tracking (the hare)
Was al his lust,° for no cost wolde he spare.   pleasure
     I seigh° his sleves y-purfiled ° at the hond   saw trimmed
With grys,° and that the fyneste of a lond;   gray fur
And for to festne his hood under his chyn

---

[10] The Monk, though a *keeper* or guardian of a local *cell* or group of monks, and an *out-rider* or supervisor of the monastery's property, no longer followed the rule of behavior incumbent upon Benedictine monks. This rule was first formulated in Italy in the sixth century by St. Benedict (*Beneit*), the originator of the order, and subsequently brought to France in the same century by his disciple St. Maur. (Two sentences are here run together:—"This . . . monk let . . . the rule . . . pass by," and "This . . . monk let old things pass by.") [11] St. Augustine (*Austyn*) of Hippo in the fifth century criticized monks for their sloth. The query *How is the world to be served* means "Who will perform worldly services such as require a cleric's education if monks withdraw themselves from the world to the life of spiritual contemplation required of them?" Throughout this portrait Chaucer acquiesces ironically with the Monk's argument.

He hadde of gold wroght a ful curious pyn;
A love knotte in the gretter° ende ther was.   larger
His heed was balled,° that shoon as any glas,   bald
And eek° his face as° he hadde been enoynt.°   also as if anointed
He was a lord ful fat and in good poynt,°   200 condition
Hise eyen stepe° and rollynge in his heed,   eyes bulging
That stemed ° as a forneys° of a leed,°   glowed furnace boiler
His bootes souple, his hors in greet estat.
   Now certeynly he was a fair prelat.
He was nat pale as a forpyned goost.°   tormented spirit
A fat swan loved he best of any roost.
His palfrey was as broun as is a berye.
   A FRERE ° ther was, a wantowne° and a merye,   friar gay
A lymytour,° a ful solempne° man.   limiter splendid
In alle the ordres foure[12] is noon that kan°   210 knows
So muche of daliaunce° and fair langage.   flirtation
He hadde maad ° ful many a mariage   arranged
Of yonge wommen at his owene cost.
   Unto his ordre he was a noble post.°   pillar
Ful wel biloved and famulier was he
With frankeleyns over-al ° in his contree   rich landholders everywhere
And with worthy wommen of the toun,
For he hadde power of confessioun,
As seyde hymself, moore than a curat,°   parish priest
For of his ordre he was licenciat.   220
Ful swetely herde he confessioun,
And pleasunt was his absolucioun.
He was an esy man to yeve° penaunce   give
Ther-as he wiste° to have a good pitaunce.°   Where he knew gift
For unto a poure ordre for to yive°   give

[12] The four orders of friars, which were all established in the thirteenth century, were intended to combat the abuses of the earlier monastic orders. Friars renounced property and undertook, when necessary, to earn money by manual labor; and they followed an active life of service to mankind rather than, as the monks did, a contemplative life. But the need of their organization became such that they were forced to become mendicants and beg for alms; and they were subsequently licensed to raise funds by hearing confessions and granting absolutions. In the fourteenth century priests came to object to the infringements on their parishes made by limiters, or friars assigned to particular limits; and reformers began to accuse them of corruption. The outspoken advocate of reform, John Wyclif, called the friars "the children of Caim, punning on the medieval form of the name of Cain, Abel's murderer, and the initial letters of the four orders: Carmelites, Augustines, Iacobins (Dominicans), and Minorites (Franciscans).

Is signe that a man is wel y-shryve;°   confessed
For if he yaf,° he dorste make avaunt,°   gave (the Friar)   dared
                                                         to avow
He wiste° that a man was repentaunt;   knew
For many a man so hard is of his herte,
He may not wepe, althogh hym° soore smerte.°   230 he smart
Therefore, in stede of wepynge and preyeres,
Men moote yeve° silver to the poure freres.   One ought to give
   His typet° was ay farsed° ful of knyves   cape always stuffed
And pynnes for to yeven faire wyves.
   And certeynly he hadde a murye note.
Wel koude he synge and pleyen on a rote;°   stringed instrument
Of yeddynges° he bar outrely° the prys.   ballads carried off
                                                         completely
His nekke whit was as the flour de lys;°   fleur-de-lis
Ther-to° he strong was as a champioun.   In addition
He knew the tavernes wel in every toun   240
And every hostiler° and tappestere°   innkeeper barmaid
Bet° than a lazar° or a beggestere,°   Better leper female
                                                         beggar
For unto swich° a worthy man as he   such
Accorded nat,° as by his facultee,°   It was not suitable ca-
                                                         pacity
To have with sike° lazars aqueyntaunce.   sick
It is nat honeste,° it may nat avaunce,°   proper benefit
For to deelen with no swich poraille°   such poor folk
But al with riche and selleres of vitaille.°   victuals
And, over-al ther-as° profit sholde arise,   everywhere where
Curteys he was and lowely of servyse.   250
Ther was no man nowher so vertuous.°   gifted
He was the beste beggere in his hous,°   friary
For thogh a wydwe° hadde noght a sho,°   widow shoe
So plesant was his *In principio*,[13]
Yet wolde he have a ferthyng er° he wente.   farthing before
His purchas° was wel ° bettre than his rente.°   pickings much regular
                                                         income
And rage° he koude as it were right° a whelpe.   frolic just like
   In lovedayes° ther koude he muchel ° helpe,   arbitration days much
For ther he was nat lyk a cloysterer
With a thredbare cope,° as is a poure scoler,   260 cloak
But he was lyk a maister° or a pope;   Master of Arts
Of double worstede was his semycope,°   short cloak
That rounded as a belle out of the presse.
   Somwhat he lipsed ° for his wantownesse°   lisped playfulness
To make his Englissh sweete upon his tonge;
And in his harpyng, whan that he hadde songe,

[13] "In the beginning"—the first words of St. John's Gospel, used in the Middle
Ages as a religious and even magic formula.

Hise eyen° twynkled in his heed aright   *eyes*
As doon the sterres in the frosty nyght.
This worthy lymytour was cleped ° Huberd.   *called*
   A MARCHANT ° was ther with a forked berd, 270   *merchant*
In motlee,° and hye on hors he sat,   *figured cloth*
Upon his heed a Flaundryssh° bevere hat,   *Flemish*
His bootes clasped faire and fetisly.°   *elegantly*
   Hise resons° he spak ful solempnely,°   *views impressively*
Sownynge° alwey the encrees of his wynnyng.°   *Relating profit*
He wolde the see were kept° for any thyng   *guarded*
Bitwixe Middelburgh° and Orewelle.°   *Middleburg (Holland) Orwell Harbor (England)*
Wel koude he in eschaunge sheeldes selle.[14]
   This worthy man ful wel his wit bisette.°   *applied*
Ther wiste° no wight° that he was in dette, 280   *knew person*
So estatly was he of his governaunce
With his bargaynes and with his chevysaunce.°   *manipulation*
   For sothe,° he was a worthy man with alle,   *Truly*
But, sooth to seyn,° I noot° how men hym calle.   *say don't know*
   A CLERK ° ther was of Oxenford ° also   *student Oxford*
That unto logyk[15] hadde longe y-go.°   *long since gone*
   As leene was his hors as is a rake,
And he was nat right° fat, I undertake,°   *particularly vow*
But looked holwe° and ther-to sobrely.   *hollow*
Ful thredbare was his overeste courtepy,° 290   *outer short coat*
For he hadde geten hym yet no benefice,°   *ecclesiastical appointment*
Ne was so worldly for to have office,°   *secular position*
For hym was levere° have at his beddes heed   *he would rather*
Twenty bookes clad in blak or reed
Of Aristotle and his philosophie
Than robes riche or fithele° or gay sautrie.°   *fiddle psaltery (harp)*
   But, al be that he was a philosophre,[16]
Yet hadde he but litel gold in cofre,°   *coffer*
But al that he myghte of his frendes hente,°   *get*

---

[14] He well knew how to sell *shields* or *écus* (French coins) in (illegal) exchange (at a profit allowed only to the royal money-changers). Presumably the Merchant was a wholesale exporter and, as such, knew how to evade foreign exchange restrictions.   [15] Medieval university courses in arts were based on a study of the Seven Arts. The B.A. required the study of the trivium, a group of three topics—grammar, logic, and rhetoric. The M.A. required further, prolonged study of the quadrivium, a group of four topics—arithmetic, geometry, music, and astronomy. . . . The Clerk was presumably engaged in completing his M.A. . . .   [16] Natural philosophy, which the Clerk probably neglected in favor of moral philosophy, embraced all the sciences, one of which was alchemy, and alchemists claimed to be able to transmute base metals into gold.

On bookes and on lernynge he it spente,   300
And bisily gan for the soules preye°   prayed (*gan . . . preye*)
Of hem that yaf ° hym wher-with to scoleye.°   gave study
   Of studie took he moost cure° and moost heede.   care
Noght oo° word spak he moore than was neede,   one
And that was seid in forme and reverence°   formally and respectfully
And short and quyk and ful of heigh sentence.°   significance
Sownynge in° moral vertu was his speche,   Tending toward
And gladly wolde he lerne and gladly teche. . . .
   A SOMNOUR ° was ther with us in that place,   constable of a church court
That hadde a fyr-reed cherubynnes face,[17]   310
For saucefleem° he was, with eyen° narwe,   pimpled eyes
As hoot he was and lecherous as a sparwe,°   sparrow
With scaled ° browes blake and piled ° berd.   scabby scanty
Of his visage children were aferd.°   afraid
Ther nas quyksilver, lytarge,° ne brymstoon,   lead ointment
Boras,° ceruce,° ne oille° of tartre noon,   Borax white lead cream
Ne oynement that wolde clense and byte,
That hym myghte helpen° of his whelkes° white,   could rid (leprous) sores
Nor of the knobbes sittynge on his chekes.
   Wel loved he garlek, oynons, and eek lekes,   320
And for to drynke strong wyn reed as blood;
Thanne wolde he speke and crye as° he were wood;°   as if mad
And whan that he wel dronken hadde the wyn,
Thanne wolde he speke no word but Latyn.
   A fewe termes hadde he, two or thre,
That he had lerned out of som decre.
No wonder is! He herde it al the day;
And eek ye knowen wel how that a jay
Kan clepen "Watte" ° as wel as kan the Pope.   call out "Walter" (like "Polly")
But who so koude in oother thyng hym grope,°   330   examine
Thanne hadde he spent al his philosophie.
Ay° "*Questio, quid juris?*" [18] wolde he crie.   Always
   He was a gentil harlot° and a kynde;   an obliging rascal
A bettre felawe sholde men noght fynde.
He wolde suffre,° for a quart of wyn,   allow
A good felawe° to have his concubyn°   A rascal mistress
A twelf monthe and excuse hym atte fulle.°   fully
Ful pryvely° a fynch eek koude he pulle;°   secretively fornicate (*pulle a fynch*)

---

[17] The Summoner had a "fire-red cherub's face," like the faces of cherubim colored red in ecclesiastical ornamentation. He evidently had, in medieval terms, a "sanguine complexion" and suffered from a leprous disease known as *alopicia*.
[18] Query, what of the law (here)? That is, "What law applies to this case?"

And if he foond owher° a good felawe,   found anywhere
He wolde techen hym to have noon awe   340
In swich caas of the ercedekenes curs°   archdeacon's curse (of excommunication)
But if° a mannes soule were in his purs,   Unless
For in his purs he sholde y-punysshed be.
"Purs is the ercedekenes helle," seyde he.
But wel I woot° he lyed right in dede;   know
Of cursyng oghte ech gilty man drede,—
For curs wol slee,° right as assoillyng° savith,—   slay   absolution
And also war hym of ° a *significavit*.°   beware   writ for arrest
  In daunger° hadde he at° his owene gyse°   subjection   in   way
The yonge gerles° of the diocise,   350   people (male and female)
And knew hir counseil,° and was al hir reed.°   their secrets   adviser of all of them
  A gerland ° hadde he set upon his heed,   garland
As greet as it were for an ale stake;°   alehouse sign
A bokeler hadde he maad hym of a cake.
  With hym ther rood a gentil PARDONER
Of Rouncival, his freend and his comper,°   comrade
That streight was comen fro the court of Rome.[19]
Ful loude he soong,° "Com hider,° love, to me."   sang   hither
This Somnour bar° to hym a stif burdoun,°   carried   strong accompaniment
Was nevere trompe° of half so greet a soun.°   360   trumpet   sound
  This Pardoner hadde heer° as yelow as wex,°   hair   wax
But smothe it heeng° as dooth a strike of flex.°   hung   hank of flax
By ounces° henge his lokkes that he hadde,   In wisps
And ther-with he his shuldres overspradde,
But thynne it lay by colpons oon and oon.°   in single strands
But hood, for jolitee,° wered ° he noon,   jauntiness   wore
For it was trussed up in his walet.
Hym thoughte he rood al of the newe jet.°   style
Dischevelee,° save his cappe he rood al bare.   With loose hair
Swiche glarynge eyen hadde he as an hare.   370
  A vernycle° hadde he sowed upon his cappe,   souvenir of St. Veronica
His walet biforn hym in his lappe,
Bret° ful of pardoun comen from Rome al hoot.°   Cram   hot
  A voys he hadde as smal as hath a goot.°   goat
No berd ° hadde he, ne nevere sholde have;   beard
As smothe it was as° it were late y-shave.°   as if   newly shaved

[19] The Pardoner evidently belonged to a fraternity located at the religious hospital of the Blessed Mary of Rouncivalle, just outside London. The pardons (remissions of punishment) which he was prepared to dispense were, allegedly at least, issued by the pope at Rome. Many of the pardoners in Chaucer's England, however, were fraudulent and unlicensed.

I trowe° he were a geldyng° or a mare.   believe   must have been a gelding

   But of his craft fro Berwyk into Ware

Ne was ther swich another pardoner,

For in his male° he hadde a pilwe-beer°   380 bag   pillowcase

Which that he seyde was Oure Lady veyl.°   Lady's veil

He seyde he hadde a gobet° of the seyl °   piece   sail

That Seint Peter hadde whan that he wente°   walked

Upon the see til Jesu Crist hym hente.° 20   caught

He hadde a croys of latoun° ful of stones,   copper alloy

And in a glas he hadde pigges bones.

But with thise relikes, whan that he fond

A poure persoun° dwellyng upon lond,°   parson (to aid him)   the country

Upon a° day he gat hym moore moneye   one

Than that the persoun gat in monthes tweye.   390

And thus with feyned flaterye and japes°   tricks

He made the persoun and the peple his apes.°   fools

   But trewely to tellen, atte laste,

He was in chirche a noble ecclesiaste.

Wel koude he rede a lessoun or a storie,°   Bible story (or saint's life)

But alderbest° he song° an offertorie,   best of all   sang

For wel he wiste° whan that song was songe,   knew

He moste° preche and wel affile° his tonge   must   make smooth

To wynne silver, as he ful wel koude.

Ther-fore he song the murierly° and loude.   400 more merrily

   Now have I told yow soothly in a clause°   truly in brief

Th' estaat, th' array, the nombre, and eek the cause

Why that assembled was this compaignye

In Southwerk at this gentil hostelrye,

That highte° the Tabard, faste° by the Belle.°   was called   close   Bell Inn

But now is tyme to yow for to telle

How that we baren us° that ilke° nyght   conducted ourselves   same

Whan we were in that hostelrie alyght;°   alighted

And after wol I telle of oure viage°   journey

And al the remenant of oure pilgrymage.   410

   But first I pray yow of youre curteisye

That ye n' arette it nat° my vileynye°   won't blame it on   boorishness

Thogh that° I pleynly speke in this matere   Even if

To telle yow hir° wordes and hir cheere°   their   behavior

Ne thogh° I speke° hir wordes proprely.°   And if   repeat   literally

For this ye knowen also° wel as I,   as

Who so shal telle° a tale after a man,   retell

He moot reherce° as neigh° as evere he kan   must repeat   closely

20 Matt. 14:29.

Everich a° word if it be in his charge, — Every single

Al° speke he nevere so rudeliche° and large,° 420 — Even though rudely broadly

Or ellis° he moot telle his tale untrewe, — else

Or feyne thyng,° or fynde wordes newe. — invent something

He may nat spare° al thogh he were his brother; — hold back

He moot° as wel seye o° word as another. — must one

Crist spak hymself ful brode° in holy writ, — freely

And wel ye woot,° no vileynye is it. — know

Eek° Plato seith, who so kan hym rede, — Also

The wordes mote° be cosyn° to the dede. — must cousin

Also, I pray yow to foryeve° it me, — forgive

Al° have I nat set folk in hir degree° 430 — Even if their order of rank

Here in this tale as that° they sholde stonde.° — just as stand

My wit is short, ye may° wel understonde. — can

Greet cheere made oure HOOST us everichon,° — for each of us

And to the soper sette he us anon.° — immediately

He served us with vitaille° at the beste. — victuals

Strong was the wyn, and wel to drynke us leste.° — it pleased

A semely° man oure Hoost was with alle — suitable

For to been a marchal in an halle.° — banquet hall

A large man he was, with eyen stepe.° — bulging

A fairer burgeys° was ther noon in Chepe,° 440 — citizen Cheapside (London)

Boold of his speche, and wys, and wel y-taught,

And of manhode hym° lakked right naught. — he

Eke ther-to he was right° a murye man, — truly

And after soper pleyen° he bigan — to joke

And spak of myrthe,° amonges othere thynges, — amusement

Whan that we hadde maad ° oure rekenynges,° — paid bills

And seyde thus, "Now, lordynges,° trewely, — sirs

Ye been° to me right welcome, hertely, — are

For by my trouthe, if that I shal not lye,

I saugh nat this yeer so murye a compaignye 450

At ones° in this herberwe° as is now. — once lodging

Fayn° wolde I doon° yow myrthe, wiste I° how. — Gladly provide if I knew

And of a myrthe I am right now bythoght

To doon yow ese,° and it shal coste noght. — comfort

"Ye goon° to Canterbury, God yow spede! — are going

The blisful martir quyte° yow youre mede!° — grant reward

And wel I woot° as ye goon by the weye, — know

Ye shapen yow to talen° and to pleye, — intend to tell tales

For trewely confort ne° myrthe is noon° — nor none

To ryde by the weye domb as a stoon. 460

And ther-fore wol I maken yow disport,° — amusement

As I seyde erst,° and doon yow som confort.   before
And if yow liketh alle by oon° assent   one
For to stonden at° my juggement   abide by
And for to werken° as I shall yow seye,   do
Tomorwe, whan ye riden by the weye,
Now, by my fader° soule, that is deed,   father's
But° ye be murye, I wol yeve yow myn heed.°   Unless   head
Hoold up youre hondes withouten moore speche."
    Oure conseil was nat longe for to seche.°   470   seek
Us thoughte it was nat worth to make it wys,°   difficult
And graunted ° hym withouten moore avys°   (we) yielded to consid-
       eration
And bad hym seye his voirdit° as hym leste.°   verdict   it pleased
    "Lordynges," quod° he, "now herkneth° for the   said   listen
    beste,
But taketh it not, I pray yow, in desdeyn.°   contemptuously
This is the poynt, to speken short and pleyn,
That ech of yow, to shorte with oure weye,°   cut short our way with
In this viage° shal telle tales tweye,°—   journey   two
To Caunterburyward° I mene it so,—   toward Canterbury
And homward he shal tellen othere two   480
Of aventures that whilom° have bifalle.   once upon a time
And which° of yow that bereth° hym best of alle,   whichever   conducts
That is to seyn, that telleth in this caas
Tales of best sentence° and moost solaas,°   significance   delight
Shal have a soper at oure aller cost°   the expense of all of us
Here in this place, sittyng by this post,
Whan that we come agayn fro Caunterbury.
And, for to make yow the moore mury,
I wol myself goodly with yow ryde
Right at myn owene cost and be your gyde;   490
And who so° wole my juggement withseye°   whosoever   resist
Shal paye al that we spende by the weye.
And if ye vouchesauf that it be so,
Tel me anoon° withouten wordes mo,°   immediately   more
And I wol erly shape° me ther-fore."   prepare
    This thyng was graunted, and oure othes swore°   sworn
With ful glad herte, and preyden° hym also   (we) begged
That he wolde vouchesauf for to do so,
And that he wolde been oure governour,
And of oure tales juge and reportour,°   500   critic
And sette a soper at a certeyn prys,
And we wol reuled been at his devys°   discretion
In heigh and lough.° And thus by oon assent   In all matters

We been acorded to his juggement;
And ther-upon the wyn was fet anoon.°   fetched immediately
We dronken,° and to reste wente echon°   drank   each one
Withouten any lenger taryynge.
   A morwe,° whan that day bigan to sprynge,   The next morning
Up roos oure Hoost and was oure aller cok°   the cock (who crowed) for us all
And gadred° us togidre° in a flok,   510   gathered   together
And forth we riden,° a° litel moore than pas,°   rode at a foot pace
Unto the wateryng° of Seint Thomas,   watering place
And there oure Hoost bigan his hors areste°   to halt
And seyde, "Lordynges, herkneth,° if yow leste.°   listen it pleases
Ye woot° youre forward° and it yow recorde.°   know agreement remember it
If evensong and morwesong acorde,°   morning song agree
Lat se° now who shal telle the firste tale.   Let's see
As evere moot° I drynke wyn or ale,   may
Who so be rebel to my juggement
Shal paye for al that by the wey is spent.   520
Now draweth cut er that we ferrer twynne.°   lots before we further depart
He which that hath the shorteste shal bigynne.
Sire Knyght," quod he, "my mayster and my lord,
Now draweth° cut, for that is myn acord.°   draw a agreement
Cometh neer," quod he, "my lady Prioresse,
And ye, sire Clerk, lat be° youre shamefastnesse,°   lay aside modesty
Ne studieth noght. Ley hond to, every man."
   Anoon° to drawen every wight bigan,   Immediately
And shortly for to tellen as it was,
Were it by aventure° or sort° or cas,°   530   chance lot destiny
The sothe° is this: the cut fil° to the Knyght,   truth fell
Of which ful blithe and glad was every wight,°   person
And telle he moste° his tale, as was resoun°   must right
By forward° and by composicioun,°   agreement compact
As ye han° herd. What nedeth wordes mo?   have
   And whan this goode man saugh that it was so,
As he that wys was and obedient
To kepe his forward by his free assent,
He seyde, "Syn° I shal bigynne the game,   Since
What,° welcome be the cut, a° Goddess name!   540   Why in
Now lat us ryde, and herkneth what I seye."
And with that word we ryden forth oure weye. . . .

The Nun's Priest's Tale

A poure widwe,° somdel stape° in age,   *widow somewhat advanced*
Was whilom° dwellynge in a narwe° cotage   *once small*
Biside a grove, stondyng° in a dale.   *standing*
This widwe of which I telle yow my tale,
Syn thilk° day that she was last a wyf,   *Since that same*
In pacience ladde a ful symple lyf,
For litel was hire catel° and hire rente.°   *property income*
By housbondrye of swich° as God hire sente   *such*
She foond° hireself and eek° hire doghtren° two.   *supported also daughters*
Thre large sowes hadde she and namo,°   10   *no more*
Thre kyn,° and eek a sheep that highte° Malle.   *cows was called*
Ful sooty was hire bour° and eek hire halle,   *bedroom*
In which she eet ful many a sklendre° meel.   *slender*
Of poynaunt° sauce hir neded° never a deel.°   *pungent she needed bit*
No deyntee morsel passed thurgh hir throte;
Hir diete was acordant to hir cote.°   *means*
Repleccioun ne made hire nevere syk;
Attempree° diete was al hir phisyk,   *Temperate*
And excercise, and hertes suffisaunce.°   *sufficiency*
The goute lette° hire no thyng° for to daunce,   20   *hindered in no way*
N'apoplexie shente nat° hir heed.°   *Nor did apoplexy trouble head*
No wyn ne drank she, neither whit ne reed.
Hir bord° was served moost with whit and blak,   *table*
Milk and broun breed, in which she foond no lak,°   *found no fault*
Seynd° bacoun, and som tyme an ey or tweye,°   *Broiled egg or two*
For she was, as it were, a maner deye.°   *sort of dairywoman*
A yeerd she hadde, enclosed al aboute
With stikkes, and a drye dych° withoute,   *ditch*
In which she hadde a cok heet° Chauntecleer.   *named*
In al the land of crowyng nas° his peer.   30   *(there) was not*
His voys was murier° than the myrie orgon   *merrier*
On massedayes that in the chirche gon.°   *plays*
Wel sikerer° was his crowyng in his logge°   *Much more accurate lodge*
Than is a clokke or any abbey orlogge.°   *horologe (clock)*
By nature he knew ech ascensioun
Of the equinoxial in thilke toun,
For whan degrees fiftene were ascended,[21]

[21] According to ancient astronomy the heavens were thought of as rotating 360° daily around the earth's equator in what was called the equinoctial circle. Thus a new sector of 15° "ascended" at each of the twenty-four hours of the day.

Thanne krew he that it myghte nat ben amended.°   so that it couldn't be
His comb was redder than the fyn coral   bettered
And batailled as° it were a castel wal.   40   battlemented as if
His byle° was blak, and as the jeet° it shoon.   bill   jet
Lyk asure were hise legges and his toon,°   toes
Hise nayles whitter than the lylye flour,
And lyk the burned° gold was his colour.   burnished
This gentil cok hadde in his governaunce°   control
Sevene hennes for to doon° al his pleasaunce,°   do   pleasure
Whiche were hise sustres° and his paramours,°   sisters (sweethearts)
                                                                       mistresses
And wonder° lyke to hym as of colours,   wonderfully
Of whiche the faireste hewed on hire throte
Was cleped° faire damoysele Pertelote.   50   called
Curteys she was, discreet, and debonaire,
And compaignable, and bar° hirself so faire   conducted
Syn thilke° day that she was seven nyght oold   Since that same
That, trewely, she hath the herte in hoold
Of Chauntecleer, loken° in every lith.°   locked   limb
He loved hire so that wel was hym ther-with.°   he was well contented
But swich a joye was it to here hem° synge,   them
Whan that the brighte sonne gan to sprynge,°   began to rise
In swete acord "My leef is faren in londe.° "   sweetheart has gone to the
                                                                       country
For thilke° tyme, as I have understonde,   60   (at) that
Beestes and briddes° koude speke and synge.   birds
     And so bifel that in a dawenynge,°   one dawn
As Chauntecleer among his wyves alle
Sat on his perche, that was in the halle,
And next hym sat this faire Pertelote,
This Chauntecleer gan gronen° in his throte   began to groan
As man that in his dreem is drecched° soore.   tormented
     And whan that° Pertelote thus herde hym rore,   when (whan that)
She was agast and seyde, "Herte deere,
What eyleth yow to grone in this manere?   70
Ye ben a verray° slepere. Fy, for shame!"   sound
     And he answerde and seyde thus: "Madame,
I prey yow that ye take it nat agrief.°   ill
By God, me mette° I was in swich meschief   I dreamed
Right now that yet° myn herte is soore afright.   still
Now God," quod° he, "my swevene recche° aright,   said   may my dream work
                                                                       out
And kepe my body out of foul prisoun.
Me mette how that° I romed up and doun   I dreamed that
Withinne oure yeerd, where-as I say° a beest,   where I saw
Was lyk an hound and wolde han maad areest°   80   have seized

Upon my body and han° had me deed.   have
His colour was bitwixe yelow and reed,
And tipped was his tayl and bothe hise erys°   ears
With blak unlik the remenaunt° of hise herys,° rest hair
His snowte smal, with glowyng eyen tweye.°   eyes two
Yet of his look for fere almoost I deye.
This caused me my gronyng, doutelees."
    "Avoy!"° quod she. "Fy on yow, hertelees!   Shame
Allas," quod she, "for, by that God above,
Now han° ye lost myn herte and al my love.   90 have
I kan nat love a coward, by my feith!
For, certes,° what so° any womman seith,   certainly whatever
We alle desiren, if it myghte be,
To han housbondes hardy, wise, and fre,°   generous
And secree,° and no nygard, ne no fool,   discreet ·
Ne hym that is agast of every tool,°   weapon
Ne noon avauntour,° by that God above.   boaster
How dorste° ye seyn, for shame, unto youre love dared
That any thyng myghte make you aferd?
Have ye no mannes herte and han a berd?°   100 beard
    "Allas, and konne ye ben agast of swevenys.° be afraid of dreams
No thyng, God woot,° but vanytee in swevene is.[22] knows
Swevenes engendren of replexions,°   are engendered from re-
                          pletion
And ofte of fume° and of complexions,°   vapor temperaments
Whan humours ben to° habundant in a wight.° are too person
    "Certes, this dreem which ye han met to-nyght° have dreamed this night
Comth of the grete superfluytee
Of youre rede colera,° pardee,°   choler certainly
Which causeth folk to dreden° in hir° dremes be frightened their
Of arwes,° and of fyr with rede lemes,°   110 arrows flames
Of rede bestes that they wol hem byte,
Of contek,° and of whelpes grete and lyte   strife
Right° as the humour of malencolie°   Just melancholy
Causeth ful many a man in sleep to crie

---

[22] Pertelote dismisses Chauntecleer's *swevene* or dream as a "natural dream" of physiological and not of supernatural origin, presumably produced by a superabundance in his "complexion" (l. 104) of one of the four "humors" or bodily fluids—choler, melancholy, phlegm, or blood. The colors involved in the dream suggest that the excess humor in his case is choler; she therefore prescribes a laxative (l. 123, ll. 142–145) to be preceded by a digestive of worms (l. 141) in order to absorb the choler and warns him against ague and the tertian fever (ll. 139–140), a fever recurring every other day, which was associated with both choler and melancholy.

For fere of blake beres,° or boles° blake, — bears bulls
Or elles blake develes, wol hem° take. — (which) will them
Of othere humours koude I telle also
That werken° many a man in sleep ful wo,° — make woeful
But I wol passe as lightly as I kan.
Lo Catoun,° which that was so wys a man, — 120 (Dionysius) Cato
Seyde he nat thus: 'Ne do no fors of° dremes'? — Pay no attention to
  "Now sire," quod she, "whan we fle fro° the — fly down from
    bemes,
For Goddes love, as taak° som laxatif. — take (as taak)
Up° peril of my soule and of my lif, — Upon
I conseille yow the beste, I wol nat lye,
That bothe of colere and of malencolye
Ye purge yow. And, for° ye shal nat tarye, — in order that
Thogh in this toun is noon° apothecarye, — no
I shal myself to herbes techen° yow — direct
That shul ben for youre heele° and for youre — cure well-being
    prow.° — 130
And in oure yerd tho° herbes shal I fynde — those
The whiche han° of hire propretee by kynde° — Which have nature
To purge yow bynethe and eek° above. — also
Foryet° nat this, for Goddes owene love: — Forget
Ye ben ful colerik of complexioun.
Ware° the sonne in his ascensioun — Beware that
Ne fynde yow nat replet of° humours hote, — overfilled with
And, if it do, I dar wel leye a grote° — groat (4 pence)
That ye shul have a fevere terciane° — tertian
Or an agu that may be youre bane.° — 140 destruction
A day or two ye shul have digestyves
Of wormes er° ye take youre laxatyves — before
Of lauriol,° centaure,° and fumetere,° — spurge laurel centaury fumitory
Or elles° of ellebor° that groweth there, — else hellebore
Of kapatpuce,° or of gaitrys beryis,° — caper spurge gay tree berries
Of herbe yve° growyng in oure yerd, ther merye is.° — ground ivy where it is pleasant
Pekke hem up right as they growe, and ete hem in.
Be myrie, housbonde, for youre fader kyn!° — father's kin
Dredeth° no dreem. I kan sey yow namoore." — Dread
  "Madame," quod he, "graunt mercy of° youre — much thanks for instruction
    loore.° — 150
But nathelees, as touchyng daun Catoun,° — as for sir Cato
That hath of widom swich° a gret renoun, — such
Thogh that he bad no dremes for to drede,
By God, men may in olde bokes rede

Of many a man moore of auctoritee
Than evere Catoun was, so mote I thee,°   *may I prosper*
That al the revers° seyn of his sentence°   *contrary   opinion*
And han wel founden° by experience   *found*
That dremes ben° significaciouns   *are*
As wel of joye as of tribulaciouns   160
That folk enduren in this lyf present.
Ther nedeth° make of this noon argument;   *There is (no) need to*
The verray preeve° sheweth it in dede.   *very proof*
   "Oon° of the gretteste auctor° that men rede   *One   author(s)*
Seith thus, that whilom° two felawes° wente   *once   companions*
On pilgrymage in a ful good entente,
And happed° so they coomen° in a toun   *it happened   came*
Where-as ther was swich° congregacioun   *such*
Of peple and eek so streit of herbergage°   *short of lodgings*
That they ne founde° as muche as a cotage   170 *didn't find*
In which they bothe myghte y-logged° be.   *lodged*
Wherfore they mosten° of necessitee,   *must*
As for° that nyght, departen° compaignye,   *For   part*
And ech of hem gooth to his hostelrye
And took his loggyng as it wolde falle.
That oon of hem° was logged in a stalle   *The one of them*
Fer in a yeerd° with oxen of the plow.   *Far off in a courtyard*
That oother man was logged wel ynow°   *enough*
As was his aventure° or his fortune,   *lot*
That us governeth alle as in commune.°   180 *all in common*
   "And so bifel that, longe er it were day,
This man mette° in his bed ther-as° he lay   *dreamed   where*
How that his felawe gan° upon hym calle   *began to*
And seyde. 'Allas, for in an oxes stalle
This nyght I shal be mordred ther° I lye.   *murdered where*
Now help me, deere brother, or I dye.
In alle haste com to me,' he sayde.
   "This man out of his sleep for feere abrayde,°   *awoke*
But whan that he was wakned of his sleep,
He turned hym and took of this no keep.°   190 *heed*
Hym thoughte° his dreem nas but° a vanytee.   *It seemed to him   was only*
Thus twies° in his slepyng dremed he,   *twice*
And atte thridde tyme yet his felawe
Cam, as hym thoughte, and seyde, 'I am now
     slawe.°   *slain*
Bihoold my blody woundes, depe and wyde.
Arys up erly in the morwe tyde,°   *morningtime*

And at the west gate of the toun,' quod he,
'A carte ful of donge° ther shaltow se,°   dung   you will see
In which my body is hid ful pryvely.°   very secretly
Do thilke° carte aresten° boldely.   200   Have that same   stopped
My gold caused my mordre, sooth to seyn';°   truth to tell
And tolde hym every poynt how he was slayn
With a ful pitous° face pale of hewe.   piteous
And truste wel his dreem he fond° ful trewe,   found
For on the morwe, as soone as it was day,
To his felawes in° he took the way,   companion's lodging
And whan that he cam to this oxes stalle,
After° his felawe he bigan to calle.   For
    "The hostiler answerde hym anon°   at once
And seyde, 'Sire, youre felawe is agon.°   gone
As soone as day he wente out of the toun.'
    "This man gan fallen° in suspecioun,   began to fall
Remembrynge on hise dremes that he mette,°   dreamed
And forth he gooth, no lenger wolde he lette,°   stay
Unto the west gate of the toun and fond
A dong carte, wente° as it were to donge° lond,   (which) went   manure
That was arrayed in the same wise
As ye han herd the dede man devyse,°   describe
And with an hardy herte he gan to crye
Vengeaunce and justice of this felonye.   220
'My felawe mordred is this same nyght,
And in this carte heere he lyth° gapyng upright.°   lies   face upward
I crye out on the mynystres,' quod he,
'That sholden kepe and reulen this citee.
Harrow,° allas! Heere lyth my felawe slayn!'   Help
What sholde I moore unto this tale sayn?
The peple out sterte° and caste the cart to grounde,   sprang
And in the myddel of the dong they founde
The dede man, that mordred was al newe.°   just recently
    "O blisful God, that are so just and trewe, 230
Lo how that thow biwreyest mordre alway°   reveal murder always
Mordre wol out, that se° we day by day.   see
Mordre is so wlatsom° and abhomynable   foul
To God, that is so just and resonable,
That he ne wol nat suffre it heled° be,   concealed
Thogh it abyde° a yeer, or two, or thre.   await
Mordre wol out, this is my conclusioun.
And right anon ministres of that toun
Han hent° the cartere and so soore hym pyned°   Have seized   tortured

And eek° the hostiler so soore engyned°   240   also   racked
That they biknewe hir° wikkednesse anon   confessed their
And were an-hanged by the nekke bon.°   bone
    "Heere may men seen that dremes ben to drede.°   are to be feared
And, certes,° in the same book I rede,   certainly
Right in the nexte chapitre after this—
I gabbe° nat, so have I° joye or blys—   exaggerate   may I have
Two men that wolde° han passed over see   wished to
For certeyn cause into a fer contree,
If that the wynd ne hadde ben contrarie,
That made hem in a citee for to tarie,   250
That stood ful myrie° upon an haven° syde.   pleasant   harbor
But on a day, agayn the even tyde,°   towards eveningtime
The wynd gan chaunge and blew right as hem
    leste.°   they wished
Jolif° and glad they wente unto hir° reste   Jolly   their
And casten hem° ful erly for to saille.   decided
    "But herkneth! To that o° man fil° a greet   one   befell
    mervaille,
That oon of hem, in slepyng as he lay,
Hym mette° a wonder° dreem agayn° the day.   Dreamed   wonderful   before
Hym thoughte° a man stood by his beddes syde,   It seemed to him
And hym comanded that he sholde abyde,   260
And seyde him thus: 'If thow tomorwe wende,°   travel
Thou shalt be dreynt.° My tale is at an ende.'   drowned
He wook, and tolde his felawe what he mette,°   dreamed
And preyde hym his viage° to lette.°   voyage   delay
As for that day, he preyde hym to abyde.
His felawe, that lay by his beddes syde,
Gan for to laughe and scorned hym ful faste.
'No dreem,' quod he, 'may so myn herte agaste°   frighten
That I wol lette for to do my thynges.°   stop doing my business
I sette nat a straw by thy dremynges,   270
For swevenes ben° but vanytees and japes.°   dreams are   follies
Men dreme alday° of owles and of apes   every day
And of many a maze° therwithal;   wonder
Men dreme of thyng that nevere was ne shal.°   nor shall (be)
But, sith° I see that thow wolt here abyde,   since
And thus forslewthen wilfully° thy tyde,°   squander willingly   time
God woot,° it reweth me,° and have good day!'   knows   I rue it
And thus he took his leve and wente his way,
But er that° he hadde half his cours y-seyled,   before

Noot I° nat why ne° what meschaunce it eyled,° 280   I don't know   nor   ailed

But casuelly° the shippes botme rente,°   by chance   burst

And ship and man under the water wente

In sighte of othere shippes it bisyde°   beside it

That with hem seyled at the same tyde.

And therfore, faire Pertelote so deere,

By swiche ensamples° olde maystow leere°   such examples   you may learn

That no man sholde been to recchelees°   too heedless

Of dremes, for I sey° thee, doutelees,   tell

That many a dream ful soore is for to dred.°   to be dreaded

   "Lo, in the lyf of Seint Kenelm I rede, 290

That was Kenulphus sone,° the noble kyng   Kenulphus' son

Of Mercenrike,° how Kenelm mette° a thyng.[23]   Mercia   dreamed

A lite er° he was mordred on a day,   little before

His mordre° in his avysioun° he say.°   murder   vision   saw

His norice° hym expowned every del°   nurse   expounded completely

His swevene,° and bad hym for to kepe hym° wel   dream   to guard himself

For° traisoun, but he nas but° sevene yeer old,   Against   was only

And therfore litel tale° hath he told°   heed   paid

Of any dreem, so holy was his herte.

By God, I hadde levere° than my sherte 300   rather

That ye hadde rad° his legende as have I.   read

Dame Pertelote, I sey yow trewely,

Macrobeus,° that writ° the avysioun°   Macrobius   writes   vision

In Affrike° of the worthy Cipioun,°   Africa   Scipio

Affermeth dremes and seith that they ben

Warnynge of thynges that men aften sen.° [24]   afterward see

And forther-moore, I pray yow, looketh wel

In the Olde Testament,[25] of Daniel,

If he heeld dremes any vanytee.

Rede eek of Joseph, and there shul ye see 310

Wher° dremes be somtyme, I sey nat alle,   Whether

Warnyge of thynges that shul after falle.

---

[23] After the death of his father, Kenulphus, in 821, seven-year-old Kenelm became heir to Mercia but was murdered by his aunt. Shortly before his death he dreamed that he climbed a tree, a friend cut it down, and he flew to heaven in the shape of a bird.   [24] The Latin author Macrobius wrote, at the end of the fourth century, a commentary on Cicero's account of the dream of Scipio Africanus Minor, which became a standard authority on dreams in the Middle Ages. [25] Daniel (according to the book of Daniel) and Joseph (Gen. 37, 40, 41) are both typical of the Old Testament seers who prophesy the future by their own dreams and the dreams of others. Joseph correctly predicted the meaning of dreams for Pharaoh and for Pharaoh's butler and baker.

Looke of Egipte° the kyng, daun Pharao,° Egypt lord Pharaoh
His bakere, and his butiller also,
Wher° they ne felt noon effect in dremes. Whether
Who-so° wol seke actes of sondry remes° whoever various realms
May rede of dremes many a wonder° thyng. wondrous
Lo Cresus,° which that was of Lyde° kyng, Croesus Lydia
Mette° he nat° that he sat upon a tree, Dreamed not
Which signified he sholde an-hanged be? 320
Lo heere Andromacha,° Ectores° wyf, Andromache Hector's
That day that Ector sholde lese° his lyf, lose
She dremed on the same nyght biforn° before
How that the lyf of Ector sholde be lorn° lost
If thilke° day he wente in to bataille. that same
She warned hym, but it myghte nat availle;
He wente for to fighte, nathelees.° nevertheless
But he was slayn anon of° Achilles. immediately by
But thilke° tale is al to° long to telle, that same too
And eek it is ny° day. I may nat dwelle. 330 near
 "Shortly I seye, as for conclusioun,
That I shal han of this avysioun
Adversitee, and I seye forther-moor
That I ne telle of laxatyves no stoor,° set no store on laxatives
For they ben venymes,° I woot° it wel. are venomous know
I hem deffye! I love hem never a del.° them not at all
 "Now lat us speke of myrthe and stynte° al this. stop
Madame Pertelote, so have I° blis, may I have
Of o° thyng God hath sent me large grace, one
For whan I se the beautee of youre face, 340
Ye ben° so scarlet reed° aboute youre eyen,° are red eyes
It maketh al my drede for to dyen,
For, also siker° as *In principio*, as sure
'*Mulier est hominis confusio.*' [26]
 "Madame, the sentence° of this Latyn is, meaning
'Womman is mannes joye and al his blis.'
For whan I feele a-nyght youre softe syde,
Al be it that I may nat on yow ryde
For that° oure perche is maad° so narwe,° allas, Because made narrow
I am so ful of joye and of solas° 350 pleasure

[26] The phrase *In principio*, "In the beginning (was the Word)," with which the Latin version of John commences, was esteemed in Chaucer's time as a formula of almost magical efficacy. The Friar, according to the General Prologue (l. 254), used it as a preliminary greeting to his victims. The widely used Latin proverb, which Chauntecleer carefully mistranslates, means "Woman is man's ruin."

That I deffye both swevene° and dreem." — vision
   And with that word he fley° doun fro the beem, — flew
For it was day, and eke° hise hennes alle. — also
And with a chuk he gan° hem for to calle, — began
For he hadde founde a corn,° lay° in the yerd. — corn-grain (which) lay
Real° he was; he was na moore aferd.° — Regal no more afraid
He fethered Pertelote twenty tyme
And trad° as ofte er that it was pryme.° — trod (her) prime (9 A.M.)
He looketh as it were° a grym leoun,° — looks like lion
And on hise toos he rometh up and doun.   360
Hym deyned° nat to sette his foot to grounde. — He deigned
He chukketh whan he hath a corn y-founde,
And to hym rennen thanne° hise wyves alle. — run then
Thus real° as a prince is in his halle — regal
Leve I this Chauntecleer in his pasture,
And after wol I telle his aventure.
   Whan that the monthe in which the world bigan,
That highte° March, whan God first maked ° man,[27] — is called made
Was complet, and passed were also,
Syn° March bigan, thritty dayes and two,   370 — Since
Bifel° that Chauntecleer in al his pryde, — It befell
Hise sevene wyves walkyng hym bisyde,
Caste up hise eyen to the brighte sonne,
That in the signe of Taurus hadde y-ronne
Twenty degrees and oon, and som-what moore,
And knew by kynde° and by noon oother loore — nature
That it was pryme,° and krew with blisful stevene.° — prime (9 A.M.) voice
"The sonne," he seyde, "is clomben° upon hevene — has climbed
Fourty degrees and oon, and moore ywis.° — indeed
Madame Pertelote, my worldes blis,   380
Herkneth° thise blisful briddes,° how they synge, — Listen to birds
And se the fresshe floures how they sprynge.
Ful is myn herte of revel and solas.° " — pleasure
But sodeynly hym fil° a sorweful cas,° — befell him happening
For evere the latter ende of joye is wo.
God woot° that worldly joye is soone ago,° — knows gone
And if a rethor° koude faire endite,° — rhetorician compose
He in a cronycle saufly myghte it write
As for a sovereyn notabilitee.° — As a supreme observation
Now every wys man, lat hym herkne° me;   390 — listen to
This storie is also° trewe, I undertake,° — as vow

[27] It was believed in the Middle Ages that the creation of the world occurred in March during the spring equinox.

As is the book of *Launcelot de Lake*,[28]
That wommen holde in ful gret reverence.
Now wol I torne agayn to my sentence.°   subject
  A colfox° ful of sly iniquitee,   coal-fox
That in the grove hadde woned° yeres three,   lived
By heigh ymaginacioun forncast,°   divine knowledge fore-
                                                                 ordained
The same nyght thurgh-out the heggs brast°   hedges burst
Into the yerd ther° Chauntecleer the faire   where
Was wont,° and eek hise wyves, to repaire,   400   accustomed
And in a bed of wortes° stille he lay   plants
Til it was passed undren° of the day,   midmorning
Waitynge his tyme on Chauntecleer to falle,
As gladly doon° thise homycides° alle   usually do   murderers
That in awayt liggen° to mordre men.   waiting lie
O false mordrour, lurkynge in thy den,
O newe Scariot,° newe Genyloun,°   Iscariot   Ganelon
False dissimilour,° O Greek Synoun,°   deceiver   Sinon
That broghtest Troye al outrely° to sorwe! [29]   utterly
O Chauntecleer, acursed be that morwe°   410   morning
That thow into the yerd flaugh° fro the bemes.   flew
Thow were ful wel y-warned by thy dremes
That thilke° day was perilous to thee.   that same
But what that God forwoot moot nedes° be   foreknows most needs
After° the opynyoun of certeyn clerkis.°   According to   scholars
Witnesse on hym that any parfit clerk is,
That in scole is greet altercacioun
In this matere and greet disputisoun,°   disputation
And hath ben of an hundred thousand men.
But I ne kan nat bulte° it to the bren°   420   sift   bran
As kan the holy doctour Augustyn°   Augustine
Or Boece,° or the bisshop Bradwardyn,°   Boethius   Bradwardine
Wheither that Goddes worthy forewityng°   excellent   foreknowing
Streyneth° me nedely° for to doon a thyng—   Constrains   necessarily
"Nedely" clepe° I symple necessitee—   call
Or ellis° if fre choys be graunted me   else
To do that same thyng or do it noght,
Though God forwoot° it er that° it was wroght;   foreknows   before
Or if his wityng streyneth never a del°   knowing constrains not at
                                                                 all

[28] An entirely fictitious romance concerning Launcelot, the lover of Guinevere,
King Arthur's wife.   [29] Judas Iscariot, the disciple, betrayed Christ. Ganelon betrayed Charlemagne's nephew Roland. Sinon, in conspiracy with the Greeks
besieging Troy, persuaded the Trojans to take the Greeks' wooden horse into their
city.

But° by necessitee condicionel.³⁰   430   Except
I wol nat han° to do of swich° matere.   have (anything) with such
My tale is of a cok, as ye may heere,
That took his conseil of his wyf with sorwe
To walken in the yerd upon that morwe°   morning
That he hadde met° the dreem that I yow tolde.   dreamed
Wommanes conseils ben° ful ofte colde.°   are   fatal
Wommanes conseil broghte us first to wo
And made Adam fro Paradys to go,
Ther-as° he was ful myrie and wel at ese.   Where
But, for I noot° to whom it myghte displese   440   since I don't know
If I conseil of wommen wolde blame,
Passe over, for I seyde it in my game.°   in jest
Rede auctours° where they trete of swich matere,   authors
And what they seyn° of wommen ye may heere.   say
Thise ben the cokkes wordes and nat myne;
I kan noon° harm of no womman devyne.°   no   imagine
    Faire in the sond° to bathe hire myrily°   sand   happily
Lith° Pertelote, and alle hir sustres° by,   Lies   sisters
Agayn the sonne;° and Chauntecleer so free   In the sun
Song° myrier than the mermayde in the see,   450   Sang
For Phisiologus seith sikerly°   says certainly
How that° they syngen wel and myrily.³¹   That
    And so bifel that, as he caste his eye
Among the wortes° on a boterflye,°   plants   butterfly
He was war° of this fox that lay ful lowe.   aware
No thyng ne liste hym thanne° for to crowe,   Not at all did he wish then
But cryde anon° "Cok, cok," and up he sterte°   at once   sprang
As man° that was affrayed° in his herte,   Like someone   frightened
For naturelly° a beest desireth flee°   by nature   to flee
Fro his contrarie,° if he may it see,   460   opposite

³⁰ God, being omniscient, must at all times have a correct foreknowledge of man's choice of action. Has man, therefore, "free choice" (l. 426) of action; and if not, to what extent is he responsible for his own good or bad actions? Among the many philosophers and theologians who have discussed this complex problem, St. Augustine of Hippo (354–430) elaborated the concept of "free choice"; Boethius in his *Consolation of Philosophy* (sixth century), translated by Chaucer, distinguished between simple (l. 425) and conditional (l. 430) necessity; and Thomas Bradwardine (l. 422), archbishop of Canterbury, who died in 1349, delivered notable lectures at Oxford on the subject. ³¹ Physiologus was the reputed author of a Greek work on natural history, composed in the second century, which gave rise to numerous later imitations known as *Bestiaries*. These notoriously unscientific works provided entertaining lore about animals and fabulous creatures, and instructive allegorical interpretations.

Though he nevere erst° hadde syn° it with his eye.	before seen
This Chauntecleer, whan he gan hym espye,°	noticed him
He wolde han fled but° that the fox anon	except
Seyde, "Gentile sire, allas! Wher wol ye gon?	
Be ye affrayed of me that am youre freend?	
Now, certes,° I were worse than a feend	certainly
If I to yow wolde° harm or vileynye.	intended
I am nat come youre conseil for t'espye,°	secret to discover
But trewely the cause of my comynge	
Was oonly for to herkne how that° ye synge, 470	hear how
For trewely ye han as myrie a stevene°	voice
As any aungel hath that is in hevene.	
Ther-with ye han in musyk moore feelynge	
Than hadde Boece³² or any that kan synge.	
My lord, youre fader—God his soule blesse!—	
And eek youre moder, of hire gentillesse,°	gentility
Han in myn hous y-ben° to my greet ese.°	been satisfaction
And, certes, sire, ful fayn° wolde I yow plese.	gladly
"But, for° men speke of syngynge, I wol seye—	since
So mote I brouke° wel myne eyen tweye!— 480	may I use
Save° yow I herde nevere man so synge	Except for
As dide youre fader in the morwenynge.	
Certes, it was of herte,° al that he song.	hearty
And for to make his voys the moore strong,	
He wolde so peyne hym° that with bothe hise eyen	strive
He moste wynke,° so loude he wolde cryen,	must shut (his eyes)
And stonden° on his tiptoon° ther-with-al,	stand tiptoes
And strecche forth his nekke long and smal.	
And eek he was of swich discrecioun	
That ther nas no° man in no regioun 490	was no
That hym in song or wisdom myghte passe.	
I have wel rad° in Daun° Burnel the Asse,	read Sir
Among his vers, how that ther was a cok,	
For° a preestes sone yaf° hym a knok	Because gave
Upon his leg, while he was yong and nyce,°	foolish
He made hym for to lese° his benefice.³³	lose
But, certeyn, ther nys no comparisoun	

³² Boethius, besides writing on philosophy, was the author of a work entitled *On Music*. ³³According to the tale in Nigel Wireker's twelfth-century Latin poem *Burnellus the Ass,* a young man named Gundulf threw a stone at a cock and broke its leg. Later, when Gundulf was to have been appointed as priest to a benefice, the cock avenged himself by failing to awaken Gundulf with his crowing in time for the ordination.

Bitwix the wisdom and discrecioun
Of youre fader and of his subtiltee.
Now syngeth, sire, for seinte° charitee!   500   holy
Lat se, konne ye youre fader countrefete?" °   imitate
    This Chauntecleer hise wynges gan° to bete   began
As man that koude his traysoun nat espie,°   perceive
So was he ravysshed with° his flaterie.   overwhelmed by
    Allas, ye lordes, many a fals flatour°   flatterer
Is in youre court, and many a losengeour,°   deceiver
That plesen° yow wel moore, by my feith,   please
Than he that soothfastnesse° unto yow seith.   truth
Redeth Ecclesiaste of° flaterye.   Ecclesiasticus on
Beth war,° ye lordes, of hir° trecherye.   510   Beware   their
This Chauntecleer stood hye upon his toos,
Strecchynge his nekke, and heeld hise eyen cloos,°   closed
And gan to crowe loude for the nones.°   occasion
And daun° Russell the fox stirte up atones,°   sir   sprang up at once
And by the gargat hente° Chauntecleer,   throat seized
And on his bak toward the wode hym beer,°   carried
For yet ne was ther no man that hym sewed.°   pursued
    O destynee, that mayst nat ben eschewed! °   be avoided
Allas that Chauntecleer fleigh° fro the bemes!   flew
Allas, his wij ne roghte nat° of dremes!   520   took no heed
And on a Friday fil at this meschaunce.
    O Venus, that art goddesse of plesaunce,°   pleasure
Syn that° thy servant was this Chauntecleer,   Since
And in thy servyce dide al his power
Moore for delit° than world to multiplie,   delight
Why woldestow suffre° hym on thy day to dye?   would you allow
    O Gaufred,° deere maister soverayn,   Geoffrey
That, whan thy worthy kyng Richard was slayn
With shot, compleynedest° his deth so soore,   lamented
Why ne hadde I now thy sentence° and thy loore°   erudition   learning
The Friday for to chide, as diden ye?   531
For on a Friday, soothly,° slayn was he.[34]   truly

---

[34] Friday, as the French word *vendredi* indicates, is the day of Venus. In his Latin verse treatise on the composition of poetry, entitled *The New Poetry* and composed at the end of the twelfth century, Goeffrey de Vinsauf offers as a sample of his highly rhetorical techniques an elegy for King Richard I, who was mortally wounded (in 1199) on a Friday. It begins: "O tearful day of Venus! O sorry star! That day was your night, and that Venus was venomous." Although Geoffrey's rhetoric was still imitated by students in Chaucer's age, Chaucer himself obviously intends the Priest's homage to be ironical.

Thanne wolde I shewe yow how that I koude
    pleyne°   lament
For Chauntecleeres drede and for his peyne.
    Certes, swich cry ne° lamentacioun   or
Was nevere of ladyes maad° whan Ylioun°   made Ilium (Troy)
Was wonne, and Pirrus° with his streite swerd°   Pyrrhus   drawn sword
Whanne he hadde hent° kyng Priam by the berd   seized
And slayn hym, as seith us *Eneydos,*°   (the) *Aeneid* tells us
As maden° alle the hennes in the cloos°   540 made enclosure
Whan they hadde seyn° of Chauntecleer the sighte. seen
But sovereynly° dame Pertelote shrighte°   especially shrieked
Ful louder than dide Hasdrubales wyf
Whan that° hire housbonde hadde lost his lyf   When
And that the Romayns hadden brend Cartage.°   burned Carthage
She was so ful of torment and of rage
That wilfully° into the fyr she sterte°   voluntarily leaped
And brende hirselven° with a stedefast herte.   burned herself
    O woful hennes, right so cryden ye
As, whan that Nero brende the citee   550
Of Rome, cryden senatours wyves
For that° hir housbondes losten alle hire° lyves.   Because   all lost their
Withouten° gilt this Nero hath hem slayn.   Without
Now wol I turne to my tale agayn.
    The sely widwe° and eek hire doghtres two   poor widow
Herden thise hennes crye and maken wo,
And out atte dores stirten° they anon,°   out of doors rushed at
                         once
And syen° the fox toward the grove gon,°   saw go
And bar° upon his bak the cok away,   carry (*lit.* carried)
And criden "Out! Harrow!" and "Weilaway! ° 560 Alas
Ha, ha, the fox!" And after hym they ran,
And eek with staves° many another man.   sticks
Ran Colle oure dogge, and Talbot, and Gerland,
And Malkyn, with a distaf in hire hand.[35]
Ran cow, and calf, and eek the verray hogges,
So fered for the berkyng° of the dogges   frightened by the barking
And showtynge° of the men and wommen eek.   shouting
They ronne° so, hem thoughte hir° herte breek.° ran they thought their
                         would break
They yelleden as fendes doon° in helle.   fiends do
The dokes° cryden as° men wolde hem quelle.° 570 ducks as if kill
The gees for feere flowen° over the trees.   flew
Out of the hyve cam the swarm of bees.

[35] *Talbot* and *Gerland* (modern *Garland*) are presumably, like *Colle,* customary
names for dogs. *Malkyn* was the name typifying a country girl. . . .

So hydous° was the noyse, A, *benedicitee,*°   hideous blessings
Certes, he Jakke Straw and his meynee°   company
Ne made nevere shoutes half so shrille
Whan that° they wolden° any Flemyng kille   When would
As thilke° day was maad upon the fox.[36]   that same
Of bras they broghten bemes,° and of box,°   brought trumpets box-
Of horn, of boon,° in whiche they blewe and   wood
    powped,°   bone puffed
And ther-with-al they skryked,° and they howped.°   shrieked whooped
It semed as that° hevene sholde falle.   581 as if
Now goode men, I prey yow, herkneth alle.

    Lo, how Fortune turneth sodeynly°   overturns suddenly
The hope and pryde eek of hire enemy.
This cok that lay upon the foxes bak
In al his drede unto the fox he spak
And seyde, "Sire, if that I were as ye,
Yit sholde I seyn,° as wys God helpe me,   say
'Turneth agayn,° ye proude cherles alle.   Turn back
A verray pestilence upon yow falle.   590
Now I am come unto this wodes° syde,   wood's
Maugree youre heed,° the cok shal here abyde.   Despite all you can do
I wol hym ete, in feith, and that anon.' "
    The fox answerde, "In feith, it shal be don."
And as he spak that word, al sodeynly
This cok brak° from his mouth delyverly,°   broke nimbly
And hye° upon a tree he fley° anon.   high flew
And whan the fox say° that he was gon,   saw
"Allas," quod he, "O Chauntecleer, allas!
I have to yow," quod he, "y-doon trespas°   600 offence
In as muche as I maked yow aferd
Whan I yow hente° and broghte out of the yerd.   seized
But, sire, I dide it in no wikke° entente.   evil
Com doun, and I shal telle yow what I mente.
I shal seye sooth° to yow, God help me so."   truth
    "Nay thanne," quod he, "I shrewe° us bothe two.   curse
And first I shrewe myself, bothe blood and bones,
If thow bigile me any ofter° than ones.   more often

---

[36] During a widespread revolt of English workers (in 1381) against the leaders of state, church, and commerce, an otherwise unknown rebel named Jack Straw, who was later executed, led a group of Kentishmen into London. There they destroyed property and murdered those whom they considered to be their exploiters, including a large number of clothmakers, recently arrived from Flanders, who had kept their superior technique secret from the native English workmen.

Thow shalt namoore thurgh° thy flaterye   no more through
Do° me to synge and wynke with° myn eye,   610   Persuade   close
For he that wynketh, whan he sholde see,
Al wilfully,° God lat hym nevere thee." °   voluntarily   prosper
   "Nay," quod the fox, "but God yeve° hym   give
     meschaunce°   misfortune
That is so undiscreet of governaunce°   self-control
That jangleth° whan he sholde holde his pees." °   chatters   peace
   Lo, swich it is for to be recchelees,°   careless
And necligent, and truste on flaterye.
   But ye that holden this tale a folye
As of° a fox, or of a cok and hen,   Concerning
Taketh the moralitee, goode men.   620
For seint Poul ° seith that al that writen is,   Paul
To oure doctryne° it is y-write,° ywis.°   instruction   written   indeed
Taketh the fruyt, and lat the chaf be stille.
Now goode God, if that it be thy wille,
As seith my lord, so make us alle goode men,
and brynge us to his heye° bliss. Amen.   high

The Pardoner's Tale

   In Flaundres whilom° was a compaignye   Flanders once
Of yonge folk that haunteden° folye,   practiced
As° riot, hasard,° stewes,° and tavernes   Such as   dicing   brothels
Where-as° with harpes, lutes, and gyternes°   Where   guitars
They daunce and pleyen at dees° bothe day and   dice
     nyght,
And ete also and drynke over hir myght,°   beyond their capacity
Thurgh which they doon° the devel sacrifise   do
Withinne that develes temple in cursed wise°   manner
By superfluytee abhomynable.
Hir othes been° so grete and so dampnable   10   Their oaths are
That it is grisly for to heere hem swere;
Oure blissed Lordes body they to-tere;°   tear apart
Hem thoughte that Jewes rente hym noght ynough! [37]

---

[37] It seemed to them that the Jews did not rend him enough! In his tale the Parson admonishes his listeners: ". . . swear not so sinfully, dismembering Christ by soul, heart, bones, and body. For certainly it would seem that you think that the cursed Jews did not dismember the precious person of Christ enough, but that you should dismember him more."

And ech° of hem at otheres synne lough.° — each laughed
And right anon thanne comen tombesteres,° — would come dancing girls
Fetys° and smale,° and yonge frutesteres,° — Trim slender fruit-sellers
Syngeres with harpes, baudes,° wafereres,° — bawds confectioners
Whiche been the verray develes officeres,
To kyndle and blowe the fyr of lecherye,
That is annexed unto glotonye.   20
The Holy Writ take I to my witnesse
That luxurie° is in wyn and dronkenesse. — excess
    Lo how that dronken Loth° unkyndely° — Lot (Gen. 19:33, 35) unnaturally
Lay by his doghtres two unwityngly.° — unknowingly
So dronke he was, he nyste° what he wroghte.° — didn't know was doing
Herodes,° whoso° wel the stories soghte, — Herod (Matt. 14) as one would know who
Whan he of wyn was replet° at his feste, — overfilled
Right at his owene table he yaf ° his heste° — gave order
To sleen° the Baptist John ful giltelees. — slay
Senec° seith a good word, doutelees.   30 — Seneca
He seith he kan no difference fynde
Bitwix a man that is out of his mynde
And a man which that is dronkelewe,° — drunken
But° that woodnesse y-fallen° in a shrewe — Except madness occurring
Persevereth lenger than dooth dronkenesse.
O glotonye, ful of cursednesse,
O cause first of oure confusioun!° — ruin
O original of oure dampnacioun,
Til Crist hadde bought us with his blood agayn! ° — redeemed (boght ... agayn)
Lo how deere,° shortly for to sayn,°   40 — dearly say
Aboght° was thilke° cursed vileynye. — aid for that same
Corrupt was al this world for glotonye.
    Adam oure fader, and his wyf also,
Fro° Paradys to labour and to wo — From
Were dryven for that vice, it is no drede.° — doubt
For whil that Adam fasted, as I rede,
He was in Paradys; and whan that he
Eet° of the fruyt defended° on the tree, — Ate forbidden
Anon° he was out cast to wo and peyne. — At once
O glotonye, on thee wel oghte us pleyne.°   50 — should we complain
O, wiste° a man how manye maladies — knew
Folwen of° excesse and of glotonyes, — Follow from
He wolde been the moore mesurable° — moderate
Of his diete, sittyng at his table.
Allas, the shorte throte, the tendre mouth,
Maketh that, est and west and north and south,

In erthe, in eyr, in water, men to swynke[38]
To gete a glotoun deyntee mete and drynke.
Of this matere, O Paul, wel kanstow° trete.   can you
"Mete unto wombe,° and wombe eek° unto mete,   belly   also
Shal God destroyen bothe," as Paulus° seith.   61 Paul (1 Cor, 6:13)
Allas, a foul thyng is it, by my feith,
To seye this word, and fouler is the dede,
Whan man so drynketh of the white and rede°   red (wine)
That of his throte he maketh his pryvee°   privy
Thurgh thilke° cursed superfluitee.   that same
    The apostle° wepyng seith ful pitously,   Paul (Phil. 3:18, 19)
"Ther walken manye of whiche yow toold have I,—
I seye it now wepyng with pitous voys—
They been° enemys of Cristes croys,   70 are
Of whiche° the ende is deth; wombe is hir° God."   whom   their
O wombe, O bely, O stynkyng cod,°   paunch
Fulfilled of donge and of corrupcioun,
At either ende of thee foul is the soun!°   sound
How greet labour and cost is thee to fynde!°   provide for
Thise cokes,° how they stampe, and streyne, and   cooks
        grynde,
And turnen substaunce into accident,[39]
To fulfillen° al thy likerous talent.°   satisfy   unrestrained
                                                                 appetite
Out of the harde bones knokke they
The mary,° for they caste noght awey   80 marrow
That may go thurgh the golet° softe and soote.°   gullet   sweet
Of spicerie of leef, and bark, and roote
Shal been his sauce y-maked, by delit°   delight
To make hym yet a newer appetit.
But, certes,° he that haunteth swiche delices°   certainly   pursues such
                                                                 delights
Is deed whil that° he lyveth in tho° vices.   dead while   those
    A lecherous thyng is wyn, and dronkenesse
Is ful of stryvyng° and of wrecchednesse.   strife
O dronke man, disfigured is thy face,
Sour is thy breeth, foul artow° to embrace,   90 are you
And thurgh thy dronke nose semeth the soun
As thogh thou seydest ay° "Sampsoun, Sampsoun."   always

---

[38] Chaucer here mixes two constructions: (1) *maketh that men swynke,* "brings about that men toil"; (2) *maketh men to swynke,* "makes men toil."   [39] . . . turn substaunce into accident; that is, convert the essential, "substantial" components which, according to contemporary philosophical teaching, were held to cause things to have appearance, into the temporary, "accidental" appearance of things.

And yet, God woot,° Sampsoun drank nevere no   *knows*
  wyn.⁴⁰
Thou fallest as it were a stiked swyn,°   *like a stuck pig*
Thy tonge is lost, and al thyn honeste cure.°   *care for honor*
For dronkenesse is verray sepulture°   *the very burial*
Of mannes wit° and his discrecioun.   *understanding*
In whom that° drynke hath dominacioun,   *whom*
He kan no conseil kepe, it is no drede.°   *doubt*
Now kepe yow fro the white and fro the rede,   100
And namely fro° the white wyn of Lepe   *particularly from*
That is to selle in Fisshstrete° or in Chepe.°   *Fish Street (London) / Cheapside*
This wyn of Spaigne⁴¹ crepeth subtilly
In othere wynes growynge faste by,°   *nearby*
Of which ther riseth swich fumositee°   *such spirituous vapors*
That, whan a man hath dronken draghtes thre,
And weneth° that he be at hoom in Chepe,   *believes*
He is in Spaigne right at the toune of Lepe,
Nat at the Rochel° ne at Burdeux° toun.   *La Rochelle / Bordeaux (France)*
And thanne wol he seyn "Sampsoun, Sampsoun."   110
  But herkneth, lordynges, o° word, I yow preye,   *one*
That alle the sovereyn actes, dar I seye,
Of victories in the Olde Testament,
Thurgh verray God, that is omnipotent,
Were doon in abstinence and in prayere.
Looketh° the Bible, and ther ye may it leere.°   *Look at / learn*
  Looke, Attila,⁴² the grete conquerour,
Deyde in his sleep with shame and dishonour,
Bledyng at his nose in dronkenesse.
A capitayn sholde lyve in sobrenesse.   120
And over al this, avyseth yow° right wel   *consider*
What was comaunded unto Lamwel° —   *Lemuel*
Nat Samuel but Lamwel, seye I.
Redeth the Bible, and fynd it expresly
Of wyn-yevyng° to hem that han justise.   *wine-giving*
Namoore of this, for it may wel suffise.

---

⁴⁰ Samson had vowed the vow of a Nazarite never to drink wine. ⁴¹ The strong wines of Lepe and of other Spanish vineyards, which were cheaper in England than the superior wines produced "faste by" in France, were evidently used to adulterate the more expensive vintages. ⁴² The Pardoner has here abruptly abandoned his generalization about Old Testament victories without attempting to provide examples. Attila, king of the Huns, died in 453, reputedly through drunkenness on his wedding night. In Proverbs, 31, the otherwise unknown King Lemuel (l. 122) is enjoined to avoid wine.

And now that I have spoken of glotonye,
Now wol I yow defenden hasardrye.°   forbid dicing
Hasard is verray moder of lesynges,°   the very mother of false-
                                                             hood
And of deceite, and cursed forswerynges,°   130   perjuries
Blaspheme° of Crist, manslaughtre, and wast° also   Blasphemy   waste
Of catel° and of tyme; and forther mo°   substance   more
It is repreve° and contrarie of honour   reproach
For to ben holde° a commune hasardour.   To be held
And evere the hyer he is of estaat,
The moore is he holden desolat.
If that a prynce useth hasardrye,
In alle governaunce and policye
He is, as by° commune opynyoun,   by (as by)
Y-holde the lasse in reputacioun.   140
    Stilbon, that was a wys embassadour,
Was sent to Corynthe in ful gret honour
Fro Lacedomye° to make hire° alliaunce;   Lacedaemon (in Greece)
                                                            their
And whan he cam, hym happed ° par chaunce   it happened to him
That alle the gretteste that were of that lond
Pleiynge atte hasard he hem fond.°   found
For which, as soone as it myghte be,
He stal° hym hoom agayn to his contree,   stole
And seyde, "Ther wol I nat lese° my name,   lose
N' I wol nat° take on me so greet defame   150   Nor will
Yow for to allie unto none hasardours.
Sendeth othere wise embassadours,
For, by my trouthe, me were levere° dye   I would rather
Than I yow sholde to hasardours allye.
For ye that been so glorious in honours
Shal nat allye yow with hasardours
As by° my wyl ne as by my tretee."   By
This wise philosophre thus seyde he.
    Looke eek that to the kyng Demetrius
The kyng of Parthes,° as the book seith us,   160   Parthia
Sente hym a paire of dees° of gold in scorn,   dice
For° he hadde used hasard ther-biforn;°   Because   previously
For which he heeld his glorie or his renoun
At no value or reputacioun.
Lordes may fynden oother manere° pley   sort of
Honeste ynow° to dryve the day awey.   enough
    Now wol I speke of oothes false and grete
A word or two, as olde bokes trete.
Greet sweryng is a thyng abhomynable,

And fals sweryng is yet moore reprevable.°   170   reprovable
The heighe God forbad sweryng at al.
Witnesse on Mathew;° but in special   Matthew 5:34
Of sweryng seith the holy Jeremye,°   Jeremiah 4:2
"Thow shalt swere sooth° thyne othes and nat lye,   truthfully
And swere in doom° and eek in rightwisnesse." °   judgment   righteousness
But ydel° sweryng is a cursednesse.   vain
Bihoold and se that, in the firste table
Of heighe Goddes Hestes° honurable,   (Ten)   Commandments
How that the Seconde Heste of hym is this:
"Take nat my name in ydel° or amys."   180   vain
Lo, rather he forbedeth swich sweryng
Than homycide or many a cursed thyng.
I seye that, as by ordre,° thus it standeth;   in order
This knowen, that hise Hestes understandeth,
How that the Seconde Heste of God is that.
And forther over, I wol thee telle al plat°   plainly
That vengeance shall nat parten° from his hous   depart (Ecclesiasticus
That of hise othes is to° outrageous.   23:11)
                                                           too
"By Goddes precious herte," and "By his nayles,"
And "By the blood of Crist that is in Hayles,"°   190   (preserved) at Hayles
Sevene is my chaunce, and thyn is cynk° and   (Gloucestershire)
      treye," °   five
                                                           three
"By Goddes armes, if thow falsly pleye,
This daggere shal thurgh out thyn herte go,"—
This fruyt cometh of the bicched bones° two,   cursed dice
Forsweryng, ire, falsnesse, homycide.
Now, for the love of Crist, that for us dyde,
Lete° youre othes, bothe grete and smale.   Restrain
But, sires, now wol I telle forth my tale.
    This riotoures° thre of whiche I telle,   profligates
Longe erst er pryme rong° of any belle,   200   before prime (9A.M.) rang
Were set hem° in a taverne to drynke;   seated
And, as they sat, they herde a belle clynke°   clang
Biforn a cors° was caried to his° grave.   corpse (which)   its
That oon° of hem gan° callen to his knave:°   One   began to   boy
"Go bet,"° quod° he, "and axe° redily   faster   said   ask
What cors is this that passeth heer forby.
And looke that thow reporte his name wel."
    "Sire," quod this boy, "it nedeth° never a del.°   is necessary   one bit
It is me told er ye cam heer two houres.
He was, pardee,° an old felawe° of youres,   210   certainly   companion
And sodeynly he was y-slayn to-nyght,°   last night

Fordronke,° as he sat on his bench upright.   Very drunk
Ther cam a pryvee° theef, men clepeth° Deeth, secretive (whom) men
                     call
That in this contree al the peple sleeth,°   slays
And with his spere he smoot his herte a-two,° in two
And wente his wey withouten wordes mo.
He hath a thousand slayn, this pestilence.
And, maister, er ye come in his presence,
Me thynketh that it were necessarie
For to be war of swich an adversarie.   220
Beth° redy for to meete hym evere moore.° Be always
Thus taughte me my dame.° I sey namoore." mother
 "By seinte Marie," seyde this taverner,°   innkeeper
"The child seith sooth, for he hath slayn this yer,
Henne° over a myle, withinne a greet village, Hence
Bothe man and womman, child, and hyne,° and page. servant
I trowe° his habitacioun be there.   believe
To been avysed° greet wisdom it were,   be prepared
Er that he dide a man a dishonour."
 "Ye,° Goddes armes!" quod this riotour. 230 Yes
"Is it swich peril with hym for to meete?
I shal hym seke by wey and eek by strete,
I make avow to Goddes digne° bones.   worthy
Herkneth, felawes. We thre been al ones.°   one
Lat ech of us holde up his hand til° oother,   to
And ech of us bicome otheres brother,°   the other's sworn brother
And we wol sleen° this false traytour Deeth. slay
He shal be slayn, he that so manye sleeth,
By Goddes dignytee, er it be nyght."
 Togidres° han thise thre hir trouthes plight° 240 Together pledged their
                      faith
To lyve and dyen ech of hem for oother,
As thogh he were his owene y-bore° brother. born
And up they stirte,° al dronken in this rage, sprang
And forth they goon towardes that village
Of which the taverner hadde spoke biforn.
And many a grisly ooth thanne han they sworn,
And Cristes blessed body they to-rente.°   tore to pieces
Deeth shal be deed, if that they may hym hente!° catch
 Whan they han goon nat fully half a myle,
Right° as they wolde han treden° over a stile, 250 Just have stepped
An old man and a poure° with hem mette.   poor
This olde man ful mekely hem grette°   greeted
And seyde thus, "Now, lordes, God yow se."° save
 The proudeste of thise riotoures thre

Answerde agayn,° "What, carl!° With sory grace!°   back churl Curse you!
Why artow° al forwrapped° save thy face?   are you wrapped up
Why lyvestow° so longe in so greet age?"   live you
  This olde man gan looke° in his visage   looked
And seyde thus: "For° I ne kan nat fynde   Because
A man, thogh that I walked into Inde,°   260 India
Neither in citee ne in no village,
That wolde chaunge his youthe for myn age.
And, therfore, moot° I han myn age stille,   must
As longe tyme as it is Goddes wille.
  "Ne Deeth, allas, ne wol nat han° my lyf.   have
Thus walke I lyk a restelees caytyf,°   wretch
And on the ground, which is my modres° gate,   mother's
I knokke with my staf bothe erly and late,
And seye, "Leeve° moder, leet me in.   Dear
Lo, how I vanysshe, flessh, and blood, and skyn. 270
Allas, whan shul my bones been at reste?
Moder, with yow wolde I chaunge my cheste,°   clothes chest
That in my chambre longe tyme hath be,°   been
Ye,° for an heyre clowt° to wrappe me!'   Yes hair rag
But yet to me she wol nat do that grace,
For which ful pale and welked° is my face.   withered
  "But, sires, to yow it is no curteisye
To speken to an old man vileynye
But° he trespase in word or elles° in dede.   Unless else
In Holy Writ ye may yourself wel rede,   280
'Agayns° an old man, hoor° upon his heed,   Before hoary (Lev.
Ye sholde arise.' Wherfore I yeve° yow reed:°   19:32)
                                                     give advice
Ne dooth° unto an old man noon harm now,   Don't do
Namoore than that ye wolde men dide to yow
In age, if that ye so longe abyde.
And God be with yow, wher° ye go° or ryde.   whether walk
I moot° go thider as° I have to go."   must where
  "Nay, olde cherl. By God, thow shalt nat so,"
Seyde this oother hasardour° anon.   gambler
"Thow partest° nat so lightly,° by seint John. 290 depart easily
Thow spak right now of thilke° traytour Deeth,   that same
That in this contree alle oure freendes sleeth.
Have here my trouthe,° as thow art his espye,°   oath spy
Telle wher he is, or thow shalt it abye,°   pay for
By God and by the holy sacrament!
For soothly thow art oon of his assent
To sleen° us yonge folk, thow false theef!"   slay

"Now, sires," quod he, "if that yow be so leef°   *eager*
To fynde Deeth, turn up this croked wey.
For in that grove I lafte° hym, by my fey,°   300   *left*   *faith*
Under a tree, and ther he wol abyde.
Nat for youre boost he wol hym° no thyng hyde.   *himself*
Se ye that ook?° Right ther ye shal hym fynde.   *oak*
God save yow, that boghte agayn° mankynde,   *redeemed*
And yow amende." Thus seyde this olde man.
And everich° of thise riotoures ran   *each*
Til they came to that tree, and ther they founde
Of floryns° fyne of gold y-coyned rounde   *florins (coins)*
Wel ny an eighte° busshels, as hem thoughte.°   *Very nearly eight*   *it seemed to*
No lenger thanne° after Deeth they soughte;   310   *then*
But ech of hem so glad was of the sighte,
For that the floryns been so faire and brighte,
That doun they sette hem° by this precious hoord.   *themselves*
The worste of hem he spak the firste word.
    "Bretheren," quod he, "taak kepe° what I seye.   *heed to*
My wit° is greet, thogh that I bourde° and pleye.   *understanding*   *jest*
This tresor hath fortune unto us yeven,°   *given*
In myrthe and jolitee oure lyf to lyven.
And lightly° as it cometh, so wol we spende.   *easily*
By Goddes precious dignytee, who wende°   320   *would have believed*
Today that we sholde han so faire a grace?
But, myghte this gold be caried fro this place
Hoom to myn hous, or ellis unto youres—
For wel ye woot° that al this gold is oures—   *know*
Thanne were we in heigh felicitee.
But, trewely, by daye it may nat be.
Men wolde seyn° that we were theves stronge°   *say*   *violent*
And for oure owene tresor doon us honge.°   *have us hanged*
This tresor moste y-carried be° by nyghte   *must be carried*
As wisly and as slyly as it myghte.   330
Wherfore I rede° that cut° among us alle   *advise*   *cuts*
Be drawe, and lat se° wher the cut wol falle.   *let see*
And he that hath the cut, with herte blithe
Shall rennc° to the toune, and that ful swithe,°   *run*   *quickly*
And brynge us breed and wyn ful pryvely.°   *secretly*
And two of us shul kepen subtilly°   *guard craftily*
This tresor wel; and if he wol nat tarie,
Whan it is nyght, we wol this tresor carie
By oon assent wher-as us thynketh° best."   *where it seems to us*
    That oon° of hem the cut broghte in his fest,°   340   *The one*   *fist*

And bad hem drawe and looke wher it wol falle,

And it fil° on the yongeste of hem alle,   fell

And forth toward the toun he wente anon.°   at once

And also° soone as that he was agon,°   as gone

That oon of hem spak thus unto that oother:

"Thow knowest wel, thow art my sworn brother.

Thy profit wol I telle thee anon.

Thow woost° wel that oure felawe is agon,   know

And heere is gold, and that ful greet plentee,

That shal departed° been among us thre.   350   divided

But, nathelees,° if I kan shape it so   nevertheless

That it departed were among us two,

Hadde I nat doon a freendes torn° to thee?"   turn

    That oother answerde, "I noot° how that may be.   don't know

He woot° that the gold is with us tweye.°   knows two

What shal we doon? What shal we to hym seye?"

    "Shal it be conseil?"° seyde the firste shrewe.°   secret wretch

"And I shal tellen in a wordes fewe

What we shul doon, and brynge it wel aboute."

    "I graunte," quod that oother, "out of doute,   360

That, by my trouthe, I wol thee nat biwreye." °   betray

    "Now," quod the firste, "thow woost° wel we be   know
        tweye,

And two of us shul strenger be than oon.

Looke, whan that he is set, that right anoon°   at once

Arys[43] as though thow woldest with hym pleye,

And I shal ryve° hym thurgh the sydes tweye,°   stab two

Whil that thow strogelest with hym as in game.

And with thy daggere looke thow do the same,

And thanne shal al this gold departed be,

My deere freend, bitwixe me and thee.   370

Thanne may we bothe oure lustes al fulfille,

And pleye at dees° right at oure owene wille."   dice

And thus acorded been thise shrewes tweye

To sleen° the thridde, as ye han herd me seye.   slay

    This yongeste, which that wente to the toun,

Ful ofte in herte he rolleth up and doun

The beautee of thise floryns newe and brighte.

"O Lord," quod he, "if so were that I myghte

Have al this tresor to myself allone,

---

[43] Chaucer here seems to have mixed two constructions: (1) *Looke that thou arise,* "see to it that you arise"; (2) *Whan that he is set, arys,* "when he is set, arise."

Ther is no man that lyveth under the trone   380
Of God that sholde lyve so myrie as I!"
And atte laste the feend, oure enemy,
Putte in his thoght that he sholde poyson beye,°   buy
With which he myghte sleen his felawes tweye,
For-why° the feend foond ° hym in swich lyvynge   Because found
That he hadde leve° hym to sorwe brynge.   permission (from God)
For this was outrely° his ful entente,   entirely
To sleen hem bothe and nevere to repente.
And forth he goth—no lenger wolde he tarie—
Into the toun unto a pothecarie,°   390 apothecary
And preyed hym that he hym wolde selle
Som poysoun that he myghte his rattes quelle,°   kill
And eek ther was a polcat° in his hawe,°   weasel hedge
That, as he seyde, his capouns° hadde y-slawe,°   capons killed
And fayn° he wolde wreke hym,° if he myghte,   gladly avenge himself
On vermyn that destroyed° hym by nyghte.   annoyed
      The pothecarie answerde, "And thow shalt have
A thyng that, also° God my soule save,   as
In al this world ther is no creature
That ete° or dronke hath of this confiture°   400 eaten preparation
Nat but the montaunce° of a corn° of whete,   quantity grain
That he ne shal his lyf anoon forlete.°   lose
Ye,° sterve° he shal, and that in lasse while   Yes die
Than thow wolt goon a paas° nat but a myle,   walk at footpace
The poysoun is so strong and violent."
      This cursed man hath in his hond y-hent°   taken
This poysoun in a box, and sith° he ran   then
Into the nexte strete unto a man
And borwed of hym large botels thre,
And in the two his poyson poured he.   410
The thridde he kepte clene for his drynke,
For al the nyght he shoop hym for to swynke°   intended to work
In cariyng of the gold out of that place.
And whan this riotuor—with sory grace!°—   curse him!
Hadde filled with wyn hise grete botels thre,
To hise felawes agayn repaireth he.
      What nedeth it to sermone of it moore?
For right as they hadde cast° his deeth bifore,   planned
Right so they han hym slayn, and that anon.
And whan that this was doon, thus spak that oon: 420
      "Now lat us sitte, and drynke, and make us
            merye,

And afterward we wol his body berye."
And with that word it happed hym par cas°   he happened by chance
To take the botel ther° the poysoun was,   where
And drank, and yaf° his felawe drynke also,   gave
For which anon they storven° bothe two.   died
    But, certes,° I suppose that Avycen   certainly
Wroot nevere in no canon ne in no fen[44]
Mo wonder signes° of empoysonyng   More wonderful symptoms
Than hadde thise wrecches two er hir° endyng.   430   before their
Thus ended been thise homicides two,
And eek the false empoysonere also.
    O cursed synne of alle cursednesse!
O traytours homicide! O wikkednesse!
O glotonye, luxurie, and hasardrye!
Thou blasphemour of Crist with vileynye
And othes grete of usage° and of pryde! °   habit   ostentation
Allas, mankynde, how may it bityde
That to thy Creatour, which that thee wroghte°   made
And with his precious herte-blood thee boghte,   440
Thow art so fals and so unkynde° allas?   unnatural
    Now, goode men, God foryeve° yow youre trespas,   forgive
And ware yow fro° the synne of avarice.   beware of
Myn holy pardoun may yow alle warice,°   cure
So° that ye offre nobles° or sterlynges,°   Providing   nobles (6 shil-
Or elles silver broches, spones, rynges.   lings, 8 pence)   silver pennies
Boweth youre heed under this holy bulle!
Cometh up, ye wyves! Offreth of youre wolle!°   wool
Youre name I entre here in my rolle anon;
Into the blisse of hevene shul ye gon.   450
I yow assoille,° by myn heigh power,   absolve
Yow that wol offre, as clene and eek as cler
As ye were born. —And lo, sires, thus I preche.
And Jesu Crist, that is or soules leche,°   leech (physician)
So graunte yow his pardoun to receyve,
For that is best. I wol yow nat deceyve.

[44] Avicenna, the eleventh-century Arabian philosopher, was the author of a widely studied work on medicine, divided into *fens* or sections, which contained the *canons* or rules of procedure appropriate to various illness, including poisoning.

Epilogue

"But, sires, o° word forgat I in my tale.	one
I have relikes and pardon in my male°	wallet
As faire as any man in Engelond,	
Whiche were me yeven by the Popes hond. 460	
If any of yow wol, of° devocioun,	out of
Offren and han myn absolucioun,	
Com forth anon, and kneleth here adoun,	
And mekely receyveth my pardoun;	
Or ellis taketh pardoun, as ye wende,°	travel
Al newe and fressh at every myles ende,	
So° that ye offren, alwey newe and newe,°	Providing again and again
Nobles or pens whiche that been goode and trewe.	
It is an honour to everich° that is heer	each one
That ye mowe° have a suffisant° pardoner 470	can adequate
T'assoille° yow, in contree as ye ryde,	To absolve
For aventures° whiche that may bityde.	incidents
Peraventure° ther may falle oon or two	Perhaps
Doun of° his hors, and breke his nekke atwo.	off
Looke which° a seuretee° is it to yow alle	what security
That I am in youre felaweship y-falle,°	fallen
That may assoille yow, bothe moore° and lasse,°	high low
Whan that the soule shal fro the body passe.	
I rede° that oure Hoost shal bigynne,	advise
For he is moost envoluped° in synne. 480	enveloped
Com forth, sire Hoost, and offre first anon,°	at once
And thow shalt kisse the relikes everychon,°	each one
Ye,° for a grote.° Unbokele anon thy purs."	Yes groat (4 pence)
"Nay, nay!" quod he. "Thanne have I Cristes curs!	
Lat be!" quod he. "It shal nat be, so thee'ch.°	may I prosper (*thee ich*)
Thow woldest make me kisse thyn olde breech,	
And swere it were a relyk of a seint,	
Thogh it were with thy fundement depeynt.°	discolored
But, by the croys which that Seint Eleyne fond,[45]	
I wolde I hadde thy coylons° in myn hond 490	testicles
In stede of relikes or of seintuarie.°	holy objects
Lat kutte hem of!° I wol thee helpe hem carie.	Have them cut off!

---

[45] by the cross which St. Helena found. Helena, the mother of Constantine, the first Christian emperor of Rome, was credited with having rediscovered the true cross in Jerusalem in 326. She was especially revered in England since local legend claimed her to be of British origin.

They shul be shryned—in an hogges toord!" °   turd
   This Pardoner answerde nat a word;
So wrooth° he was, no word ne wolde he seye.   wrathful
   "Now," quod oure Hoost, "I wol no lenger pleye
With thee, ne with noon° oother angry man."   nor with any
But right anon the worthy Knyght bigan,
Whan that he saugh that al the people lough,°   were laughing
"Namoore of this, for it is right ynough.   500
Sire Pardoner, be glad and murye° of cheere.   merry
And ye, sire Hoost, that been to me so deere,
I pray yow that ye kisse the Pardoner.
And, Pardoner, I pray thee, drawe thee neer.
And, as we diden, lat us laughe and pleye."
Anon they kiste, and ryden° forth hir weye.   rode

François Rabelais

FROM Gargantua and Pantagruel

TRANSLATED BY JACQUES LE CLERQ

François Rabelais (1494?–1553)

THE FIRST HALF OF THE SIXTEENTH CENTURY WAS A TIME OF unrest in France. The Reformation was undermining the authority of the Catholic Church, while the ruling hierarchy was still confident of its own unlimited power. It is a tribute to Rabelais' genius for survival that his attacks on the prevailing order, as well as his rejection of the more puritanical reformers, did not cause him greater difficulty than they did. Still, some of his luck in remaining a relatively free man was certainly the result of his having influential friends, who were able to intercede on his behalf with kings and popes.

From an early age, his consuming desire was the study of classical literature, a desire frustrated by his superiors at school and at the monastery to which he was sent when he first took Franciscan orders. Through the intervention of a powerful friend, Rabelais was eventually released from his vows by the pope. He then studied medicine, and for several years he was a very able lecturer in this field. His central interests were eventually served when, in the early 1530's, he began to compose *Gargantua and Pantagruel*, a work modeled on contemporary popular French tales concerning giants, and thus so superficially nonsensical that Rabelais was able to hide his serious purposes and immense learning behind a surface of buffoonery. The work is primarily an attack upon the Church as an opponent of new knowledge, but it also throws almost all authoritarian practices and beliefs into doubt. At various times, parts of the work (which appeared in five books over a period of twenty years) were condemned by the censors of the Sorbonne, but its popularity made certain that it would always remain in print.

Gargantua and Pantagruel

The Author's Prologue

Hail, O most valiant and illustrious drinkers! Your health, my precious pox-ridden comrades! To you alone, I dedicate my writings. Suffer me, therefore, to draw your attention to a dialogue of Plato's called *The Banquet*.

In this work, Alcibiades, praising his master Socrates (undoubtedly the prince of philosophers), happens, among other things, to liken him to sileni.

Sileni, in the days of yore, were small boxes such as you may see nowadays at your apothecary's. They were named for Silenus, foster father to Bacchus. The outside of these boxes bore gay, fantastically painted figures of harpies, satyrs, bridled geese, hares with gigantic horns, saddled ducks, winged goats in flight, harts in harness and many other droll fancies. They were pleasurably devised to inspire just the sort of laughter Silenus, Bacchus' master, inspired.

But inside these sileni, people kept priceless drugs such as balsam of Mecca, ambergris from the sperm whale, amomum from the cardamon, musk from the deer and civet from the civet's arsehole—not to mention various sorts of precious stones, used for medical purposes, and other invaluable possessions.

Well, Alcibiades likened Socrates to these boxes, because, judging by his exterior, you would not have given an onion skin for him. He was ill-shaped, ridiculous in carriage, with a nose like a knife, the gaze of a bull and the face of a fool. His ways stamped him a simpleton, his clothes a bumpkin. Poor in fortune, unlucky when it came to women, hopelessly unfit for all office in the republic, forever laughing, forever drinking neck to neck with his friends, forever hiding his divine knowledge under a mask of mockery. . . .

Yet had you opened this box, you would have found in it all sorts of priceless, celestial drugs: immortal understanding, wondrous virtue, indomitable courage, unparalleled sobriety, unfailing serenity, perfect assurance and a heroic contempt for whatever moves humanity to watch, to bustle, to toil, to sail ships overseas and to engage in warfare.

Alcibiades? Socrates? The sileni? Why all this introductory flourish? Let me explain to you only, O my beloved disciples, and to such other idlers and idiots as read my works. Having noted the flippant titles of certain books of my invention—*Gargantua, Pantagruel, Drownbottle, The Dignity of Cod-pieces and Trouserflies, Of Peas and Bacon, with Tables and Sauce Material,* etc.—you jump to the conclusion that these tomes are filled with mere jests, vulgarities and buffoonery. Alas! you leap at the outward and visible sign; you swallow the title in a spirit of levity and derision without pausing to make further inquiry. How unseemly to consider so frivolously the works of humankind! Is it you who profess that clothes do not make the man nor robes the monk? Do I quote you when I declare that a fellow most monasterially apparelled may turn out to be a downright infidel whereas another, draped in a Spanish cloak, may possess every virtue on earth except Castilian pride and daring? Well then, you see why you should look beyond my title, open my book and seriously weigh its subject matter. The spice secreted within the box is more precious, far, than its exterior promised. In other words, the topics treated are not so foolish as the title suggested at first hand.

Again, supposing you find enough tomfoolery to live up to the title, must you tarry there, as Ulysses tarried at the song of the sirens?[1] Certainly not. Instead you should lend a loftier sense to what you first believed written in the exuberance of humor.

Have you ever uncorked a bottle of wine? God help us, do you remember the look on your face?

Or have you ever seen a dog fall on a marrow bone? (The dog, I may add, is, as Plato says in Book II of the *Republic,* the most philosophic beast in the world.) If you have seen my dog, you may recall how intently he scrutinizes his bone, how solicitously he guards it, how fervently he clutches it, how warily he bites his way into it, how passionately he breaks it, how diligently he sucks it. What force moves him to act so, what hope fosters such zealous pains, what recompense does he aspire to? Nothing but a little marrow. (To be sure this little is more toothsome than large quantities of any other meat, for—as Galen[2] testifies in Chapter III of his *Concerning the Natural Faculties,* and Chapter XI of *Concerning the Uses of the Various Parts of the Human Body*—marrow is the most perfect food elaborated by nature.)

Modelling yourself upon the dog, you should be wise to scent, to feel and to prize these fine, full-flavored volumes. You should be fleet in your pursuit of them, resolute in your attack. Then, by diligent reading and prolonged meditation, you should break the bone of my symbols to suck out the marrow of my meaning—for I make use of allegory as freely as Pythagoras[3] did. As you read, you must confidently expect to become valiant and

[1] In Homer's account (*Odyssey,* Bk. XII) Ulysses was not detained by the Sirens. Rabelais seems to share the medieval opinion that Ulysses was detained.
[2] ancient Greek medical authority. [3] Greek philosopher and mathematician of the sixth century B.C.

wise. For here you will find a novel savor, a most abstruse doctrine; here you will learn the deepest mysteries, the most agonizing problems of our religion, our body politic, our economic life.

Do you honestly believe that Homer, penning his *Iliad* or *Odyssey,* ever dreamed of the allegorical patchwork subsequently inflicted upon him by Plutarch, by Heraclides Ponticus, by Eustathius, by Cornutus the Stoic, or by Politian, the Italian who filched his criticism from the lot of them? [4]

If you *do,* you are miles away from my opinion, for *I* hold that Homer no more dreamed of all this allegorical fustian[5] than Ovid in his *Metamorphoses* dreamed of the Gospel. Yet whenever he met folk as witless as himself, a certain Friar Jobbernowl, a true glutton for bacon and misinformation, strove to establish the Christianity of Ovid. Fit lids, that audience, for such a pot, say I, quoting the old saw.

If you agree with the Friar, why refuse the same consideration to my own original mirthful chronicles? Yes, even though I, writing them, gave the matter no more thought than you, who were probably also drinking. I may add that in composing this masterpiece I have not spent or wasted more leisure than is required for my bodily refection—food and drink to you! Is that not the proper time to commit to the page such sublime themes and such profound wisdom? Homer, the paragon of all philologists, knew it perfectly well and Ennius also, the father of the Latin poets, as Horace testifies, though a certain sorry clown has said that his poems smelled more of wine than of oil.

So, too, spoke a third-rate cynic about my books, but a ripe turd to the fellow! Oh, the sweet fragrance of wine! How much more reconciling, smiling and beguiling wine is than oil! Let the world say I spent more on wine than on oil: I shall glory in it, like Demosthenes[6] when they accused him of the opposite. For my part, I consider it honorable and noble to be reputed a sportsman and a wit, for as such I am welcome wherever two or three Pantagruelists are gathered together. Did not a certain surly bore denounce Demosthenes because his *Orations* smelled like a filthy rag in an oil can. Not so, I!

Accordingly, take in perfect part all I write and do; revere the cheese-shaped brain which feeds you this noble flummery; strive diligently to keep me ever jocund.

And now, my hearties, be gay, and gayly read the rest, with ease of body and in the best of kidney! And you, donkey-pizzles, hark!—may a canker rot you!—remember to drink to me gallantly, and I will counter with a toast at once!

[4] Rabelais here mentions some of the major commentators on Homer from antiquity to his own day. Each of them had interpreted Homer's two works in a highly ethical or allegorical fashion. [5] high-sounding nonsense. [6] Athenian orator of the fourth century B.C.

CHAPTER VII

How Gargantua Came By His
Name and How He
Swilled Down the Wine

That excellent man Grangousier was drinking and making merry with the others, when he heard a horrible tumult. It was his son emerging into the light of this world, bellowing, "Drink, drink, drink!"

At once Grangousier exclaimed: *"Que grand tu as le gousier"* or "What a great gullet you have!" Hearing this, the company declared that the child should indeed be named *"grand tu as"*: Gargantua or Greatgullet. Were these not the first sounds the father had uttered after the child's birth? And was this not an ancient Hebrew custom well worth following? Grangousier assented; Gargamelle was delighted with the idea.

Next, to quiet the babe, they made him drink till his throat almost burst. Then, carrying him to the font, they baptized him, as is the custom among all good Christians.

Shortly after, they appointed seventeen thousand nine hundred and thirteen cows from Pontille and Bréhémont to furnish him with milk in ordinary, for, considering his enormous needs, it was impossible to find a satisfactory nurse in all the country. Nevertheless, certain learned doctors, disciples of Duns Scotus,[7] have affirmed that his own mother suckled him. She could, they say, draw from her breasts two thousand one hundred and three hogsheads and eighteen pints at one time. This seems scarcely probable. Indeed, this point has been condemned by the Sorbonne[8] as mammarily scandalous and reeking with heresy.

Gargantua was thus looked after until he was twenty-two months old. Then, on the advice of the physicians, they began to carry him, and Jean Denyau built a special ox-drawn cart for him. They drove him about in it here, there and everywhere with the greatest pleasure; and a fine sight he was, too, with a great, open face and almost eighteen chins! He cried very little but he beshitted himself at all times. For he was wondrously phlegmatic of bum, as much by natural complexion as from an accidental predisposition, due to exaggerated quaffing of the juices of Septembral mash. Yet he never touched a drop without good reason; for whenever he happened to be out of sorts, vexed, angry or melancholy, if he stamped, wept or shouted, they brought him a drink. This invariably restored his native good humor and at once made him as quiet and happy as before.

[7] thirteenth-century scholastic philosopher.   [8] Center of French theological study at the University of Paris, the Sorbonne is attacked by Rabelais fiercely, frequently, and not without peril.

One of his governesses told me on oath what a rooted habit this tippling had become. Indeed, the mere clinking of pints and flagons sent him off into the ecstasy of one who tastes the joys of Paradise. Accordingly, in view of this divine character, they used to delight him every morning by making music on glasses with knives, on bottles with their stoppers, and on pots with their lids. At this he would turn gay, thrill with joy, wag his head and rock from side to side, monochording with his fingers and barytoning through his tail.

CHAPTER VIII

How They Arrayed
Gargantua

When he was twenty-two months old, his father ordered clothes for him made in his own livery, which was white and blue. Going to work with a will, the tailors soon cut, sewed and produced his apparel according to the current fashion. From ancient records in the Chamber of Accounts at Montsoreau,[9] I learn that he was arrayed in the following manner:

To make Gargantua one shirt, they cut off nine hundred ells[10] of Châtellerault linen and two hundred more for the gussets, which were square and placed under the armpits for comfort. His shirt was not pleated, for the pleating of shirts was only discovered later. That was when certain seamstresses, who had broken the point of their needles, turned up their holes and put their tails to work.

For Gargantua's doublet they used eight hundred and thirteen ells of white satin, and for his aglets—the laces that held it together—fifteen hundred and nine and one-half dogs' skins. This was the period when men began to tie their breeches to their doublets and not their doublets to their breeches the latter habit being contrary to nature, as William of Ockham[11] explained at length in his comment upon the *Exponabilia* of Monsieur Hautechaussade and Master Highbreecham.

Eleven hundred and five and one-third ells of the finest white broadcloth were used for the breeches. They were cut in the form of columns, pinked and grooved behind so as not to overheat his reins: from within the slashes, as much blue damask puffed out as was needful. Note, too, that he had very fine legs, perfectly in proportion to the rest of his body.

The tailoring of Gargantua's codpiece (here was no modern degenerate

[9] small French town, which, if it kept any municipal records at all, surely kept none such as these.   [10] obsolete measure of cloth, about 27 inches.   [11] fourteenth-century scholastic philosopher.

fly!) required sixteen and one-quarter ells of the same cloth. In shape, it resembled a buttress; it was most gallantly fastened to two handsome golden buckles, caught up by two enamelled clasps. Each had a large emerald, the size of an orange, set in it. As Orpheus points out in his treatise on precious stones, *Liber de Lapidibus,* and Pliny in the last book of his *Natural History,* emeralds exert a highly erective and bracing influence upon the natural member.[12] The gibbosity or bulge of the codpiece stretched out about five and one-half feet; it was jagged and pinked, with flaring blue damask, like the breeches.

Had you seen the delicate embroidery of the gold thread and the priceless network of laces, adorned, by the goldsmith's art, with rare diamonds, rich rubies, precious turquoises, splendid emeralds and choice Persian pearls, what would you have done? Inevitably you would have compared it to some proud cornucopia such as you see on ancient monuments, or such as Rhea gave to the nymphs Adrasta and Ida, nurses to her son Jupiter.

You recall the tale, doubtless. The goat, whose milk nourished the divine infant, happened one day to break one of her horns against a rock. Straightway the nymphs filled it with fruit and flowers to present to Jove, who made of this horn a source of eternal abundance.

Well, Gargantua's codpiece was like that horn: forever lively, succulent and resinous; forever flourishing, pollening and fructifying; full of juice, aflower with pistils and teeming with fruit, in short (but it was never that!), a compendium of delights. May I never meet my God if it was not a brave spectacle to behold! But I reserve the right to deal with it at greater length in a book I have written upon *The Dignity of Codpieces.* One thing, however, I shall disclose: if it was extremely long and extraordinarily expansive, it was also fully stocked and inexhaustible within. Hence it was in no wise comparable to the hypocritical codpieces of a heap of noodles, which are crammed with only wind, to the great prejudice of the female sex.

Gargantua's shoes—calling for four hundred and six ells of dazzling blue velvet—were most stylishly slashed by parallel lines, crossed by uniform cylinders. The soles alone required eleven hundred hides of brown cows, cut like the tail of a codfish.

For his coat, they bespoke eighteen hundred ells of blue velvet, dyed in grain, with elegantly embroidered vine leaves and branches around the border and, in the middle, pint goblets stitched in silver, intermingled with bars of gold and many pearls. The branches, goblets and bars indicated that Gargantua was destined to be a wine-punisher and bottle-flogger of the first . . . water!

Three hundred and one-half ells of silken rep, half blue and half white, unless I err, went to make up Gargantua's belt.

---

[12] Neither of these Greek texts makes any such claim.

His sword was not of Valencia, nor his dagger from Saragossa, for his father abominated those *hidalgos, borrachos* and *moriscos*—braggarts, sots and Moorish Jew mongrels—as cordially as you hate the devil. No: Gargantua had a noble sword made of wood and a dagger of boiled leather, both as richly painted and gilt as any man could wish.

His purse was fashioned out of the ballock of an elephant, given him by My Lord Pracontal, Proconsul of Africa.

For Gargantua's gown, they employed nine thousand six hundred ells less two-thirds of blue velvet as before. But they decorated it diagonally with such a wealth of gold purling that, seen in proper perspective, it bore that indefinable tint you may observe on the necks of turtledoves. It afforded the eye much pleasure.

His hat used up three hundred and two ells and one-quarter of white velvet. It was wide and round, fitting very close to his head, for his father declared that caps à la Morisco, shaped like pie-crusts, would some day visit ill-fortune upon the shavepates that wore them.

The plume in his hat was a splendid, wide, blue one, plucked from an onocrotal—which we call pelican—in Hircania, that wild vast land in Central Asia. Very proudly, very smartly it swept down over his right ear.

The emblem in his hat? Against a base of gold weighing over forty pounds was an enamel figure very much in keeping. It portrayed a man's body with two heads facing one another, four arms, four feet, a pair of arses and a brace of sexual organs, male and female. Such, according to Plato's *Symposium*, was human nature in its mystical origins. Around the emblem ran a motto in Greek script: Ἀγάπη οὐ ζητεῖ τὰ ἑαυτῆς, Charity seeketh not her own,[13] or more freely, the only virtuous person is one who does good to another whilst profiting himself. . . .

CHAPTER IX

Gargantua's Colors
and Livery

Gargantua's colors were white and blue, as I have indicated above. By these colors, his father wished to signify that the lad was a heavenly joy to him. White expresses joy, pleasure, delight and rejoicing; blue denotes things celestial.

I realize quite well that, as you read these words, you are laughing at the old toper, for you believe this symbolic use of colors to be crude and extrava-

[13] from 1 Cor. 13:5.

gant. White, you say, stands for faith, and blue for strength. But without getting excited, losing your temper, flying into a rage or working yourself into a tongue-parched passion—the weather is dangerous—tell me one thing! I shall exercise no compulsion upon you or any one else—I shall merely point to the bottle and trust you will drink with me.

What moves, impels or induces you to believe what you do? Who told you that white means faith, and blue strength?

"A shoddy book," you reply, "sold by peddlers in remote mountain hamlets and by weatherbeaten hawkers God knows where. Its title? *In Praise of Colors.*" [14]

Who wrote it; do you know? Whoever did, had sense enough not to put his name to it. And I cannot tell which I should rather admire: his presumption or his stupidity.

His presumption? Without cause, reason or evidence, he dares to prescribe by his private authority what this color or that shall mean. Such is the practice of tyrants who impose their arbitrary will instead of justice, not of the wise and learned who satisfy their readers by obvious proofs.

His stupidity? The fellow actually believes that the world will interpret its devices according to his inept charlatanry without demanding further demonstration or a more valid argument! . . .

These equivokes are so ineffectual, so dull, so crude and so barbarous that we should pin a fox's tail to the coat of the offender and fashion a mask of cow dung for whosoever should attempt this in the realm of France after the renascence of learning.

For like reasons—if reason may be used here rather than folly—I shall have a *panier* or basket painted to attest that I am in *pain,* and a pot of *moutarde* or *mustard* because I am *moult tard* or *much tardy.* Similarly, since a pisspot is sometimes more politely known in French as an *official,* and a bishop is an *official* of the Church, if I am a *bishop,* I shall exhibit a thundermug upon my coat-of-arms rather than a *mitre.* Again, the *seat of my breeches* is a harbor full of poops or a vessel full of *farthings;* my *cod piece* is *a fish* swimming in a *sea of urine;* and a dog's *turd* is the *alluring turret* wherein lies the love of my sweetheart.

In the olden days, the sages of Egypt ordered matters better when they wrote in what they called hieroglyphics. No man understood these unless he were familiar with the virtue, property and nature of the things represented. By the same token, all who were conversant could readily decipher these mysterious symbols. Their lore has been dealt with in two volumes in Greek by Orus Apollo the grammarian, and further exposed by Polyphilus in his *Dream of Love.* In France you have a fragment of this science in the device of My Lord Admiral, which he borrowed from Octavian Augustus: a dol-

---

[14] actual fifteenth-century manual.

phin (signifying speed) upon an anchor (signifying steadfastness), the picture being a symbol of moderation.[15]

But my skiff will adventure no further among these uninviting shoals and shallows: I turn back to call at the haven whence I came. Yet I hope one day to write at greater length upon this subject and to demonstrate—both by philosophical arguments and by time-hallowed authorities—what colors are in nature, how many there are and what every one of them may mean. This, if God preserve my head, for, as my grandam was wont to say, the mould of your cap[16] is your best wine pot.

CHAPTER X

What the Colors White and Blue Signify

White, then, signifies joy, solace and gladness—not at random but by unimpeachable authority. You may easily convince yourselves of this if you set aside your prejudices and consent to give ear to what I shall presently expound.

Aristotle proves this. Take two opposites—say, good and evil, virtue and vice, hot and cold, white and black, joy and grief, pleasure and pain, and so on. Couple them so as to make a contrary of one comparison agree reasonably with its fellow in the next comparison. Then inevitably the contrasted contraries to which you have compared them will, in turn, correspond. Thus *virtue* and *vice,* are opposites in one kind; so are *good* and *evil.* Now if one of the contraries of the first kind agrees (like *virtue* and *good,* for we know virtue to be good), then the remaining set of qualities—*vice* and *evil*—will in turn agree, since we know vice to be evil.

Having mastered this logical rule, take one pair of opposites, *joy* and *sorrow,* and couple it with another, *white* and *black*—for they are physically contrary—well then, if *black* signifies mourning, then *white* rightly signifies *joy.*

This signification is neither imposed nor instituted by one man. On the contrary, it is admitted by general consent of all men, in accordance with what the philosophers call *jus gentium,* universal law, which rules in all climes.

As you doubtless know, all peoples and nations, whatever their tongues

---

[15] This actually was the emblem of Guillaume Gouffier, admiral of France who died in 1525. *Festine lente,* "hurry slowly," was the motto of Augustus Caesar.
[16] that is, your head.

(save the ancient Syracusans and certain other Greeks with contrary souls!), expressed their grief outwardly by wearing black clothes. All mourning therefore was done in black. Any such universal consent is not given without nature supplying certain arguments and reasons which any man may forthwith acknowledge without outside intervention. This we call natural law.

By the same natural token, white has always meant joy, pleasure, solace, gladness and delight. In past ages, the men of Thrace and Crete marked their happy and propitious days by white stones and their sad, inauspicious ones by black.

Is not night mournful, gloomy, melancholy? It is black and obscure for want of light. Does not light bear joy to all the world? Is it not whiter than any other thing on earth? I might, to prove my point, refer you to the book written by the Italian humanist, Laurentius Valla, against the fourteenth-century jurist, Bartolus. But the testimony of the Bible will doubtless content you. It is said in *Matthew,* xvii, that at the Transfiguration of Our Lord *"vestimenta ejus facta sunt alba sicut lux,"* his raiment was white as the light." By this luminous whiteness, He wished to convey to His three apostles the idea and figure of eternal joy. Light, it is, gladdens all human beings. You have, in support of this statement, the words of the old woman who, with never a tooth in her head, yet exclaimed: *"Bona Lux!* Light is good!"* [17] And in the *Book of Tobit,* Chapter V, we learn that when Tobit, blinded by sparrows "muting warm dung into his eyes," was greeted by Raphael:

"Alas," he answered, "what joy can I know, who may not see the light of Heaven?"

White, too, was the color used by the angels to betoken the joy of the entire universe at the resurrection of Our Saviour (*John,* XX) and at His Ascension (*Acts,* I), whilst vestments of the same hue apparelled the faithful whom St. John the Evangelist saw entering into the blessed and heavently city of Jerusalem (*Revelation,* chapters IV and VII).

I urge you further to read the ancient histories, both Greek and Roman. In the latter you will learn that the city of Alba,[18] the earliest pattern of Rome, was not only built on the spot where Aeneas found a white sow among thirty young boars, but also named for the beast.

You will learn, too, that whenever a victorious general was, by senatorial decree, allowed the honors of a triumphal entry into Rome, his chariot was drawn by white horses. In the lesser triumphs—allowed by ovation—white was likewise customary, for the people could not by any other sign or color more clearly express their joy at the hero's homecoming.

---

[17] words of Stultitia (Folly) in Eramus' *Praise of Folly* (1514), a work which was one of the major influences on Rabelais.   [18] *alba:* "white" in Latin.

In Greek history, you will read how Pericles, the Athenian leader, ordered those of his soldiers who had drawn white beans by lot to spend the whole day in joy, comfort and rest, while the others went into battle. How easily I could cite a thousand further examples and proofs if this were only the proper place for it!

If you understand the above, you can readily solve a problem considered insoluble by by Alexander Aphrodiseus, a contemporary of Marcus Aurelius. "Why," asks this commentator on Aristotle, "does a lion, whose mere roar terrifies all animals, fear and respect only the white rooster?" Because the virtues of the sun are present—as Proclus Diadochus, Platonic philosopher of the fifth century, points out in his *De Sacrificio et Magia, Of Sacrifice and Magic*. The sun is the organ and receptacle of all terrestrial and sidereal light. Its virtues are better expressed and symbolized by the white rooster than by the lion, both because of the rooster's color and because of his essential attributes. Devils, this authority adds, have often appeared in the form of lions who suddenly vanished at the sight of a white rooster.

That is why the *Galli*—the French were so named because they are by nature white as milk, which in Greek is γάλα or *gala*—are pleased to wear white feathers in their caps. Are they not naturally gay, candid, gracious and popular? Is it surprising therefore to find that their symbol and sign is the whitest flower on earth: the lily?

Do you ask me how nature would convey joy and gladness to us through the color white? I reply that it is thus by analogy and conformity. For white reflects the rays of the light; it obviously dissolves the visual spirits, according to Aristotle, in his *Problems,* and other students of optics. You may best discover the truth of this yourselves when you pass snow-covered mountains and complain that you cannot see clearly. (Xenophon attests that this happened to his soldiers and Galen treats of the subject at length in Book X of his *De usu Partium, Of the Use of the Parts of the Body.*)

Precisely so the heart. Joy may dilate it and excess of joy actually make it suffer. Indeed, a frenzy of gladness may so dissolve the vital spirits that life itself is snuffed out. This destructive excess of joy is called *perichareia;* Galen discusses it in Book XII, *De Methodo Medendi* or *Of the Method of Healing;* in Book V, *De Locis Affectis, Of the Portions Affected;* and in Book II, *De Symptomatum Causis, Of the Causes of Symptoms.*

That excessive joy has killed men is attested by witnesses in ancient times: Marcus Tullius Cicero, Book I of the *Tuscan Questions;* Marcus Verrius Flaccus, the Latin grammarian cited by Pliny on unnatural deaths; Aristotle; Livy in his account of what happened after the Battle of Cannae; Pliny in his *Natural History,* Book VII, Chapters XXXII and LIII; Aulus Gellius in his *Attic Nights,* Book III, Chapter XV.

Examples of men who perished of joy include Diagoras of Rhodes, who gave up the ghost when his three sons were crowned victors in the Olympics . . . Chilo, in like circumstances . . . Sophocles and Dionysius, the tyrant of Sicily, when they learned of their triumph in the Tragedy contests . . . Philippides and Philemon, both comic poets, in much the same way . . . Polycrata, when she saw her countrymen of Naxos conquering her abductors and advancing to crown her . . . Philistion, who laughed himself to death . . . M. Juventius Thalva, when he received favorable tidings from the Roman Senate. . . .

Avicenna in Book II of his *De Viribus Cordis, Of the Heart's Strength,* says that saffron so stimulates the heart that, taken to excess, it may cause death through extreme dilation and resolution. This, indeed, applies as much to joy. In this connection, consult Alexander Aphrodiseus, Book I of his *Problems,* Chapter XIX. So much for that!

Enough! I seem to have gone further into this question than I first intended. So I shall strike sail now, referring the rest of this to the book in which I propose to treat of such matters at length. Meanwhile I hasten to add that blue most certainly signifies Heaven and all heavenly things, by the same token and symbols that white signifies joy and pleasure.

CHAPTER XI

Of Gargantua's Adolescence

From three to five years of age, Gargantua was, by his father's orders, brought up and instructed in all proper discipline. He spent his time like other small children; namely, in drinking, eating and sleeping; in eating, sleeping and drinking; in sleeping, drinking and eating.

He was forever wallowing in dirt, covering his nose with filth and begriming his face. He wore his shoes down to a frazzle, lay with his mouth gaping to catch heaven knows what, and delighted in chasing butterflies—an infidel tribe over which his father ruled. He used to piddle on his shoes, brown up his shirt-tails, wipe his nose on his sleeve, clear his nostrils into his soup, and dive headlong into the foulest muck at hand. He was wont to drink from his slipper, scratch his belly with a wicker basket and sharpen his teeth on a wooden shoe. When he washed his hands, he did so in his soup; he combed his hair with a drinking cup, fell flat on his rump between two stools, blew hot and cold, cut blocks with a razor and drank while he ate his broth. His bread he consumed without dough; he bit laughing and laughed biting. Often he coughed up, figuratively and literally. Fat? another ounce of wind and he would have exploded. Appreciative? He would piss, full-bladdered, at the sun. Cautious? He used to hide under water for fear of the rain.

Among Gargantua's other pursuits were striking on the iron while it was cold; going woolgathering; shamming Abraham or playing the hypocrite; throwing up his food or flaying the fox, as the saying goes; reciting the monkey's paternoster or letting his teeth chatter like a baboon's. If he had wandered from the point, he invariably followed the Judge's advice to Pathelin, and came back to his sheep[19] . . . he turned his hogs to hay or, as some say, took the wrong sow by the ear . . . he beat the dog for the lion or thrashed the slave to teach the master a lesson . . . he put the cart before the horse and locked the stable door after the mare was stolen. . . . He did not self-flatteringly scratch himself where he itched, but unexpectedly enough where he did not. He would pump people and bite off more than he could chew, leap before he looked, milk the ram and tickle himself to make himself laugh. A fine trencherman, withal, he plied a tireless knife and fork.

Among his other accomplishments were stealing pigs and giving the feet to God . . . having the magnificat sung at matins and considering it perfectly seasonable . . . eating red cabbage and voiding white beets . . . knowing black from white and spotting a fly in a bowl of milk . . . cooling his heels . . . pouring water into sieves. . . . He would scribble on papers, mess up parchments and save his bacon by taking French leave. He collected hairs from the dog that bit him, tossed the pot, threw up and reckoned without his host. He beat about the bush without stirring the birds; he thought the moon was made of green cheese and bladders were lanterns.

He feathered his nest; had two strings to his bow and two linings to his purse; he would play the ass if he could get a sack of bran out of it and he made a mallet of his fist. With the greatest ease, he caught weasels asleep and washed blackamoors white; and, throwing in his lot with such as believe Rome was not built in a day, he held that some roads led elsewhere.

Gargantua was also inclined to look a gift horse in the mouth . . . tell cock and bull stories . . . throw the helve after the hatchet . . . rob Peter to pay Paul . . . fence in the cuckoo to preserve the summer and keep the moon safe from the wolves . . . hope, if the heavens fell, to catch larks . . . make a virtue of necessity . . . cut his coat according to his cloth . . . split no hairs and care as little for the shaven as for the shorn. . . .

Every morning Gargantua retched, spewed, flayed the fox. He ate out of the same dish as his father's puppies: he would bite their ears, they

[19] reference to the famous refrain in a fifteenth-century French comedy, *The Farce of Master Pierre Pathelin*. It has come to mean "let's get back to the subject."

would scratch his nose, and he blow into their arseholes whilst they licked his chops.

Do you know what else he did, my brave lads? May the drunkard's pip rot your guts if the little lecher wasn't forever groping his nurses upside-down, arsey-turvy, *hirdie-girdie, giddy-up, whoah, Hinny!*—and if he wasn't beginning to bring his codpiece into play and turn it to account. Every morning his governesses prinked and dizened it with lovely nosegays and fine silken tassels. Their favorite pastime was to feel and finger his organ, to knead and mould it lovingly as pharmacists handle ointment and salve to make a large, solidified cylindrical suppository. Then they would burst out laughing for joy at the sport as, under their skilled hands, it would prick up its ears.

One called it her darling faucet, another her corking pin, a third her coral branch, a fourth her bungpeg, a fifth her stopgap. Others named it variously their ramrod, their spikebit, their swagdangle, their trunnion, their private hardware because it must be hard where they stocked· it, their lever, their borer, their little ruddy sausage, their nutty little booby prize.

"It belongs to me!" one cried.

"No, it's mine!" another protested.

"What about me?" piped up a third. "Shall I have no share in it? By my faith, I'll cut it off then."

"Ha!" said the other. "You would hurt him, Madame, if you cut it off. Do you propose to cut a child's penial utensil? He'd be Master Bobtail, then!"

And so that he might play like other little children they made him a fine whirligig with the wings from a windmill in the Mirebelais region of the Poitou.

The following characters span Gargantua's education, first under the medieval system of rote learning, then under the new Humanist disciplines. He proceeds to Paris, whence he is called home (after a series of delightful adventures) by his father, Grangousier, who is faced with a war against the forces of the venomous King Picrochole. Gargantua leads his father's side to victory, aided by the least monkish of all monks, Friar John of the Funnels. As a reward for his vigorous assistance, Gargantua offers John the abbot's position at the monastery of his choice.

CHAPTER LII

How Gargantua Had
the Abbey of Thélème
Built for the Monk

There remained only the monk to provide for. Gargantua offered him the Abbey of Seuilly: he refused. What about the Benedictine abbeys of Bourgueil or St. Florent, among the richest in France: he might have either or both? Again, the offer met with a flat refusal: Friar John of the Funnels answered peremptorily that he did not seek the charge or government of monks.

"For," he explained, "how shall I govern others when I cannot possibly govern myself?" There was a pause. "But—" he hesitated. "But if you believe I have given and can give you good service, let me found an abbey after my own heart."

The notion delighted Gargantua: he forthwith offered his estate of Thélème, by the Loire, two leagues away from Port Huault. Thélème in Greek means free will, an auspicious name for Friar John's abbey. Here indeed he could institute a religious order contrary to all others.

"First," said Gargantua, "you must not build a wall around it, for all other abbeys are solidly enclosed."

"Quite so," agreed the monk, "for where there are *mures*, walls, before, and *mures*, walls, behind, we have *murmures*, murmurs of envy and plotting."

Now in certain monasteries it is a rule that if any women enter (I mean honest and chaste ones) the ground they tread upon must be swept over. Therefore it was decreed that if a monk or nun should by any chance enter Thélème, every place that religious passed through should be thoroughly disinfected.

Similarly because all monasteries and convents on earth are compassed, limited and regulated by hours, at Thélème no clock or dial of any sort should be tolerated. On the contrary, their time here would be governed by what occasions and opportunities might arise. As Gargantua sagaciously commented:

"I can conceive of no greater waste of time than to count the hours. What good comes of it? To order your life by the toll of a bell instead of by reason or common sense is the veriest piece of asininity imaginable."

By the same token, they established the qualifications for entrance into their order. Was it not true that at present women took the veil only if they were wall-eyed, lame, hunchbacked, ill-favored, misshapen, half-witted, unreasonable or somewhat damaged? That only such men entered monasteries as were cankered, ill-bred idiots or plain nuisances?

("Incidentally," said Friar John, "if the woman is neither fair nor good, of what use is the cloth?"

"Let the clot hump her," Gargantua replied.

"I said 'cloth' not 'clot.' "

"Well, what's the answer?"

"To cover her face or her arse with!")

Accordingly, they decided to admit into the new order only such women as were beautiful, shapely, pleasing of form and nature, and such men as were handsome, athletic and personable.

Again, because men entered the convents of this world only by guile and stealth, it was decreed that no women would be in Thélème unless men were there also, and vice-versa.

Moreover, since both men in monasteries and women in convents were forced after their year of noviciate to stay there perpetually, Gargantua and Friar John decided that the Thélèmites, men or women, might come and go whenever they saw fit.

Further, since the religious usually made the triple vow of chastity, poverty and obedience, at Thélème all had full leave to marry honestly, to enjoy wealth and to live in perfect freedom.

As for the age of initiation, they stipulated that women were admissible between the ages of ten and fifteen, men between twelve and eighteen.

CHAPTER LV

How the Monks and Nuns
Lived at Thélème

In the middle of the lower court stood a magnificent alabaster fountain, surmounted by the Three Graces[20] holding cornucopias and spouting water through their breasts, mouths, ears, eyes and other orifices. The buildings above this court stood upon great pillars of chalcedony and porphyry, forming classical arches about lengthy wide galleries adorned with paintings and trophies of various animals: the horns of bucks, unicorns and hippopotami, elephants' tusks and sundry other curiosities.

The ladies' quarters ran from *Arctice*[21] all the way to the *Mesembrine* Gate; the rest of the abbey was reserved for men. In front of this part, between the outer two towers, lay the recreational facilities: the tilting yard, the riding school, the theatre and the natatorium which included wonderful swimming pools on three different levels, with every sort of equipment and myrtle water aplenty.

[20] Greek sister goddesses who confer grace and beauty.   [21] *Artice* and the following three italicized names are those of four of the six towers of the abbey.

Near the river was the fine pleasure garden, with, in the middle, a maze. Tennis courts and football fields spread out between the next two towers. Close to *Cryere*, an orchard offered a mass of fruit trees laid out in quincunxes, with, at its end, a sizy park abounding in venison.

The space between the third pair of towers was reserved for the shooting ranges: here were targets and butts for harquebuss, long bow and crossbow. The servants' quarters, one storey high, were situated outside *Hesperia*. Beyond was the falconry, managed by expert falconers and hawk trainers and annually supplied by the Cretans, Venetians and Sarmatian Poles with all manner of birds. There were priceless eagles for hunting hares, foxes and cranes. There were gerfalcons, goshawks, sakers for hunting wild geese, herons and bitterns. There were falcons, lanners, sparhawks and merlins for hunting larks and partridges. Other birds there were, too, in great quantities, so well trained that when they flew afield for their own sport they never failed to catch every bird they encountered. . . . The venery with its hounds and beagles stood a little further along towards the park.

All the halls, apartments and chambers were richly hung with tapestries varying with the season; the floors were covered with green cloth, the beds all embroidered. Each rear chamber boasted a pier glass set in a heavy gold frame adorned with pearls. Near the exits of the ladies' halls were the perfumers and hairdressers who ministered to the gentlemen before the latter visited the ladies. These attendants furnished the ladies' rooms with rose water, orange-flower water and angelica, supplying a precious small atomizer to give forth the most exquisite aromatic perfumes.

CHAPTER LVII

How Those of Thélème Were Governed in Their Manner of Living

Their whole life was ordered not by law, statute or rule, but according to their free will and pleasure. They arose when they pleased. They ate, drank, worked and slept when the spirit moved them. No one awoke them, forced food or drink upon them or *made* them do anything else. Gargantua's plan called for perfect liberty. The only rule of the house was:

DO AS THOU WILT

because men that are free, of gentle birth, well-bred and at home in civilized company possess a natural instinct that inclines them to virtue and saves them from vice. This instinct they name their honor. Sometimes they may be depressed or enslaved by subjection or constraint; for we all long for forbidden fruit and covet what is denied us. But they usually apply the fine forces that tend to virtue in such a way as to shake off the yoke of servitude.

The Thélèmites, thanks to their liberty, knew the virtues of emulation. All wished to do what they saw pleased one of their number. Let some lad or maid say "Let us drink" and all of them drank, "Let us play" and all of them played, "Let us frolic in the fields" and all of them frolicked. When falconry or hawking were in order, the ladies sat high upon their saddles on fine nags, a sparhawk, lanner or merlin on one daintily gloved wrist, while the men bore other kinds of hawks.

They were so well-bred that none, man or woman, but could read, write, sing, play several instruments, speak five or six languages and readily compose verse and prose in any of them. Never had earth known knights so proud, so gallant, so adroit on horseback and on foot, so athletic, so lively, so well-trained in arms as these. Never were ladies seen so dainty, so comely, so winsome, so deft at handwork and needlework, so skilful in feminine arts, so frank and so free as these.

Thus when the time came for a man to leave the abbey (either at his parents' request or for some other reason) he took with him one of the ladies—the particular one who had chosen him for her knight—and they were married. And though they had lived in devotion and friendship at Thélème, their marriage relations proved even more tender and agreeable. Indeed to the end of their lives they loved one another as they had on the day of their wedding. . . .

Book II of Gargantua and Pantagruel *was actually written two years before Book I, in 1532. The following pages, as far as is known, were the first that Rabelais wrote of his* Pantagrueline Chronicle. *It is perhaps for this reason that this first chapter parodies the first books of both the Old and the New Testaments, Genesis and Matthew.*

CHAPTER I

Of the Origin and Antiquity of the Great Pantagruel

It will not be amiss, since we have the leisure, to acquaint you with the primeval origin of our good Pantagruel. I know that all good historiographers have handled their chronicles thus, not only Arabs, Barbarians and Latins, but also Greeks and Gentiles (great drinkers these!) and finally writers of Holy Scripture like St. Luke and St. Matthew. You must therefore remember that I speak of the beginning of the world, of long ages since, of more than forty times forty nights ago, to reckon as the Druids did.[22]

A little while after Cain slew his brother Abel, the earth, imbued with the blood of the just, was one year extremely fertile in all fruits. Medlars were particularly plentiful and large, just three to the bushel. So that year was recorded in the memory of men as the year of the great medlars.

That year, too, the Greek kalends[23] first figured in the almanacs, March coincided with Lent, it was mid-August in May. The week famed in the *Annals,* the week of the three Thursdays, fell in October—or September, to exclude all possibility of error, since I am bound to remain scrupulously accurate. Three Thursdays it had, because of the irregular bissextile. The sun swerved a little towards the left, like a debtor ducking the bailiffs. The moon shifted about five fathoms off her course. The firmament called Aplanes (the heaven of fixed stars surrounding the seven heavens of planets) showed distinct signs of trepidation. As a result, the middle Pleïad abandoned her fellows and declined toward the equinox. The star called Spica, in the constellation of the Virgin, moved over to the neighboring constellation of the Balance or Libra. Dreadful events these, matters too hard for astrologians to set their teeth in, even if the latter could have reached so high.

You may be certain that every one ate most heartily of these medlars, which were beautiful to see and delicious to taste.

Now you recall Noah, that holy man to whom we are so eternally grateful for planting the vine whence we obtain that nectarian, delicious, precious, heavenly, joyful and deific liquor known as bibbage. Noah drank of it and he was mocked, for he was unaware of its great powers and virtues. Even so, now in the year of the medlars, men and women enjoyed eating that fat juicy fruit. But many and divers accidents befell them. Alas! one and all suffered a most terrible swelling in their bodies, though not each in the same place.

Some swelled in the belly, their paunches sticking out in front of them like great tuns. Of these it is written *Ventrem omnipotentem:* honest ventripotent men, these, and merry blades. St. Paunchard, St. Fatgulch and Mardigras are of their company.

Others swelled at the shoulders, growing so hunchbacked that they were called Montifers or Hummock-bearers. You still see some of these of either sex in various stations of life; Æsop, whose noble words and deeds you have in writings, was of that ilk.

---

[22] Julius Caesar reported that the Druids reckoned time by nights, not by days.
[23] *Calends* was a Roman term, not a Greek one. Throughout this paragraph Rabelais ridicules the elaborate and inaccurate calendar calculations necessitated by Ptolemaic astronomy.

The expansion of others occurred lengthwise in that member we call the husbandman of nature. This appendage of joy grew amazingly long, stout, fat, muscular and crested in the old fashion; its crest, in point of fact, rose on the least provocation. It was crested, too, in the new fashion; its bearer was prominent and certainly had a handle to his name. Men used their tools as girdles, winding them five or six times around their waists. If you could have seen these fellows with their members full cocked or spooming along with a fair wind behind them, you would have sworn they were knights with their lances settled on their rests, about to run at the ring, or tilt at quintain. Of these, the race is utterly spent and lost, as the women tell you when they continually lament:

> There aren't any more great gyratory diddly-whackers,
> Elongated, diathermal, bumgut-tickling kidney-crackers, etc. etc.

You know the rest of the song.

Others incrassated so enormously in the ballocks that the organic trio filled a large hogshead. From these come the nuts of Lorraine which never fit snug into a codpiece but draggle down to the bottom of the breeches.

Others grew in the legs: they looked like cranes or flamingos or people walking on stilts. Others grew in the feet, and snotty schoolboys called them Spondees because there were two long feet.

In others, the nose stretched so far that it looked like the beak of an alembic, all bediapered and bespangled with pimples, pullulant and be-purpled with nobs, enamelled, buttoned and embroidered with gules and crimson. Of such are Ganon Panzoult or Potgut, and Piedeboys or Wooden-foot, the physician of Angers. Few of this race cared for broths and brews of herb or plant; all were devotees of the septembral juice. Publius Ovidius Naso and the poet Ovid [24] were two sprung from that race, as were all those of whom it is written: *the Noes have it!*

Others put forth greater ears to such lengths that the right would have supplied material for a doublet, a pair of breeches and a jacket, while the left availed to bury its owner as in a Spanish cloak. This race, they say, still exists in Bourbonnais; such ears are known as Bourbons.

Others, finally, grew in length of body. Of these came the giants; of them Pantagruel.

And the first was Chalbroth,[25] who begat Sarabroth, who begat Fari-broth, who begat Hurtali, a brave eater of pottage who reigned in the time of the flood. He sat on the roof of the Ark and Noah passed food to him through a trapdoor.

[24] Ovid's full name was Publius Ovidius Naso. Rabelais is punning here on *nose* and *Naso* (*nasus* in Latin).   [25] Here follows Rabelais' parody of the genealogy of Jesus in the first chapter of Matthew.

Hurtali begat Nembroth, who begat Atlas, whose shoulders kept the skies from falling. And Atlas begat Goliath, who begat Eryx, inventor of the game of Tippling, who begat Titus. And Titus begat Badeloury, who killed seven cows that he might eat of their livers; and Badeloury begat Eryon, who begat Polyphemus, who begat Cacus, who begat Etion, the first man ever afflicted with the pox, and that for failing to drink fresh in summer or closing his mouth when he slept, as Bartachin the Italian commentator on the *Pandect* testifies.

Cacus begat Enceladus, who begat Ceus, who begat Typhœus, who begat Aloeus, who begat Othus, who begat Aegeon. Aegeon begat Briareus, who had a hundred hands; who begat Porphyrio, who begat Adamastor, who begat Anteus, who begat Agatho, who begat Porus, against whom Alexander the Great waged war.

And Porus begat Aranthas, who begat Gabbara. Gabbara, the tallest man under the Emperor Claudius, was nine feet nine; he invented the drinking of toasts and begat Goliath of Secundilla, who lived in the reign of Augustus and was ten feet three. He in turn begat Offot, terribly well-nosed for drinking at the barrelhead; who begat Artachaeus, who begat Oromedon, who begat Gemmagog, the inventor of Poland shoes, which are open on the foot and tied over the instep with a latchet.

From him sprang Sisyphus, who begat the Titans, of whom Hercules was born, who begat Enay, the most skilful man that ever was known at extracting fleshworms from under his fingernails.

And Enay begat Fierabras, vanquished by Oliver, a peer of France and Roland's comrade in arms. Fierabras begat Morgan, the first in the world to wear spectacles when he diced and the hero celebrated by Pulci in *Il Morgante Maggiore*; Morgan begat Fracassus, celebrated by Merlin Coccaius, the monk Teofilo Folengo,[26] learned author of *Opus Macaronicum*. Of Fracassus was born Ferragus; who begat Hapmouche or Swallow-fly, the first to dry tongues in the chimney, for hitherto people had salted them, as they now salt hams.

And Hapmouche begat Bolivorax, who begat Longis, who begat Gayoffo, whose ballocks were poplar and his rod service wood; he begat Mâchefain or Crunchneat, who begat Brûlefer or Ironburner, who begat Engoulevent the Windsucker, who begat Galehault, the inventor of flagons.

The last begat Mirelangaut, who begat Gallaffre, who begat Falourdin, who begat Roboast, who begat Sortibrant of Coïmbra in Portugal, who begat Brûlant, the Fire Eater of Mommiré; who begat Bruyer that was overcome by Ogier the Dane, a peer of France. Bruyer begat Maubrun of Aigremalée, a Saracen, who begat Foutanon or Donkeyphucker, who begat

---

[26] writer from whom a great deal of Rabelais' material for *Gargantua and Pantagruel* derives.

Haquelebac or Brangleferry, who begat Graincock or Vitdegrain, who begat
Grangousier, who begat Gargantua, who begat the noble Pantagruel, my[27]
master.

I know that as you read this passage, you will retain a learned doubt.
Quite rightly, too. How can this account possibly be true, you will argue,
when the entire universe perished at the flood save Noah and seven others
in the Ark? (Hurtali, mentioned above, is not cited among the latter.)

Your point is, of course, reasonable and obvious; but my answer will
satisfy you, or I am an idiot. Since I was not alive at the time, I can tell
you nothing on my own authority; I shall therefore cite the Massorets, a
learned group of commentators. Good ballocking lads, these, and fine Hebrew bagpipers, who assert that Hurtali was certainly never inside Noah's
Ark. How indeed could he have got in? He was much too big! Well, he
straddled it, one leg to the right, one to the left, like a child riding a
hobby-horse, or like the soldier they call the great bull of Berne. (He,
it was, sounded the attack on the bull's horn; in the battle of Marignano
he sought to spike the enemy's guns and perished, sprawled over a great
mortar. A pretty mount, undoubtedly, an easy, pleasant ambler!)

Hurtali, perched in this posture, was responsible for the salvation of the
Ark—after God, that is! For with his legs, he gave it the necessary balance,
and with his feet, he turned it whichever way he wished, like a ship's
rudder. Those within sent him up victuals aplenty through a trapdoor;
they were grateful for the service he did them. And sometimes they conversed as the philosopher Icaromenippus did with Jupiter, when, according
to Lucian, he merely gazed at the trapdoors through which the prayers of
men reached the ear of the Almighty.

Have you understood all this perfectly clearly? Then drink a good deep
draught without water. Now if you don't believe me—

"No, truly I do not," quoth she, to cite a popular song—

Then all the worse for you.

CHAPTER 11

Of the Nativity
of the Most Redoubtable
Pantagruel

At the age of four hundred fourscore and forty-four years, Gargantua
begat his son Pantagruel upon his wife named Badebec, daughter to the
king of the dimly-seen Amaurotes in Utopia. She died in the throes of

[27] Here, and again at the end of Book II, Rabelais uses the device of an interior
narrator.

childbirth. Alas! Pantagruel was so extraordinarily large and heavy that he could not possibly come to light without suffocating his mother.

If you would fully understand how he came to be christened Pantagruel, you must remember that a terrible drought raged that year throughout the land of Africa. For thirty-six months, three weeks, four days, thirteen hours and even longer, there was no drop of rain. And the sun blazed so fiercely that the whole earth was parched.

Even in the days of Elijah, the soil was no drier, for now no tree on earth bore leaf or flower. The grass had no verdure; rivers and springs ran dry; the luckless fishes, abandoned by their element, crawled on solid earth, crying and screaming most horribly. Birds fell from the air for want of moisture; wolves, foxes, harts, wild boars, fallow deer, hares, rabbits, weasels, martens, badgers and other beasts were found dead in the fields, their mouths agape.

As for the men, their state was very piteous. You should have seen them with their tongues dangling like a hound's after a run of six hours. Not a few threw themselves into the wells. Others lay under a cow's belly to enjoy the shade—these it is whom Homer calls *Alibantes,* the desiccated. The whole country was at a standstill. The strenuous efforts of mortals against the vehemence of this drought was a horrible spectacle. It was hard enough, God knows, to save the holy water in the churches from being wasted; but My Lords the Cardinals and our Holy Father laid down such strict rules that no man dared take more than a lick of it. In the churches, scores of parched, unhappy wretches followed the priest who distributed it, their jaws yawning for one tiny driblet. Like the rich man in *Luke,* who cried for Lazarus to dip his fingers in water, they were tormented by a flame, and would not suffer the slightest drop to be wasted. Ah! thrice happy that year the man who had a cool, wellplenished wine cellar underground!

In discussing the question: "Why is sea water salty?" the philosopher Aristotle, after Empedocles,[28] supplies the following reason. When Phœbus gave the reins of his luminous chariot to Phaëton, his son, the latter, unskilled in the art of driving, was incapable of following the ecliptic lines between the two tropics of the sun's sphere. Accordingly, he strayed from the appointed path and came so close to earth that he dried up all the countries under his course. He also burnished that great portion of heaven which philosophers call *Via Lactea* or the Milky Way, and good drinkers St. James' Way, since it is the starry line that guides pilgrims to Santiago de Compostella. (On the other hand, poets declare that it is here Juno's milk dropped while she was suckling Hercules.)

Earth at that time was so excessively heated that it broke into an enor-

[28] Greek philosopher of the fifth century B.C.

mous sweat which ran over the sea, making the latter salty, since all sweat is salt. If you do not admit this last statement, then taste of your own sweat. Or savor the perspiration of your pox-stricken friends when they are put in sweatboxes for treatment. It is all one to me.

Practically the same thing happened the year I am speaking of. On a certain Friday, all the people were intent upon their devotions. A noble procession was in progress with plenty of litanies and fine preachings. Supplications arose toward Almighty God beseeching Him to cast His eye of mercy upon them in their affliction. Suddenly they clearly saw some great drops of water stand out upon the ground, exactly as from a person sweating copiously.

The wretched populace began to rejoice as though here were a great blessing. Some declared that, since the air lacked all moisture, earth was supplying the deficiency. Other scientists asseverated that it was a shower of the Antipodes, as described by Seneca in *Quaestiones Naturales,* Book IV, where he treats of the Nile's source, attributing its floods to distant rains washed underground into the river. But they were thoroughly deceived. For, the procession done, when each sought to gather up this dew and drink it up by the bowlful, they found it was only pickle, far saltier than the saltiest water of the sea.

Another great mishap befell Gargantua that week. A dungchafing lout, bearing two great bags of salt and a hambone in his game-pouch, walked into poor Gargantua's mouth as the giant lay snoring. The clod spilled a quantity of salt in Gargantua's throat. Gargantua, crazy with a thirst he could not slake, angrily snapped his mouth shut. He gnashed his teeth fiercely; they ground like millstones. Later the rascal told me he was so terrified you could have stopped up his nose with a bale of hay. He fell flat on his face like a dead man, dropping the two saltbags that had tormented Gargantua. They were at once swallowed up and entombed.

My rogue vowed vengeance. Thrusting his hand in his game-pouch, he drew out a great hambone, highly salted, still covered with hair, and twenty-eight inches long. Ragefully he rammed it down Gargantua's throat. The giant, drier than ever, felt the pig's hair tickling his belly and, willy-nilly, spewed up all he had. Eighteen tumbrils could not have drawn away the rich nauseous yield. My dungchafer, hidden in the cavity of one of his teeth, was forced to take French leave in such pitiful condition that all who saw him were horrified. Gargantua, looking down, noticed this jackpudding whirling about in a great puddle.

"Here is some worm that sought to sting me in the belly," he mused, happy to have expelled him from his body.

Because he was born that very day, his father called him Pantagruel or All-Athirst, a name derived from the Greek *panta* meaning all, and the

Hagarene or Saracen *gruel* meaning athirst. Gargantua inferred thereby that at his son's birth the entire universe was wholly parched. Prophetically, too, he realized that some day Pantagruel would become Supreme Lord of the Thirsty, a fact indicated even more surely by a further portent.

For while his mother Badebec was bringing him forth and the midwives stood by ready to receive him, there first issued from her belly seventy-eight salt-vendors, each leading a salt-laden mule by the halter. They were followed by nine dromedaries, bearing hams and smoked oxtongues; seven camels bearing chitterlings; twenty-five cartloads of leeks, garlic, onions and chives. This terrified some midwives, but others said:

"Here is good provision! As it is, we drink but lazily, instead of vigorously. This must be a good omen, since these victuals are spurs to bibbing wine!"

As they were tattling away, out pops Pantagruel, hairy as a bear! At which, prophetically, one of them exclaimed:

"God help us, he is born hair and all, straight from the arse of Satan in flight. He will do terrible wonders. If he lives, he will grow to a lusty age!"

Of Pantagruel's race are those who drink so heavily in the evening that they must rise at night to drink again, quenching the coals of fire and blistering thirst in their throats. This form of thirst is called Pantagruel, in memory of the giant.

CHAPTER III

Of Gargantua's Grief
at the Demise
of His Wife Badebec

At Pantagruel's birth, none was more amazed and perplexed than his father Gargantua. On one hand, he saw his wife Badebec dead, on the other, his son Pantagruel, large as life and much noisier. He was at a complete loss what to say or do. A terrible doubt racked his brain: should he weep over the death of his wife or rejoice over the birth of his son? On either hand, sophistical arguments arose to choke him. He could frame them capitally *in modo et figura*, according to the modes and figures of the syllogism in formal logic. But he could not resolve them. So there he was, fretting like a mouse caught in a trap, or a kite snared in a gin.

"Shall I weep?" he cried. "Ay! . . . And why? Because my dear wife is dead! She was the most *this* and the most *that* who ever lived! I shall never see her again, I shall never know her like, I have suffered an irreparable loss! O God! what have I done to Thee to be thus punished? Why didst Thou not snatch me away before her, when to live without her is but to languish! Ah, Badebec, my darling, my love, my sweetheart, my dainty follicle (yet in area it was a good five and a half acres!), my tender mistress, my codpiece darling, my favorite pump, my dearest slipper, never shall I see you again! Alas, poor Pantagruel, you have lost your blessed mother, your indulgent nurse, your beloved lady! Ha, false Death, how outrageously evil to rob me of one that should by rights have been immortal. . . ."

As he spoke, he cried like a cow. But suddenly, struck by the thought of Pantagruel, he began to laugh like a calf.

"Ha, my little son!" he said, "my ballocky darling, my adorable fartlet, how lusty you are! How grateful I am to God for granting me a son so handsome, so sprightly, so gay and so spirited! Ho, ho, ho, ho, how happy I am! Let us drink, ho! and put away our melancholy! Bring out the best wine, rinse the glasses, lay the table, drive out those dogs, poke up this fire, light the candles, close that door there, cut the bread in sippets for our pottage, send away these beggar folk but give them anything they ask for! You, there, hold my gown! I shall strip to my doublet to entertain the gossips better!"

As he said this, he heard the priests chanting litanies and mementos as they bore his wife off to burial. All his glee suddenly evaporated; he was transported to the opposite extreme of emotion.

"Lord God," said Gargantua, "must I cry myself blind? This is the torment of hell! I am no longer young, I grow old, the weather is dangerous: I might easily fall ill of a fever. Already I am beside myself. Upon my faith as a gentleman, it were better I weep less and drink more. My wife is dead; well then, by God—*da jurandi veniam,* excuse my language—my tears will not resurrect her. It is well with her . . . she is in Paradise at least, if no higher . . . she is praying to God for us . . . she is happy, beyond the reach of our miseries and calamities. . . . The same fate stares us all in the face. God help the survivor, I must think of finding me another wife.

"But here is what *you* must do—" He turned to the midwives. "Midwives, sages-femmes! (Where are they, good people, I cannot see them? Who ever saw a *femme* who was really *sage!* [29]) Go, go to my wife's funeral whilst I stay here holding my son, for I feel somewhat out of sorts and dare not expose myself to sickness. Down a good drink first, too! You will be all the better for it, I assure you."

Doing as they were bid, they attended Badebec's funeral, while poor

[29] French for "well-behaved."

Gargantua remained at home, composing the following epitaph to be engraved upon her tombstone:

> Here lies sweet Badebec, snatched in the middle
> Of bearing child. What a metathesis! [30]
> Her face was like the carving on a fiddle,
> Her body Spanish and her belly Swiss,
> Pray God if she wrought anything amiss,
> He pardon her and she be sanctified.
> Here lies her body that expired, I wis,
> The very year and day wherein she died.

Gargantua packs Pantagruel off to Paris, since he wishes to send his son to the center of learning to gain an education. The letter he writes to his son, as perhaps no other text in all of Rabelais' work, puts forward what we have come to know as the essential precepts of Renaissance Humanism. While there are a number of sly, ironic moments in this text, this letter surpasses everything else in Gargantua and Pantagruel *in its earnestness of tone and its lack of gross humor.*

CHAPTER VIII

How Pantagruel in Paris
Received a Letter From
His Father Gargantua

As you may suppose, Pantagruel studied very hard and profited much by his study, for his intelligence was naturally active and his memory as full as twelve casks of olives. While in Paris, he received the following letter from his father:

My beloved son,

Among the gifts, graces and prerogatives with which our sovereign Creator, God Almighty, blessed and enriched humanity from the beginning, there is one that I deem supreme. By its means, though we be mortal, we can yet achieve a sort of immortality; through it, we may, in the course of our transitory lives, yet perpetuate our name and race.

To be sure, what we gain by a progeny born of lawful wedlock

---

[30] interchange.

cannot make up for what we lost through the sin of our first parents. Adam and Eve disobeyed the commandments of the Lord their God: mortality was their punishment. By death the magnificent mould in which Man was fashioned vanished into the dust of oblivion.

However, thanks to seminal propagation, what a man loses his children revive and, where they fail, their children prevail. So it has gone, and so it shall be, from generation to generation, until the Day of Judgment, when Christ shall restore to God the Father His kingdom pacified, secured and cleansed of all sin. Then all generation and corruption shall cease, for the elements will have completed their continuous transmutations. The peace humanity has craved so anxiously will have been attained; all things will have been reduced to their appointed end and period.

I therefore have reason to give thanks to God, my Saviour, for having granted me the joy of beholding my old age blossom anew in your youth. When, by His pleasure, which rules and orders everything, my soul must abandon this human habitation, I shall not believe I am dying utterly, but rather passing from one place to another. For in you my visible image will continue to live on earth; by you, I shall go on frequenting honorable men and true friends, as I was wont to do.

My associations have not been without sin, I confess. We all transgress and must continually beseech God to forgive us our trespasses. But they have been without reproach in the eyes of men.

That is why if, beside my bodily image, my soul did not likewise shine in you, you would not be accounted worthy of guarding the precious immortality of my name. In that case, the least part of me (my body) would endure. Scant satisfaction, that, when the best part (my soul, which should keep my name blessed among men) had degenerated and been bastardized. I say this not through any doubt as to your virtue, which I have already often tested, but to encourage you to go on doing ever better and profiting by your constant improvement.

My purpose is not so much to keep you absolutely on your present virtuous course as to make you rejoice that you have kept and are keeping on it. I seek to quicken your heart with resolutions for the future. To help you make and carry these out, remember that I have spared nothing. I have helped you as though my sole treasure on earth were once in my lifetime to see you well-bred and accomplished in honesty and valor as well as in knowledge and civility. Ay, I have longed to leave you after my death as a mirror of your father's personality. The reflection may not prove perfect in practice, but certainly I could not more studiously wish for its perfection.

My late father Grangousier, of blessed memory, made every effort that I might achieve mental, moral and technical excellence. The fruit of my studies and labors matched, indeed surpassed, his dearest wish. But you can realize that conditions were not as favorable to learning as they are to-day. Nor had I such gifted teachers as you. We were still in the dark ages; we still walked in the shadow of the dark clouds of ignorance; we suffered the calamitous consequences of the destruction of good literature by the Goths. Now, by God's grace, light and dignity have been restored to letters, and I have lived to see it. Indeed, I have watched such a revolution in learning that I, not erroneously reputed in my manhood the leading scholar of the century, would find it difficult to enter the bottom class in a grammar school.

I tell you all this not through boastfulness, though in writing to you I might be proud with impunity. Does not Marcus Tullius[31] authorize it in his book *Of Old Age,* and Plutarch in *How a Man May Praise Himself without Envy?* Both authors recognize that such pride is useful in fostering the spirit of emulation. No—I do it simply to give you a proof of my love and affection.

To-day, the old sciences are revived, knowledge is systematized, discipline reëstablished. The learned languages are restored: Greek, without which a man would be ashamed to consider himself educated; Hebrew, Chaldean and Latin. Printing is now in use, an art so accurate and elegant that it betrays the divine inspiration of its discovery, which I have lived to witness. Alas! Conversely, I was not spared the horror of such diabolic works as gunpowder and artillery.

To-day, the world is full of learned men, brilliant teachers and vast libraries: I do not believe that the ages of Plato, Cicero or Papinian[32] afforded such facilities for culture. From now on, it is unthinkable to come before the public or move in polite circles without having worshipped at Minerva's[33] shrine. Why, the robbers, hangmen, adventurers and jockeys of to-day are infinitely better educated than the doctors and preacheres of my time. More, even women and girls aspire to the glory, the heavenly manna of learning. Thus, at my advanced age, I have been forced to take up Greek. Not that I had despised it, like Cato;[34] I never had the opportunity to learn it. Now I delight in reading Plutarch's *Morals,* Plato's noble *Dialogues,* the *Monuments* of Pausanias and the *Antiquities* of Athenæus, as I await the hour when it shall please God, my Creator, to call me back to His bosom.

That is why, my dear son, I urge you to spend your youth making

[31] Cicero.
[32] Roman jurist of the second and third centuries A.D. [33] Roman goddess of wisdom. [34] Cato the Elder, who vigorously opposed the dissemination of Greek culture in ancient Rome.

the most of your studies and developing your moral sense. You are in Paris, which abounds in noble men upon whom to pattern yourself; you have Epistemon, an admirable tutor, who can inspire you by direct oral teaching. But I demand more of you. I insist you learn languages perfectly! Greek first, as old Quintilian prescribes; then Latin; then Hebrew for the sake of the Holy Scripture; then Chaldee and Arabic, too. Model your Greek style on Plato, your Latin on Cicero. Let no history slip your memory; cultivate cosmography, for you will find its texts helpful.

As for the liberal arts of geometry, arithmetic and music, I gave you a taste of them when you were a little lad of five or six. Proceed further in them yourself, learning as much as you can. Be sure to master all the rules of astronomy; but dismiss astrology and the divinatory art of Lullius as but vanity and imposture. Of civil law, I would have you know the texts of the Code by heart, then compare them with philosophy.

A knowledge of nature is indispensable; devote yourself to this study with unflagging curiosity. Let there be no sea, river or fountain but you know the fish that dwell in it. Be familiar with all the shrubs, bushes and trees in forest or orchard, all the plants, herbs and flowers that grow on the ground, all the birds of the air, all the metals in the bowels of earth, all the precious stones in the orient and the south. In a word, be well informed in everything that concerns the physical world we live in.

Then carefully consult the works of Greek, Arabian and Latin physicians, without slighting the Jewish doctors, Talmudists and Cabbalists. By frequent exercises in dissection[35] acquire a perfect knowledge of that other world, which is man.

Devote a few hours a day to the study of Holy Writ. Take up the New Testament and the Epistles in Greek; then, the Old Testament in Hebrew. Strive to make your mind an inexhaustible storehouse of knowledge. For you are growing to manhood now: soon you will have to give up your studious repose to lead a life of action. You will have to learn to bear arms, to achieve knighthood, so as to defend my house and help our allies frustrate the attacks of evildoers.

Further, I wish you soon to test what profit you have gained from your education. This you can best do by public discussion and debate on all subjects against all comers, and by frequenting learned men both in Paris and elsewhere.

But remember this. As Solomon says, wisdom entereth not into a

---

[35] Rabelais himself, as a medical student, is reputed to have been present at the first cadaver dissections performed in France.

malicious soul, and science without conscience spells but destruction of the spirit. Therefore serve, love and fear God, on Him pin all your thoughts and hopes; by faith built of charity, cling to Him so closely that never a sin come between you. Hold the abuses of the world in just suspicion. Set not your heart upon vanity, for this life is a transitory thing, but the Word of God endureth forever. Be serviceable to your neighbor, love him as you do yourself. Honor your teachers. Shun the company of all men you would not wish to resemble; receive not in vain the favors God has bestowed upon you.

When you realize that you have acquired all the knowledge Paris has to offer, come back so I may see you and give you my blessing before I die.

My son, the peace and grace of Our Lord be with you. Amen.

Your father,
Gargantua

From Utopia, the seventeenth day of September.

Having read this letter, Pantagruel, greatly encouraged, strove more ardently than ever to profit in his work. Had you seen him studying vigorously, practically and tirelessly, you would have compared his spirit moving among his books to flames blazing through a bonfire of dry branches.

Book II, as does the later Book I, takes its hero home from Paris to fight in a just war on behalf of his father's kingdom. The war is on the point of being won when the author is swallowed by the hero.

CHAPTER XXXII

How Pantagruel Covered
a Whole Army
With His Tongue
and What the Author Saw
in His Mouth

Pantagruel's progress through Dipsody was one continuous triumph, the inhabitants greeting him joyfully and surrendering on the spot. Of their own accord, the citizens would come out to meet him bearing the keys of the city he was approaching. The Almyrodes or Dirtyones alone sought to resist, replying to his heralds that they would surrender only on the best terms.

"What better terms could we have been on than sitting together with my hand on the pot and their glasses in their fists?" Pantagruel grumbled. "Oh, well, come along, let us go sock them."

So he drew up his army in battle formation, and they proceeded against the enemy. As they were passing by extensive meadowlands, suddenly they were caught by a heavy rain, which made them shiver, worry, and crowd together. Pantagruel bade their captains assure them it was nothing serious. Could he not see over the top of the clouds? He could, he did and all he made out up there was a little dew. At all events, let them draw up in close order and he would shelter them. So they formed a serried line and Pantagruel, putting out his tongue, covered them as a hen covers her chicks.

Meanwhile, I, who am simply reporting cold fact, had sought cover under a burdock leaf almost as large as the arch of the Montrible Bridge. When I saw Pantagruel's men in their snug refuge, I decided to join them. But they were too numerous; there was no room for me. After all, a foot is a foot and not thirteen inches, as the saying goes. The best I could do, therefore, was to climb on to Pantagruel's tongue and make for his mouth, which I finally reached after a two leagues' journey.

But O gods and goddesses of high heaven, what did I behold? May Jupiter confound me with his three-pronged lightning if I lie!

I walked in there as people walk into the church of St. Sophia at Constantinople. And I saw tall rocks looming up like the mountains of Scandinavia (his teeth, I fancy) . . . endless green fields . . . extensive forests . . . massive cities, fortified, and no less populous than Lyons or Poitiers. . . .

The first person I met was a goodman planting cabbages. Amazed, I asked:

"What are you doing here, friend?"

"Planting cabbages!"

"Why? How?"

"Faith, sir, we can't all sport ballocks as heavy as mortars and we can't all be rich. *I* earn *my* living planting cabbages *here* and selling them in market in the city yonder."

"Good Lord, is this a new world?"

"No, no, there's nothing new about this place. Though they do say there is a world beyond here somewhere—a new world too—with a sun and a moon in it and all sorts of fine jobs for a man. Maybe so, maybe not. At any rate, *this* is the *old* world!"

"Really?" I pondered the question a moment. Then: "This city where you sell your cabbages—what do they call it?"

"It's called Aspharage;[36] the citizens are good Christians and friendly souls. They will give you a rousing welcome."

[36] from the Greek words for "throat" thus meaning "Gulletsville."

On his recommendation, I decided to go. On my way, I came upon a man lying in wait for pigeons.

"Good morning, friend. Those pigeons you get—where do they come from?"

"From the other world."

I concluded that when Pantagruel yawned, the pigeons, believing his throat to be a dovecote, doubtless flew in in flocks. Presently I reached the city which I found to be picturesque, strongly fortified and prosperous in appearance. At the gate, the sentries stopped me for my pass. Amazed, I cried:

"What is the matter, gentlemen? Is there an epidemic of the plague?"

"My Lord!" they groaned. "We've had so many deaths hereabouts that the tumbrils drive through incessantly."

"Hereabouts, you say? Where?"

They told me the plague was raging in Larynx and Pharynx, large and bustling cities like Rouen and Nantes. It was due, apparently, to a noxious, malodorous and infectious exhalation which had been rising out of the abyss for some time now. Within seven days, more than twenty-two hundred and seventy-six thousand and sixteen people had perished. As I thought back, reckoning the dates, I realized that it was the unsavory breath emanating from Pantagruel's belly, since he had eaten the garlic-strewn stews that illustrated [37] King Anarchus' wedding.

Leaving hastily, I passed among the rocks of his teeth and kept walking until I got to the top of one. Here I found the fairest pleasure resort in the world, with large tennis courts, spacious galleries, sweet meadows, plentiful vines and an infinity of pretty houses, built Italian-fashion in the midst of delightful verdure. Here I spent a good four months and never fared better in my life.

Then I went down by the back teeth towards the jaws, but I was robbed by footpads in a great forest near the ears. Coming down again, I stopped at a small village the name of which I have forgotten. Here I did even better than before; I actually managed to make a little money to live on. Do you know how? By sleeping.

I am not lying: in this extraordinary place, the inhabitants hire people to sleep and pay them five or six sous a day. Heavy snorers get as much as seven and a half.

I told the senators how I had been robbed in the valley. They explained that the folk in those parts were lowlifes and by nature inclined to brigandry. From which I concluded, just as we have countries Cisalpine and Transalpine, they have countries Cidentine and Tradentine. But it is better living on this side because the air is purer.

[37] made bright.

I began to appreciate the truth of the axiom *Not half the world knows how the other half lives.* Imagine: no one has yet described this country though it includes more than twenty-five populous kingdoms, vast stretches of desert and a great arm of the sea. But I have written a voluminous book upon the subject. The title is *History of the Gorgians.* I named them so because they live in the throat of my master Pantagruel.

At last I returned via the beard, cast myself on his shoulders and thence made my way to *terra firma.* I fell right in front of him. Seeing me:

"Where the devil have you been, Alcofribas?" [38] he asked.

"In your throat, sir."

"How long, may I ask?"

"Ever since you set out against the Almyrodes."

"That was six months ago," he said. "And how did you live?"

"Handsomely, I thank you."

"What did you find to eat?"

"Plenty."

"To drink?"

"My Lord, I ate and drank just as you did, for I took my toll of the daintiest morsels and most toothsome wines that passed through your throat."

"Indeed, indeed. . . . But where did you cack?"

"Down your throat, My Lord."

"Ha, ha, what a wag you are!" he roared. "Well, since you left, with God's help we conquered all of Dipsody. I will give you the domain of Salmagundi for your part."

"I thank you, My Lord, you reward me beyond my deserts."

CHAPTER XXXIII

How Pantagruel Fell Ill and How He Was Cured

Shortly after, Pantagruel was taken ill. He suffered so severely from stomach trouble that he could neither eat nor drink. As afflictions never come singly, something else rose to torment him more cruelly than you can possibly imagine. What happened was this: a stroke of misfortune caused the pale-yellow fluid secreted by his kidneys, stored in his bladder and discharged by his urethra, to burn like the geysers of hell.

Fortunately, his physicians treated him with great skill, and thanks to

[38] Alcofribas Nasier was Rabelais' *nom de plume,* an anagram of his own name, François Rabelais.

various lenitives and diuretics, he voided his ailment and urine simultaneously.

The latter was so hot that it has not cooled off yet. According to the course it took, you can still find it in France and Italy in so-called watering-places or thermal springs. Such spas are Luchon in the Pyrenées and Cauterets, near by . . . Dax in Gascony . . . Balaruc near Montpellier . . . Néris in Bourbonnais . . . Bourbonne-Lancy in Burgundy. . . . Jets of Pantagruel's penial flood landed in Italy at Appona, St. Peter in Padua, St. Helena, Casanova, St. Bartolomeo, and, in the county of Bologna, at Porretta, and in a thousand other places.

That a horde of foolish scientists and physicians waste their time arguing about the origin of these boiling springs is, to me, an amazing phenomenon. Some vow it is borax, others, alum. Still others champion the cause of saltpetre. Tommyrot, all of it. They would do far better to rub their scuts with thistles than consume their energy discussing a matter they know nothing about. The answer is crystal clear. The only possible conclusion is that these watering places are hot because they came from water made by Pantagruel when a slight misadventure caused that water to flow hot.

To cure his principal ailment, he took the following purgative: four hundredweights of scammony from Colophon near Ephesus, one hundred and thirty-eight cartloads of casaia, eleven thousand nine hundred pounds of rhubarb, not to mention other incredible pharmaceutical hotchpots. After lengthy consultations, his physicians determined that whatever was disturbing his stomach must be removed. To this effect, engineers built seventeen huge copper globes as tall as Virgil's Obelisk in Rome, each fitted with trapdoors opening or closing automatically.

A servant went into one of these globes with a lantern and a lighted torch; Pantagruel swallowed it as you would a small pill. Three brawny peasants, armed with picks, climbed into each of five more globes; other stalwart varlets with huge shovels filled an additional three. The rest were manned by hosts of lumbermen with enormous baskets, and all went down Pantagruel's gullet like so many pills.

Once in his belly, they released the springs and emerged through the trapdoors, the lantern-bearer in the van. Doggedly they forged ahead more than half a league through a gulf of corruption more fulsome and putrid than Mephitis, goddess of Sulphur . . . more fetid than the marshes of Camerina, mentioned by Virgil . . . more putrid than the rank lake of Sorbona, cited by Strabo. . . . Had they not thoroughly antidoted their hearts, their stomachs and the winepots we call noddles, they would have been asphyxiated by these nauseous fumes. Oh, what perfumes, what evaporations to coprocontaminate and scatoscandalize the pretty little snouts of adolescent punks!

Groping and sounding their way through the stench, these heroes approached the fæcal matter and the corrupt humors, finally discovering a heap of ordure. The picks struck valiantly to break it loose, the shovels did double duty filling the baskets. When the pit was thoroughly scoured, the men reëntered their globes, closing the trapdoors behind them.

Pantagruel then forced himself to vomit, and thus brought them back to earth very easily. Rising, they made no more show in his throat than a fart in yours. As they emerged from their globes, they looked for all the world like the Greeks leaping out from the Trojan horse.

Thus Pantagruel was cured and restored to his usual good health and spirits.

CHAPTER XXXIV

The Conclusion of This Book
and the Author's Apology

Gentlemen, you have now heard the beginning of the horrendous story of My Lord and Master Pantagruel. I will leave off here because my head aches a little and I realize that the registers of my brain are somewhat blurred by this septembral mash. (As you well know, new wine is heady!)

But I promise you the continuation next spring at the time of the Frankfort Fair. In it you will read how Panurge was married and cuckolded within a week . . . how Pantagruel found the philosopher's stone . . . how once found, it should be used . . . how Pantagruel crossed the Caspian Mountains between Armenia and Media . . . how he navigated the Atlantic Ocean . . . how he vanquished the Cannibals and conquered the Isles of Perlas in the West Indies . . . how he married the daughter of Prester John, King of India . . . how he fought against the devils, burned five chambers of hell, sacked the great black apartment, tossed Persephone into the fire and drubbed Lucifer, breaking four of his teeth and the horn in his scut . . . how he visited the regions of the moon to ascertain if it were whole or if women bore three-quarters of it in their heads. . . . Ay, you shall learn a thousand other authentic and very humorous facts, brave things, truly, gospel texts set down in French.

Good night, gentles all. *Perdonate mi*, as the Italians say; forgive me and do not dwell so long upon my faults that you forget your own.

Do I hear you saying: "Master, it scarcely seems sensible of you to be writing such jocose twaddle!" My reply is that you are no more sensible to waste your time reading it.

But if you do so as a gay pastime—which was the spirit in which I wrote—then you and I are less reprehensible than a rabble of unruly monks, critters and hypocritters, sophists and double-fists, humbugs and other bugs, and all folk of the same water and kidney who skulk under religious robes the better to gull the world. For they seek to persuade ordinary people that they are intent solely upon contemplation, devotion, fasts, maceration of their sensualities—and that merely to sustain the petty fragility of their humanity! Whereas, quite to the contrary, they were roistering, and God knows how they roister! As Juvenal has it: *"Et Curios simulant sed bacchanalia vivant,* they play the austere Curius yet revel in bacchanalian orgies."* You may read the record of their dissipation in great letters of illuminated script upon their florid snouts and their pendulous bellies unless they perfume themselves with sulphur.

As for their studies, they read only Pantagrueline books, not so much to pass the time merrily as to hurt some one mischievously. How so? By fouling and befouling, by twiddling their dry fingers and fingering their dry twiddlers, by twisting wry necks, by bumming, arsing and ballocking, by devilscutting, in a word by calumniating. Rapt in this task, they are like nothing so much as the brutish village clods who in the cherry season stir up the ordures of little children to find kernels to sell to druggists for pomander oil.

Flee these rascals at sight, hate and abhor them as I do myself, and, by my faith, you will be the better for it. Would you be good Pantagruelists? That is, would you live peaceful, happy, healthy and forever content? Then never trust in people who peep through holes, especially through the opening of a monk's hood.

HERE END THE CHRONICLES OF PANTAGRUEL, KING OF THE DIPSODES, RESTORED TO THEIR TRUE NATURE, TOGETHER WITH HIS DEEDS AND HORRENDOUS FEATS, SET DOWN BY THE LATE[39] MONSIEUR ALCOFRIBAS, ABSTRACTOR OF QUINTESSENCE.

[39] The transparent pretense is that the author is dead and thus out of the reach of any potential persecutors.

William Shakespeare

Othello

THE TEXT AND NOTES ARE
BY G. B. HARRISON

William Shakespeare (1564–1616)

QUEEN ELIZABETH I GAVE HER NAME TO A PERIOD OF INTENSE theatrical activity in England. The second half of the sixteenth century, in which Shakespeare rose to his position of eminence not only as England's greatest playwright but eventually as her most celebrated poet, saw a proliferation of dramatic writing and performance. Little is known of Shakespeare's youth and young manhood in the town of Stratford-on-Avon. By the early 1590s he was a known playwright and actor in London, as well as a poet. His early success on the stage was sufficient for him to return to Stratford in 1596 to help his father out of debt and to purchase the house to which he eventually retired in about 1610.

Although his sonnet sequence is certainly a major work, it is through some two dozen of his thirty-eight plays that Shakespeare has become one of the giants of literature. He was master of all forms of the drama, excelling in comedy, tragedy, history, and romance. *Othello,* which was first performed in 1604, borrows its plot from one of the *Hecatommithi* (1566), a collection of one hundred tales by the Italian writer Giraldi Cinthio, loosely modeled after Boccaccio's *Decameron.* From the more melodramatic *Hecatommithi* Shakespeare constructed one of his tightest plots, putting the emphasis on inner conflict rather than outward action, ridding his play of all extraneous detail. *Othello* has long puzzled its audience because of the apparent lack of motivation for the behavior of Iago, one of literature's most malicious villains.

Othello

DUKE OF VENICE
BRABANTIO, *a Senator*
OTHER SENATORS
GRATIANO, *brother to Brabantio*
LODOVICO, *kinsman to Brabantio*
OTHELLO, *a noble Moor in the service of the Venetian state*
CASSIO, *his lieutenant*
IAGO, *his ancient*
MONTANO, *Othello's predecessor in the government of Cyprus*
RODERIGO, *A Venetian gentleman*
CLOWN, *servant to Othello*
DESDEMONA, *daughter to Brabantio and wife to Othello*
EMILIA, *wife to Iago*
BIANCA, *mistress to Cassio*
SAILOR, MESSENGER, HERALD, OFFICERS, GENTLEMEN, MUSI-
    CIANS, *and* ATTENDANTS

SCENE—*Venice: a seaport in Cyprus.*

SCENE I. *Venice. A street.*

[*Enter* RODERIGO *and* IAGO.]

RODERIGO. Tush, never tell me. I take it much unkindly
  That thou, Iago, who hast had° my purse
  As if the strings were thine, shouldst know of this.
IAGO. 'Sblood,° but you will not hear me.
  If ever I did dream of such a matter,
  Abhor me.
RODERIGO. Thou told'st me thou didst hold him in thy hate.
IAGO. Despise me if I do not. Three great ones of the city,
  In personal suit° to make me his Lieutenant,
  Off-capped° to him. And, by the faith of man,   10
  I know my price, I am worth no worse a place.
  But he, as loving his own pride and purposes,
  Evades them, with a bombast circumstance°
  Horribly stuffed with epithets of war.°
  And, in conclusion,
  Nonsuits° my mediators, for, "Certes,"° says he,
  "I have already chose my officer."
  And what was he?
  Forsooth, a great arithmetician,°
  One Michael Cassio, a Florentine,   20
  A fellow almost damned in a fair wife,°
  That never set a squadron in the field,
  Nor the division of a battle° knows
  More than a spinster, unless the bookish theoric,°
  Wherein the toged° Consuls° can propose
  As masterly as he—mere prattle without practice

ACT I, SCENE I: 2. *had:* used. 4. *'Sblood:* by God's blood. 9. *In . . . suit:* making this request in person. 10. *Off-capped:* stood cap in hand. 13. *bombast circumstance:* bombastic phrases. Bombast is cotton padding used to stuff out a garment. 14. *stuffed . . . war:* padded out with military terms. 16. *Nonsuits:* rejects the petition of; *Certes:* assuredly. 19. *arithmetician:* Contemporary books on military tactics are full of elaborate diagrams and numerals to explain military formations. Cassio is a student of such books. 21. *almost . . . wife:* a much-disputed phrase. There is an Italian proverb, "You have married a fair wife? You are damned." If Iago has this in mind, he means by *almost* that Cassio is about to marry. 23. *division . . . battle:* organization of an army. 24. *bookish theoric:* student of war; not a practical soldier. 25. *toged:* wearing a toga; *Consuls:* councilors (see I.ii. 43).

Is all his soldiership. But he, sir, had the election.
And I, of whom his eyes had seen the proof
At Rhodes, at Cyprus, and on other grounds
Christian and heathen, must be beeled° and calmed   30
By debitor and creditor. This countercaster,°
He, in good time,° must his Lieutenant be,
And I—God bless the mark!°—his Moorship's Ancient.°

RODERIGO. By Heaven, I rather would have been his hangman.

IAGO. Why, there's no remedy. 'Tis the curse of service,
Preferment goes by letter and affection,
And not by old gradation,° where each second
Stood heir to the first. Now, sir, be judge yourself
Whether I in any just term am affined°
To love the Moor.

RODERIGO.   I would not follow him, then.   40

IAGO. Oh, sir, content you,
I follow him to serve my turn upon him.
We cannot all be masters, nor all masters
Cannot be truly followed. You shall mark
Many a duteous and knee-crooking knave
That doting on his own obsequious bondage
Wears out his time, much like his master's ass,
For naught but provender, and when he's old, cashiered.°
Whip me such honest knaves. Others there are
Who, trimmed in forms and visages of duty,°   50
Keep yet their hearts attending on themselves,
And throwing but shows of service° on their lords
Do well thrive by them, and when they have lined their coats
Do themselves homage.° These fellows have some soul,
And such a one do I profess myself. For, sir,
It is as sure as you are Roderigo,
Were I the Moor, I would not be Iago.
In following him, I follow but myself.

---

30. *beeled*: placed on the lee (or unfavorable) side.   31. *countercaster*: calculator (repeating the idea of arithmetician). Counters were used in making calculations.   32. *in . . . time*: a phrase expressing indigation.   33. *God . . . mark*: an exclamation of impatience; *Ancient*: ensign, the third officer in the company of which Othello is Captain and Cassio Lieutenant.   36–37. *Preferment . . . gradation*: Promotion comes through private recommendation and favoritism and not by order of seniority.   39. *affined*: tied by affection.   48. *cashiered*: dismissed. The word at this time did not imply dishonorable discharge.   50. *trimmed . . . duty*: decking themselves out with the outward forms of loyal service.   52. *throwing . . . service*: serving merely in outward show.   54. *Do . . . homage*: serve themselves; *homage*: an outward act signifying obedience.

Heaven is my judge, not I for love and duty,
But seeming so, for my peculiar° end.   60
For when my outward action doth demónstrate
The native act and figure of my heart°
In compliment extern,° 'tis not long after
But I will wear my heart upon my sleeve
For daws° to peck at. I am not what I am.°
RODERIGO. What a full fortune° does the thick-lips owe°
    If he can carry 't thus! °
IAGO.   Call up her father,
    Rouse him. Make after him, poison his delight,
    Proclaim him in the streets. Incense her kinsmen,
    And though he in a fertile climate dwell,   70
    Plague him with flies. Though that his joy be joy,
    Yet throw such changes of vexation on 't
    As it may lose some color.°
RODERIGO. Here is her father's house, I'll call aloud.
IAGO. Do, with like timorous° accent and dire yell
    As when, by night and negligence, the fire
    Is spied in populous cities.
RODERIGO. What ho, Brabantio! Signior Brabantio, ho!
IAGO. Awake! What ho, Brabantio! Thieves! Thieves! Thieves!
    Look to your house, your daughter and your bags! °   80
    Thieves! Thieves!
            [BRABANTIO appears above, at a window.]
BRABANTIO. What is the reason of this terrible summons?
    What is the matter there?
RODERIGO. Signior, is all your family within?
IAGO. Are your doors locked?
BRABANTIO.   Why, wherefore ask you this?
IAGO. 'Zounds,° sir, you're robbed. For shame, put on your gown,°
    Your heart is burst, you have lost half your soul.
    Even now, now, very now, an old black ram
    Is tupping° your white ewe. Arise, arise,
    Awake the snorting° citizens with the bell,   90

---

60. *peculiar:* particular, personal. 62. *native . . . heart:* natural actions and shape of my secret designs. 63. *extern:* outward. 65. *daws:* jackdaws; that is, fools; *I . . . am:* I am in secret a devil. 66. *full fortune:* overflowing good luck; *owe:* own. 67. *carry't thus:* that is, bring off this marriage. 72–73. *throw . . . color:* cause him some annoyance by way of variety to tarnish his joy. 75. *timorous:* terrifying. 80. *bags:* moneybags. 86. *'Zounds:* by God's wounds; *gown:* dressing gown. 89. *tupping:* covering. 90. *snorting:* snoring.

Or else the Devil ° will make a grandsire of you.
   Arise, I say.
BRABANTIO.   What, have you lost your wits?
RODERIGO. Most reverend signior, do you know my voice?
BRABANTIO. Not I. What are you?
RODERIGO. My name is Roderigo.
BRABANTIO.   The worser welcome.
   I have charged thee not to haunt about my doors.
   In honest plainness thou hast heard me say
   My daughter is not for thee, and now, in madness,
   Being full of supper and distempering draughts, °
   Upon malicious bravery° dost thou come   100
   To start° my quiet.
RODERIGO. Sir, sir, sir——
BRABANTIO.   But thou must needs be sure
   My spirit and my place have in them power
   To make this bitter to thee.
RODERIGO.   Patience, good sir.
BRABANTIO. What tell'st thou me of robbing? This is Venice,
   My house is not a grange. °
RODERIGO.   Most grave Brabantio,
   In simple and pure soul I come to you.
IAGO. 'Zounds, sir, you are one of those that will not serve God if the
   Devil bid you. Because we come to do you service and you think
   we are ruffians, you'll have your daughter covered with a Bar-   110
   bary° horse, you'll have your nephews° neigh to you, you'll have
   coursers for cousins,° and jennets° for germans. °
BRABANTIO. What profane wretch art thou?
IAGO. I am one, sir, that comes to tell you your daughter and the Moor
   are now making the beast with two backs.
BRABANTIO. Thou art a villain.
IAGO.   You are—a Senator.
BRABANTIO. This thou shalt answer. I know thee, Roderigo.
RODERIGO. Sir, I will answer anything. But I beseech you
   If 't be your pleasure and most wise consent,
   As partly I find it is, that your fair daughter,   120
   At this odd-even° and dull ° watch o' the night,

---

91. *Devil:* The Devil in old pictures and woodcuts was represented as black. *99.*
distempering draughts: liquor that makes senseless. *100. bravery:* defiance. *101.*
start: startle. *106. grange:* lonely farm. *111. Barbary:* Moorish. *112. nephews:*
grandsons. *113. cousins:* near relations; *jennets:* Moorish ponies. *114. germans:*
kinsmen. *124. odd-even:* about midnight; *dull:* heavy, sleepy.

Transported with no worse nor better guard
But with a knave of common hire, a gondolier,
To the gross clasps of a lascivious Moor—
If this be known to you, and your allowance,°
We then have done you bold and saucy wrongs.
But if you know not this, my manners tell me
We have your wrong rebuke. Do not believe
That from the sense of all civility°
I thus would play and trifle with your reverence.   130
Your daughter, if you have not given her leave,
I say again, hath made a gross revolt,°
Tying her duty, beauty, wit, and fortunes
In an extravagant° and wheeling° stranger
Of here and everywhere. Straight satisfy yourself.
If she be in her chamber or your house,
Let loose on me the justice of the state
For thus deluding you.
BRABANTIO.   Strike on the tinder,° ho!
Give me a taper!° Call up all my people!
This accident is not unlike my dream.   140
Belief of it oppresses me already.
Light, I say! Light!   [*Exit above.*]
IAGO.   Farewell, for I must leave you.
It seems not meet, nor wholesome to my place,°
To be produced—as if I stay I shall—
Against the Moor. For I do know the state,
However this may gall° him with some check,°
Cannot with safety cast° him. For he's embarked
With such loud reason to the Cyprus wars,
Which even now stand in act,° that, for their souls,
Another of his fathom° they have none   150
To lead their business. In which regard,
Though I do hate him as I do Hell pains,
Yet for necessity of present life

---

128. *your allowance:* by your permission.   132. *from . . . civility:* disregarding
all sense of decent behavior.   135. *gross revolt:* indecent rebellion.   137. *extravagant:* vagabond; *wheeling:* wandering.   141. *tinder:* the primitive method of making fire, used before the invention of matches. A spark, made by striking flint on
steel, fell on the tinder, some inflammable substance such as charred linen, which
was blown into flame.   142. *taper:* candle.   146. *place:* that is, as Othello's officer.
149. *gall:* make sore; *check:* rebuke.   150. *cast:* dismiss from service.   152. *stand
in act:* are on the point of beginning.   153. *fathom:* depth.

I must show out a flag° and sign of love,
Which is indeed but sign. That you shall surely find him,
Lead to the Sagittary° the raisèd search,
And there will I be with him. So farewell.   [*Exit.*]
    [*Enter, below,* BRABANTIO, *in his nightgown, and*
                SERVANTS *with torches.*]
BRABANTIO. It is too true an evil. Gone she is,
  And what's to come of my despisèd time°
  Is naught but bitterness. Now, Roderigo,   160
  Where didst thou see her? Oh, unhappy girl!
  With the Moor, say'st thou? Who would be a father!
  How didst thou know 'twas she? Oh, she deceives me
  Past thought! What said she to you? Get more tapers.
  Raise all my kindred. Are they married, think you?
RODERIGO. Truly, I think they are.
BRABANTIO. Oh Heaven! How got she out? Oh, treason of the blood! °
  Fathers, from hence trust not your daughters' minds
  By what you see them act. Are there not charms°
  By which the property° of youth and maidhood   170
  May be abused?° Have you not read, Roderigo,
  Of some such thing?
RODERIGO.   Yes, sir, I have indeed.
BRABANTIO. Call up my brother. Oh, would you had had her!
  Some one way, some another. Do you know
  Where we may apprehend her and the Moor?
RODERIGO. I think I can discover him, if you please
  To get good guard and go along with me.
BRABANTIO. Pray you, lead on. At every house I'll call,
  I may command° at most. Get weapons, ho!
  And raise some special officers of night.   180
  On, good Roderigo, I'll deserve your pains.°
                      [*Exeunt.*]

---

157. *flag:* a sign of welcome.   159. *Sagittary:* presumably some building in Venice,
not identified, used as a meeting place for the Council.   162. *what's . . . time:*
the rest of my wretched life.   170. *treason . . . blood:* treachery of my own
child.   172. *charms:* magic spells.   173. *property:* nature.   174. *abused:* deceived.
182. *command:* find supporters.   184. *deserve . . . pains:* reward your labor.

SCENE II. *Another street.*

[*Enter* OTHELLO, IAGO, *and* ATTENDANTS,
with torches.]

IAGO. Though in the trade of war I have slain men,
    Yet do I hold it very stuff° o' the conscience
    To do no contrivèd° murder. I lack iniquity
    Sometimes to do me service. Nine or ten times
    I had thought to have yerked° him here under the ribs.
OTHELLO. 'Tis better as it is.
IAGO.   Nay, but he prated
    And spoke such scurvy and provoking terms
    Against your honor
    That, with the little godliness I have,
    I did full hard forbear him.° But I pray you, sir,   10
    Are you fast° married? Be assured of this,
    That the Magnifico° is much beloved,
    And hath in his effect° a voice potential
    As double as° the Duke's. He will divorce you,
    Or put upon you what restraint and grievance
    The law, with all his might to enforce it on,
    Will give him cable.°
OTHELLO.   Let him do his spite.
    My services which I have done the signiory°
    Shall outtongue his complaints. 'Tis yet to know°—
    Which, when I know that boasting is an honor,   20
    I shall promulgate°—I fetch my life and being°
    From men of royal siege,° and my demerits°
    May speak unbonneted° to as proud a fortune
    As this that I have reached. For know, Iago,
    But that I love the gentle Desdemona,
    I would not my unhousèd° free condition
    Put into circumscription and confine°

SCENE II: 2. *stuff:* material, nature. 3. *contrived:* deliberately planned. 5. *yerked:* jabbed. 10. *full . . . him:* had a hard job to keep my hands off him. 11. *fast:* securely. 12. *Magnifico:* the title of the chief men of Venice. 13. *in . . . effect:* what he can do. 13–14. *potential . . . as:* twice as powerful as. 17. *cable:* rope. 18. *signiory:* the state of Venice. 19. '*Tis . . . know:* it has still to be made known. 21. *promulgate:* proclaim; *fetch . . . being:* am descended. 22. *royal siege:* throne; *demerits:* deserts. 23. *unbonneted:* A disputed phrase. Usually it means "without a cap"; that is, in sign that the wearer is standing before a superior. But Othello means that his merits are such that he need show deference to no man. 26. *unhoused:* unmarried. 27. *confine:* confinement.

For the sea's worth. But look! What lights come yond?
IAGO. Those are the raisèd father and his friends.
  You were best go in.
OTHELLO.   Not I, I must be found.   30
  My parts,° my title, and my perfect° soul
  Shall manifest me rightly. Is it they?
IAGO. By Janus,° I think no.
          [Enter CASSIO, and certain OFFICERS with torches.]
OTHELLO. The servants of the Duke, and my Lieutenant.
  The goodness of the night upon you, friends!
  What is the news?
CASSIO.   The Duke does greet you, General,
  And he requires your haste-posthaste° appearance,
  Even on the instant.
OTHELLO.   What is the matter, think you?
CASSIO. Something from Cyprus, as I may divine.
  It is a business of some heat. The galleys°   40
  Have sent a dozen sequent° messengers
  This very night at one another's heels,
  And many of the consuls, raised and met,
  Are at the Duke's already. You have been hotly called for
  When, being not at your lodging to be found,
  The Senate hath sent about three several° quests
  To search you out.
OTHELLO.   'Tis well I am found by you.
  I will but spend a word here in the house
  And go with you.   [Exit.]
CASSIO.   Ancient, what makes he here?
IAGO. Faith, he tonight hath boarded a land carrack.°   50
  If it prove lawful prize, he's made forever.
CASSIO. I do not understand.
IAGO.   He's married.
CASSIO.   To who?
              [Re-enter OTHELLO.]
IAGO. Marry,° to——Come, Captain, will you go?
OTHELLO.   Have with you.

31. *parts:* abilities; *perfect:* ready.   33. *Janus:* the two-faced God of Romans, an appropriate deity for Iago.   37. *haste-posthaste:* with the quickest possible speed. When it was necessary to urge the postboy to greater speed than usual, the letter or dispatch was inscribed "haste, posthaste."   40. *galleys:* Venetian ships manned and rowed by slaves; the fastest of craft.   41. *sequent:* following one after another. 46. *several:* separate.   50. *carrack:* the largest type of Spanish merchant ship.   53. *Marry:* Mary, by the Virgin—with a pun.

CASSIO. Here comes another troop to seek for you.

IAGO. It is Brabantio. General, be advised,°

    He comes to bad intent.

        [*Enter* BRABANTIO, RODERIGO, *and* OFFICERS *with*
          torches and weapons.]

OTHELLO.   Holloa! Stand there!

RODERIGO. Signior, it is the Moor.

BRABANTIO.   Down with him, thief!

        [*They draw on both sides.*]

IAGO. You, Roderigo! Come, sir, I am for you.

OTHELLO. Keep up° your bright swords, for the dew will rust them.

    Good signior, you shall more command with years   60

    Than with your weapons.

BRABANTIO. O thou foul thief, where hast thou stowed my daughter?

    Damned as thou art, thou hast enchanted her.

    For I'll refer me to all things of sense°

    If she in chains of magic were not bound,

    Whether a maid so tender, fair, and happy,

    So opposite to marriage that she shunned

    The wealthy curlèd darlings of our nation,

    Would ever have, to incur a general mock,

    Run from her guardage° to the sooty bosom   70

    Of such a thing as thou, to fear, not to delight.

    Judge me the world if 'tis not gross in sense°

    That thou hast practiced on her with foul charms,

    Abused her delicate youth with drugs or minerals

    That weaken motion.° I'll have 't disputed on,°

    'Tis probable, and palpable° to thinking.

    I therefore apprehend and do attach° thee

    For an abuser of the world, a practicer

    Of arts inhibited and out of warrant.°

    Lay hold upon him. If he do resist,   80

    Subdue him at his peril.

OTHELLO.   Hold your hands,

    Both you of my inclining and the rest.

    Were it my cue to fight, I should have known it

    Without a prompter. Where will you that I go

---

55. *advised:* careful. 59. *Keep up:* sheathe. 64. *refer . . . sense:* that is, by every rational consideration. 70. *guardage:* guardianship. 72. *gross in sense:* that is, plain to the perception. 75. *motion:* sense; *disputed on:* argued in the courts of law. 76. *palpable:* clear. 77. *attach:* arrest. 79. *arts . . . warrant:* forbidden and illegal acts; that is, magic and witchcraft.

To answer this your charge?
BRABANTIO.   To prison, till fit time
Of law and course of direct session°
Call thee to answer.
OTHELLO.   What if I do obey?
How may the Duke be therewith satisfied,
Whose messengers are here about my side
Upon some present° business of the state   90
To bring me to him?
1. OFFICER.   'Tis true, most worthy signior.
The Duke's in Council, and your noble self
I am sure is sent for.
BRABANTIO.   How! The Duke in Council!
In this time of the night! Bring him away.
Mine's not an idle° cause. The Duke himself,
Or any of my brothers of the state,
Cannot but feel this wrong as 'twere their own.
For if such actions may have passage free,°
Bondslaves and pagans shall our statesmen be.

                                                    [*Exeunt.*]

SCENE III. *A council chamber.*

[*The* DUKE *and* SENATORS *sitting at a table,* OFFICERS
attending.]
DUKE. There is no composition° in these news°
That gives them credit.
1. SENATOR.   Indeed they are disproportioned.
My letters say a hundred and seven galleys.
DUKE. And mine, a hundred and forty.
2. SENATOR.   And mine, two hundred.
But though they jump not on a just account°—
As in these cases, where the aim reports,°
'Tis oft with difference—yet do they all confirm

---

86. *course . . . session:* trial in the ordinary courts, where witches and other
criminals are tried—and not by special commission as a great man. 90. *present:*
immediate. 95. *idle:* trivial. 98. *have . . . free:* be freely allowed.
SCENE III: 1. *composition:* agreement; *news:* reports. 5. *jump . . . account:* do
not agree with an exact estimate. 6. *aim reports:* that is, intelligence reports of
an enemy's intention often differ in details.

A Turkish fleet, and bearing up° to Cyprus.
DUKE. Nay, it is possible enough to judgment.
    I do not so secure me in the error,°   10
    But the main article° I do approve
    In fearful° sense.
SAILOR [*within*]   What ho! What ho! What ho!
1. OFFICER. A messenger from the galleys.
               [*Enter* SAILOR.]
DUKE.   Now, what's the business?
SAILOR. The Turkish preparation makes for Rhodes.
    So was I bid report here to the state
    By Signior Angelo.
DUKE. How say you by this change?
1. SENATOR.   This cannot be,
    By no assay of reason.° 'Tis a pageant°
    To keep us in false gaze.° When we consider
    The importancy of Cyprus to the Turk,   20
    And let ourselves again but understand
    That as it more concerns the Turk than Rhodes,
    So may he with more facile question bear° it,
    For that it stands not in such warlike brace°
    But altogether lacks the abilities
    That Rhodes is dressed° in—if we make thought of this,
    We must not think the Turk is so unskillful
    To leave that latest which concerns him first,
    Neglecting an attempt of ease and gain
    To wake and wage° a danger profitless.   30
DUKE. Nay, in all confidence, he's not for Rhodes.
1. OFFICER. Here is more news.
            [*Enter a* MESSENGER.]
MESSENGER. The Ottomites,° Reverend and Gracious,
    Steering with due course toward the isle of Rhodes,
    Have there injointed° them with an after-fleet.°
1. SENATOR. Aye, so I thought. How many, as you guess?
MESSENGER. Of thirty sail. And now they do restem°
    Their backward course, bearing with frank appearance°

8. *bearing up:* making course for.   10. *I . . . error:* I do not consider myself free from danger, because the reports may not all be accurate.   11. *main article:* general purport.   12. *fearful:* to be feared.   18. *assay of reason:* reasonable test; *pageant:* show.   19. *false gaze:* looking the wrong way.   23. *with . . . bear:* take it more easily.   24. *brace:* state of defense.   26. *dressed:* prepared.   30. *wage:* risk.   33. *Ottomites:* Turks.   35. *injointed:* joined; *after-fleet:* following, second fleet.   37. *restem:* steer again.   38. *frank appearance:* no attempt at concealment.

Their purposes toward Cyprus. Signior Montano,
Your trusty and most valiant servitor,   40
With his free duty recommends you thus,°
And prays you to believe him.
DUKE. 'Tis certain then for Cyprus.
Marcus Luccicos, is not he in town?
1. SENATOR. He's now in Florence.
DUKE. Write from us to him, post-posthaste dispatch.
1. SENATOR. Here comes Barbantio and the valiant Moor.
            [*Enter* BRABANTIO, OTHELLO, IAGO, RODERIGO,
                        and OFFICERS.]
DUKE. Valiant Othello, we must straight employ you
Against the general enemy Ottoman.
[*To* BRABANTIO] I did not see you. Welcome, gentle signior.   50
We lacked your counsel and your help tonight.
BRABANTIO. So did I yours. Good your Grace, pardon me.
Neither my place nor aught I heard of business
Hath raised me from my bed, nor doth the general care
Take hold on me. For my particular° grief
Is of so floodgate° and o'erbearing nature
That it engluts° and swallows other sorrows,
And it is still itself.
DUKE.   Why, what's the matter?
BRABANTIO. My daughter! Oh, my daughter!
ALL.   Dead?
BRABANTIO.   Aye, to me.
She is abused, stol'n from me and corrupted   60
By spells and medicines bought of mountebanks.°
For nature so preposterously to err,
Being not deficient, blind, or lame of sense,
Sans° witchcraft could not.
DUKE. Whoe'er he be that in this foul proceeding
Hath thus beguiled your daughter of herself °
And you of her, the bloody book of law
You shall yourself read in the bitter letter
After your own sense—yea, though our proper° son
Stood in your action.
BRABANTIO.   Humbly I thank your Grace.   70

---

41. *With . . . thus:* with all due respect thus advises.   55. *particular:* personal.
56. *floodgate:* that is, like water rushing through an opened sluice.   57. *engluts:*
swallows.   61. *mountebanks:* quack doctors, who dealt in poisons and love po-
tions.   64. *Sans:* without.   66. *beguiled . . . herself:* cheated your daughter of
herself; that is, caused her to be "beside herself."   69. *proper:* own.

Here is the man, this Moor, whom now, it seems,
Your special mandate for the state affairs
Hath hither brought.
ALL.   We are very sorry for 't.
DUKE [to OTHELLO]. What in your own part can you say to this?
BRABANTIO. Nothing but this is so.
OTHELLO. Most potent, grave, and reverend signiors,
My very noble and approved° good masters,
That I have ta'en away this old man's daughter,
It is most true—true, I have married her.
The very head and front° of my offending   80
Hath this extent, no more. Rude° am I in my speech,
And little blest with the soft phrase of peace.
For since these arms of mine had seven years' pith°
Till now some nine moons wasted, they have used
Their dearest° action in the tented field.
And little of this great world can I speak,
More than pertains to feats of broil and battle,
And therefore little shall I grace my cause
In speaking for myself. Yet, by your gracious patience,
I will a round unvarnished tale° deliver   90
Of my whole course of love—what drugs, what charms,
What conjuration and what mighty magic—
For such proceeding I am charged withal—
I won his daughter.
BRABANTIO.   A maiden never bold,
Of spirit so still and quiet that her motion
Blushed at herself,° and she—in spite of nature,
Of years, of country, credit,° everything—
To fall in love with what she feared to look on!
It is a judgment maimed and most imperfect
That will confess° perfection so could err   100
Against all rules of nature, and must be driven
To find out practices° of cunning Hell
Why this should be. I therefore vouch° again
That with some mixtures° powerful o'er the blood,°
Or with some dram conjured° to this effect,

77. *approved:* tested; that is, found good masters by experience. 80. *front:* forehead. 81. *Rude:* rough, uncultured. 83. *pith:* marrow. 85. *dearest:* most important. 90. *round . . . tale:* direct, unadorned account. 95–96. *Of . . . herself:* she was so shy that she blushed at the slightest cause; *motion:* outward behavior. 97. *credit:* reputation. 100. *will confess:* would believe. 102. *practices:* plots. 103. *vouch:* declare. 104. *mixtures:* drugs; *blood:* passions. 105. *conjured:* mixed with spells.

He wrought upon her.
DUKE.   To vouch this is no proof
Without more certain and more overt° test
Than these thin habits° and poor likelihoods°
Of modern seeming° do prefer° against him.
1. SENATOR. But, Othello, speak.   110
Did you by indirect and forcèd° courses
Subdue and poison this young maid's affections?
Or came it by request, and such fair question
As soul to soul affordeth?
OTHELLO.   I do beseech you
Send for the lady to the Sagittary,
And let her speak of me before her father.
If you do find me foul in her report,
The trust, the office I do hold of you,
Not only take away, but let your sentence
Even fall upon my life.
DUKE.   Fetch Desdemona hither.   120
OTHELLO. Ancient, conduct them, you best know the place.
                    [*Exeunt* IAGO *and* ATTENDANTS.]
And till she come, as truly as to Heaven
I do confess the vices of my blood,
So justly to your grave ears I'll present
How I did thrive in this fair lady's love
And she in mine.
DUKE.   Say it, Othello.
OTHELLO. Her father loved me, oft invited me,
Still° questioned me the story of my life
From year to year, the battles, sieges, fortunes,
That I have passed.   130
I ran it through, even from my boyish days
To the very moment that he bade me tell it.
Wherein I spake of most disastrous chances,°
Of moving accidents° by flood and field,
Of hairbreadth 'scapes i' the imminent deadly breach,°
Of being taken by the insolent foe
And sold to slavery, of my redemption thence,
And portance° in my travels' history.

---

107. *overt:* open.   108. *thin habits:* slight evidence; lit., thin clothes; *poor like-lihoods:* unconvincing charges.   109. *modern seeming:* slight suspicion; *prefer:* make a charge against.   111. *forcèd:* unnatural.   129. *Still:* always, continu-ally.   133. *chances:* accidents.   134. *accidents:* occurrences.   135. *breach:* as-sault on a city.   138. *portance:* bearing.

Wherein of antres° vast and deserts idle,°
Rough quarries, rocks, and hills whose heads touch heaven,   140
It was my hint° to speak—such was the process.°
And of the cannibals that each other eat,
The anthropophagi,° and men whose heads
Do grow beneath their shoulders. This to hear
Would Desdemona seriously incline.
But still the house affairs would draw her thence,
Which ever as she could with haste dispatch,
She'd come again, and with a greedy ear
Devour up my discourse. Which I observing,
Took once a pliant° hour and found good means   150
To draw from her a prayer of earnest heart
That I would all my pilgrimage dilate,°
Whereof by parcels° she had something heard,
But not intentively.° I did consent,
And often did beguile her of° her tears
When I did speak of some distressful stroke
That my youth suffered. My story being done,
She gave me for my pains a world of sighs.
She swore, in faith, 'twas strange, 'twas passing strange,
'Twas pitiful, 'twas wondrous pitiful.   160
She wished she had not heard it, yet she wished
That Heaven had made her° such a man. She thanked me,
And bade me, if I had a friend that loved her,
I should but teach him how to tell my story
And that would woo her. Upon this hint I spake.
She loved me for the dangers I had passed,
And I loved her that she did pity them.
This only is the witchcraft I have used.
Here comes the lady, let her witness it.
            [*Enter* DESDEMONA, IAGO, *and* ATTENDANTS.]
DUKE. I think this tale would win my daughter too.   170
      Good Brabantio,
      Take up this mangled matter at the best.°
      Men do their broken weapons rather use
      Than their bare hands.

---

139. antres: caves; *idle:* worthless.   *141. hint:* occasion; *process:* proceeding,
order.   *143. anthropophagi:* cannibals.   *150. pliant:* suitable.   *152. dilate:* relate at length.   *153. parcels:* portions.   *154. intentively:* intently.   *155. beguile
. . . of:* draw from her.   *162. her:* for her.   *172. Take . . . best:* make the
best settlement you can of this confused business.

BRABANTIO.   I pray you hear her speak.
If she confess that she was half the wooer,
Destruction on my head if my bad blame
Light on the man! Come hither, gentle mistress.
Do you perceive in all this noble company
Where most you owe obedience?

DESDEMONA.   My noble Father,
I do perceive here a divided duty.   180
To you I am bound for life and education,
My life and education both do learn° me
How to respect you, you are the lord of duty,°
I am hitherto your daughter. But here's my husband,
And so much duty as my mother showed
To you, preferring you before her father
So much I challenge that I may profess
Due to the Moor my lord.

BRABANTIO.   God be with you! I have done.
Please it your Grace, on to the state affairs.
I had rather to adopt a child than get° it.   190
Come hither, Moor.
I here do give thee that with all my heart
Which, but thou hast already, with all my heart
I would keep from thee. For your sake, jewel,
I am glad at soul I have no other child,
For thy escape would teach me tyranny,
To hang clogs on them. I have done, my lord.

DUKE. Let me speak like yourself, and lay a sentence°
Which, as a grise° or step, may help these lovers
Into your favor.   200
When remedies are past, the griefs are ended
By seeing the worst, which late on hopes depended.°
To mourn a mischief that is past and gone
Is the next way to draw new mischief on.
What cannot be preserved when fortune takes,
Patience her injury a mockery makes.°
The robbed that smiles steals something from the thief.
He robs himself that spends a bootless° grief.

---

182. *learn:* teach.   183. *lord of duty:* the man to whom I owe duty.   190. *get:* beget.   198. *sentence:* proverbial saying.   199. *grise:* degree, step.   201–02. *When . . . depended:* our anxieties end when the feared event happens.   206. *Patience . . . makes:* that is, when we are not unduly disturbed by our misfortunes, we mock Fortune.   208. *bootless:* vain.

BRABANTIO. So° let the Turk of Cyprus us beguile,
    We lose it not so long as we can smile. 210
    He bears the sentence well that nothing bears
    But the free comfort which from thence he hears.
    But he bears both the sentence and the sorrow
    That, to pay grief, must of poor patience borrow.
    These sentences, to sugar or to gall,
    Being strong on both sides, are equivocal.
    But words are words. I never yet did hear
    That the bruisèd heart was piercèd through the ear.
    I humbly beseech you, proceed to the affairs of state.
DUKE. The Turk with a most mighty preparation makes for Cyprus. 220
    Othello, the fortitude of the place is best known to you, and
    though we have there a substitute° of most allowed° suffi-
    ciency,° yet opinion, a sovereign mistress of effects, throws a
    more safer voice on you.° You must therefore be content to
    slubber° the gloss of your new fortunes with this more stubborn
    and boisterous expedition.
OTHELLO. The tyrant custom, most grave Senators,
    Hath made the flinty and steel couch of war
    My thrice-driven° bed of down. I do agnize°
    A natural and prompt alacrity 230
    I find in hardness,° and do undertake
    These present wars against the Ottomites.
    Most humbly therefore bending to your state,
    I crave fit disposition for my wife,
    Due reference of place° and exhibition,°
    With such accommodation and besort°
    As levels with her breeding.°
DUKE.   If you please,
    Be 't at her father's.
BRABANTIO.   I'll not have it so.
OTHELLO. Nor I.

209–18. So . . . ear: Brabantio retaliates sarcastically with a few "sentences"
of his own: Let the Turk take Cyprus; it is no loss if we smile at it. It is
easy enough to produce sententious consolation, it costs nothing; but the man
who has to endure both consolation and the sorrow itself must needs be patient.
These sentences work both ways; mere words hurt no one. 222. *substitute:*
deputy commander; *allowed:* admitted; *sufficiency:* efficiency. 223–24. *yet . . .
you:* yet public opinion, which controls our actions, is such that we regard you
as a safer choice. 225. *slubber:* tarnish. 229. *thrice-driven:* three times refined;
agnize: confess. 231. *hardness:* hardship. 235. *Due . . . place:* that is, that
she shall be treated as becomes my wife; *exhibition:* allowance. 236. *besort:*
attendants. 237. *levels . . . breeding:* as suits her birth.

DESDEMONA.   Nor I. I would not there reside
    To put my father in impatient thoughts   240
    By being in his eye. Most gracious Duke,
    To my unfolding° lend your prosperous° ear,
    And let me find a charter° in your voice
    To assist my simpleness.
DUKE. What would you, Desdemona?
DESDEMONA. That I did love the Moor to live with him,
    My downright violence and storm of fortunes
    May trumpet to the world. My heart's subdued
    Even to the very quality of my lord.°
    I saw Othello's visage in his mind,   250
    And to his honors and his valiant parts
    Did I my soul and fortunes consecrate.
    So that, dear lords, if I be left behind,
    A moth of peace,° and he go to the war,
    The rites for which I love him are bereft me,
    And I a heavy interim° shall support
    By his dear absence. Let me go with him.
OTHELLO. Let her have your voices.
    Vouch° with me, Heaven, I therefore beg it not
    To please the palate of my appetite,   260
    Nor to comply with heat—the young affects
    In me defunct°—and proper satisfaction,
    But to be free and bounteous° to her mind.°
    And Heaven defend° your good souls, that you think
    I will your serious and great business scant
    For she is with me. No, when light-winged toys°
    Of feathered Cupid seel° with wanton dullness
    My speculative and officed instruments,°
    That my disports° corrupt and taint my business,
    Let housewives make a skillet° of my helm,   270
    And all indign° and base adversities

---

242. *unfolding:* plan; literally, revealing; *prosperous:* favorable.   243. *charter:*
privilege.   246–49. *That . . . lord:* my love for the Moor is publicly shown by
the way in which I have violently taken my fortunes in my hands; my heart has
become a soldier like my husband; *quality:* profession.   254. *moth of peace:* a
useless creature living in luxury.   256. *interim:* interval.   259. *Vouch:* certify.
261–62. *young . . . defunct:* in me the passion of youth is dead.   263. *bounteous:* generous; *to . . . mind:* Othello repeats Desdemona's claim that this is a
marriage of minds.   264. *defend:* forbid.   266. *toys:* trifles.   267. *seel:* close up;
a technical term from falconry.   268. *speculative . . . instruments:* powers of
sight and action; that is, my efficiency as your general.   269. *disports:* amusements.   270. *skillet:* saucepan.   271. *indign:* unworthy.

Make head against° my estimation! °

DUKE. Be it as you shall privately determine,
Either for her stay or going. The affair cries haste,
And speed must answer 't. You must hence tonight.

DESDEMONA. Tonight, my lord?

DUKE.   This night.

OTHELLO.   With all my heart.

DUKE. At nine i' the morning here we'll meet again.
Othello, leave some officer behind,
And he shall our commission° bring to you,
With such things else of quality and respect   280
As doth import you.°

OTHELLO.   So please your Grace, my Ancient,
A man he is of honesty and trust.
To his conveyance I assign my wife,
With what else needful your good grace shall think
To be sent after me.

DUKE.   Let it be so.
Good night to everyone. [*To* BRABANTIO] And, noble signior,
If virtue no delighted beauty lack,
Your son-in-law is far more fair than black.°

1. SENATOR. Adieu, brave Moor. Use Desdemona well.

BRABANTIO. Look to her, Moor, if thou hast eyes to see.   290
She has deceived her father, and may thee.°
                    [*Exeunt* DUKE, SENATORS, OFFICERS, *etc.*]

OTHELLO. My life upon her faith! Honest Iago,
My Desdemona must I leave to thee.
I prithee, let thy wife attend on her,
And bring them after in the best advantage.°
Come, Desdemona, I have but an hour
Of love, of worldly matters and direction,
To spend with thee. We must obey the time.
                    [*Exeunt* OTHELLO *and* DESDEMONA.]

RODERIGO. Iago!

IAGO. What say'st thou, noble heart?   300

RODERIGO. What will I do, thinkest thou?

272. *Make . . . against:* overcome; *estimation:* reputation. 279. *commission:* formal document of appointment. 280–81. *With . . . you:* with other matters that concern your position and honor. 287–88. *If . . . black:* if worthiness is a beautiful thing in itself, your son-in-law, though black, has beauty. 290–91. *Look . . . thee:* Iago in the background takes note of these words, and later reminds Othello of them with deadly effect (see III.iii.210). 295. *in . . . advantage:* at the best opportunity.

IAGO. Why, go to bed and sleep.
RODERIGO. I will incontinently° drown myself.
IAGO. If thou dost, I shall never love thee after.
Why, thou silly gentleman!
RODERIGO. It is silliness to live when to live is torment, and then have
we a prescription to die when death is our physician.
IAGO. Oh, villainous! I have looked upon the world for four times
seven years, and since I could distinguish betwixt a benefit and
an injury I never found man that knew how to love himself. 310
Ere I would say I would drown myself for the love of a guinea
hen, I would change my humanity with a baboon.
RODERIGO. What should I do? I confess it is my shame to be so fond,°
but it is not in my virtue° to amend it.
IAGO. Virtue! A fig! 'Tis in ourselves that we are thus or thus. Our
bodies are gardens, to the which our wills° are gardeners. So that
if we will plant nettles or sow lettuce, set hyssop and weed up
thyme, supply it with one gender° of herbs or distract it with
many, either to have it sterile with idleness or manured with industry—why, the power and corrigible° authority of this lies in 320
our wills. If the balance of our lives had not one scale of reason
to poise° another of sensuality, the blood and baseness of our
natures would conduct us to most preposterous conclusions. But
we have reason to cool our raging motions, our carnal stings,° our
unbitted° lusts, whereof I take this that you call love to be a
sect or scion.°
RODERIGO. It cannot be.
IAGO. It is merely a lust of the blood and a permission of the will.
Come, be a man. Drown thyself! Drown cats and blind puppies.
I have professed me thy friend, and I confess me knit to thy de- 330
serving with cables of perdurable° toughness. I could never better stead° thee than now. Put money in thy purse, follow thou
the wars, defeat thy favor with an usurped beard°—I say put
money in thy purse. It cannot be that Desdemona should long
continue her love to the Moor—put money in thy purse—nor he
his to her. It was a violent commencement, and thou shalt see an
answerable sequestration°—put but money in thy purse. These

303. *incontinently:* immediately. 313. *fond:* foolishly in love. 314. *virtue:*
manhood. 316. *wills:* desires. 318. *gender:* kind. 320. *corrigible:* correcting,
directing. 322. *poise:* weigh. 324. *carnal stings:* fleshly desires. 325. *un-
bitted:* uncontrolled. 326. *sect of scion:* Both words mean a slip taken from a
tree and planted to produce a new growth. 331. *perdurable:* very hard. 332.
stead: help. 332–33. *defeat . . . beard:* disguise your face by growing a beard.
337. *answerable sequestration:* corresponding separation; that is, reaction.

Moors are changeable in their wills.—Fill thy purse with money.
The food that to him now is as luscious as locusts° shall be to
him shortly as bitter as coloquintida.° She must change for youth.   340
When she is sated with his body, she will find the error of her
choice. She must have change, she must—therefore put money
in thy purse. If thou wilt needs damn thyself, do it a more delicate way than drowning. Make all the money thou canst.° If
sanctimony and a frail vow betwixt an erring° barbarian and a
supersubtle Venetian be not too hard for my wits and all the
tribe of Hell, thou shalt enjoy her—therefore make money. A
pox of drowning thyself! It is clean out of the way. Seek thou
rather to be hanged in compassing° thy joy than to be drowned
and go without her.   350

RODERIGO. Wilt thou be fast to my hopes if I depend on the issue?

IAGO. Thou art sure of me. Go, make money. I have told thee often,
and I retell thee again and again, I hate the Moor. My cause is
hearted,° thine hath no less reason. Let us be conjunctive° in our
revenge against him. If thou canst cuckold° him, thou dost thyself a pleasure, me a sport. There are many events in the womb
of time, which will be delivered. Traverse,° go, provide thy
money. We will have more of this tomorrow. Adieu.

RODERIGO. Where shall we meet i' the morning?

IAGO. At my lodging.   360

RODERIGO. I'll be with thee betimes.°

IAGO. Go to, farewell. Do you hear, Roderigo?

RODERIGO. What say you?

IAGO. No more of drowning, do you hear?

RODERIGO. I am changed. I'll go sell all my land.   [Exit.]

IAGO. Thus do I ever make my fool my purse,
    For I mine own gained knowledge should profane
    If I would time expend with such a snipe
    But for my sport and profit. I hate the Moor,
    And it is thought abroad that 'twixt my sheets   370
    He has done my office. I know not if 't be true,
    But I for mere suspicion in that kind
    Will do as if for surety. He holds me well,
    The better shall my purpose work on him.

339. *locusts:* It is not known what fruit was called a locust.   340. *coloquintida:*
known as "bitter apple," a form of gherkin from which a purge was made.
344. *Make . . . canst:* turn all you can into ready cash.   345. *erring:* vagabond.   349. *compassing:* achieving.   354. *hearted:* heartfelt; *conjunctive:* united.
355. *cuckold:* make him a cuckold.   357. *Traverse:* quickstep.   361. *betimes:*
in good time, early.

Cassio's a proper° man. Let me see now,
To get his place, and to plume up° my will
In double knavery——How, how?—Let's see.—
After some time, to abuse Othello's ear
That he is too familiar with his wife.
He hath a person and a smooth dispose   380
To be suspected,° framed to make women false.
The Moor is of a free and open nature
That thinks men honest that but seem to be so,
And will as tenderly be led by the nose
As asses are.
I have 't. It is engendered.° Hell and night
Must bring this monstrous birth to the world's light.   [*Exit.*]

ACT II

SCENE I. *A seaport in Cyprus. An open place near the wharf.*

[*Enter* MONTANO *and two* GENTLEMEN.]
MONTANO. What from the cape can you discern at sea?
1. GENTLEMAN. Nothing at all. It is a high-wrought flood.°
    I cannot 'twixt the heaven and the main°
    Descry a sail.
MONTANO. Methinks the wind hath spoke aloud at land,
    A fuller blast ne'er shook our battlements.
    If it hath ruffianed° so upon the sea,
    What ribs of oak, when mountains melt on them,
    Can hold the mortise? ° What shall we hear of this?
2. GENTLEMAN. A segregation° of the Turkish fleet.   10
    For do but stand upon the foaming shore,
    The chidden billow seems to pelt the clouds,
    The wind-shaked surge, with high and monstrous mane,
    Seems to cast water on the burning Bear,°
    And quench the guards of the ever-fixèd Pole.°
    I never did like molestation° view
    On the enchafèd° flood.
MONTANO.   If that the Turkish fleet

375. *proper:* handsome. 376. *plume up:* glorify. 380–81. *He . . . suspected:*
an easy way with him that is naturally suspected. 386. *engendered:* conceived.
ACT II, SCENE I: 2. *high-wrought flood:* heavy sea. 3. *main:* sea. 7. *ruffianed:*
played the ruffian. 9. *hold . . . mortise:* remain fast joined. 10. *segregation:*
separation. 14. *Bear:* the Great Bear. 15. *guards . . . Pole:* stars in the "tail"
of the Little Bear constellation. 16. *molestation:* disturbance. 17. *enchafed:*
angry.

Be not ensheltered and embayed,° they are drowned.
It is impossible to bear it out.
                    [*Enter a* THIRD GENTLEMAN]
3. GENTLEMAN. News, lads! Our wars are done.   20
    The desperate tempest hath so banged the Turks
    That their designment halts.° A noble ship of Venice
    Hath seen a grievous wreck and sufferance°
    On most part of their fleet.
MONTANO. How! Is this true?
3. GENTLEMAN.   The ship is here put in,
    A Veronesa. Michael Cassio,
    Lieutenant to the warlike Moor Othello,
    Is come on shore, the Moor himself at sea,
    And is in full commission° here for Cyprus.
MONTANO. I am glad on 't. 'Tis a worthy governor.   30
3. GENTLEMAN. But this same Cassio, though he speak of comfort
    Touching the Turkish loss, yet he looks sadly
    And prays the Moor be safe, for they were parted
    With foul and violent tempest.
MONTANO.   Pray Heavens he be,
    For I have served him, and the man commands
    Like a full° soldier. Let's to the seaside, ho!
    As well to see the vessel that's come in
    As to throw out our eyes for brave Othello,
    Even till we make the main and the aerial blue
    An indistinct regard.°
3. GENTLEMAN.   Come, let's do so.   40
    For every minute is expectancy
    Of more arrivance.°
                    [*Enter* CASSIO.]
CASSIO. Thanks, you the valiant of this warlike isle
    That so approve the Moor! Oh, let the heavens
    Give him defense against the elements,
    For I have lost him on a dangerous sea.
MONTANO. Is he well shipped? °
CASSIO. His bark is stoutly timbered, and his pilot
    Of very expert and approved allowance.°

---

18. embayed: anchored in some bay.   *22. designment halts:* plan is made lame.
23. sufferance: damage.   *29. in* . . . *commission:* with full powers (see I.iii.278–
79).   *36. full:* perfect.   *39–40. Even* . . . *regard:* until we can no longer distinguish between sea and sky.   *41–42. For* . . . *arrivance:* every minute more
arrivals are expected.   *47. well shipped:* in a good ship.   *49. approved allowance:*
proved skill.

Therefore my hopes, not surfeited° to death,   50
Stand in bold cure.°   [*A cry within:* "A sail, a sail, a sail!"]
                [*Enter a* FOURTH GENTLEMAN.]
CASSIO. What noise?
4. GENTLEMAN. The town is empty. On the brow o' the sea
    Stand ranks of people, and they cry "A sail!"
CASSIO. My hopes do shape° him for the governor.
                  [*Guns heard.*]
2. GENTLEMAN. They do discharge their shot of courtesy.
    Our friends, at least.
CASSIO.   I pray you, sir, go forth,
    And give us truth who 'tis that is arrived.
2. GENTLEMAN. I shall.   [*Exit.*]
MONTANO. But, good Lieutenant, is your General wived?   60
CASSIO. Most fortunately. He hath achieved° a maid
    That paragons° description and wild fame,
    One that excels the quirks of blazoning pens
    And in the essential vesture of creation
    Does tire the ingener.°
              [*Re-enter* SECOND GENTLEMAN.]
    How now! Who has put in?
2. GENTLEMAN. 'Tis one Iago, Ancient to the General.
CASSIO. He has had most favorable and happy speed.
    Tempests themselves, high seas, and howling winds,
    The guttered° rocks, and congregated sands,   70
    Traitors ensteeped° to clog the guiltless keel,
    As having sense of beauty, do omit
    Their mortal natures,° letting go safely by
    The divine Desdemona.
MONTANO.   What is she?
CASSIO. She that I spake of, our great Captain's captain,
    Left in the conduct° of the bold Iago,
    Whose footing° here anticipates our thoughts
    A sennight's° speed. Great Jove, Othello guard,
    And swell his sail with thine own powerful breath,

---

50. *surfeited:* sickened.   51. *Stand . . . cure:* have every hope of cure.   55.
shape: imagine.   61. *achieved:* won.   62. *paragons:* surpasses.   63–65. *One . . .*
ingener: one that is too good for the fancy phrases (*quirks*) of painting
pens (i.e., poets) and in her absolute perfection wearies the artist (i.e., the
painter). Cassio is full of gallant phrases and behavior, in contrast to Iago's
bluntness; *ingener:* inventor.   70. *guttered:* worn into channels.   71. *ensteeped:*
submerged.   72–73. *omit . . . natures:* forbear their deadly nature.   76. *con-*
duct: escort.   77. *footing:* arrival.   78. *sennight:* week.

That he may bless this bay with his tall ship,   80
Make love's quick pants in Desdemona's arms,
Give renewed fire to our extincted° spirits,
And bring all Cyprus comfort.
      [*Enter* DESDEMONA, EMILIA, IAGO, RODERIGO, *and* ATTENDANTS.]
                                Oh, behold,
The riches of the ship is come on shore!
Ye men of Cyprus, let her have your knees.
Hail to thee, lady! And the grace of Heaven,
Before, behind thee, and on every hand,
Enwheel° thee round!
DESDEMONA.   I thank you, valiant Cassio.
What tidings can you tell me of my lord?
CASSIO. He is not yet arrived, nor know I aught   90
But that he's well and will be shortly here.
DESDEMONA. Oh, but I fear——How lost you company?
CASSIO. The great contention of the sea and skies
Parted our fellowship.°—But, hark! A sail.
                [*A cry within:* "A sail, a sail!" *Guns heard.*]
2. GENTLEMAN. They give their greeting to the citadel.
This likewise is a friend.
CASSIO.   See for the news.   [*Exit* GENTLEMAN.]
Good Ancient, you are welcome. [*To* EMILIA] Welcome, mistress.
Let it not gall your patience, good Iago,
That I extend my manners.° 'Tis my breeding°
That gives me this bold show of courtesy.° [*Kissing her.*]   100
IAGO. Sir, would she give you so much of her lips
As of her tongue she oft bestows on me,
You'd have enough.
DESDEMONA.   Alas, she has no speech.
IAGO. In faith, too much,
I find it still° when I have list° to sleep.
Marry, before your ladyship, I grant,
She puts her tongue a little in her heart
And chides with thinking.
EMILIA. You have little cause to say so.
IAGO. Come on, come on. You are pictures° out of doors,   110

82. *extincted:* extinguished.   88. *Enwheel:* encompass.   94. *fellowship:* company.
99. *extend my manners:* that is, salute your wife; *breeding:* bringing-up.   100.
bold . . . courtesy: that is, of saluting your wife with a kiss—a piece of presumptuous behavior which indicates that Cassio regards himself as Iago's social
superior.   105. *still:* continuously; *list:* desire.   110. *pictures:* that is, painted
and dumb.

Bells° in your parlors, wildcats in your kitchens,
Saints in your injuries,° devils being offended,
Players in your housewifery, and housewives in your beds.
DESDEMONA. Oh, fie upon thee, slanderer!
IAGO. Nay, it is true, or else I am a Turk.°
You rise to play, and go to bed to work.
EMILIA. You shall not write my praise.
IAGO.   No, let me not.
DESDEMONA. What wouldst thou write of me if thou shouldst praise
me?
IAGO. O gentle lady, do not put me to 't,
For I am nothing if not critical.°   120
DESDEMONA. Come, on, assay.°—There's one gone to the harbor?
IAGO. Aye, madam.
DESDEMONA. I am not merry, but I do beguile
The thing I am by seeming otherwise.
Come, how wouldst thou praise me?
IAGO. I am about it, but indeed my invention
Comes from my pate as birdlime does from frieze°—
It plucks out brains and all. But my Muse labors,
And thus she is delivered.
If she be fair and wise, fairness and wit,   130
The one's for use, the other useth it.
DESDEMONA. Well praised! How if she be black and witty?
IAGO. If she be black, and thereto have a wit,
She'll find a white° that shall her blackness fit.
DESDEMONA. Worse and worse.
EMILIA. How if fair and foolish?
IAGO. She never yet was foolish that was fair,
For even her folly helped her to an heir.
DESDEMONA. These are old fond paradoxes° to make fools laugh i' the
alehouse. What miserable praise hast thou for her that's foul and   140
foolish?
IAGO. There's none so foul, and foolish thereunto,
But does foul pranks which fair and wise ones do.
DESDEMONA. Oh, heavy ignorance! Thou praisest the worst best. But
what praise couldst thou bestow on a deserving woman indeed,

---

111. Bells: i.e., ever clacking. *112. Saints . . . injuries:* saints when you hurt
anyone else. *115. Turk:* heathen. *120. critical:* bitter. *121. assay:* try. *126–
27. my . . . frieze:* my literary effort (*invention*) is as hard to pull out of my head
as frieze (cloth with a nap) stuck to birdlime. *134. white:* with a pun on *wight*
(l.158). man, person. *139. fond paradoxes:* foolish remarks, contrary to general
opinion.

one that in the authority of her merit did justly put on the vouch
of very malice itself? °
IAGO. She that was ever fair and never proud,
    Had tongue at will° and yet was never loud,
    Never lacked gold and yet went never gay,   150
    Fled from her wish and yet said "Now I may."
    She that, being angered, her revenge being nigh,
    Bade her wrong stay and her displeasure fly.
    She that in wisdom never was so frail
    To change the cod's head for the salmon's tail.°
    She that could think and ne'er disclose her mind,
    See suitors following and not look behind.
    She was a wight, if ever such wight were——
DESDEMONA. To do what?
IAGO. To suckle fools and chronicle small beer.°   160
DESDEMONA. Oh, most lame and impotent conclusion! Do not learn
    of him, Emilia, though he be thy husband. How say you, Cassio?
    If he not a most profane and liberal° counselor?
CASSIO. He speaks home,° madam. You may relish° him more in the
    soldier than in the scholar.
IAGO [aside]. He° takes her by the palm. Aye, well said, whisper.
    With as little a web as this will I ensnare as great a fly as Cassio.
    Aye, smile upon her, do, I will gyve° thee in thine own courtship.
    You say true, 'tis so indeed. If such tricks as these strip you out of
    your Lieutenantry, it had been better you had not kissed your
    three fingers° so oft, which now again you are most apt to play
    the sir° in. Very good, well kissed! An excellent courtesy! 'Tis so
    indeed. Yet again your fingers to your lips? Would they were
    clyster pipes° for your sake! [Trumpet within.] The Moor! I
    know his trumpet.
CASSIO. 'Tis truly so.
DESDEMONA. Let's meet him and receive him.
CASSIO. Lo where he comes!
          [Enter OTHELLO and ATTENDANTS.]
OTHELLO. O my fair warrior! °

146–47. one . . . itself: one so deserving that even malice would declare her good.
149. tongue . . . will: a ready flow of words.￼ 155. To . . . tail: to prefer
the tail end of a good thing to the head of a poor thing.￼ 160. chronicle . . .
beer: write a whole history about trifles (small beer: thin drink).￼ 163. liberal:
gross.￼ 164. home: to the point; relish: appreciate.￼ 166–74. He . . . sake:
As so often, Shakespeare without using elaborate stage directions exactly indicates
the action in the dialogue.￼ 168. gyve: fetter.￼ 170–71. kissed . . . fingers: a
gesture of gallantry.￼ 171–72. play . . . sir: act the fine gentleman.￼ 174. clyster
pipes: an enema syringe.￼ 179. warrior: because she is a soldier's wife (see I.iii.
249).

DESDEMONA.   My dear Othello!

OTHELLO. It gives me wonder great as my content   180
　　　To see you here before me. O my soul's joy!
　　　If after every tempest come such calms,
　　　May the winds blow till they have wakened death!
　　　And let the laboring bark climb hills of seas
　　　Olympus-high,° and duck again as low
　　　As Hell's from Heaven! If it were now to die,
　　　'Twere now to be most happy, for I fear
　　　My soul hath her content so absolute
　　　That not another comfort like to this
　　　Succeeds in unknown fate.

DESDEMONA.   The Heavens forbid   190
　　　But that our loves and comforts should increase,
　　　Even as our days do grow!

OTHELLO.   Amen to that, sweet powers!
　　　I cannot speak enough of this content.
　　　It stops me here,° it is too much of joy.
　　　And this, and this, the greatest discords be [*kissing her*]
　　　That e'er our hearts shall make!

IAGO [*aside*].   Oh, you are well tuned now,
　　　But I'll set down the pegs° that make this music,
　　　As honest as I am.

OTHELLO.   Come, let us to the castle.
　　　News, friends. Our wars are done, the Turks are drowned.
　　　How does my old acquaintance of this isle?   200
　　　Honey, you shall be well desired in Cyprus,
　　　I have found great love amongst them. O my sweet,
　　　I prattle out of fashion,° and I dote
　　　In mine own comforts. I prithee, good Iago,
　　　Go to the bay and disembark my coffers.°
　　　Bring thou the master° to the citadel.
　　　He is a good one, and his worthiness
　　　Does challenge° much respect. Come, Desdemona,
　　　Once more well met at Cyprus.
　　　　　　[*Exeunt all but* IAGO *and* RODERIGO.]

IAGO. Do thou meet me presently° at the harbor. Come hither. If thou   210
　　beest valiant—as they say base men being in love have then a
　　nobility in their natures more than is native to them—list me.

---

185. *Olympus-high:* high as Olympus, the highest mountain in Greece.   194.
here: that is, in the heart.   197. *set . . . pegs:* that is, make you sing in a different key. A stringed instrument was tuned by the pegs.   203. *prattle . . . fashion:*
talk idly.   205. *coffers:* trunks.   206. *master:* captain of the ship.   208. *challenge:* claim.   210. *presently:* immediately.

The Lieutenant tonight watches on the court of guard.° First, I
must tell thee this. Desdemona is directly in love with him.
RODERIGO. With him! Why, 'tis not possible.
IAGO. Lay thy finger thus,° and let thy soul be instructed. Mark me
with what violence she first loved the Moor, but for° bragging
and telling her fantastical lies. And will she love him still for
prating? Let not thy discreet heart think it. Her eye must be fed,   230
and what delight shall she have to look on the Devil? ° When
the blood is made dull with the act of sport, there should be,
again to inflame it and to give satiety a fresh appetite, loveliness
in favor,° sympathy in years, manners, and beauties, all which
the Moor is defective in. Now, for want of these required con-
veniences, her delicate tenderness will find itself abused, begin to
heave the gorge,° disrelish and abhor the Moor. Very nature
will instruct her in it and compel her to some second choice.
Now, sir, this granted—as it is a most pregnant and unforced
position°—who stands so eminently in the degree of this fortune   220
as Cassio does? A knave very voluble, no further conscionable°
than in putting on the mere form of civil and humane seeming°
for the better compassing of his salt° and most hidden loose
affection? Why, none, why, none. A slipper° and subtle knave, a
finder-out of occasions, that has an eye can stamp and counterfeit
advantages,° though true advantage never present itself. A
devilish knave! Besides, the knave is handsome, young, and hath
all those requisites in him that folly and green° minds look after.
A pestilent complete knave, and the woman hath found him
already.
RODERIGO. I cannot believe that in her. She's full of most blest   240
condition.°
IAGO. Blest fig's-end! ° The wine she drinks is made of grapes. If she
had been blest, she would never have loved the Moor. Blest
pudding! Didst thou not see her paddle° with the palm of his
hand? Didst not mark that?
RODERIGO. Yes, that I did, but that was but courtesy.

213. watches . . . guard: is on duty with the guard. The court of guard meant
both the guard itself and the guardroom.   216. finger thus: that is, on the lips.
217. but for: only for.   220. Devil: See I.i.91,n.   223. favor: face.   226. heave
. . . gorge: retch; gorge: throat.   228–29. pregnant . . . position: very significant and probable argument.   230. no . . . conscionable: who has no more
conscience.   231. humane seeming: courteous appearance.   232. salt: lecherous.
233. slipper: slippery.   234–35. stamp . . . advantages: forge false opportunities.
237. green: inexperienced, foolish.   241. condition: disposition.   242. Blest fig's-
end: blest nonsense, a phrase used as a substitute in contempt for a phrase just
used, as is also blest pudding (l.243).   244. paddle: play.

IAGO. Lechery, by this hand, an index° and obscure prologue to the
history of lust and foul thoughts. They met so near with their
lips that their breaths embraced together. Villainous thoughts,
Roderigo! When these mutualities° so marshal the way, hard at   250
hand comes the master and main exercise, the incorporate° conclusion. Pish! But, sir, be you ruled by me. I have brought you
from Venice. Watch you tonight. For the command, I'll lay 't
upon you. Cassio knows you not. I'll not be far from you. Do you
find some occasion to anger Cassio, either by speaking too loud,
or tainting° his discipline, or from what other course you please
which the time shall more favorably minister.°

RODERIGO. Well.

IAGO. Sir, he is rash and very sudden in choler,° and haply° may
strike at you. Provoke him, that he may, for even out of that will   260
I cause these of Cyprus to mutiny, whose qualification° shall
come into no true taste again but by the displanting° of Cassio.
So shall you have a shorter journey to your desires by the means
I shall then have to prefer° them, and the impediment most
profitably removed without the which there were no expectation
of our prosperity.

RODERIGO. I will do this, if I can bring it to any opportunity.

IAGO. I warrant thee. Meet me by and by at the citadel. I must fetch
his necessaries ashore. Farewell.

RODERIGO. Adieu.   [Exit.]   270

IAGO. That Cassio loves her, I do well believe it.
That she loves him, 'tis apt and of great credit.°
The Moor, howbeit that I endure him not,
Is of a constant, loving, noble nature,
And I dare think he'll prove to Desdemona
A most dear husband. Now, I do love her too,
Not out of absolute lust, though peradventure
I stand accountant for as great a sin,
But partly led to diet° my revenge
For that I do suspect the lusty Moor   280
Hath leaped into my seat. The thought whereof
Doth like a poisonous mineral° gnaw my inwards.
And nothing can or shall content my soul
Till I am evened with him, wife for wife.

---

247. *index:* table of contents.   250. *mutualities:* mutual exchanges.   251. *in-
corporate:* bodily.   256. *tainting:* disparaging.   257. *minister:* provide.   259.
choler: anger; *haply:* perhaps.   261. *qualification:* appeasement.   262. *displant-
ing:* removal.   264. *prefer:* promote.   272. *apt . . . credit:* likely and very
credible.   279. *diet:* feed.   282. *poisonous mineral:* corrosive poison (see I.ii.74).

Or failing so, yet that I put the Moor
At least into a jealousy so strong
That judgment° cannot cure. Which thing to do,
If this poor trash of Venice, whom I trash°
For his quick hunting, stand the putting-on,°
I'll have our Michael Cassio on the hip,   290
Abuse him to the Moor in the rank garb°—
For I fear Cassio with my nightcap too—
Make the Moor thank me, love me, and reward me
For making him egregiously° an ass
And practicing upon° his peace and quiet
Even to madness. 'Tis here, but yet confused.
Knavery's plain face is never seen till used.   [*Exit.*]

SCENE II. *A street.*

[*Enter a* HERALD *with a proclamation,* PEOPLE *following.*]
HERALD. It is Othello's pleasure, our noble and valiant General, that
upon certain tidings now arrived, importing the mere perdition°
of the Turkish fleet, every man put himself into triumph°—some
to dance, some to make bonfires, each man to what sport and
revels his addiction° leads him. For, besides these beneficial
news, it is the celebration of his nuptial. So much was his
pleasure should be proclaimed. All offices° are open, and there is
full liberty of feasting from this present hour of five till the bell
have told eleven. Heaven bless the isle of Cyprus and our noble
General Othello!   [*Exeunt.*]   10

SCENE III. *A hall in the castle.*

[*Enter* OTHELLO, DESDEMONA, CASSIO, *and* ATTENDANTS.]
OTHELLO. Good Michael, look you to the guard tonight.
    Let's teach ourselves that honorable stop,
    Not to outsport discretion.°

---

287. *judgment:* reason. 288. *trash . . . trash:* rubbish . . . discard. 289.
putting-on: encouraging. 291. *rank garb:* gross manner; that is, by accusing him
of being Desdemona's lover. 294. *egregiously:* notably. 295. *practicing upon:*
plotting against.
SCENE ii: 2. *mere perdition:* absolute destruction. 3. *put . . . triumph:* celebrate. 5. *addiction:* inclination. 7. *offices:* the kitchen and buttery—that is,
free food and drink for all.
SCENE iii: 3. *outsport discretion:* let the fun go too far.

CASSIO. Iago hath direction what to do,
But notwithstanding with my personal eye
Will I look to 't.
OTHELLO.   Iago is most honest.
Michael, good night. Tomorrow with your earliest°
Let me have speech with you. Come, my dear love,
The purchase made, the fruits are to ensue—
That profit's yet to come 'tween me and you.   10
Good night.
        [*Exeunt* OTHELLO, DESDEMONA, *and* ATTENDANTS.]
                    [*Enter* IAGO.]
CASSIO. Welcome, Iago. We must to the watch.
IAGO. Not this hour, Lieutenant, 'tis not yet ten o' the clock. Our
General cast° us thus early for the love of his Desdemona, who
let us not therefore blame. He hath not yet made wanton the
night with her, and she is sport for Jove.
CASSIO. She's a most exquisite lady.
IAGO. And, I'll warrant her, full of game.
CASSIO. Indeed she's a most fresh and delicate creature.
IAGO. What an eye she has! Methinks it sounds a parley to provo-   20
cation.°
CASSIO. An inviting eye, and yet methinks right modest.
IAGO. And when she speaks, is it not an alarum° to love?
CASSIO. She is indeed perfection.
IAGO. Well, happiness to their sheets! Come, Lieutenant, I have a
stoup° of wine, and here without are a brace of Cyprus gallants
that would fain° have a measure to the health of black Othello.
CASSIO. Not tonight, good Iago. I have very poor and unhappy brains
for drinking. I could well wish courtesy would invent some other
custom of entertainment.   30
IAGO. Oh, they are our friends. But one cup—I'll drink for you.
CASSIO. I have drunk but one cup tonight, and that was craftily
qualified° too, and behold what innovation° it makes here. I am
unfortunate in the infirmity, and dare not task° my weakness
with any more.
IAGO. What, man! 'Tis a night of revels. The gallants desire it.
CASSIO. Where are they?
IAGO. Here at the door. I pray you call them in.
CASSIO. I'll do 't, but it dislikes° me.   [*Exit.*]

7. *with . . . earliest:* very early.   14. *cast:* dismissed.   20–21. *sounds . . . provo-
ocation:* invites to a love talk.   23. *alarum:* call to arms.   26. *stoup:* large
drinking vessel.   27. *fain:* gladly.   33. *craftily qualified:* cunningly mixed;
innovation: revolution, disturbance.   34. *task:* burden.   39. *dislikes:* dis-
pleases.

IAGO. If I can fasten but one cup upon him,   40
  With that which he hath drunk tonight already
  He'll be as full of quarrel and offense
  As my young mistress' dog. Now my sick fool Roderigo,
  Whom love hath turned almost the wrong side out,
  To Desdemona hath tonight caroused°
  Potations pottle-deep,° and he's to watch.
  Three lads of Cyprus, noble swelling° spirits
  That hold their honors in a wary distance,°
  The very elements° of this warlike isle,
  Have I tonight flustered with flowing cups,   50
  And they watch too. Now, 'mongst this flock of drunkards,
  Am I to put our Cassio in some action
  That may offend the isle. But here they come.
  If consequence do but approve my dream,°
  My boat sails freely, both with wind and stream.
    [*Re-enter* CASSIO, *with him* MONTANO *and* GENTLEMEN,
      SERVANTS *following with wine.*]
CASSIO. 'Fore God, they have given me a rouse° already.
MONTANO. Good faith, a little one—not past a pint, as I am a soldier.
IAGO. Some win, ho! [*Sings*]
        "And let me the cannikin° clink, clink,
        And let me the cannikin clink.   60
        A soldier's a man,
        A life's but a span.°
        Why, then let a soldier drink."
  Some wine, boys!
CASSIO. 'Fore God, an excellent song.
IAGO. I learned it in England, where indeed they are most potent in
  potting.° Your Dane, your German, and your swag-bellied°
  Hollander—Drink, ho!—are nothing to your English.
CASSIO. Is your Englishman so expert in his drinking?
IAGO. Why, he drinks you with facility your Dane dead drunk, he   70
  sweats not° to overthrow your Almain,° he gives your Hollander
  a vomit° ere the next pottle can be filled.

45. *caroused:* drunk healths.   46. *pottle-deep:* "bottoms up"; a pottle held two
quarts.   47. *swelling:* bursting with pride.   48. *hold . . . distance:* "have a chip
on their shoulders."   49. *very elements:* typical specimens.   54. *If . . . dream:*
if what follows proves my dream true.   56. *rouse:* a deep drink.   59. *cannikin:*
large drinking pot.   62. *span:* literally, the measure between the thumb and
little finger of the outstretched hand; about 9 inches.   66–67. *potent in potting:*
desperate drinkers.   67. *swag-bellied:* with loose bellies.   85. *sweats not:* has no
need to labor excessively.   71. *Almain:* German.   71–72. *gives . . . vomit:*
drinks as much as will make a Dutchman throw up.

CASSIO. To the health of our General!

MONTANO. I am for it, Lieutenant, and I'll do you justice.

IAGO. O sweet England! [*Sings*]

    "King Stephen was a worthy peer,
        His breeches cost him but a crown.
    He held them sixpence all too dear,°
        With that he called the tailor lown.°

    "He was a wight of high renown,   80
        And thou art but of low degree.
    'Tis pride that pulls the country down.
        Then take thine auld cloak about thee."

    Some wine, ho!

CASSIO. Why, this is a more exquisite song than the other.

IAGO. Will you hear 't again?

CASSIO. No, for I hold him to be unworthy of his place that does those
things. Well, God's above all, and there be souls must be saved
and there be souls must not be saved.

IAGO. It's true, good Lieutenant.   90

CASSIO. For mine own part—no offense to the General, nor any man
of quality°—I hope to be saved.

IAGO. And so do I too, Lieutenant.

CASSIO. Aye, but, by your leave, not before me. The Lieutenant is to
be saved before the Ancient. Let's have no more of this, let's to
our affairs. God forgive us our sins! Gentlemen, let's look to our
business. Do not think, gentlemen, I am drunk. This is my
Ancient, this is my right hand and this is my left. I am not
drunk now, I can stand well enough and speak well enough.

ALL. Excellent well.   100

CASSIO. Why, very well, then, you must not think then that I am
drunk.   [*Exit.*]

MONTANO. To the platform,° masters. Come, let's set the watch.°

IAGO. You see this fellow that is gone before.

    He is a soldier fit to stand by Caesar
    And give direction. And do but see his vice.
    'Tis to his virtue a just equinox,°
    The one as long as the other. 'Tis pity of him.
    I fear the trust Othello puts him in
    On some odd time° of his infirmity   110

---

78. *sixpence . . . dear:* too dear by sixpence.   79. *lown:* lout.   92. *quality:*
rank.   103. *platform:* the level place on the ramparts where the cannon were
mounted; *set . . . watch:* mount guard.   107. *just equinox:* exact equal.   110.
some . . . time: some time or other.

Will shake this island.

MONTANO.   But is he often thus?

IAGO. 'Tis evermore the prologue to his sleep.
He'll watch the horologe a double set,°
If drink rock not his cradle.

MONTANO.   It were well
The General were put in mind of it.
Perhaps he sees it not, or his good nature
Prizes the virtue that appears in Cassio
And looks not on his evils. Is not this true?

                              [Enter RODERIGO.]

IAGO [aside to him]. How now, Roderigo! I pray you, after the Lieu-
        tenant. Go.

                                        [Exit RODERIGO.]

MONTANO. And 'tis great pity that the noble Moor   120
Should hazard such a place as his own second
With one of an ingraft° infirmity.
It were an honest action to say
So to the Moor.

IAGO.   Not I, for this fair island.
I do love Cassio well, and would do much
To cure him of this evil—But, hark! What noise?

                [A cry within: "Help! help!"]
        [Re-enter CASSIO, driving in RODERIGO.]

CASSIO. 'Zounds! You rogue! You rascal!

MONTANO.   What's the matter, Lieutenant?

CASSIO. A knave teach me my duty!
But I'll beat the knave into a wicker bottle.°

RODERIGO. Beat me!   130

CASSIO. Dost thou prate, rogue? [Striking RODERIGO.]

MONTANO.   Nay, good Lieutenant, [staying him]
I pray you, sir, hold your hand.

CASSIO.   Let me go, sir,
Or I'll knock you o'er the mazzard.°

MONTANO.   Come, come, you're drunk.

CASSIO. Drunk!   [They fight.]

IAGO. [aside to RODERIGO]. Away, I say. Go out and cry a mutiny.°

                                        [Exit RODERIGO.]

113. watch . . . set: stay awake the clock twice round.   122. ingraft: engrafted, firmly fixed.   129. But . . . bottle: one of those bad-tempered threatening phrases which have no very exact meaning, like "I'll knock him into a cocked hat."   wicker bottle: large bottle covered with wicker, demijohn.   133. mazzard: head, a slang word.   135. cry . . . mutiny: cry that a mutiny has broken out; i.e., raise a riot.

Nay, good Lieutenant! God's will, gentlemen!
Help, ho!—Lieutenant—sir—Montano—sir—
Help, masters!—Here's a goodly watch indeed!
          [*A bell rings.*]
Who's that that rings the bell?—Diablo,° ho!
The town will rise. God's will, Lieutenant, hold—   140
You will be shamed forever.
      [*Re-enter* OTHELLO *and* ATTENDANTS.]
OTHELLO.   What is the matter here?
MONTANO. 'Zounds, I bleed still, I am hurt to the death.   [*Faints.*]
OTHELLO. Hold, for your lives!
IAGO. Hold, ho! Lieutenant—sir—Montano—gentlemen—
Have you forgot all sense of place and duty?
Hold! The General speaks to you. Hold, hold, for shame!
OTHELLO. Why, how now, ho! From whence ariseth this?
Are we turned Turks, and to ourselves do that
Which Heaven hath forbid the Ottomites?
For Christian shame, put by this barbarous brawl.   150
He that stirs next to carve for his own rage°
Holds his soul light, he dies upon his motion.°
Silence that dreadful bell. It frights the isle
From her propriety.° What is the matter, masters?
Honest Iago, that look'st dead with grieving,
Speak, who began this? On thy love, I charge thee.
IAGO. I do not know. Friends all but now, even now,
In quarter and in terms like bride and groom
Devesting° them for bed. And then, but now,
As if some planet had unwitted men,°   160
Swords out, and tilting° one at other's breast
In opposition bloody. I cannot speak
Any beginning to this peevish odds,°
And would in action glorious I had lost
Those legs that brought me to a part of it!
OTHELLO. How comes it, Michael, you are thus forgot? °
CASSIO. I pray you, pardon me, I cannot speak.
OTHELLO. Worthy Montano, you were wont be civil.°
The gravity and stillness° of your youth
The world hath noted, and your name is great   170

---

139. *Diablo:* the Devil. *151. carve . . . rage:* to satisfy his hunger for rage.
152. upon . . . motion: at his first movement. *154. propriety:* natural behavior.
159. Devesting: taking off their clothes. *160. planet . . . men:* as if some evil
star had made men mad. *161. tilting:* thrusting. *163. peevish odds:* silly dis-
agreement. *166. are . . . forgot:* have so forgotten yourself. *168. civil:* well
behaved. *169. stillness:* staid behavior.

In mouths of wisest censure.° What's the matter
That you unlace° your reputation thus,
And spend your rich opinion° for the name
Of a night brawler? Give me answer to it.

MONTANO. Worthy Othello, I am hurt to danger.
Your officer, Iago, can inform you—
While I spare speech, which something now offends me—
Of all that I do know. Nor know I aught
By me that's said or done amiss this night,
Unless self-charity° be sometimes a vice,   180
And to defend ourselves it be a sin
When violence assails us.

OTHELLO.   Now, by Heaven,
My blood begins my safer guides to rule,
And passion, having my best judgment collied,°
Assays to lead the way. If I once stir,
Or do but lift this arm, the best of you
Shall sink in my rebuke. Give me to know
How this foul rout° began, who set it on,
And he that is approved° in this offense,
Though he had twinned with me, both at a birth,   190
Shall lose me. What! In a town of war,
Yet wild, the people's hearts brimful of fear,
To manage° private and domestic quarrel,
In night, and on the court and guard of safety!
'Tis monstrous. Iago, who began 't?

MONTANO. If partially affined, or leagued in office,
Thou dost deliver° more or less than truth,
Thou art no soldier.

IAGO.   Touch me not so near.
I had rather have this tongue cut from my mouth
Than it should do offense to Michael Cassio.   200
Yet I persuade myself to speak the truth
Shall nothing wrong him. Thus it is, General.
Montano and myself being in speech,
There comes a fellow crying out for help,
And Cassio following him with determined sword
To execute upon him. Sir, this gentleman

---

171. *censure:* judgment.   172. *unlace:* undo.   173. *spend . . . opinion:* lose
your good reputation.   180. *self-charity:* love for oneself.   184. *collied:* darkened.
188. *rout:* riot, uproar.   189. *approved:* proved guilty.   193. *manage:* be concerned with.   196–97. *If . . . deliver:* if, because you are influenced by partiality
or because he is your fellow officer, you report; *affined:* bound.

Steps in to Cassio and entreats his pause.°
Myself the crying fellow did pursue,
Lest by his clamor—as it so fell out—
The town might fall in fright. He, swift of foot,   210
Outran my purpose, and I returned the rather
For that I heard the clink and fall of swords,
And Cassio high in oath, which till tonight
I ne'er might say before. When I came back—
For this was brief—I found them close together,
At blow and thrust, even as again they were
When you yourself did part them.
More of this matter cannot I report.
But men are men, the best sometimes forget.
Though Cassio did some little wrong to him,   220
As men in rage strike those that wish them best,
Yet surely Cassio, I believe, received
From him that fled some strange indignity,
Which patience could not pass.
OTHELLO.   I know, Iago,
Thy honesty and love doth mince this matter,
Making it light to Cassio. Cassio, I love thee,
But never more be officer of mine.
[Re-enter DESDEMONA, attended.]
Look, if my gentle love be not raised up!
I'll make thee an example.
DESDEMONA.   What's the matter?
OTHELLO. All's well now, sweeting.° Come away to bed.   230
              [To MONTANO, who is led off]
Sir, for your hurts, myself will be your surgeon.
Lead him off.
Iago, look with care about the town,
And silence those whom this vile brawl distracted.
Come, Desdemona. 'Tis the soldiers' life
To have their balmy slumbers waked with strife.
              [Exeunt all but IAGO and CASSIO.]
IAGO. What, are you hurt, Lieutenant?
CASSIO. Aye, past all surgery.
IAGO. Marry, Heaven forbid!
CASSIO. Reputation, reputation, reputation! Oh, I have lost my repu-   240
tation! I have lost the immortal part of myself, and what remains
is bestial. My reputation, Iago, my reputation!

207. *entreats . . . pause:* begs him to stop.   230. *sweeting:* sweetheart.

IAGO. As I am an honest man, I thought you had received some bodily wound. There is more sense in that than in reputation. Reputation is an idle and most false imposition,° oft got without merit and lost without deserving. You have lost no reputation at all unless you repute yourself such a loser. What, man! There are ways to recover the General again. You are but now cast in his mood,° a punishment more in policy° than in malice—even so as one would beat his offenseless dog to affright an imperious lion.°   250 Sue to him again and he's yours.

CASSIO. I will rather sue to be despised than to deceive so good a commander with so slight, so drunken, and so indiscreet an officer. Drunk? And speak parrot?° And squabble? Swagger? Swear? And discourse fustian° with one's own shadow? O thou invisible spirit of wine, if thou hast no name to be known by, let us call thee devil!

IAGO. What was he that you followed with your sword? What had he done to you?

CASSIO. I know not.   260

IAGO. Is 't possible?

CASSIO. I remember a mass of things, but nothing distinctly—a quarrel, but nothing wherefore. Oh God, that men should put an enemy in their mouths to steal away their brains! That we should, with joy, pleasance,° revel, and applause, transform ourselves into beasts!

IAGO. Why, but you are now well enough. How came you thus recovered?

CASSIO. It hath pleased the devil drunkenness to give place to the devil wrath. One unperfectness shows me another, to make me frankly   270 despise myself.

IAGO. Come, you are too severe a moraler.° As the time, the place, and the condition of this country stands, I could heartily wish this had not befallen. But since it is as it is, mend it for your own good.

CASSIO. I will ask him for my place again, he shall tell me I am a drunkard! Had I as many mouths as Hydra,° such an answer would stop them all. To be now a sensible man, by and by a fool,

---

245. *imposition*: a quality laid on a man by others. 248. *cast . . . mood*: dismissed because he is in a bad mood. 249. *in policy*: that is, because he must appear to be angry before the Cypriots. 249–50. *even . . . lion*: a proverb meaning that when the lion sees the dog beaten, he will know what is coming to him. 254. *speak parrot*: babble. 255. *fustian*: nonsense; literally, cheap cloth. 265. *pleasance*: a gay time. 272. *moraler*: moralizer. 277. *Hydra*: a hundred-headed beast slain by Hercules.

and presently a beast! Oh, strange! Every inordinate° cup is
unblest, and the ingredient is a devil.   280
IAGO. Come, come, good wine is a good familiar creature, if it be well
    used. Exclaim no more against it. And, good Lieutenant, I think
    you think I love you.
CASSIO. I have well approved it, sir. I drunk!
IAGO. You or any man living may be drunk at some time, man. I'll tell
    you what you shall do. Our General's wife is now the General. I
    may say so in this respect, for that he hath devoted and given up
    himself to the contemplation, mark, and denotement° of her
    parts and graces. Confess yourself freely to her, importune her
    help to put you in your place again. She is of so free, so kind, so   290
    apt,° so blessed a disposition, she holds it a vice in her goodness
    not to do more than she is requested. This broken joint between
    you and her husband entreat her to splinter° and, my fortunes
    against any lay° worth naming, this crack of your love shall grow
    stronger than it was before.
CASSIO. You advise me well.
IAGO. I protest, in the sincerity of love and honest kindness.
CASSIO. I think it freely, and betimes in the morning I will beseech the
    virtuous Desdemona to undertake for me. I am desperate of
    my fortunes if they check me here.°   300
IAGO. You are in the right. Good night, Lieutenant, I must to the
    watch.
CASSIO. Good night, honest Iago.   [*Exit.*]
IAGO. And what's he then that says I play the villain?
    When this advice is free I give and honest,
    Probal° to thinking, and indeed the course
    To win the Moor again? For 'tis most easy
    The inclining Desdemona to subdue
    In any honest suit. She's framed° as fruitful
    As the free elements.° And then for her   310
    To win the Moor, were 't to renounce his baptism,
    All seals and symbols of redeemèd sin,
    His soul is so enfettered to her love
    That she may make, unmake, do what she list,
    Even as her appetite shall play the god
    With his weak function.° How am I then a villain
    To counsel Cassio to this parallel course,

279. *inordinate:* excessive. 288. *denotement:* careful observation. 291. *apt:*
ready. 293. *splinter:* put in splints. 294. *lay:* bet. 299–300. *I . . . here:* I
despair of my future if my career is stopped short here. 306. *Probal:* probable.
309. *framed:* made. 310. *free elements:* that is, the air. 316. *function:* intelligence.

Directly to his good? Divinity of Hell!
When devils will the blackest sins put on,
They do suggest° at first with heavenly shows,   320
As I do now. For whiles this honest fool
Plies° Desdemona to repair his fortunes,
And she for him pleads strongly to the Moor,
I'll pour this pestilence into his ear,
That she repeals° him for her body's lust.
And by how much she strives to do him good,
She shall undo her credit with the Moor.
So will I turn her virtue into pitch,
And out of her own goodness make the net
That shall enmesh them all.
                    [*Enter* RODERIGO.]
                    How now, Roderigo!   330
RODERIGO. I do follow here in the chase, not like a hound that hunts
but one that fills up the cry.° My money is almost spent, I have
been tonight exceedingly well cudgeled, and I think the issue
will be I shall have so much experience for my pains and so, with
no money at all and a little more wit, return again to Venice.
IAGO. How poor are they that have not patience!
What wound did ever heal but by degrees?
Thou know'st we work by wit and not by witchcraft,
And wit depends on dilatory Time.°
Does 't not go well? Cassio hath beaten thee,   340
And thou by that small hurt hast cashiered Cassio.
Though other things grow fair against the sun,
Yet fruits that blossom first will first be ripe.°
Content thyself awhile. By the mass, 'tis morning.
Pleasure and action make the hours seem short.
Retire thee, go where thou art billeted.
Away, I say. Thou shalt know more hereafter.
Nay, get thee gone.
                    [*Exit* RODERIGO.]
                    Two things are to be done:
My wife must move for° Cassio to her mistress,
I'll set her on,   350

---

320. *suggest:* seduce. 322. *Plies:* vigorously urges. 325. *repeals:* calls back.
332. *one . . . cry:* that is, one of the pack chosen merely for its bark. 339.
And . . . Time: and cleverness must wait for Time, who is in no hurry. 341–
43. *Though . . . ripe:* Though the fruit ripens in the sun, yet the first fruit to
ripen will come from the earliest blossoms; that is, our first plan—to get Cassio
cashiered—has succeeded, the rest will soon follow. 349. *move for:* petition for.

Myself the while to draw the Moor apart
And bring him jump° when he may Cassio find
Soliciting his wife. Aye, that's the way.
Dull not device° by coldness and delay.   [*Exit.*]

A C T   I I I

SCENE I. *Before the castle.*

[*Enter* CASSIO *and some* MUSICIANS.]
CASSIO. Masters, play here, I will content your pains°—
    Something that's brief, and bid "Good morrow, General." °
                                              [*Music.*]
                    [*Enter* CLOWN.]
CLOWN. Why, masters, have your instruments been in Naples,° that
    they speak i' the nose thus?
1. MUSICIAN. How, sir, how?
CLOWN. Are these, I pray you, wind instruments?
1. MUSICIAN. Aye, marry are they, sir.
CLOWN. Oh, thereby hangs a tail.
1. MUSICIAN. Whereby hangs a tale, sir?
CLOWN. Marry, sir, by many a wind instrument that I know. But,   10
    masters, here's money for you. And the General so likes your
    music that he desires you, for love's sake, to make no more noise
    with it.
1. MUSICIAN. Well, sir, we will not.
CLOWN. If you have any music that may not be heard, to 't again. But,
    as they say, to hear music the General does not greatly care.
1. MUSICIAN. We have none such, sir.
CLOWN. Then put up your pipes in your bag, for I'll away. Go, vanish
    into air, away!
                          [*Exeunt* MUSICIANS.]
CASSIO. Dost thou hear, my honest friend?   20
CLOWN. No, I hear not your honest friend, I hear you.
CASSIO. Prithee keep up thy quillets.° There's a poor piece of gold for
    thee. If the gentlewoman that attends the General's wife be

---

352. *jump:* at the moment, just.   354. *Dull . . . device:* do not spoil the plan.
ACT III, SCENE I: *1. content . . . pains:* reward your labor.   *2. bid . . . General:* It was a common custom to play or sing a song beneath the bedroom window of a distinguished guest or of a newly wedded couple on the morning after their wedding night.   *3. in Naples:* a reference to the Neapolitan (i.e., venereal) disease.   *22. keep . . . quillets:* Put away your wisecracks.

stirring, tell her there's one Cassio entreats her a little favor of
speech. Wilt thou do this?

CLOWN. She is stirring, sir. If she will stir hither, I shall seem to notify
unto her.

CASSIO. Do, good my friend.   [Exit CLOWN.]

[Enter IAGO.]

In happy time,° Iago.

IAGO. You have not been abed, then?

CASSIO. Why, no, the day had broke   30
Before we parted. I have made bold, Iago,
To send in to your wife. My suit to her
Is that she will to virtuous Desdemona
Procure me some access.

IAGO.   I'll send her to you presently,
And I'll devise a mean to draw the Moor
Out of the way, that your convérse and business
May be more free.

CASSIO. I humbly thank you for 't.   [Exit IAGO.]
I never knew
A Florentine more kind° and honest.

[Enter EMILIA.]

EMILIA. Good morrow, good Lieutenant. I am sorry   40
For your displeasure,° but all will sure be well.
The General and his wife are talking of it,
And she speaks for you stoutly. The Moor replies
That he you hurt is of great fame in Cyprus
And great affinity,° and that in wholesome wisdom
He might not but° refuse you. But he protests he loves you,
And needs no other suitor but his likings°
To take the safest occasion by the front
To bring you in° again.

CASSIO.   Yet I beseech you,
If you think fit, or that it may be done,   50
Give me advantage of some brief discourse
With Desdemona alone.

EMILIA.   Pray you, come in.
I will bestow you where you shall have time

28. In . . . time: that is, I am glad to see you.   39. Florentine . . . kind: Iago
is a Venetian. Cassio means: even one of my own people could not have been
kinder.   41. your displeasure: that is, that Othello is displeased with you.   45.
affinity: kindred.   46. might . . . but: that is, he must.   47. likings: affections.
48–49. safest . . . in: to take the first opportunity to restore you to your position;
front: forehead; that is, to take time by the forelock.

To speak your bosom freely.°

CASSIO.   I am much bound to you.

                                                    [*Exeunt.*]

SCENE II. *A room in the castle.*

[*Enter* OTHELLO, IAGO, *and* GENTLEMEN.]

OTHELLO. These letters give, Iago, to the pilot,
   And by him do my duties° to the Senate.
   That done, I will be walking on the works.°
   Repair there to me.

IAGO.   Well, my good lord, I'll do 't.

OTHELLO. This fortification, gentlemen, shall we see 't?

GENTLEMEN. We'll wait upon your lordship.   [*Exeunt.*]

SCENE III. *The garden of the castle.*

[*Enter* DESDEMONA, CASSIO, *and* EMILIA.]

DESDEMONA. Be thou assured, good Cassio, I will do
   All my abilities in thy behalf.

EMILIA. Good madam, do. I warrant it grieves my husband
   As if the case were his.

DESDEMONA. Oh, that's an honest fellow. Do not doubt, Cassio,
   But I will have my lord and you again
   As friendly as you were.

CASSIO.   Bounteous madam,
   Whatever shall become of Michael Cassio,
   He's never anything but your true servant.

DESDEMONA. I know 't. I thank you. You do love my lord.   10
   You have known him long, and be you well assured
   He shall in strangeness stand no farther off
   Than in a politic distance.°

CASSIO.   Aye, but, lady,
   That policy may either last so long,
   Or feed upon such nice and waterish diet,°
   Or breed itself so out of circumstance,°
   That, I being absent and my place supplied,°

55. *speak . . . freely:* declare what is on your mind.
SCENE ii: 2. *do . . . duties:* express my loyalty. 3. *works:* fortifications.
SCENE iii: 12–13. *He . . . distance:* that is, his apparent coldness to you shall only be so much as his official position demands for reasons of policy. 15. *nice . . . diet:* have such weak encouragement. 16. *breed . . . circumstance:* become so used to the situation. 17. *supplied:* filled by another.

My General will forget my love and service.

DESDEMONA. Do not doubt° that. Before Emilia here
    I give thee warrant of thy place.° Assure thee,   20
    If I do vow a friendship, I'll perform it
    To the last article. My lord shall never rest.
    I'll watch him tame° and talk him out of patience,
    His bed shall seem a school, his board a shrift.°
    I'll intermingle every thing he does
    With Cassio's suit. Therefore be merry, Cassio,
    For thy solicitor shall rather die
    Than give thy cause away.
                  [Enter OTHELLO *and* IAGO, *at a distance.]*

EMILIA. Madam, here comes my lord.

CASSIO. Madam, I'll take my leave.   30

DESDEMONA. Nay, stay and hear me speak.

CASSIO. Madam, not now. I am very ill at ease,
    Unfit for mine own purposes.°

DESDEMONA. Well, do your discretion.
                         [Exit CASSIO.]*

IAGO. Ha! I like not that.

OTHELLO. What dost thou say?

IAGO. Nothing, my lord. Or if—I know not what.

OTHELLO. Was not that Cassio parted from my wife?

IAGO. Cassio, my lord! No, sure, I cannot think it,
    That he would steal away so guilty-like,   40
    Seeing you coming.

OTHELLO.   I do believe 'twas he.

DESDEMONA. How now, my lord!
    I have been talking with a suitor here,
    A man that languishes in your displeasure.

OTHELLO. Who is 't you mean?

DESDEMONA. Why, your Lieutenant, Cassio. Good my lord,
    If I have any grace or power to move you,
    His present reconciliation take.°
    For if he be not one that truly loves you,
    That errs in ignorance and not in cunning,°   50
    I have no judgment in an honest face.

---

19. doubt: fear.   *20. give . . . place:* guarantee that you will be restored to your position.   *23. watch . . . tame:* as wild hawks are made tame by keeping them from sleep.   *24. shrift:* place of confession and absolution.   *33. Unfit . . . purposes:* in no condition to plead my own cause.   *48. His . . . take:* accept his immediate apology and forgive him.   *50. in cunning:* knowingly.

I prithee call him back.

OTHELLO.   Went he hence now?

DESDEMONA. Aye, sooth, so humbled
    That he hath left part of his grief with me,
    To suffer with him. Good love, call him back.

OTHELLO. Not now, sweet Desdemona, some other time.

DESDEMONA. But shall 't be shortly?

OTHELLO.   The sooner, sweet, for you.

DESDEMONA. Shall 't be tonight at supper?

OTHELLO.   No, not tonight.

DESDEMONA. Tomorrow dinner then?

OTHELLO.   I shall not dine at home.
    I meet the captains at the citadel.   60

DESDEMONA. Why, then tomorrow night or Tuesday morn,
    On Tuesday noon, or night, on Wednesday morn.
    I prithee name the time, but let it not
    Exceed three days. In faith, he's penitent,
    And yet his trespass, in our common reason°—
    Save that, they say, the wars must make examples
    Out of their best—is not almost° a fault
    To incur a private check.° When shall he come?
    Tell me, Othello. I wonder in my soul
    What you would ask me that I should deny,   70
    Or stand so mammering° on. What! Michael Cassio,
    That came a-wooing with you, and so many a time
    When I have spoke of you dispraisingly
    Hath ta'en your part—to have so much to do
    To bring him in! Trust me, I could do much——

OTHELLO. Prithee, no more. Let him come when he will.
    I will deny thee nothing.

DESDEMONA.   Why, this is not a boon.°
    'Tis as I should entreat you wear your gloves,
    Or feed on nourishing dishes, or keep you warm,
    Or sue to you to do a peculiar° profit   80
    To your own person. Nay, when I have a suit
    Wherein I mean to touch your love indeed,
    It shall be full of poise° and difficult weight,°
    And fearful to be granted.°

OTHELLO.   I will deny thee nothing.

65. *common reason:* common sense. 67. *not almost:* hardly. 68. *check:* rebuke.
71. *mammering:* hesitating. 77. *boon:* great favor. 80. *peculiar:* particular.
83. *poise:* weight in the scales; *difficult weight:* hard to estimate. 84. *fearful
. . . granted:* only granted with sense of fear.

Whereon I do beseech thee grant me this,
To leave me but a little to myself.
DESDEMONA. Shall I deny you? No. Farewell, my lord.
OTHELLO. Farewell, my Desdemona. I'll come to thee straight.
DESDEMONA. Emilia, come. Be as your fancies teach you.°
  Whate'er you be, I am obedient. 90
                      [*Exeunt* DESDEMONA *and* EMILIA.]
OTHELLO. Excellent wretch! Perdition catch my soul
  But I do love thee! And when I love thee not,
  Chaos° is come again.
IAGO. My noble lord——
OTHELLO   What dost thou say, Iago?
IAGO. Did Michael Cassio, when you wooed my lady,
  Know of your love?
OTHELLO. He did, from first to last. Why dost thou ask?
IAGO. But for a satisfaction of my thought,
  No further harm.
OTHELLO.   Why of thy thought, Iago?
IAGO. I did not think he had been acquainted with her. 100
OTHELLO. Oh yes, and went between us very oft.
IAGO. Indeed!
OTHELLO. Indeed! Aye, indeed. Discern'st thou aught in that?
  Is he not honest?
IAGO. Honest, my lord!
OTHELLO. Honest! Aye, honest.
IAGO. My lord, for aught I know.
OTHELLO. What dost thou think?
IAGO. Think, my lord!
OTHELLO. Think, my lord! By Heaven, he echoes me 110
  As if there were some monster in his thought
  Too hideous to be shown. Thou dost mean something.
  I heard thee say even now thou likedst not that
  When Cassio left my wife. What didst not like?
  And when I told thee he was of my counsel
  In my whole course of wooing, thou criedst "Indeed!"
  And didst contract and purse thy brow together
  As if thou then hadst shut up in thy brain
  Some horrible conceit.° If thou dost love me,
  Show me thy thought. 120
IAGO. My lord, you know I love you.

---

89. *Be . . . you:* please yourself. 93. *Chaos:* the utter confusion that existed before order was established in the universe. *119. conceit:* conception, notion.

OTHELLO.   I think thou dost,
And for° I know thou'rt full of love and honesty
And weigh'st thy words before thou givest them breath,
Therefore these stops of thine fright me the more.
For such things in a false disloyal knave
Are tricks of custom, but in a man that's just
They're close delations,° working from the heart,
That passion cannot rule.
IAGO.   For Michael Cassio,
I dare be sworn I think that he is honest.
OTHELLO. I think so too.
IAGO.   Men should be what they seem,   130
Or those that be not, would they might seem none! °
OTHELLO. Certain, men should be what they seem.
IAGO. Why, then I think Cassio's an honest man.
OTHELLO. Nay, yet there's more in this.
I prithee speak to me as to thy thinkings,
As thou dost ruminate and give thy worst of thoughts
The worst of words.
IAGO.   Good my lord, pardon me.
Though I am bound to every act of duty,
I am not bound to that all slaves are free to.
Utter my thoughts? Why, say they are vile and false,   140
As where's that palace whereinto foul things
Sometimes intrude not? Who has a breast so pure
But some uncleanly apprehensions
Keep leets and law days, and in session sit
With meditations lawful?°
OTHELLO. Thou dost conspire against thy friend, Iago,
If thou but think'st him wronged and makest his ear
A stranger to thy thoughts.
IAGO.   I do beseech you—
Though I perchance am vicious in my guess,
As, I confess, it is my nature's plague   150
To spy into abuses, and oft my jealousy°
Shapes faults that are not—that your wisdom yet,
From one that so imperfectly conceits,°

122. *for:* since.   127. *close delations:* concealed accusations.   131. *seem none:* that is, not seem to be honest men.   142–45. *Who . . . lawful:* whose heart is so pure but that some foul suggestion will sit on the bench alongside lawful thoughts; that is, foul thoughts will rise even on the most respectable occasions; *leet:* court held by the lord of the manor; *law days:* days when courts sit; *session:* sitting of the court.   151. *jealousy:* suspicion.   153. *conceits:* conceives, imagines.

Would take no notice, nor build yourself a trouble
Out of his scattering° and unsure observance.°
It were not for your quiet nor your good,
Nor for my manhood, honesty, or wisdom,
To let you know my thoughts.
OTHELLO.   What dost thou mean?
IAGO. Good name in man and woman, dear my lord,
    Is the immediate° jewel of their souls.   160
    Who steals my purse steals trash—'tis something, nothing,
    'Twas mine, 'tis his, and has been slave to thousands—
    But he that filches from me my good name
    Robs me of that which not enriches him
    And makes me poor indeed.
OTHELLO. By Heaven, I'll know thy thoughts.
IAGO.You cannot if my heart were in your hand,
    Nor shall not whilst 'tis in my custody.
OTHELLO. Ha!
IAGO.   Oh, beware, my lord, of jealousy.
    It is the green-eyed monster which doth mock°   170
    The meat° it feeds on. That cuckold lives in bliss
    Who, certain of his fate, loves not his wronger.°
    But, oh, what damnèd minutes tells he o'er
    Who dotes, yet doubts, suspects, yet strongly loves!
OTHELLO. Oh, misery!
IAGO. Poor and content is rich, and rich enough,
    But riches fineless° is as poor as winter
    To him that ever fears he shall be poor.
    Good Heaven, the souls of all my tribe defend
    From jealousy!
OTHELLO.   Why, why is this?   180
    Think'st thou I'd make a life of jealousy,
    To follow still the changes of the moon
    With fresh suspicions? No, to be once in doubt
    Is once to be resolved.° Exchange me for a goat
    When I shall turn the business of my soul
    To such exsufflicate and blown surmises,
    Matching thy inference.° 'Tis not to make me jealous

---

155. *scattering:* scattered, casual; *observance:* observation.   160. *immediate:* most
valuable.   170. *doth mock:* makes a mockery of.   171. *meat:* i.e., victim.   171–
72. *That . . . wronger:* that is, the cuckold who hates his wife and knows her
falseness is not tormented by suspicious jealousy.   177. *fineless:* limitless.
183–84. *to . . . resolved:* whenever I find myself in doubt, I at once seek out
the truth.   185–87. *When . . . inference:* when I shall allow that which concerns me most dearly to be influenced by such trifling suggestions as yours;
exsufflicate: blown up, like a bubble.

To say my wife is fair, feeds well, loves company,
Is free of speech, sings, plays, and dances well.
Where virtue is, these are more virtuous.   190
Nor from mine own weak merits will I draw
The smallest fear or doubt of her revolt,°
For she had eyes, and chose me. No, Iago,
I'll see before I doubt, when I doubt, prove,
And on the proof, there is no more but this—
Away at once with love or jealousy!
IAGO. I am glad of it, for now I shall have reason
To show the love and duty that I bear you
With franker spirit. Therefore, as I am bound,
Receive it from me. I speak not yet of proof.   200
Look to your wife. Observe her well with Cassio.
Wear your eye thus, not jealous nor secure.°
I would not have your free and noble nature
Out of self-bounty° be abused, look to 't.
I know our country disposition well.
In Venice° they do let Heaven see the pranks
They dare not show their husbands. Their best conscience
Is not to leave 't undone, but keep 't unknown.
OTHELLO. Dost thou say so?
IAGO. She did deceive her father,° marrying you,   210
And when she seemed to shake and fear your looks,
She loved them most.
OTHELLO.   And so she did.
IAGO.   Why, go to, then.
She that so young could give out such a seeming
To seel° her father's eyes up close as oak——
He thought 'twas witchcraft—but I am much to blame.
I humbly do beseech you of your pardon
For too much loving you.
OTHELLO.   I am bound to thee forever.
IAGO. I see this hath a little dashed your spirits.
OTHELLO. Not a jot, not a jot.
IAGO.   I' faith, I fear it has.
I hope you will consider what is spoke   220
Comes from my love, but I do see you're moved.
I am to pray you not to strain my speech

192. *revolt:* faithlessness.   202. *secure:* overconfident.   204. *self-bounty:* natural
goodness.   206. *In Venice:* Venice was notorious for its loose women; the Venetian courtesans were among the sights of Europe and were much commented upon
by travelers.   210. *She . . . father:* Iago deliberately echoes Brabantio's parting
words (see I.iii.290–91).   214. *seel:* blind (see I.iii.267,n.).

To grosser issues° nor to larger reach°
Than to suspicion.
OTHELLO. I will not.
IAGO.   Should you do so, my lord,
My speech should fall into such vile success°
As my thoughts aim not at. Cassio's my worthy friend.—
My lord, I see you're moved.
OTHELLO.   No, not much moved.
I do not think but Desdemona's honest.°
IAGO. Long live she so! And long live you to think so!   230
OTHELLO. And yet, how nature erring from itself——
IAGO. Aye, there's the point. As—to be bold with you—
Not to affect° many proposed matches°
Of her own clime, complexion, and degree,
Whereto we see in all things nature tends°——
Foh! One may smell in such a will most rank,°
Foul disproportion, thoughts unnatural.
But pardon me. I do not in position
Distinctly speak of her, though I may fear
Her will, recoiling to her better judgment,   240
May fall to match° you with her country forms,°
And happily° repent.
OTHELLO.   Farewell, farewell.
If more thou dost perceive, let me know more.
Set on thy wife to observe. Leave me, Iago.
IAGO [going]. My lord, I take my leave.
OTHELLO. Why did I marry? This honest creature doubtless
Sees and knows more, much more, than he unfolds.
IAGO [returning]. My lord, I would I might entreat your honor
To scan this thing no further. Leave it to time.
Though it be fit that Cassio have his place,   250
For sure he fills it up with great ability,
Yet if you please to hold him off awhile,
You shall by that perceive him and his means.
Note if your lady strain his entertainment°

---

223. *grosser issues:* worse conclusions; *larger reach:* that is, more widely. 226.
success: result. 229. *honest:* When applied to Desdemona, "honest" means
"chaste," but applied to Iago it has the modern meaning of "open and sincere."
233. *affect:* be inclined to; *proposed matches:* offers of marriage. 235. *in . . .
tends:* that is, a woman naturally marries a man of her own country, color, and
rank. 236. *will . . . rank:* desire most lustful. 241. *match:* compare; *country
forms:* the appearance of her countrymen; that is, white men. 242. *happily:*
haply, by chance. 254. *strain . . . entertainment:* urge you to receive him.

With any strong or vehement importunity—
Much will be seen in that. In the meantime,
Let me be thought too busy in my fears—
As worthy cause I have to fear I am—
And hold her free, I do beseech your Honor.

OTHELLO. Fear not my government.°   260
IAGO. I once more take my leave.   [*Exit.*]
OTHELLO. This fellow's of exceeding honesty,
  And knows all qualities,° with a learned spirit,
  Of human dealings.° If I do prove her haggard,
  Though that her jesses were my dear heartstrings,
  I'd whistle her off and let her down the wind
  To prey at fortune.° Haply, for I am black
  And have not those soft parts of conversation
  That chamberers° have, or for I am declined
  Into the vale of years—yet that's not much—   270
  She's gone, I am abused, and my relief
  Must be to loathe her. Oh, curse of marriage,
  That we can call these delicate creatures ours,
  And not their appetites! I had rather be a toad
  And live upon the vapor of a dungeon
  Than keep a corner in the thing I love
  For others' uses. Yet, 'tis the plague of great ones,
  Prerogatived° are they less than the base.
  'Tis destiny unshunnable, like death.
  Even then this forkèd plague° is fated to us   280
  When we do quicken.° Desdemona comes.
              [*Re-enter* DESDEMONA *and* EMILIA.]
  If she be false, oh, then Heaven mocks itself!
  I'll not believe 't.
DESDEMONA.   How now, my dear Othello!
  Your dinner, and the generous° islanders
  By you invited, do attend your presence.
OTHELLO. I am to blame.
DESDEMONA.   Why do you speak so faintly?
  Are you not well?

---

260. *government:* self-control.   263. *qualities:* different kinds.   263–64. *with . . .
dealings:* with wide experience of human nature.   264–67. *If . . . fortune: . . .
If I find that she is wild, I'll whistle her off the game and let her go where she
will, for she's not worth keeping . . . haggard:* a wild hawk; *jesses:* the straps
attached to a hawk's legs.   269. *chamberers:* playboys.   278. *Prerogatived:* privi-
leged.   280. *forkèd plague:* that is, to be a cuckold.   281. *quicken:* stir in our
mother's womb.   284. *generous:* noble, of gentle blood.

OTHELLO. I have a pain upon my forehead here.
DESDEMONA. Faith, that's with watching,° 'twill away again.
Let me but bind it hard, within this hour 290
It will be well.
OTHELLO.   Your napkin° is too little.
[*He puts the handkerchief from him, and she drops it.*]
Let it alone. Come, I'll go in with you.
DESDEMONA. I am very sorry that you are not well.
[*Exeunt* OTHELLO *and* DESDEMONA.]
EMILIA. I am glad I have found this napkin.
This was her first remembrance from the Moor.
My wayward° husband hath a hundred times
Wooed me to steal it, but she so loves the token,
For he conjured° her she should ever keep it,
That she reserves it evermore about her
To kiss and talk to. I'll have the work ta'en out,° 300
And give 't Iago. What he will do with it
Heaven knows, not I.
I nothing but to please his fantasy.°
[*Re-enter* IAGO.]
IAGO. How now! What do you here alone?
EMILIA. Do not you chide, I have a thing for you.
IAGO. A thing for me? It is a common thing——
EMILIA. Ha!
IAGO. To have a foolish wife.
EMILIA. Oh, is that all? What will you give me now
For that same handkerchief?
IAGO.   What handkerchief? 310
EMILIA. What handkerchief!
Why, that the Moor first gave to Desdemona,
That which so often you did bid me steal.
IAGO. Hast stol'n it from her?
EMILIA. No, faith, she let it drop by negligence,
And, to the advantage,° I being here took 't up.
Look, here it is.
IAGO.   A good wench. Give it me.
EMILIA. What will you do with 't, that you have been so earnest
To have me filch it?

289. *watching:* lack of sleep. 291. *napkin:* handkerchief. 296. *wayward:* un-
accountable. 298. *conjured:* begged with an oath. 300. *work . . . out:* pattern copied. 303. *fantasy:* whim. 316. *to . . . advantage:* thereby giving me
the opportunity.

IAGO [*snatching it*]. Why, what's that to you? 320
EMILIA. If 't be not for some purpose of import,
    Give 't me again. Poor lady, she'll run mad
    When she shall lack it.
IAGO. Be not acknown on 't,° I have use for it.
    Go, leave me.
                              [*Exit* EMILIA.]
    I will in Cassio's lodging lose this napkin,
    And let him find it. Trifles light as air
    Are to the jealous confirmations strong
    As proofs of Holy Writ. This may do something.
    The Moor already changes with my poison. 330
    Dangerous conceits are in their natures poisons,
    Which at the first are scarce found to distaste,°
    But with a little° act upon the blood
    Burn like the mines of sulphur. I did say so.°
    Look where he comes!
                [*Re-enter* OTHELLO.]
              Not poppy,° nor mandragora,°
    Nor all the drowsy syrups of the world,
    Shall ever medicine thee to that sweet sleep
    Which thou owedst° yesterday.
OTHELLO.   Ha! Ha! False to me?
IAGO. Why, how now, General! No more of that.
OTHELLO. Avaunt!° Be gone! Thou hast set me on the rack.° 340
    I swear 'tis better to be much abused
    Than but to know 't a little.
IAGO.   How now, my lord!
OTHELLO. What sense had I of her stol'n hours of lust?
    I saw 't not, thought it not, it harmed not me.
    I slept the next night well, was free and merry.
    I found not Cassio's kisses on her lips.
    He that is robbed, not wanting° what is stol'n,
    Let him not know 't and he's not robbed at all.
IAGO. I am sorry to hear this.
OTHELLO. I had been happy if the general camp, 350

---

324. *Be . . . on't:* know nothing about it.   332. *distaste:* taste unpleasantly.
333. *with a little:* in a little while.   334. *I . . . so:* As Iago says this, Othello
enters from the back of the stage, with all the signs of his agitation outwardly
visible.   335. *poppy:* opium; *mandragora:* called also mandrake, a root used as a
drug to bring sleep.   338. *owedst:* owned, possessed.   340. *Avaunt:* be off!
on . . . rack: that is, in torment.   347. *wanting:* missing.

Pioners° and all, had tasted her sweet body,
So I had nothing known. Oh, now forever
Farewell the tranquil mind! Farewell content!
Farewell the plumèd° troop and the big wars
That make ambition virtue! Oh, farewell,
Farewell the neighing steed and the shrill trump,
The spirit-stirring drum, the ear-piercing fife,
The royal banner and all quality,°
Pride, pomp, and circumstance of glorious war!
And, O you mortal engines,° whose rude throats   360
The immortal Jove's dread clamors counterfeit,°
Farewell! Othello's occupation's gone!
IAGO. Is 't possible, my lord?
OTHELLO. Villain, be sure thou prove my love a whore,
Be sure of it, give me the ocular proof.
Or by the worth of man's eternal soul,
Thou hadst been better have been born a dog
Than answer my waked wrath!
IAGO.   Is 't come to this?
OTHELLO. Make me to see 't, or at the least so prove it
That the probation° bear no hinge nor loop   370
To hang a doubt on, or woe upon thy life!
IAGO. My noble lord——
OTHELLO. If thou dost slander her and torture me,
Never pray more, abandon all remorse.°
On horror's head horrors accumulate,
Do deeds to make Heaven weep, all earth amazed,
For nothing canst thou to damnation add
Greater than that.
IAGO.   Oh, grace! Oh, Heaven defend me!
Are you a man? Have you a soul or sense?
God be wi' you, take mine office. O wretched fool,   380
That livest to make thine honesty a vice!
O monstrous world! Take note, take note, O world,
To be direct and honest is not safe.
I thank you for this profit,° and from hence
I'll love no friend, sith° love breeds such offense.
OTHELLO. Nay, stay. Thou shouldst be honest.
IAGO. I should be wise, for honesty's a fool.

351. *Pioners:* pioneers, the lowest type of soldier.   354. *plumed:* wearing plumes
in the helmet.   358. *quality:* military rank.   360. *mortal engines:* deadly cannon.
361. *counterfeit:* imitate.   370. *probation:* proof.   374. *remorse:* pity.   384. *profit:* profitable lesson.   385. *sith:* since.

And loses that it works for.
OTHELLO.   By the world,
    I think my wife be honest, and think she is not.
    I think that thou art just, and think thou art not.   390
    I'll have some proof. Her name, that was as fresh
    As Dian's° visage, is now begrimed and black
    As mine own face. If there be cords, or knives,
    Poison, or fire, or suffocating streams,
    I'll not endure it. Would I were satisfied!
IAGO. I see, sir, you are eaten up with passion.
    I do repent me that I put it to you.
    You would be satisfied?
OTHELLO.   Would! Nay, I will.
IAGO. And may, but, how? How satisfied, my lord?
    Would you, the supervisor,° grossly gape on?   400
    Behold her topped?
OTHELLO.   Death and damnation! Oh!
IAGO. It were a tedious difficulty, I think,
    To bring them to that prospect.° Damn them then,
    If ever mortal eyes do see them bolster°
    More than their own! What then? How then?
    What shall I say? Where's satisfaction?
    It is impossible you should see this,
    Were they as prime° as goats, as hot as monkeys,
    As salt° as wolves in pride,° and fools as gross
    As ignorance made drunk. But yet I say   410
    If imputation° and strong circumstances,
    Which lead directly to the door of truth,
    Will give you satisfaction, you may have 't.
OTHELLO. Give me a living° reason she's disloyal.
IAGO. I do not like the office.
    But sith I am entered in this cause so far,
    Pricked° to 't by foolish honesty and love,
    I will go on. I lay with Cassio lately,
    And being troubled with a raging tooth,
    I could not sleep.   420
    There are a kind of men so loose of soul
    That in their sleeps will mutter their affairs.
    One of this kind is Cassio.

---

392. *Dian:* Diana, goddess of chastity.   400. *supervisor:* looker-on.   403. *prospect:* sight.   404. *bolster:* sleep together.   408. *prime:* lustful.   409. *salt:* eager; *in pride:* in heat.   411. *imputation:* probability.   414. *living:* tangible.   417. *Pricked:* spurred on.

In sleep I heard him say "Sweet Desdemona,
Let us be wary, let us hide our loves."
And then, sir, would he gripe° and wring my hand,
Cry "O sweet creature!" and then kiss me hard,
As if he plucked up kisses by the roots
That grew upon my lips. Then laid his leg
Over my thigh, and sighed and kissed, and then   430
Cried "Cursed fate that gave thee to the Moor!"
OTHELLO. Oh, monstrous! Monstrous!
IAGO.   Nay, this was but his dream.
OTHELLO. But this denoted a foregone conclusion.
　'Tis a shrewd doubt,° though it be but a dream.
IAGO. And this may help to thicken other proofs
　That do demónstrate thinly.
OTHELLO.   I'll tear her all to pieces.
IAGO. Nay, but be wise. Yet we see nothing done.
　She may be honest yet. Tell me but this:
　Have you not sometimes seen a handkerchief
　Spotted with strawberries° in your wife's hand?   440
OTHELLO. I gave her such a one, 'twas my first gift.
IAGO. I know not that. But such a handkerchief—
　I am sure it was your wife's—did I today
　See Cassio wipe his beard with.
OTHELLO.   If it be that——
IAGO. If it be that, or any that was hers,
　It speaks against her with the other proofs.
OTHELLO. Oh, that the slave had forty thousand lives!
　One is too poor, too weak, for my revenge.
　Now do I see 'tis true. Look here, Iago,
　All my fond love thus do I blow to Heaven—   450
　'Tis gone.
　Arise, black Vengeance, from thy hollow cell!
　Yield up, O Love, thy crown and hearted° throne
　To tyrannous hate! Swell, bosom, with thy fraught,°
　For 'tis of aspics'° tongues!
IAGO.   Yet be content.
OTHELLO. Oh, blood, blood, blood!
IAGO. Patience, I say. Your mind perhaps may change.
OTHELLO. Never, Iago. Like to the Pontic Sea,
　Whose icy current and compulsive course

---

426. *gripe:* grip.　434. *shrewd doubt:* bitter suspicion.　440. *with strawberries:*
with a pattern of strawberries.　453. *hearted:* in my heart.　454. *fraught:* fright,
load.　455. *aspic:* asp, a small poisonous snake.

Ne'er feels retiring ebb but keeps due on   460
To the Propontic and the Hellespont;°
Even so my bloody thoughts, with violent pace,
Shall ne'er look back, ne'er ebb to humble love,
Till that capable° and wide revenge
Swallow them up. Now, by yond marble Heaven,
In the due reverence of a sacred vow [kneels]
I here engage° my words.
IAGO.   Do not rise yet. [Kneels.]
Witness, you ever burning lights above,
You elements that clip° us round about,
Witness that here Iago doth give up   470
The execution of his wit, hands, heart,
To wronged Othello's service! Let him command,
And to obey shall be in me remorse,°
What bloody business ever.
                              [They rise.]
OTHELLO.   I greet thy love,
Not with vain thanks, but with acceptance bounteous,
And will upon the instant put thee to 't.°
Within these three days let me hear thee say
That Cassio's not alive.
IAGO. My friend is dead. 'Tis done at your request.
But let her live.   480
OTHELLO. Damn her, lewd minx! Oh, damn her!
Come, go with me apart. I will withdraw,
To furnish me with some swift means of death
For the fair devil. Now art thou my Lieutenant.
IAGO. I am your own forever.
                                        [Exeunt.]

SCENE IV. Before the castle.

[Enter DESDEMONA, EMILIA, and CLOWN.]
DESDEMONA. Do you know, sirrah, where Lieutenant Cassio lies?
CLOWN. I dare not say he lies anywhere.

458–61. Like . . . Hellespont: In Pliny's Natural History, translated by Philemon
Holland in 1601, it was noted that "the sea Pontus (Black Sea) evermore floweth
and runneth out into Propontis (Sea of Marmora) but the sea never returneth
back again within Pontus." Hellespont: the Dardanelles. 464. capable: compre-
hensive, complete. 467. engage: pledge. 469. elements . . . clip: skies that
embrace, surround. 473. remorse: solemn obligation. 476. put . . . to't: put
you to the proof.

DESDEMONA. Why, man?

CLOWN. He's a soldier, and for one to say a soldier lies is stabbing.

DESDEMONA. Go to. Where lodges he?

CLOWN. To tell you where he lodges is to tell you where I lie.

DESDEMONA. Can anything be made of this?

CLOWN. I know not where he lodges, and for me to devise a lodging,
and say he lies here or he lies there, were to lie in mine own
throat.   10

DESDEMONA. Can you inquire him out and he edificed by report? °

CLOWN. I will catechize the world for him; that is, make questions and
by them answer.

DESDEMONA. Seek him, bid him come hither. Tell him I have moved
my lord on his behalf and hope all will be well.

CLOWN. To do this is within the compass of man's wit, and therefore
I will attempt the doing it.   [Exit.]

DESDEMONA. Where should I lose that handkerchief, Emilia?

EMILIA. I know not, madam.

DESDEMONA. Believe me, I had rather have lost my purse   20
Full of crusados.° And, but my noble Moor
Is true of mind and made of no such baseness
As jealous creatures are, it were enough
To put him to ill thinking.

EMILIA.   Is he not jealous?

DESDEMONA. Who, he? I think the sun where he was born
Drew all such humors° from him.

EMILIA.   Look where he comes.

DESDEMONA. I will not leave him now till Cassio
Be called to him.

[Enter OTHELLO.]
How is 't with you, my lord?

OTHELLO. Well, my good lady. [Aside.] Oh, hardness to dissemble!
How do you, Desdemona?

DESDEMONA.   Well, my good lord.   30

OTHELLO. Give me your hand. This hand is moist,° my lady.

DESDEMONA. It yet has felt no age nor known no sorrow.

OTHELLO. This argues fruitfulness and liberal heart.
Hot, hot, and moist—this hand of yours requires
A sequester° from liberty, fasting and prayer,

SCENE IV: *11. edificed by report:* enlightened by the information. Desdemona
speaks with mock pomposity. *21. crusados:* small gold Portuguese coins. *26.
humors:* moods; literally, dampnesses. *31. moist:* a hot moist palm was believed
to show desire. *35. sequester:* separation.

Much castigation, exercise devout.
For here's a young and sweating devil here,
That commonly rebels. 'Tis a good hand,
A frank one.
DESDEMONA.   You may indeed say so,
For 'twas that hand that gave away my heart.   40
OTHELLO. A liberal° hand. The hearts of old gave hands,
But our new heraldry is hands, not hearts.°
DESDEMONA. I cannot speak of this. Come now, your promise.
OTHELLO. What promise, chuck? °
DESDEMONA. I have sent to bid Cassio come speak with you.
OTHELLO. I have a salt and sorry rheum° offends me.
Lend me thy handkerchief.
DESDEMONA. Here, my lord.
OTHELLO. That which I gave you.
DESDEMONA. I have it not about me.   50
OTHELLO. Not?
DESDEMONA. No indeed, my lord.
OTHELLO. That's a fault. That handkerchief
Did an Egyptian° to my mother give.
She was a charmer, and could almost read
The thoughts of people. She told her while she kept it
'Twould make her amiable and subdue my father
Entirely to her love, but if she lost it
Or made a gift of it, my father's eye
Should hold her loathed and his spirits should hunt   60
After new fancies. She dying gave it me,
And bid me, when my fate would have me wive,
To give it her. I did so. And take heed on 't,
Make it a darling like your precious eye.
To lose 't or give 't away were such perdition
As nothing else could match.
DESDEMONA.   Is 't possible?
OTHELLO. 'Tis true. There's magic in the web of it.
A sibyl° that had numbered in the world
The sun to course two hundred compasses
In her prophetic fury° sewed the work.   70

41. *liberal:* overgenerous.   41–42. *The . . . hearts:* Once love and deeds went
together, but now it is all deeds (i.e., faithfulness) and no love. . . .   44. *chuck:*
a term of affection, but not the kind of word with which a person of Othello's
dignity would normally address his wife. He is beginning to treat her with contemptuous familiarity (see IV.ii.24).   46. *rheum:* common cold.   54. *Egyptian:*
gypsy.   68. *sibyl:* prophetess.   70. *fury:* inspiration.

The worms were hallowed that did breed the silk,
And it was dyed in mummy° which the skillful
Conserved° of maidens' hearts.
DESDEMONA.   Indeed! Is 't true?
OTHELLO. Most veritable, therefore look to 't well.
DESDEMONA. Then would to God that I had never seen 't.
OTHELLO. Ha! Wherefore?
DESDEMONA. Why do you speak so startlingly and rash?
OTHELLO. Is 't lost? Is 't gone? Speak, is it out o' the way?
DESDEMONA. Heaven bless us!
OTHELLO. Say you?   80
DESDEMONA. It is not lost, but what an if it were?
OTHELLO. How!
DESDEMONA. I say it is not lost.
OTHELLO. Fetch 't, let me see it.
DESDEMONA. Why, so I can, sir, but I will not now.
     This is a trick to put me from my suit.
     Pray you let Cassio be received again.
OTHELLO. Fetch me the handkerchief. My mind misgives.
DESDEMONA. Come, come,
     You'll never meet a more sufficient man.   90
OTHELLO. The handkerchief!
DESDEMONA.   I pray talk me of Cassio.
OTHELLO. The handkerchief!
DESDEMONA.   A man that all his time
     Hath founded his good fortunes on your love,
     Shared dangers with you——
OTHELLO. The handkerchief!
DESDEMONA. In sooth, you are to blame.
OTHELLO. Away!   [*Exit.*]
EMILIA. Is not this man jealous?
DESDEMONA. I ne'er saw this before.
     Sure there's some wonder in this handkerchief.   100
     I am most unhappy in the loss of it.
EMILIA. 'Tis not a year or two shows us a man.°
     They are all but stomachs and we all but food.
     They eat us hungerly, and when they are full
     They belch us. Look you, Cassio and my husband.
          [*Enter* CASSIO *and* IAGO.]
IAGO. There is no other way, 'tis she must do 't.

72. *mummy:* a concoction made from Egyptian mummies.   73. *Conserved:* prepared.   102. *'Tis . . . man:* It does not take a couple of years for us to discover the nature of a man; that is, he soon shows his real nature.

And, lo, the happiness!° Go and impórtune her.
DESDEMONA. How now, good Cassio! What's the news with you?
CASSIO. Madam, my former suit. I do beseech you
    That by your virtuous means I may again   110
    Exist, and be a member of his love
    Whom I with all the office of my heart
    Entirely honor. I would not be delayed.
    If my offense be of such mortal kind
    That nor my service past nor present sorrows
    Nor purposed merit in futurity°
    Can ransom me into his love again,
    But to know so must be my benefit.
    So shall I clothe me in a forced content
    And shut myself up in some other course   120
    To Fortune's alms.°
DESDEMONA.   Alas, thrice-gentle Cassio!
    My advocation° is not now in tune.
    My lord is not my lord, nor should I know him
    Were he in favor as in humor altered.°
    So help me every spirit sanctified,
    As I have spoken for you all my best
    And stood within the blank° of his displeasure
    For my free speech! You must awhile be patient.
    What I can do I will, and more I will
    Than for myself I dare. Let that suffice you.   130
IAGO. Is my lord angry?
EMILIA.   He went hence but now,
    And certainly in strange unquietness.
IAGO. Can he be angry? I have seen the cannon
    When it hath blown his ranks into the air,
    And, like the Devil, from his very arm
    Puffed his own brother, and can he be angry?
    Something of moment then. I will go meet him.
    There's matter in 't indeed if he be angry.
DESDEMONA. I prithee do so.
                            [*Exit* IAGO.]
           Something sure of state,

107. *And . . . happiness:* What good luck, here she is. 116. *Nor . . . futurity:* nor my good resolutions for the future. 118–21. *But . . . alms:* If I know that Othello will not restore me to my position, it will have this benefit: I shall force myself to be contented and try my luck elsewhere; *Fortune's alms:* what Fortune may give me. 122. *advocation:* advocacy, pleading. 124. *favor . . . altered:* as changed in face as in mood. 127. *blank:* aim. The blank is the bull's-eye of a target.

Either from Venice, or some unhatched practice   140
Made demonstrable° here in Cyprus to him,
Hath puddled° his clear spirit. And in such cases
Men's natures wrangle with inferior things,
Though great ones are their object.° 'Tis even so,
For let our finger ache and it indues°
Our other healthful members even to that sense
Of pain. Nay, we must think men are not gods,
Nor of them look for such observancy
As fits the bridal.° Beshrew me° much, Emilia,
I was, unhandsome warrior° as I am,   150
Arraigning his unkindness with my soul,
But now I find I had suborned the witness,°
And he's indicted falsely.
EMILIA. Pray Heaven it be state matters, as you think,
And no conception nor no jealous toy°
Concerning you.
DESDEMONA. Alas the day, I never gave him cause!
EMILIA. But jealous souls will not be answered so.
They are not ever jealous for the cause,
But jealous for they are jealous. 'Tis a monster   160
Begot upon itself, born on itself.
DESDEMONA. Heaven keep that monster from Othello's mind!
EMILIA. Lady, amen.
DESDEMONA. I will go seek him. Cassio, walk hereabout.
If I do find him fit, I'll move your suit,
And seek to effect it to my uttermost.
CASSIO. I humbly thank your ladyship.

                         [*Exeunt* DESDEMONA *and* EMILIA.]
                         [*Enter* BIANCA.]
BIANCA. Save you, friend Cassio!
CASSIO.   What make you from° home?
How is it with you, my most fair Bianca?
I' faith, sweet love, I was coming to your house.   170
BIANCA. And I was going to your lodging, Cassio.
What, keep a week away? Seven days and nights?

140–41. *unhatched . . . demonstrable*: some plot, not yet matured, which has
been revealed.   142. *puddled*: muddied, stirred up.   142–44. *in . . . object*:
When men are disturbed by great matters, they show their temper in small things.
145. *indues*: endows, pervades.   148. *bridal*: honeymoon; *Beshrew me*: plague on
me.   150. *unhandsome warrior*: clumsy soldier. Desdemona continually thinks of
herself as Othello's companion in arms (see I.iii.246ff.).   152. *suborned . . .
witness*: corrupted the evidence; that is, it is my fault, not his.   155. *jealous toy*:
silly suspicion.   168. *make . . . from*: are you doing away from.

Eightscore eight hours? And lovers' absent hours,
More tedious than the dial eightscore times?°
Oh, weary reckoning!

CASSIO.   Pardon me, Bianca.
I have this while with leaden thoughts been pressed,
But I shall in a more continuate time°
Strike off this score of absence. Sweet Bianca
                    [*giving her* DESDEMONA's *handkerchief*],
Take me this work out.°

BIANCA.   O Cassio, whence came this?
This is some token from a newer friend.   180
To the felt absence now I feel a cause.
Is 't come to this? Well, well.

CASSIO.   Go to, woman!
Throw your vile guesses in the Devil's teeth,
From whence you have them. You are jealous now
That this is from some mistress, some remembrance.
No, by my faith, Bianca.

BIANCA.   Why, whose is it?

CASSIO. I know not, sweet. I found it in my chamber.
I like the work well. Ere it be demanded—
As like enough it will—I'd have it copied.
Take it, and do 't, and leave me for this time.   190

BIANCA. Leave you! Wherefore?

CASSIO. I do attend here on the General,
And think it no addition,° nor my wish,
To have him see me womaned.°

BIANCA.   Why, I pray you?

CASSIO. Not that I love you not.

BIANCA.   But that you do not love me.
I pray you bring me on the way a little,
And say if I shall see you soon at night.

CASSIO. 'Tis but a little way that I can bring you,
For I attend here. But I'll see you soon.

BIANCA. 'Tis very good, I must be circumstanced.°   200

                    [*Exeunt.*]

173–174. *And . . . times:* When one's lover is absent for a week, does it not seem far longer than a hundred and sixty clock hours?   177. *continuate time:* that is, when my time is not continually being interrupted.   179. *Take . . . out:* copy this pattern.   193. *addition:* honor.   194. *womaned:* with a girl.   200. *circumstanced:* put off.

ACT   IV

SCENE 1. *Cyprus. Before the castle.*

[*Enter* OTHELLO *and* IAGO.]

IAGO. Will you think so?

OTHELLO.   Think so, Iago!

IAGO.   What,
    To kiss in private?

OTHELLO.   An unauthorized kiss.

IAGO. Or to be naked with her friend in bed
    An hour or more, not meaning any harm?

OTHELLO. Naked in bed, Iago, and not mean harm!
    It is hypocrisy against the Devil.°
    They that mean virtuously and yet do so,
    The Devil their virtue tempts and they tempt Heaven.°

IAGO. So° they do nothing, 'tis a venial° slip.
    But if I give my wife a handkerchief——   10

OTHELLO. What then?

IAGO. Why, then, 'tis hers, my lord, and being hers,
    She may, I think, bestow 't on any man.

OTHELLO. She is protectress of her honor too.
    May she give that?

IAGO. Her honor is an essence that's not seen.
    They have it very oft that have it not.°
    But for the handkerchief——

OTHELLO. By Heaven, I would most gladly have forgot it.
    Thou said'st—oh, it comes o'er my memory,   20
    As hoth the raven o'er the infected house,°
    Boding° to all—he had my handkerchief.

IAGO. Aye, what of that?

OTHELLO.   That's not so good now.

IAGO.   What,
    If I had said I had seen him do you wrong?
    Or heard him say—as knaves be such abroad,
    Who having, by their own importunate suit,
    Or voluntary dotage° of some mistress,

ACT IV, SCENE i:6. *hypocrisy . . . Devil:* "double-crossing the Devil"; that is, they are behaving in a most suspicious way. 7–8. *They . . . Heaven:* that is, those who go to bed together and mean no harm are asking the Devil to tempt them, and they make God suspect their innocence. 9. *So:* so long as; *venial:* pardonable. 17. *They . . . not:* that is, many are honored who have no honor. 21. *As . . . house:* that is, as a bird of prey waits for its victim to die. 22. *Boding:* foretelling evil. 27. *dotage:* infatuation.

Convincèd or supplied° them, cannot choose
But they must blab——
OTHELLO.   Hath he said anything?
IAGO. He hath, my lord, but be you well assured,   30
No more than he'll unswear.
OTHELLO.   What hath he said?
IAGO. Faith, that he did——I know not what he did.
OTHELLO. What? What?
IAGO. Lie——
OTHELLO.   With her?
IAGO.   With her, on her, what you will.
OTHELLO. Lie° with her! Lie on her!—We say lie on her when they
belie her.—Lie with her! 'Zounds, that's fulsome! ° Handker-
chief—confessions—handkerchief!—To confess, and be hanged
for his labor. First to be hanged, and then to confess. I tremble
at it. Nature would not invest herself in such shadowing passion
without some instruction.° It is not words that shake me thus.   40
Pish! Noses, ears, and lips. Is 't possible?—Confess?—Handker-
chief?—Oh, devil!   [Falls in a trance.]
IAGO. Work on,
My medicine, work! Thus credulous fools are caught,
And many worthy and chaste dames even thus,
All guiltless, meet reproach. What ho! My lord!
My lord, I say! Othello!
                         [Enter CASSIO.]
                    How now, Cassio!
CASSIO. What's the matter?
IAGO. My lord is fall'n into an epilepsy.
This is his second fit, he had one yesterday.   50
CASSIO. Rub him about the temples.
IAGO.   No, forbear,
The lethargy° must have his quiet course.
If not, he foams at mouth and by and by
Breaks out to savage madness. Look, he stirs.
Do you withdraw yourself a little while,
He will recover straight. When he is gone,
I would on great occasion speak with you.
                              [Exit CASSIO.]

---

28. *Convinced or supplied:* overcome or satisfied their desires.   35–42. *Lie . . .
devil:* Othello breaks into incoherent muttering before he falls down in a fit.
36. *fulsome:* disgusting.   39–40. *Nature . . . instruction:* Nature would not fill
me with such overwhelming emotion unless there was some cause.   52. *lethargy:*
epileptic fit.

How is it, General? Have you not hurt your head? °
OTHELLO. Dost thou mock me?
IAGO.   I mock you! No, by Heaven.
   Would you would bear your fortune like a man!   60
OTHELLO. A hornèd man's a monster and a beast.
IAGO. There's many a beast, then, in a populous city,
   And many a civil° monster.
OTHELLO. Did he confess it?
IAGO.   Good sir, be a man.
   Think every bearded fellow that's but yoked°
   May draw with you.° There's millions now alive
   That nightly lie in those unproper beds
   Which they dare swear peculiar.° Your case is better.
   Oh, 'tis the spite of Hell, the Fiend's archmock,
   To lip° a wanton in a secure couch°   70
   And to suppose her chaste! No, let me know,
   And knowing what I am, I know what she shall be.
OTHELLO. Oh, thou art wise, 'tis certain.
IAGO.   Stand you awhile apart,
   Confine yourself but in a patient list.°
   Whilst you were here o'erwhelmèd with your grief—
   A passion most unsuiting such a man—
   Cassio came hither. I shifted him away,
   And laid good 'scuse upon your ecstasy,°
   Bade him anon return and here speak with me,
   The which he promisèd. Do but encave° yourself,   80
   And mark the fleers,° the gibes, and notable scorns,
   That dwell in every region of his face.
   For I will make him tell the tale anew,
   Where, how, how oft, how long ago, and when
   He hath and is again to cope° your wife.
   I say but mark his gesture. Marry, patience,
   Or I shall say you are all in all in spleen,°
   And nothing of a man.
OTHELLO.   Dost thou hear, Iago?
   I will be found most cunning in my patience,

---

58. *Have . . . head:* With brutal cynicism Iago asks whether Othello is suffering from cuckold's headache. 63. *civil:* sober, well-behaved citizen. 65. *yolked:* married. 66. *draw . . . you:* literally, be your yoke fellow, share your fate. 67–68. *That . . . peculiar:* that lie nightly in beds which they believe are their own but which others have shared. 70. *lip:* kiss; *secure couch:* literally, a carefree bed; that is, a bed which has been used by the wife's lover, but secretly. 74. *patient list:* confines of patience. 78. *ecstasy:* fit. 80. *encave:* hide. 81. *fleers:* scornful grins. 85. *cope:* encounter. 87. *spleen:* hot temper.

But—dost thou hear?—most bloody.

IAGO.   That's not amiss,   90
But yet keep time in all. Will you withdraw?

[OTHELLO *retires.*]

Now will I question Cassio of Bianca,
A housewife° that by selling her desires
Buys herself bread and clothes. It is a creature
That dotes on Cassio, as 'tis the strumpet's plague
To beguile many and be beguiled by one.
He, when he hears of her, cannot refrain
From the excess of laughter. Here he comes.

[*Re-enter* CASSIO.]

As he shall smile, Othello shall go mad,
And his unbookish° jealousy must construe°   100
Poor Cassio's smiles, gestures, and light behavior
Quite in the wrong. How do you now, Lieutenant?

CASSIO. The worser that you give me the addition°
Whose want even kills me.

IAGO. Ply° Desdemona well, and you are sure on 't.
Now, if this suit lay in Bianca's power,
How quickly should you speed!

CASSIO.   Alas, poor caitiff! °

OTHELLO. Look how he laughs already!

IAGO. I never knew a woman love man so.

CASSIO. Alas, poor rogue! I think, i' faith, she loves me.   110

OTHELLO. Now he denies it faintly and laughs it out.

IAGO. Do you hear, Cassio?

OTHELLO.   Now he impórtunes him
To tell it o'er. Go to. Well said, well said.

IAGO. She gives it out that you shall marry her.
Do you intend it?

CASSIO. Ha, ha, ha!

OTHELLO. Do you triumph, Roman? ° Do you triumph?

CASSIO. I marry her! What, a customer! ° I prithee bear some charity
to my wit. Do not think it so unwholesome. Ha, ha, ha!

OTHELLO. So, so, so, so. They laugh that win.°   120

IAGO. Faith, the cry goes that you shall marry her.

CASSIO. Prithee say true.

IAGO. I am a very villain else.

---

93. *housewife:* hussy.   100. *unbookish:* unlearned, simple; *construe:* interpret.
103. *addition:* title (Lieutenant) which he has lost.   105. *Ply:* urge.   107. *caitiff:*
wretch.   117. *triumph, Roman:* The word "triumph" suggests "Roman" because
the Romans celebrated their victories with triumphs, elaborate shows, and processions.   118. *customer:* harlot.   120. *They . . . win:* a proverbial saying.

OTHELLO. Have you scored° me? Well.

CASSIO. This is the monkey's own giving out. She is persuaded I will marry her out of her own love and flattery, not out of my promise.

OTHELLO. Iago beckons me, now he begins the story.

CASSIO. She was here even now. She haunts me in every place. I was the other day talking on the sea bank with certain Venetians, 130 and thither comes the bauble,° and, by this hand, she falls me thus about my neck——

OTHELLO. Crying "O dear Cassio!" as it were. His gesture imports it.

CASSIO. So hangs and lolls and weeps upon me, so hales° and pulls me. Ha, ha, ha!

OTHELLO. Now he tells how she plucked him to my chamber. Oh, I see that nose of yours, but not that dog I shall throw it to.

CASSIO. Well, I must leave her company.

IAGO. Before me! ° Look where she comes.

CASSIO. 'Tis such another fitchew! ° Marry, a perfumed one.   140

[*Enter* BIANCA.]

What do you mean by this haunting of me?

BIANCA. Let the Devil and his dam° haunt you! What did you mean by that same handkerchief you gave me even now? I was a fine fool to take it. I must take out the work? A likely piece of work, that you should find it in your chamber and not know who left it there! This is some minx's token, and I must take out the work? There, give it your hobbyhorse.° Wheresoever you had it, I'll take out no work on 't.

CASSIO. How now, my sweet Bianca! How now! How now!

OTHELLO. By Heaven, that should be my handkerchief!   150

BIANCA. An° you'll come to supper tonight, you may. An you will not, come when you are next prepared for.   [*Exit.*]

IAGO. After her, after her.

CASSIO. Faith, I must, she'll rail i' the street else.

IAGO. Will you sup there?

CASSIO. Faith, I intend so.

IAGO. Well, I may chance to see you, for I would very fain° speak with you.

CASSIO. Prithee, come, will you?

IAGO. Go to. Say no more.   160

[*Exit* CASSIO.]

124. *scored:* marked, as with a blow from a whip.   131. *bauble:* toy, plaything.
134. *hales:* hauls, drags.   139. *Before me:* by my soul, a mild oath.   140. *fit-chew:* polecat, a creature most demonstrative in the mating season.   142. *dam:* mother.   147. *hobbyhorse:* harlot.   151. *An:* if.   157. *fain:* gladly.

OTHELLO [*advancing*]. How shall I murder him, Iago?

IAGO. Did you perceive how he laughed at his vice?

OTHELLO. Oh, Iago!

IAGO. And did you see the handkerchief?

OTHELLO. Was that mine?

IAGO. Yours, by this hand. And to see how he prizes the foolish woman your wife! She gave it him, and he hath given it his whore.

OTHELLO. I would have him nine years a-killing. A fine woman! A fair woman! A sweet woman!

IAGO. Nay, you must forget that. 170

OTHELLO. Aye, let her rot, and perish, and be damned tonight, for she shall not live. No, my heart is turned to stone, I strike it and it hurts my hand. Oh, the world hath not a sweeter creature. She might lie by an emperor's side, and command him tasks.

IAGO. Nay, that's not your way.°

OTHELLO. Hang her! I do but say what she is, so delicate with her needle, an admirable musician—oh, she will sing the savageness out of a bear—of so high and plenteous wit and invention—

IAGO. She's the worse for all this.

OTHELLO. Oh, a thousand thousand times. And then, of so gentle a 180 condition! °

IAGO. Aye, too gentle.

OTHELLO. Nay, that's certain. But yet the pity of it, Iago! O Iago, the pity of it, Iago!

IAGO. If you are so fond° over her iniquity, give her patent° to offend, for if it touch not you, it comes near nobody.

OTHELLO. I will chop her into messes.° Cuckold me!

IAGO. Oh, 'tis foul in her.

OTHELLO. With mine officer!

IAGO. That's fouler. 190

OTHELLO. Get me some poison, Iago, this night. I'll not expostulate° with her, lest her body and beauty unprovide° my mind again. This night, Iago.

IAGO. Do it not with poison, strangle her in her bed, even the bed she hath contaminated.

OTHELLO. Good, good. The justice of it pleases. Very good.

IAGO. And for Cassio let me be his undertaker.° You shall hear more by midnight.

---

175. *Nay . . . way:* that is, don't get soft thoughts about her. 181. *condition:* nature. 185. *fond:* foolish; *patent:* a grant by the King of some special privilege. 187. *messes:* little pieces. 191. *expostulate:* argue. 192. *unprovide:* weaken. 197. *be . . . undertaker:* undertake to manage his business. In Shakespeare's plays the word does *not* mean "mortician."

OTHELLO. Excellent good. [*A trumpet within.*] What trumpet is that same? 200
IAGO. Something from Venice, sure. 'Tis Lodovico
Come from the Duke. And see, your wife is with him.
[*Enter* LODOVICO, DESDEMONA, *and* ATTENDANTS.]
LODOVICO. God save the worthy General!
OTHELLO. With all my heart, sir.
LODOVICO. The Duke and Senators of Venice greet you
[*Gives him a letter.*]
OTHELLO. I kiss the instrument° of their pleasures
[*Opens the letter, and reads.*]
DESDEMONA. And what's the news, good Cousin Lodovico?
IAGO. I am very glad to see you, signior.
Welcome to Cyprus.
LODOVICO. I thank you. How does Lieutenant Cassio?
IAGO. Lives, sir. 210
DESDEMONA. Cousin, there's fall'n between him and my lord
An unkind breach, but you shall make all well.
OTHELLO. Are you sure of that?
DESDEMONA. My lord?
OTHELLO [*reads*]. "This fail you not to do, as you will——"
LODOVICO. He did not call, he's busy in the paper.
Is there division 'twixt my lord and Cassio?
DESDEMONA. A most unhappy one. I would do much
To atone° them, for the love I bear to Cassio.
OTHELLO. Fire and brimstone!
DESDEMONA. My lord?
OTHELLO. Are you wise? ° 220
DESDEMONA. What, is he angry?
LODOVICO. Maybe the letter moved him,
For, as I think, they do command him home,
Deputing Cassio in his government.°
DESDEMONA. By my troth,° I am glad on 't.
OTHELLO. Indeed!
DESDEMONA. My lord?
OTHELLO. I am glad to see you mad.
DESDEMONA. Why, sweet Othello?
OTHELLO. Devil! [*Striking her.*]
DESDEMONA. I have not deserved this.
LODOVICO. My lord, this would not be believed in Venice

---

205. *instrument:* that is, the official letter which he has just received.   219. *atone:* reconcile.   220. *Are . . . wise:* that is, in saying you bear love to Cassio.   223. *in . . . government:* in his place as governor.   224. *troth:* truth.

Though I should swear I saw 't. 'Tis very much.°
Make her amends, she weeps.
OTHELLO.   O devil, devil!   230
　　If that the earth could teem with a woman's tears,
　　Each drop she falls would prove a crocodile.°
　　Out of my sight!
DESDEMONA.   I will not stay to offend you.   [*Going.*]
LODOVICO. Truly, an obedient lady.
　　I do beseech your lordship, call her back.
OTHELLO. Mistress!
DESDEMONA. My lord?
OTHELLO. What would you with her, sir?
LODOVICO.   Who, I, my lord?
OTHELLO. Aye, you did wish that I would make her turn.
　　Sir, she can turn and turn, and yet go on   240
　　And turn again. And she can weep, sir, weep.
　　And she's obedient, as you say, obedient,
　　Very obedient. Proceed you in your tears.
　　Concerning this, sir—oh, well-painted passion! °—
　　I am commanded home. Get you away.
　　I'll send for you anon. Sir, I obey the mandate,
　　And will return to Venice. Hence, avaunt!
                                         [*Exit* DESDEMONA.]
　　Cassio shall have my place. And, sir, tonight,
　　I do entreat that we may sup together.
　　You are welcome, sir, to Cyprus. Goats and monkeys!   [*Exit.*]   250
LODOVICO. Is this the noble Moor whom our full Senate
　　Call all-in-all sufficient? This the nature
　　Whom passion could not shake? Whose solid virtue
　　The shot of accident nor dart of chance
　　Could neither graze nor pierce?
IAGO.   He is much changed.
LODOVICO. Are his wits safe? Is he not light of brain?
IAGO. He's that he is. I may not breathe my censure°
　　What he might be. If what he might he is not,
　　I would to Heaven he were! °
LODOVICO.   What, strike his wife!

229. *'Tis . . . much:* this is too much. 231–32. *If . . . crocodile:* If the earth
could breed from woman's tears, each tear that she lets fall would become a
crocodile. It was believed that the crocodile would cry and sob to attract the
sympathetic passer-by, who was then snapped up. 244. *well-painted passion:*
cleverly imitated emotion; *passion* is any violent emotion. 257. *censure:* opinion,
judgment. 259. *I . . . were:* I wish he were the man he ought to be. Once
more Iago hints that he is holding back some unpleasant fact.

IAGO. Faith, that was not so well, yet would I knew   260
    That stroke would prove the worst!
LODOVICO.   Is it his use? °
    Or did the letters work upon his blood,
    And new-create this fault?
IAGO.   Alas, alas!
    It is not honesty in me to speak
    What I have seen and known. You shall observe him,
    And his own courses° will denote him so
    That I may save my speech. Do but go after,
    And mark how he continues.
LODOVICO. I am sorry that I am deceived in him.

                                          [Exeunt.]

SCENE II. *A room in the castle.*

[*Enter* OTHELLO *and* EMILIA.]
OTHELLO. You have seen nothing, then?
EMILIA. Nor ever heard, nor ever did suspect.
OTHELLO. Yes, you have seen Cassio and she together.
EMILIA. But then I saw no harm, and then I heard
    Each syllable that breath made up between them.
OTHELLO. What, did they never whisper?
EMILIA.   Never, my lord.
OTHELLO. Nor send you out o' the way?
EMILIA. Never.
OTHELLO. To fetch her fan, her gloves, her mask, nor nothing?
EMILIA. Never, my lord.   10
OTHELLO. That's strange.
EMILIA. I durst, my lord, to wager she is honest,
    Lay down my soul at stake.° If you think other,
    Remove your thought, it doth abuse your bosom.
    If any wretch have put this in your head,
    Let Heaven requite it with the serpent's curse! °
    For if she be not honest, chaste, and true,
    There's no man happy, the purest of their wives
    Is foul as slander.
OTHELLO.   Bid her come hither. Go.

                                  [Exit EMILIA.]

---

261. *Is . . . use:* Does he always behave like this?   266. *courses:* ways, behavior.
SCENE ii: 13. *at stake:* as the stake, the bet.   16. *serpent's curse:* that is, the
curse laid on the serpent in the Garden of Eden.

She says enough. Yet she's a simple bawd°   20
That cannot say as much. This is a subtle whore,
A closet° lock and key of villainous secrets.
And yet she'll kneel and pray, I have seen her do 't.
              [*Enter* DESDEMONA *with* EMILIA.]
DESDEMONA. My lord, what is your will?
OTHELLO.   Pray, chuck,° come hither.
DESDEMONA. What is your pleasure?
OTHELLO.   Let me see your eyes.
    Look in my face.
DESDEMONA.   What horrible fancy's this?
OTHELLO [*to* EMILIA]. Some of your function,° mistress.
    Leave procreants alone and shut the door,
    Cough, or cry hem, if anybody come.
    Your mystery,° your mystery. Nay, dispatch.°   30
                  [*Exit* EMILIA.]
DESDEMONA. Upon my knees, what doth your speech import?
    I understand a fury in your words,
    But not the words.
OTHELLO. Why, what art thou?
DESDEMONA. Your wife, my lord, your true and loyal wife.
OTHELLO. Come, swear it, damn thyself,
    Lest, being like one of Heaven,° the devils themselves
    Should fear to seize thee. Therefore be double-damned.
    Swear thou art honest.
DESDEMONA.   Heaven doth truly know it.
OTHELLO. Heaven truly knows that thou art false as Hell.   40
DESDEMONA. To whom, my lord? With whom? How am I false?
OTHELLO. O Desdemona! Away! Away! Away!
DESDEMONA. Alas the heavy day! Why do you weep?
    Am I the motive of these tears, my lord?
    If haply you my father do suspect
    An instrument of this your calling-back,
    Lay not your blame on me. If you have lost him,
    Why, I have lost him too.
OTHELLO.   Had it pleased Heaven
    To try me with affliction, had they rained
    All kinds of sores and shames on my bare head,   50
    Steeped me in poverty to the very lips,

20. *bawd:* keeper of a brothel.   22. *closet:* box in which secret papers are kept.
24. *chuck:* See III.iv.44,n.   27. *Some . . . function:* Get about your business;
that is, prostitution. Othello pretends that Emilia is keeper of a brothel and
Desdemona *one* of the women.   30. *mystery:* profession; *dispatch:* be quick.   37.
being . . . Heaven: because you look like an angel.

Given to captivity me and my utmost hopes,
I should have found in some place of my soul
A drop of patience. But, alas, to make me
A fixèd figure for the time of scorn
To point his slow unmoving finger at! °
Yet could I bear that too, well, very well.
But there where I have garnered up my heart,°
Where either I must live or bear no life,
The fountain from the which my current runs   60
Or else dries up—to be discarded thence!
Or keep it as a cistern for foul toads
To knot and gender° in! Turn thy complexion there,
Patience, thou young and rose-lipped cherubin—
Aye, there, look grim as Hell!
DESDEMONA. I hope my noble lord esteems me honest.
OTHELLO. Oh, aye, as summer flies are in the shambles,°
    That quicken even with blowing.° O thou weed,
    Who art so lovely fair and smell'st so sweet
    That the sense aches at thee, would thou hadst ne'er been born!   70
DESDEMONA. Alas, what ignorant sin have I committed?
OTHELLO. Was this fair paper,° this most goodly book,
    Made to write "whore" upon? What committed!
    Committed! O thou public commoner! °
    I should make very forges of my cheeks°
    That would to cinders burn up modesty
    Did I but speak thy deeds. What committed!
    Heaven stops the nose at it, and the moon winks.
    The bawdy wind, that kisses all it meets,
    Is hushed within the hollow mine° of earth   80
    And will not hear it. What committed!
    Impudent strumpet!
DESDEMONA.   By Heaven, you do me wrong.
OTHELLO. Are not you a strumpet?
DESDEMONA.   No, as I am a Christian
    If to preserve this vessel for my lord

55–56. *At . . . at:* a difficult image, much discussed. . . . Probably it means "a perpetual mark for scorn to point at with motionless finger." *time of scorn:* (perhaps) scorn for all time.   58. *garnered . . . heart:* stored the harvest of my love.   63. *gender:* mate.   67. *shambles:* slaughterhouse.   68. *quicken . . . blowing:* come to life as soon as the eggs are laid.   72. *fair paper:* that is, her white body.   74. *public commoner:* one who offers herself to all comers.   75. *I . . . cheeks:* that is, my cheeks would be as hot as a forge if I told the truth.   80. *hollow mine:* that is, the cave where the winds were supposed to be kept.

From any other foul unlawful touch
Be not to be a strumpet, I am none.
OTHELLO. What, not a whore?
DESDEMONA.   No, as I shall be saved.
OTHELLO. Is 't possible?
DESDEMONA. Oh, Heaven forgive us!
OTHELLO.   I cry you mercy, then.
I took you for that cunning whore of Venice   90
That married with Othello. [*Raising his voice.*] You, mistress,
That have the office opposite to Saint Peter,°
And keep the gate of Hell!
              [*Re-enter* EMILIA.]
                    You, you, aye, you!
We have done our course, there's money for your pains.
I pray you turn the key, and keep our counsel.°   [*Exit.*]
EMILIA. Alas, what does this gentleman conceive? °
How do you, madam? How do you, my good lady?
DESDEMONA. Faith, half-asleep.
EMILIA. Good madam, what's the matter with my lord?
DESDEMONA. With who?   100
EMILIA. Why, with my lord, madam.
DESDEMONA. Who is thy lord?
EMILIA.   He that is yours, sweet lady.
DESDEMONA. I have none. Do not talk to me, Emilia.
I cannot weep, nor answer have I none
But what should go by water.° Prithee tonight
Lay on my bed my wedding sheets. Remember,
And call thy husband hither.
EMILIA.   Here's a change indeed!   [*Exit.*]
DESDEMONA. 'Tis meet I should be used so, very meet.
How have I been behaved that he might stick
The small'st opinion on my least misuse? °   110
          [*Re-enter* EMILIA *with* IAGO.]
IAGO. What is your pleasure, madam? How is 't with you?
DESDEMONA. I cannot tell. Those that do teach young babes
Do it with gentle means and easy tasks.
He might have chid me so, for, in good faith,
I am a child to chiding.
IAGO.   What's the matter, lady?

92. *office . . . Peter:* St. Peter kept the keys to Heaven. 95. *counsel:* that is, secret. 96. *conceive:* imagine. 105. *should . . . water:* be expressed in tears. 109–110. *How . . . misuse:* What have I done that he could find the smallest reason to find fault with my least mistake?

EMILIA. Alas, Iago, my lord hath so bewhored her,
    Thrown such despite and heavy terms upon her,
    As true hearts cannot bear.
DESDEMONA. Am I that name, Iago?
IAGO.   What name, fair lady?
DESDEMONA. Such as she says my lord did say I was.   120
EMILIA. He called her whore. A beggar in his drink
    Could not have laid such terms upon his callet.°
IAGO. Why did he so?
DESDEMONA. I do not know. I am sure I am none such.
IAGO. Do not weep, do not weep. Alas the day!
EMILIA. Hath she forsook so many noble matches,
    Her father and her country and her friends,
    To be called whore? Would it not make one weep?
DESDEMONA. It is my wretched fortune.
IAGO.   Beshrew him for 't!
    How comes this trick upon him?
DESDEMONA.   Nay, Heaven doth know.   130
EMILIA. I will be hanged if some eternal villain,
    Some busy and insinuating rogue,
    Some cogging, cozening° slave, to get some office,
    Have not devised this slander. I'll be hanged else.
IAGO. Fie, there is no such man, it is impossible.
DESDEMONA. If any such there be, Heaven pardon him!
EMILIA. A halter pardon him! And Hell gnaw his bones!
    Why should he call her whore? Who keeps her company?
    What place? What time? What form? What likelihood?
    The Moor's abused by some most villainous knave,   140
    Some base notorious knave, some scurvy fellow.
    O Heaven, that such companions° Thou'dst unfold,°
    And put in every honest hand a whip
    To lash the rascals naked through the world
    Even from the east to the west!
IAGO.   Speak withindoor.°
EMILIA. Oh, fie upon them! Some such squire° he was
    That turned your wit the seamy side without,
    And made you to suspect me with the Moor.
IAGO. You are a fool. Go to.°
DESDEMONA.   O good Iago,

---

122. *laid . . . callet:* used such words about his moll.   133. *cogging, cozening:*
deceiving, cheating.   142. *companions:* low creatures, *unfold:* bring to light.
145. *Speak withindoor:* Don't shout so loud that all the street will hear you.
146. *squire:* fine fellow.   149. *Go to:* an expression of derision.

What shall I do to win my lord again?   150
Good friend, go to him, for, by this light of Heaven,
I know not how I lost him. Here I kneel.
If e'er my will did trespass 'gainst his love
Either in discourse of thought or actual deed,
Or that mine eyes, mine ears, or any sense
Delighted them in any other form,
Or that I do not yet, and ever did,
And ever will, though he do shake me off
To beggarly divorcement, love him dearly,
Comfort forswear° me! Unkindness may do much,   160
And this unkindness may defeat° my life,
But never taint my love. I cannot say "whore,"
It doth abhor me now I speak the word.
To do the act that might the addition° earn
Not the world's mass of vanity° could make me.
IAGO. I pray you be content, 'tis but his humor.
    The business of the state does him offense,
    And he does chide with you.
DESDEMONA. If 'twere no other——
IAGO. 'Tis but so, I warrant.   170
                    [*Trumpets within.*]
    Hark how these instruments summon to supper!
    The messengers of Venice stay the meat.°
    Go in, and weep not, all things shall be well.
                    [*Exeunt* DESDEMONA *and* EMILIA.]
                    [*Enter* RODERIGO.]
    How now, Roderigo!
RODERIGO. I do not find that thou dealest justly with me.
IAGO. What in the contrary?
RODERIGO. Every day thou daffest° me with some device, Iago, and
    rather, as it seems to me now, keepest from me all conveniency°
    than suppliest me with the least advantage of hope. I will indeed
    no longer endure it, nor am I yet persuaded to put up in peace   180
    what already I have foolishly suffered.
IAGO. Will you hear me, Roderigo?
RODERIGO. Faith, I have heard too much, for your words and perform-
    ances are no kin together.
IAGO. You charge me most unjustly.
RODERIGO. With naught but truth. I have wasted myself out of my

160. forswear: repudiate. *161. defeat:* destroy. *164. addition:* title. *165.
vanity:* that is, riches. *172. meat:* serving of supper. *177. thou daffest:* you
put me aside. *178. conveniency:* opportunity.

means. The jewels you have had from me to deliver to Desdemona would half have corrupted a votarist.° You have told me
she hath received them, and returned me expectations and comforts of sudden respect and acquaintance, but I find none.   190
IAGO. Well, go to, very well.
RODERIGO. Very well! Go to! I cannot go to, man, nor 'tis not very
well. By this hand, I say 'tis very scurvy, and begin to find myself
fopped° in it.
IAGO. Very well.
RODERIGO. I tell you 'tis not very well. I will make myself known to
Desdemona. If she will return me my jewels, I will give over my
suit and repent my unlawful solicitation. If not, assure yourself I
will seek satisfaction of you.
IAGO. You have said now.°   200
RODERIGO. Aye, and said nothing but what I protest intendment of
doing.
IAGO. Why, now I see there's mettle° in thee, and even from this
instant do build on thee a better opinion than ever before. Give
me thy hand, Roderigo. Thou hast taken against me a most just
exception,° but yet I protest I have dealt most directly in thy
affair.
RODERIGO. It hath not appeared.
IAGO. I grant indeed it hath not appeared, and your suspicion is not
without wit° and judgment. But, Roderigo, if thou hast that in   210
thee indeed which I have greater reason to believe now than ever
—I mean purpose, courage, and valor—this night show it. If
thou the next night following enjoy not Desdemona, take me
from this world with treachery and devise engines° for my life.
RODERIGO. Well, what is it? Is it within reason and compass?
IAGO. Sir, there is especial commission come from Venice to depute
Cassio in Othello's place.
RODERIGO. Is that true? Why, then Othello and Desdemona return
again to Venice.
IAGO. Oh, no. He goes into Mauritania, and takes away with him the   220
fair Desdemona, unless his abode be lingered here by some acci-
dent. Wherein none can be so determinate° as the removing of
Cassio.
RODERIGO. How do you mean, "removing of" him?

---

188. votarist: one who has taken a vow, here a nun.   *194. fopped:* fooled.   *200.
You . . . now:* or in modern slang, "Oh yeah."   *203. mettle:* metal, good stuff.
206. just exception: reasonable grievance.   *210. wit:* wisdom.   *214. engines:*
instruments of torture.   *222. determinate:* decisive.

IAGO. Why, by making him uncapable° of Othello's place, knocking out his brains.

RODERIGO. And that you would have me to do?

IAGO. Aye, if you dare do yourself a profit and a right. He sups tonight with a harlotry,° and thither will I go to him. He knows not yet of his honorable fortune. If you will watch his going thence, 330 which I will fashion to fall out between twelve and one, you may take him at your pleasure. I will be near to second your attempt, and he shall fall between us. Come, stand not amazed at it, but go along with me. I will show you such a necessity in his death that you shall think yourself bound to put it on him. It is now high suppertime, and the night grows to waste. About it.

RODERIGO. I will hear further reason for this.

IAGO. And you shall be satisfied.

[*Exeunt.*]

SCENE III. *Another room in the castle.*

[*Enter* OTHELLO, LODOVICO, DESDEMONA, EMILIA, *and*
ATTENDANTS.]

LODOVICO. I do beseech you, sir, trouble yourself no further.

OTHELLO. Oh, pardon me, 'twill do me good to walk.

LODOVICO. Madam, good night. I humbly thank your ladyship.

DESDEMONA. Your Honor is most welcome.

OTHELLO.   Will you walk, sir?
Oh—Desdemona——

DESDEMONA. My lord?

OTHELLO. Get you to bed on the instant, I will be returned forthwith. Dismiss your attendant there. Look it be done.

DESDEMONA. I will, my lord.

[*Exeunt* OTHELLO, LODOVICO, *and* ATTENDANTS.]

EMILIA. How goes it now? He looks gentler than he did.   10

DESDEMONA. He says he will return incontinent.°
He hath commanded me to go to bed,
And bade me to dismiss you.

EMILIA.   Dismiss me!

DESDEMONA. It was his bidding, therefore, good Emilia,
Give me my nightly wearing,° and adieu.
We must not now displease him.

EMILIA. I would you had never seen him!

225. *uncapable:* unable to take.   229. *harlotry:* harlot.
SCENE iii: *11. incontinent:* immediately.   *15. nightly wearing:* nightgown.

DESDEMONA. So would not I. My love doth so approve° him
   That even his stubbornness, his checks, his frowns—
   Prithee, unpin me—have grace and favor in them.   20
EMILIA. I have laid those sheets you bade me on the bed.
DESDEMONA. All's one. Good faith, how foolish are our minds!
   If I do die before thee, prithee shroud me
   In one of those same sheets.
EMILIA.   Come, come, you talk.
DESDEMONA. My mother had a maid called Barbara.
   She was in love, and he she loved proved mad
   And did forsake her. She had a song of "willow" °—
   An old thing 'twas, but it expressed her fortune,
   And she died singing it. That song tonight
   Will not go from my mind. I have much to do   30
   But to go hang my head all at one side
   And sing it like poor Barbara. Prithee, dispatch.
EMILIA. Shall I go fetch your nightgown?
DESDEMONA.   No, unpin me here.
   This Lodovico is a proper man.
EMILIA. A very handsome man.
DESDEMONA. He speaks well.
EMILIA. I know a lady in Venice would have walked barefoot to Pales-
   tine for a touch of his nether° lip.
DESDEMONA [singing].
      "The poor soul sat sighing by a sycamore tree,
         Sing all a green willow.   40
      Her hand on her bosom, her head on her knee,
         Sing willow, willow, willow.
      The fresh streams ran by her, and murmured her moans,
         Sing willow, willow, willow.
      Her salt tears fell from her, and softened the stones—"
   Lay by these—[singing]
      "Sing willow, willow, willow."
   Prithee, hie thee, he'll come anon.°—[singing]
      "Sing all a green willow must be my garland.
         Let nobody blame him, his scorn I approve——"   50
   Nay, that's not next. Hark! Who is 't that knocks?
EMILIA. It's the wind.
DESDEMONA [singing].
      "I called my love false love, but what said he then?
         Sing willow, willow, willow.

18. approve: commend.   27. willow: the emblem of the forlorn lover.   38. nether:
lower.   48. anon: soon.

If I court moe° women, you'll couch with moe men."
So get thee gone, good night. Mine eyes do itch.
Doth that bode weeping?
EMILIA.   'Tis neither here nor there.
DESDEMONA. I have heard it said so. Oh, these men, these men!
Dost thou in conscience think—tell me, Emilia—
That there be women do abuse their husbands   60
In such gross kind?
EMILIA.   There be some such, no question.
DESDEMONA. Wouldst thou do such a deed for all the world?
EMILIA. Why, would not you?
DESDEMONA.   No, by this heavenly light!
EMILIA. Nor I neither by this heavenly light. I might do 't as well i'
the dark.
DESDEMONA. Wouldst thou do such a deed for all the world?
EMILIA. The world's a huge thing. It is a great price
For a small vice.
DESDEMONA.   In troth, I think thou wouldst not.
EMILIA. In troth, I think I should, and undo 't when I had done.
Marry, I would not do such a thing for a joint ring,° nor for   70
measures of lawn,° nor for gowns, petticoats, nor caps, nor any
petty exhibition;° but for the whole world—why, who would not
make her husband a cuckold to make him a monarch? I should
venture Purgatory for 't.
DESDEMONA. Beshrew me if I would do such a wrong
For the whole world.
EMILIA. Why, the wrong is but a wrong i' the world, and having the
world for your labor, 'tis a wrong in your own world and you
might quickly make it right.
DESDEMONA. I do not think there is any such woman.   80
EMILIA. Yes, a dozen, and as many to the vantage° as would store° the
world they played for.
But I do think it is their husbands' faults
If wives do fall. Say that they slack their duties
And pour our treasures into foreign laps,
Or else break out in peevish jealousies,
Throwing restraint° upon us, or say they strike us,
Or scant our former having in despite,°

---

55. moe: more. 70. joint ring: ring made in two pieces, a lover's gift. 71. measures of lawn: lengths of finest lawn, or as a modern woman would say, "sheer
nylon." 72. petty exhibition: small allowance of money. 81. as . . . vantage:
and more too; vantage is that added to the exact weight to give generous measure;
store: stock, fill up. 86. Throwing restraint: putting restraints. 87. scant
. . . despite: for spite cut down our allowance.

Why, we have galls,° and though we have some grace,
Yet have we some revenge. Let husbands know
Their wives have sense like them. They see and smell   90
And have their palates both for sweet and sour,
As husbands have. What is it that they do
When they change us for others? Is it sport?
I think it is. And doth affection breed it?
I think it doth. Is 't frailty that thus errs?
It is so too. And have not we affections,
Desires for sport, and frailty, as men have?
Then let them use us well. Else let them know
The ills we do, their ills instruct us so.
DESDEMONA. Good night, good night. Heaven me such uses° send,   100
Not to pick bad from bad, but my bad mend!

                                           [*Exeunt.*]

A C T   V

SCENE I. *Cyprus. A street.*

[*Enter* IAGO *and* RODERIGO.]
IAGO. Here, stand behind this bulk,° straight° will he come.
Wear thy good rapier bare, and put it home.
Quick, quick, fear nothing, I'll be at thy elbow.
It makes us, or it mars us. Think on that,
And fix most firm thy resolution.
RODERIGO. Be near at hand, I may miscarry in 't.
IAGO. Here, at thy hand. Be bold, and take thy stand.   [*Retires.*]
RODERIGO. I have no great devotion to the deed,
And yet he hath given me satisfying reasons.
'Tis but a man gone. Forth, my sword. He dies.   10
IAGO. I have rubbed this young quat° almost to the sense,°
And he grows angry. Now, whether he kill Cassio,
Or Cassio him, or each do kill the other,
Every way makes my gain. Live Roderigo,
He calls me to a restitution large°
Of gold and jewels that I bobbed° from him
As gifts to Desdemona.

88. *galls:* bile, the cause of bitterness.   100. *uses:* practices.
ACT V, SCENE i: *1. bulk:* stall outside a shop; *straight:* straightway.   *11. quat:*
pimple; *to . . . sense:* to the quick, to the raw.   *15. large:* full.   *16. bobbed:*
cheated.

It must not be. If Cassio do remain,
He hath a daily beauty in his life
That makes me ugly,° and besides, the Moor   20
May unfold° me to him. There stand I in much peril.
No, he must die. Be 't so. I hear him coming.
[*Enter* CASSIO.]
RODERIGO. I know his gait, 'tis he. Villain, thou diest!
[*Makes a pass at* CASSIO.]
CASSIO. That thrust had been mine enemy indeed
But that my coat is better than thou know'st.°
I will make proof of thine.
[*Draws, and wounds* RODERIGO.]
RODERIGO.   Oh, I am slain!
[IAGO *from behind wounds* CASSIO *in the leg, and exit.*]
CASSIO. I am maimed for ever. Help, ho! Murder! Murder!   [*Falls.*]
[*Enter* OTHELLO.]
OTHELLO. The voice of Cassio. Iago keeps his word.
RODERIGO. Oh, villain that I am!
OTHELLO.   It is even so.
CASSIO. Oh, help, ho! Light! A surgeon!   30
OTHELLO. 'Tis he. O brave Iago, honest and just,
That hast such noble sense of thy friend's wrong!
Thou teachest me. Minion,° your dear lies dead,
And your unblest fate hies.° Strumpet, I come!
Forth of my heart those charms, thine eyes, are blotted.
Thy bed lust-stained shall with lust's blood be spotted.   [*Exit.*]
[*Enter* LODOVICO *and* GRATIANO.]
CASSIO. What ho! No watch? ° No passage? ° Murder! Murder!
GRATIANO. 'Tis some mischance, the cry is very direful.
CASSIO. Oh, help!
LODOVICO. Hark!   40
RODERIGO. Oh, wretched villain!
LODOVICO. Two or three groan. It is a heavy° night.
These may be counterfeits.° Let's think 't unsafe
To come in to the cry without more help.
RODERIGO. Nobody come? Then shall I bleed to death.
LODOVICO. Hark!
[*Re-enter* IAGO, *with a light.*]

19-20. *He . . . ugly:* by comparison with him I am a poor thing. Iago is conscious of his lack of social graces.   21. *unfold:* expose.   25. *coat . . . know'st:* that is, I wear mail under my coat.   33. *Minion;* darling, in a bad sense.   34. *hies:* comes on quickly.   37. *watch:* citizen police force; *No passage:* "Is nobody passing by?"   42. *heavy:* thick.   43. *counterfeits:* fakes.

GRATIANO. Here's one comes in his shirt, with light and weapons.

IAGO. Who's there? Whose noise is this that cries on° murder?

LODOVICO. We do not know.

IAGO.   Did not you hear a cry?

CASSIO. Here, here! For Heaven's sake, help me!

IAGO.   What's the matter?   50

GRATIANO. This is Othello's Ancient, as I take it.

LODOVICO. The same indeed, a very valiant fellow.

IAGO. What are you here that cry so grievously?

CASSIO. Iago? Oh, I am spoiled, undone by villains!
     Give me some help.

IAGO. Oh me, Lieutenant! What villains have done this?

CASSIO. I think that one of them is hereabout,
     And cannot make away.

IAGO.   Oh, treacherous villains!
     [*To* LODOVICO *and* GRATIANO] What are you there? Come in
     and give some help.

RODERIGO. Oh, help me here!   60

CASSIO. That's one of them.

IAGO. Oh, murderous slave! Oh, villain!   [*Stabs* RODERIGO.]

RODERIGO. Oh, damned Iago! Oh, inhuman dog!

IAGO. Kill men i' the dark! Where be these bloody thieves?
     How silent is this town! Ho! Murder! Murder!
     What may you be? Are you of good or evil?

LODOVICO. As you shall prove us, praise us.

IAGO. Signior Lodovico?

LODOVICO. He, sir.

IAGO. I cry you mercy. Here's Cassio hurt by villains.   70

GRATIANO. Cassio!

IAGO. How is 't, brother?

CASSIO. My leg is cut in two.

IAGO.   Marry, Heaven forbid!
     Light, gentlemen. I'll bind it with my shirt.
                              [*Enter* BIANCA.]

BIANCA. What is the matter, ho? Who is 't that cried?

IAGO. Who is 't that cried!

BIANCA. Oh, my dear Cassio! My sweet Cassio! Oh, Cassio, Cassio,
     Cassio!

IAGO. Oh, notable strumpet! Cassio, may you suspect
     Who they should be that have thus mangled you?

CASSIO. No.   80

GRATIANO. I am sorry to find you thus. I have been to seek you.

47. *cries on:* cries out.

IAGO. Lend me a garter. So. Oh, for a chair,
    To bear him easily hence!
BIANCA. Alas, he faints! Oh, Cassio, Cassio, Cassio!
IAGO. Gentlemen all, I do suspect this trash
    To be a party in this injury.
    Patience awhile, good Cassio. Come, come,
    Lend me a light. Know we this face or no?
    Alas, my friend and my dear countryman
    Roderigo? No—yes, sure. Oh Heaven! Roderigo.   90
GRATIANO. What, of Venice?
IAGO. Even he, sir. Did you know him?
GRATIANO.   Know him! Aye.
IAGO. Signior Gratiano? I cry you gentle pardon.°
    These bloody accidents must excuse my manners,
    That so neglected you.
GRATIANO.   I am glad to see you.
IAGO. How do you, Cassio? Oh, a chair, a chair!
GRATIANO. Roderigo!
IAGO. He, he, 'tis he.
            [*A chair is brought in.*]
        Oh, that's well said, the chair.
    Some good man bear him carefully from hence.
    I'll fetch the General's surgeon. [*To* BIANCA] For you, mistress,   100
    Save you your labor. He that lies slain here, Cassio,
    Was my dear friend. What malice was between you?
CASSIO. None in the world, nor do I know the man.
IAGO [*to* BIANCA]. What, look you pale? Oh, bear him out o' the air.
        [CASSIO *and* RODERIGO *are borne off.*]
    Stay you, good gentlemen. Look you pale, mistress?
    Do you perceive the gastness° of her eye?
    Nay, if you stare, we shall hear more anon.
    Behold her well, I pray you look upon her.
    Do you see, gentlemen? Nay, guiltiness will speak,
    Though tongues were out of use.   110
             [*Enter* EMILIA.]
EMILIA. 'Las, what's the matter? What's the matter, husband?
IAGO. Cassio hath here been set on in the dark
    By Roderigo, and fellows that are 'scaped.
    He's almost slain, and Roderigo dead.
EMILIA. Alas, good gentlemen! Alas, good Cassio!
IAGO. This is the fruit of whoring. Pithee, Emilia,
    Go know of Cassio where he supped tonight.

93. *I . . . pardon:* I beg you kindly pardon me.   106. *gastness:* ghastly look.

What, do you shake at that?
BIANCA. He supped at my house, but I therefore shake not.
IAGO. Oh, did he so? I charge you, go with me.   120
EMILIA. Fie, fie upon thee, strumpet!
BIANCA. I am no strumpet, but of life as honest
    As you that thus abuse me.
EMILIA.   As I! Foh! Fie upon thee!
IAGO. Kind gentlemen, let's go see poor Cassio dressed.°
    Come, mistress, you must tell 's another tale.
    Emilia, run you to the citadel,
    And tell my lord and lady what hath happed!
    Will you go on? I pray. [Aside.] This is the night
    That either makes me or fordoes° me quite.

                                        [Exeunt.]

SCENE II. *A bedchamber in the castle.*
DESDEMONA *in bed asleep, a light burning.*

                    [Enter OTHELLO.]
OTHELLO. It is the cause,° it is the cause, my soul.
    Let me not name it to you, you chaste stars!
    It is the cause. Yet I'll not shed her blood,
    Nor scar that whiter skin of hers than snow
    And smooth as monumental alabaster.°
    Yet she must die, else she'll betray more men.
    Put out the light, and then put out the light.
    If I quench thee, thou flaming minister,°
    I can again thy former light restore,
    Should I repent me. But once put out thy light,   10
    Thou cunning'st° pattern of excelling nature,
    I know not where is that Promethean heat°
    That can thy light relume.° When I have plucked the rose,
    I cannot give it vital growth again,
    It needs must wither. I'll smell it on the tree   [Kissing her].

---

124. *dressed:* that is, his wound dressed. 129. *fordoes:* ruins.
SCENE ii: 1. *It . . . cause:* The meaning of the opening lines of this speech has
been much discussed. The *cause* is Desdemona's supposed faithlessness; Othello,
at this moment, sees himself as embodied vengeance, the venger of man betrayed
by woman. 5. *monumental alabaster:* Alabaster is white translucent stone, much
used for memorial effigies on Elizabethan tombs. 8. *minister:* servant. 11. *cunning'st:* most skillfully made. 12. *Promethean heat:* fire from Heaven. Prometheus
stole fire from Heaven and first gave it to man. 13. *relume:* relight.

Ah, balmy breath, that dost almost persuade
Justice to break her sword! One more, one more.
Be thus when thou art dead, and I will kill thee,
And love thee after. One more, and this the last.
So sweet was ne'er so fatal. I must weep,   20
But they are cruel tears. This sorrow's heavenly,
It strikes where it doth love. She wakes.

DESDEMONA. Who's there? Othello?

OTHELLO   Aye, Desdemona.

DESDEMONA. Will you come to bed, my lord?

OTHELLO. Have you prayed tonight, Desdemona?

DESDEMONA. Aye, my lord.

OTHELLO. If you bethink yourself of any crime
Unreconciled as yet to Heaven and grace,
Solicit for it straight.

DESDEMONA. Alas, my lord, what may you mean by that?   30

OTHELLO. Well, do it, and be brief. I will walk by.
I would not kill thy unpreparèd spirit.
No, Heaven forfend! I would not kill thy soul.°

DESDEMONA. Talk you of killing?

OTHELLO. Aye, I do.

DESDEMONA. Then Heaven have mercy on me!

OTHELLO. Amen, with all my heart!

DESDEMONA. If you say so, I hope you will not kill me.

OTHELLO. Hum!

DESDEMONA. And yet I fear you, for you are fatal° then   40
When your eyes roll so. Why I should fear I know not,
Since guiltiness I know not, but yet I feel I fear.

OTHELLO. Think on thy sins.

DESDEMONA.   They are loves I bear to you.

OTHELLO. Aye, and for that thou diest.

DESDEMONA. That death's unnatural that kills for loving.
Alas, why gnaw you so your nether lip?
Some bloody passion shakes your very frame.
These are portents,° but yet I hope, I hope,
They do not point on me.

OTHELLO.   Peace, and be still!

DESDEMONA. I will so. What's the matter?   50

OTHELLO. That handkerchief which I so loved and gave thee
Thou gavest to Cassio.

27–33. *If . . . soul:* Othello will be a merciful murderer. *forfend:* forbid. 40.
fatal: deadly. *48. portents:* signs foretelling disaster.

DESDEMONA.   No, by my life and soul!
    Send for the man, and ask him.
OTHELLO.   Sweet soul, take heed,
    Take heed of perjury, thou art on thy deathbed.
DESDEMONA. Aye, but not yet to die.
OTHELLO.   Yes, presently.°
    Therefore confess thee freely of thy sin,
    For to deny each article with oath
    Cannot remove nor choke the strong conception°
    That I do groan withal. Thou art to die.
DESDEMONA. Then Lord have mercy on me!
OTHELLO.   I say amen.   60
DESDEMONA. And have you mercy too! I never did
    Offend you in my life, never loved Cassio
    But with such general warranty° of Heaven
    As I might love. I never gave him token.
OTHELLO. By Heaven, I saw my handkerchief in 's hand.
    O perjured woman! Thou dost stone° my heart,
    And makest me call what I intend to do
    A murder, which I thought a sacrifice.
    I saw the handkerchief.
DESDEMONA.   He found it, then,
    I never gave it him. Send for him hither.   70
    Let him confess a truth.
OTHELLO.   He hath confessed.
DESDEMONA. What, my lord?
OTHELLO. That he hath used thee.
DESDEMONA.   How? Unlawfully?
OTHELLO. Aye.
DESDEMONA. He will not say so.
OTHELLO.   No, his mouth is stopped.
    Honest Iago hath ta'en order for 't.
DESDEMONA. Oh, my fear interprets! What, is he dead?
OTHELLO. Had all his hairs been lives, my great revenge
    Had stomach for them all.
DESDEMONA. Alas, he is betrayed, and I undone!   80
OTHELLO. Out, strumpet! Weep'st thou for him to my face?
DESDEMONA. Oh, banish me, my lord, but kill me not!
OTHELLO. Down, strumpet!
DESDEMONA. Kill me tomorrow, let me live tonight!
OTHELLO. Nay, if you strive——

55. *presently*: at once.   58. *conception*: thought.   63. *warranty*: permission.   66.
stone: turn to stone.

DESDEMONA. But half an hour!
OTHELLO.   Being done, there is no pause.
DESDEMONA. But while I say one prayer!
OTHELLO.   It is too late. [*He stifles her.*]
EMILIA [*within*]. My lord, my lord! What ho! My lord, my lord!
OTHELLO. What noise is this? Not dead? Not yet quite dead?
   I that am cruel am yet merciful,   90
   I would not have thee linger in thy pain.
   So, so.
EMILIA [*within*]. What ho! My lord, my lord!
OTHELLO.   Who's there?
EMILIA [*within*]. Oh, good my lord, I would speak a word with you!
OTHELLO. Yes, 'tis Emilia. By and by. She's dead.
   'Tis like she comes to speak of Cassio's death.
   The noise was here. Ha! No more moving?
   Still as the grave. Shall she come in? Were 't good?
   I think she stirs again. No. What's best to do?
   If she come in, she'll sure speak to my wife.   100
   My wife! My wife! What wife? I have no wife.
   Oh, insupportable! Oh, heavy hour!
   Methinks it should be now a huge eclipse
   Of sun and moon, and that the affrighted globe
   Should yawn at alteration.°
EMILIA [*within*].   I do beseech you
   That I may speak with you, O good my lord!
OTHELLO. I had forgot thee. Oh, come in, Emilia.
   Soft, by and by. Let me the curtains° draw.
   Where art thou?   [*Unlocks the door.*]
               [*Enter* EMILIA.]
   What's the matter with thee now?
EMILIA. Oh, my good lord, yonder 's foul murders done!   110
OTHELLO. What, now?
EMILIA. But now, my lord.
OTHELLO. It is the very error° of the moon.
   She comes more nearer earth than she was wont
   And makes men mad.
EMILIA. Cassio, my lord, hath killed a young Venetian
   Called Roderigo.
OTHELLO.   Roderigo killed!
   And Cassio killed!

---

105. yawn at alteration: gape with wonder at some monstrous change.   *108.
curtains:* that is, of the bed.   *113. error:* wandering out of her proper course.

EMILIA.   No, Cassio is not killed.
OTHELLO. Not Cassio killed! Then murder's out of tune,
    And sweet revenge grows harsh.   120
DESDEMONA. Oh, falsely, falsely murdered!
EMILIA.   Alas, what cry is that?
OTHELLO. That! What?
EMILIA. Out and alas! That was my lady's voice.
    Help! Help, ho! Help! O lady, speak again!
    Sweet Desdemona! O sweet mistress, speak!
DESDEMONA. A guiltless death I die.
EMILIA. Oh, who hath done this deed?
DESDEMONA. Nobody, I myself. Farewell.
    Commend me to my kind lord. Oh, farewell!   [*Dies.*]
OTHELLO. Why, how should she be murdered?   130
EMILIA. Alas, who knows?
OTHELLO. You heard her say herself it was not I.
EMILIA. She said so. I must needs report the truth.
OTHELLO. She's like a liar gone to burning Hell.
    'Twas I that killed her.
EMILIA.   Oh, the more angel she,
    And you the blacker devil!
OTHELLO. She turned to folly,° and she was a whore.
EMILIA. Thou dost belie her, and thou art a devil.
OTHELLO. She was false as water.
EMILIA.   Thou art rash as fire to say
    That she was false. Oh, she was heavenly true!   140
OTHELLO. Cassio did top her, ask thy husband else.
    Oh, I were damned beneath all depth in Hell
    But that I did proceed upon just grounds
    To this extremity. Thy husband knew it all.
EMILIA. My husband!
OTHELLO. Thy husband.
EMILIA. That she was false to wedlock?
OTHELLO. Aye, with Cassio. Nay, had she been true,
    If Heaven would make me such another world
    Of one entire and perfect chrysolite,°   150
    I'd not have sold her for it.
EMILIA. My husband!
OTHELLO.   Aye, 'twas he that told me first.
    An honest man he is, and hates the slime
    That sticks on filthy deeds.

---

137. folly: lewdness.   *150. chrysolite:* a semiprecious stone, usually green in color.

EMILIA. My husband!

OTHELLO. What needs this iteration,° woman? I say thy husband.

EMILIA. Oh, mistress, villainy hath made mocks with love!
My husband say that she was false!

OTHELLO. He, woman.
I say thy husband. Dost understand the word?
My friend, thy husband, honest, honest Iago.

EMILIA. If he say so, may his pernicious soul   160
Rot half a grain a day! He lies to the heart.
She was too fond of her most filthy bargain.

OTHELLO. Ha!

EMILIA. Do thy worst.
This deed of thine is no more worthy Heaven
Than thou wast worthy her.

OTHELLO. Peace, you were best.

EMILIA. Thou hast not half that power to do me harm
As I have to be hurt. O gull! ° O dolt! °
As ignorant as dirt! Thou hast done a deed——
I care not for thy sword, I'll make thee known,   170
Though I lost twenty lives. Help! Help, ho! Help!
The Moor hath killed my mistress! Murder! Murder!

[*Enter* MONTANO, GRATIANO, IAGO, *and others.*]

MONTANO. What is the matter? How now, General!

EMILIA. Oh, are you come, Iago? You have done well,
That men must lay their murders on your neck.

GRATIANO. What is the matter?

EMILIA. Disprove this villain, if thou be'st a man.
He says thou told'st him that his wife was false.
I know thou didst not, thou'rt not such a villain.
Speak, for my heart is full.   180

IAGO. I told him what I thought, and told no more
Than what he found himself was apt° and true.

EMILIA. But did you ever tell him she was false?

IAGO. I did.

EMILIA. You told a lie, an odious, damnèd lie,
Upon my soul, a lie, a wicked lie!
She false with Cassio! Did you say with Cassio?

IAGO. With Cassio, mistress. Go to, charm your tongue.°

EMILIA. I will not charm my tongue, I am bound to speak.
My mistress here lies murdered in her bed.   190

ALL. Oh, Heavens forfend!

155. *iteration:* repetition.   168. *gull:* dupe; *dolt:* dull-witted ass.   182. *apt:* likely.
188. *charm . . . tongue:* be silent.

EMILIA. And your reports have set the murder on.

OTHELLO. Nay, stare not, masters. It is true indeed.

GRATIANO. 'Tis a strange truth.

MONTANO. Oh, monstrous act!

EMILIA.   Villainy, villainy, villainy!
    I think upon 't. I think I smell 't. Oh, villainy!
    I thought so then.° I'll kill myself for grief.
    Oh, villainy, villainy!

IAGO. What, are you mad? I charge you, get you home.

EMILIA. Good gentlemen, let me have leave to speak.   200
    'Tis proper I obey him, but not now.
    Perchance, Iago, I will ne'er go home.

OTHELLO. Oh! Oh! Oh!   [Falling on the bed.]

EMILIA.   Nay, lay thee down and roar,
    For thou hast killed the sweetest innocent
    That e'er did lift up eye.

OTHELLO [rising].   Oh, she was foul!
    I scarce did know you, Uncle. There lies your niece,
    Whose breath indeed these hands have newly stopped.
    I know this act shows horrible and grim.

GRATIANO. Poor Desdemona! I am glad thy father's dead.
    Thy match was mortal° to him, and pure grief   210
    Shore his old thread in twain.° Did he live now,
    This sight would make him do a desperate turn—
    Yea, curse his better angel from his side,
    And fall to reprobation.°

OTHELLO. 'Tis pitiful, but yet Iago knows
    That she with Cassio hath the act of shame
    A thousand times committed. Cassio confessed it.
    And she did gratify his amorous works
    With that recognizance° and pledge of love
    Which I first gave her, I saw it in his hand.   220
    It was a handkerchief, an antique token
    My father gave my mother.

EMILIA. Oh, heaven! Oh, heavenly powers!

IAGO. 'Zounds! Hold your peace.

EMILIA.   'Twill out, 'twill out. I peace!
    No, I will speak as liberal as the north.°

197. I . . . then: that is, I suspected this earlier—as for example when Iago took
the handkerchief (see III.iii.320). 210. match . . . mortal: that is, grief at this
marriage killed him. 211. Shore . . . twain: cut his thread of life in two. 214.
reprobation: damnation; that is, by self-murder. 219. recognizance: badge, token.
226. liberal . . . north: as freely as the north wind, which is loud and bitter.

Let Heaven and men and devils, let them all,
All, all, cry shame against me, yet I'll speak.
IAGO. Be wise, and get you home.
EMILIA.   I will not.
                  [IAGO *offers to stab* EMILIA.]
GRATIANO.   Fie!
    Your sword upon a woman!
EMILIA. O thou dull Moor! That handkerchief thou speak'st of   230
    I found by fortune and did give my husband,
    For often with a solemn earnestness,
    More than indeed belonged to such a trifle,
    He begged of me to steal it.
IAGO.   Villainous whore!
EMILIA. She give it Cassio! No, alas, I found it,
    And I did give 't my husband.
IAGO.   Filth, thou liest!
EMILIA. By Heaven, I do not, I do not, gentlemen.
    Oh, murderous coxcomb! ° What should such a fool
    Do with so good a wife?
OTHELLO.   Are there no stones° in Heaven
    But what serve for the thunder? Precious villain!   240
        [*He runs at* IAGO. IAGO, *from behind, stabs* EMILIA, *and exits.*]
GRATIANO. The woman falls. Sure, he hath killed his wife.
EMILIA. Aye, aye. Oh, lay me by my mistress' side.
GRATIANO. He's gone, but his wife's killed.
MONTANO. 'Tis a notorious villain. Take you this weapon,
    Which I have here recovered from the Moor.
    Come, guard the door without, let him not pass,
    But kill him rather. I'll after that same villain,
    For 'tis a damnèd slave.
                  [*Exeunt all but* OTHELLO *and* EMILIA.]
OTHELLO.   I am not valiant neither.
    But every puny whipster° gets my sword.
    But why should honor outlive honesty?   250
    Let it go all.
EMILIA.   What did thy song bode, lady?
    Hark, canst thou hear me? I will play the swan,
    And die in music.° [*Singing*]
                  "Willow, willow, willow."
    Moor, she was chaste. She loved thee, cruel Moor,

---

238. *coxcomb:* conceited fool.   239. *stones:* thunderbolts.   249. *whipster:* whip-persnapper.   252–53. *play . . . music:* that is, I will sing at my death. It was believed that swans sang once only, just before they died.

So come my soul to bliss as I speak true.
So speaking as I think, I die, I die.   [*Dies.*]
OTHELLO. I have another weapon in this chamber.
    It is a sword of Spain,° the ice brook's temper.°—
    Oh, here it is. Uncle, I must come forth.
GRATIANO [*within*]. If thou attempt it, it will cost thee dear.   260
    Thou hast no weapon, and perforce must suffer.
OTHELLO. Look in upon me then, and speak with me,
    Or, naked ° as I am, I will assault thee.
                    [*Re-enter* GRATIANO.]
GRATIANO. What is the matter?
OTHELLO.   Behold, I have a weapon,
    A better never did itself sustain
    Upon a soldier's thigh. I have seen the day
    That with this little arm and this good sword
    I have made my way through more impediments
    Than twenty times your stop. But, oh, vain boast!
    Who can control his fate? 'Tis not so now.   270
    Be not afraid, though you do see me weaponed.
    Here is my journey's end, here is my butt°
    And very sea mark of my utmost sail.°
    Do you go back dismayed? 'Tis a lost fear.
    Man but a rush° against Othello's breast,
    And he retires. Where should Othello go?
    Now, how dost thou look now? O ill-starred wench!
    Pale as thy smock! When we shall meet at compt,°
    This look of thine will hurl my soul from Heaven
    And fiends will snatch at it. Cold, cold, my girl!   280
    Even like thy chastity. Oh, cursèd slave!
    Whip me, ye devils,
    From the possession of this heavenly sight!
    Blow me about in winds! Roast me in sulphur!
    Wash me in steep-down gulfs° of liquid fire!
    O Desdemona! Desdemona! Dead!
    Oh! Oh! Oh!
            [*Enter* LODOVICO, MONTANO, CASSIO *carried in a chair,*
                and OFFICERS *with* IAGO, *prisoner.*]

---

258. *sword of Spain*: Spanish swords and rapiers, from Toledo or Bilbao, were
famous; *ice . . . temper*: hardened in ice-cold water. 263. *naked*: unarmed.
272. *butt*: aim. 273. *And . . . sail*: the mark that I have reached the end of
my voyage; *sea mark*: a conspicuous object by which the mariner checks his
course. 275. *Man . . . rush*: attack with only a reed. 278. *compt*: account;
that is, the Day of Judgment. 285. *steep-down gulfs*: sheer whirlpools.

LODOVICO. Where is this rash and most unfortunate man?

OTHELLO. That's he that was Othello. Here I am.

LODOVICO. Where is that viper? Bring the villain forth.   290

OTHELLO. I look down toward his feet,° but that's a fable.
        If that thou be'st a devil,° I cannot kill thee.   [*Wounds* IAGO.]

LODOVICO. Wrench his sword from him.

IAGO.   I bleed, sir, but not killed.

OTHELLO. I am not sorry neither. I'd have thee live,
        For, in my sense, 'tis happiness to die.

LODOVICO. O thou Othello, that wert once so good,
        Fall'n in the practice° of a damnèd slave,
        What shall be said to thee?

OTHELLO.   Why, anything.
        An honorable murderer, if you will,
        For naught did I in hate, but all in honor.   300

LODOVICO. This wretch hath part confessed his villainy.
        Did you and he consent in Cassio's death?

OTHELLO. Aye.

CASSIO. Dear General, I never gave you cause.

OTHELLO. I do believe it, and I ask your pardon.
        Will you, I pray, demand that demidevil
        Why he hath thus ensnared my soul and body?

IAGO. Demand me nothing. What you know, you know.
        From this time forth I never will speak word.

LODOVICO. What, not to pray?

GRATIANO.   Torments will ope your lips.   310

OTHELLO. Well, thou dost best.

LODOVICO. Sir, you shall understand what hath befall'n,
        Which, as I think, you know not. Here is a letter
        Found in the pocket of the slain Roderigo,
        And here another. The one of them imports
        The death of Cassio to be undertook
        By Roderigo.

OTHELLO. Oh, villain!

CASSIO.   Most heathenish and most gross!

LODOVICO. Now here's another discontented paper,
        Found in his pocket too. And this, it seems,   320
        Roderigo meant to have sent this damnèd villain
        But that, belike, Iago in the interim
        Came in and satisfied him.

---

291. *toward . . . feet:* that is, to see if he has the cloven hoof of a devil. 292.
If . . . devil: if you are an evil spirit and no man. 297. *Fall'n . . . practice:*
destroyed by the plotting.

OTHELLO.   Oh, the pernicious caitiff!
How came you, Cassio, by that handkerchief
That was my wife's?
CASSIO.   I found it in my chamber.
And he himself confessed but even now
That there he dropped it for a special purpose
Which wrought to his desire.
OTHELLO.   O fool! Fool! Fool!
CASSIO. There is besides in Roderigo's letter
How he upbraids Iago, that he made him   330
Brave° me upon the watch, whereon it came
That I was cast.° And even but now he spake
After long seeming dead, Iago hurt him,
Iago set him on.
LODOVICO. You must forsake this room, and go with us.
Your power and your command is taken off,
And Cassio rules in Cyprus. For this slave,   ɪ
If there be any cunning cruelty
That can torment him much and hold him long,°
It shall be his. You shall close prisoner rest   340
Till that the nature of your fault be known
To the Venetian state. Come, bring away.
OTHELLO. Soft you,° a word or two before you go.
I have done the state some service, and they know 't.
No more of that. I pray you, in your letters,
When you shall these unlucky deeds relate,
Speak of me as I am, nothing extenuate,
Nor set down aught in malice. Then must you speak
Of one that loved not wisely but too well,
Of one not easily jealous, but, being wrought,   350
Perplexed in the extreme, of one whose hand,
Like the base Indian, threw a pearl away
Richer than all his tribe—of one whose subdued eyes,
Albeit unusèd to the melting mood,
Drop tears as fast as the Arabian trees
Their medicinal gum. Set you down this,
And say besides that in Aleppo once,
Where a malignant and a turbaned Turk
Beat a Venetian and traduced° the state,
I took by the throat the circumcisèd dog   360
And smote him, thus.   [*Stabs himself.*]

331. *Brave:* dare, insult.   332. *cast:* dismissed.   339. *hold . . . long:* that is, in
dying.   343. *Soft you:* pause awhile.   359. *traduced:* insulted.

LODOVICO. Oh, bloody period!
GRATIANO.   All that's spoke is marred.°
OTHELLO. I kissed thee ere I killed thee. No way but this,
    Killing myself, to die upon a kiss.   [*Falls on the bed, and dies.*]
CASSIO. This did I fear, but thought he had no weapon.
    For he was great of heart.
LODOVICO [*to* IAGO].   O Spartan° dog,
    More fell° than anguish, hunger, or the sea!
    Look on the tragic loading° of this bed,
    This is thy work. The object poisons sight,
    Let it be hid.° Gratiano, keep the house,   370
    And seize upon the fortunes of the Moor,
    For they succeed on you. To you, Lord Governor,
    Remains the censure of this hellish villain,
    The time, the place, the torture.
    Oh, enforce it!
    Myself will straight aboard, and to the state
    This heavy act with heavy heart relate.
                                              [*Exeunt.*]

362. *marred:* spoiled.   366. *Spartan:* that is, hardhearted.   367. *fell:* cruel.   368.
loading: burden—the bodies of Desdemona and Othello.   370. *Let . . . hid:*
At these words the curtains are closed across the inner stage (or chamber, if this
scene was acted aloft), concealing all three bodies.

/

Miguel Cervantes

FROM Don Quixote

TRANSLATION AND NOTES BY JOHN ORMSBY

Miguel Cervantes (1547–1616)

CERVANTES, SON OF AN APOTHECARY-SURGEON, BEGAN HIS career as a soldier. He was seriously wounded while serving as a marine infantryman at the battle of Lepanto in 1571. His tour of duty over, he was attempting to return to Spain in 1575 when he was captured by pirates and sold into slavery in Algiers. There he remained for five years, despite several brave attempts to escape, which earned him the admiration of his captors. Finally his family was able to raise enough money to ransom him. On his return to Spain he took up playwriting with some success, but not enough to make his fortune. His further attempts at a career in government service met with disaster; he was charged with mismanagement of funds and served at least one brief prison sentence. It was only with the publication of Part I of *Don Quixote* in 1605 and its enormous public success that Cervantes' life became bearable again, although he was forced to finish the last fourteen chapters of Part II with furious speed when someone else, capitalizing on *Don Quixote*'s success, published a false second part.

Don Quixote is frequently described as the first novel, although in its own time it was not taken as such. The formal criteria for the genre that Cervantes had invented did not yet exist, and thus the means for adequately judging the book were not available. Even today what its author accomplished is still difficult to judge. At first *Don Quixote* might seem to be only what its author frequently claimed it was—an attack on chivalric romances. (*Amadis of Gaul,* so often referred to in the text, is the major example in the novel of those fantastic tales in which incredible feats of arms are constant occurrences.) Yet the scope of *Don Quixote* is much greater than its obviously limited satirical purpose. At any rate, Cervantes may be said to have transcended his own stated goals in creating a work of fiction that many readers consider to be the highest expression of the very possibilities of fiction itself.

Don Quixote

Part One

Which Treats of the Character
and Pursuits of the Famous Gentleman
Don Quixote of La Mancha.

In a village of La Mancha, the name of which I have no desire to call to mind,[1] there lived not long since one of those gentlemen that keep a lance in the lance-rack, an old buckler, a lean hack, and a greyhound for coursing. An olla[2] of rather more beef than mutton, a salad on most nights, scraps on Saturdays, lentils on Fridays, and a pigeon or so extra on Sundays, made away with three-quarters of his income. The rest of it went in a doublet of fine cloth and velvet breeches and shoes to match for holidays, while on week-days he made a brave figure in his best homespun. He had in his house a housekeeper past forty, a niece under twenty, and a lad for the field and market-place, who used to saddle the hack as well as handle the bill-hook. The age of this gentleman of ours was bordering on fifty, he was of a hardy habit, spare, gaunt-featured, a very early riser and a great sportsman. They will have it his surname was Quixada or Quesada (for here there is some difference of opinion among the authors who write on the subject), although from reasonable conjectures it seems plain that he was called Quixana. This, however, is of but little importance to our tale; it will be enough not to stray a hair's breadth from the truth in the telling of it.

You must know, then, that the above-named gentleman whenever he was at leisure (which was mostly all the year round) gave himself up to reading

---

[1] Argamasilla is the village that Cervantes does not name. Also, it seems likely that Cervantes had a grudge of some kind against the town. [2] The national dish, the *olla,* is a stew with beef, bacon, sausage, chickpeas, and cabbage for its prime constituents, and for ingredients any other meat or vegetable that may be available. There is nothing exceptional in Don Quixote's *olla* being more a beef than a mutton one, for mutton is scarce in Spain, except in the mountain districts.

books of chivalry with such ardor and avidity that he almost entirely neglected the pursuit of his field-sports, and even the management of his property; and to such a pitch did his eagerness and infatuation go that he sold many an acre of tillage-land to buy books of chivalry to read, and brought home as many of them as he could get. But of all there were none he liked so well as those of the famous Feliciano de Silva's composition, for their lucidity of style and complicated conceits were as pearls in his sight, particularly when in his reading he came upon courtships and cartels, where he often found passages like *"the reason of the unreason with which my reason is afflicted so weakens my reason that with reason I murmur at your beauty;"* or again, *"the high heavens, that of your divinity divinely fortify you with the stars, render you deserving of the desert your greatness deserves."* [3] Over conceits of this sort the poor gentleman lost his wits, and used to lie awake striving to understand them and worm the meaning out of them; what Aristotle himself could not have made out or extracted had he come to life again for that special purpose. He was not at all easy about the wounds which Don Belianis[4] gave and took, because it seemed to him that, great as were the surgeons who had cured him, he must have had his face and body covered all over with seams and scars. He commended, however, the author's way of ending his book with the promise of that interminable adventure, and many a time was he tempted to take up his pen and finish it properly as is there proposed, which no doubt he would have done, and made a successful piece of work of it too, had not greater and more absorbing thoughts prevented him.

Many an argument did he have with the curate of his village (a learned man, and a graduate of Siguenza[5]) as to which had been the better knight, Palmerin of England or Amadis of Gaul. Master Nicholas, the village barber, however, used to say that neither of them came up to the Knight of Phœbus, and that if there was any that could compare with *him* it was Don Galaor, the brother of Amadis of Gaul, because he had a spirit that was equal to every occasion, and was no finikin knight, nor lachrymose like his brother, while in the matter of valor he was not a whit behind him. In short, he became so absorbed in his books that he spent his nights from sunset to sun-

---

[3] The first passage quoted is from the *Chronicle of Don Florisel de Niquea,* by Feliciano de Silva, the volumes of which appeared in 1532, 1536, and 1551, and from the tenth and eleventh books of the *Amadis* series. The second is from *Olivante de Laura,* by Torquemada (1564). Clemencha points out that the first passage had been previously picked out as a sample of the absurdity of the school by Diego Hurtado de Mendoza.   [4] *The History of Belianis de Grecia,* by the Licentiate Jerónimo Fernández, 1547. It has been by some included in the *Amadis* series, but it is in reality an independent romance.   [5] Siguenza was one of the *Universidades menores,* the degrees of which were often laughed at by Spanish humorists.

rise, and his days from dawn to dark, poring over them; and what with little sleep and much reading his brains got so dry that he lost his wits. His fancy grew full of what he used to read about in his books, enchantments, quarrels, battles, challenges, wounds, wooings, loves, agonies and all sorts of impossible nonsense; and it so possessed his mind that the whole fabric of invention and fancy he read of was true, that to him no history in the world had more reality in it. He used to say the Cid Ruy Diaz was a very good knight, but that he was not to be compared with the Knight of the Burning Sword who with one back-stroke cut in half two fierce and monstrous giants. He thought more of Bernardo del Carpio because at Roncesvalles he slew Roland in spite of enchantments,[6] availing himself of the artifice of Hercules when he strangled Antæus the son of Terra in his arms. He approved highly of the giant Morgante, because, although of the giant breed which is always arrogant and ill-conditioned, he alone was affable and well-bred. But above all he admired Reinaldos of Montalban, especially when he saw him sallying forth from his castle and robbing every one he met, and when beyond the seas he stole that image of Mahomet which, as his history says, was entirely of gold. And to have a bout of kicking at that traitor of a Ganelon[7] he would have given his housekeeper, and his niece into the bargain.

In short, his wits being quite gone, he hit upon the strangest notion that ever madman in this world hit upon, and that was that he fancied it was right and requisite, as well for the support of his own honor as for the service of his country, that he should make a knight-errant of himself, roaming the world over in full armor and on horseback in quest of adventures, and putting in practice himself all that he had read of as being the usual practices of knights-errant; righting every kind of wrong, and exposing himself to peril and danger from which, in the issue, he was to reap eternal renown and fame. Already the poor man saw himself crowned by the might of his arm Emperor of Trebizond[8] at least; and so, led away by the intense enjoyment he found in these pleasant fancies, he set himself forthwith to put his scheme into execution.

The first thing he did was to clean up some armor that had belonged to his great-grandfather, and had been for ages lying forgotten in a corner eaten with rust and covered with mildew. He scoured and polished it as best he could, but he perceived one great defect in it, that it had no closed helmet, nothing but a simple morion.[9] This deficiency, however, his in-

[6] The Spanish tradition of the battle of Roncesvalles is, of course, at variance with the *Chanson de Roland*, but it is somewhat nearer historical truth, inasmuch as the slaughter of Roland and the rearguard of Charlemagne's army was effected not by Saracens, but by the Basque mountaineers. [7] *Ganelon*, the archtraitor of the Charlemagne legend. [8] like Reinaldos, or Rinaldo, who came to be Emperor of Trebizond. [9] that is, a simple headpiece without either visor or beaver.

genuity supplied, for he contrived a kind of half-helmet of pasteboard which, fitted on to the morion, looked like a whole one. It is true that, in order to see if it was strong and fit to stand a cut, he drew his sword and gave it a couple of slashes, the first of which undid in an instant what had taken him a week to do. The ease with which he had knocked it to pieces disconcerted him somewhat, and to guard against that danger he set to work again, fixing bars of iron on the inside until he was satisfied with its strength; and then, not caring to try any more experiments with it, he passed it and adopted it as a helmet of the most perfect construction.

He next proceeded to inspect his hack, which, with more quartos than a real[10] and more blemishes than the steed of Gonela, that *"tantum pellis et ossa fuit,"* [11] surpassed in his eyes the Bucephalus of Alexander or the Babieca of the Cid. Four days were spent in thinking what name to give him, because (as he said to himself) it was not right that a horse belonging to a knight so famous, and one with such merits of his own, should be without some distinctive name, and he strove to adapt it so as to indicate what he had been before belonging to a knight-errant, and what he then was; for it was only reasonable that, his master taking a new character, he should take a new name, and that it should be a distinguished and full-sounding one, befitting the new order and calling he was about to follow. And so, after having composed, struck out, rejected, added to, unmade, and remade a multitude of names out of his memory and fancy, he decided upon calling him Rocinante, a name, to his thinking, lofty, sonorous, and significant of his condition as a hack before he became what he now was, the first and foremost of all the hacks in the world.[12]

Having got a name for his horse so much to his taste, he was anxious to get one for himself, and he was eight days more pondering over this point, till at last he made up his mind to call himself Don Quixote,[13] whence, as has been already said, the authors of this veracious history have inferred

---

[10] an untranslatable pun on the word *quarto,* which means a sand crack in a horse's hoof, as well as the coin equal to one-eighth of the real. Gonela, or Gonnella, was a jester in the service of Borso, Duke of Ferrara (1450–1470). A book of the jests attributed to him was printed in 1568, the year before Cervantes went to Italy. [11] was so much skin and bone.—Ed. [12] *Rocin* is a horse employed in labor, as distinguished from one kept for pleasure, the chase, or personal use generally; the word therefore may fairly be translated "hack." *Ante* is an old form of *antes =* "before," whether in time or in order. [13] *Quixote*—or, as it is now written, *Quijote*—means the piece of armor that protects the thigh (*cuissau, cuish*). Smollett's "Sir Lancelot Greaves" is a kind of parody on the name. *Quixada* and *Quesada* were both distinguished family names. The Governor of the Goletta, who was one of the passengers on board the unfortunate *Sol* galley, was a Quesada; and the faithful major-domo of Charles V and guardian of Don John of Austria was a Quixada. [*Quixana,* on the other hand, seems to be taken from the Spanish word for "jawbone."]

that his name must have been beyond a doubt Quixada, and not Quesada as others would have it. Recollecting, however, that the valiant Amadis was not content to call himself curtly Amadis and nothing more, but added the name of his kingdom and country to make it famous, and called himself Amadis of Gaul, he, like a good knight, resolved to add on the name of his, and to style himself Don Quixote of La Mancha, whereby, he considered, he described accurately his origin and country, and did honor to it in taking his surname from it.

So then, his armor being furbished, his morion turned into a helmet, his hack christened, and he himself confirmed, he came to the conclusion that nothing more was needed now but to look out for a lady to be in love with; for a knight-errant without love was like a tree without leaves or fruit, or a body without a soul. As he said to himself, "If, for my sins, or by my good fortune, I come across some giant hereabouts, a common occurrence with knights-errant, and overthrow him in one onslaught, or cleave him asunder to the waist, or, in short, vanquish and subdue him, will it not be well to have some one I may send him to as a present, that he may come in and fall on his knees before my sweet lady, and in a humble, submissive voice say, 'I am the giant Caraculiambro, lord of the island of Malindrania, vanquished in single combat by the never sufficiently extolled knight Don Quixote of La Mancha, who has commanded me to present myself before your Grace, that your Highness dispose of me at your pleasure?'" Oh, how our good gentleman enjoyed the delivery of this speech, especially when he had thought of some one to call his Lady! There was, so the story goes, in a village near his own a very good-looking farm girl with whom he had been at one time in love, though, so far as is known, she never knew it nor gave a thought to the matter. Her name was Aldonza Lorenzo, and upon her he thought fit to confer the title of Lady of his Thoughts; and after some search for a name which should not be out of harmony with her own, and should suggest and indicate that of a princess and great lady, he decided upon calling here Dulcinea del Toboso—she being of El Toboso—a name, to his mind, musical, uncommon, and significant, like all those he had already bestowed upon himself and the things belonging to him.

CHAPTER II

Which Treats of the
First Sally the Ingenious Don Quixote
Made from Home.

These preliminaries settled, he did not care to put off any longer the execution of his design, urged on to it by the thought of all the world was losing by his delay, seeing what wrongs he intended to right, grievances to redress, injustices to repair, abuses to remove, and duties to discharge. So, without giving notice of his intention to any one, and without anybody seeing him, one morning before the dawning of the day (which was one of the hottest of the month of July) he donned his suit of armor, mounted Rocinante with his patched-up helmet on, braced his buckler, took his lance, and by the back door of the yard sallied forth upon the plain in the highest contentment and satisfaction at seeing with what ease he had made a beginning with his grand purpose. But scarcely did he find himself upon the open plain, when a terrible thought struck him, one all but enough to make him abandon the enterprise at the very outset. It occurred to him that he had not been dubbed a knight, and that according to the law of chivalry he neither could nor ought to bear arms against any knight; and that even if he had been, still he ought, as a novice knight, to wear white armor,[14] without a device upon the shield until by his prowess he had earned one. These reflections made him waver in his purpose, but his craze being stronger than any reasoning he made up his mind to have himself dubbed a knight by the first one he came across, following the example of others in the same case, as he had read in the books that brought him to this pass. As for white armor, he resolved, on the first opportunity, to scour his until it was whiter than an ermine; and so comforting himself he pursued his way, taking that which his horse chose, for in this he believed lay the essence of adventures.

Thus setting out, our new-pledged adventurer paced along, talking to himself and saying, "Who knows but that in time to come, when the veracious history of my famous deeds is made known, the sage who writes it, when he has to set forth my first sally in the early morning, will do it after this fashion? 'Scarce had the rubicund Apollo spread o'er the face of the broad spacious earth the golden threads of his bright hair, scarce had the little birds of painted plumage attuned their notes to hail with dulcet and mellifluous harmony the coming of the rosy Dawn, that, deserting the soft couch of her jealous spouse, was appearing to mortals at the gates and balconies of the Manchegan horizon, when the renowned knight Don

[14] properly, *blank armor,* but Don Quixote takes the word in its common sense of *white.*

Quixote of La Mancha, quitting the lazy down, mounted his celebrated steed Rocinante and began to traverse the ancient and famous Campo de Montiel;'" which in fact he was actually traversing.[15] "Happy the age, happy the time," he continued, "in which shall be made known my deeds of fame, worthy to be moulded in brass, carved in marble, limned in pictures, for a memorial forever. And thou, O sage magician,[16] whoever thou art, to whom it shall fall to be the chronicler of this wondrous history, forget not, I entreat thee, my good Rocinante, the constant companion of my ways and wanderings." Presently he broke out again, as if he were love-stricken in earnest, "O Princess Dulcinea, lady of this captive heart, a grievous wrong hast thou done me to drive me forth with scorn, and with inexorable obduracy banish me from the presence of thy beauty. O lady, deign to hold in remembrance this heart, thy vassal, that thus in anguish pines for love of thee."

So he went on stringing together these and other absurdities, all in the style of those his books had taught him, imitating their language as well as he could; and all the while he rode so slowly and the sun mounted so rapidly and with such fervor that it was enough to melt his brains if he had any. Nearly all day he travelled without anything remarkable happening to him, at which he was in despair, for he was anxious to encounter some one at once upon whom to try the might of his strong arm.

Writers there are who say the first adventure he met with was that of Puerto Lápice; others say it was that of the windmills; but what I have ascertained on this point, and what I have found written in the annals of La Mancha, is that he was on the road all day, and towards nightfall his hack and he found themselves dead tired and hungry, when, looking all around to see if he could discover any castle or shepherd's shanty where he might refresh himself and relieve his sore wants, he perceived not far out of his road an inn, which was welcome as a star guiding him to the portals, if not the palaces, of his redemption; and quickening his pace he reached it just as night was setting in. At the door were standing two young women, girls of the district as they call them, on their way to Seville with some carriers who had chanced to halt that night at the inn; and as, happen what might to our adventurer, everything he saw or imagined seemed to him to be and to happen after the fashion of what he had read of, the moment he saw the inn he pictured it to himself as a castle with its four turrets and pinnacles of shining silver, not forgetting the drawbridge and moat and

---

[15] The Campo de Montiel was "famous" as being the scene of the battle, in 1369, in which Pedro the Cruel was defeated by his brother Henry of Trastamara supported by Du Guesclin. The actual battlefield, however, lies some considerable distance to the south of Argamasilla. . . . [16] In the later romances of chivalry, a sage or a magician or some such personage was frequently introduced as the original source of the history.

all the belongings usually ascribed to castles of the sort. To this inn, which to him seemed a castle, he advanced, and at a short distance from it he checked Rocinante, hoping that some dwarf would show himself upon the battlements, and by sound of trumpet give notice that a knight was approaching the castle. But seeing that they were slow about it, and that Rocinante was in a hurry to reach the stable, he made for the inn door, and perceived the two gay damsels who were standing there, and who seemed to him to be two fair maidens or lovely ladies taking their ease at the castle gate.

At this moment it so happened that a swineherd who was going through the stubbles collecting a drove of pigs (for, without any apology, that is what they are called) gave a blast of his horn to bring them together, and forthwith it seemed to Don Quixote to be what he was expecting, the signal of some dwarf announcing his arrival; and so with prodigious satisfaction he rode up to the inn and to the ladies, who, seeing a man of this sort approaching in full armor and with lance and buckler, were turning in dismay into the inn, when Don Quixote, guessing their fear by their flight, raising his pasteboard visor, disclosed his dry, dusty visage,[17] and with courteous bearing and gentle voice addressed them, "Your ladyships need not fly or fear any rudeness, for that it belongs not to the order of knighthood which I profess to offer to any one, much less to high-born maidens as your appearance proclaims you to be." The girls were looking at him and straining their eyes to make out the features which the clumsy visor obscured, but when they heard themselves called maidens, a thing so much out of their line, they could not restrain their laughter, which made Don Quixote wax indignant, and say, "Modesty becomes the fair, and moreover laughter that has little cause is great silliness; this, however, I say not to pain or anger you, for my desire is none other than to serve you."

The incomprehensible language and the unpromising looks of our cavalier only increased the ladies' laughter, and that increased his irritation, and matters might have gone farther if at that moment the landlord had not come out, who, being a very fat man, was a very peaceful one. He, seeing this grotesque figure clad in armor that did not match any more than his saddle, bridle, lance, buckler, or corselet, was not at all indisposed to join the damsels in their manifestations of amusement; but, in truth, standing in awe of such a complicated armament, he thought it best to speak him fairly, so he said, "Señor Caballero, if your worship wants lodging, bating[18]

---

[17] The commentators are somewhat exercised by the contradiction here. If Don Quixote raised his visor and disclosed his visage, how was it that the girls were unable "to make out the features which the clumsy visor obscured"? Cervantes probably was thinking of the makeshift pasteboard visor (*mala visera*, as he calls it), which could not be put up completely, and so kept the face behind it in the shade. . . .   [18] excepting—Ed.

the bed (for there is not one in the inn) there is plenty of everything else here." Don Quixote, observing the respectful bearing of the Alcaide of the fortress (for so innkeeper and inn seemed in his eyes), made answer, "Sir Castellan, for me anything will suffice, for

> My armor is my only wear,
> My only rest the fray."

The host fancied he called him Castellan because he took him for a "worthy of Castile,"[19] though he was in fact an Andalusian, and one from the Strand of San Lucar, as crafty a thief as Cacus[20] and as full of tricks as a student or a page. "In that case," said he,

> "Your bed is on the flinty rock,
> Your sleep to watch alway;[21]

and if so, you many dismount and safely reckon upon my quantity of sleeplessness under this roof for a twelvemonth, not to say for a single night." So saying, he advanced to hold the stirrup for Don Quixote, who got down with great difficulty and exertion (for he had not broken his fast all day), and then charged the host to take great care of his horse as he was the best bit of flesh that ever ate bread in this world. The landlord eyed him over, but did not find him as good as Don Quixote said, nor even half as good, and putting him up in the stable, he returned to see what might be wanted by his guest, whom the damsels, who had by this time made their peace with him, were now relieving of his armor. They had taken off his breastplate and backpiece, but they neither knew nor saw how to open his gorget or remove his make-shift helmet, for he had fastened it with green ribbons, which, as there was no untying the knots, required to be cut. This, however, he would not by any means consent to, so he remained all the

---

[19] *Sano de Castilla*—a slang phrase from the Germania dialect for a thief in disguise. . . . "Castellano" and "alcaide" both mean governor of a castle or fortress, but the former means also a Castilian. [20] in Greek mythology, the thieving centaur—Ed. [21] The lines quoted by Don Quixote and the host are, in the original:

> Mis arreos son las armas,
> Mi descanso el pelear,
> Mi cama, las duras peñas,
> Mi dormir, siempre velar.

They occur first in the old, probably fourteenth century, ballad of *Moriana en un Castillo,* and were afterwards adopted as the beginning of a serenade. In England it would be a daring improbability to represent the landlord of a roadside alehouse capping verses with his guest out of *Chevy Chase* or *Sir Andrew Barton,* but in Spain familiarity with the old national ballad poetry and proverbs is an accomplishment that may, even to this day, be met in quarters as unpromising.

evening with his helmet on, the drollest and oddest figure that can be imagined; and while they were removing his armor, taking the baggages who were about it for ladies of high degree belonging to the castle, he said to them with great sprightliness:

> "Oh, never, surely, was there knight
> So served by hand of dame,
> As served was he, Don Quixote hight,
> When from his town he came;
> With maidens waiting on himself,
> Princesses on his back[22]—

—or Rocinante, for that, ladies mine, is my horse's name, and Don Quixote of La Mancha is my own; for though I had no intention of declaring myself until my achievements in your service and honor had made me known, the necessity of adapting that old ballad of Lancelot to the present occasion has given you the knowledge of my name altogether prematurely. A time, however, will come for your ladyships to command and me to obey, and then the might of my arm will show my desire to serve you."

The girls, who were not used to hearing rhetoric of this sort, had nothing to say in reply: they only asked him if he wanted anything to eat. "I would gladly eat a bit of something," said Don Quixote, "for I feel it would come very seasonably." The day happened to be a Friday, and in the whole inn there was nothing but some pieces of the fish they call in Castile "abadejo," in Andalusia "bacallao," and in some places "curadillo," and in others "troutlet;" so they asked him if he thought he could eat troutlet, for there was no other fish to give him. "If there be troutlets enough," said Don Quixote, "they will be the same thing as a trout; for it is all one to me whether I am given eight reals in small change or a piece of eight; moreover, it may be that these troutlets are like veal, which is better than beef, or kid, which is better than goat. But whatever it be let it come quickly, for the burden and pressure of arms cannot be borne without support to the inside." They laid a table for him at the door of the inn for the sake of the air, and the host brought him a portion of ill-soaked and worse cooked stockfish, and a piece of bread as black and mouldy as his own armor; but a laughable sight it was to see him eating, for having his helmet on and the beaver up,[23] he could not with his own hands put any-

---

[22] a parody of the opening lines of the ballad of *Lancelot of the Lake*. Their chief attraction for Cervantes was, no doubt, the occurrence of *rocino* (*rocín*) in the last line.   [23] The original has, *la visera alzada,* "the visor up," in which case Don Quixote would have found no difficulty in feeding himself. . . . [But] *Babera* "beaver" . . . removes the difficulty and is consistent with what follows; when the landlord "poured wine into him" it must have been *over* the beaver, not *under* the visor.

thing into his mouth unless some one else placed it there, and this service one of the ladies rendered him. But to give him anything to drink was impossible, or would have been so had not the landlord bored a reed, and putting one end in his mouth poured the wine into him through the other; all which he bore with patience rather than sever the ribbons of his helmet.

While this was going on there came up to the inn a pig-gelder, who, as he approached, sounded his reed pipe four or five times, and thereby completely convinced Don Quixote that he was in some famous castle, and that they were regaling him with music, and that the stockfish was trout, the bread the whitest, the wenches ladies, and the landlord the castellan of the castle; and consequently he held that his enterprise and sally had been to some purpose. But it still distressed him to think he had not been dubbed a knight, for it was plain to him he could not lawfully engage in any adventure without receiving the order of knighthood.

CHAPTER III

Wherein Is Related the Droll Way
in Which Don Quixote
Had Himself Dubbed a Knight.

Harassed by this reflection, he made haste with his scanty pothouse supper,[24] and having finished it called the landlord, and shutting himself into the stable with him, fell on his knees before him, saying, "From this spot I rise not, valiant knight, until your courtesy grants me the boon I seek, one that will redound to your praise and the benefit of the human race." The landlord, seeing his guest at his feet and hearing a speech of this kind, stood staring at him in bewilderment, not knowing what to do or say, and entreating him to rise, but all to no purpose until he had agreed to grant the boon demanded of him. "I looked for no less, my lord, from your High Magnificence," replied Don Quixote, "and I have to tell you that the boon I have asked and your liberality has granted is that you shall dub me knight to-morrow morning, and that to-night I shall watch my arms in the chapel of this your castle; thus to-morrow, as I have said, will be accomplished what I so much desire, enabling me lawfully to roam through all the four quarters of the world seeking adventures on behalf of those in distress, as is the duty of chivalry and of knights-errant like myself, whose ambition is directed to such deeds."

The landlord, who, as has been mentioned, was something of a wag,

---

[24] "pothouse"—*venteril*, i.e., such as only a *venta* could produce.

and had already some suspicion of his guest's want of wits, was quite convinced of it on hearing talk of this kind from him, and to make sport for
the.night he determined to fall in with his humor. So he told him he was
quite right in pursuing the object he had in view, and that such a motive
was natural and becoming in cavaliers as distinguished as he seemed and his
gallant bearing showed him to be; and that he himself in his younger days
had followed the same honorable calling, roaming in quest of adventures in
various parts of the world, among others the Curing-grounds of Malaga, the
Isles of Riaran, the Precinct of Seville, the Little Market of Segovia, the
Olivera of Valencia, the Rondilla of Granada, the Strand of San Lucar,
the Colt of Cordova, the Taverns of Toledo,[25] and divers other quarters,
where he had proved the nimbleness of his feet and the lightness of his
fingers doing many wrongs, cheating many widows, ruining maids and
swindling minors, and in short, bringing himself under the notice of almost
every tribunal and court of justice in Spain; until at last he had retired to
this castle of his, where he was living upon his property and upon that of
others; and where he received all knights-errant, of whatever rank or condition they might be, all for the great love he bore them and that they might
share their substance with him in return for his benevolence. He told him,
moreover, that in this castle of his there was no chapel in which he could
watch his armor, as it had been pulled down in order to be rebuilt, but that
in a case of necessity it might, he knew, be watched anywhere, and he might
watch it that night in a courtyard of the castle, and in the morning, God
willing, the requisite ceremonies might be performed so as to have him
dubbed a knight, and so thoroughly dubbed that nobody could be more so.
He asked if he had any money with him, to which Don Quixote replied that
he had not a farthing, as in the histories of knights-errant he had never read
of any of them carrying any. On this point the landlord told him he was
mistaken; for, though not recorded in the histories, because in the author's
opinion there was no need to mention anything so obvious and necessary as
money and clean shirts, it was not to be supposed therefore that they did not
carry them, and he might regard it as certain and established that all
knights-errant (about whom there were so many full and impeachable
books) carried well-furnished purses in case of emergency, and likewise carried shirts and a little box of ointment to cure the wounds they received.
For in those plains and deserts where they engaged in combat and came out
wounded, it was not always that there was some one to cure them, unless indeed they had for a friend some sage magician to succor them at once by
fetching through the air upon a cloud some damsel or dwarf with a vial of
water of such virtue that by tasting one drop of it they were cured of their

[25] The localities here mentioned were, and some of them still are, haunts of the
rogue and vagabond, or what would be called in Spain the *pícaro* class. . . .

hurts and wounds in an instant and left as sound as if they had not received any damage whatever. But in case this should not occur, the knights of old took care to see that their squires were provided with money and other requisites, such as lint and ointments for healing purposes; and when it happened that knights had no squires (which was rarely and seldom the case) they themselves carried everything in cunning saddle-bags that were hardly seen on the horse's croup, as if it were something else of more importance, because, unless for some such reason, carrying saddle-bags was not very favorably regarded among knights-errant. He therefore advised him (and, as his godson so soon to be, he might even command him) never from that time forth to travel without money and the usual requirements, and he would find the advantage of them when he least expected it.

Don Quixote promised to follow his advice scrupulously, and it was arranged forthwith that he should watch his armor in a large yard at one side of the inn; so, collecting it all together, Don Quixote placed it on a trough that stood by the side of a well, and bracing his buckler on his arm he grasped his lance and began with a stately air to march up and down in front of the trough, and as he began his march night began to fall.

The landlord told all the people who were in the inn about the craze of his guest, the watching of the armor, and the dubbing ceremony he contemplated. Full of wonder at so strange a form of madness, they flocked to see it from a distance, and observed with what composure he sometimes paced up and down, or sometimes, leaning on his lance, gazed on his armor without taking his eyes off it for ever so long; and as the night closed in with a light from the moon so brilliant that it might vie with his that lent it, everything the novice knight did was plainly seen by all.

Meanwhile one of the carriers who were in the inn thought fit to water his team, and it was necessary to remove Don Quixote's armor as it lay on the trough; but he seeing the other approach hailed him in a loud voice, "O thou, whoever thou art, rash knight that comest to lay hands on the armor of the most valorous errant that ever girt on sword, have a care what thou dost; touch it not unless thou wouldst lay down thy life as the penalty of thy rashness." The carrier gave no heed to these words (and he would have done better to heed them if he had been heedful of his health), but seizing it by the straps flung the armor some distance from him. Seeing this, Don Quixote raised his eyes to heaven, and fixing his thoughts, apparently, upon his lady Dulcinea, exclaimed, "Aid me, lady mine, in this the first encounter that presents itself to this breast which thou holdest in subjection; let not thy favor and protection fail me in this first jeopardy;" and, with these words and others to the same purpose, dropping his buckler he lifted his lance with both hands and with it smote such a blow on the carrier's head that he stretched him on the ground so stunned that had he followed it up with a second there would have been no need of a surgeon to cure him. This done, he picked up his armor and returned to his beat with the same serenity as before.

Shortly after this, another, not knowing what had happened (for the carrier still lay senseless), came with the same object of giving water to his mules, and was proceeding to remove the armor in order to clear the trough, when Don Quixote, without uttering a word or imploring aid from any one, once more dropped his buckler and once more lifted his lance, and without actually breaking the second carrier's head into pieces, made more than three of it, for he laid it open in four.[26] At the noise all the people of the inn ran to the spot, and among them the landlord. Seeing this, Don Quixote braced his buckler on his arm, and with his hand on his sword exclaimed, "O Lady of Beauty, strength and support of my faint heart, it is time for thee to turn the eyes of thy greatness on this thy captive knight on the brink of so mighty an adventure." By this he felt himself so inspirited that he would not have flinched if all the carriers in the world had assailed him. The comrades of the wounded perceiving the plight they were in began from a distance to shower stones on Don Quixote, who screened himself as best he could with his buckler, not daring to quit the trough and leave his armor unprotected. The landlord shouted to them to leave him alone, for he had already told them that he was mad, and as a madman he would not be accountable even if he killed them all. Still louder shouted Don Quixote, calling them knaves and traitors, and the lord of the castle, who allowed knights-errant to be treated in this fashion, a villain and a low-born knight whom, had he received the order of knighthood, he would call to account for his treachery. "But of you," he cried, "base and vile rabble, I make no account; fling, strike, come on, do all ye can against me, ye shall see what the reward of your folly and insolence will be." This he uttered with so much spirit and boldness that he filled his assailants with a terrible fear, and as much for this reason as at the persuasion of the landlord they left off stoning him, and he allowed them to carry off the wounded, and with the same calmness and composure as before resumed the watch over his armor.

But these freaks of his guest were not much to the liking of the landlord, so he determined to cut matters short and confer upon him at once the unlucky order of knighthood before any further misadventure could occur; so, going up to him, he apologized for the rudeness which, without his knowledge, had been offered to him by these low people, who, however, had been well punished for their audacity. As he had already told him, he said, there was no chapel in the castle, nor was it needed for what remained to be done, for, as he understood the ceremonial of the order, the whole point of being dubbed a knight lay in the accolade and in the slap on the

---

[26] that is, inflicting two cuts that formed a cross.

shoulder, and that could be administered in the middle of a field; and that he had now done all that was needful as to watching the armor, for all requirements were satisfied by a watch of two hours only, while he had been more than four about it. Don Quixote believed it all, and told him he stood there ready to obey him, and to make an end of it with as much despatch as possible; for, if he were again attacked, and felt himself to be a dubbed knight, he would not, he thought, leave a soul alive in the castle, except such as out of respect he might spare at his bidding.

Thus warned and menaced, the castellan forthwith brought out a book in which he used to enter the straw and barley he served out to the carriers, and, with a lad carrying a candle-end, and the two damsels already mentioned, he returned to where Don Quixote stood, and bade him kneel down. Then, reading from his account-book as if he were repeating some devout prayer, in the middle of his delivery he raised his hand and gave him a sturdy blow on the neck, and then, with his own sword, a smart slap on the shoulder, all the while muttering between his teeth as if he were saying his prayers. Having done this, he directed one of the ladies to gird on his sword, which she did with great self-possession and gravity, and not a little was required to prevent a burst of laughter at each stage of the ceremony; but what they had already seen of the novice knight's prowess kept their laughter within bounds. On girding him with the sword the worthy lady said to him, "May God make your worship a very fortunate knight, and grant you success in battle." Don Quixote asked her name in order that he might from that time forward know to whom he was beholden for the favor he had received, as he meant to confer upon her some portion of the honor he acquired by the might of his arm. She answered with great humility that she was called La Tolosa, and that she was a daughter of a cobbler of Toledo who lived in the stalls of Sanchobienaya,[27] and that wherever she might be she would serve and esteem him as her lord. Don Quixote said in reply that she would do him a favor if thenceforward she assumed the "Don" and called herself Doña Tolosa. She promised she would, and then the other buckled on his spur, and with her followed almost the same conversation as with lady of the sword. He asked her name, and she said it was La Molinera,[28] and that she was the daughter of a respectable miller of Antequera; and of her likewise Don Quixote requested that she would adopt the "Don" and call herself Doña Molinera, making offers to her of further services and favors.

Having thus, with hot haste and speed, brought to a conclusion these never-till-now-seen ceremonies, Don Quixote was on thorns until he saw himself on horseback sallying forth in quest of adventures; and saddling Rocinante at once he mounted, and embracing his host, as he returned

[27] an old *plaza* in Toledo. . . .   [28] that is, the Milleress.

thanks for his kindness in knighting him, he addressed him in language so extraordinary that it is impossible to convey an idea of it or report it. The landlord, to get him out of the inn, replied with no less rhetoric though with shorter words, and without calling upon him to pay the reckoning, let him go with a Godspeed.

CHAPTER IV

Of What Happened to Our Knight
When He Left the Inn.

Day was dawning when Don Quixote quitted the inn, so happy, so gay, so exhilarated at finding himself dubbed a knight, that his joy was like to burst his horse-girths. However, recalling the advice of his host as to the requisites he ought to carry with him, especially that referring to money and shirts, he determined to go home and provide himself with all, and also with a squire, for he reckoned upon securing a farm-laborer,[29] a neighbor of his, a poor man with a family, but very well qualified for the office of squire to a knight. With this object he turned his horse's head towards his village, and Rocinante, thus reminded of his old quarters, stepped out so briskly that he hardly seemed to tread the earth.

He had not gone far, when out of a thicket on his right there seemed to come feeble cries as of some one in distress, and the instant he heard them he exclaimed, "Thanks be to Heaven for the favor it accords me, that it so soon offers me an opportunity of fulfilling the obligation I have undertaken, and gathering the fruit of my ambition. These cries, no doubt, come from some man or woman in want of help, and needing my aid and protection;" and wheeling, he turned Rocinante in the direction whence the cries seemed to proceed. He had gone but a few paces into the wood, when he saw a mare tied to an oak, and tied to another, and stripped from the waist upward, a youth of about fifteen years of age, from whom the cries came. Nor were they without cause, for a lusty farmer was flogging him with a belt and following up every blow with scoldings and commands, repeating, "Your mouth shut and your eyes open!" while the youth made answer, "I won't do it again, master mine; by God's passion I won't do it again, and I'll take more care of the flock another time."

Seeing what was going on, Don Quixote said in an angry voice, "Dis-

[29] *Labrador,* the word used here to describe the status of Sancho means, generally, a tiller of the soil and includes farmers employing laborers, like Juan Haldudo the Rich, who is so described later on, as well as those who tilled their land themselves or worked for others. Sancho was one of the latter class, as appears from a remark of his own in Part Two.

courteous knight, it ill becomes you to assail one who cannot defend himself; mount your steed and take your lance" (for there was a lance leaning against the oak to which the mare was tied), "and I will make you know that you are behaving as a coward." The farmer, seeing before him this figure in full armor brandishing a lance over his head, gave himself up for dead, and made answer meekly, "Sir Knight, this youth that I am chastising is my servant, employed by me to watch a flock of sheep that I have hard by, and he is so careless that I lose one every day, and when I punish him for his carelessness and knavery he says I do it out of niggardliness, to escape paying him the wages I owe him, and before God, and on my soul, he lies."

"Lies before me, base clown!" said Don Quixote. "By the sun that shines on us I have a mind to run you through with this lance. Pay him at once without another word; if not, by the God that rules us I will make an end of you, and annihilate you on the spot; release him instantly."

The farmer hung his head, and without a word untied his servant, of whom Don Quixote asked how much his master owed him.

He replied, nine months at seven reals a month. Don Quixote added it up, found that it came to sixty-three reals, and told the farmer to pay it down immediately, if he did not want to die for it.

The trembling clown replied that as he lived and by the oath he had sworn (though he had not sworn any) it was not so much; for there were to be taken into account and deducted three pairs of shoes he had given him, and a real for two blood-lettings when he was sick.

"All that is very well," said Don Quixote; "but let the shoes and the blood-lettings stand as a set-off against the blows you have given him without any cause; for if he spoiled the leather of the shoes you paid for, you have damaged that of his body, and if the barber took blood from him when he was sick[30] you have drawn it when he was sound; so on that score he owes you nothing."

"The difficulty is, Sir Knight, that I have no money here; let Andres come home with me, and I will pay him all, real by real."

"I go with him!" said the youth. "Nay, God forbid! no, señor, not for the world; for once alone with me, he would flay me like a Saint Bartholomew."

"He will do nothing of the kind," said Don Quixote; "I have only to command, and he will obey me; and as he has sworn to me by the order of knighthood which he has received, I leave him free, and I guarantee the payment."

"Consider what you are saying, señor," said the youth; "this master of mine is not a knight, nor has he received any order of knighthood; for he is Juan Haldudo the Rich, of Quintanar."

[30] Barbers performed many of the functions of doctors, especially that of letting blood—Ed.

"That matters little," replied Don Quixote; "there may be Haldudos[31] knights; moreover, every one is the son of his works."

"That is true," said Andres; "but this master of mine—of what works is he the son, when he refuses me the wages of my sweat and labor?"

"I do not refuse, brother Andres," said the farmer; "be good enough to come along with me, and I swear by all the orders of knighthood there are in the world to pay you as I have agreed, real by real, and perfumed." [32]

"For the perfumery I excuse you," said Don Quixote; "give it to him in reals, and I shall be satisfied; and see that you do as you have sworn; if not, by the same oath I swear to come back and hunt you out and punish you; and I shall find you though you should lie closer than a lizard. And if you desire to know who it is lays this command upon you, that you may be more firmly bound to obey it, know that I am the valorous Don Quixote of La Mancha, the undoer of wrongs and injustices; and so, God be with you, and keep in mind what you have promised and sworn under those penalties that have been already declared to you."

So saying, he gave Rocinante the spur and was soon out of reach. The farmer followed him with his eyes, and when he saw that he had cleared the wood and was no longer in sight, he turned to his boy Andres, and said, "Come here, my son, I want to pay you what I owe you, as that undoer of wrongs has commanded me."

"My oath on it," said Andres, "your worship will be well advised to obey the command of that good knight—may he live a thousand years—for, as he is a valiant and just judge, by Roque,[33] if you do not pay me, he will come back and do as he said."

"My oath on it, too," said the farmer; "but as I have a strong affection for you, I want to add to the debt in order to add to the payment;" and seizing him by the arm, he tied him up to the oak again, where he gave him such a flogging that he left him for dead.

"Now, Master Andres," said the farmer, "call on the undoer of wrongs; you will find he won't undo that, though I am not sure that I have quite done with you, for I have a good mind to flay you alive as you feared." But at last he untied him, and gave him leave to go look for his judge in order to put the sentence pronounced into execution.

Andres went off rather down in the mouth, swearing he would go to look for the valiant Don Quixote of La Mancha and tell him exactly what had happened, and that all would have to be repaid him sevenfold; but for all that, he went off weeping, while his master stood laughing.

Thus did the valiant Don Quixote right that wrong, and, thoroughly satisfied with what had taken place, as he considered he had made a very

[31] *Haldudos*, wearers of long skirts.　[32] *perfumed*: a way of expressing completeness or perfection of condition.　[33] an obscure oath, of which there is no satisfactory explanation. . . .

happy and noble beginning with his knighthood, he took the road towards his village in perfect self-content, saying in a low voice, "Well mayest thou this day call thyself fortunate above all on earth, O Dulcinea del Toboso, fairest of the fair! since it has fallen to thy lot to hold subject and submissive to thy full will and pleasure a knight so renowned as is and will be Don Quixote of La Mancha, who, as all the world knows, yesterday received the order of knighthood, and hath to-day righted the greatest wrong and grievance that ever injustice conceived and cruelty perpetrated: who hath to-day plucked the rod from the hand of yonder ruthless oppressor so wantonly lashing that tender child."

He now came to a road branching in four directions, and immediately he was reminded of those cross-roads where knights-errant used to stop to consider which road they should take. In imitation of them he halted for a while, and after having deeply considered it, he gave Rocinante his head, submitting his own will to that of his hack, who followed out his first intention, which was to make straight for his own stable. After he had gone about two miles Don Quixote perceived a large party of people, who, as afterwards appeared, were some Toledo traders, on their way to buy silk at Murcia. There were six of them coming along under their sunshades, with four servants mounted, and three muleteers on foot. Scarcely had Don Quixote descried them when the fancy possessed him that this must be some new adventure; and to help him to imitate as far as he could those passages[34] he had read of in his books, here seemed to come one made on purpose, which he resolved to attempt. So with a lofty bearing and determination he fixed himself firmly in his stirrups, got his lance ready, brought his buckler before his breast, and planting himself in the middle of the road, stood waiting the approach of these knights-errant, for such he now considered and held them to be; and when they had come near enough to see and hear, he exclaimed with a haughty gesture, "All the world stand, unless all the world confess that in all the world there is no maiden fairer than the Empress of La Mancha, the peerless Dulcinea del Toboso."

The traders halted at the sound of this language and the sight of the strange figure that uttered it, and from both figure and language at once guessed the craze of their owner; they wished, however, to learn quietly what was the object of this confession that was demanded of them, and one of them, who was rather fond of a joke and was very sharp-witted, said to him, "Sir Knight, we do not know who this good lady is that you speak of; show her to us, for, if she be of such beauty as you suggest, with all our hearts and without any pressure we will confess the truth that is on your part required of us."

"If I were to show her to you," replied Don Quixote, "what merit would

[34] not passages of the book, but passages of arms like that of Suero de Quiñones on the bridge of Orbigo in the reign of John II.

you have in confessing a truth so manifest? The essential point is that without seeing her you must believe, confess, affirm, swear, and defend it; else ye have to do with me in battle, ill-conditioned, arrogant rabble that ye are; and come ye on, one by one as the order of knighthood requires, or all together as is the custom and vile usage of your breed, here do I bide and await you, relying on the justice of the cause I maintain."

"Sir Knight," replied the trader, "I entreat your worship in the name of this present company of princes, that, to save us from charging our consciences with the confession of a thing we have never seen or heard of, and one moreover so much to the prejudice of the Empresses and Queens of the Alcarria and Estremadura,[35] your worship will be pleased to show us some portrait of this lady, though it be no bigger than a grain of wheat; for by the thread one gets at the ball,[36] and in this way we shall be satisfied and easy, and you will be content and pleased; nay, I believe we are already so far agreed with you that even though her portrait should show her blind of one eye, and distilling vermilion and sulphur from the other, we would nevertheless, to gratify your worship, say all in her favor that you desire."

"She distils nothing of the kind, vile rabble," said Don Quixote, burning with rage, "nothing of the kind, I say, only ambergis and civet in cotton;[37] nor is she one-eyed or hump backed, but straighter than a Guadarrama spindle: but ye must pay for the blasphemy ye have uttered against beauty like that of my lady."

And so saying, he charged with levelled lance against the one who had spoken, with such fury and fierceness that, if luck had not contrived that Rocinante should stumble midway and come down, it would have gone hard with the rash trader. Down went Rocinante, and over went his master, rolling along the ground for some distance; and when he tried to rise he was unable, so encumbered was he with lance, buckler, spurs, helmet, and the weight of his old armor; and all the while he was struggling to get up, he kept saying, "Fly not, cowards and caitiffs! stay, for not by my fault, but my horse's, am I stretched here."

One of the muleteers in attendance, who could not have had much good nature in him, hearing the poor prostrate man blustering in this style, was unable to refrain from giving him an answer on his ribs; and coming up to him he seized his lance, and having broken it in pieces, with one of them he began so to belabor our Don Quixote that, notwithstanding and in spite of his armor, he milled him like a measure of wheat. His masters called out

---

[35] The *Alcarria* is a bare, thinly populated district, in the upper valley of the Tagus, stretching from Guadalajara to the confines of Aragon. Estremadura is the most backward of all the provinces of Spain. In elevating these two regions into the rank of empires, the waggish trader falls in with the craze of Don Quixote. [36] . . . [that is, the ball] on which it is wound.   [37] *Civet* was the perfume most in request at the time and was imported packed in cotton.

not to lay on so hard and to leave him alone, but the muleteer's blood was up, and he did not care to drop the game until he had vented the rest of his ·wrath, and, gathering up the remaining fragments of the lance, he finished with a discharge upon the unhappy victim, who all through the storm of sticks that rained on him never ceased threatening heaven, and earth, and the brigands, for such they seemed to him. At last the muleteer was tired, and the traders continued their journey, taking with them matter for talk about the poor fellow who had been cudgelled. He when he found himself alone made another effort to rise; but if he was unable when whole and sound, how was he to rise after having been thrashed and well-nigh knocked to pieces? And yet he esteemed himself fortunate, as it seemed to him that this was a regular knight-errant's mishap, and entirely, he considered, the fault of his horse. However, battered in body as he was, to rise was beyond his power.

In Chapter V the battered Don Quixote is discovered by a neighbor, a peasant from his village, who leads him home. There Don Quixote's niece, the town barber, and the priest marvel at the loss of reason in a man who had been known for his keen understanding. Blaming the insanity on the chivalric romances in Don Quixote's library, the priest resolves to burn them on the following day. Chapter VI describes the "inquisition" conducted by the priest and the barber. They put the worst of the chivalric romances aside for burning and preserve those that seem to them the best of the genre—a doubly irrational act, since by preserving the best, they seem to preserve the very works that have the most power to draw men like Don Quixote into madness. As Chapter VII begins, Don Quixote is awakening from a sleep in which he has dreamed of chivalric action.

CHAPTER VII

Of the Second Sally of Our
Worthy Knight
Don Quixote of La Mancha.

. . . When they reached Don Quixote he was already out of bed, and was still shouting and raving, and slashing and cutting all round, as wide awake as if he had never slept.

They closed with him and by force got him back to bed, and when he had become a little calm, addressing the curate, he said to him, "Of a truth,

Señor Archbishop Turpin,[38] it is a great disgrace for us who call ourselves the Twelve Peers, so carelessly to allow the knights of the Court to gain the victory in this tourney, we the adventurers having carried off the honor on the three former days."

"Hush, gossip," said the curate; "please God, the luck may turn, and what is lost to-day may be won to-morrow; for the present let your worship have a care of your health, for it seems to me that you are over-fatigued, if not badly wounded."

"Wounded no," said Don Quixote, "but bruised and battered no doubt, for that bastard Don Roland has cudgelled me with the trunk of an oak tree, and all for envy, because he sees that I alone rival him in his achievements. But I should not call myself Reinaldos of Montalvan did he not pay me for it in spite of all his enchantments as soon as I rise from this bed. For the present let them bring me something to eat, for that, I feel, is what will be more to my purpose, and leave it to me to avenge myself."

They did as he wished; they gave him something to eat, and once more he fell asleep, leaving them marvelling at his madness.

That night the housekeeper burned to ashes all the books that were in the yard and in the whole house; and some must have been consumed that deserved preservation in everlasting archives, but their fate and the laziness of the examiner did not permit it, and so in them was verified the proverb that sometimes the innocent suffer for the guilty.

One of the remedies which the curate and the barber immediately applied to their friend's disorder was to wall up and plaster the room where the books were, so that when he got up he should not find them (possibly the cause being removed, the effect might cease), and they might say that a magician had carried them off, room and all; and this was done with all despatch. Two days later Don Quixote got up, and the first thing he did was to go and look at his books, and not finding the room where he had left it, he wandered from side to side looking for it. He came to the place where the door used to be, and tried it with his hands, and turned and twisted his eyes in every direction without saying a word; but after a good while he asked his housekeeper whereabouts was the room that held his books.

The housekeeper, who had been already well instructed in what she was to answer, said, "What room or what nothing is it that your worship is looking for? There are neither room nor books in this house now, for the devil himself has carried all away."

"It was not the devil," said the niece, "but a magician who came on a cloud one night after the day your worship left this, and dismounting from a serpent that he rode he entered the room, and what he did there I know not,

---

[38] *Turpin* (or *Tilpin*), Charlemagne's chaplain, and archbishop of Rheims: according to the *Chanson de Roland*, one of those slain at Roncesvalles. . . .

but after a little while he made off, flying through the roof, and left the house full of smoke; and when we went to see what he had done we saw neither book nor room; but we remember very well, the housekeeper and I, that on leaving, the old villain said in a loud voice that, for a private grudge he owed the owner of the books and the room, he had done mischief in that house that would be discovered by and by: he said too that his name was the Sage Muñaton."

"He must have said Friston," [39] said Don Quixote.

"I don't know whether he called himself Friston or Friton," said the housekeeper, "I only know that his name ended with 'ton.'"

"So it does," said Don Quixote, "and he is a sage magician, a great enemy of mine, who has a spite against me because he knows by his arts and lore that in process of time I am to engage in single combat with a knight whom he befriends and that I am to conquer, and he will be unable to prevent it; and for this reason he endeavors to do me all the ill turns that he can; but I promise him it will be hard for him to oppose or avoid what is decreed by Heaven."

"Who doubts that?" said the niece; "but, uncle, who mixes you up in these quarrels? Would it not be better to remain at peace in your own house instead of roaming the world looking for better bread than ever came of wheat, never reflecting that many go for wool and come back shorn?"

"Oh, niece of mine," replied Don Quixote, "how much astray art thou in thy reckoning; ere they shear me I shall have plucked away and stripped off the beards of all who would dare to touch only the tip of a hair of mine."

The two were unwilling to make any further answer, as they saw that his anger was kindling.

In short, then, he remained at home fifteen days very quietly without showing any signs of a desire to take up with his former delusions, and during this time he held lively discussions with his two gossips, the curate and the barber, on the point he maintained, that knights-errant were what the world stood most in need of, and that in him was to be accomplished the revival of knight-errantry. The curate sometimes contradicted him, sometimes agreed with him, for if he had not observed this precaution he would have been unable to bring him to reason.

Meanwhile Don Quixote worked upon a farm-laborer, a neighbor of his, an honest man (if indeed that title can be given to him who is poor), but with very little wit in his pate. In a word, he so talked him over, and with such persuasions and promises, that the poor clown made up his mind to sally forth with him and serve him as esquire. Don Quixote, among other things, told him he ought to be ready to go with him gladly, because any moment an adventure might occur that might win an island in the twin-

[39] Friston, a magician, the reputed author of *Belianis de Grecia*.

kling of an eye and leave him governor of it. On these and the like promises
Sancho Panza (for so the laborer was called) left wife and children, and
engaged himself as esquire to his neighbor. Don Quixote next set about
getting some money; and selling one thing and pawning another, and
making a bad bargain in every case, he got together a fair sum. He provided
himself with a buckler, which he begged as a loan from a friend, and,
restoring his battered helmet as best he could, he warned his squire Sancho
of the day and hour he meant to set out, that he might provide himself with
what he thought most needful. Above all, he charged him to take alforjas[40]
with him. The other said he would, and that he meant to take also a very
good ass he had, as he was not much given to going on foot. About the ass,
Don Quixote hesitated a little, trying whether he could call to mind any
knight-errant taking with him an esquire mounted on ass-back, but no
instance occurred to his memory. For all that, however, he determined to
take him, intending to furnish him with a more honorable mount when a
chance of it presented itself, by appropriating the horse of the first dis-
courteous knight he encountered. Himself he provided with shirts and
such other things as he could, according to the advice the host had given
him; all which being settled and done, without taking leave, Sancho Panza
of his wife and children, or Don Quixote of his housekeeper and niece,
they sallied forth unseen by anybody from the village one night, and made
such good way in the course of it that by daylight they held themselves safe
from discovery, even should search be made for them.

Sancho rode on his ass like a patriarch with his alforjas and bota,[41] and
longing to see himself soon governor of the island his master had promised
him. Don Quixote decided upon taking the same route and road he had
taken on his first journey, that over the Campo de Montiel, which he
travelled with less discomfort than on the last occasion, for, as it was early
morning and the rays of the sun fell on them obliquely, the heat did not
distress them.

And now said Sancho Panza to his master, "Your worship will take care,
Señor Knight-errant, not to forget about the island you have promised me,
for be it ever so big I'll be equal to governing it."

To which Don Quixote replied, "Thou must know, friend Sancho Panza,
that it was a practice very much in vogue with the knights-errant of old
to make their squires governors of the islands or kingdoms they won,[42] and
I am determined that there shall be no failure on my part in so liberal a
custom; on the contrary, I mean to improve upon it, for they sometimes,

[40] . . . a sort of double wallet serving for saddlebags but more frequently carried
slung across the shoulder.   [41] The *bota* is the leathern wine bag which is as much
a part of the Spanish wayfarer's paraphernalia as the *alforjas*. It cannot, of course,
be properly translated "bottle."   [42] Amadis, for instance, made his squire Gandalin
governor of the Insula Firme.

and perhaps most frequently, waited until their squires were old and then when they had had enough of service and hard days and worse nights, they gave them some title or other, of count, or at the most marquis, of some valley or province more or less; but if thou livest and I live, it may well be that before six days are over, I may have won some kingdom that has others dependent upon it, which will be just the thing to enable thee to be crowned king of one of them. Nor needst thou count this wonderful, for things and chances fall to the lot of such knights in ways so unexampled and unexpected that I might easily give thee even more than I promise thee."

"In that case," said Sancho Panza, "if I should become a king by one of those miracles your worship speaks of, even Juana Gutierrez, my old woman, would come to be queen and my children infantes."

"Well, who doubts it?" said Don Quixote.

"I doubt it," replied Sancho Panza, "because for my part I am persuaded that though God should shower down kingdoms upon earth, not one of them would fit the head of Mari Gutierrez. Let me tell you, señor, she is not worth two maravedís for a queen; countess will fit her better, and that only with God's help."

"Leave it to God, Sancho," returned Don Quixote, "for he will give her what suits her best; but do not undervalue thyself so much as to come to be content with anything less than being governor of a province."

"I will not, señor," answered Sancho, "especially as I have a man of such quality for a master in your worship, who will be able to give me all that will be suitable for me and that I can bear."

CHAPTER VIII

Of the Good Fortune Which
the Valiant Don Quixote Had
in the Terrible and Undreamed of Adventure
of the Windmills, with Other Occurrences
Worthy to Be Fitly Recorded.

At this point they came in sight of thirty or forty windmills that there are on that plain,[43] and as soon as Don Quixote saw them he said to his squire, "Fortune is arranging matters for us better than we could have shaped our desires ourselves, for look there, friend Sancho Panza, where

[43] These famous windmills had not been very long set up and owed their existence to the failure of water power in the Zaneara, an affluent of the Guadiana, about thirty years before *Don Quixote* was written. . . .

thirty or more monstrous giants present themselves, all of whom I mean to engage in battle and slay, and with whose spoils we shall begin to make our fortunes; for this is righteous warfare, and it is God's good service to sweep so evil a breed from off the face of the earth."

"What giants?" said Sancho Panza.

"Those thou seest there," answered his master, "with the long arms, and some have them nearly two leagues long."

"Look, your worship," said Sancho; "what we see there are not giants but windmills, and what seem to be their arms are the sails that turned by the wind make the millstone go."

"It is easy to see," replied Don Quixote, "that thou art not used to this business of adventures; those are giants; and if thou art afraid, away with thee out of this and betake thyself to prayer while I engage them in fierce and unequal combat."

So saying, he gave the spur to his steed Rocinante, heedless of the cries his squire Sancho sent after him, warning him that most certainly they were windmills and not giants he was going to attack. He, however, was so positive they were giants that he neither heard the cries of Sancho, nor perceived, near as he was, what they were, but made at them shouting, "Fly not, cowards and vile beings, for it is a single knight that attacks you."

A slight breeze at this moment sprang up, and the great sails began to move, seeing which Don Quixote exclaimed, "Though ye flourish more arms than the giant Briareus, ye have to reckon with me."

So saying, and commending himself with all his heart to his lady Dulcinea, imploring her to support him in such a peril, with lance in rest and covered by his buckler, he charged at Rocinante's fullest gallop and fell upon the first mill that stood in front of him; but as he drove his lance-point into the sail the wind whirled it round with such force that it shivered the lance to pieces, sweeping with it horse and rider, who went rolling over on the plain, in a sorry condition. Sancho hastened to his assistance as fast as his ass could go, and when he came up found him unable to move, with such a shock had Rocinante fallen with him.

"God bless me!" said Sancho, "did I not tell your worship to mind what you were about, for they were only windmills? and no one could have made any mistake about it but one who had something of the same kind in his head."

"Hush, friend Sancho," replied Don Quixote, "the fortunes of war more than any other are liable to frequent fluctuations; and moreover I think, and it is the truth, that that same sage Friston who carried off my study and books, has turned these giants into mills in order to rob me of the glory of vanquishing them, such is the enmity he bears me; but in the end his wicked arts will avail but little against my good sword."

"God order it as he may," said Sancho Panza, and helping him to rise got him up again on Rocinante, whose shoulder was half out; and then, discussing the late adventure, they followed the road to Puerto Lápice, for there, said Don Quixote, they could not fail to find adventures in abundance and variety, as it was a great thoroughfare.[44] For all that, he was much grieved at the loss of his lance, and saying so to his squire, he added, "I remember having read how a Spanish knight, Diego Perez de Vargas by name, having broken his sword in battle, tore from an oak a ponderous bough or branch, and with it did such things that day, and pounded so many Moors, that he got the surname of Machuca,[45] and he and his descendants from that day forth were called Vargas y Machuca. I mention this because from the first oak[46] I see I mean to rend such another branch, large and stout like that, with which I am determined and resolved to do such deeds that thou mayest deem thyself very fortunate in being found worthy to come and see them, and be an eye-witness of things that will with difficulty be believed."

"Be that as God will," said Sancho, "I believe it all as your worship says it; but straighten yourself a little, for you seem all on one side, maybe from the shaking of the fall."

"That is the truth," said Don Quixote, "and if I make no complaint of the pain it is because knights-errant are not permitted to complain of any wound, even though their bowels be coming out through it."

"If so," said Sancho, "I have nothing to say; but God knows I would rather your worship complained when anything ailed you. For my part, I confess I must complain however small the ache may be; unless indeed this rule about not complaining extends to the squires of knights-errant also."

Don Quixote could not help laughing at his squire's simplicity, and he assured him he might complain whenever and however he chose, just as he liked, for, so far, he had never read of anything to the contrary in the order of knighthood.

Sancho bade him remember it was dinner-time, to which his master answered that he wanted nothing himself just then, but that he might eat when he had a mind. With this permission Sancho settled himself as comfortably as he could on his beast, and taking out of the alforjas what he had stowed away in them, he jogged along behind his master munching deliberately, and from time to time taking a pull at the bota with a relish that the thirstiest tapster in Malaga might have envied; and while he went on in this way, gulping down draught after draught, he never gave a thought

[44] being a stage on the great high road from Madrid to Seville. [45] from *machucar* or *machacar*, "to pound." The feat referred to by Don Quixote was performed at the seige of Jerez under Alfonso X in 1264. . . . [46] In the ballad it is an olive tree, but the olive does not flourish in La Mancha, so Don Quixote substitutes oak.

to any of the promises his master had made him, nor did he rate it as hardship but rather as recreation going in quest of adventures, however dangerous they might be. Finally they passed the night among some trees, from one of which Don Quixote plucked a dry branch to serve him after a fashion as a lance, and fixed on it the head he had removed from the broken one. All that night Don Quixote lay awake thinking of his lady Dulcinea, in order to conform to what he had read in his books, how many a night in the forests and deserts knights used to lie sleepless supported by the memory of their mistresses. Not so did Sancho Panza spend it, for having his stomach full of something stronger than chiccory water he made but one sleep of it, and, if his master had not called him, neither the rays of the sun beating on his face nor all the cheery notes of the birds welcoming the approach of day would have had power to waken him. On getting up he tried the bota and found it somewhat less full than the night before, which grieved his heart because they did not seem to be on the way to remedy the deficiency readily. Don Quixote did not care to break his fast, for, as has been already said, he confined himself to savory recollections for nourishment. . . .

After several further adventures, Don Quixote and Sancho spend a night in the woods, terrified by mysterious sounds that Don Quixote believes are made by some horrific foe. In morning's light they discover that the sounds issue from the mechanical process of a nearby mill.

CHAPTER XXI

Which Treats of the Exalted Adventure and Rich Prize of Mambrino's Helmet, Together with Other Things That Happened to Our Invincible Knight.

It now began to rain a little, and Sancho was for going into the fulling[47] mills, but Don Quixote had taken such a disgust to them on account of the late joke that he would not enter them on any account; so turning aside to the right they came upon another road, different from that which they had taken the night before. Shortly afterwards Don Quixote perceived a man on horseback who wore on his head something that shone like gold, and the moment he saw him he turned to Sancho and said, "I think,

[47] process of thickening cloth by beating and washing—Ed.

Sancho, there is no proverb that is not true, all being maxims drawn from experience itself, the mother of all the sciences, especially that one that says, 'Where one door shuts, another opens.' I say so because if last night fortune shut the door of the adventure we were looking for against us, cheating us with the fulling mills, it now opens wide another one for another better and more certain adventure, and if I do not contrive to enter it, it will be my own fault, and I cannot lay it to my ignorance of fulling mills, or the darkness of the night. I say this because, if I mistake not, there comes toward us one who wears on his head the helmet of Mambrino, concerning which I took the oath thou rememberest."

"Mind what you say, your worship, and still more what you do," said Sancho, "for I don't want any more fulling mills to finish off fulling and knocking our senses out."

"The devil take thee, man," said Don Quixote; "what has a helmet to do with fulling mills?"

"I don't know," replied Sancho, "but, faith, if I might speak as I used, perhaps I could give such reasons that your worship would see you were mistaken in what you say."

"How can I be mistaken in what I say, unbelieving traitor?" returned Don Quixote; "tell me, seest thou not yonder knight coming towards us on a dappled gray steed, who has upon his head a helmet of gold?"

"What I see and make out," answered Sancho, "is only a man on a gray ass like my own, who has something that shines on his head."

"Well, that is the helmet of Mambrino," said Don Quixote; "stand to one side and leave me alone with him; thou shalt see how, without saying a word, to save time, I shall bring this adventure to an issue and possess myself of the helmet I have so longed for."

"I will take care to stand aside," said Sancho; "but God grant, I say once more, that it may be marjoram and not fulling mills."

"I have told thee, brother, on no account to mention those fulling mills to me again," said Don Quixote, "or I vow—and I say no more—I'll full the soul out of you."

Sancho held his peace in dread lest his master should carry out the vow he had hurled like a bowl at him.

The fact of the matter as regards the helmet, steed, and knight that Don Quixote saw, was this. In that neighborhood there were two villages, one of them so small that it had neither apothecary's shop, nor barber, which the other that was close to it had, so the barber of the larger served the smaller, and in it there was a sick man who required to be bled and another man who wanted to be shaved, and on this errand the barber was going, carrying with him a brass basin; but as luck would have it, as he was on the way it began to rain, and not to spoil his hat, which probably was a new one, he put the basin on his head, and being clean it glittered at half a league's distance. He rode upon a gray ass, as Sancho said, and this was what made it seem to Don Quixote to be a dapple-gray steed and a knight and a golden helmet; for everything he saw he made to fall in with his crazy chivalry and ill errant notions; and when he saw the poor knight draw near, without entering into any parley with him, at Rocinante's top speed he bore down upon him with the pike pointed low, fully determined to run him through and through, and as he reached him, without checking the fury of his charge, he cried to him, "Defend thyself, miserable being, or yield me of thine own accord that which is so reasonably my due."

The barber, who without any expectation or apprehension of it saw this apparition coming down upon him, had no other way of saving himself from the stroke of the lance but to let himself fall off his ass; and no sooner had he touched the ground than he sprang up more nimbly than a deer and sped away across the plain faster than the wind.

He left the basin on the ground, with which Don Quixote contented himself, saying that the pagan had shown his discretion and imitated the beaver, which finding itself pressed by the hunters bites and cuts off with its teeth that for which, by its natural instinct, it knows it is pursued.

He told Sancho to pick up the helmet, and he taking it in his hands said, "By God the basin is a good one, and worth a real of eight if it is worth a maravedí," and handed it to his master, who immediately put it on his head, turning it round, now this way, now that, in search of the visor, and not finding it he said, "Clearly the pagan to whose measure this famous head-piece was first forged must have had a very large head; but the worst of it is half of it is wanting."

When Sancho heard him call the basin a head-piece he was unable to restrain his laughter, but remembering his master's wrath he checked himself in the midst of it.

"What art thou laughing at, Sancho?" said Don Quixote.

"I am laughing," said he, "to think of the great head the pagan must have had who owned this helmet, for it looks exactly like a regular barber's basin."

"Dost thou know what I suspect, Sancho?" said Don Quixote; "that this wonderful piece of this enchanted helmet must by some strange accident have come into the hands of some one who was unable to recognize or realize its value, and who, not knowing what he did, and seeing it to be of the purest gold, must have melted down one half for the sake of what it might be worth, and of the other made this which is like a barber's basin as thou sayest; but be it as it may, to me who recognize it, its transformation makes no difference, for I will set it to rights at the first village where there is a blacksmith, and in such style that that helmet the god of smithies forged for the god of battles shall not surpass it or even come up to it; and in the meantime I will wear it as well as I can, for something is better than nothing; all the more as it will be quite enough to protect me from any chance blow of a stone."

"That is," said Sancho, "if it is not shot with a sling as they were in the battle of the two armies, when they signed the cross on your worship's grinders and smashed the flask with that blessed draught that made me vomit my bowels up."

"It does not grieve me much to have lost it," said Don Quixote, "for thou knowest, Sancho, that I have the receipt in my memory."

"So have I," answered Sancho, "but if ever I make it, or try it again as long as I live, may this be my last hour; moreover, I have no intention of putting myself in the way of wanting it, for I mean, with all my five senses, to keep myself from being wounded or from wounding any one: as to being blanketed [48] again I say nothing, for it is hard to prevent mishaps of that sort, and if they come there is nothing for it but to squeeze our shoulders together, hold our breath, shut our eyes, and let ourselves go where luck and the blanket may send us."

"Thou art a bad Christian, Sancho," said Don Quixote on hearing this, "for once an injury has been done thee thou never forgettest it: but know that it is the part of noble and generous hearts not to attach importance to trifles. What lame leg hast thou got by it, what broken rib, what cracked head, that thou canst not forget that jest? For jest and sport it was, properly regarded, and had I not seen it in that light I would have returned and done more mischief in revenging thee than the Greeks did for the rape of Helen, who, if she were alive now, or if my Dulcinea had lived then, might depend upon it she would not be so famous for her beauty as she is;" and here he heaved a sigh and sent it aloft; and said Sancho, "Let it pass for a jest as it can not be revenged in earnest, but I know what sort of jest and earnest it was, and I know it will never be rubbed out of my memory any more than off my shoulders. But putting that aside, will your worship tell me what are we to do with this dapple-gray steed that looks like a gray ass, which that Martino[49] that your worship overthrew has left deserted here? for, from the way he took to his heels and bolted, he is not likely ever to come back for it; and by my beard but the gray is a good one."

"I have never been in the habit," said Don Quixote, "of taking spoil of those whom I vanquish, nor is it the practice of chivalry to take away their horses and leave them to go on foot, unless indeed it be that the victor have lost his own in the combat, in which case it is lawful to take that of the vanquished as a thing won in lawful war; therefore, Sancho, leave this horse, or ass, or whatever thou wilt have it to be; for when its owner sees us gone hence he will come back for it."

"God knows I should like to take it," returned Sancho, "or at least to

[48] Sancho had been tossed in a blanket by an irate innkeeper, whom Don Quixote had neglected to pay—Ed.   [49] a blunder of Sancho's for Mambrino.

change it for my own, which does not seem to me as good a one; verily the laws of chivalry are strict, since they can not be stretched to let one ass be changed for another; I should like to know if I might at least change trappings."

"On that head I am not quite certain," answered Don Quixote, "and the matter being doubtful, pending better information, I say thou mayest change them, if so be thou hast urgent need of them."

"So urgent is it," answered Sancho, "that if they were for my own person I could not want them more;" and forthwith, fortified by this license, he effected the *mutatio capparum*,[50] and rigged out his beast to the ninety-nines, making quite another thing of it. This done, they broke their fast on the remains of the spoils of war plundered from the sumpter mule, and drank of the brook that flowed from the fulling mills, without casting a look in that direction, in such loathing did they hold them for the alarm they had caused them; and, all anger and gloom removed, they mounted and, without taking any fixed road (not to fix upon any being the proper thing for true knights-errant), they set out, guided by Rocinante's will, which carried along with it that of his master, not to say that of the ass, which always followed him wherever he led, lovingly and sociably; nevertheless they returned to the high road, and pursued it at a venture without any other aim. . . .

Part One ends when after many more adventures, Don Quixote and Sancho return home, the knight exhausted from the adventures, his squire still eager to go forth. Whether Cervantes intended to continue the story is not certain. However, Part Two of Don Quixote *appeared ten years later, in 1615, only shortly before Cervantes' death. He was apparently in some hurry to finish the work, furious because another writer, hoping to exploit the enormous popularity of Cervantes' creation, had published his own sequel to* Don Quixote *the preceding year.*

Preface

God bless me, gentle[51] (or it may be plebeian) reader, how eagerly must thou be looking forward to this preface, expecting to find there retaliation, scolding, and abuse against the author of the second Don Quixote—I mean him who was, they say, begotten at Tordesillas and born at Tarra-

---

[50] The *mutatio capparum* was the change of hoods authorized by the Roman ceremonial when the cardinals exchanged the fur-lined hoods worn in winter for lighter ones of silk. There is a certain audacity of humor in the application of the phrase here. [51] that is, noble—Ed.

gona! [52] Well then, the truth is, I am not going to give thee that satisfaction; for, though injuries stir up anger in humbler breasts, in mine the
rule must admit of an exception. Thou wouldst have me call him ass, fool,
and malapert, but I have no such intention; let his offense be his punishment, with his bread let him eat it, and there 's an end of it. What I can
not help taking amiss is, that he charges me with being old and one-handed,
as if it had been in my power to keep time from passing over me, or as
if the loss of my hand had been brought about in some tavern, and not
on the grandest occasion the past or present has seen, or the future can
hope to see. If my wounds have no beauty to the beholder's eye, they are,
at least, honorable in the estimation of those who know where they were
received; for the soldier shows to greater advantage dead in battle than
alive in flight; and so strongly is this my feeling, that if now it were proposed to perform an impossibility for me, I would rather have had my share
in that mighty action, than be free from my wounds this minute without
having been present at it. Those the soldier shows on his face and breast,
are stars that direct others to the heaven of honor and ambition of merited
praise; and moreover it is to be observed that it is not with gray hairs that
one writes, but with the understanding, and that commonly improves
with years. I take it amiss, too, that he calls me envious, and explains to
me, as if I were ignorant, what envy is; for really and truly, of the two
kinds there are, I only know that which is holy, noble, and high minded;
and if that be so, as it is, I am not likely to attack a priest, above all if,
in addition, he holds the rank of familiar of the Holy Office. And if he
said what he did on account of him on whose behalf it seems he spoke,
he is entirely mistaken; for I worship the genius of that person, and admire his works and his unceasing and strenuous industry.[53] After all, however, I am grateful to this gentleman, the author, for saying that my novels
are more satirical than exemplary, but that they are good; for they could
not be that unless there was a little of everything in them.

I suspect thou wilt say that I am taking a very humble line, and keeping myself too much within the bounds of my moderation, from a feeling
that additional suffering should not be inflicted upon a sufferer, and that
what this gentleman has to endure must doubtless be very great, as he
does not dare to come out into the open field and broad daylight, but hides
his name and disguises his country as if he had been guilty of some lese
majesty. If perchance thou shouldst come to know him, tell him from me
that I do not hold myself aggrieved; for I know well what the temptations

---

[52] The spurious "Second Part," which came out in the autumn of 1614, was
described on the title page as the work of Alonso Fernandez de Avellaneda, of
Tordesillas, and was licensed and printed at Tarragona.   [53] Avellaneda, in his coarse
and scurrilous preface, charged Cervantes with attacking Lope de Vega. . . .

of the devil are, and that one of the greatest is putting it into a man's head
that he can write and print a book by which he will get as much fame as
money, and as much money as fame; and to prove it I will beg of you,
in your own sprightly, pleasant way, to tell him this story.

There was a madman in Seville who took to one of the drollest absurdities
and vagaries that ever madman in the world gave way to. It was this: he
made a tube of reed sharp at one end, and catching a dog in the street, or
wherever it might be, he with his foot held one of its legs fast, and with
his hand lifted up the other, and as best he could fixed the tube where,
by blowing, he made the dog as round as a ball; then holding it in this
position, he gave it a couple of slaps on the belly, and let it go, saying to
the bystanders (and there were always plenty of them): "Do your worships think, now, that it is an easy thing to blow up a dog?"—Does your
worship think now, that it is an easy thing to write a book?

And if this story does not suit him, you may, dear reader, tell him this
one, which is likewise of a madman and a dog.

In Cordova there was another madman, whose way it was to carry a piece
of marble slab or a stone, not of the lightest, on his head, and when he
came upon any unwary dog he used to draw close to him and let the weight
fall right on top of him; on which the dog in a rage, barking and howling,
would run three streets without stopping. It so happened, however, that
one of the dogs he discharged his load upon was a cap-maker's dog, of
which his master was very fond. The stone came down hitting it on the
head, the dog raised a yell at the blow, the master saw the affair and was
wroth, and snatching up a measuring-yard rushed out at the madman and
did not leave a sound bone in his body, and at every stroke he gave him
he said, "You dog, you thief! my lurcher! [54] Don't you see, you brute, that
my dog is a lurcher?" and so, repeating the word "lurcher" again and again,
he sent the madman away beaten to a jelly. The madman took the lesson
to heart, and vanished, and for more than a month never once showed
himself in public; but after that he came out again with his old trick and
a heavier load than ever. He came up to where there was a dog, and, examining it very carefully without venturing to let the stone fall, he said:
"This is a lurcher; ware!" In short, all the dogs he came across, be they
mastiffs or terriers, he said were lurchers; and he discharged no more stones.
May be it will be the same with this historian; that he will not venture
another time to discharge the weight of his wit in books, which, being bad,
are harder than stones. Tell him, too, that I do not care a farthing for the
threat he holds out to me of depriving me of my profit by means of his
book; for, to borrow from the famous interlude of "The Perendenga," I say
in answer to him, "Long life to my lord the Veintiquatro, and Christ be

[54] *podenco,* a kind of small greyhound, hunting by nose as well as by sight, and
generally used for rabbits.

with us all." [55] Long life to the great Conde de Lemos, whose Christian charity and well-known generosity support me against all the strokes of my curst fortune; and long life to the supreme benevolence of His Eminence of Toledo, Don Bernardo de Sandoval y Rojas;[56] and what matter if there be no printing-presses in the world, or if they print more books against me than there are letters in the verses of Mingo Revulgo! [57] These two princes, unsought by any adulation or flattery of mine, of their own goodness alone, have taken it upon them to show me kindness and protect me, and in this I consider myself happier and richer than if Fortune had raised me to her greatest height in the ordinary way. The poor man may retain honor, but not the vicious; poverty may cast a cloud over nobility, but can not hide it altogether; and as virtue of itself sheds a certain light, even though it be through the straits and chinks of penury, it wins the esteem of lofty and noble spirits, and in consequence their protection. Thou needst say no more to him, nor will I say anything more to thee, save to tell thee to bear in mind that this Second Part of "Don Quixote" which I offer thee is cut by the same craftsman and from the same cloth as the First, and that in it I present thee Don Quixote continued, and at length dead and buried, so that no one may dare to bring forward any further evidence against him, for that already produced is sufficient, and suffice it, too, that some reputable person should have given an account of all these shrewd lunacies of his without going into the matter again; for abundance, even of good things, prevents them from being valued; and scarcity, even in the case of what is bad, confers a certain value. I was forgetting to tell thee that thou mayest expect the "Persiles," which I am now finishing, and also the Second Part of "Galatea."

[55] the municipal authorities of Seville, Cordova, and Granada were called *Vientiquatros*, from being twenty-four in number. The passage is, of course, a quotation from some popular interlude of the day. [56] *Bernardo de Sandoval y Rojas* was Cardinal-Archbishop of Toledo, Primate of Spain, and brother of the Duke of Lerma, the Prime Minister. [57] *Las Coplas de Mingo Revulgo* is the title given to an old versified satire on the reign of Henry IV. . . .

Part Two

CHAPTER I

Of the Interview the Curate
and the Barber Had with Don Quixote
about His Malady.

Cid Hamet Benengeli, in the Second Part of this history, and third sally
of Don Quixote, says that the curate and the barber remained nearly a
month without seeing him, lest they should recall or bring back to his
recollection what had taken place. They did not, however, omit to visit his
niece and housekeeper, and charge them to be careful to treat him with
attention, and give him comforting things to eat, and such as were good
for the heart and the brain, whence, it was plain to see, all his misfortune
proceeded. The niece and housekeeper replied that they did so, and meant
to do so with all possible care and assiduity, for they could perceive that
their master was now and then beginning to show signs of being in his
right mind. This gave great satisfaction to the curate and the barber, for
they concluded they had taken the right course in carrying him off enchanted on the ox-cart, as has been described in the First Part of this great
as well as accurate history, in the last chapter thereof. So they resolved to
pay him a visit and test the improvement in his condition, although they
thought it almost impossible that there could be any; and they agreed not
to touch upon any point connected with knight-errantry, so as not to run
the risk of re-opening wounds which were still so tender.

They came to see him consequently, and found him sitting up in bed
in a green baize waistcoat and a red Toledo cap, and so withered and
dried up that he looked as if he had been turned into a mummy. They
were very cordially received by him; they asked him after his health, and
he talked to them about it and about himself very naturally and in very
well chosen language. In the course of their conversation they fell to discussing what they call State-craft and systems of government, correcting this
abuse and condemning that, reforming one practice and abolishing another,
each of the three setting up for a new legislator, a modern Lycurgus, or a
brand-new Solon; and so completely did they remodel the State, that they
seemed to have thrust it into a furnace and taken out something quite different from what they had put in; and on all the subjects they dealt with,
Don Quixote spoke with such good sense that the pair of examiners were
fully convinced that he was quite recovered and in his full senses.

The niece and housekeeper were present at the conversation and could not find words enough to express their thanks to God at seeing their master so clear in his mind; the curate, however, changing his original plan, which was to avoid touching upon matters of chivalry, resolved to test Don Quixote's recovery thoroughly, and see whether it were genuine or not; and so, from one subject to another, he came at last to talk of the news that had come from the capital, and, among other things, he said it was considered certain that the Turk was coming down with a powerful fleet, and that no one knew what his purpose was, or when the great storm would burst; and that all Christendom was in apprehension of this, which almost every year calls us to arms, and that his Majesty had made provision for the security of the coasts of Naples and Sicily and the island of Malta.

To this Don Quixote replied, "His Majesty has acted like a prudent warrior in providing for the safety of his realms in time, so that the enemy may not find him unprepared; but if my advice were taken I would recommend him to adopt a measure which at present, no doubt, his Majesty is very far from thinking of."

The moment the curate heard this he said to himself, "God keep thee in his hand, poor Don Quixote, for it seems to me thou art precipitating thyself from the height of thy madness into the profound abyss of thy simplicity."

But the barber, who had the same suspicion as the curate, asked Don Quixote what would be his advice as to the measures that he said ought to be adopted; for perhaps it might prove to be one that would have to be added to the list of the many impertinent suggestions that people were in the habit of offering to princes.

"Mine, master shaver," said Don Quixote, "will not be impertinent, but, on the contrary, pertinent."

"I don't mean that," said the barber, "but that experience has shown that all or most of the expedients which are proposed to his Majesty are either impossible, or absurd, or injurious to the King and to the kingdom."

"Mine, however," replied Don Quixote, "is neither impossible nor absurd, but the easiest, the most reasonable, the readiest and most expeditious that could suggest itself to any projector's mind."

"You take a long time to tell it, Señor Don Quixote," said the curate.

"I don't choose to tell it here, now," said Don Quixote, "and have it reach the ears of the lords of the council to-morrow morning, and some other carry off the thanks and rewards of my trouble."

"For my part," said the barber, "I give my word here and before God that I will not repeat what your worship says, to King, Rook,[58] or earthly

[58] *ni Rey ni Roque*—neither king nor rook—a popular phrase somewhat like *gentle or simple*, or *high or low*. According to Clemencin probably derived from the game of chess, rook or rock (Persian *rokh*) being the same thing as the castle.

man—an oath I learned from the ballad of the curate, who, in the prelude, told the king of the thief who had robbed him of the hundred gold crowns and his pacing mule."

"I am not versed in stories," said Don Quixote; "but I know the oath is a good one, because I know the barber to be an honest fellow."

"Even if he were not," said the curate, "I will go bail and answer for him that in this matter he will be as silent as a dummy, under pain of paying any penalty that may be pronounced."

"And who will be security for you, señor curate?" said Don Quixote.

"My profession," replied the curate, "which is to keep secrets."

"Ods body!" [59] said Don Quixote at this, "what more has his Majesty to do but to command, by public proclamation, all the knights-errant that are scattered over Spain to assemble on a fixed day in the capital, for even if no more than half a dozen come, there may be one among them who alone will suffice to destroy the entire might of the Turk. Give me your attention and follow me. Is it, pray, any new thing for a single knight-errant to demolish an army of two hundred thousand men, as if they all had but one throat or were made of sugar-paste? Nay, tell me, how many histories are there filled with these marvels? If only (in an evil hour for me: I don't speak for any one else) the famous Don Belianis were alive now, or any one of the innumerable progeny of Amadis of Gaul! If any of these were alive to-day, and were to come face to face with the Turk, by my faith, I would not give much for the Turk's chance. But God will have regard for his people, and will provide some one, who, if not so valiant as the knights-errant of yore, at least will not be inferior to them in spirit; but God knows what I mean, and I say no more."

"Alas!" exclaimed the niece at this, "may I die if my master does not want to turn knight-errant again;" to which Don Quixote replied, "A knight-errant I shall die, and let the Turk come down or go up when he likes, and in as strong force as he can, once more I say, God knows what I mean." But here the barber said, "I ask your worships to give me leave to tell a short story of something that happened in Seville, which comes so pat to the purpose just now that I should like greatly to tell it." Don Quixote gave him leave, and the rest prepared to listen, and he begun thus:

"In the madhouse at Seville there was a man whom his relations had placed there as being out of his mind. He was a graduate of Osuna in canon law; but even if he had been of Salamanca, it was the opinion of most people that he would have been mad all the same. This graduate, after some years of confinement, took it into his head that he was sane and in his full senses, and under this impression wrote to the Archbishop, en-

---

[59] *Cuerpo de tal*—like the English—a less irreverent form of God's body!

treating him earnestly, and in very correct language, to have him released
from the misery in which he was living; for by God's mercy he had now
recovered his lost reason, though his relations, in order to enjoy his property, kept him there, and, in spite of the truth, would make him out to be
mad until his dying day. The Archbishop, moved by repeated sensible,
well-written letters, directed one of his chaplains to make inquiry of the
governor of the madhouse as to the truth of the licentiate's statements, and
to have an interview with the madman himself, and, if it should appear
that he was in his senses, to take him out and restore him to liberty. The
chaplain did so, and the governor assured him that the man was still mad,
and that though he often spoke like a highly intelligent person, he would
in the end break out into nonsense that in quantity and quality counter-
balanced all the sensible things he had said before, as might be easily tested
by talking to him. The chaplain resolved to try the experiment, and obtaining access to the madman conversed with him for an hour or more,
during the whole of which time he never uttered a word that was incoherent or absurd, but, on the contrary, spoke so rationally that the chaplain
was compelled to believe him to be sane. Among other things, he said the
governor was against him, not to lose the presents his relations made him
for reporting him still mad but with lucid intervals; and that the worst foe
he had in his misfortune was his large property; for in order to enjoy it
his enemies disparaged and threw doubts upon the mercy our Lord had
shown him in turning him from a brute beast into a man. In short, he spoke
in such a way that he cast suspicion on the governor, and made his relations appear covetous and heartless, and himself so rational that the chaplain
determined to take him away with him that the Archbishop might see him,
and ascertain for himself the truth of the matter. Yielding to this conviction,
the worthy chaplain begged the governor to have the clothes in which the
licentiate had entered the house given to him. The governor again bade
him beware of what he was doing, as the licentiate was beyond a doubt
still mad; but all his cautions and warnings were unavailing to dissuade the
chaplain from taking him away. The governor, seeing that it was the order
of the Archbishop, obeyed, and they dressed the licentiate in his own
clothes, which were new and decent. He, as soon as he saw himself clothed
like one in his senses, and divested of the appearance of a madman, entreated the chaplain to permit him in charity to go and take leave of his
comrades the madmen. The chaplain said he would go with him to see
what madmen there were in the house; so they went upstairs, and with
them some of those who were present. Approaching a cage in which there
was a furious madman, though just at that moment calm and quiet, the
licentiate said to him, 'Brother, think if you have any commands for me,
for I am going home, as God has been pleased, in his infinite goodness and
mercy, without any merit of mine, to restore me my reason. I am now

cured and in my senses, for with God's power nothing is impossible. Have strong hope and trust in him, for as he has restored me to my original condition, so likewise he will restore you if you trust in him. I will take care to send you some good things to eat; and be sure you eat them; for I would have you know I am convinced, as one who has gone through it, that all this madness of ours comes of having the stomach empty and the brains full of wind. Take courage! take courage! for despondency in misfortune breaks down health and brings on death.'

"To all these words of the licentiate another madman in a cage opposite that of the furious one was listening; and raising himself up from an old mat on which he lay stark naked, he asked in a loud voice who it was that was going away cured and in his senses. The licentiate answered, 'It is I, brother, who am going; I have now no need to remain here any longer, for which I return infinite thanks to Heaven that has had so great mercy upon me.'

" 'Mind what you are saying, licentiate; don't let the devil deceive you,' replied the madman. 'Keep quiet, stay where you are, and you will save yourself the trouble of coming back.'

" 'I know I am cured,' returned the licentiate, 'and that I shall not have to go stations again.' [60]

" 'You cured!' said the madman; 'well, we shall see; God be with you; but I swear to you by Jupiter, whose majesty I represent on earth, that for this crime alone, which Seville is committing to-day in releasing you from this house, and treating you as if you were in your senses, I shall have to inflict such a punishment on it as will be remembered for ages and ages, amen. Dost thou not know, thou miserable little licentiate, that I can do it, being, as I say, Jupiter the Thunderer, who hold in my hands the fiery bolts with which I am able and am wont to threaten and lay waste the world? But in one way only will I punish this ignorant town, and that is by not raining upon it, nor on any part of its district or territory, for three whole years, to be reckoned from the day and moment when this threat is pronounced. Thou free, thou cured, thou in thy senses! and I mad, I disordered, I bound! I will as soon think of sending rain as of hanging myself.'

"Those present stood listening to the words and exclamations of the madman; but our licentiate, turning to the chaplain and seizing him by the hands, said to him, 'Be not uneasy, señor; attach no importance to what this madman has said; for if he is Jupiter and will not send rain, I, who am Neptune, the father and god of the waters, will rain as often as it pleases me and may be needful.'

"The governor and the bystanders laughed, and at their laughter the

[60] *Andar estaciones* properly means to visit certain churches, for the purpose of offering up the prayers required to obtain indulgences.

chaplain was half ashamed, and he replied, 'For all that, Señor Neptune, it will not do to vex Señor Jupiter; remain where you are, and some other day, when there is a better opportunity and more time, we will come back for you.' So they stripped the licentiate, and he was left where he was; and that's the end of the story."

"So that's the story, master barber," said Don Quixote, "which came in so pat to the purpose that you could not help telling it? Master shaver, master shaver! how blind is he who can not see through a sieve. Is it possible that you do not know that comparisons of wit with wit, valor with valor, beauty with beauty, birth with birth, are always odious and unwelcome? I, master barber, am not Neptune the god of the waters, nor do I try to make any one take me for an astute man, for I am not one. My only endeavor is to convince the world of the mistake it makes in not reviving in itself the happy time when the order of knight-errantry was in the field. But our depraved age does not deserve to enjoy such a blessing as those ages enjoyed when knights-errant took upon their shoulders the defence of kingdoms, the protection of damsels, the succor of orphans and minors, the chastisement of the proud, and the recompense of the humble. With the knights of these days, for the most part, it is the damask, brocade, and rich stuffs they wear, that rustle as they go, not the chain mail of their armor; no knight now-a-days sleeps in the open field exposed to the inclemency of heaven, and in full panoply from head to foot; no one now takes a nap, as they call it, without drawing his feet out of the stirrups, and leaning upon his lance, as the knights-errant used to do; no one now, issuing from the wood, penetrates yonder mountains, and then treads the barren, lonely shore of the sea—mostly a tempestuous and stormy one—and finding on the beach a little bark without oars, sail, mast, or tackling of any kind, in the intrepidity of his heart flings himself into it and commits himself to the wrathful billows of the deep sea, that one moment lift him up to heaven and the next plunge him into the depths; and opposing his breast to the irresistible gale, finds himself, when he least expects it, three thousand leagues and more away from the place where he embarked; and leaping ashore in a remote and unknown land has adventures that deserve to be written, not on parchment, but on brass. But now sloth triumphs over energy, indolence over exertion, vice over virtue, arrogance over courage, and theory over practice in arms, which flourished and shone only in the golden ages and in knights-errant. For tell me, who was more virtuous and more valiant than the famous Amadis of Gaul? Who more discreet than Palmerin of England? Who more gracious and easy than Tirante el Blanco? Who more courtly than Lisuarte of Greece? Who more slashed or slashing than Don Belianis? Who more intrepid than Perion of Gaul? Who more ready to face danger than Felixmarte of Hircania? Who more sincere than Esplandian? Who more impetuous than Don Cirongilio of Thrace? Who more bold than Rodamonte? Who more prudent than King Sobrino? Who more daring than Reinaldos? Who more invincible than Roland? and who more gallant and courteous than Ruggiero, from whom the Dukes of Ferrara of the present day are descended, according to Turpin in his 'Cosmography'? [61] All these knights, and many more that I could name, señor curate, were knights-errant, the light and glory of chivalry. These, or such as these, I would have to carry out my plan and in that case his Majesty would find himself well served and would save great expense, and the Turk would be left tearing his beard. And so I will stay where I am, as the chaplain does not take me away; and if Jupiter, as the barber has told us, will not send rain, here am I, and I will rain when I please. I say this that Master Basin may know that I understand him."

"Indeed, Señor Don Quixote," said the barber, "I did not mean it in that way, and, so help me God, my intention was good, and your worship ought not to be vexed."

"As to whether I ought to be vexed or not," returned Don Quixote, "I myself am the best judge."

Hereupon the curate observed, "I have hardly said a word as yet; and I would gladly be relieved of a doubt, arising from what Don Quixote has said, that worries and works my conscience."

"The señor curate has leave for more than that," returned Don Quixote, "so he may declare his doubt, for it is not pleasant to have a doubt on one's conscience."

"Well then, with that permission," said the curate, "I say my doubt is that, all I can do, I can not persuade myself that the whole pack of knights-errant you, Señor Quixote, have mentioned, were really and truly persons of flesh and blood, that ever lived in the world; on the contrary, I suspect it to be all fiction, fable, and falsehood, and dreams told by men awakened from sleep, or rather still half asleep."

"That is another mistake," replied Don Quixote, "into which many have fallen who do not believe that there ever were such knights in the world, and I have often, with divers people and on divers occasions, tried to expose this almost universal error to the light of truth. Sometimes I have not been successful in my purpose, sometimes I have, supporting it upon the shoulders of the truth; which truth is so clear that I can almost say I have with my own eyes seen Amadis of Gaul, who was a man of lofty stature, fair complexion, with a handsome though black beard, of a countenance between gentle and stern in expression, sparing of words, slow to anger, and quick to put it away from him; and as I have depicted Amadis,

[61] The first nine are heroes of Spanish chivalric romance; the others are from Boiardo and Ariosto. There never was any such books as Turpin's *Cosmography*; it was Ariosto himself who traced the descent of the Dukes of Ferrara from Ruggiero.

so I could, I think, portray and describe all the knights-errant that are in all the histories in the world; for by the perception I have that they were what their histories describe, and by the deeds they did and the dispositions they displayed, it is possible, with the aid of sound philosophy, to deduce their features, complexion, and stature."

"How big, in your worship's opinion, may the giant Morgante have been, Señor Don Quixote?" asked the barber.

"With regard to giants," replied Don Quixote, "opinions differ as to whether there ever were any or not in the world; but the Holy Scripture, which can not err by a jot from the truth, shows us that there were, when it gives us the history of that big Philistine, Goliath, who was seven cubits and a half in height, which is a huge size. Likewise, in the island of Sicily, there have been found leg-bones and arm-bones so large that their size makes it plain that their owners were giants, and as tall as great towers; geometry puts this fact beyond a doubt. But, for all that, I can not speak with certainty as to the size of Morgante, though I suspect he can not have been very tall; and I am inclined to be of this opinion because I find in the history[62] in which his deeds are particularly mentioned, that he frequently slept under a roof; and as he found houses to contain him, it is clear that his bulk could not have been anything excessive."

"That is true," said the curate, and yielding to the enjoyment of hearing such nonsense, he asked him what was his notion of the features of Reinaldos of Montalban, and Don Roland and the rest of the Twelve Peers of France, for they were all knights-errant.

"As for Reinaldos," replied Don Quixote, "I venture to say that he was broad-faced, of ruddy complexion, with roguish and somewhat prominent eyes, excessively punctilious and touchy, and given to the society of thieves and scapegraces. With regard to Roland, or Rotolando, or Orlando (for the histories call him by all these names), I am of opinion, and hold, that he was of middle height, broad-shouldered, rather bow-legged, swarthy-complexioned, red-bearded, with a hairy body and a severe expression of countenance, a man of few words, but very polite and well-bred."

"If Roland was not a more graceful person than your worship has described," said the curate, "it is no wonder that the fair Lady Angelica rejected him and left him for the gayety, liveliness, and grace of that budding-bearded little Moor to whom she surrendered herself; and she showed her sense in falling in love with the gentle softness of Medoro rather than the roughness of Roland."

"That Angelica, señor curate," returned Don Quixote, "was a giddy damsel, flighty and somewhat wanton, and she left the world as full of her

---

[62] that is, the *Morgante Maggiore* of Pulci. The account of the bones found in Sicily is in the *Jardín de Flores Curiosos* of Antonio de Torquemada.

vagaries as the fame of her beauty. She treated with scorn a thousand gentlemen, men of valor and wisdom, and took up with a smooth-faced sprig of
a page, without fortune or fame, except such reputation for gratitude as
the affection he bore his friend got for him.[63] The great poet who sang her
beauty, the famous Ariosto, not caring to sing her adventures after her
contemptible surrender (which probably were not over and above credit-
able), dropped her where he says:

> How she received the sceptre of Cathay,
> Some bard of defter quill may sing some day;[64]

and this was no doubt a kind of prophecy, for poets are also called *vates,*
that is to say diviners; and its truth was made plain; for since then a famous
Andalusian poet has lamented and sung her tears, and another famous and
rare poet, a Castilian, has sung her beauty." [65]

"Tell me, Señor Don Quixote," said the barber here, "among all those
who praised her, has there been no poet to write a satire on this Lady
Angelica?"

"I can well believe," replied Don Quixote, "that if Sacripante or Roland
had been poets they would have given the damsel a trimming; for it is
naturally the way with poets who have been scorned and rejected by their
ladies, whether fictitious or not, in short by those whom they select as the
ladies of their thoughts, to avenge themselves in satires and libels—a vengeance, to be sure, unworthy of generous hearts; but up to the present I
have not heard of any defamatory verse against the Lady Angelica, who
turned the world upside down."

"Strange," said the curate; but at this moment they heard the housekeeper
and the niece, who had previously withdrawn from the conversation, exclaiming aloud in the courtyard, and at the noise they all ran out.

---

[63] The friend was his master, Dardinel, beside whose body he received the wound
of which he was cured by Angelica.   [64] Cervantes misquotes Ariosto's lines, which
are:

> E dell' India a Medor desse lo scettro,
> Forse altri canterà con miglior plettro.
>
> *Orlando Furioso,* xxx. 16.

[65] The Andalusian was Barahona de Soto, who wrote the *Primera parte de la
Angélica* (not *Lágrimas de Angélica,* as Cervantes calls it in Chapter VI Part I).
It appeared at Granada in 1586. The Castilian was Lope de Vega, whose *Hermo-
sura de Angélica* formed the first part of his *Rimas,* printed at Madrid in 1602.

CHAPTER II

Which Treats of the Notable Altercation
which Sancho Panza Had with
Don Quixote's Niece and Housekeeper,
Together with Other Droll Matters.

The history relates that the outcry Don Quixote, the curate, and the
barber heard came from the niece and the housekeeper exclaiming to
Sancho, who was striving to force his way in to see Don Quixote while they
held the door against him, "What does the vagabond want in this house?
Be off to your own, brother, for it is you, and no one else, that delude my
master, and lead him astray, and take him tramping about the country."

To which Sancho replied, "Devil's own housekeeper! it is I who am
deluded, and led astray, and taken tramping about the country, and not thy
master! He has carried me all over the world, and you are mightily mistaken. He enticed me away from home by a trick, promising me an island,
which I am still waiting for."

"May evil islands choke thee, thou detestable Sancho," said the niece;
"what are islands? Is it something to eat, glutton and gormandizer that
thou art?"

"It is not something to eat," replied Sancho, "but something to govern
and rule, and better than four cities or four judgeships at court."

"For all that," said the housekeeper, "you don't enter here, you bag of
mischief and sack of knavery; go govern your house and dig your seed-patch,
and give over looking for islands or shylands." [66]

The curate and the barber listened with great amusement to the words
of the three; but Don Quixote, uneasy lest Sancho should blab and blurt
out a whole heap of mischievous stupidities, and touch upon points that
might not be altogether to his credit, called to him and made the other two
hold their tongues and let him come in. Sancho entered, and the curate and
the barber took their leave of Don Quixote, of whose recovery they despaired
when they saw how wedded he was to his crazy ideas, and how saturated
with the nonsense of his unlucky chivalry; and said the curate to the barber,
"You will see, gossip, that when we are least thinking of it, our gentleman
will be off once more for another flight."

"I have no doubt of it," returned the barber; "but I do not wonder so
much at the madness of the knight as at the simplicity of the squire, who has
such a firm belief in all that about the island, that I suppose all the ex-
posures that could be imagined would not get it out of his head."

[66] in the original *insulas ni insulos. Insula*, the word always used in the *Amadis*,
and by Don Quixote, instead of *isla*, is a puzzle to the niece and housekeeper.

"God help them," said the curate; "and let us be on the look-out to see
what comes of all these absurdities of the said knight and squire, for it
seems as if they had both been cast in the same mould, and the madness
of the master without the simplicity of the man would not be worth a
farthing."

"That is true," said the barber, "and I should like very much to know
what the pair are talking about at this moment."

"I promise you," said the curate, "the niece or the housekeeper will tell
us by-and-by, for they are not the ones to forget to listen."

Meanwhile Don Quixote shut himself up in his room with Sancho, and
when they were alone he said to him, "It grieves me greatly, Sancho, that
thou shouldst have said, and sayest, that I took thee out of thy cottage,
when thou knowest I did not remain in my house. We sallied forth together,
we took the road together, we wandered abroad together; we have had the
same fortune and the same luck; if they blanketed thee once, they be-
labored me a hundred times, and that is the only advantage I have of thee."

"That was only reasonable," replied Sancho, "for, by what your worship
says, misfortunes belong more properly to knights-errant than to their
squires."

"Thou art mistaken, Sancho," said Don Quixote, "according to the
maxim *quando caput dolet,* etc."

"I don't understand any language but my own," said Sancho.

"I mean to say," said Don Quixote, "that when the head suffers all the
members suffer; and so, being thy lord and master, I am thy head, and thou
a part of me as thou art my servant; and therefore any evil that affects or
shall affect me should give thee pain, and what affects thee give pain to me."

"It should be so," said Sancho; "but when I was blanketed as a member,
my head was on the other side of the wall, looking on while I was flying
through the air, and did not feel any pain whatever; and if the members
are obliged to feel the suffering of the head, it should be obliged to feel
their sufferings."

"Dost thou mean to say now, Sancho," said Don Quixote, "that I did not
suffer when they were blanketing thee? If thou dost, thou must not say so
or think so, for I felt more pain then in spirit than thou didst in body.
But let us put that aside for the present, for we shall have opportunities
enough for considering and settling the point; tell me, Sancho my friend,
what do they say about me in the village here? What do the common people
think of me? What do the hidalgos? What do the caballeros? [67] What do
they say of my valor; of my achievements; of my courtesy? How do they
treat the task I have undertaken in reviving and restoring to the world
the now forgotten order of chivalry? In short, Sancho, I would have thee

[67] that is, the gentry by birth and the gentry by position.

tell me all that has come to thine ears on this subject; and thou art to tell me, without adding anything to the good or taking away anything from the bad; for it is the duty of loyal vassals to tell the truth to their lords just as it is and in its proper shape, not allowing flattery to add to it or any idle deference to lessen it. And I would have thee know, Sancho, that if the naked truth, undisguised by flattery, came to the ears of princes, times would be different, and other ages would be reckoned iron ages more than ours, which I hold to be the golden of these latter days. Profit by this advice, Sancho, and report to me clearly and faithfully the truth of what thou knowest touching what I have demanded of thee."

"That I will do with all my heart, master," replied Sancho, "provided your worship will not be vexed at what I say, as you wish me to say it out in all its nakedness, without putting any more clothes on it than it came to my knowledge in."

"I will not be vexed at all," returned Don Quixote; "thou mayest speak freely, Sancho, and without any beating about the bush."

"Well then," said he, "first of all, I have to tell you that the common people consider your worship a mighty great madman, and me no less a fool. The hidalgos say that, not keeping within the bounds of your quality of gentleman, you have assumed the 'Don,' [68] and made a knight of yourself at a jump, with four vine-stocks and a couple of acres of land, and never a shirt to your back. The caballeros say they do not want to have hidalgos setting up in opposition to them, particularly squire hidalgos who polish their own shoes and darn their black stockings with green silk."

"That," said Don Quixote, "does not apply to me, for I always go well dressed and never patched; ragged I may be, very likely, but ragged more from the wear and tear of arms than of time."

"As to your worship's valor, courtesy, achievements, and task, there is a variety of opinions. Some say, 'mad but droll;' others, 'valiant but unlucky;' others, 'courteous but meddling;' and then they go into such a number of things that they don't leave a whole bone either in your worship or in myself."

"Recollect, Sancho," said Don Quixote, "that wherever virtue exists in an eminent degree it is persecuted. Few or none of the famous men that have lived escaped being calumniated by malice. Julius Cæsar, the boldest, wisest, and bravest of captains, was charged with being ambitious, and not particularly cleanly in his dress, or pure in his morals. Of Alexander, whose deeds won him the name of Great, they say that he was somewhat of a drunkard. Of Hercules, him of the many labors, it is said that he was lewd and luxurious. Of Don Galaor, the brother of Amadis of Gaul, it was whispered that he was quarrelsome, and of his brother that he was lachry-

[68] In the time of Cervantes, the title of *Don* was much more restricted than nowadays, when it is by courtesy given to every one.

mose. So that, O Sancho, amongst all these calumnies against good men, mine may be let pass, since they are no more than thou hast said."

"That's just where it is, body of my father!" returned Sancho.

"Is there more, then?" asked Don Quixote.

"There's the tail to be skinned yet," said Sancho; "all so far is cakes and fancy bread; but if your worship wants to know all about the calumnies they bring against you, I will fetch you one this instant who can tell you the whole of them without missing an atom; for last night the son of Bartholomew Carrasco, who has been studying at Salamanca, came home after having been made a bachelor, and when I went to welcome him, he told me that your worship's history is already abroad in books, with the title of 'The Ingenious Gentleman Don Quixote of La Mancha;' and he says they mention me in it by my own name of Sancho Panza, and the lady Dulcinea del Toboso too, and divers things that happened to us when we were alone; so that I crossed myself in my wonder how the historian who wrote them down could have known them."

"I promise thee, Sancho," said Don Quixote, "the author of our history will be some sage enchanter; for to such nothing that they choose to write about is hidden."

"What!" said Sancho, "a sage and an enchanter! Why, the bachelor Samson Carrasco (that is the name of him I spoke of) says the author of the history is called Cid Hamet Berengena."

"That is a Moorish name," said Don Quixote.

"May be so," replied Sancho; "for I have heard say that the Moors are mostly great lovers of berengenas." [69]

"Thou must have mistaken the surname of this 'Cid'—which means in Arabic 'Lord'—Sancho," observed Don Quixote.

"Very likely," replied Sancho, "but if your worship wishes me to fetch the bachelor I will go for him in a twinkling."

"Thou wilt do me a great pleasure, my friend," said Don Quixote, "for what thou hast told me has amazed me, and I shall not eat a morsel that will agree with me until I have heard all about it."

"Then I am off for him," said Sancho; and leaving his master he went in quest of the bachelor, with whom he returned in a short time, and, all three together, they had a very droll colloquy.

After several chapters of conversation, Don Quixote and Sancho resolve to take to the road once more. Among the many adventures in Part II, perhaps Don Quixote's descent into the Cave of Montesinos best illustrates Cervantes' handling of the extensive implications of his hero's subjective vision of the world.

[69] *berengena*—the aubergine or egg plant.

Wherein Is Related the Grand Adventure of the Cave of Montesinos in the Heart of La Mancha Which the Valiant Don Quixote Brought to a Happy Termination.

. . . In this and other pleasant conversation the day went by, and that night they put up at a small hamlet whence it was not more than two· leagues to the cave of Montesinos, so the cousin[70] told Don Quixote, adding that if he was bent upon entering it, it would be requisite for him to provide himself with ropes, so that he might be tied and lowered into its depths. Don Quixote said that even if it reached to the bottomless pit he meant to see where it went to; so they bought about a hundred fathoms of rope, and next day at two in the afternoon they arrived at the cave, the mouth of which is spacious and wide, but full of thorn and wild-fig bushes and brambles and briers, so thick and matted that they completely close it up and cover it over.[71]

On coming within sight of it the cousin, Sancho, and Don Quixote dismounted, and the first two immediately tied the latter very firmly with the ropes, and as they were girding and swathing him Sancho said to him, "Mind what you are about, master mine; don't go burying yourself alive, or putting yourself where you'll be like a bottle put to cool in a well; it's no affair or business of your worship's to become the explorer of this, which must be worse than a Moorish dungeon."

"Tie me and hold thy peace," said Don Quixote, "for an emprise like this, friend Sancho, was reserved for me;" [72] and said the guide, "I beg of you, Señor Don Quixote, to observe carefully and examine with a hundred eyes everything that is within there; perhaps there may be some things for me to put into my book of transformations."

[70] He is the cousin of a character who has briefly appeared shortly before. The cousin, at his appearance, has announced that he is a humanist author, currently preparing (among other things) a work to be entitled *The Metamorphoses or the Spanish Ovid*—Ed.   [71] The hamlet referred to is clearly that of Ruidera, about five leagues southeast of Argamasilla, near the Laguna del Rey, the lowest of the chain of lakes from which the waters of the Guadiana flow into the plain of La Mancha. From thence across the hills it is about two leagues to the cave of Montesinos, which lies a little to the north of the ruins of the castle of Rocafria. . . . There can be no doubt that Cervantes visited the spot, but he has somewhat exaggerated the dimensions of the cave. The mouth is not more than eight or ten feet wide, nor the depth more than fifty or sixty; nor is the descent so steep as to make a rope requisite. It is, in all probability, an ancient mine of Roman or possibly Carthaginian origin. . . .   [72] a line from the ballad in the *Guerras Civiles de Granada*, "Estanda el Rey Don Fernando."

"The drum is in hands that will know how to beat it well enough," said Sancho Panza.

When he had said this and finished the tying (which was not over the armor, but only over the doublet) Don Quixote observed, "It was careless of us not to have provided ourselves with a small cattle-bell to be tied on the rope close to me, the sound of which would show that I was still descending and alive; but as this is out of the question now, in God's hand be it to guide me;" and forthwith he fell on his knees and in a low voice offered up a prayer to Heaven, imploring God to aid him and grant him success in this to all appearance perilous and untried adventure, and then exclaimed aloud, "O mistress of my actions and movements, illustrious and peerless Dulcinea del Toboso, if so be the prayers and supplications of this thy fortunate lover can reach thy ears, by thy incomparable beauty I entreat thee to listen to them, for they but ask thee not to refuse me thy favor and protection now that I stand in such need of them. I am about to precipitate, to sink, to plunge myself into the abyss that is here before me, only to let the world know that while thou dost favor me there is no impossibility I will not attempt and accomplish." With these words he approached the cavern, and perceived that it was impossible to let himself down or effect an entrance except by sheer force or cleaving a passage; so drawing his sword he began to demolish and cut away the brambles at the mouth of the cave, at the noise of which a vast multitude of crows and choughs flew out of it so thick and so fast that they knocked Don Quixote down; and if he had been as much of a believer in augury as he was a Catholic Christian he would have taken it as a bad omen and declined to bury himself in such a place. He got up, however, and as there came no more crows, or night-birds like the bats that flew out at the same time with the crows, the cousin and Sancho giving him rope, he lowered himself into the depths of the dread cavern; and as he entered it Sancho sent his blessing after him, making a thousand crosses over him and saying, "God, and the Peña de Francia, and the Trinity of Gaeta[73] guide thee, O flower and cream of knights-errant. There thou goest, thou dare-devil of the earth, heart of steel, arm of brass; once more, God guide thee and send thee back safe, and sound, and unhurt to the light of this world thou art leaving to bury thyself in the darkness thou art seeking there;" and the cousin offered up almost the same prayers and supplications.

Don Quixote kept calling to them to give him rope and more rope, and they gave it out little by little, and by the time the calls, which came out of the cave as out of a pipe, ceased to be heard they had let down the hundred

---

[73] The *Peña de Francia* is a mountain near Ciudad Rodrigo, and one of the holy places of Spain in consequence of the discovery of an image of the Virgin there in the fifteenth century. The *Trinity of Gaeta* is the chapel dedicated to the Trinity above the harbor of Gaeta.

fathoms of rope. They were inclined to pull Don Quixote up again, as they could give him no more rope; however, they waited about half an hour, at the end of which time they began to gather in the rope again with great ease and without feeling any weight, which made them fancy Don Quixote was remaining below; and persuaded that it was so, Sancho wept bitterly, and hauled away in great haste in order to settle the question. When, however, they had come to, as it seemed, rather more than eighty fathoms they felt a weight, at which they were greatly delighted; and at last, at ten fathoms more, they saw Don Quixote distinctly, and Sancho called out to him, saying, "Welcome back, señor, for we had begun to think you were going to stop there to found a family." But Don Quixote answered not a word, and drawing him out entirely they perceived he had his eyes shut and every appearance of being fast asleep.

They stretched him on the ground and untied him, but still he did not awake; however, they rolled him back and forwards and shook and pulled him about, so that after some time he came to himself, stretching himself just as if he were waking up from a deep and sound sleep, and looking about him as if scared he said, "God forgive you, friends; ye have taken me away from the sweetest and most delightful existence and spectacle that ever human being enjoyed or beheld. Now indeed do I know that all the pleasures of this life pass away like a shadow and a dream, or fade like the flower of the field. O ill-fated Montesinos! O sore-wounded Durandarte! O unhappy Belerma! O tearful Guadiana, and ye O hapless daughters of Ruidera who show in your waves the tears that flowed from your beauteous eyes!"

The cousin and Sancho Panza listened with deep attention to the words of Don Quixote, who uttered them as though with immense pain he drew them up from his very bowels. They begged of him to explain himself, and tell them what he had seen in that hell down there.

"Hell do you call it?" said Don Quixote; "call it by no such name, for it docs not deserve it, as ye shall soon see."

He then begged them to give him something to eat, as he was very hungry. They spread the cousin's sack-cloth on the grass, and put the stores of the alforjas into requisition, and all three sitting down lovingly and sociably, they made a luncheon and a supper of it all in one; and when the sack-cloth was removed, Don Quixote of La Mancha said, "Let no one rise; and attend to me, my sons, both of you."

CHAPTER XXIII

Of the Wonderful Things
the Incomparable Don Quixote Said
He Saw in the Profound Cave of Montesinos,
the Impossibility and Magnitude of Which
Cause this Adventure
to Be Deemed Apocryphal.

It was about four in the afternoon when the sun, veiled in clouds, with subdued light and tempered beams, enabled Don Quixote to relate, without heat or inconvenience, what he had seen in the cave of Montesinos to his two illustrious hearers, and he began as follows:

"A matter of some twelve or fourteen times a man's height down in this pit, on the left-hand side, there is a recess or space, roomy enough to contain a large cart with its mules. A little light reaches it through some chinks or crevices, communicating with it and open to the surface of the earth. This recess or space I perceived when I was already growing weary and disgusted at finding myself hanging suspended by the rope, travelling downwards into that dark region without any certainty or knowledge of where I was going to, so I resolved to enter it and rest myself for a while. I called out, telling you not to let out more rope until I bade you, but you can not have heard me. I then gathered in the rope you were sending me, and making a coil or pile of it I seated myself upon it, ruminating and considering what I was to do to lower myself to the bottom, having no one to hold me up; and as I was thus deep in thought and perplexity, suddenly and without provocation a profound sleep fell upon me, and when I least expected it, I know not how, I awoke and found myself in the midst of the most beautiful, delicious, delightful meadow that nature could produce or the most lively human imagination conceive. I opened my eyes, I rubbed them, and found I was not asleep, but thoroughly awake. Nevertheless, I felt my head and breast to satisfy myself whether it was I myself who was there or some empty delusive phantom; but touch, feeling, the collected thoughts that passed through my mind, all convinced me that I was the same then and there that I am this moment. Next there presented itself to my sight a stately royal palace or castle, with walls that seemed built of clear transparent crystal; and through two great doors that opened wide therein, I saw coming forth and advancing towards me a venerable old man, clad in a long gown of mulberry-colored serge that trailed upon the ground. On his shoulders and breast he had a green satin collegiate hood, and covering his head a black Milanese bonnet, and his snow-white beard fell below his girdle. He carried no arms whatever, nothing but a rosary of beads bigger than fair-sized filberts, each tenth bead being like a moderate ostrich egg; his bearing, his gait, his dignity and imposing presence held me spellbound and wondering. He approached me, and the first thing he did was to embrace me closely, and then he said to me, 'For a long time now, O valiant knight Don Quixote of La Mancha, we who are here enchanted in these solitudes have been hoping to see thee, that thou mayest make known to the world what is shut up and concealed in this deep cave, called the cave of Montesinos, which thou hast entered, an achievement reserved for thy invincible heart and stupendous courage alone to attempt. Come with me, illustrious sir, and I will show thee the marvels hidden within this transparent castle, whereof I am the alcaide and perpetual warden; for I am Montesinos himself, from whom the cave takes it name.' [74]

"The instant he told me he was Montesinos, I asked him if the story they told in the world above here was true, that he had taken out the heart of his great friend Durandarte from his breast with a little dagger, and carried it to the Lady Belerma, as his friend when at the point of death had commanded him. He said in reply that they spoke the truth in every respect except as to the dagger, for it was not a dagger, nor little, but a burnished poniard sharper than an awl."

"That poniard must have been made by Ramon de Hoces the Sevillian," said Sancho.

"I do not know," said Don Quixote; "it could not have been by that poniard maker, however, because Ramon de Hoces was a man of yesterday, and the affair of Roncesvalles, where this mishap occurred, was long ago; but the question is of no great importance, nor does it affect or make any alteration in the truth or substance of the story."

"That is true," said the cousin; "continue, Señor Don Quixote, for I am listening to you with the greatest pleasure in the world."

"And with no less do I tell the tale," said Don Quixote; "and so, to proceed—the venerable Montesinos led me into the palace of crystal, where, in a lower chamber, strangely cool and entirely of alabaster, was an elaborately wrought marble tomb, upon which I beheld, stretched at full length, a knight, not of bronze, or marble, or jasper, as are seen on other tombs, but of actual flesh and bone. His right hand (which seemed to me somewhat hairy and sinewy, a sign of great strength in its owner) lay on the side of his heart; but before I could put any question to Montesinos, he, seeing me gazing at the tomb in amazement, said to me. 'This is my friend Durandarte, flower and mirror of the true lovers and valiant knights of his time. He is held enchanted here, as I myself and many others are, by that French en-

[74] Montesinos is the hero of half a dozen ballads belonging to the Carlovingian cycle but does not figure in any of the French romances. According to the ballads he was one of the Peers, and son of Count Grimaltos, or Grimaldos, by a daughter of Charlemagne. . . .

chanter Merlin, who, they say, was the devil's son;[75] but my belief is, not that he was the devil's son, but that he knew, as the saying is, a point more than the devil. How or why he enchanted us, no one knows, but time will tell, and I suspect that time is not far off. What I marvel at is, that I know it to be as sure as that it is now day, that Durandarte ended his life in my arms, and that, after his death, I took out his heart with my own hands; and indeed it must have weighed more than two pounds, for, according to naturalists, he who has a large heart is more largely endowed with valor than he who has a small one. Then, as this is the case, and as the knight did really die, how comes it that he now moans and sighs from time to time, as if he were still alive?'

"As he said this, the wretched Durandarte cried out in a loud voice:

> O cousin Montesinos!
>   'T was my last request of thee,
> When my soul hath left the body,
>   And that lying dead I be,
> With thy poniard or thy dagger
>   Cut the heart from out my breast,
> And bear it to Belerma.
>   This was my last request.

On hearing which, the venerable Montesinos fell on his knees before the unhappy knight, and with tearful eyes exclaimed, 'Long since, O Señor Durandarte, my beloved cousin, long since have I done what you bade me on that sad day when I lost you; I took out your heart as well as I could, not leaving an atom of it in your breast, I wiped it with a lace handkerchief, and I took the road to France with it, having first laid you in the bosom of the earth with tears enough to wash and cleanse my hands of the blood that covered them after wandering among your bowels; and more by token, O cousin of my soul, at the first village I came to after leaving Roncevalles, I sprinkled a little salt upon your heart to keep it sweet, and bring it, if not fresh, at least pickled, into the presence of the lady Belerma, whom, together with you, myself, Guadiana your squire, the duenna Ruidera and her seven daughters and two nieces, and many more of your friends and acquaintances, the sage Merlin has been keeping here these many years; and although more than five hundred have gone by, not one of us has died; Ruidera and her daughters and nieces alone are missing, and these, because of the tears they shed, Merlin, out of the compassion he seems to have felt for them, changed into so many lakes, which to this day in the world of the living, and in the province of La Mancha, are called the lakes

---

[75] Merlin has been claimed by the Bretons as one of themselves, but of course he was a Welshman. In Malloy's *Arthur* he is called "a devil's son."

of Ruidera. The seven daughters belong to the kings of Spain, and the two nieces to the knights of a very holy order called the Order of St. John. Guadiana your squire, likewise bewailing your fate, was changed into a river of his own name, but when he came to the surface and beheld the sun of another heaven, so great was his grief at finding he was leaving you, that he plunged into the bowels of the earth; however, as he can not help following his natural course, he from time to time comes forth and shows himself to the sun and the world. The lakes aforesaid send him their waters, and with these, and others that come to him, he makes a grand and imposing entrance into Portugal; but for all that, go where he may, he shows his melancholy and sadness, and takes no pride in breeding dainty choice fish, only coarse and tasteless sorts, very different from those of the golden Tagus.[76] All this that I tell you now, O cousin mine, I have told you many times before, and as you make no answer, I fear that either you believe me not, or do not hear me, whereat I feel God knows what grief. I have now news to give you, which, if it serves not to alleviate your sufferings, will not in any wise increase them. Know that you have here before you (open your eyes and you will see) that great knight of whom the sage Merlin has prophesied such great things; that Don Quixote of La Mancha I mean, who has again, and to better purpose than in past times, revived in these days knight-errantry, long since forgotten, and by whose intervention and aid it may be we shall be disenchanted; for great deeds are reserved for great men.'

" 'And if that may not be,' said the wretched Durandarte in a low and feeble voice, 'if that may not be, then, O my cousin, I say "patience and shuffle;" ' and turning over on his side, he relapsed into his former silence without uttering another word.

"And now there was heard a great outcry and lamentation, accompanied by deep sighs and bitter sobs. I looked round, and through the crystal wall I saw passing through another chamber a procession of two lines of fair damsels all clad in mourning, and with white turbans of Turkish fashion on their heads. Behind, in the rear of these, there came a lady, for so from her dignity she seemed to be, also clad in black, with a white veil so long and ample that it swept the ground. Her turban was twice as large as the largest of any of the others; her eybrows met, her nose was rather flat, her mouth was large but with ruddy lips, and her teeth, of which at times she allowed a glimpse, were seen to be sparse, and ill-set, though as white as peeled almonds. She carried in her hands a fine cloth, and in it, as well as I could make out, a heart that had been mummied, so parched and dried was it. Montesinos told me that all those forming the procession were the

---

[76] The Guadiana, after issuing from the Ruidera valley near the picturesque old castle of Peñaroya, traverses the plain of La Mancha and disappears from sight a little to the north of Argamasilla, to reappear seven or eight leagues off at the Ojos de la Guadiana, near Daimiel. . . .

attendants of Durandarte and Belerma, who were enchanted there with their master and mistress, and that the last, she who carried the heart in the cloth, was the lady Belerma, who, with her damsels, four days in the week went in procession singing, or rather weeping, dirges over the body and miserable heart of his cousin; and that if she appeared to me somewhat ill-favored, or not so beautiful as fame reported her, it was because of the bad nights and worse days that she passed in that enchantment, as I could see by the great dark circles round her eyes, and her sickly complexion; 'her sallowness, and the rings round her eyes,' said he, 'are not caused by the periodical ailment usual with women, for it is many months and even years since she has had any, but by the grief her own heart suffers because of that which she holds in her hand perpetually, and which recalls and brings back to her memory the sad fate of her lost lover; were it not for this, hardly would the great Dulcinea del Toboso, so celebrated in all these parts, and even in all the world, come up to her for beauty, grace, and gayety.'

" 'Hold hard!' said I at this, 'tell your story as you ought, Señor Don Montesinos, for you know very well that all comparisons are odious, and there is no occasion to compare one person with another; the peerless Dulcinea del Toboso is what she is, and the lady Doña Belerma is what *she* is and has been, and that's enough.' To which he made answer, 'Forgive me, Señor Don Quixote; I own I was wrong and spoke unadvisedly in saying that the lady Dulcinea could scarcely come up to the lady Belerma; for it were enough for me to have learned, by what means I know not, that you are her knight, to make me bite my tongue out before I compared her to anything save heaven itself.' After this apology which the great Montesinos made me, my heart recovered itself from the shock I had received in hearing my lady compared with Belerma."

"Still I wonder," said Sancho, "that your worship did not get upon the old fellow and bruise every bone of him with kicks, and pluck his beard until you didn't leave a hair in it."

"Nay, Sancho, my friend," said Don Quixote, "it would not have been right in me to do that, for we are all bound to pay respect to the aged, even though they be not knights, but especially those who are, and who are enchanted; I only know I gave him as good as he brought in the many other questions and answers we exchanged."

"I can not understand, Señor Don Quixote," remarked the cousin here, "how it is that your worship, in such a short space of time as you have been below there, could have seen so many things, and said and answered so much."

"How long is it since I went down?" asked Don Quixote.

"Little better than an hour," replied Sancho.

"That can not be," returned Don Quixote, "because night overtook me while I was there, and day came, and it was night again and day again three times; so that, by my reckoning, I have been three days in those remote regions beyond our ken."

"My master must be right," replied Sancho; "for as everything that has happened to him is by enchantment, maybe what seems to us an hour would seem three days and nights there."

"That's it," said Don Quixote.

"And did your worship eat anything all that time, señor?" asked the cousin.

"I never touched a morsel," answered Don Quixote, "nor did I even feel hunger, or think of it."

"And do the enchanted eat?" said the cousin.

"They neither eat," said Don Quixote; "nor are they subject to the greater excrements, though it is thought that their nails, beards, and hair grow."

"And do the enchanted sleep, now, señor?" asked Sancho.

"Certainly not," replied Don Quixote; "at least, during those three days I was with them not one of them closed an eye, nor did I either."

"The proverb, 'Tell me what company thou keepest and I'll tell thee what thou art,' is to the point here," said Sancho; "your worship keeps company with enchanted people that are always fasting and watching; what wonder is it, then, that you neither eat nor sleep while you are with them? But forgive me, señor, if I say that of all this you have told us now, may God take me—I was just going to say the devil—if I believe a single particle."

"What!" said the cousin, "has Señor Don Quixote, then, been lying? Why, even if he wished it he has not had time to imagine and put together such a host of lies."

"I don't believe my master lies," said Sancho.

"If not, what dost thou believe?" asked Don Quixote.

"I believe," replied Sancho, "that this Merlin, or those enchanters who enchanted the whole crew your worship says you saw and discoursed with down there, stuffed your imagination or your mind with all this rigmarole you have been treating us to, and all that is still to come."

"All that might be, Sancho," replied Don Quixote; "but it is not so, for everything that I have told you I saw with my own eyes, and touched with my own hands. But what will you say when I tell you now how, among the countless other marvellous things Montesinos showed me (of which at leisure and at the proper time I will give thee an account in the course of our journey, for they would not be all in place here), he showed me three country girls who went skipping and capering like goats over the pleasant fields there, and the instant I beheld them I knew one to be the peerless Dulcinea del Toboso, and the other two those same country girls that were with her and that we spoke to on the road from El Toboso! I asked Montesinos if he knew them, and he told me he did not, but he thought they must be some enchanted ladies of distinction, for it was only a few days before that they had made their appearance in those meadows; but I was not to be surprised at that, because there were a great many other ladies there of times past and present, enchanted in various strange shapes, and among them he had recognized Queen Guinevere and her dame Quintañona, she who poured out the wine for Lancelot when he came from Britain."

When Sancho Panza heard his master say this he was ready to take leave of his senses, or die with laughter; for, as he knew the real truth about the pretended enchantment of Dulcinea, in which he himself had been the enchanter and concocter of all the evidence,[77] he made up his mind at last that, beyond all doubt, his master was out of his wits and stark mad, so he said to him, "It was an evil hour, a worse season, and a sorrowful day, when your worship, dear master mine, went down to the other world, and an unlucky moment when you met with Señor Montesinos, who has sent you back to us like this. You were well enough here above in your full senses, such as God had given you, delivering maxims and giving advice at every turn, and not as you are now, talking the greatest nonsense that can be imagined."

"As I know thee, Sancho," said Don Quixote, "I heed not thy words."

"Nor I your worship's," said Sancho, "whether you beat me or kill me for those I have spoken, and will speak if you don't correct and mend your own. But tell me, while we are still at peace, how or by what did you recognize the lady our mistress; and if you spoke to her, what did you say, and what did she answer?"

"I recognized her," said Don Quixote, "by her wearing the same garments she wore when thou didst point her out to me. I spoke to her, but she did not utter a word in reply; on the contrary, she turned her back on me and took to flight, at such a pace that a crossbow bolt could not have overtaken her. I wished to follow her, and would have done so had not Montesinos recommended me not to take the trouble as it would be useless, particularly as the time was drawing near when it would be necessary for me to quit the cavern. He told me, moreover, that in course of time he would let me know how he and Belerma, and Durandarte, and all who were there, were to be disenchanted. But of all I saw and observed down there, what gave me most pain was, that while Montesinos was speaking to me, one of the two companions of the hapless Dulcinea approached me on one side, without my having seen her coming, and with tears in her eyes said to me, in a low, agitated voice, 'My lady Dulcinea del Toboso kisses your worship's hands, and entreats you to do her the favor of letting her know how you are; and,

---

[77] In Chapter X of Part II Sancho has convinced Don Quixote that a peasant girl is Dulcinea. When she fails to reverence her knight, Don Quixote decides she has been put under the spell of an evil enchanter. Sancho, of course, knows the facts of the case, since it is he who has created them—Ed.

being in great need, she also entreats your worship as earnestly as she can to be so good as to lend her half a dozen reals, or as much as you may have about you, on this new dimity petticoat that I have here; and she promises to repay them very speedily.' I was amazed and taken aback by such a message, and turning to Señor Montesinos I asked him, 'Is it possible, Señor Montesinos, that persons of distinction under enchantment can be in need?' To which he replied, 'Believe me, Señor Don Quixote, that which is called need is to be met with everywhere, and penetrates all quarters and reaches every one, and does not spare even the enchanted; and as the lady Dulcinea del Toboso sends to beg those six reals, and the pledge is to all appearance a good one, there is nothing for it but to give them to her, for no doubt she must be in some great strait.' 'I will take no pledge of her,' I replied, 'nor yet can I give her what she asks, for all I have is four reals;' which I gave (they were those which thou, Sancho, gavest me the other day to bestow in alms upon the poor I met along the road), and I said, 'Tell your mistress, my dear, that I am grieved to the heart because of her distresses, and wish I was a Fucar[78] to remedy them, and that I would have her know that I can not be, and ought not be, in health while deprived of the happiness of seeing her and enjoying her discreet conversation, and that I implore her as earnestly as I can, to allow herself to be seen and addressed by this her captive servant and forlorn knight. Tell her, too, that when she least expects it she will hear it announced that I have made an oath and vow after the fashion of that which the Marquis of Mantua made to avenge his nephew Baldwin, when he found him at the point of death in the heart of the mountains, which was, not to eat bread off a table-cloth, and the other trifling matters which he added, until he had avenged him; and I will make the same to take no rest, and to roam the seven regions of the earth more thoroughly than the Infante Don Pedro of Portugal ever roamed them,[79] until I have disenchanted her.' 'All that, and more, you owe my lady,' was the damsel's answer to me, and taking the four reals, instead of making me a courtesy she cut a caper, springing two full yards into the air."

"O blessed God!" exclaimed Sancho aloud at this, "is it possible that such things can be in the world, and that enchanters and enchantments can have such power in it as to have changed my master's right senses into a craze so full of absurdity! O señor, señor, for God's sake, consider yourself, have a care for your honor, and give no credit to this silly stuff that has left you scant and short of wits."

"Thou talkest in this way because thou lovest me, Sancho," said Don

---

[78] the Spanish form of Fugger, the name of the great Augsburg capitalists of the sixteenth century.   [79] *The Travels of the Infante Don Pedro of Portugal through the Four Quarters of the World*, "written by Juan Gómez de Sanestevan," Saragossa, 1570, was a popular book and passed through several editions.

Quixote; "and not being experienced in the things of the world, everything that has some difficulty about it, seems to thee impossible; but time will pass, as I said before, and I will tell thee some of the things I saw down there which will make thee believe what I have related now, the truth of which admits of neither reply nor question."

The eventful wanderings of Don Quixote and Sancho Panza continue until the Don is unhorsed by the Knight of the White Moon—actually Quixote's neighbor, the Bachelor Carrasco, in disguise—and agrees to return home. On the way back he and Sancho conspire to become shepherds for the duration of the year, throughout which Quixote has pledged to refrain from knightly activity.

CHAPTER LXXIV

Of How Don Quixote Fell Sick, and of the Will He Made, and How He Died.

As nothing that is man's can last forever, but all tends ever downwards from its beginning to its end, and above all man's life, and as Don Quixote's enjoyed no special dispensation from Heaven to stay its course, its end and close came when he least looked for it. For—whether it was of the dejection the thought of his defeat produced, or of Heaven's will that so ordered it—a fever settled upon him and kept him in his bed for six days, during which he was often visited by his friends the curate, the bachelor, and the barber, while his good squire Sancho Panza never quitted his bedside. They, persuaded that it was grief at finding himself vanquished, and the object of his heart, the liberation and disenchantment of Dulcinea, unattained, that kept him in this state, strove by all the means in their power to cheer him up; the bachelor bidding him take heart and get up to begin his pastoral life, for which he himself, he said, had already composed an eclogue that would take the shine out of all Sannazaro[80] had ever written, and had bought with his own money two famous dogs to guard the flock, one called Barcino and the other Butron, which a herdsman of Quintanar had sold him.

But for all this Don Quixote could not shake off his sadness. His friends called in the doctor, who felt his pulse and was not very well satisfied with

[80] Jacopo Sannazaro, the Neapolitan poet (1458–1530), author of the *Arcadia*.

it, and said that in any case it would be well for him to attend to the
health of his soul, as that of his body was in a bad way. Don Quixote heard
this calmly; but not so his housekeeper, his niece, and his squire, who fell
weeping bitterly, as if they had him lying dead before them. The doctor's
opinion was that melancholy and depression were bringing him to his end.
Don Quixote begged them to leave him to himself, as he had a wish to
sleep a little. They obeyed, and he slept at one stretch, as the saying is, more
than six hours, so that the housekeeper and niece thought he was going to
sleep forever. But at the end of that time he woke up, and in a loud voice
exclaimed, "Blessed be Almighty God, who has shown me such goodness.
In truth his mercies are boundless, and the sins of men can neither limit
them nor keep them back!"

The niece listened with attention to her uncle's words, and they struck
her as more coherent than what usually fell from him, at least during his
illness, so she asked, "What are you saying, señor? Has anything strange
occurred? What mercies or what sins of men are you talking of?"

"The mercies, niece," said Don Quixote, "are those that God has this
moment shown me, and with him, as I said, my sins are no impediment to
them. My reason is now free and clear, rid of the dark shadows of ignorance
that my unhappy constant study of those detestable books of chivalry cast
over it. Now I see through their absurdities and deceptions, and it only
grieves me that this destruction of my illusions has come so late that it
leaves me no time to make some amends by reading other books that might
be a light to my soul. Niece, I feel myself at the point of death, and I would
fain meet it in such a way as to show that my life has not been so ill that I
should leave behind me the name of a madman; for though I have been
one, I would not that the fact should be made plainer at my death. Call in
to me, my dear, my good friends the Curate, the Bachelor Samson Carrasco,
and Master Nicholas the barber, for I wish to confess and make my will."
But his niece was saved the trouble by the entrance of the three. The instant Don Quixote saw them he exclaimed, "Good news for you, good sirs,
that I am no longer Don Quixote of La Mancha, but Alonso Quixano,[81]
whose way of life won for him the name of Good. Now am I the enemy of
Amadis of Gaul and of the whole countless troop of his descendants; odious
to me now are all the profane stories of knight-errantry; now I perceive my
folly, and the peril into which reading them brought me; now, by God's
mercy schooled into my right senses, I loathe them."

When the three heard him speak in this way, they had no doubt whatever that some new craze had taken possession of him; and said Samson,
"What? Señor Don Quixote! Now that we have intelligence of the lady

---

[81] In the first chapter of Part I, the reader may remember, the name is given as
Quixana.

Dulcinea being disenchanted, are you taking this line; now, just as we are on the point of becoming shepherds, to pass our lives singing, like princes, are you thinking of turning hermit? Hush for Heaven's sake, be rational, and let's have no more nonsense."

"All that nonsense," said Don Quixote, "that until now has been a reality to my hurt, my death will, with Heaven's help, turn to my good. I feel, sirs, that I am rapidly drawing near death; a truce to jesting; let me have a confessor to confess me, and a notary to make my will; for in extremities like this, man must not trifle with his soul; and while the curate is confessing me let some one, I beg, go for the notary."

They looked at one another, wondering at Don Quixote's words; but, though uncertain, they were inclined to believe him, and one of the signs by which they came to the conclusion he was dying was this so sudden and complete return to his senses after having been mad; for to the words already quoted he added much more, so well expressed, so devout, and so rational, as to banish all doubt and convince them that he was sound of mind. The curate turned them all out, and left alone with him confessed him. The bachelor went for the notary and returned shortly afterwards with him and with Sancho, who, having already learned from the bachelor the condition his master was in, and finding the housekeeper and niece weeping, began to blubber and shed tears.

The confession over, the curate came out saying, "Alonso Quixano the Good is indeed dying, and is indeed in his right mind; we may now go in to him while he makes his will."

This news gave a tremendous impulse to the brimming eyes of the housekeeper, the niece, and Sancho Panza his good squire, making the tears burst from their eyes and a host of sighs from their hearts; for of a truth, as has been said more than once, whether as plain Alonso Quixano the Good, or as Don Quixote of La Mancha, Don Quixote was always of a gentle disposition and kindly in all his ways, and hence he was beloved, not only by those of his own house, but by all who knew him.

The notary came in with the rest, and as soon as the preamble of the will had been set out and Don Quixote had commended his soul to God with all the devout formalities that are usual, coming to the bequests, he said, "Item, it is my will that, touching certain moneys in the hands of Sancho Panza (whom in my madness I made my squire), inasmuch as between him and me there have been certain accounts and debits and credits, no claim be made against him, nor any account demanded of him in respect of them; but that if anything remain over and above, after he has paid himself what I owe him, the balance, which will be but little, shall be his, and much good may it do him; and if, as when I was mad I had a share in giving him the government of an island, so, now that I am in my senses, I could give him that of a kingdom, it should be his, for the simplicity of his character and the fidelity of his conduct deserve it." And then, turning to Sancho, he said, "Forgive me, my friend, that I led thee to seem as mad as myself, making thee fall into the same error I myself fell into, that there were and still are knights-errant in the world."

"Ah!" said Sancho weeping, "don't die, master, but take my advice and live many years; for the foolishest thing a man can do in this life is to let himself die without rhyme or reason, without anybody killing him, or any hands but melancholy's making an end of him. Come, don't be lazy, but get up from your bed and let us take to the fields in shepherd's trim as we agreed. Perhaps behind some bush we shall find the lady Dulcinea disenchanted, as fine as fine can be. If it be that you are dying of vexation at having been vanquished, lay the blame on me, and say you were overthrown because I had girthed Rocinante badly; besides you must have seen in your books of chivalry that it is a common thing for knights to upset one another, and for him who is conquered to-day to be conqueror to-morrow."

"Very true," said Samson, "and good Sancho Panza's view of these cases is quite right."

"Sirs, not so fast," said Don Quixote, "'in last year's nests there are no birds this year.' I was mad, now I am in my senses; I was Don Quixote of La Mancha, I am now, as I said, Alonso Quixano the Good; and may my repentance and sincerity restore me to the esteem you used to have for me; and now let Master Notary proceed.

"Item, I leave all my property absolutely to Antonia Quixana my niece, here present, after all has been deducted from the most available portion of it that may be required to satisfy the bequests I have made. And the first disbursement I desire to be made is the payment of the wages I owe for the time my housekeeper has served me, with twenty ducats, over and above for a gown. The curate and the bachelor Samson Carrasco, now present, I appoint my executors.

"Item, it is my wish that if Antonia Quixana, my niece, desires to marry, she shall marry a man of whom it shall be first of all ascertained by information taken that he does not know what books of chivalry are; and if it should be proved that he does, and if, in spite of this, my niece insists upon marrying him, and does marry him, then that she shall forfeit the whole of what I have left her, which my executors shall devote to works of charity as they please.

"Item, I entreat the aforesaid gentlemen my executors, that if any happy chance should lead them to discover the author who is said to have written a history now going about under the title of 'Second Part of the Achievements of Don Quixote of La Mancha,' they beg of him on my behalf as earnestly as they can to forgive me for having been, without intending it, the cause of his writing so many and such monstrous absurdities as he has written in it; for I am leaving the world with a feeling of compunction at having provoked him to write them."

With this he closed his will, and a faintness coming over him he stretched himself out at full length on the bed. All were in a flutter and made haste to relieve him, and during the three days he lived after that on which he made his will he fainted away very often. The house was all in confusion; but still the niece ate and the housekeeper drank and Sancho Panza enjoyed himself; for inheriting property wipes out or softens down in the heir the feeling of grief the dead man might be expected to leave behind him.

At last Don Quixote's end came, after he had received all the sacraments, and had in full and forcible terms expressed his detestation of books of chivalry. The notary was there at the time, and he said that in no book of chivalry had he ever read of any knight-errant dying in his bed so calmly and so like a Christian as Don Quixote, who amid the tears and lamentations of all present yielded up his spirit, that is to say died. On perceiving it the curate begged the notary to bear witness that Alonso Quixano the Good, commonly called Don Quixote of La Mancha, had passed away from this present life, and died naturally; and said he desired this testimony in order to remove the possibility of any other author save Cid Hamet Benengeli bringing him to life again falsely and making interminable stories out of his achievements.

Such was the end of the Ingenious Gentleman of La Mancha, whose village Cid Hamet would not indicate precisely, in order to leave all the towns and villages of La Mancha to contend among themselves for the right to adopt him and claim him as a son, as the seven cities of Greece contended for Homer. The lamentations of Sancho and the niece and housekeeper are omitted here, as well as the new epitaphs upon his tomb; Samson Carrasco, however, put the following:

> A doughty gentleman lies here;
> A stranger all his life to fear;
> Nor in his death could Death prevail,
> In that lost hour, to make him quail.
>
> He for the world but little cared;
> And at his feats the world was scared;
> A crazy man his life he passed,
> But in his senses died at last.

And said most sage Cid Hamet to his pen, "Rest here, hung up by this brass wire, upon this shelf, O my pen, whether of skilful make or clumsy cut I know not; here shalt thou remain long ages hence, unless presumptuous or malignant story-tellers take thee down to profane thee. But ere they touch thee warn them, and, as best thou canst, say to them:

> Hold off! ye weaklings; hold your hands!
> Adventure it let none,
> For this emprise, my lord the king,
> Was meant for me alone.[82]

For me alone was Don Quixote born, and I for him; it was his to act, mine to write; we two together make but one, nothwithstanding and in spite of that pretended Tordesillesque writer who has ventured or would venture with his great, coarse, ill-trimmed ostrich quill to write the achievements of my valiant knight;—no burden for his shoulders, nor subject for his frozen wit: whom, if perchance thou shouldst come to know him, thou shalt warn to leave at rest where they lie the weary mouldering bones of Don Quixote, and not to attempt to carry him off, in opposition to all the privileges of death, to Old Castile,[83] making him rise from the grave where in reality and truth he lies stretched at full length, powerless to make any third expedition or new sally; for the two that he has already made, so much to the enjoyment and approval of everybody to whom they have become known, in this as well as in foreign countries, are quite sufficient for the purpose of turning into ridicule the whole of those made by the whole set of the knights-errant; and so doing shalt thou discharge thy Christian calling, giving good counsel to one that bears ill-will to thee. And I shall remain satisfied, and proud to have been the first who has ever enjoined the fruit of his writings as fully as he could desire; for my desire has been no other than to deliver over to the detestation of mankind the false and foolish tales of the books of chivalry, which, thanks to that of my true Don Quixote, are even now tottering, and doubtless doomed to fall forever.[84] Farewell."

[82] The two last lines occur in one of the ballads on the death of Alonso de Aguilar in the *Guerras Civiles de Granada,* Part I, Chapter XVII.   [83] At the end of his last chapter Avellaneda speaks of a tradition in La Mancha that Don Quixote recovered his senses and made a journey through Old Castile by Salamanca, Avila, and Valladolid.   [84] The bibliography of chivalric romance shows that this was no vainglorious boast on the part of Cervantes. All through the sixteenth century, romances of chivalry, new or reprints, continued to pour from the press in a steady stream, but no new romance was produced after the appearance of Don Quixote, and only one or two of the swarm of old ones [were] reprinted. . . .

Molière (Jean-Baptiste Poquelin)

FROM *The Misanthrope*

TRANSLATED BY RICHARD WILBUR

Molière (1622–1673)

Jean-baptiste poquelin, the son of an upholsterer who was attached to the French court, was intended by his father to continue in the same profession. However, at the age of twenty-three Poquelin renounced his right to his royal appointment in order to follow, under the name Molière, a life of the theater. After initial failure in Paris, he enjoyed twelve years of success in the provinces of France. Returning to Paris as leader of his acting troupe, he gained the immediate favor of the king, Louis XIV, who served as his patron and protector until Molière's death.

France's greatest comic playwright, Molière employed his satirical gifts to denounce whatever human foolishness violated the social norm. For him that norm coincided with life at the court of Louis XIV, where the rules for self-preservation in a dangerously polite society were quickly learned or one paid the cost of failure. Molière generally set his comedies in middle-class family situations, thus avoiding any direct commentary on the ways of the court. *The Misanthrope,* on which he labored longer than on any other of his plays, is an exception in that its characters are aristocrats. Thus Molière, insofar as his voice may have been identified with that of Alceste, ran the risk of royal censure for attacking the shallow hypocrisy of life at court. However, if that was his intention, he covered his tracks well and in a number of ways. For example, Molière himself played the part of Alceste; it was always his habit to play the role of the buffoon in his own plays. He further discredited Alceste with the subtitle of the play, "The Bilious Lover." Thus modern readers who might tend to agree with Jean-Jacques Rousseau's indignant insistence that in this play only Alceste is worthy of our respect are warned that the author has shielded his work rather carefully against this interpretation.

The Misanthrope

ALCESTE, *in love with Célimène*
PHILINTE, *Alceste's friend*
ORONTE, *in love with Célimène*
CELIMENE, *Alceste's beloved*
ELIANTE, *Célimène's cousin*
ARSINOE, *a friend of Célimène's*
ACASTE
CLITANDRE } *marquesses*
BASQUE, *Célimène's servant*
A GUARD *of the Marshalsea*
DUBOIS, *Alceste's valet*

The scene throughout is in Célimène's house at Paris.

ACT I

SCENE I
PHILINTE, ALCESTE

PHILINTE. Now, what's got into you?
ALCESTE [seated].   Kindly leave me alone.
PHILINTE. Come, come, what is it? This lugubrious tone . . . .
ALCESTE. Leave me, I said; you spoil my solitude.
PHILINTE. Oh, listen to me, now, and don't be rude.
ALCESTE. I choose to be rude, Sir, and to be hard of hearing.
PHILINTE. These ugly moods of yours are not endearing;
      Friends though we are, I really must insist . . . .
ALCESTE [abruptly rising]. Friends? Friends, you say? Well, cross me off
          your list.
      I've been your friend til now, as you well know;
      But after what I saw a moment ago   10
      I tell you flatly that our ways must part.
      I wish no place in a dishonest heart.
PHILINTE. Why, what have I done, Alceste? Is this quite just?
ALCESTE. My God, you ought to die of self-disgust.
      I call your conduct inexcusable, Sir,
      And every man of honor will concur.
      I see you almost hug a man to death,
      Exclaim for joy until you're out of breath,
      And supplement these loving demonstrations
      With endless offers, vows, and protestations;   20
      Then when I ask you "Who was that?", I find
      That you can barely bring his name to mind!
      Once the man's back is turned, you cease to love him,
      And speak with absolute indifference of him!
      By God, I say it's base and scandalous
      To falsify the heart's affections thus;
      If I caught myself behaving in such a way,
      I'd hang myself for shame, without delay.
PHILINTE. It hardly seems a hanging matter to me;
      I hope that you will take it graciously   30
      If I extend myself a slight reprieve,
      And live a little longer, by your leave.
ALCESTE. How dare you joke about a crime so grave?
PHILINTE. What crime? How else are people to behave?

354

ALCESTE. I'd have them be sincere, and never part
    With any word that isn't from the heart.
PHILINTE. When someone greets us with a show of pleasure,
    It's but polite to give him equal measure,
    Return his love the best that we know how,
    And trade him offer for offer, vow for vow.   40
ALCESTE. No, no, this formula you'd have me follow,
    However fashionable, is false and hollow,
    And I despise the frenzied operations
    Of all these barterers of protestations,
    These lavishers of meaningless embraces,
    These utterers of obliging commonplaces,
    Who court and flatter everyone on earth
    And praise the fool no less than the man of worth.
    Should you rejoice that someone fondles you,
    Offers his love and service, swears to be true,   50
    And fills your ears with praises of your name,
    When to the first damned fop he'll say the same?
    No, no: no self-respecting heart would dream
    Of prizing so promiscuous an esteem;
    However high the praise, there's nothing worse
    Than sharing honors with the universe.
    Esteem is founded on comparison:
    To honor all men is to honor none.
    Since you embrace this indiscriminate vice,
    Your friendship comes at far too cheap a price;   60
    I spurn the easy tribute of a heart
    Which will not set the worthy man apart:
    I choose, Sir, to be chosen; and in fine,
    The friend of mankind is no friend of mine.
PHILINTE. But in polite society, custom decrees
    That we show certain outward courtesies. . . .
ALCESTE. Ah, no! we should condemn with all our force
    Such false and artificial intercourse.
    Let men behave like men; let them display
    Their inmost hearts in everything they say;   70
    Let the heart speak, and let our sentiments
    Not mask themselves in silly compliments.
PHILINTE. In certain cases it would be uncouth
    And most absurd to speak the naked truth;
    With all respect for your exalted notions,
    It's often best to veil one's true emotions.
    Wouldn't the social fabric come undone

If we were wholly frank with everyone?
Suppose you met with someone you couldn't bear;
Would you inform him of it then and there?   80
ALCESTE. Yes.
PHILINTE.   Then you'd tell old Emilie it's pathetic
The way she daubs her features with cosmetic
And plays the gay coquette at sixty-four?
ALCESTE. I would.
PHILINTE.   And you'd call Dorilas a bore,
And tell him every ear at court is lame
From hearing him brag about his noble name?
ALCESTE. Precisely.
PHILINTE.   Ah, you're joking.
ALCESTE.   *Au contraire:*°
In this regard there's none I'd choose to spare.
All are corrupt; there's nothing to be seen
In court or town but aggravates my spleen.   90
I fall into deep gloom and melancholy
When I survey the scene of human folly,
Finding on every hand base flattery,
Injustice, fraud, self-interest, treachery. . . .
Ah, it's too much; mankind has grown so base,
I mean to break with the whole human race.
PHILINTE. This philosophic rage is a bit extreme;
You've no idea how comical you seem;
Indeed, we're like those brothers in the play
Called *School for Husbands,*° one of whom was prey   100
ALCESTE. Enough, now! None of your stupid similes.
PHILINTE. Then let's have no more tirades, if you please.
The world won't change, whatever you say or do;
And since plain speaking means so much to you,
I'll tell you plainly that by being frank
You've earned the reputation of a crank,
And that you're thought ridiculous when you rage
And rant against the manners of the age.
ALCESTE. So much the better; just what I wish to hear.
No news could be more greatful to my ear.   110
All men are so detestable in my eyes,
I should be sorry if they thought me wise.
PHILINTE. Your hatred's very sweeping, is it not?
ALCESTE. Quite right: I hate the whole degraded lot.

87. *Au contraire:* (French) on the contrary.   100. *School for Husbands:* earlier
play by Molière.

PHILINTE. Must all poor human creatures be embraced,
    Without distinction, by your vast distaste?
    Even in these bad times, there are surely a few . . . .
ALCESTE. No, I include all men in one dim view:
    Some men I hate for being rogues; the others
    I hate because they treat the rogues like brothers,   120
    And, lacking a virtuous scorn for what is vile,
    Receive the villain with a complaisant smile.
    Notice how tolerant people choose to be
    Toward that bold rascal who's at law with me.
    His social polish can't conceal his nature;
    One sees at once that he's a treacherous creature;
    No one could posibly be taken in
    By those soft speeches and that sugary grin.
    The whole world knows the shady means by which
    The low-brow's grown so powerful and rich,   130
    And risen to rank so bright and high
    That virtue can but blush, and merit sigh.
    Whenever his name comes up in conversation,
    None will defend his wretched reputation;
    Call him knave, liar, scoundrel, and all the rest,
    Each head will nod, and no one will protest.
    And yet his smirk is seen in every house,
    He's greeted everywhere with smiles and bows,
    And when there's any honor that can be got
    By pulling strings, he'll get it, like as not.   140
    My God! It chills my heart to see the ways
    Men come to terms with evil nowadays;
    Sometimes, I swear, I'm moved to flee and find
    Some desert land unfouled by humankind.
PHILINTE. Come, let's forget the follies of the times
    And pardon mankind for its petty crimes;
    Let's have an end of rantings and of railings,
    And show some leniency toward human failings.
    This world requires a pliant rectitude;
    Too stern a virtue makes one stiff and rude;   150
    Good sense views all extremes with detestation,
    And bids us to be noble in moderation.
    The rigid virtues of the ancient days
    Are not for us; they jar with all our ways
    And ask of us too lofty a perfection.
    Wise men accept their times without objection,
    And there's no greater folly, if you ask me,

Than trying to reform society.
Like you, I see each day a hundred and one
Unhandsome deeds that might be better done,   160
But still, for all the faults that meet my view,
I'm never known to storm and rave like you.
I take men as they are, or let them be,
And teach my soul to bear their frailty;
And whether in court or town, whatever the scene,
My phlegm's as philosophic as your spleen.°
ALCESTE. This phlegm which you so eloquently commend,
Does nothing ever rile it up, my friend?
Suppose some man you trust should treacherously
Conspire to rob you of your property,   170
And do his best to wreck your reputation?
Wouldn't you feel a certain indignation?
PHILINTE. Why, no. These faults of which you so complain
Are part of human nature, I maintain,
And it's no more a matter for disgust
That men are knavish, selfish and unjust,
Than that the vulture dines upon the dead,
And wolves are furious, and apes ill-bred.
ALCESTE. Shall I see myself betrayed, robbed, torn to bits,
And not. . . . Oh, let's be still and rest our wits.   180
Enough of reasoning, now. I've had my fill.
PHILINTE. Indeed, you would do well, Sir, to be still.
Rage less at your opponent, and give some thought
To how you'll win this lawsuit that he's brought.
ALCESTE. I assure you I'll do nothing of the sort.
PHILINTE. Then who will plead your case before the court?
ALCESTE. Reason and right and justice will plead for me.
PHILINTE. Oh, Lord. What judges do you plan to see?
ALCESTE. Why, none. The justice of my cause is clear.
PHILINTE. Of course, man; but there's politics to fear. . . . 190
ALCESTE. No, I refuse to lift a hand. That's flat.
I'm either right, or wrong.
PHILINTE.   Don't count on that.
ALCESTE. No, I'll do nothing.
PHILINTE.   Your enemy's influence
Is great, you know . . . .

---

166. *phlegm . . . spleen:* Phlegm and *spleen* were physiological terms for two
of the four humors of the body. *Phlegm* was thought to cause sluggishness (here
equanimity); *spleen,* another term for bile, was supposed to cause anger.

ALCESTE.   That makes no difference.

PHILINTE. It will; you'll see.

ALCESTE.   Must honor bow to guile?
    If so, I shall be proud to lose the trial.

PHILINTE. Oh, really . . . .

ALCESTE.   I'll discover by this case
    Whether or not men are sufficiently base
    And impudent and villainous and perverse
    To do me wrong before the universe.   200

PHILINTE. What a man!

ALCESTE.   Oh, I could wish, whatever the cost,
    Just for the beauty of it, that my trial were lost.

PHILINTE. If people heard you talking so, Alceste,
    They'd split their sides. Your name would be a jest.

ALCESTE. So much the worse for jesters.

PHILINTE.   May I enquire
    Whether this rectitude you so admire,
    And these hard virtues you're enamored of
    Are qualities of the lady whom you love?
    It much surprises me that you, who seem
    To view mankind with furious disesteem,   210
    Have yet found something to enchant your eyes
    Amidst a species which you so despise.
    And what is more amazing, I'm afraid,
    Is the most curious choice your heart has made.
    The honest Eliante is fond of you,
    Arsinoé, the prude, admires you too;
    And yet your spirit's been perversely led
    To choose the flighty Célimène instead,
    Whose brittle malice and coquettish ways
    So typify the manners of our days.   220
    How is it that the traits you most abhor
    Are bearable in this lady you adore?
    Are you so blind with love that you can't find them?
    Or do you contrive, in her case, not to mind them?

ALCESTE. My love for that young widow's not the kind
    That can't perceive defects; no, I'm not blind.
    I see her faults, despite my ardent love,
    And all I see I fervently reprove.
    And yet I'm weak; for all her falsity,
    That woman knows the art of pleasing me,   230
    And though I never cease complaining of her,
    I swear I cannot manage not to love her.

Her charm outweighs her faults; I can but aim
To cleanse her spirit in my love's pure flame.
PHILINTE. That's no small task; I wish you all success.
You think then that she loves you?
ALCESTE.   Heavens, yes!
I wouldn't love her did she not love me.
PHII INTE. Well, if her taste for you is plain to see,
Why do these rivals cause you such despair?
ALCESTE. True love, Sir, is possessive, and cannot bear   240
To share with all the world. I'm here today
To tell her she must send that mob away.
PHILINTE. If I were you, and had your choice to make,
Eliante, her cousin, would be the one I'd take;
That honest heart, which cares for you alone,
Would harmonize far better with your own.
ALCESTE. True, true: each day my reason tells me so;
But reason doesn't rule in love, you know.
PHILINTE. I fear some bitter sorrow is in store;
This love . . . .

SCENE II
ORONTE, ALCESTE, PHILINTE

ORONTE [*to* ALCESTE]. The servants told me at the door   250
That Eliante and Célimène were out,
But when I heard, dear Sir, that you were about,
I came to say, without exaggeration,
That I hold you in the vastest admiration,
And that it's always been my dearest desire
To be the friend of one I so admire.
I hope to see my love of merit requited,
And you and I in friendship's bond united.
I'm sure you won't refuse—if I may be frank—
A friend of my devotedness—and rank.   260
    [*During this speech of* ORONTE'*s,* ALCESTE *is abstracted,
    and seems unaware that he is being spoken to. He only
    breaks off his reverie when* ORONTE *says:*]
It was for you, if you please, that words were intended.
ALCESTE. For me, Sir?
ORONTE.   Yes, for you. You're not offended?
ALCESTE. By no means. But this much surprises me. . . .
    The honor comes most unexpectedly. . . .
ORONTE. My high regard should not astonish you;

The whole world feels the same. It is your due.

ALCESTE. Sir . . . .

ORONTE.   Why, in all the State there isn't one
Can match your merits; they shine, Sir, like the sun.

ALCESTE. Sir . . . .

ORONTE.   You are higher in my estimation
Than all that's most illustrious in the nation.   270

ALCESTE. Sir . . . .

ORONTE.   If I lie, may heaven strike me dead!
To show you that I mean what I have said,
Permit me, Sir, to embrace you most sincerely,
And swear that I will prize our friendship dearly.
Give me your hand. And now, Sir, if you choose,
We'll make our vows.

ALCESTE.   Sir . . . .

ORONTE.   What! You refuse?

ALCESTE. Sir, it's very great honor you extend:
But friendship is a sacred thing, my friend;
It would be profanation to bestow
The name of friend on one you hardly know.   280
All parts are better played when well-rehearsed;
Let's put off friendship, and get acquainted first.
We may discover it would be unwise
To try to make our natures harmonize.

ORONTE. By heaven! You're sagacious to the core;
This speech has made me admire you even more.
Let time, then, bring us closer day by day;
Meanwhile, I shall be yours in every way.
If, for example, there should be anything
You wish at court, I'll mention it to the King.   290
I have his ear, of course; it's quite well known
That I am much in favor with the throne.
In short, I am your servant. And now, dear friend,
Since you have such fine judgment, I intend
To please you, if I can, with a small sonnet
I wrote not long ago. Please comment on it,
And tell me whether I ought to publish it.

ALCESTE. You must excuse me, Sir; I'm hardly fit
To judge such matters.

ORONTE.   Why not?

ALCESTE.   I am, I fear,
Inclined to be unfashionably sincere.   300

ORONTE. Just what I ask; I'd take no satisfaction

In anything but your sincere reaction.
I beg you not to dream of being kind.
ALCESTE. Since you desire it, Sir, I'll speak my mind.
ORONTE. *Sonnet.* It's a sonnet . . . . *Hope* . . . . The poem's ad-
    dressed
To a lady who wakened hopes within my breast.
Hope . . . this is not the pompous sort of thing,
Just modest little verses, with a tender ring.
ALCESTE. Well, we shall see.
ORONTE.   *Hope* . . . . I'm anxious to hear
Whether the style seems properly smooth and clear,   310
And whether the choice of words is good or bad.
ALCESTE. We'll see, we'll see.
ORONTE.   Perhaps I ought to add
That it took me only a quarter-hour to write it.
ALCESTE. The time's irrelevant, Sir: kindly recite it.

ORONTE [*reading*]. *Hope comforts us awhile, t'is true,*
    Lulling our cares with careless laughter,
    And yet such joy is full of rue,
    My Phyllis, if nothing follows after.

PHILINTE. I'm charmed by this already; the style's delightful.
ALCESTE [*sotto voce,° to* PHILINTE]. How can you say that? Why, the
    thing is frightful.   320

ORONTE. *Your fair face smiled on me awhile,*
    But was it kindness so to enchant me?
    'Twould have been fairer not to smile,
    If hope was all you meant to grant me.

PHILINTE. What a clever thought! How handsomely you phrase it!
ALCESTE [*sotto voce, to* PHILINTE]. You know the thing is trash. How
    dare you praise it?

ORONTE. *If it's to be my passion's fate*
    Thus everlastingly to wait,
    Then death will come to set me free:
    For death is fairer than the fair;   330
    Phyllis, to hope is to despair
    When one must hope eternally.

319. *sotto voce:* (Italian) in an undertone.

PHILINTE. The close is exquisite—full of feeling and grace.

ALCESTE [*sotto voce, aside*]. Oh, blast the close; you'd better close
      your face
  Before you send your lying soul to hell.

PHILINTE. I can't remember a poem I've liked so well.

ALCESTE [*sotto voce, aside*]. Good Lord!

ORONTE. [*to* PHILINTE].   I fear you're flattering me a
      bit.

PHILINTE. Oh, no!

ALCESTE [*sotto voce, aside*]. What else d'you call it, you hypocrite?

ORONTE [*to* ALCESTE]. But you, Sir, keep your promise now: don't
      shrink
  From telling me sincerely what you think.   340

ALCESTE. Sir, these are delicate matters; we all desire
  To be told that we've the true poetic fire.
  But once, to one whose name I shall not mention,
  I said, regarding some verse of his invention,
  That gentlemen should rigorously control
  That itch to write which often afflicts the soul;
  That one should curb the heady inclination
  To publicize one's little avocation;
  And that in showing off one's works of art
  One often plays a very clownish part.   350

ORONTE. Are you suggesting in a devious way
  That I ought not . . . .

ALCESTE.   Oh, that I do not say.
  Further, I told him that no fault is worse
  Than that of writing frigid, lifeless verse,
  And that the merest whisper of such a shame
  Suffices to destroy a man's good name.

ORONTE. D'you mean to say my sonnet's dull and trite?

ALCESTE. I don't say that. But I went on to cite
  Numerous cases of once-respected men
  Who came to grief by taking up the pen.   360

ORONTE. And am I like them? Do I write so poorly?

ALCESTE. I don't say that. But I told this person, "Surely
  You're under no necessity to compose;
  Why you should wish to publish, heaven knows.
  There's no excuse for printing tedious rot
  Unless one writes for bread, as you do not.
  Resist temptation, then, I beg of you;
  Conceal your pastimes from the public view;
  And don't give up, on any provocation,

Your present high and courtly reputation,   370
To purchase at a greedy printer's shop
The name of silly author and scribbling fop."
These were the points I tried to make him see.
ORONTE. I sense that they are also aimed at me;
  But now—about my sonnet—I'd like to be told . . . .
ALCESTE. Frankly, that sonnet should be pigeonholed.
  You've chosen the worst models to imitate.
  The style's unnatural. Let me illustrate:

  For example, *Your fair face smiled on me awhile,*
  Followed by, *'Twould have been fairer not to smile!*   380
  Or this: *such joy is full of rue;*
  Or this: *For death is fairer than the fair;*
  Or, *Phyllis, to hope is to despair*
    When one must hope eternally!

This artificial style, that's all the fashion,
Has neither taste, nor honesty, nor passion;
It's nothing but a sort of wordy play,
And nature never spoke in such a way.
What, in this shallow age, is not debased?
Our fathers, though less refined, had better taste;   390
I'd barter all that men admire today
For one old love-song I shall try to say:

    If the King had given me for my own
    Paris, his citadel,
    And I for that must leave alone
    Her whom I love so well,
    I'd say then to the Crown,
    Take back your glittering town;
    My darling is more fair, I swear,
    My darling is more fair.   400

The rhyme's not rich, the style is rough and old,
But don't you see that it's the purest gold
Beside the tinsel nonsense now preferred,
And that there's passion in its every word?

    If the King had given me for my own
    Paris, his citadel,
    And I for that must leave alone

Her whom I love so well,
I'd say then to the Crown,
Take back your glittering town;   410
My darling is more fair, I swear,
My darling is more fair.

There speaks a loving heart. [*to* PHILINTE] You're laughing, eh?
Laugh on, my precious wit. Whatever you say,
I hold that song's worth all the bibelots°
That people hail today with ah's and oh's.
ORONTE. And I maintain my sonnet's very good.
ALCESTE. It's not at all surprising that you should.
    You have your reasons; permit me to have mine
    For thinking that you cannot write a line.   420
ORONTE. Others have praised my sonnet to the skies.
ALCESTE. I lack their art of telling pleasant lies.
ORONTE. You seem to think you've got no end of wit.
ALCESTE. To praise your verse, I'd need still more of it.
ORONTE. I'm not in need of your approval, Sir.
ALCESTE. That's good; you couldn't have it if you were.
ORONTE. Come now, I'll lend you the subject of my sonnet;
    I'd like to see you try to improve upon it.
ALCESTE. I might, by chance, write something just as shoddy;
    But then I wouldn't show it to everybody.   430
ORONTE. You're most opinionated and conceited.
ALCESTE. Go find your flatterers, and be better treated.
ORONTE. Look here, my little fellow, pray watch your tone.
ALCESTE. My great big fellow, you'd better watch your own.
PHILINTE [*stepping between them*]. Oh, please, please, gentlemen!
    This will never do.
ORONTE. The fault is mine, and I leave the field to you.
    I am your servant, Sir, in every way.
ALCESTE. And I, Sir, am your most abject valet.

SCENE III
PHILINTE, ALCESTE

PHILINTE. Well, as you see, sincerity in excess
    Can get you into a very pretty mess;   440
    Oronte was hungry for appreciation. . . .
ALCESTE. Don't speak to me.

415. *bibelots*: showy but worthless things.

PHILINTE.   What?
ALCESTE.   No more conversation.
PHILINTE. Really, now . . . .
ALCESTE.   Leave me alone.
PHILINTE.   If I . . . .
ALCESTE.   Out of my
          sight!
PHILINTE. But what . . . .
ALCESTE.   I won't listen.
PHILINTE.   But . . . .
ALCESTE.   Silence!
PHILINTE.   Now, is it
          polite . . . .
ALCESTE. By heaven, I've had enough. Don't follow me.
PHILINTE. Ah, you're just joking. I'll keep you company.

ACT II

SCENE I
ALCESTE, CELIMENE

ALCESTE. Shall I speak plainly, Madam? I confess
          Your conduct gives me infinite distress,
          And my resentment's grown too hot to smother.
          Soon, I foresee, we'll break with one another.   450
          If I said otherwise, I should deceive you;
          Sooner or later, I shall be forced to leave you,
          And if I swore that we shall never part,
          I should misread the omens of my heart.
CELIMENE. You kindly saw me home, it would appear,
          So as to pour invectives in my ear.
ALCESTE. I've no desire to quarrel. But I deplore
          Your inability to shut the door
          On all these suitors who beset you so.
          There's what annoys me, if you care to know.   460
CELIMENE. Is it my fault that all these men pursue me?
          Am I to blame if they're attracted to me?
          And when they gently beg an audience,
          Ought I to take a stick and drive them hence?
ALCESTE. Madam, there's no necessity for a stick;
          A less responsive heart would do the trick.
          Of your attractiveness I don't complain;

But those your charms attract, you then detain
By a most melting and receptive manner,
And so enlist their hearts beneath your banner. 470
It's the agreeable hopes which you excite
That keep these lovers round you day and night;
Were they less liberally smiled upon,
That sighing troop would very soon be gone.
But tell me, Madam, why it is that lately
This man Clitandre interests you so greatly?
Because of what high merits do you deem
Him worthy of the honor of your esteem?
Is it that your admiring glances linger
On the splendidly long nail of his little finger? 480
Or do you share the general deep respect
For the blond wig he chooses to affect?
Are you in love with his embroidered hose?
Do you adore his ribbons and his bows?
Or is it that this paragon bewitches
Your tasteful eye with his vast German breeches?
Perhaps his giggle, or his falsetto voice,
Makes him the latest gallant of your choice?
CELIMENE. You're much mistaken to resent him so.
Why I put up with him you surely know: 490
My lawsuit's very shortly to be tried,
And I must have his influence on my side.
ALCESTE. Then lose your lawsuit, Madam, or let it drop;
Don't torture me by humoring such a fop.
CELIMENE. You're jealous of the whole world, Sir.
ALCESTE.   That's true,
Since the whole world is well-received by you.
CELIMENE. That my good nature is so unconfined
Should serve to pacify your jealous mind;
Were I to smile on one, and scorn the rest,
Then you might have some cause to be distressed. 500
ALCESTE. Well, if I mustn't be jealous, tell me, then,
Just how I'm better treated than other men.
CELIMENE. You know you have my love. Will that not do?
ALCESTE. What proof have I that what you say is true?
CELIMENE. I would expect, Sir, that my having said it
Might give the statement a sufficient credit.
ALCESTE. But how can I be sure that you don't tell
The selfsame thing to other men as well?
CELIMENE. What a gallant speech! How flattering to me!

What a sweet creature you make me out to be!   510
Well then, to save you from the pangs of doubt,
All that I've said I hereby cancel out;
Now, none but yourself shall make a monkey of you:
Are you content?
ALCESTE.   Why, why am I doomed to love you?
I swear that I shall bless the blissful hour
When this poor heart's no longer in your power!
I make no secret of it: I've done my best
To exorcise this passion from my breast;
But thus far all in vain; it will not go;
It's for my sins that I must love you so.   520
CELIMENE. Your love for me is matchless, Sir; that's clear.
ALCESTE. Indeed, in all the world it has no peer;
Words can't describe the nature of my passion,
And no man ever loved in such a fashion.
CELIMENE. Yes, it's a brand-new fashion, I agree:
You show your love by castigating me,
And all your speeches are enraged and rude.
I've never been so furiously wooed.
ALCESTE. Yet you could calm that fury, if you chose.
Come, shall we bring our quarrels to a close?   530
Let's speak with open hearts, then, and begin . . . .

SCENE II
CELIMENE, ALCESTE, BASQUE

CELIMENE. What is it?
BASQUE.   Acaste is here.
CELIMENE.   Well, send him in.

SCENE III
CELIMENE, ALCESTE

ALCESTE. What! Shall we never be alone at all?
You're always ready to receive a call,
And you can't bear, for ten ticks of the clock,
Not to keep open house for all who knock.
CELIMENE. I couldn't refuse him: he'd be most put out.
ALCESTE. Surely that's not worth worrying about.
CELIMENE. Acaste would never forgive me if he guessed
That I consider him a dreadful pest.   540

ALCESTE. If he's a pest, why bother with him then?
CELIMENE. Heavens! One can't antagonize such men;
Why, they're the chartered gossips of the court,
And have a say in things of every sort.
One must receive them, and be full of charm;
They're no great help, but they can do you harm,
And though your influence be ever so great,
They're hardly the best people to alienate.
ALCESTE. I see, dear lady, that you could make a case
For putting up with the whole human race;   550
These friendships that you calculate so nicely . . . .

SCENE IV

ALCESTE, CELIMENE, BASQUE

BASQUE. Madam, Clitandre is here as well.
ALCESTE.   Precisely.
CELIMENE. Where are you going?
ALCESTE.   Elsewhere.
CELIMENE.   Stay.
ALCESTE.   No, no.
CELIMENE. Stay, Sir.
ALCESTE.   I can't.
CELIMENE.   I wish it.
ALCESTE.   No, I must go.
I beg you, Madam, not to press the matter;
You know I have no taste for idle chatter.
CELIMENE. Stay: I command you.
ALCESTE.   No, I cannot stay.
CELIMENE. Very well; you have my leave to go away.

SCENE V

ELIANTE, PHILINTE, ACASTE, CLITANDRE, ALCESTE,
CELIMENE, BASQUE

ELIANTE [to CELIMENE]. The Marquesses have kindly come to call.
Were they announced?
CELIMENE.   Yes. Basque, bring chairs for all.   560
[BASQUE provides the chairs, and exits.]
[To ALCESTE] You haven't gone?
ALCESTE.   No; and I shan't depart

Till you decide who's foremost in your heart.

CELIMENE. Oh, hush.

ALCESTE. It's time to choose; take them, or me.

CELIMENE. You're mad.

ALCESTE. I'm not, as you shall shortly see.

CELIMENE. Oh?

ALCESTE. You'll decide.

CELIMENE. You're joking now, dear friend.

ALCESTE. No, no; you'll choose; my patience is at an end.

CLITANDRE. Madam, I come from court, where poor Cléonte
Behaved like a perfect fool, as is his wont.
Has he no friend to counsel him, I wonder,
And teach him less unerringly to blunder? 570

CELIMENE. It's true, the man's a most accomplished dunce;
His gauche behavior charms the eye at once;
And every time one sees him, on my word,
His manner's grown a trifle more absurd.

ACASTE. Speaking of dunces, I've just now conversed
With old Damon, who's one of the very worst;
I stood a lifetime in the broiling sun
Before his dreary monologue was done.

CELIMENE. Oh, he's a wondrous talker, and has the power
To tell you nothing hour after hour: 580
If, by mistake, he ever came to the point,
The shock would put his jawbone out of joint.

ELIANTE [to PHILINTE]. The conversation takes its usual turn,
And all our dear friends' ears will shortly burn.

CLITANDRE. Timante's a character, Madam.

CELIMENE. Isn't he, though?
A man of mystery from top to toe,
Who moves about in a romantic mist
On secret missions which do not exist.
His talk is full of eyebrows and grimaces;
How tired one gets of his momentous faces; 590
He's always whispering something confidential
Which turns out to be quite inconsequential;
Nothing's too slight for him to mystify;
He even whispers when he says "good-by."

ACASTE. Tell us about Géralde.

CELIMENE. That tiresome ass.
He mixes only with the titled class,
And fawns on dukes and princes, and is bored
With anyone who's not at least a lord.

The man's obsessed with rank, and his discourses
Are all of hounds and carriages and horses;   600
He uses Christian names with all the great,
And the word Milord, with him, is out of date.
CLITANDRE. He's very taken with Bélise, I hear.
CELIMENE. She is the dreariest company, poor dear.
    Whenever she comes to call, I grope about
    To find some topic which will draw her out,
    But, owing to her dry and faint replies,
    The conversation wilts, and droops, and dies.
    In vain one hopes to animate her face
    By mentioning the ultimate commonplace;   610
    But sun or shower, even hail or frost
    Are matters she can instantly exhaust.
    Meanwhile her visit, painful though it is,
    Drags on and on through mute eternities,
    And though you ask the time, and yawn, and yawn,
    She sits there like a stone and won't be gone.
ACASTE. Now for Adraste.
CELIMENE.   Oh, that conceited elf
    Has a gigantic passion for himself;
    He rails against the court, and cannot bear it
    That none will recognize his hidden merit;   620
    All honors given to others give offense
    To his imaginary excellence.
CLITANDRE. What about young Cléon? His house, they say,
    Is full of the best society, night and day.
CELIMENE. His cook has made him popular, not he:
    It's Cléon's table that people come to see.
ELIANTE. He gives a splendid dinner, you must admit.
CELIMENE. But must he serve himself along with it?
    For my taste, he's a most insipid dish
    Whose presence sours the wine and spoils the fish.   630
PHILINTE. Damis, his uncle, is admired no end.
    What's your opinion, Madam?
CELIMENE.   Why, he's my friend.
PHILINTE. He seems a decent fellow, and rather clever.
CELIMENE. He works too hard at cleverness, however.
    I hate to see him sweat and struggle so
    To fill his conversation with bons mots.°
    Since he's decided to become a wit

636. *bons mots:* (French) witty remarks.

His taste's so pure that nothing pleases it;
He scolds at all the latest books and plays,
Thinking that wit must never stoop to praise,   640
That finding fault's a sign of intellect,
That all appreciation is abject,
And that by damning everything in sight
One shows oneself in a distinguished light.
He's scornful even of our conversations:
Their trivial nature sorely tries his patience;
He folds his arms, and stands above the battle,
And listens sadly to our childish prattle.
ACASTE. Wonderful, Madam! You've hit him off precisely.
CLITANDRE. No one can sketch a character° so nicely.   650
ALCESTE. How bravely, Sirs, you cut and thrust at all
    These absent fools, till one by one they fall:
    But let one come in sight, and you'll at once
    Embrace the man you lately called a dunce,
    Telling him in a tone sincere and fervent
    How proud you are to be his humble servant.
CLITANDRE. Why pick on us? Madam's been speaking, Sir,
    And you should quarrel, if you must, with her.
ALCESTE. No, no, by God, the fault is yours, because
    You lead her on with laughter and applause,   660
    And make her think that she's the more delightful
    The more her talk is scandalous and spiteful.
    Oh, she would stoop to malice far, far less
    If no such claque approved her cleverness.
    It's flatterers like you whose foolish praise
    Nourishes all the vices of these days.
PHILINTE. But why protest when someones ridicules
    Those you'd condemn, yourself, as knaves or fools?
CELIMENE. Why, Sir? Because he loves to make a fuss.
    You don't expect him to agree with us,   670
    When there's an opportunity to express
    His heaven-sent spirit of contrariness?
    What other people think, he can't abide;
    Whatever they say, he's on the other side;
    He lives in deadly terror of agreeing;
    'Twould make him seem an ordinary being.
    Indeed, he's so in love with contradiction,
    He'll turn against his most profound conviction

650. *character:* The verbal caricature was very much the rage as a parlor game
in this period.

And with a furious eloquence deplore it,
If only someone else is speaking for it. 680
ALCESTE. Go on, dear lady, mock me as you please;
You have your audience in ecstasies.
PHILINTE. But what she says is true: you have a way
Of bridling at whatever people say;
Whether they praise or blame, your angry spirit
Is equally unsatisfied to hear it.
ALCESTE. Men, Sir, are always wrong, and that's the reason
That righteous anger's never out of season;
All that I hear in all their conversation
Is flattering praise or reckless condemnation. 690
CELIMENE. But . . . .
ALCESTE.   No, no, Madam, I am forced to state
That you have pleasures which I deprecate,
And that these others, here, are much to blame
For nourishing the faults which are your shame.
CLITANDRE. I shan't defend myself, Sir; but I vow
I'd thought this lady faultless until now.
ACASTE. I see her charms and graces, which are many;
But as for faults, I've never noticed any.
ALCESTE. I see them, Sir; and rather than ignore them,
I strenuously criticize her for them. 700
The more one loves, the more one should object
To every blemish, every least defect.
Were I this lady, I would soon get rid
Of lovers who approved of all I did,
And by their slack indulgence and applause
Endorsed my follies and excused my flaws.
CELIMENE. If all hearts beat according to your measure,
The dawn of love would be the end of pleasure;
And love would find its perfect consummation
In ecstasies of rage and reprobation. 710
ELIANTE. Love, as a rule, affects men otherwise,
And lovers rarely love to criticize.
They see their lady as a charming blur,
And find all things commendable in her.
If she has any blemish, fault, or shame,
They will redeem it by a pleasing name.
The pale-faced lady's lily-white, perforce;
The swarthy one's a sweet brunette, of course;
The spindly lady has a slender grace;
The fat one has a most majestic pace; 720

The plain one, with her dress in disarray,
They classify as *beauté négligée;*°
The hulking one's a goddess in their eyes,
The dwarf, a concentrate of Paradise;
The haughty lady has a noble mind;
The mean one's witty, and the dull one's kind;
The chatterbox has liveliness and verve,
The mute one has a virtuous reserve.
So lovers manage, in their passion's cause,
To love their ladies even for their flaws.   730
ALCESTE. But I still say . . . .
CELIMENE.   I think it would be nice
To stroll around the gallery once or twice.
What! You're not going, Sirs?
CLITANDRE AND ACASTE.   No, Madam, no.
ALCESTE. You seem to be in terror lest they go.
Do what you will, Sirs; leave, or linger on,
But I shan't go till after you are gone.
ACASTE. I'm free to linger, unless I should perceive
Madame is tired, and wishes me to leave.
CLITANDRE. And as for me, I needn't go today
Until the hour of the King's *coucher.*°   740
CELIMENE [*to* ALCESTE]. You're joking, surely?
ALCESTE.   Not in the least; we'll see
Whether you'd rather part with them, or me.

SCENE VI
ALCESTE, CELIMENE, ELIANTE, ACASTE,
PHILINTE, CLITANDRE, BASQUE

BASQUE [*to* ALCESTE]. Sir, there's a fellow here who bids me state
That he must see you, and that it can't wait.
ALCESTE. Tell him that I have no such pressing affairs.
BASQUE. It's a long tailcoat that this fellow wears,
With gold all over.
CELIMENE [*to* ALCESTE]. You'd best go down and see.
Or—have him enter.

722. *beauté négligée:* (French) unstudied loveliness.   740. *coucher:* (French)
afternoon reception, held in the King's bedchamber.

SCENE VII

ALCESTE, CELIMENE, ELIANTE, ACASTE, PHILINTE,
CLITANDRE, A GUARD *of the Marshalsea*[1]

ALCESTE [*confronting the guard*]. Well, what do you want with me?
    Come in, Sir.
GUARD.   I've a word, Sir, for your ear.
ALCESTE. Speak it aloud, Sir; I shall strive to hear.   750
GUARD. The Marshals have instructed me to say
    You must report to them without delay.
ALCESTE. Who? Me, Sir?
GUARD.   Yes, Sir; you.
ALCESTE.   But what do they want?
PHILINTE [*to* ALCESTE]. To scotch your silly quarrel with Oronte.
CELIMENE [*to* PHILINTE]. What quarrel?
PHILINTE.   Oronte and he have fallen out
    Over some verse he spoke his mind about;
    The Marshals wish to arbitrate the matter.
ALCESTE. Never shall I equivocate or flatter!
PHILINTE. You'd best obey their summons; come, let's go.
ALCESTE. How can they mend our quarrel, I'd like to know?   760
    Am I to make a cowardly retraction,
    And praise those jingles to his satisfaction?
    I'll not recant; I've judged that sonnet rightly.
    It's bad.
PHILINTE.   But you might say so more politely. . . .
ALCESTE. I'll not back down; his verses make me sick.
PHILINTE. If only you could be more politic!
    But come, let's go.
ALCESTE.   I'll go, but I won't unsay
    A single word.
PHILINTE.   Well, let's be on our way.
ALCESTE. Till I am ordered by my lord the King
    To praise that poem, I shall say the thing   770
    Is scandalous, by God, and that the poet
    Ought to be hanged for having the nerve to show it.
    [*To* CLITANDRE *and* ACASTE, *who are laughing*]
    By heaven, Sirs, I really didn't know
    That I was being humorous.

---

[1] *Marshalsea:* court overseen by the King's marshals, who formed a tribunal that gave judgments in disputes of honor among gentlemen.

CELIMENE.   Go, Sir, go;
    Settle your business.
ALCESTE.   I shall, and when I'm through,
    I shall return to settle things with you.

ACT III

SCENE I
CLITANDRE, ACASTE

CLITANDRE. Dear Marquess, how contented you appear;
    All things delight you, nothing mars your cheer.
    Can you, in perfect honesty, declare
    That you've a right to be so debonair?   780
ACASTE. By Jove, when I survey myself, I find
    No cause whatever for distress of mind.
    I'm young and rich; I can in modesty
    Lay claim to an exalted pedigree;
    And owing to my name and my condition
    I shall not want for honors and position.
    Then as to courage, that most precious trait,
    I seem to have it, as was proved of late
    Upon the field of honor, where my bearing,
    They say, was very cool and rather daring.   790
    I've wit, of course; and taste in such perfection
    That I can judge without the least reflection,
    And at the theater, which is my delight,
    Can make or break a play on opening night,
    And lead the crowd in hisses or bravos,
    And generally be known as one who knows.
    I'm clever, handsome, gracefully polite;
    My waist is small, my teeth are strong and white;
    As for my dress, the world's astonished eyes
    Assure me that I bear away the prize.   800
    I find myself in favor everywhere,
    Honored by men, and worshiped by the fair;
    And since these things are so, it seems to me
    I'm justified in my complacency.
CLITANDRE. Well, if so many ladies hold you dear,
    Why do you press a hopeless courtship here?

ACASTE. Hopeless, you say? I'm not the sort of fool
    That likes his ladies difficult and cool.
    Men who are awkward, shy, and peasantish
    May pine for heartless beauties, if they wish,   810
    Grovel before them, bear their cruelties,
    Woo them with tears and sighs and bended knees,
    And hope by dogged faithfulness to gain
    What their poor merits never could obtain.
    For men like me, however, it makes no sense
    To love on trust, and foot the whole expense.
    Whatever any lady's merits be,
    I think, thank God, that I'm as choice as she;
    That if my heart is kind enough to burn
    For her, she owes me something in return;   820
    And that in any proper love affair
    The partners must invest an equal share.
CLITANDRE. You think, then, that our hostess favors you?
ACASTE. I've reason to believe that that is true.
CLITANDRE. How did you come to such a mad conclusion?
    You're blind, dear fellow. This is sheer delusion.
ACASTE. All right, then: I'm deluded and I'm blind.
CLITANDRE. Whatever put the notion in your mind?
ACASTE. Delusion.
CLITANDRE.   What persuades you that you're right?
ACASTE. I'm blind.
CLITANDRE.   But have you any proofs to cite?   830
ACASTE. I tell you I'm deluded.
CLITANDRE.   Have you, then,
    Received some secret pledge from Célimène?
ACASTE. Oh, no: she scorns me.
CLITANDRE.   Tell me the truth, I beg.
ACASTE. She just can't bear me.
CLITANDRE.   Ah, don't pull my leg.
    Tell me what hope she's given you, I pray.
ACASTE. I'm hopeless, and it's you who win the day.
    She hates me thoroughly, and I'm so vexed
    I mean to hang myself on Tuesday next.
CLITANDRE. Dear Marquess, let us have an armistice
    And make a treaty. What do you say to this?   840
    If ever one of us can plainly prove
    That Célimène encourages his love,
    The other must abandon hope, and yield,
    And leave him in possession of the field.

ACASTE. Now, there's a bargain that appeals to me;
　　With all my heart, dear Marquess, I agree.
　　But hush.

SCENE II

CELIMENE, ACASTE, CLITANDRE

CELIMENE.　　　Still here?
CLITANDRE.　　　　　　'Twas love that stayed our feet.
CELIMENE. I think I heard a carriage in the street.
　　Whose is it? D'you know?

SCENE III

CELIMENE, ACASTE, CLITANDRE, BASQUE

BASQUE. Arsinoé is here, *Madame*.
CELIMENE.　　　　　Arsinoé, you say?
　　　Oh, dear.   850
BASQUE. Eliante is entertaining her below.
CELIMENE. What brings the creature here, I'd like to know?
ACASTE. They say she's dreadfully prudish, but in fact
　　I think her piety . . . .
CELIMENE.　　　　　It's all an act.
　　At heart she's worldly, and her poor success
　　In snaring men explains her prudishness.
　　It breaks her heart to see the beaux and gallants
　　Engrossed by other women's charms and talents,
　　And so she's always in a jealous rage
　　Against the faulty standards of the age.   860
　　She lets the world believe that she's a prude
　　To justify her loveless solitude,
　　And strives to put a brand of moral shame
　　On all the graces that she cannot claim.
　　But still she'd love a lover; and Alceste
　　Appears to be the one she'd love the best.
　　His visits here are poison to her pride;
　　She seems to think I've lured him from her side;
　　And everywhere, at court or in the town,
　　The spiteful, envious woman runs me down.   870
　　In short, she's just as stupid as can be,
　　Vicious and arrogant in the last degree,
　　And . . . .

SCENE IV
ARSINOE, CELIMENE, CLITANDRE, ACASTE

CELIMENE. Ah! What happy chance has brought you here?
I've thought about you ever so much, my dear.
ARSINOE. I've come to tell you something you should know.
CELIMENE. How good of you to think of doing so!
[CLITANDRE *and* ACASTE *go out, laughing.*]

SCENE V
ARSINOE, CELIMENE

ARSINOE. It's just as well those gentlemen didn't tarry.
CELIMENE. Shall we sit down?
ARSINOE. That won't be necessary.
Madam, the flame of friendship ought to burn
Brightest in matters of the most concern,   880
And as there's nothing which concerns us more
Than honor, I have hastened to your door
To bring you, as your friend, some information
About the status of your reputation.
I visited, last night, some virtuous folk,
And, quite by chance, it was of you they spoke;
There was, I fear, no tendency to praise
Your light behavior and your dashing ways.
The quantity of gentlemen you see
And your by now notorious coquetry   890
Were both so vehemently criticized
By everyone, that I was much surprised.
Of course, I needn't tell you where I stood;
I came to your defense as best I could,
Assured them you were harmless, and declared
Your soul was absolutely unimpaired.
But there are some things, you must realize,
One can't excuse, however hard one tries,
And I was forced at last into conceding
That your behavior, Madam, is misleading,   900
That it makes a bad impression, giving rise
To ugly gossip and obscene surmise,
And that if you were more *overtly* good,
You wouldn't be so much misunderstood.
Not that I think you've been unchaste—no! no!

The saints preserve me from a thought so low!
But mere good conscience never did suffice:
One must avoid the outward show of vice.
Madam, you're too intelligent, I'm sure,
To think my motives anything but pure   910
In offering you this counsel—which I do
Out of a zealous interest in you.
CELIMENE. Madam, I haven't taken you amiss;
I'm very much obliged to you for this;
And I'll at once discharge the obligation
By telling you about *your* reputation.
You've been so friendly as to let me know
What certain people say of me, and so
I mean to follow your benign example
By offering you a somewhat similar sample.   920
The other day, I went to an affair
And found some most distinguished people there
Discussing piety, both false and true.
The conversation soon came round to you.
Alas! Your prudery and bustling zeal
Appeared to have a very slight appeal.
Your affectation of a grave demeanor,
Your endless talk of virtue and of honor,
The aptitude of your suspicious mind
For finding sin where there is none to find,   930
Your towering self-esteem, that pitying face
With which you contemplate the human race,
Your sermonizings and your sharp aspersions
On people's pure and innocent diversions—
All these were mentioned, Madam, and, in fact,
Were roundly and concertedly attacked.
"What good," they said, "are all these outward shows,
When everything belies her pious pose?
She prays incessantly; but then, they say,
She beats her maids and cheats them of their pay;   940
She shows her zeal in every holy place,
But still she's vain enough to paint her face;
She holds that naked statues are immoral,
But with a naked *man* she'd have no quarrel."
Of course, I said to everybody there
That they were being viciously unfair;
But still they were disposed to criticize you,
And all agreed that someone should advise you

To leave the morals of the world alone,
And worry rather more about your own.   950
They felt that one's self-knowledge should be great
Before one thinks of setting others straight;
That one should learn the art of living well
Before one threatens other men with hell,
And that the Church is best equipped, no doubt,
To guide our souls and root our vices out.
Madam, you're too intelligent, I'm sure,
To think my motives anything but pure
In offering you this counsel—which I do
Out of a zealous interest in you.   960
ARSINOE. I dared not hope for gratitude, but I
Did not expect so acid a reply;
I judge, since you've been so extremely tart,
That my good counsel pierced you to the heart.
CELIMENE. Far from it, Madam. Indeed, it seems to me
We ought to trade advice more frequently.
One's vision of oneself is so defective
That it would be an excellent corrective.
If you are willing, Madam, let's arrange
Shortly to have another frank exchange   970
In which we'll tell each other, *entre nous,*°
What you've heard tell of me, and I of you.
ARSINOE. Oh, people never censure you, my dear;
It's me they criticize. Or so I hear.
CELIMENE. Madam, I think we either blame or praise
According to our taste and length of days.
There is a time of life for coquetry,
And there's a season, too, for prudery.
When all one's charms are gone, it is, I'm sure,
Good strategy to be devout and pure: 980
It makes one seem a little less forsaken.
Some day, perhaps, I'll take the road you've taken:
Time brings all things. But I have time aplenty,
And see no cause to be a prude at twenty.
ARSINOE. You give your age in such a gloating tone
That one would think I was an ancient crone;
We're not so far apart, in sober truth,
That you can mock me with a boast of youth!
Madam, you baffle me. I wish I knew

971. *entre nous:* (French) just between us.

What moves you to provoke me as you do.   990
CELIMENE. For my part, Madam, I should like to know
    Why you abuse me everywhere you go.
    Is it my fault, dear lady, that your hand
    Is not, alas, in very great demand?
    If men admire me, if they pay me court
    And daily make me offers of the sort
    You'd dearly love to have them make to you,
    How can I help it? What would you have me do?
    If what you want is lovers, please feel free
    To take as many as you can from me.   1000
ARSINOE. Oh, come. D'you think the world is losing sleep
    Over that flock of lovers which you keep,
    Or that we find it difficult to guess
    What price you pay for their devotedness?
    Surely you don't expect us to suppose
    Mere merit could attract so many beaux?
    It's not your virtue that they're dazzled by;
    Nor is it virtuous love for which they sigh.
    You're fooling no one, Madam; the world's not blind;
    There's many a lady heaven has designed   1010
    To call men's noblest, tenderest feelings out,
    Who has no lovers dogging her about;
    From which it's plain that lovers nowadays
    Must be acquired in bold and shameless ways,
    And only pay one court for such reward
    As modesty and virtue can't afford.
    Then don't be quite so puffed up, if you please,
    About your tawdry little victories;
    Try, if you can, to be a shade less vain,
    And treat the world with somewhat less disdain.   1020
    If one were envious of your amours,
    One soon could have a following like yours;
    Lovers are no great trouble to collect
    If one prefers them to one's self-respect.
CELIMENE. Collect them then, my dear; I'd love to see
    You demonstrate that charming theory;
    Who knows, you might . . . .
ARSINOE.   Now, Madam, that will do;
    It's time to end this trying interview.
    My coach is late in coming to your door,
    Or I'd have taken leave of you before.   1030
CELIMENE. Oh, please don't feel that you must rush away;

I'd be delighted, Madam, if you'd stay.
However, lest my conversation bore you,
Let me provide some better company for you;
This gentleman, who comes most apropos,
Will please you more than I could do, I know.

SCENE VI
ALCESTE, CELIMENE, ARSINOE

CELIMENE. Alceste, I have a little note to write
   Which simply must go out before tonight;
   Please entertain *Madame;* I'm sure that she
   Will overlook my incivility.   1040

SCENE VII
ALCESTE, ARSINOE

ARSINOE. Well, Sir, our hostess graciously contrives
   For us to chat until my coach arrives;
   And I shall be forever in her debt
   For granting me this little tête-à-tête.
   We women very rightly give our hearts
   To men of noble character and parts,
   And your especial merits, dear Alceste,
   Have roused the deepest sympathy in my breast.
   Oh, how I wish they had sufficient sense
   At court, to recognize your excellence!   1050
   They wrong you greatly, Sir. How it must hurt you
   Never to be rewarded for your virtue!
ALCESTE. Why, Madam, what cause have I to feel aggrieved?
   What great and brilliant thing have I achieved?
   What service have I rendered to the King
   That I should look to him for anything?
ARSINOE. Not everyone who's honored by the State
   Has done great services. A man must wait
   Till time and fortune offer him the chance.
   Your merit, Sir, is obvious at a glance,   1060
   And . . . .
ALCESTE.   Ah, forget my merit; I'm not neglected.
   The court, I think, can hardly be expected
   To mine men's souls for merit, and unearth

Our hidden virtues and our secret worth.
ARSINOE. *Some* virtues, though, are far too bright to hide;
Yours are acknowledged, Sir, on every side.
Indeed, I've heard you warmly praised of late
By persons of considerable weight.
ALCESTE. This fawning age has praise for everyone,
And all distinctions, Madam, are undone.   1070
All things have equal honor nowadays,
And no one should be gratified by praise.
To be admired, one only need exist,
And every lackey's on the honors list.
ARSINOE. I only wish, Sir, that you had your eye
On some position at court, however high;
You'd only have to hint at such a notion
For me to set the proper wheels in motion;
I've certain friendships I'd be glad to use
To get you any office you might choose.   1080
ALCESTE. Madam, I fear that any such ambition
Is wholly foreign to my disposition.
The soul God gave me isn't of the sort
That prospers in the weather of a court.
It's all too obvious that I don't possess
The virtues necessary for success.
My one great talent is for speaking plain;
I've never learned to flatter or to feign;
And anyone so stupidly sincere
Had best not seek a courtier's career.   1090
Outside the court, I know, one must dispense
With honors, privilege, and influence;
But still one gains the right, foregoing these,
Not to be tortured by the wish to please.
One needn't live in dread of snubs and slights,
Nor praise the verse that every idiot writes,
Nor humor silly Marquesses, nor bestow
Politic sighs on Madam So-and-So.
ARSINOE. Forget the court, then; let the matter rest.
But I've another cause to be distressed   1100
About your present situation, Sir.
It's to your love affair that I refer.
She whom you love, and who pretends to love you,
Is, I regret to say, unworthy of you.
ALCESTE. Why, Madam! Can you seriously intend
To make so grave a charge against your friend?

ARSINOE. Alas, I must. I've stood aside too long
　　And let that lady do you grievous wrong;
　　But now my debt to conscience shall be paid:
　　I tell you that your love has been betrayed.　　　　　　1110
ALCESTE. I thank you, Madam; you're extremely kind.
　　Such words are soothing to a lover's mind.
ARSINOE. Yes, though she *is* my friend, I say again
　　You're very much too good for Célimène.
　　She's wantonly misled you from the start.
ALCESTE. You may be right; who knows another's heart?
　　But ask yourself if it's the part of charity
　　To shake my soul with doubts of her sincerity.
ARSINOE. Well, if you'd rather be a dupe than doubt her,
　　That's your affair. I'll say no more about her.　　　　1120
ALCESTE. Madam, you know that doubt and vague suspicion
　　Are painful to a man in my position;
　　It's most unkind to worry me this way
　　Unless you've some real proof of what you say.
ARSINOE. Sir, say no more: all doubt shall be removed,
　　And all that I've been saying shall be proved.
　　You've only to escort me home, and there
　　We'll look into the heart of this affair.
　　I've ocular evidence which will persuade you
　　Beyond a doubt, that Célimène's betrayed you.　　　　1130
　　Then, if you're saddened by that revelation,
　　Perhaps I can provide some consolation.

ACT IV

SCENE I

ELIANTE, PHILINTE

PHILINTE. Madam, he acted like a stubborn child;
　　I thought they never would be reconciled;
　　In vain we reasoned, threatened, and appealed;
　　He stood his ground and simply would not yield.
　　The Marshals, I feel sure, have never heard
　　An argument so splendidly absurd.
　　"No, gentlemen," said he, "I'll not retract.
　　His verse is bad: extremely bad, in fact.　　　　　　1140
　　Surely it does the man no harm to know it.

Does it disgrace him, not to be a poet?
A gentleman may be respected still,
Whether he writes a sonnet well or ill.
That I dislike his verse should not offend him;
In all that touches honor, I commend him;
He's noble, brave, and virtuous—but I fear
He can't in truth be called a sonneteer.
I'll gladly praise his wardrobe; I'll endorse
His dancing, or the way he sits a horse;   1150
But, gentlemen, I cannot praise his rhyme.
In fact, it ought to be a capital crime
For anyone so sadly unendowed
To write a sonnet, and read the thing aloud."
At length he fell into a gentler mood
And, striking a concessive attitude,
He paid Oronte the following courtesies:
"Sir, I regret that I'm so hard to please,
And I'm profoundly sorry that your lyric
Failed to provoke me to a panegyric." °   1160
After these curious words, the two embraced,
And then the hearing was adjourned—in haste.

ELIANTE. His conduct has been very singular lately;
    Still, I confess that I respect him greatly.
    The honesty in which he takes such pride
    Has—to my mind—its noble, heroic side.
    In this false age, such candor seems outrageous;
    But I could wish that it were more contagious.

PHILINTE. What most intrigues me in our friend Alceste
    Is the grand passion that rages in his breast.   1170
    The sullen humors he's compounded of
    Should not, I think, dispose his heart to love;
    But since they do, it puzzles me still more
    That he should choose your cousin to adore.

ELIANTE. It does, indeed, belie the theory
    That love is born of gentle sympathy,
    And that the tender passion must be based
    On sweet accords of temper and of taste.

PHILINTE. Does she return his love, do you suppose?

ELIANTE. Ah, that's a difficult question, Sir. Who knows?   1180
    How can we judge the truth of her devotion?
    Her heart's a stranger to its own emotion.

1160. *panegyric:* formal speech of praise.

Sometimes it thinks it loves, when no love's there;
At other times it loves quite unaware.
PHILINTE. I rather think Alceste is in for more
Distress and sorrow than he's bargained for;
Where he of my mind, Madam, his affection
Would turn in quite a different direction,
And we would see him more responsive to
The kind regard which he receives from you.   1190
ELIANTE. Sir, I believe in frankness, and I'm inclined,
In matters of the heart, to speak my mind.
I don't oppose his love for her; indeed,
I hope with all my heart that he'll succeed,
And were it in my power, I'd rejoice
In giving him the lady of his choice.
But if, as happens frequently enough
In love affairs, he meets with a rebuff—
If Célimène should grant some rival's suit—
I'd gladly play the role of substitute;   1200
Nor would his tender speeches please me less
Because they'd once been made without success.
PHILINTE. Well, Madam, as for me, I don't oppose
Your hopes in this affair; and heaven knows
That in my conversations with the man
I plead your cause as often as I can.
But if those two should marry, and so remove
All chance that he will offer you his love,
Then I'll declare my own, and hope to see
Your gracious favor pass from him to me.   1210
In short, should you be cheated of Alceste,
I'd be most happy to be second best.
ELIANTE. Philinte, you're teasing.
PHILINTE.   Ah, Madam, never fear;
No words of mine were ever so sincere,
And I shall live in fretful expectation
Till I can make a fuller declaration.

SCENE II

ALCESTE, ELIANTE, PHILINTE

ALCESTE. Avenge me, Madam! I must have satisfaction,
　　Or this great wrong will drive me to distraction!
ELIANTE. Why, what's the matter? What's upset you so?
ALCESTE. Madam, I've had a mortal, mortal blow.　　　　　1220
　　If Chaos repossessed the universe,°
　　I swear I'd not be shaken any worse.
　　I'm ruined. . . . I can say no more. . . . My soul . . . .
ELIANTE. Do try, Sir, to regain your self-control.
ALCESTE. Just heaven! Why were so much beauty and grace
　　Bestowed on one so vicious and so base?
ELIANTE. Once more, Sir, tell us. . . .
ALCESTE.　　　　　　　　　　My world has gone to wrack;
　　I'm—I'm betrayed; she's stabbed me in the back:
　　Yes, Célimène (who would have thought it of her?)
　　Is false to me, and has another lover.　　　　　　　　1230
ELIANTE. Are you quite certain? Can you prove these things?
PHILINTE. Lovers are prey to wild imaginings
　　And jealous fancies. No doubt there's some mistake. . . .
ALCESTE. Mind your own business, Sir, for heaven's sake.
　　[To ELIANTE]
　　Madam, I have the proof that you demand
　　Here in my pocket, penned by her own hand.
　　Yes, all the shameful evidence one could want
　　Lies in this letter written to Oronte—
　　Oronte! whom I felt sure she couldn't love,
　　And hardly bothered to be jealous of.　　　　　　　　1240
PHILINTE. Still, in a letter, appearances may deceive;
　　This may not be so bad as you believe.
ALCESTE. Once more I beg you, Sir, to let me be;
　　Tend to your own affairs; leave mine to me.
ELIANTE. Compose yourself; this anguish that you feel . . . .
ALCESTE. Is something, Madam, you alone can heal.
　　My outraged heart, beside itself with grief,
　　Appeals to you for comfort and relief.
　　Avenge me on your cousin, whose unjust
　　And faithless nature has deceived my trust;　　　　　1250

1221. *Chaos . . . universe:* In Greek creation myths, Chaos existed before the orderly creation of the universe. (The translator has added this allusion, which is not present in the original French.)

Avenge a crime your pure soul must detest.
ELIANTE. But how, Sir?
ELIANTE.   Madam, this heart within my breast
    Is yours; pray take it; redeem my heart from her,
    And so avenge me on my torturer.
    Let her be punished by the fond emotion,
    The ardent love, the bottomless devotion,
    The faithful worship which this heart of mine
    Will offer up to yours as to a shrine.
ELIANTE. You have my sympathy, Sir, in all you suffer;
    Nor do I scorn the noble heart you offer;   1260
    But I suspect you'll soon be mollified,
    And this desire for vengeance will subside.
    When some beloved hand has done us wrong
    We thirst for retribution—but not for long;
    However dark the deed that she's committed,
    A lovely culprit's very soon acquitted.
    Nothing's so stormy as an injured lover,
    And yet no storm so quickly passes over.
ALCESTE. No, Madam, no—this is no lovers' spat;
    I'll not forgive her; it's gone too far for that;   1270
    My mind's made up; I'll kill myself before
    I waste my hopes upon her any more.
    Ah, here she is. My wrath intensifies.
    I shall confront her with her tricks and lies,
    And crush her utterly, and bring you then
    A heart no longer slave to Célimène.

                        SCENE III
                    CELIMENE, ALCESTE

ALCESTE [aside]. Sweet heaven, help me to control my passion.
CELIMENE [aside, to ALCESTE]. Oh, Lord. Why stand there staring in that
        fashion?
    And what d'you mean by those dramatic sighs,
    And that malignant glitter in your eyes?   1280
ALCESTE. I mean that sins which cause the blood to freeze
    Look innocent beside your treacheries;
    That nothing Hell's or Heaven's wrath could do
    Ever produced so bad a thing as you.
CELIMENE. Your compliments were always sweet and pretty.
ALCESTE. Madam, it's not the moment to be witty.

No, blush and hang your head; you've ample reason,
Since I've the fullest evidence of your treason.
Ah, this is what my sad heart prophesied;
Now all my anxious fears are verified;   1290
My dark suspicion and my gloomy doubt
Divined the truth, and now the truth is out.
For all your trickery, I was not deceived;
It was my bitter stars that I believed.
But don't imagine that you'll go scot-free;
You shan't misuse me with impunity.
I know that love's irrational and blind;
I know the heart's not subject to the mind,
And can't be reasoned into beating faster;
I know each soul is free to choose its master;   1300
Therefore had you but spoken from the heart,
Rejecting my attentions from the start,
I'd have no grievance, or at any rate
I could complain of nothing but my fate.
Ah, but so falsely to encourage me—
That was a treason and a treachery
For which you cannot suffer too severely,
And you shall pay for that behavior dearly.
Yes, now I have no pity, not a shred;
My temper's out of hand; I've lost my head;   1310
Shocked by the knowledge of your double-dealings,
My reason can't restrain my savage feelings;
A righteous wrath deprives me of my senses,
And I won't answer for the consequences.
CELIMENE. What does this outburst mean? Will you please explain?
Have you, by any chance, gone quite insane?
ALCESTE. Yes, yes, I went insane the day I fell
A victim to your black and fatal spell,
Thinking to meet with some sincerity
Among the treacherous charms that beckoned me.   1320
CELIMENE. Pooh. Of what treachery can you complain?
ALCESTE. How sly you are, how cleverly you feign!
But you'll not victimize me any more.
Look: here's a document you've seen before.
This evidence, which I acquired today,
Leaves you, I think, without a thing to say.
CELIMENE. Is this what sent you into such a fit?
ALCESTE. You should be blushing at the sight of it.
CELIMENE. Ought I to blush? I truly don't see why.

ALCESTE. Ah, now you're being bold as well as sly;   1330
    Since there's no signature, perhaps you'll claim . . . .
CELIMENE. I wrote it, whether or not it bears my name.
ALCESTE. And you can view with equanimity
    This proof of your disloyalty to me!
CELIMENE. Oh, don't be so outrageous and extreme.
ALCESTE. You take this matter lightly, it would seem.
    Was it no wrong to me, no shame to you,
    That you should send Oronte this billet-doux?
CELIMENE. Oronte! Who said it was for him?
ALCESTE.   Why, those
    Who brought me this example of your prose.   1340
    But what's the difference? If you wrote the letter
    To someone else, it pleases me no better.
    My grievance and your guilt remain the same.
CELIMENE. But need you rage, and need I blush for shame,
    If this was written to a *woman* friend?
ALCESTE. Ah! Most ingenious. I'm impressed no end;
    And after that incredible evasion
    Your guilt is clear. I need no more persuasion.
    How dare you try so clumsy a deception?
    D'you think I'm wholly wanting in perception?   1350
    Come, come, let's see how brazenly you'll try
    To bolster up so palpable a lie:
    Kindly construe this ardent closing section
    As nothing more than sisterly affection!
    Here, let me read it. Tell me, if you dare to,
    That this is for a woman . . . .
CELIMENE.   I don't care to.
    What right have you to badger and berate me,
    And so highhandedly interrogate me?
ALCESTE. Now, don't be angry; all I ask of you
    Is that you justify a phrase or two   1360
CELIMENE. No, I shall not. I utterly refuse,
    And you may take those phrases as you choose.
ALCESTE. Just show me how this letter could be meant
    For a woman's eyes, and I shall be content.
CELIMENE. No, no, it's for Oronte; you're perfectly right.
    I welcome his attentions with delight,
    I prize his character and his intellect,
    And everything is just as you suspect.
    Come, do your worst now; give your rage free rein;
    But kindly cease to bicker and complain.   1370

ALCESTE [*aside*]. Good God! Could anything be more inhuman?
　　Was ever a heart so mangled by a woman?
　　When I complain of how she has betrayed me,
　　She bridles, and commences to upbraid me!
　　She tries my tortured patience to the limit;
　　She won't deny her guilt; she glories in it!
　　And yet my heart's too faint and cowardly
　　To break these chains of passion, and be free,
　　To scorn her as it should, and rise above
　　This unrewarded, mad, and bitter love.   1380
　　[*To* CELIMENE]
　　Ah, traitress, in how confident a fashion
　　You take advantage of my helpless passion,
　　And use my weakness for your faithless charms
　　To make me once again throw down my arms!
　　But do at least deny this black transgression;
　　Take back that mocking and perverse confession;
　　Defend this letter and your innocence,
　　And I, poor fool, will aid in your defense.
　　Pretend, pretend, that you are just and true,
　　And I shall make myself believe in you.   1390
CELIMENE. Oh, stop it. Don't be such a jealous dunce,
　　Or I shall leave off loving you at once.
　　Just why should I *pretend*? What could impel me
　　To stoop so low as that? And kindly tell me
　　Why, if I loved another, I shouldn't merely
　　Inform you of it, simply and sincerely!
　　I've told you where you stand, and that admission
　　Should altogether clear me of suspicion;
　　After so generous a guarantee,
　　What right have you to harbor doubts of me?   1400
　　Since women are (from natural reticence)
　　Reluctant to declare their sentiments,
　　And since the honor of our sex requires
　　That we conceal our amorous desires,
　　Ought any man for whom such laws are broken
　　To question what the oracle has spoken?
　　Should he not rather feel an obligation
　　To trust that most obliging declaration?
　　Enough, now. Your suspicions quite disgust me;
　　Why should I love a man who doesn't trust me?   1410
　　I cannot understand why I continue,
　　Fool that I am, to take an interest in you.

I ought to choose a man less prone to doubt,
And give you something to be vexed about.
ALCESTE. Ah, what a poor enchanted fool I am;
    These gentle words, no doubt, were all a sham;
    But destiny requires me to entrust
    My happiness to you, and so I must.
    I'll love you to the bitter end, and see
    How false and treacherous you dare to be.   1420
CELIMENE. No, you don't really love me as you ought.
ALCESTE. I love you more than can be said or thought;
    Indeed, I wish you were in such distress
    That I might show my deep devotedness.
    Yes, I could wish that you were wretchedly poor,
    Unloved, uncherished, utterly obscure;
    That fate had set you down upon the earth
    Without possessions, rank, or gentle birth;
    Then, by the offer of my heart, I might
    Repair the great injustice of your plight;   1430
    I'd raise you from the dust, and proudly prove
    The purity and vastness of my love.
CELIMENE. This is a strange benevolence indeed!
    God grant that I may never be in need. . . .
    Ah, here's Monsieur Dubois, in quaint disguise.

SCENE IV
CELIMENE, ALCESTE, DUBOIS

ALCESTE. Well, why this costume? Why those frightened eyes?
    What ails you?
DUBOIS.   Well, Sir, things are most mysterious.
ALCESTE. What do you mean?
DUBOIS.   I fear they're very serious.
ALCESTE. What?
DUBOIS.   Shall I speak more loudly?
ALCESTE.   Yes; speak out.
DUBOIS. Isn't there someone here, Sir?
ALCESTE.   Speak, you lout!   1440
    Stop wasting time.
DUBOIS.   Sir, we must slip away.
ALCESTE. How's that?
DUBOIS.   We must decamp without delay.
ALCESTE. Explain yourself.

DUBOIS. I tell you we must fly.

ALCESTE. What for?

DUBOIS. We mustn't pause to say good-by.

ALCESTE. Now what d'you mean by all of this, you clown?

DUBOIS. I mean, Sir, that we've got to leave this town.

ALCESTE. I'll tear you limb from limb and joint from joint
    If you don't come more quickly to the point.

DUBOIS. Well, Sir, today a man in a black suit,
    Who wore a black and ugly scowl to boot, 1450
    Left us a document scrawled in such a hand
    As even Satan couldn't understand.
    It bears upon your lawsuit, I don't doubt;
    But all hell's devils couldn't make it out.

ALCESTE. Well, well, go on. What then? I fail to see
    How this event obliges us to flee.

DUBOIS. Well, Sir: an hour later, hardly more,
    A gentleman who's often called before
    Came looking for you in an anxious way.
    Not finding you, he asked me to convey 1460
    (Knowing I could be trusted with the same)
    The following message. . . . Now, what *was* his name?

ALCESTE. Forget his name, you idiot. What did he say?

DUBOIS. Well, it was one of your friends, Sir, anyway.
    He warned you to begone, and he suggested
    That if you stay, you may well be arrested.

ALCESTE. What? Nothing more specific? Think, man, think!

DUBOIS. No, Sir. He had me bring him pen and ink,
    And dashed you off a letter which, I'm sure,
    Will render things distinctly less obscure. 1470

ALCESTE. Well—let me have it!

CELIMENE. What *is* this all about?

ALCESTE. God knows; but I have hopes of finding out.
    How long am I to wait, you blitherer?

DUBOIS [*after a protracted search for the letter*]. I must have left it
        on your table, Sir.

ALCESTE. I ought to . . . .

CELIMENE. No, no, keep your self-control;
    Go find out what's behind his rigmarole.

ALCESTE. It seems that fate, no matter what I do,
    Has sworn that I may not converse with you;
    But, Madam, pray permit your faithful lover
    To try once more before the day is over. 1480

ACT V

SCENE I
ALCESTE, PHILINTE

ALCESTE. No, it's too much. My mind's made up, I tell you.
PHILINTE. Why should this blow, however hard, compel you . . . .
ALCESTE. No, no, don't waste your breath in argument;
    Nothing you say will alter my intent;
    This age is vile, and I've made up my mind
    To have no further commerce with mankind.
    Did not truth, honor, decency, and the laws
    Oppose my enemy and approve my cause?
    My claims were justified in all men's sight;
    I put my trust in equity and right;   1490
    Yet, to my horror and the world's disgrace,
    Justice is mocked, and I have lost my case!
    A scoundrel whose dishonesty is notorious
    Emerges from another lie victorious!
    Honor and right condone his brazen fraud,
    While rectitude and decency applaud!
    Before his smirking face, the truth stands charmed,
    And virtue conquered, and the law disarmed!
    His crime is sanctioned by a court decree!
    And not content with what he's done to me,   1500
    The dog now seeks to ruin me by stating
    That I composed a book now circulating,
    A book so wholly criminal and vicious
    That even to speak its title is seditious!
    Meanwhile Oronte, my rival, lends his credit
    To the same libelous tale, and helps to spread it!
    Oronte! a man of honor and of rank,
    With whom I've been entirely fair and frank;
    Who sought me out and forced me, willy-nilly,
    To judge some verse I found extremely silly;   1510
    And who, because I properly refused
    To flatter him, or see the truth abused,
    Abets my enemy in a rotten slander!
    There's the reward of honesty and candor!
    The man will hate me to the end of time
    For failing to commend his wretched rhyme!
    And not this man alone, but all humanity

Do what they do from interest and vanity;
They prate of honor, truth, and righteousness,
But lie, betray, and swindle nonetheless.   1520
Come then: man's villainy is too much to bear;
Let's leave this jungle and this jackal's lair.
Yes! treacherous and savage race of men,
You shall not look upon my face again.
PHILINTE. Oh, don't rush into exile prematurely;
Things aren't as dreadful as you make them, surely.
It's rather obvious, since you're still at large,
That people don't believe your enemy's charge.
Indeed, his tale's so patently untrue
That it may do more harm to him than you.   1530
ALCESTE. Nothing could do that scoundrel any harm:
His frank corruption is his greatest charm,
And, far from hurting him, a further shame
Would only serve to magnify his name.
PHILINTE. In any case, his bald prevarication
Has done no injury to your reputation,
And you may feel secure in that regard.
As for your lawsuit, it should not be hard
To have the case reopened, and contest
This judgment . . . .
ALCESTE.   No, no, let the verdict rest.   1540
Whatever cruel penalty it may bring,
I wouldn't have it changed for anything.
It shows the times' injustice with such clarity
That I shall pass it down to our posterity
As a great proof and signal demonstration
Of the black wickedness of this generation.
It may cost twenty thousand francs; but I
Shall pay their twenty thousand, and gain thereby
The right to storm and rage at human evil,
And send the race of mankind to the devil.   1550
PHILINTE. Listen to me. . . .
ALCESTE.   Why? What can you possibly say?
Don't argue, Sir; your labor's thrown away.
Do you propose to offer lame excuses
For men's behavior and the times' abuses?
PHILINTE. No, all you say I'll readily concede:
This is a low, dishonest age indeed;
Nothing but trickery prospers nowadays,
And people ought to mend their shabby ways.

Yes, man's a beastly creature; but must we then
Abandon the society of men? 1560
Here in the world, each human frailty
Provides occasion for philosophy,
And that is virtue's noblest exercise;
If honesty shone forth from all men's eyes,
If every heart were frank and kind and just,
What could our virtues do but gather dust
(Since their employment is to help us bear
The villainies of men without despair)?
A heart well-armed with virtue can endure. . . .
ALCESTE. Sir, you're a matchless reasoner, to be sure; 1570
Your words are fine and full of cogency;
But don't waste time and eloquence on me.
My reason bids me go, for my own good.
My tongue won't lie and flatter as it should;
God knows what frankness it might next commit,
And what I'd suffer on account of it.
Pray let me wait for Célimène's return
In peace and quiet. I shall shortly learn,
By her response to what I have in view,
Whether her love for me is feigned or true. 1580
PHILINTE. Till then, let's visit Eliante upstairs.
ALCESTE. No, I am too weighed down with somber cares.
Go to her, do; and leave me with my gloom
Here in the darkened corner of this room.
PHILINTE. Why, that's no sort of company, my friend;
I'll see if Eliante will not descend.

SCENE II
CELIMENE, ORONTE, ALCESTE

ORONTE. Yes, Madam, if you wish me to remain
Your true and ardent lover, you must deign
To give me some more positive assurance.
All this suspense is quite beyond endurance. 1590
If your heart shares the sweet desires of mine,
Show me as much by some convincing sign;
And here's the sign I urgently suggest:
That you no longer tolerate Alceste,
But sacrifice him to my love, and sever
All your relations with the man forever.

CELIMENE. Why do you suddenly dislike him so?
    You praised him to the skies not long ago.
ORONTE. Madam, that's not the point. I'm here to find
    Which way your tender feelings are inclined.   1600
    Choose, if you please, between Alceste and me,
    And I shall stay or go accordingly.
ALCESTE [emerging from the corner]. Yes, Madam, choose; this
          gentleman's demand
    Is wholly just, and I support his stand.
    I too am true and ardent; I too am here
    To ask you that you make your feelings clear.
    No more delays, now; no equivocation;
    The time has come to make your declaration.
ORONTE. Sir, I've no wish in any way to be
    An obstacle to your felicity.   1610
ALCESTE. Sir, I've no wish to share her heart with you;
    That may sound jealous, but at least it's true.
ORONTE. If, weighing us, she leans in your direction . . . .
ALCESTE. If she regards you with the least affection . . . .
ORONTE. I swear I'll yield her to you there and then.
ALCESTE. I swear I'll never see her face again.
ORONTE. Now, Madam, tell us what we've come to hear.
ALCESTE. Madam, speak openly and have no fear.
ORONTE. Just say which one is to remain your lover.
ALCESTE. Just name one name, and it will all be over.   1620
ORONTE. What! Is it possible that you're undecided?
ALCESTE. What! Can your feelings possibly be divided?
CELIMENE. Enough: this inquisition's gone too far:
    How utterly unreasonable you are!
    Not that I couldn't make the choice with ease;
    My heart has no conflicting sympathies;
    I know full well which one of you I favor,
    And you'd not see me hesitate or waver.
    But how can you expect me to reveal
    So cruelly and bluntly what I feel?   1630
    I think it altogether too unpleasant
    To choose between two men when both are present;
    One's heart has means more subtle and more kind
    Of letting its affections be divined,
    Nor need one be uncharitably plain
    To let a lover know he loves in vain.
ORONTE. No, no, speak plainly; I for one can stand it.
    I beg you to be frank.

ALCESTE.   And I demand it.
   The simple truth is what I wish to know,
   And there's no need for softening the blow.   1640
   You've made an art of pleasing everyone,
   But now your days of coquetry are done:
   You have no choice now, Madam, but to choose,
   For I'll know what to think if you refuse;
   I'll take your silence for a clear admission
   That I'm entitled to my worst suspicion.
ORONTE. I thank you for this ultimatum, Sir,
   And I may say I heartily concur.
CELIMENE. Really, this foolishness is very wearing:
   Must you be so unjust and overbearing?   1650
   Haven't I told you why I must demur?
   Ah, here's Eliante; I'll put the case to her.

SCENE III

ELIANTE, PHILINTE, CELIMENE, ORONTE, ALCESTE

CELIMENE. Cousin, I'm being persecuted here
   By these two persons, who, it would appear,
   Will not be satisfied till I confess
   Which one I love the more, and which the less,
   And tell the latter to his face that he
   Is henceforth banished from my company.
   Tell me, has ever such a thing been done?
ELIANTE. You'd best not turn to me; I'm not the one   1660
   To back you in a matter of this kind:
   I'm all for those who frankly speak their mind.
ORONTE. Madam, you'll search in vain for a defender.
ALCESTE. You're beaten, Madam, and may as well surrender.
ORONTE. Speak, speak, you must; and end this awful strain.
ALCESTE. Or don't, and your position will be plain.
ORONTE. A single word will close this painful scene.
ALCESTE. But if you're silent, I'll know what you mean.

SCENE IV

ARSINOE, CELIMENE, ELIANTE, ALCESTE,
PHILINTE, ACASTE, CLITANDRE, ORONTE

ACASTE [to CELIMENE]. Madam, with all due deference, we two
    Have come to pick a little bone with you.   1670
CLITANDRE [to ORONTE and ALCESTE]. I'm glad you're present, Sirs; as
       you'll soon learn,
    Our business here is also your concern.
ARSINOE [to CELIMENE]. Madam, I visit you so soon again
    Only because of these two gentlemen,
    Who came to me indignant and aggrieved
    About a crime too base to be believed.
    Knowing your virtue, having such confidence in it,
    I couldn't think you guilty for a minute,
    In spite of all their telling evidence;
    And, rising above our little difference,   1680
    I've hastened here in friendship's name to see
    You clear yourself of this great calumny.
ACASTE. Yes, Madam, let us see with what composure
    You'll manage to respond to this disclosure.
    You lately sent Clitandre this tender note.
CLITANDRE. And this one, for Acaste, you also wrote.
ACASTE [to ORONTE and ALCESTE]. You'll recognize this writing, Sirs,
       I think;
    The lady is so free with pen and ink
    That you must know it all too well, I fear.
    But listen: this is something you should hear.   1690

    "How absurd you are to condemn my lightheartedness in
society, and to accuse me of being happiest in the company of
others. Nothing could be more unjust; and if you do not come to
me instantly and beg pardon for saying such a thing, I shall never
forgive you as long as I live. Our big bumbling friend the Vis-
count. . . ."

What a shame that he's not here.

    "Our big bumbling friend the Viscount, whose name stands
first in your complaint, is hardly a man to my taste; and ever
since the day I watched him spend three-quarters of an hour   1700
spitting into a well, so as to make circles in the water, I have been
unable to think highly of him. As for the little Marquess . . . ."

In all modesty, gentlemen, that is I.

"As for the little Marquess, who sat squeezing my hand for such a long while yesterday, I find him in all respects the most trifling creature alive; and the only things of value about him are his cape and his sword. As for the man with the green ribbons . . . ."

[*To* ALCESTE]
It's your turn now, Sir.

"As for the man with the green ribbons, he amuses me now   1710
and then with his bluntness and his bearish ill-humor; but there are many times indeed when I think him the greatest bore in the world. And as for the sonneteer . . . ."

[*To* ORONTE]
Here's your helping.

"And as for the sonneteer, who has taken it into his head to be witty, and insists on being an author in the teeth of opinion, I simply cannot be bothered to listen to him, and his prose wearies me quite as much as his poetry. Be assured that I am not always so well-entertained as you suppose; that I long for your company, more than I dare to say, at all these entertainments to which   1720
people drag me; and that the presence of those one loves is the true and perfect seasoning to all one's pleasures."

CLITANDRE. And now for me.

"Clitandre, whom you mention, and who so pesters me with his saccharine speeches, is the last man on earth for whom I could feel any affection. He is quite mad to suppose that I love him, and so are you, to doubt that you are loved. Do come to your senses; exchange your suppositions for his; and visit me as often as possible, to help me bear the annoyance of his unwelcome attentions."   1730

It's a sweet character that these letters show,
And what to call it, Madam, you well know.
Enough. We're off to make the world acquainted
With this sublime self-portrait that you've painted.
ACASTE. Madam, I'll make you no farewell oration;
No, you're not worthy of my indignation.
Far choicer hearts than yours, as you'll discover,
Would like this little Marquess for a lover.

SCENE V

CELIMENE, ELIANTE, ARSINOE, ALCESTE, ORONTE, PHILINTE

ORONTE. So! After all those loving letters you wrote,
    You turn on me like this, and cut my throat!   1740
    And your dissembling, faithless heart, I find,
    Has pledged itself by turns to all mankind!
    How blind I've been! But now I clearly see;
    I thank you, Madam, for enlightening me.
    My heart is mine once more, and I'm content;
    The loss of it shall be your punishment.
    [*To* ALCESTE]
    Sir, she is yours; I'll seek no more to stand
    Between your wishes and this lady's hand.

SCENE VI

CELIMENE, ELIANTE, ARSINOE, ALCESTE, PHILINTE

ARSINOE [*to* CELIMENE]. I'm forced to speak. I'm far too stirred
    To keep my counsel, after what I've heard.   1750
    I'm shocked and staggered by your want of morals.
    It's not my way to mix in others' quarrels;
    But really, when this fine and noble spirit,
    This man of honor and surpassing merit,
    Laid down the offering of his heart before you,
    How *could* you . . . .
ALCESTE.   Madam, permit me, I implore you,
    To represent myself in this debate.
    Don't bother, please, to be my advocate.
    My heart, in any case, could not afford
    To give your services their due reward;   1760
    And if I chose, for consolation's sake,
    Some other lady, 'twould not be you I'd take.
ARSINOE. What makes you think you could, Sir? And how dare you
    Imply that I've been trying to ensnare you?
    If you can for a moment entertain
    Such flattering fancies, you're extremely vain.
    I'm not so interested as you suppose
    In Célimène's discarded gigolos.
    Get rid of that absurd illusion, do.
    Women like me are not for such as you.   1770

Stay with this creature, to whom you're so attached;
I've never seen two people better matched.

SCENE VII
CELIMENE, ELIANTE, ALCESTE, PHILINTE

ALCESTE [*to* CELIMENE]. Well, I've been still throughout this exposé, ·
    Till everyone but me has said his say.
    Come, have I shown sufficient self-restraint?
    And may I now . . . .
CELIMENE.   Yes, make your just complaint.
    Reproach me freely, call me what you will;
    You've every right to say I've used you ill.
    I've wronged you, I confess it; and in my shame
    I'll make no effort to escape the blame.   1780
    The anger of those others I could despise;
    My guilt toward you I sadly recognize.
    Your wrath is wholly justified, I fear;
    I know how culpable I must appear,
    I know all things bespeak my treachery,
    And that, in short, you've grounds for hating me.
    Do so; I give you leave.
ALCESTE.   Ah, traitress—how,
    How should I cease to love you, even now?
    Though mind and will were passionately bent
    On hating you, my heart would not consent.   1790
    [*To* ELIANTE *and* PHILINTE]
    Be witness to my madness, both of you;
    See what infatuation drives one to;
    But wait; my folly's only just begun,
    And I shall prove to you before I'm done
    How strange the human heart is, and how far
    From rational we sorry creatures are.
    [*To* CELIMENE]
    Woman, I'm willing to forget your shame,
    And clothe your treacheries in a sweeter name;
    I'll call them youthful errors, instead of crimes,
    And lay the blame on these corrupting times.   1800
    My one condition is that you agree
    To share my chosen fate, and fly with me
    To that wild, trackless, solitary place
    In which I shall forget the human race.

Only by such a course can you atone
For those atrocious letters; by that alone
Can you remove my present horror of you,
And make it possible for me to love you.
CELIMENE. What! *I* renounce the world at my young age,
And die of boredom in some hermitage?   1810
ALCESTE. Ah, if you really loved me as you ought,
You wouldn't give the world a moment's thought;
Must you have me, and all the world beside?
CELIMENE. Alas, at twenty one is terrified
Of solitude. I fear I lack the force
And depth of soul to take so stern a course.
But if my hand in marriage will content you,
Why, there's a plan which I might well consent to,
And . . . .
ALCESTE.   No, I detest you now. I could excuse
Everything else, but since you thus refuse   1820
To love me wholly, as a wife should do,
And see the world in me, as I in you,
Go! I reject your hand, and disenthrall
My heart from your enchantments, once for all.

SCENE VIII

ELIANTE, ALCESTE, PHILINTE

ALCESTE [*to* ELIANTE]. Madam, your virtuous beauty has no peer;
Of all this world, you only are sincere;
I've long esteemed you highly, as you know;
Permit me ever to esteem you so,
And if I do not now request your hand,
Forgive me, Madam, and try to understand.   1830
I feel unworthy of it; I sense that fate
Does not intend me for the married state,
That I should do you wrong by offering you
My shattered heart's unhappy residue,
And that in short . . . .
ELIANTE.   Your argument's well taken:
Nor need you fear that I shall feel forsaken.
Were I to offer him this hand of mine,
Your friend Philinte, I think, would not decline.
PHILINTE. Ah, Madam, that's my heart's most cherished goal,
For which I'd gladly give my life and soul.   1840

ALCESTE [*to* ELIANTE *and* PHILINTE]. May you be true to all you now
        profess,
  And so deserve unending happiness.
  Meanwhile, betrayed and wronged in everything,
  I'll flee this bitter world where vice is king,
  And seek some spot unpeopled and apart
  Where I'll be free to have an honest heart.
PHILINTE. Come, Madam, let's do everything we can
  To change the mind of this unhappy man.

John Milton

FROM *Paradise Lost*

NOTES BY ALEXANDER M. WITHERSPOON

John Milton (1608–1674)

AN ACCOMPLISHED STUDENT AND AUTHOR SINCE BOYHOOD, Milton made a mark with his superb intellectual gifts while attending Cambridge University, writing in Latin as well as in English. After Cambridge his father supported him during six years of leisure in the country while he prepared himself for a literary career. This aim was furthered by a one-year tour of the Continent, spent mainly in Italy. When he heard news of the impending civil turmoil at home, he broke short this sojourn, one of the most pleasant times in his life, and returned to England. Upon his return, he engaged in polemics concerning the religious questions of the day. In 1649, after King Charles I was beheaded by the victorious forces of Cromwell, Milton accepted a post in the new government. In 1652 he became totally blind. The death of Cromwell and the consequent failure of the Protectorate he had established to govern England led to the restoration of the monarchy in 1660. Milton was spared death as a traitor to the king and the world was allowed to have *Paradise Lost*, the great poem its author had been preparing to compose for most of his life. It was published first in 1667 and then in its final, expanded form in 1674, shortly before Milton's death.

Milton lived a life of amazing activity, despite the personal difficulty and sorrow of his three marriages, his blindness, and the turmoil of revolution. He left a body of other major works as well—pamphlets on education, divorce, and censorship, two great elegies for friends who died young, *Paradise Regained* (the sequel to his epic), and *Samson Agonistes*. Yet, though many of his other works are still read, it is *Paradise Lost* which continues to draw the audience Milton hoped for.

Paradise Lost

The Verse*

The measure is English heroic verse without rime, as that of Homer in Greek, and of Virgil in Latin—rime being no necessary adjunct or true ornament of poem or good verse, in longer works especially, but the invention of a barbarous age, to set off wretched matter and lame metre; graced indeed since by the use of some famous modern poets, carried away by custom, but much to their own vexation, hindrance, and constraint to express many things otherwise, and for the most part worse, than else they would have expressed them. Not without cause, therefore, some both Italian and Spanish poets of prime note have rejected rime both in longer and shorter works, as have also long since our best English tragedies, as a thing of itself, to all judicious ears, trivial and of no true musical delight; which consists only in apt numbers, fit quantity of syllables, and the sense variously drawn out from one verse into another, not in the jingling sound of like endings—a fault avoided by the learned ancients both in poetry and all good oratory. This neglect then of rime so little is to be taken for a defect, though it may seem so perhaps to vulgar readers, that it rather is to be esteemed an example set, the first in English, of ancient liberty recovered to heroic poem from the troublesome and modern bondage of riming.

BOOK I

The Argument**

This First Book proposes, first in brief, the whole subject: Man's disobedience, and the loss thereupon of Paradise, wherein he was placed: then

* Milton's forthright statement of why his verse is unrhymed was not in the first edition of 1667, but was added in 1668. It contains obvious hits at Dryden, who was the chief defender of rhyme. Milton's contention that his epic is the first important English poem of a nondramatic type written in blank verse is substantially true, as only a few scattered nondramatic pieces in unrhymed pentameter had appeared before Paradise Lost. ** The Argument, the subject matter of what follows.

touches the prime cause of his fall—the Serpent, or rather Satan in the
Serpent; who, revolting from God, and drawing to his side many legions of
Angels, was by the command of God driven out of Heaven with all his crew
into the great Deep. Which action passed over, the poem hastens into the
midst of things; presenting Satan with his Angels now fallen into Hell—described here, not in the Center (for Heaven and Earth may be supposed as
yet not made, certainly not yet accursed), but in a place of utter darkness,
fitliest called Chaos: here Satan with his Angels lying on the burning lake,
thunder-struck and astonished, after a certain space recovers, as from confusion; calls up him who, next in order and dignity, lay by him; they confer
of their miserable fall. Satan awakens all his legions, who lay till then in the
same manner confounded. They rise: their numbers, array of battle, their
chief leaders named, according to the idols known afterwards in Canaan and
the countries adjoining. To these Satan directs his speech; comforts them
with hope yet of regaining Heaven; but tells them lastly of a new world and
new kind of creature to be created, according to an ancient prophecy or
report in Heaven; for that Angels were long before this visible creation was
the opinion of many ancient Fathers. To find out the truth of this prophecy,
and what to determine thereon, he refers to a full council. What his asso-
ciates thence attempt. Pandemonium, the palace of Satan, rises, suddenly
built out of the Deep: the infernal peers there sit in council.

      Of man's first disobedience, and the fruit
      Of that forbidden tree, whose mortal° taste
      Brought death into the world, and all our woe,
      With loss of Eden, till one greater Man
      Restore us, and regain the blissful seat,°
      Sing, Heavenly Muse,° that, on the secret° top
      Of Oreb or of Sinai,° didst inspire
      That shepherd,° who first taught the chosen seed
      In the beginning how the Heavens and Earth
      Rose out of Chaos;° or, if Sion° hill   10
      Delight thee more, and Siloa's brook that flowed

2. *mortal:* deadly. 5. *seat:* abode. 6. *Sing, Heavenly Muse:* The invocation,
or address to the Muse of poetry, is an epic convention, which Milton borrows
from Virgil and the classic authors. Milton identifies the Muse of the classical
epics with the Holy Spirit of the Bible and Christian theology; *secret:* remote,
and therefore mysterious. 7. *Oreb . . . Sinai: Oreb* (Horeb) and *Sinai* are
mountains or mountain ranges on which Moses received communications from
God. 8. *That shepherd:* Moses (see Exodus 3 and 19–31). 9–10. *In . . .
Chaos:* (See Genesis 1.) The first five books of the Bible were supposed to
have been written by Moses; *Sion:* one of the hills on which Jerusalem was
built, and thus the abode of David, the "sweet singer of Israel."

Fast by° the oracle° of God, I thence
Invoke thy aid to my adventurous song,
That with no middle flight intends to soar
Above the Aonian mount,° while it pursues
Things unattempted yet in prose or rhyme.°
And chiefly thou, O Spirit,° that dost prefer
Before all temples the upright heart and pure,
Instruct me, for thou know'st; thou from the first
Wast present, and, with mighty wings outspread,   20
Dove-like sat'st brooding° on the vast Abyss,
And mad'st it pregnant: what in me is dark,
Illumine; what is low, raise and support;
That to the highth° of this great argument°
I may assert° Eternal Providence,
And justify the ways of God to men.
    Say first—for Heaven hides nothing from Thy view,
Nor the deep tract of Hell—say first what cause
Moved our grand° parents, in that happy state,
Favoured of Heaven so highly, to fall off   30
From their Creator, and transgress his will
For° one restraint, lords of the world besides.°
Who first seduced them to that foul revolt?
    The infernal Serpent;° he it was, whose guile,
Stirred up with envy and revenge, deceived
The Mother of Mankind, what time° his pride
Had cast him out from Heaven, with all his host
Of rebel Angels, by whose aid, aspiring
To set himself in glory above his peers,°
He trusted to have equalled the Most High,   40
If he opposed; and with ambitious aim

12. *Fast by:* Close by; *oracle:* Solomon's temple.   15. *Aonian mount:* Helicon,
the mountain of the classic Muses. Milton is contrasting his great theme with
the more earthly subjects of the classic poets.   16. *rhyme:* Milton seems to distinguish between *rhyme* as meaning "verse" and *rime,* . . . "the jingling sound
of like endings."   17. *thou, O Spirit:* the Holy Spirit of the New Testament.
21. *Dove-like sat'st brooding:* happy combination of the New Testament conception of the Holy Spirit "descending like a dove" (Matt. 3:16) and the
statement in Gen. 1:2, "the Spirit of God moved upon the face of the waters."
24. *highth:* older form of the word. *argument:* subject.   25. *assert:* vindicate,
defend.   29. *grand:* first, original.   32. *For:* because of; *besides:* in all other respects.   34. *The infernal Serpent:* Milton is here anticipating the final condition
and appearance of Satin, a very different appearance from that of the great archangel of Books I and II.   36. *what time:* at the time when.   39. *his peers:* his
equals, the other archangels.

Against the throne and monarchy of God
Raised impious war in Heaven, and battle proud,
With vain attempt. Him the Almighty Power
Hurled headlong flaming from the ethereal sky,
With hideous ruin and combustion, down
To bottomless perdition; there to dwell
In adamantine chains and penal fire,
Who durst defy the Omnipotent to arms.
    Nine times the space that measures day and night   50
To mortal men, he with his horrid crew
Lay vanquished, rolling in the fiery gulf,
Confounded, though immortal.° But his doom°
Reserved him to more wrath; for now the thought
Both of lost happiness and lasting pain
Torments him; round he throws his baleful° eyes,
That witnessed huge affliction and dismay,
Mixed with obdúrate pride and stedfast hate.
At once, as far as Angels ken,° he views
The dismal situation waste and wild: 60
A dungeon horrible on all sides round
As one great furnace flamed; yet from those flames
No light; but rather darkness visible
Served only to discover sights of woe,
Regions of sorrow, doleful shades, where peace
And rest can never dwell, hope never comes
That comes to all; but torture without end
Still urges,° and a fiery deluge, fed
With ever-burning sulphur unconsumed.
Such place Eternal Justice had prepared   70
For those rebellious; here their prison ordained
In utter° darkness, and their portion set,
As far removed from God and light of Heaven,
As from the center thrice to the utmost pole.°
Oh, how unlike the place from whence they fell! . . .

50–53. *Nine . . . immortal:* Milton in Book VI, l. 871, represents the angels as having fallen for nine days, after which for nine days they lay vanquished; *doom:* judgment. 56. *baleful:* woeful, full of pain. 59. *as . . . ken:* as far as the knowledge and perceptive faculties of angels extend. 68. *urges:* afflicts, presses on. 72. *utter:* outer. Milton represents Hell as being at the farthest remove from Heaven. 74. *from . . . pole:* Milton seems to imply that the distance from Heaven (or the Empyrean) to the gate of Hell is three times the radius of the starry universe. The vast and indeterminate region called Chaos is represented as extending round below the universe. Hell, the region "prepared for the devil and his angels," is at the bottom of Chaos.

BOOK II

The Argument

The consultation begun, Satan debates whether another battle be to be hazarded for the recovery of Heaven: some advise it, others dissuade. A third proposal is preferred, mentioned before by Satan, to search the truth of that prophecy or tradition in Heaven concerning another world, and another kind of creature, equal or not much inferior to themselves, about this time to be created. Their doubt who shall be sent on this difficult search; Satan, their chief, undertakes alone the voyage; is honoured and applauded. The council thus ended, the rest betake them several ways and to several employments, as their inclinations lead them, to entertain the time till Satan return. He passes on his journey to Hell Gates, finds them shut, and who sat there to guard them; by whom at length they are opened, and discover to him the great gulf between Hell and Heaven; with what difficulty he passes through, directed by Chaos, the Power of that place, to the sight of this new World which he sought.

  High on a throne of royal state, which far
Outshone the wealth of Ormus° and of Ind,°
Or where the gorgeous East, with richest hand,
Showers on her kings barbaric° pearl and gold,
Satan exalted sat, by merit raised
To that bad eminence; and, from despair
Thus high uplifted beyond hope, aspires
Beyond thus high, insatiate to pursue
Vain war with Heaven, and, by success° untaught,
His proud imaginations thus displayed: 10
  "Powers and Dominions,° Deities of Heaven!
For, since no deep within her gulf can hold
Immortal vigour, though oppressed and fallen,
I give not Heaven for lost.° From this descent
Celestial Virtues° rising will appear
More glorious and more dread° than from no fall,
And trust themselves to fear no second fate.

2. *Ormus:* town on an island in the Persian Gulf, famous for its diamond trade; *Ind:* India. 4. *barbaric:* barbarously magnificent. 9. *success:* issue, result, experience. 11. *Powers and Dominions:* two of the angelic orders. Milton uses the titles in the general sense of "powers of Heaven." 14. *give . . . lost:* consider as lost. 15. *Virtues:* one of the orders of angels; used here in a general sense. 16. *dread:* to be dreaded.

Me, though just right, and the fixed laws of Heaven,
Did first create your leader, next, free choice,
With what besides, in council or in fight,   20
Hath been achieved of merit, yet this loss,
Thus far at least recovered, hath much more
Established in a safe unenvied throne,
Yielded with full consent. The happier state
In Heaven, which follows dignity, might draw
Envy from each inferior; but who here
Will envy whom the highest place exposes
Foremost to stand against the Thunderer's aim
Your bulwark, and condemns to greatest share
Of endless pain? Where there is then no good   30
For which to strive, no strife can grow up there
From faction; for none sure will claim in Hell
Precedence, none whose portion is so small
Of present pain, that with ambitious mind
Will covet more. With this advantage then
To union, and firm faith, and firm accord,
More than can be in Heaven, we now return
To claim our just inheritance of old,
Surer to prosper than prosperity
Could have assured us; and by what best way,   40
Whether of open war or covert guile,
We now debate; who can advise may speak."
    He ceased; and next him Moloch,° sceptred king,
Stood up, the strongest and the fiercest spirit
That fought in Heaven, now fiercer by despair.
His trust was with the Eternal to be deemed
Equal in strength, and rather than be less
Cared not to be at all; with that care lost
Went all his fear: of God, or Hell, or worse,
He recked° not, and these words thereafter spake: 50
    "My sentence° is for open war. Of wiles,
More unexpert,° I boast not: them let those
Contrive who need, or when they need; not now.
For while they sit contriving, shall the rest—
Millions that stand in arms, and longing wait

43. *Moloch:* sun god worshipped in the form of a bull (see Psalm 106:36–38;
Jer. 7:31; and Ezek. 16:21)—Ed. 50. *recked:* cared. 51. *sentence* vote,
opinion. 52. *More unexpert:* less experienced in wiles; without skill in speech
and theoretical strategy.

The signal to ascend—sit lingering here,
Heaven's fugitives, and for their dwelling-place
Accept this dark opprobrious den of shame,
The prison of his tyranny who reigns
By our delay? No! let us rather choose,   60
Armed with Hell flames and fury, all at once
O'er Heaven's high towers to force resistless way,
Turning our tortures into horrid arms
Against the Torturer; when to meet the noise
Of his almighty engine° he shall hear
Infernal thunder, and for lightning see
Black fire and horror shot with equal rage
Among his Angels, and his throne itself
Mixed° with Tartarean sulphur and strange fire,
His own invented torments. But perhaps   70
The way seems difficult and steep to scale
With upright wing against a higher foe.
Let such bethink them, if the sleepy drench°
Of that forgetful lake benumb not still,
That in our proper motion° we ascend
Up to our native seat; descent and fall
To us is adverse.° Who but felt of late,
When the fierce foe hung on our broken rear
Insulting, and pursued us through the deep,
With what compulsion and laborious flight   80
We sunk thus low? The ascent is easy then.
The event° is feared: should we again provoke
Our stronger, some worse way his wrath may find
To our destruction—if there be in Hell
Fear to be worse destroyed! What can be worse
Than to dwell here, driven out from bliss, condemned
In this abhorrèd deep to utter woe;
Where pain of unextinguishable fire
Must exercise° us, without hope of end,
The vassals of his anger, when the scourge   90
Inexorably, and the torturing hour,
Calls us to penance? More destroyed than thus,
We should be quite abolished, and expire.
What° fear we then? what doubt we to incense

65. *engine:* thunderbolt.   69. *Mixed:* convulsed.   73. *sleepy drench:* sleep-pro-
ducing draught.   75. *proper motion:* motion "proper" or natural to us.   77.
adverse: unnatural.   82. *event:* outcome.   89. *exercise:* torment.   94. *What:*
why.

His utmost ire? which, to the highth enraged,
Will either quite consume us, and reduce
To nothing this essential°—happier far
Than miserable to have eternal being!
Or if our substance be indeed divine,
And cannot cease to be, we are at worst   100
On this side nothing;° and by proof we feel
Our power sufficient to disturb his Heaven,
And with perpetual inroads to alarm,
Though inaccessible, his fatal° throne;
Which, if not victory, is yet revenge."
   He ended frowning, and his look denounced°
Desperate revenge, and battle dangerous
To less than gods. On the other side up rose
Belial,° in act more graceful and humane;°
A fairer person lost not heaven; he seemed   110
For dignity composed and high exploit.
But all was false and hollow; though his tongue
Dropt manna,° and could make the worse appear
The better reason, to perplex and dash°
Maturest counsels: for his thoughts were low,
To vice industrious, but to nobler deeds
Timorous and slothful. Yet, he pleased the ear,
And with persuasive accent thus began:
   "I should be much for open war, O Peers!
As not behind in hate, if what was urged   120
Main reason to persuade immediate war
Did not dissuade me most, and seem to cast
Ominous conjecture on the whole success;
When he who most excels in fact° of arms,
In what he counsels and in what excels
Mistrustful, grounds his courage on despair
And utter dissolution, as the scope
Of all his aim, after some dire revenge.
First, what revenge? The towers of Heaven are filled
With armèd watch, that render all access   130
Impregnable; oft on the bordering Deep

97. *essential:* existence, essence.   *100–01. at . . . nothing:* at the worst possible
point short of annihilation.   *104. fatal:* ordained by fate.   *106. denounced:*
proclaimed, threatened.   *109. Belial:* not, strictly speaking, a god, but in the
original Hebrew an abstract term signifying worthlessness, baseness—Ed.; *humane:*
urbane, polished.   *113. manna:* honey.   *114. dash:* frustrate.   *124. fact:* feat.

Encamp their legions, or with òbscure° wing
Scout far and wide into the realm of Night,
Scorning surprise. Or could we break our way
By force, and at our heels all Hell should rise
With blackest insurrection, to confound
Heaven's purest light, yet our great Enemy,
All incorruptible, would on his throne
Sit unpolluted, and the ethereal mould,°
Incapable of stain, would soon expel   140
Her mischief, and purge off the baser fire,
Victorious. Thus repulsed, our final hope
Is flat despair: we must exasperate
The Almighty Victor to spend all his rage;
And that must end us, that must be our cure—
To be no more. Sad cure! for who would lose,
Though full of pain, this intellectual being,
Those thoughts that wander through eternity,
To perish rather, swallowed up and lost
In the wide womb of uncreated Night,   150
Devoid of sense and motion? And who knows,
Let this be° good, whether our angry Foe
Can give it, or will ever? How he can
Is doubtful; that he never will is sure.
Will he, so wise, let loose at once his ire,
Belike° through impotence,° or unaware,°
To give his enemies their wish, and end
Them in his anger, whom his anger saves
To punish endless? 'Wherefore cease we, then?'
Say they who counsel war; 'we are decreed,   160
Reserved, and destined to eternal woe;
Whatever doing, what can we suffer more,
What can we suffer worse?' Is this then worst,
Thus sitting, thus consulting, thus in arms?
What when we fled amain,° pursued and strook°
With Heaven's afflicting thunder, and besought
The Deep to shelter us? This Hell then seemed
A refuge from those wounds. Or when we lay
Chained on the burning lake? That sure was worse.

132. *òbscure:* invisible.   139. *mould:* substance.   152. *Let this be:* grant this
to be.   156. *Belike:* used ironically, in the sense of "Doubtless!" *impotence:*
inability to restrain himself; *unaware:* in ignorance of his enemies' desires.
165. *amain:* with all speed; *strook:* struck.

What if the breath that kindled those grim fires,   170
Awaked, should blow them into sevenfold rage,
And plunge us in the flames? or, from above,
Should intermitted° vengeance arm again
His red right hand to plague us? What if all
Her stores° were opened, and this firmament
Of Hell should spout her cataracts of fire,
Impendent° horrors, threatening hideous fall
One day upon our heads? while we, perhaps,
Designing or exhorting glorious war,
Caught in a fiery tempest, shall be hurled,   180
Each on his rock transfixed, the sport and prey
Of racking° whirlwinds, or for ever sunk
Under yon boiling ocean, wrapt in chains,
There to converse° with everlasting groans,
Unrespited, unpitied, unreprieved,
Ages of hopeless end! This would be worse.
War therefore, open or concealed, alike
My voice dissuades; for what can force° or guile
With him, or who deceive his mind, whose eye
Views all things at one view? He from Heaven's highth   190
All these our motions° vain sees and derides;
Not more almighty to resist our might
Than wise to frustrate all our plots and wiles.
Shall we then live thus vile, the race of Heaven
Thus trampled, thus expelled, to suffer here
Chains and these torments? Better these than worse,
By my advice; since fate inevitable
Subdues us, and omnipotent decree,
The Victor's will. To suffer,° as to do,
Our strength is equal, nor the law unjust   200
That so ordains. This was at first resolved,
If we were wise, against so great a foe
Contending, and so doubtful what might fall.°
I laugh, when those who at the spear are bold
And venturous, if that fail them, shrink, and fear
What yet they know must follow—to endure
Exile, or ignominy, or bonds, or pain,
The sentence of their conqueror. This is now

---

173. *intermitted:* temporarily suspended.   175. *Her stores:* those of Hell.
177. *Impendent:* overhanging.   182. *racking:* torturing.   184. *converse:* dwell
with.   188. *what can force:* what can force achieve?   191. *motions:* schemes.
199. *suffer:* endure.   203. *fall:* befall, happen.

Our doom; which if we can sustain and bear,
Our Sùpreme Foe in time may much remit   210
His anger, and perhaps, thus far removed,
Not mind us not offending, satisfied
With what is punished; whence these raging fires
Will slacken, if his breath stir not their flames.
Our purer essence then will overcome
Their noxious vapour, or, inured,° not feel;
Or, changed at length, and to the place conformed
In temper and in nature, will receive
Familiar° the fierce heat; and, void of pain,
This horror will grow mild, this darkness light;   220
Besides what hope the never-ending flight
Of future days may bring, what chance, what change
Worth waiting,°—since our present lot appears
For happy though but ill, for ill not worst,
If we procure not to ourselves more woe."
   Thus Belial, with words clothed in reason's garb,
Counselled ignoble ease, and peaceful sloth,
Not peace; and after him thus Mammon° spake:
   "Either to disenthrone the King of Heaven
We war, if war be best, or to regain   230
Our own right lost. Him to unthrone we then
May hope, when everlasting Fate shall yield
To fickle Chance, and Chaos judge the strife.
The former, vain to hope, argues° as vain
The latter; for what place can be for us
Within Heaven's bound, unless Heaven's Lord Supreme
We overpower? Suppose he should relent,
And publish grace to all, on promise made
Of new subjection; with what eyes could we
Stand in his presence humble, and receive   240
Strict laws imposed, to celebrate his throne
With warbled hymns, and to his Godhead sing
Forced halleluiahs; while he lordly sits
Our envied sovran, and his altar breathes
Ambrosial odours and ambrosial flowers,
Our servile offerings? This must be our task
In Heaven, this our delight. How wearisome

---

216. *inured:* accustomed to it.   219. *Familiar:* as familiar, and thus not uncomfortable.   223. *waiting,* waiting for.   228. *Mammon:* Like Belial, Mammon
is taken by Milton as a god, although the name is not that of a god, but a
Chaldaic abstract term for "riches." See Matthew 6:24—Ed.   234. *argues:* shows.

Eternity so spent, in worship paid
To whom we hate! Let us not then pursue°
By force impossible, by leave obtained   250
Unàcceptable, though in Heaven, our state
Of splendid vassalage; but rather seek
Our own good from ourselves, and from our own
Live to ourselves, though in this vast recess,
Free and to none accountable, preferring
Hard liberty before the easy yoke
Of servile pomp. Our greatness will appear
Then most conspicuous, when great things of small,
Useful of hurtful, prosperous of adverse,
We can create; and in what place soe'er   260
Thrive under evil, and work ease out of pain
Through labour and endurance. This deep world
Of darkness do we dread? How oft amidst
Thick clouds and dark doth Heaven's all-ruling Sire
Choose to reside, his glory unobscured,
And with the majesty of darkness round
Covers his throne, from whence deep thunders roar
Mustering their rage, and Heaven resembles Hell?
As he our darkness, cannot we his light
Imitate when we please? This desert soil   270
Wants° not her hidden lustre, gems and gold;
Nor want we skill or art, from whence to raise
Magnificence; and what can Heaven show more?
Our torments also may in length of time
Become our elements,° these piercing fires
As soft as now severe, our temper changed
Into their temper; which must needs remove
The sensible° of pain. All things invite
To peaceful counsels, and the settled state
Of order, how in safety best we may   280
Compose our present evils, with regard
Of what we are and where, dismissing quite
All thoughts of war. Ye have what I advise."
    He scarce had finished, when such murmur filled
The assembly, as when hollow rocks retain
The sound of blustering winds, which all night long
Had roused the sea, now with hoarse cadence lull

249. *pursue:* strive to regain. 271. *Wants:* lacks. 275. *elements:* congenial
surroundings. 278. *sensible:* sensibility.

Seafaring men o'erwatched,° whose bark by chance,
Or pinnace, anchors in a craggy bay
After the tempest: such applause was heard   290
As Mammon ended, and his sentence° pleased,
Advising peace; for such another field
They dreaded worse than Hell; so much the fear
Of thunder and the sword of Michaël°
Wrought still within them; and no less desire
To found this nether° empire, which might rise
By policy, and long process of time,
In emulation opposite to Heaven.
Which when Beëlzebub° perceived, than whom,
Satan except, none higher sat, with grave   300
Aspèct he rose, and in his rising seemed
A pillar of state; deep on his front° engraven
Deliberation sat and public care;
And princely counsel in his face yet shone,
Majestic, though in ruin. Sage he stood,
With Atlantean° shoulders fit to bear
The weight of mightiest monarchies; his look
Drew audience and attention still as night
Or summer's noon-tide air, while thus he spake:
    "Thrones and Imperial Powers, offspring of Heaven,   310
Ethereal Virtues! or these titles now
Must we renounce, and, changing style,° be called
Princes of Hell? for so the popular vote
Inclines, here to continue, and build up here
A growing empire; doubtless, while we dream,
And know not that the King of Heaven hath doomed
This place our dungeon, not our safe retreat
Beyond his potent arm, to live exempt
From Heaven's high jurisdiction, in new league
Banded against his throne, but to remain   320
In strictest bondage, though thus far removed
Under the inevitable curb, reserved
His captive multitude. For he, be sure,
In highth or depth, still first and last will reign
Sole King, and of his kingdom lose no part

288. *o'erwatched:* weary with watching. 291. *sentence:* opinion, advice. 294.
Michaël: leader of the heavenly army. "Michael" means "the sword of God."
296. *nether:* lower. 299. *Beëlzebub:* Syrian god whose epithet is "lord of the
flies." 302. *front:* countenance. 306. *Atlantean:* Atlas, one of the Titans, was
condemned to bear heaven upon his shoulders. 312. *style:* title.

By our revolt, but over Hell extend
His empire, and with iron sceptre rule
Us here, as with his golden those in Heaven.
What° sit we then projecting peace and war?
War hath determined° us, and foiled with loss   330
Irreparable; terms of peace yet none
Vouchsafed or sought; for what peace will be given
To us enslaved, but custody severe,
And stripes, and arbitrary punishment
Inflicted? and what peace can we return,
But, to° our power, hostility and hate,
Untamed reluctance,° and revenge, though slow,
Yet ever plotting how the Conqueror least
May reap his conquest, and may least rejoice
In doing what we most in suffering feel?   340
Nor will occasion want,° nor shall we need
With dangerous expedition to invade
Heaven, whose high walls fear no assault or siege,
Or ambush from the Deep. What if we find
Some easier enterprise? There is a place
(If ancient and prophetic fame° in Heaven
Err not), another World, the happy seat
Of some new race called Man, about this time
To be created like to us, though less
In power and excellence, but favoured more   350
Of him who rules above; so was his will
Pronounced among the gods, and by an oath,
That shook Heaven's whole circumference, confirmed.
Thither let us bend all our thoughts, to learn
What creatures there inhabit, of what mould
Or substance, how endued, and what their power,
And where their weakness, how attempted° best,
By force or subtlety. Though Heaven be shut,
And Heaven's high Arbitrator sit secure
In his own strength, this place may lie exposed,   360
The utmost border of his kingdom, left
To their defence who hold it. Here perhaps
Some advantageous act may be achieved
By sudden onset: either with Hell fire

329. *What:* why.   330. *determined:* put an end to.   336. *to:* according to.
337. *reluctance:* resistance.   341. *want:* be lacking.   346. *fame:* report, rumor.
357. *attempted:* attacked.

To waste° his whole creation, or possess
All as our own, and drive, as we were driven,
The puny° habitants; or, if not drive,
Seduce them to our party, that their God
May prove their foe, and with repenting hand
Abolish his own works. This would surpass   370
Common revenge, and interrupt his joy
In our confusion, and our joy upraise
In his disturbance; when his darling sons,
Hurled headlong to partake with us, shall curse
Their frail original,° and faded bliss,
Faded so soon. Advise,° if this be worth
Attempting, or to sit in darkness here
Hatching vain empires." Thus Beëlzebub
Pleaded his devilish counsel, first devised
By Satan, and in part proposed; for whence,   380
But from the author of all ill, could spring
So deep a malice, to confound° the race
Of mankind in one root, and Earth with Hell
To mingle and involve, done all to spite
The great Creator? But their spite still serves
His glory to augment. The bold design
Pleased highly those infernal States, and joy
Sparkled in all their eyes: with full assent
They vote; whereat his speech he thus renews:
  "Well have ye judged, well ended long debate,   390
Synod of gods! and, like to what ye are,
Great things resolved; which from the lowest deep
Will once more lift us up, in spite of fate,
Nearer our ancient seat—perhaps in view
Of those bright confines, whence, with neighbouring arms
And opportune excursion, we may chance
Re-enter Heaven; or else in some mild zone
Dwell not unvisited of Heaven's fair light,
Secure, and at the brightening orient beam
Purge off this gloom; the soft delicious air,   400
To heal the scar of these corrosive fires,
Shall breathe her balm. But first, whom shall we send
In search of this new World? whom shall we find

365. *waste:* lay waste. 367. *puny:* younger, and therefore weaker. 375.
original: him who was their origin, Adam. 376. *Advise:* consider. 382. *confound:* ruin utterly.

Sufficient? who shall tempt° with wandering feet
The dark, unbottomed, infinite Abyss,
And through the palpable obscure° find out
His uncouth° way, or spread his aery flight,
Upborne with indefatigable wings
Over the vast abrupt,° ere he arrive°
The happy isle?° What strength, what art, can then   410
Suffice, or what evasion bear him safe
Through the strict senteries° and stations thick
Of Angels watching round? Here he had need
All circumspection: and we now° no less
Choice in our suffrage;° for on whom we send,
The weight of all, and our last hope, relies."
    This said, he sat; and expectation held
His look suspense,° awaiting who appeared
To second, or oppose, or undertake
The perilous attempt; but all sat mute,   420
Pondering the danger with deep thoughts; and each
In other's countenance read his own dismay,
Astonished. None among the choice and prime
Of those Heaven-warring champions could be found
So hardy as to proffer or accept,
Alone, the dreadful voyage; till at last
Satan,·whom now transcendent glory raised
Above his fellows, with monarchal pride
Conscious of highest worth, unmoved thus spake:
    "O Progeny of Heaven! Empyreal Thrones!   430
With reason hath deep silence and demur°
Seized us, though undismayed. Long is the way
And hard, that out of Hell leads up to light;
Our prison strong, this huge convex of fire,
Outrageous to devour, immures us round
Ninefold; and gates of burning adamant,
Barred over us, prohibit all egress.
These passed, if any pass, the void profound
Of unessential° Night receives him next,

404. *tempt:* attempt, essay.   406. *palpable obscure:* "darkness which may be felt," as in the Egyptian plague (see Exod. 10:21).   407. *uncouth:* unknown. 409. *abrupt:* abyss of Chaos; *arrive,* arrive at.   410. *The happy isle?* The reference is, of course, not to the earth but to the universe, of the structure of which the fallen angels have as yet no knowledge.   412. *senteries:* old spelling of *sentries.*   414. *we now:* we now need.   415. *Choice . . . suffrage:* care in our voting.   418. *suspense:* fixed in suspense.   431. *demur:* delay.   439. *unessential:* without substance.

Wide-gaping, and with utter loss of being   440
Threatens him, plunged in that abortive gulf.
If thence he scape into whatever world,
Or unknown region, what remains° him less
Than unknown dangers and as hard escape?
But I should ill become this throne, O Peers,
And this imperial sovranty, adorned
With splendour, armed with power, if aught proposed
And judged of public moment, in the shape
Of difficulty or danger, could deter
Me from attempting. Wherefore do I assume   450
These royalties, and not refuse to reign,
Refusing to accept as great a share
Of hazard as of honour, due alike
To him who reigns, and so much to him due
Of hazard more, as he above the rest
High honoured sits? Go, therefore, mighty Powers,
Terror of Heaven, though fallen! intend° at home,
While here shall be our home, what best may ease
The present misery, and render Hell
More tolerable; if there be cure or charm   460
To respite, or deceive,° or slack the pain
Of this ill mansion. Intermit no watch
Against a wakeful foe, while I abroad
Through all the coasts of dark destruction seek
Deliverance for us all. This enterprise
None shall partake with me." Thus saying, rose
The Monarch, and prevented° all reply;
Prudent,° lest, from his resolution raised,°
Others among the chief might offer now
(Certain to be refused) what erst° they feared;   470
And, so refused, might in opinion° stand
His rivals, winning cheap the high repute,
Which he, through hazard huge, must earn. But they
Dreaded not more the adventure than his voice
Forbidding; and at once with him they rose.
Their rising all at once was as the sound
Of thunder heard remote. Towards him they bend
With awful° reverence prone; and as a god

443. *remains:* awaits.   457. *intend:* consider.   461. *deceive:* beguile.   467. *pre-vented:* forestalled.   468. *Prudent:* watchful; *from . . . raised:* encouraged by his fortitude.   470. *erst:* at first.   471. *opinion:* public opinion.   478. *awful:* full of awe.

Extol him equal to the Highest in Heaven:
Nor failed they to express how much they praised   480
That for the general safety he despised
His own; for neither do the spirits damned
Lose all their virtue; lest bad men should boast
Their specious° deeds on Earth, which glory° excites,
Or close° ambition varnished o'er with zeal.
   Thus they their doubtful consultations dark
Ended, rejoicing in their matchless Chief;
As when from the mountain-tops the dusky clouds
Ascending, while the North wind sleeps, o'erspread
Heaven's cheerful face, the louring element°   490
Scowls o'er the darkened landskip° snow or shower;
If chance the radiant sun with farewell sweet
Extend his evening beam, the fields revive,
The birds their notes renew, and bleating herds
Attest their joy, that hill and valley rings.
O shame to men! Devil with devil damned
Firm concord holds; men only disagree
Of creatures rational, though under hope
Of heavenly grace; and, God proclaiming peace,
Yet live in hatred, enmity, and strife   500
Among themselves, and levy cruel wars,
Wasting the Earth, each other to destroy:
As if (which might induce us to accord)
Man had not hellish foes enow° besides,
That day and night for his destruction wait!
   The Stygian° council thus dissolved; and forth
In order came the grand Infernal Peers;
Midst came their mighty Paramount,° and seemed
Alone the antagonist° of Heaven, nor less
Than Hell's dread Emperor, with pomp supreme,   510
And god-like imitated state; him round
A globe of fiery Seraphim° enclosed
With bright emblazonry, and horrent° arms.
Then of their session ended they bid cry
With trumpet's regal sound the great result:

---

484. specious: seemingly virtuous; *glory:* love of glory. *485. close:* secret.
490. element: sky. *491. landskip:* landscape—Ed. *504. enow:* enough. *506.*
Stygian: infernal—Ed. *508. Paramount:* supreme lord. *508–09. seemed . . .*
antagonist: seemed in himself alone to be a sufficient antagonist. *512. globe . . .*
Seraphim: solid military formation of angels—Ed. *513. horrent:* bristling.

Toward the four winds four speedy Cherubim°
Put to their mouths the sounding alchymy,°
By harald's voice explained; the hollow Abyss
Heard far and wide, and all the host of Hell
With deafening shout returned them loud acclaim. . . .   520

BOOK III

The Argument

God, sitting on his throne, sees Satan flying towards this World, then
newly created; shows him to the Son, who sat at his right hand; foretells the
success of Satan in perverting mankind; clears his own justice and wisdom
from all imputation, having created Man free, and able enough to have
withstood his Tempter; yet declares his purpose of grace towards him, in
regard he fell not of his own malice, as did Satan, but by him seduced.
The Son of God renders praises to his Father for the manifestation of his
gracious purpose towards Man: but God again declares that Grace cannot be
extended towards Man without the satisfaction of Divine Justice; Man hath
offended the majesty of God by aspiring to Godhead, and therefore, with
all his progeny, devoted to death, must die, unless some one can be found
sufficient to answer for his offence, and undergo his punishment. The Son
of God freely offers himself a ransom for man: the Father accepts him,
ordains his incarnation, pronounces his exaltation above all Names in
Heaven and Earth; commands all the Angels to adore him. They obey,
and, hymning to their harps in full choir, celebrate the Father and the Son.
Meanwhile Satan alights upon the bare convex of this World's outermost
orb; where wandering he first finds a place since called the Limbo of Vanity;
what persons and things fly up thither: thence comes to the gate of Heaven,
described ascending by stairs, and the waters above the firmament that flow
about it. His passage thence to the orb of the Sun: he finds there Uriel, the
regent of that orb, but first changes himself into the shape of a meaner Angel,
and, pretending a zealous desire to behold the new Creation, and Man whom
God had placed here, inquires of him the place of his habitation, and is
directed: alights first on Mount Niphates.

516. Cherubim: angels—Ed.   517. sounding alchymy: brass trumpets.

BOOK IV

The Argument

Satan, now in prospect of Eden, and nigh the place where he must now attempt the bold enterprise which he undertook alone against God and Man, falls into many doubts with himself, and many passions—fear, envy, and despair; but at length confirms himself in evil; journeys on to Paradise, whose outward prospect and situation is described; overleaps the bounds; sits, in the shape of a cormorant, on the Tree of Life, as highest in the Garden, to look about him. The Garden described; Satan's first sight of Adam and Eve; his wonder at their excellent form and happy state, but with resolution to work their fall; overhears their discourse: thence gathers that the Tree of Knowledge was forbidden them to eat of under penalty of death, and thereon intends to found his temptation by seducing them to transgress; then leaves them a while, to know further of their state by some other means. Meanwhile Uriel, descending on a sun-beam, warns Gabriel, who had in charge the gate of Paradise, that some evil spirit had escaped the Deep, and passed at noon by his sphere, in the shape of a good Angel, down to Paradise, discovered after by his furious gestures in the mount. Gabriel promises to find him ere morning. Night coming on, Adam and Eve discourse of going to their rest: their bower described; their evening worship. Gabriel, drawing forth his band of night-watch to walk the round of Paradise, appoints two strong Angels to Adam's bower, lest the evil Spirit should be there doing some harm to Adam or Eve sleeping: there they find him at the ear of Eve, tempting her in a dream, and bring him, though unwilling, to Gabriel; by whom questioned, he scornfully answers; prepares resistance; but, hindered by a sign from Heaven, flies out of Paradise.

BOOK V

The Argument

Morning approached, Eve relates to Adam her troublesome dream; he likes it not, yet comforts her: they come forth to their day labours: their morning hymn at the door of their bower. God, to render Man inexcusable, sends Raphael to admonish him of his obedience, of his free estate, of his enemy near at hand, who he is, and why his enemy, and whatever else may avail Adam to know. Raphael comes down to Paradise; his appearance described; his coming discerned by Adam afar off, sitting at the door of his bower; he goes out to meet him, brings him to his lodge, entertains him with the choicest fruits of Paradise, got together by Eve; their discourse at table. Raphael performs his message, minds Adam of his state and of his enemy; relates, at Adam's request, who that enemy is, and how he come to be so, beginning from his first revolt in Heaven, and the occasion thereof; how he drew his legions after him to the parts of the North, and there incited them to rebel with him, persuading all but Abdiel, a Seraph, who in argument dissuades and opposes him, then forsakes him.

BOOK VI

The Argument

Raphael continues to relate how Michael and Gabriel were sent forth to battle against Satan and his Angels. The first fight described: Satan and his Powers retire under night. He calls a council; invents devilish engines, which, in the second day's fight, put Michael and his Angels to some disorder; but they at length, pulling up mountains, overwhelmed both the force and machines of Satan. Yet, the tumult not so ending, God, on the third day, sends Messiah his Son, for whom he had reserved the glory of that victory. He, in the power of his Father, coming to the place, and causing all his legions to stand still on either side, with his chariot and thunder driving into the midst of his enemies, pursues them, unable to resist, towards the wall of Heaven; which opening, they leap down with horror and confusion into the place of punishment prepared for them in the Deep. Messiah returns with triumph to his Father.

BOOK VII

The Argument

Raphael, at the request of Adam, relates how and wherefore this World was first created: that God, after the expelling of Satan and his Angels out of Heaven, declared his pleasure to create another World, and other creatures to dwell therein; sends his Son with glory, and attendance of Angels, to perform the work of Creation in six days: the Angels celebrate with hymns the performance thereof, and his reascension into Heaven.

BOOK VIII

The Argument

Adam inquires concerning celestial motions; is doubtfully answered, and exhorted to search rather things more worthy of knowledge. Adam assents, and, still desirous to detain Raphael, relates to him what he remembered since his own creation—his placing in Paradise; his talk with God concerning solitude and fit society; his first meeting and nuptials with Eve. His discourse with the Angel thereupon; who, after admonitions repeated, departs.

BOOK IX *

The Argument

Satan, having compassed the Earth, with meditated guile returns as a mist by night into Paradise; enters into the Serpent sleeping. Adam and Eve in the morning go forth to their labours, which Eve proposes to divide in several places, each labouring apart: Adam consents not, alleging the danger lest that enemy of whom they were forewarned should attempt her found alone. Eve, loth to be thought not circumspect or firm enough, urges her going apart, the rather desirous to make trial of her strength; Adam at last yields. The Serpent finds her alone: his subtle approach, first gazing, then speaking, with much flattery extolling Eve above all other creatures. Eve, wondering to hear the Serpent speak, asks how he attained to human speech and such understanding not till now; the Serpent answers that by tasting of a certain tree in the Garden he attained both to speech and reason, till then void of both. Eve requires him to bring her to that tree, and finds it to be the Tree of Knowledge forbidden: the Serpent, now grown bolder, with many wiles and arguments induces her at length to eat. She, pleased with the taste, deliberates a while whether to impart thereof to Adam or not; at last brings him of the fruit; relates what persuaded her to eat thereof. Adam, at first amazed, but perceiving her lost, resolves, through vehemence of love, to perish with her, and, extenuating the trespass, eats also of the fruit. The effects thereof in them both; they seek to cover their nakedness; then fall to variance and accusation of one another.

> "What may this mean? Language of Man pronounced
> By tongue of brute, and human sense expressed!
> The first at least of these I thought denied
> To beasts, whom God on their creation-day

* The selection from Book IX comprises lines 553–1004 of Milton's text.

Created mute to all articulate sound;
The latter I demur,° for in their looks
Much reason, and in their actions, oft appears.
Thee, Serpent, subtlest beast of all the field
I knew, but not with human voice endued;
Redouble, then, this miracle, and say, 10
How cam'st thou speakable of mute,° and how
To me so friendly grown above the rest
Of brutal kind that daily are in sight:
Say, for such wonder claims attention due."
　　To whom the guileful Tempter thus replied:
"Empress of this fair World, resplendent Eve!
Easy to me it is to tell thee all
What thou command'st, and right thou shouldst be obeyed.
I was at first as other beasts that graze
The trodden herb, of abject thoughts and low, 20
As was my food, nor aught but food discerned
Or sex, and apprehended nothing high:
Till on a day, roving the field, I chanced
A goodly tree far distant to behold,
Loaden with fruit of fairest colours mixed,
Ruddy and gold: I nearer drew to gaze;
When from the boughs a savoury odour blown,
Grateful to appetite, more pleased my sense
Than smell of sweetest fennel, or the teats°
Of ewe or goat dropping with milk at even, 30
Unsucked of lamb or kid, that tend their play.
To satisfy the sharp desire I had
Of tasting those fair apples, I resolved
Not to defer; hunger and thirst at once,
Powerful persuaders, quickened at the scent
Of that alluring fruit, urged me so keen.
About the mossy trunk I wound me soon;
For, high from ground, the branches would require
Thy utmost reach, or Adam's: round the tree
All other beasts that saw, with like desire 40
Longing and envying stood, but could not reach.
Amid the tree now got, where plenty hung
Tempting so nigh, to pluck and eat my fill

---

6. *demur:* have doubts about (whether reason is denied to brutes). *11. of mute:* from being mute. *29. fennel . . . teats:* popular belief had it that fennel was a favorite food of serpents, and that they sucked the teats of sheep.

I spared not; for such pleasure till that hour
At feed or fountain never had I found.
Sated at length, ere long I might perceive
Strange alteration in me, to degree
Of reason° in my inward powers, and speech
Wanted not long, though to this shape retained.
Thenceforth to speculations high or deep   50
I turned my thoughts, and with capacious mind
Considered all things visible in Heaven,
Or Earth, or Middle,° all things fair and good.
But all that fair and good in thy divine
Semblance and in thy beauty's heavenly ray,
United I beheld—no fair° to thine
Equivalent or second; which compelled
Me thus, though importune perhaps, to come
And gaze, and worship thee of right declared
Sovran of creatures, universal Dame!" °   60
    So talked the spirited° sly Snake; and Eve,
Yet more amazed, unwary thus replied:
    "Serpent, thy overpraising leaves in doubt
The virtue of that fruit, in thee first proved.
But say, where grows the tree? from hence how far?
For many are the trees of God that grow
In Paradise, and various, yet unknown
To us; in such abundance lies our choice
As leaves a greater store of fruit untouched,
Still hanging incorruptible, till men   70
Grow up to their provision, and more hands
Help to disburden Nature of her bearth." °
    To whom the wily Adder, blithe and glad:—
"Empress, the way is ready, and not long—
Beyond a row of myrtles, on a flat,
Fast by a fountain, one small thicket past
Of blowing° myrrh and balm. If thou accept
My conduct, I can bring thee thither soon."
    "Lead, then," said Eve. He, leading, swiftly rolled
In tangles, and made intricate seem straight,   80
To mischief swift. Hope elevates, and joy

47–48. *to . . . reason:* to the extent of inducing in me some degree of reason.
53. *Middle:* the air.   56. *fair:* fairness, beauty.   60. *Dame:* mistress (of the universe).   61. *spirited:* inspired (by Satan).   72. *bearth:* that which she bears; fruit.   77. *blowing:* blossoming.

Brightens his crest. As when a wandering fire,°
Compact° of unctuous° vapour, which the night
Condenses, and the cold environs round,
Kindled through agitation to a flame
(Which oft, they say, some evil spirit attends),
Hovering and blazing with delusive light,
Misleads the amazed night-wandered from his way
To bogs and mires, and oft through pond or pool,
There swallowed up and lost, from succour far: 90
So glistered° the dire Snake, and into fraud°
Led Eve, our credulous mother, to the Tree
Of Prohibition,° root of all our woe;
Which when she saw, thus to her guide she spake:
    "Serpent, we might have spared our coming hither,
Fruitless to me, though fruit be here to excess,
The credit of whose virtue rest with thee°—
Wondrous, indeed, if cause of such effects!
But of this tree we may not taste nor touch;
God so commanded, and left that command   100
Sole daughter of his voice: the rest,° we live
Law to ourselves; our reason is our law."
    To whom the Tempter guilefully replied:
"Indeed! Hath God then said that of the fruit
Of all these garden-trees ye shall not eat,
Yet lords declared of all in earth or air?"
    To whom thus Eve, yet sinless: "Of the fruit
Of each tree in the garden we may eat;
But of the fruit of this fair tree, amidst
The garden, God hath said, 'Ye shall not eat   110
Thereof, nor shall ye touch it, lest ye die.' "
    She scarce had said, though brief, when now more bold
The Tempter, but with show of zeal and love
To Man, and indignation at his wrong,
New part puts on,° and, as to passion moved,
Fluctuates° disturbed, yet comeely, and in act
Raised, as of some great matter to begin.
As when of old some orator renowned

82. *wandering fire:* will-o'-the-wisp, jack-o'-lantern.   83. *Compact:* composed;
unctuous: oily.   91. *glistered:* glittered; *fraud:* harm, evil-doing.   92–93. *Tree
of Prohibition:* the Forbidden Tree.   97. *The . . . thee:* the proof of whose
wonder-working powers may be retained by thee alone.   101. *the rest:* as for
the rest (of the trees).   115. *New . . . on:* assumes a new role.   116. *Fluc-
tuates:* moves his body to and fro.

In Athens or free Rome, where eloquence
Flourished, since mute, to some great cause addressed,   120
Stood in himself collected, while each part,°
Motion, each act, won audience° ere the tongue
Sometimes in highth° began, as no delay
Of preface brooking° through his zeal of right:
So standing, moving, or to highth upgrown,
The Tempter, all impassioned, thus began:
    "O sacred, wise, and wisdom-giving Plant,
Mother of science!° now I feel thy power
Within me clear, not only to discern
Things in their causes, but to trace the ways   130
Of highest agents, deemed however wise.
Queen of this Universe! do not believe
Those rigid threats of death; ye shall not die.
How should ye? by the fruit? it gives you life
To knowledge.° By the Threatener? look on me,
Me who have touched and tasted, yet both live,
And life more perfect have attained than Fate
Meant me, by venturing higher than my lot.
Shall that be shut to Man which to the Beast
Is open? or will God incense° his ire   140
For such a petty trespass, and not praise
Rather your dauntless virtue, whom the pain
Of death denounced,° whatever thing Death be,
Deterred not from achieving what might lead
To happier life, knowledge of Good and Evil?
Of good, how just! of evil—if what is evil
Be real, why not known, since easier shunned?
God therefore cannot hurt ye, and be just;
Not just, not God; not feared then, nor obeyed;
Your fear itself of death removes the fear.   150
Why, then, was this forbid? Why but to awe,
Why but to keep ye low and ignorant,
His worshippers? He knows that in the day
Ye eat thereof your eyes, that seem so clear,
Yet are but dim, shall perfectly be then
Opened and cleared, and ye shall be as Gods,
Knowing both good and evil, as they know.

---

121. part: of the body.   *122. audience:* hearing.   *123. highth:* of feeling.   *124. brooking:* enduring, "putting up with."   *128. science:* knowledge.   *135. To knowledge:* in addition to knowledge.   *140. incense:* kindle.   *143. denounced:* proclaimed, threatened.

That ye should be as Gods,° since I as Man,
Internal Man,° is but proportion meet—
I, of brute, human; ye, of human, Gods.   160
So ye shall die perhaps, by putting off
Human, to put on° Gods—death to be wished,
Though threatened, which no worse than this can bring!
And what are Gods, that Man may not become
As they, participating god-like food?
The Gods are first, and that advantage use
On our belief, that all from them proceeds.
I question it; for this fair Earth I see,
Warmed by the Sun, producing every kind;
Then nothing. If they° all things, who enclosed   170
Knowledge of good and evil in this tree,
That whoso eats thereof forthwith attains
Wisdom without their leave? and wherein lies
The offence, that Man should thus attain to know?
What can your knowledge hurt him, or this tree
Impart against his will, if all be his?
Or is it envy? and can envy dwell
In heavenly breasts? These, these and many more
Causes import° your need of this fair fruit.
Goddess humane,° reach, then, and freely taste!"   180
    He ended; and his words, replete with guile,
Into her heart too easy entrance won:
Fixed on the fruit she gazed, which to behold
Might tempt alone; and in her ears the sound
Yet rung of his persuasive words, impregned°
With reason, to her seeming, and with truth.
Meanwhile the hour of noon drew on, and waked
An eager appetite, raised by the smell
So savoury of that fruit, which with desire,
Inclinable° now grown to touch or taste,   190
Solicited her longing eye; yet first,
Pausing a while, thus to herself she mused:
    "Great are thy virtues, doubtless, best of fruits,
Though kept from Man, and worthy to be admired,

158. *Gods:* "Satan speaks like a polytheist, and Eve later falls into the same idolatrous and pagan way of thought."—Hanford. *159. Internal Man:* internally, with manlike faculties, though externally a serpent. *162. put on:* assume the nature of. *170. If they:* if they produced. *179. import:* indicate. *180. humane:* gentle, gracious. *185. impregned:* impregnated. *190. Inclinable:* easily inclined.

Whose taste, too long forborne, at first assay
Gave elocution to the mute, and taught
The tongue not made for speech to speak thy praise.
Thy praise he also who forbids thy use
Conceals not from us, naming thee the Tree
Of Knowledge, knowledge both of good and evil;   200
Forbids us then to taste; but his forbidding
Commends thee more, while it infers° the good
By thee communicated, and our want;
For good unknown sure is not had, or, had
And yet unknown, is as not had at all.
In plain,° then, what forbids he but to know,
Forbids us good, forbids us to be wise?
Such prohibitions bind not. But, if Death
Bind us with after-bands, what profits then
Our inward freedom? In the day we eat   210
Of this fair fruit, our doom is we shall die!
How dies the Serpent? He hath eaten, and lives,
And knows, and speaks, and reasons, and discerns,
Irrational till then. For us alone
Was death invented? or to us denied
This intellectual food, for beasts reserved?
For beasts it seems; yet that one beast which first
Hath tasted envies not, but brings with joy
The good befallen him, author unsuspect,°
Friendly to Man, far from deceit or guile.   220
What fear I, then? rather, what know to fear
Under this ignorance of good and evil,
Of God or Death, of law or penalty?
Here grows the cure of all, this fruit divine,
Fair to the eye, inviting to the taste,
Of virtue° to make wise. What hinders, then,
To reach, and feed at once both body and mind?"
     So saying, her rash hand in evil hour
Forth reaching to the fruit, she plucked, she eat.°
Earth felt the wound, and Nature from her seat,   230
Sighing through all her works, gave signs of woe
That all was lost. Back to the thicket slunk
The guilty Serpent, and well might, for Eve,

202. *infers:* implies.   206. *In plain:* in plain terms.   219. *author unsuspect:* the
authority for which information (that is, the serpent), not to be suspected.   226.
virtue: power.   229. *eat:* past tense (pronounced et).

Intent now only on her taste, naught else
Regarded; such delight till then, as seemed,
In fruit she never tasted, whether true,
Or fancied so through expectation high
Of knowledge; nor was Godhead from her thought.
Greedily she ingorged without restraint,
And knew not eating° death. Satiate at length,   240
And heightened as with wine, jocund and boon,°
Thus to herself she pleasingly began:
   "O sovran,° virtuous, precious of all trees
In Paradise! of operation blest
To sapience,° hitherto obscured, infamed,°
And thy fair fruit let hang, as to no end
Created! but henceforth my early care,
Not without song, each morning, and due praise,
Shall tend thee, and the fertile burden ease
Of thy full branches, offered free to all;   250
Till, dieted by thee, I grow mature
In knowledge, as the Gods who all things know.
Though others envy what they cannot give—
For, had the gift been theirs, it had not here
Thus grown! Experience, next to thee I owe,
Best guide: not following thee, I had remained
In ignorance; thou open'st Wisdom's way,
And giv'st access, though secret she retire.
And I perhaps am secret: Heaven is high—
High, and remote to see from thence distinct   260
Each thing on Earth; and other care perhaps
May have diverted from continual watch
Our great Forbidder, safe with all his spies
About him. But to Adam in what sort
Shall I appear? Shall I to him make known
As yet my change, and give him to partake
Full happiness with me, or rather not,
But keep the odds of knowledge in my power
Without copartner? so to add what wants
In female sex, the more to draw his love,   270
And render me more equal, and perhaps—
A thing not undesirable—sometime

---

240. *knew not eating:* knew not that she was eating. 241. *boon:* gay. 243.
sovran: most sovereign. 244–45. *blest To sapience:* blest with the power of
conferring wisdom; *infamed:* not known (or, perhaps, falsely reputed).

Superior; for, inferior, who is free?
This may be well; but what if God have seen,
And death ensue? Then I shall be no more;
And Adam, wedded to another Eve,
Shall live with her enjoying, I extinct!
A death to think! Confirmed, then, I resolve
Adam shall share with me in bliss or woe.
So dear I love him that with him all deaths   280
I could endure, without him live no life."
 So saying, from the tree her step she turned,
But first low reverence done, as to the power°
That dwelt within, whose presence had infused
Into the plant sciential° sap, derived
From nectar, drink of Gods. Adam the while,
Waiting desirous her return, had wove
Of choicest flowers a garland, to adorn
Her tresses, and her rural labours crown,
As reapers oft are wont their harvest queen.   290
Great joy he promised to his thoughts, and new
Solace in her return, so long delayed;
Yet oft his heart, divine of° something ill,
Misgave him. He the faltering measure° felt,
And forth to meet her went, the way she took
That morn when first they parted; by the Tree
Of Knowledge he must pass; there he her met,
Scarce from the tree returning; in her hand
A bough of fairest fruit, that downy smiled,
New gathered, and ambrosial smell diffused.   300
To him she hasted; in her face excuse
Came prologue,° and apology to prompt,
Which, with bland words at will, she thus addressed:
 "Hast thou not wondered, Adam, at my stay?
Thee I have missed, and thought it long, deprived
Thy presence—agony of love till now
Not felt, nor shall be twice; for never more
Mean I to try, what rash untried I sought,°
The pain of absence from thy sight. But strange

---

283. *low . . . power:* first manifestation of idolatry. 285. *sciential:* conferring knowledge. 293. *divine of:* divining, foreboding. 294. *faltering measure:* irregular beat. 301–02. *excuse Came prologue:* The expression on her face was a suitable prologue to the apology and the hypocritical scene she was about to rehearse. 308. *what . . . sought:* what I rashly sought after because it was untried and therefore not experienced.

Hath been the cause, and wonderful to hear.   310
This tree is not, as we are told, a tree
Of danger tasted,° nor to evil unknown
Opening the way, but of divine effect
To open eyes, and make them Gods who taste;
And hath been tasted such.° The Serpent wise,
Or not restrained as we, or not obeying,
Hath eaten of the fruit, and is become
Not dead, as we are threatened, but thenceforth
Endued with human voice and human sense,
Reasoning to admiration,° and with me   320
Persuasively hath so prevailed that I
Have also tasted, and have also found
The effects to correspond—opener mine eyes,
Dim erst,° dilated spirits, ampler heart,
And growing up to Godhead; which for thee°
Chiefly I sought, without thee can despise.
For bliss, as thou hast part, to me is bliss;
Tedious, unshared with thee, and odious soon.
Thou, therefore, also taste, that equal lot
May join us, equal joy, as equal love;   330
Lest, thou not tasting, different degree
Disjoin us, and I then too late renounce°
Deity for thee, when fate will not permit."
   Thus Eve with countenance blithe her story told;
But in her cheek distemper flushing glowed.
On the other side, Adam, soon as he heard
The fatal trespass done by Eve, amazed,
Astonied stood and blank, while horror chill
Ran through his veins, and all his joints relaxed.
From his slack hand the garland wreathed for Eve   340
Down dropt, and all the faded roses shed.
Speechless he stood and pale, till thus at length
First to himself he inward silence broke:
   "O fairest of Creation, last and best
Of all God's works, creature in whom excelled
Whatever can to sight or thought be formed,
Holy, divine, good, amiable, or sweet!
How art thou lost! how on a sudden lost,

312. *tasted:* when tasted.   315. *tasted such:* found by tasting to be such.   320.
to admiration: in a manner to be wondered at.   324. *erst:* formerly.   325. ff.
which for thee: Eve now adds a palpable falsehood to her sins.   332. *renounce:*
try to renounce.

Defaced, deflowered, and now to death devote! °
Rather, how hast thou yielded to transgress   350
The strict forbiddance, how to violate
The sacred fruit forbidden? Some cursèd fraud
Of enemy hath beguiled thee, yet unknown,
And me with thee hath ruined; for with thee
Certain my resolution is to die.
How can I live without thee? how forgo
Thy sweet converse and love so dearly joined,
To live again in these wild woods forlorn?
Should God create another Eve, and I
Another rib afford, yet loss of thee   360
Would never from my heart. No, no! I feel
The link of nature draw me: flesh of flesh,
Bone of my bone° thou art, and from thy state
Mine never shall be parted, bliss or woe."
    So having said, as one from sad dismay
Recomforted, and, after thoughts disturbed,
Submitting to what seemed remediless,
Thus in calm mood his words to Eve he turned:
    "Bold deed thou hast presumed, adventurous Eve,
And peril great provoked, who thus hast dared,   370
Had it been only coveting to eye
That sacred fruit, sacred to abstinence,
Much more to taste it, under ban to touch.
But past who can recall, or done undo?
Not God Omnipotent, nor Fate! Yet so
Perhaps thou shalt not die; perhaps the fact°
Is not so heinous now—foretasted fruit,
Profaned first by the Serpent, by him first
Made common and unhallowed ere our taste,
Nor yet on him found deadly; he yet lives—   380
Lives, as thou saidst, and gains to live, as Man,
Higher degree of life: inducement strong
To us, as likely, tasting, to attain
Proportional ascent; which cannot be
But to be Gods, or Angels, demi-gods.
Nor can I think that God, Creator wise,
Though threatening, will in earnest so destroy
Us, his prime creatures, dignified so high,

349. *devote:* doomed.   362–63. *flesh . . . bone:* See Genesis 2:23.   376. *fact:*
deed.

Set over all his works; which, in our fall,
For us created, needs with us must fail,   390
Dependent made. So God shall uncreate,
Be frustrate, do, undo, and labour lose—
Not well conceived of God,° who, though his power
Creation could repeat, yet would be loth
Us to abolish, lest the Adversary
Triumph and say: 'Fickle their state whom God
Most favours; who can please him long? Me first
He ruined, now Mankind; whom will he next?'
Matter of scorn not to be given the Foe.
However, I with thee have fixed my lot,   400
Certain° to undergo like doom. If death
Consort with thee, death is to me as life;
So forcible within my heart I feel
The bond of Nature draw me to my own—
My own in thee; for what thou art is mine.
Our state cannot be severed; we are one,
One flesh; to lose thee were to lose myself."
    So Adam; and thus Eve to him replied:
"O glorious trial of exceeding love,
Illustrious evidence, example high!   410
Engaging me to emulate; but, short
Of thy perfection, how shall I attain,
Adam? from whose dear side I boast me sprung,
And gladly of our union hear thee speak,
One heart, one soul in both; whereof good proof
This day affords, declaring thee resolved,
Rather than death, or aught than death more dread,
Shall separate us, linked in love so dear,
To undergo with me one guilt, one crime,
If any be, of tasting this fair fruit;   420
Whose virtue (for of good still good proceeds,
Direct, or by occasion) hath presented
This happy trial of thy love, which else
So eminently never had been known.
Were it I thought death menaced would ensue
This my attempt, I would sustain alone
The worst, and not persuade thee—rather die
Deserted than oblige° thee with a fact

393. *Not . . . God:* That is, it is not easily conceivable that God should undo and lose his work. *401. Certain:* resolved. *428: oblige:* involve.

Pernicious to thy peace, chiefly assured
Remarkably so late of thy so true, 430
So faithful, love unequalled. But I feel
Far otherwise the event°—not death, but life
Augmented, opened eyes, new hopes, new joys,
Taste so divine that what of sweet before
Hath touched my sense, flat seems to this and harsh.
On my experience, Adam, freely taste,
And fear of death deliver to the winds."
    So saying, she embraced him, and for joy
Tenderly wept, much won that he his love
Had so ennobled as of choice to incur 440
Divine displeasure for her sake, or death.
In recompense (for such compliance bad
Such recompense best merits), from the bough
She gave him of that fair enticing fruit
With liberal hand. He scrupled not to eat,
Against his better knowledge, not deceived,
But fondly overcome with female charm.
Earth trembled from her entrails, as again
In pangs, and Nature gave a second groan;
Sky loured, and, muttering thunder, some sad drops 450
Wept at completing of the mortal sin
Original; . . .

BOOK X

The Argument

Man's transgression known, the guardian Angels forsake Paradise, and return up to Heaven to approve their vigilance, and are approved; God declaring that the entrance of Satan could not be by them prevented. He sends his Son to judge the transgressors; who descends, and gives sentence accordingly; then, in pity, clothes them both, and reascends. Sin and Death, sitting till then at the gates of Hell, by wondrous sympathy feeling the success of Satan in this new World, and the sin by Man there committed, resolve to sit no longer confined in Hell, but to follow Satan, their sire, up to the place of Man. To make the way easier from Hell to this World to and fro, they pave a broad highway or bridge over Chaos, according to the track that Satan first made; then, preparing for Earth, they meet him, proud of

432. *event:* outcome.

his success, returning to Hell; their mutual gratulation. Satan arrives at Pandemonium; in full assembly relates, with boasting, his success against Man; instead of applause is entertained with a general hiss by all his audience, transformed, with himself also, suddenly into Serpents, according to his doom given in Paradise; then, deluded with a show of the Forbidden Tree springing up before them, they, greedily reaching to take of the fruit, chew dust and bitter ashes. The proceedings of Sin and Death: God foretells the final victory of his Son over them, and the renewing of all things; but, for the present, commands his Angels to make several alterations in the Heavens and elements. Adam, more and more perceiving his fallen condition, heavily bewails, rejects the condolement of Eve; she persists, and at length appeases him: then, to evade the curse likely to fall on their offspring, proposes to Adam violent ways; which he approves not, but, conceiving better hope, puts her in mind of the late promise made them, that her seed should be revenged on the Serpent, and exhorts her, with him, to seek peace of the offended Deity, by repentance and supplication.

BOOK XI

The Argument

The Son of God presents to his Father the prayers of our first parents now repenting, and intercedes for them. God accepts them, but declares that they must no longer abide in Paradise; sends Michael with a band of Cherubim to dispossess them, but first to reveal to Adam future things: Michael's coming down. Adam shows to Eve certain ominous signs: he discerns Michael's approach; goes out to meet him: the Angel denounces[1] their departure. Eve's lamentation. Adam pleads, but submits: The Angel leads him up to a high hill; sets before him in vision what shall happen till the Flood.

BOOK XII

The Argument*

The Angel Michael continues, from the Flood, to relate what shall succeed; then, in the mention of Abraham, comes by degrees to explain who that Seed of the Woman shall be which was promised Adam and Eve in the Fall: his Incarnation, Death, Resurrection, and Ascension; the state of the

---

[1] *denounces:* announces, proclaims.   * The selection from Book XII comprises lines 552–649 of Milton's text.

Church till his second coming. Adam, greatly satisfied and recomforted by
these relations and promises, descends the hill with Michael; wakens Eve,
who all this while had slept, but with gentle dreams composed to quietness
of mind and submission. Michael in either hand leads them out of Paradise,
the fiery sword waving behind them, and the Cherubim taking their stations
to guard the place.

. . . He° ended; and thus Adam last° replied:
"How soon hath thy prediction, Seer blest,
Measured° this transient World, the race of Time,
Till Time stand fixed! Beyond is all abyss—
Eternity, whose end no eye can reach.
Greatly instructed I shall hence depart,
Greatly in peace of thought, and have my fill
Of knowledge, what this vessel° can contain;
Beyond which was my folly to aspire.
Henceforth I learn that to obey is best,   10
And love with fear the only God, to walk
As in his presence, ever to observe
His providence, and on him sole depend,
Merciful over all his works, with good
Still overcoming evil, and by small
Accomplishing great things—by things deemed weak
Subverting worldly strong, and worldly wise
By simply meek; that suffering for Truth's sake
Is fortitude to highest victory,
And to the faithful death the gate of life—   20
Taught this by his example whom I now
Acknowledge my Redeemer ever blest."
    To whom thus also the Angel last replied:
"This having learned, thou hast attained the sum
Of wisdom; hope no higher, though all the stars
Thou knew'st by name, and all the ethereal powers,
All secrets of the Deep, all Nature's works,
Or works of God in heaven, air, earth, or sea.
And all the riches of this world enjoy'dst,
And all the rule, one empire. Only add   30
Deeds to thy knowledge answerable; add faith;
Add virtue, patience, temperance; add love,

1. *He*: the Angel Michael; *last*: for the last time.   3. *Measured*: surveyed.   8.
this vessel: this mind.

By name to come called Charity,° the soul
Of all the rest: then wilt thou not be loth
To leave this Paradise, but shalt possess
A Paradise within thee, happier far.
Let us descend now, therefore, from this top
Of speculation;° for the hour precise
Exacts our parting hence; and, see! the guards,
By me encamped on yonder hill, expect   40
Their motion, at whose front a flaming sword,
In signal of remove, waves fiercely round.
We may no longer stay. Go, waken Eve;
Her also I with gentle dreams have calmed,
Portending good, and all her spirits composed
To meek submission: thou, at season fit,
Let her with thee partake what thou hast heard—
Chiefly what may concern her faith to know,
The great deliverance by her seed to come
(For by the Woman's Seed) on all mankind—   50
That ye may live, which will be many days,°
Both in one faith unanimous; though sad
With cause for evils past, yet much more cheered
With meditation on the happy end."
      He ended, and they both descend the hill.
Descended, Adam to the bower where Eve
Lay sleeping ran before, but found her waked;
And thus with words not sad she him received:
      "Whence thou return'st and whither went'st I know;
For God is also in sleep, and dreams advise,   60
Which he hath sent propitious, some great good
Presaging, since, with sorrow and heart's distress
Wearied, I fell asleep: but now lead on;
In me is no delay; with thee to go
Is to stay here; without thee here to stay
Is to go hence unwilling; thou to me
Art all things under Heaven, all places thou,
Who for my wilful crime art banished hence.
This further consolation yet secure
I carry hence: though all by me is lost,   70
Such favour I unworthy am vouchsafed,

33. *Charity:* See I Corinthians 13.   37–38. *top Of speculation: Top* is used in
a double sense. *Speculation* means observation (from the Latin *specula,* "watch-
tower").   51. *many days:* allusion to Adam's long life of 930 years (see **Gen.**
5:5).

By me the Promised Seed shall all restore."
   So spake our mother Eve; and Adam heard
Well pleased, but answered not; for now too nigh
The Archangel stood, and from the other hill
To their fixed station, all in bright array
The Cherubim descended, on the ground
Gliding meteorous,° as evening mist,
Risen from a river, o'er the marish° glides,
And gathers ground fast at the labourer's heel   80
Homeward returning. High in front advanced,
The brandished sword of God before them blazed
Fierce as a comet, which with torrid heat,
And vapour as the Libyan air adust,°
Began to parch that temperate clime; whereat
In either hand the hast'ning Angel caught
Our lingering parents, and to the eastern gate
Led them direct, and down the cliff as fast
To the subjected° plain; then disappeared.
They, looking back, all the eastern side beheld   90
Of Paradise, so late their happy seat,
Waved over by that flaming brand, the gate
With dreadful faces thronged and fiery arms:
Some natural tears they dropped, but wiped them soon;
The world was all before them, where to choose
Their place of rest, and Providence their guide:
They, hand in hand, with wandering steps and slow,
Through Eden took their solitary way.

The End

78. *meteorous:* like meteors   79. *marish:* marsh.   84. *adust:* scorched.   89. *subjected:* lying below.

Jonathan Swift

FROM *Gulliver's Travels*

BOOK FOUR

Jonathan Swift (1667–1745)

SWIFT'S LIFE WAS MADE UNHAPPY BY ALMOST EVERY DIFFI-
culty an ambitious man of extraordinary energy and talent might find in
his path. He was born in Ireland shortly after the death of his father. He
completed his studies at Trinity College, Dublin, with less than distinction.
Although fortunate to be taken ino the household of Sir William Temple,
Swift left when he felt his patron was not acting quickly enough in his
behalf. After some years of success in London in the first decade of the
eighteenth century among the leading men of letters and the Tory ministers Bolingbroke and Oxford, Swift's personal hopes were dashed when
Queen Anne sent him back to Dublin as Dean of St. Patrick's in 1713.
A year later, with the queen's death and the fall of the Tories, Swift knew
his ambitions for a political career in England were finished. His life in
Ireland, though almost made unbearable at first by his isolation and exile
from London, eventually came to be of use to the people he had been
appointed to serve. Several of his pamphlets saved the Irish from even
greater financial distress than the English usually placed upon them. He
gradually became loved by his countrymen.

Almost all of Swift's major works were satirical, *Gulliver's Travels* being
the most noteworthy of his many excellent productions in this vein. The
first two books show Gulliver, first as a giant among pygmies, then as a
pygmy among giants. The third, which gives over the play on relative sizes,
is more openly political in intent, severely criticizing most English institutions of his day. The fourth and final book moves beyond the confines of
political satire to chastise the foolish pride of all mankind.

Gulliver's Travels

A VOYAGE TO THE COUNTRY
OF THE HOUYHNHNMS

CHAPTER I

THE AUTHOR SETS OUT AS CAPTAIN OF A SHIP. HIS MEN CONSPIRE
AGAINST HIM, CONFINE HIM A LONG TIME TO HIS CABIN, SET HIM ON
SHORE IN AN UNKNOWN LAND. HE TRAVELS UP IN THE COUNTRY. THE
YAHOOS, A STRANGE SORT OF ANIMAL, DESCRIBED. THE AUTHOR MEETS
TWO HOUYHNHNMS.

I continued at home with my wife and children about five months in
a very happy condition, if I could have learned the lesson of knowing when
I was well. I left my poor wife big with child, and accepted an advantageous
offer made me to be captain of the *Adventure,* a stout merchantman of
350 tons: for I understood navigation well, and being grown weary of a
surgeon's employment at sea, which however I could exercise upon occasion, I took a skilful young man of that calling, one Robert Purefoy, into
my ship. We set sail from Portsmouth upon the 7th day of September,
1710; on the 14th, we met with Captain Pocock of Bristol, at Tenariff,[1]
who was going to the bay of Campechy,[2] to cut logwood. On the 16th, he
was parted from us by a storm; I heard since my return that his ship
foundered, and none escaped, but one cabin-boy. He was an honest man,
and a good sailor, but a little too positive in his own opinions, which was
the cause of his destruction, as it hath been of several others. For if he had
followed my advice, he might at this time have been safe at home with
his family as well as myself.

I had several men die in my ship of calentures[3] so that I was forced to
get recruits out of Barbadoes, and the Leeward Islands, where I touched

[1] Tenariff, one of the Canary Islands. [2] on the coast of Yucatan. [3] tropical
fever.

by the direction of the merchants who employed me, which I had soon too much cause to repent; for I found afterwards that most of them had been buccaneers. I had fifty hands on board, and my orders were, that I should trade with the Indians in the South Sea, and make what discoveries I could. These rogues whom I had picked up debauched my other men, and they all formed a conspiracy to seize the ship and secure me; which they did one morning, rushing into my cabin, and binding me hand and foot, threatening to throw me overboard, if I offered to stir. I told them, I was their prisoner, and would submit. This they made me swear to do, and then unbound me, only fastening one of my legs with a chain near my bed, and placed a sentry at my door with his piece charged, who was commanded to shoot me dead if I attempted my liberty. They sent me down victuals and drink, and took the government of the ship to themselves. Their design was to turn pirates, and plunder the Spaniards, which they could not do till they got more men. But first they resolved to sell the goods in the ship, and then go to Madagascar for recruits, several among them having died since my confinement. They sailed many weeks, and traded with the Indians, but I knew not what course they took, being kept close prisoner in my cabin, and expecting nothing less than to be murdered, as they often threatened me.

Upon the 9th day of May, 1711, one James Welch came down to my cabin; and said he had orders from the captain to set me ashore. I expostulated with him, but in vain; neither would he so much as tell me who their new captain was. They forced me into the long-boat, letting me put on my best suit of clothes, which were as good as new, and a small bundle of linen, but no arms except my hanger;[4] and they were so civil as not to search my pockets, into which I conveyed what money I had, with some other little necessaries. They rowed about a league, and then set me down on a strand. I desired them to tell me what country it was. They all swore, they knew no more than myself, but said, that the captain (as they called him) was resolved, after they had sold the lading, to get rid of me in the first place where they discovered land. They pushed off immediately, advising me to make haste, for fear of being overtaken by the tide, and bade me farewell.

In this desolate condition I advanced forward, and soon got upon firm ground, where I sat down on a bank to rest myself, and consider what I had best to do. When I was a little refreshed I went up into the country, resolving to deliver myself to the first savages I should meet, and purchase my life from them by some bracelets, glass rings, and other toys, which sailors usually provide themselves with in those voyages, and whereof I had some about me: the land was divided by long rows of trees, not regulary

---

[4] short sword.

planted, but naturally growing; there was great plenty of grass, and several fields of oats. I walked very circumspectly for fear of being surprised, or suddenly shot with an arrow from behind or on either side. I fell into a beaten road, where I saw many tracks of human feet, and some of cows, but most of horses. At last I beheld several animals in a field, and one or two of the same kind sitting in trees. Their shape was very singular, and deformed, which a little discomposed me, so that I lay down behind a thicket to observe them better. Some of them coming forward near the place where I lay, gave me an opportunity of distinctly marking their form. Their heads and breasts were covered with a thick hair, some frizzled and others lank; they had beards like goats, and a long ridge of hair down their backs, and the foreparts of their legs and feet, but the rest of their bodies were bare, so that I might see their skins, which were of a brown buff colour. They had no tails, nor any hair at all on their buttocks, except about the anus; which, I presume, nature had placed there to defend them as they sat on the ground; for this posture they used, as well as lying down, and often stood on their hind feet. They climbed high trees, as nimbly as a squirrel, for they had strong extended claws before and behind, terminating in sharp points, and hooked. They would often spring, and bound, and leap with prodigious agility. The females were not so large as the males; they had long lank hair on their heads, and only a sort of down on the rest of their bodies, except about the anus, and pudenda. Their dugs hung between their fore-feet, and often reached almost to the ground as they walked. The hair of both sexes was of several colours, brown, red, black, and yellow. Upon the whole, I never beheld in all my travels so disagreeable an animal, or one against which I naturally conceived so strong antipathy. So that thinking I had seen enough, full of contempt and aversion, I got up and pursued the beaten road, hoping it might direct me to the cabin of some Indian. I had not gone far when I met one of these creatures full in my way, and coming up directly to me. The ugly monster, when he saw me, distorted several ways every feature of his visage, and stared as at an object he had never seen before; then approaching nearer, lifted up his forepaw, whether out of curiosity or mischief, I could not tell. But I drew my hanger, and gave him a good blow with the flat side of it, for I durst not strike him with the edge, fearing the inhabitants might be provoked against me, if they should come to know that I had killed or maimed any of their cattle. When the beast felt the smart, he drew back, and roared so loud, that a herd of at least forty came flocking about me from the next field, howling and making odious faces; but I ran to the body of a tree, and leaning my back against it, kept them off, by waving my hanger. Several of this cursed brood getting hold of the branches behind leaped up into the tree, from whence they began to discharge their excrements on my head: however, I escaped pretty well, by sticking close to the stem of a tree, but was almost stifled with the filth, which fell about me on every side.

In the midst of this distress, I observed them all to run away on a sudden as fast as they could, at which I ventured to leave the tree, and pursue the road, wondering what it was that could put them into this fright. But looking on my left hand, I saw a horse walking softly in the field, which my persecutors having sooner discovered, was the cause of their flight. The horse started a little when he came near me, but soon recovering himself, looked full in my face with manifest tokens of wonder: he viewed my hands and feet, walking round me several times. I would have pursued my journey, but he placed himself directly in the way, yet looking with a very mild aspect, never offering the least violence. We stood gazing at each other for some time; at last I took the boldness to reach my hand towards his neck, with a design to stroke it, using the common style and whistle of jockeys when they are going to handle a strange horse. But this animal, seeming to receive my civilities with disdain, shook his head, and bent his brows, softly raising up his left forefoot to remove my hand. Then he neighed three or four times, but in so different a cadence, that I almost began to think he was speaking to himself in some language of his own.

While he and I were thus employed, another horse came up; who applying himself to the first in a very formal manner, they gently struck each other's right hoof before, neighing several times by turns, and varying the sound, which seemed to be almost articulate. They went some paces off, as if it were to confer together, walking side by side, backward and forward, like persons deliberating upon some affair of weight, but often turning their eyes towards me, as it were to watch that I might not escape. I was amazed to see such actions and behaviour in brute beasts, and concluded with myself, that if the inhabitants of this country were endued with a proportionable degree of reason, they must needs be the wisest people upon earth. This thought gave me so much comfort, that I resolved to go forward until I could discover some house or village, or meet with any of the natives, leaving the two horses to discourse together as they pleased. But the first, who was a dapple grey, observing me to steal off, neighed after me in so expressive a tone, that I fancied myself to understand what he meant; whereupon I turned back, and came near him, to expect his farther commands. But concealing my fear as much as I could, for I began to be in some pain, how this adventure might terminate; and the reader will easily believe I did not much like my present situation.

The two horses came up close to me, looking with great earnestness upon my face and hands. The grey steed rubbed my hat all round with his right fore-hoof, and discomposed it so much, that I was forced to adjust it better, by taking it off, and settling it again; whereat both he and his companion (who was a brown bay) appeared to be much surprised; the latter felt the lappet[5] of my coat, and finding it to hang loose about me, they both looked with new signs of wonder. He stroked my right hand, seeming to admire the softness, and colour; but he squeezed it so hard between his hoof and his pastern,[6] that I was forced to roar; after which they both touched me with all possible tenderness. They were under great perplexity about my shoes and stockings, which they felt very often, neighing to each other, and using various gestures, not unlike those of a philosopher, when he would attempt to solve some new and difficult phænomenon.

Upon the whole, the behaviour of these animals was so orderly and rational, so acute and judicious, that I at last concluded, they must needs be magicians, who had thus metamorphosed themselves upon some design, and seeing a stranger in the way, were resolved to divert themselves with him; or perhaps were really amazed at the sight of a man so very different in habit, feature, and complexion from those who might probably live in so remote a climate. Upon the strength of this reasoning, I ventured to address them in the following manner: Gentlemen, if you be conjurers, as I have good cause to believe, you can understand any language; therefore I make bold to let your Worships know, that I am a poor distressed English man, driven by his misfortunes upon your coast, and I entreat one of you, to let me ride upon his back, as if he were a real horse, to some house or village, where I can be relieved. In return of which favour, I will make you a present of this knife and bracelet (taking them out of my pocket). The two creatures stood silent while I spoke, seeming to listen with great attention; and when I had ended, they neighed frequently towards each other, as if they were engaged in serious conversation. I plainly observed, that their language expressed the passions very well, and the words might with little pains be resolved into an alphabet more easily than the Chinese.

I could frequently distinguish the word *yahoo*, which was repeated by each of them several times; and although it was impossible for me to conjecture what it meant, yet while the two horses were busy in conversation, I endeavoured to practice this word upon my tongue; and as soon as they were silent, I boldly pronounced *yahoo* in a loud voice, imitating, at the same time, as near as I could, the neighing of a horse; at which they were both visibly surprised, and the grey repeated the same word twice, as if he meant to teach me the right accent, wherein I spoke after him as well as I could, and found myself perceivably to improve every time, although very far from any degree of perfection. Then the bay tried me with a second word, much harder to be pronounced; but reducing it to the English orthography, may be spelt thus, *Houyhnhnm*.[7] I did not succeed in

[5] loose fold.   [6] part of a horse's foot between the fetlock and the hoof.   [7] generally accepted as suggesting the whinny of a horse.

this so well as the former, but after two or three farther trials, I had better fortune; and they both appeared amazed at my capacity.

After some farther discourse, which I then conjectured might relate to me, the two friends took their leaves, with the same compliment of striking each other's hoof; and the grey made me signs that I should walk before him, wherein I thought it prudent to comply, till I could find a better director. When I offered to slacken my pace, he would cry *hhuun, hhuun;* I guessed his meaning, and gave him to understand, as well as I could, that I was weary, and not able to walk faster; upon which he would stand a while to let me rest.

CHAPTER II

THE AUTHOR CONDUCTED BY A HOUYHNHNM TO HIS HOUSE. THE HOUSE DESCRIBED. THE AUTHOR'S RECEPTION. THE FOOD OF THE HOUYHN-HNMS. THE AUTHOR IN DISTRESS FOR WANT OF MEAT, IS AT LAST RE-LIEVED. HIS MANNER OF FEEDING IN THAT COUNTRY.

Having travelled about three miles, we came to a long kind of building, made of timber stuck in the ground, and wattled across; the roof was low, and covered with straw. I now began to be a little comforted, and took out some toys, which travellers usually carry for presents to the savage In-dians of America and other parts, in hopes the people of the house would be thereby encouraged to receive me kindly. The horse made me a sign to go in first; it was a large room with a smooth clay floor, and a rack and manger extending the whole length on one side. There were three nags, and two mares, not eating, but some of them sitting down upon their hams, which I very much wondered at; but wondered more to see the rest em-ployed in domestic business. They seemed but ordinary cattle; however, this confirmed my first opinion, that a people who could so far civilize brute animals must needs excel in wisdom all the nations of the world. The grey came in just after, and thereby prevented any ill treatment which the others might have given me. He neighed to them several times in a style of authority, and received answers.

Beyond this room there were three others, reaching the length of the house, to which you passed through three doors, opposite to each other, in the manner of a vista; we went through the second room towards the third; here the grey walked in first, beckoning me to attend: I waited in the sec-ond room, and got ready my presents for the master and mistress of the house: they were two knives, three bracelets of false pearl, a small looking-glass and a bead necklace. The horse neighed three or four times, and I waited to hear some answers in a human voice, but I heard no other returns than in the same dialect, only one or two a little shriller than his. I began to think that this house must belong to some person of great note among them, because there appeared so much ceremony before I could gain admittance. But that a man of quality should be served all by horses was beyond my comprehension. I feared my brain was disturbed by my sufferings and misfortunes: I roused myself, and looked about me in the room where I was left alone; this was furnished as the first, only after a more elegant manner. I rubbed my eyes often, but the same objects still occurred. I pinched my arms and sides, to awake myself, hoping I might be in a dream. I then absolutely concluded, that all these appearances could be nothing else but necromancy and magic. But I had no time to pursue these reflections; for the grey horse came to the door, and made me a sign to follow him into the third room, where I saw a very comely mare, together with a colt and foal, sitting on their haunches, upon mats of straw, not unartfully made, and perfectly neat and clean.

The mare, soon after my entrance, rose from her mat, and coming up close, after having nicely observed my hands and face, gave me a most contemptuous look; then turning to the horse, I heard the word *yahoo* often repeated betwixt them; the meaning of which word I could not then comprehend, although it were the first I had learned to pronounce; but I was soon better informed, to my everlasting mortification: for the horse beckoning to me with his head, and repeating the word *hhuun, hhuun*, as he did upon the road, which I understood was to attend him, led me out into a kind of court, where was another building at some distance from the house. Here we entered, and I saw three of those detestable creatures, which I first met after my landing, feeding upon roots, and the flesh of some animals, which I afterwards found to be that of asses and dogs, and now and then a cow dead by accident or disease. They were all tied by the neck with strong withes, fastened to a beam; they held their food between the claws of their forefeet, and tore it with their teeth.

The master horse ordered a sorrel nag, one of his servants, to untie the largest of these animals, and take him into the yard. The beast and I were brought close together, and our countenances diligently compared, both by master and servant, who thereupon repeated several times the word *yahoo*. My horror and astonishment are not to be described, when I observed, in this abominable animal, a perfect human figure; the face of it indeed was flat and broad, the nose depressed, the lips large, and the mouth wide. But these differences are common to all savage nations, where the lineaments of the countenance are distorted by the natives suffering their infants to lie grovelling on the earth, or by carrying them on their backs, nuzzling with their face against the mother's shoulders. The forefeet of the yahoo differed from my hands in nothing else but the length of the nails, the coarseness and brownness of the palms, and the hairiness on the backs. There was the same resemblance between our feet, with the same differences, which I knew very well, although the horses did not, because of my shoes and stockings; the same in every part of our bodies, except as to hairiness and colour, which I have already described.

The great difficulty that seemed to stick with the two horses, was to see the rest of my body so very different from that of a yahoo, for which I was obliged to my clothes, whereof they had no conception: the sorrel nag offered me a root, which he held (after their manner, as we shall describe in its proper place) between his hoof and pastern; I took it in my hand, and having smelt it, returned it to him as civilly as I could. He brought out of the yahoo's kennel a piece of ass's flesh, but it smelt so offensively that I turned from it with loathing: he then threw it to the yahoo, by whom it was greedily devoured. He afterwards showed me a wisp of hay, and a fetlock full of oats; but I shook my head, to signify, that neither of these were food for me. And indeed, I now apprehended, that I must absolutely starve, if I did not get to some of my own species: for as to those filthy yahoos, although there were few greater lovers of mankind, at that time, than myself, yet I confess I never saw any sensitive being so detestable on all accounts; and the more I came near them, the more hateful they grew, while I stayed in that country. This the master horse observed by my behaviour, and therefore sent the yahoo back to his kennel. He then put his fore-hoof to his mouth, at which I was much surprised, although he did it with ease, and with a motion that appeared perfectly natural, and made other signs to know what I would eat; but I could not return him such an answer as he was able to apprehend; and if he had understood me, I did not see how it was possible to contrive any way for finding myself nourishment. While we were thus engaged, I observed a cow passing by, whereupon I pointed to her, and expressed a desire to let me go and milk her. This had its effect; for he led me back into the house, and ordered a mare-servant to open a room, where a good store of milk lay in earthen and wooden vessels, after a very orderly and cleanly manner. She gave me a large bowl full, of which I drank very heartily, and found myself well refreshed.

About noon I saw coming towards the house a kind of vehicle drawn like a sledge by four yahoos. There was in it an old steed, who seemed to be of quality; he alighted with his hind feet forward, having by accident got a hurt in his left forefoot. He came to dine with our horse, who received him with great civility. They dined in the best room, and had oats boiled in milk for the second course, which the old horse eat warm, but the rest cold. Their mangers were placed circular in the middle of the room, and divided into several partitions, round which they sat on their haunches upon bosses of straw. In the middle was a large rack with angles answering to every partition of the manger. So that each horse and mare eat their own hay, and their own mash of oats and milk, with much decency and regularity. The behaviour of the young colt and foal appeared very modest, and that of the master and mistress extremely cheerful and complaisant to their guest. The grey ordered me to stand by him, and much discourse passed between him and his friend concerning me, as I found by the stranger's often looking on me, and the frequent repetition of the word *yahoo*.

I happened to wear my gloves, which the master grey observing, seemed perplexed, discovering signs of wonder what I had done to my forefeet; he put his hoof three or four times to them, as if he would signify, that I should reduce them to their former shape, which I presently did, pulling off both my gloves, and putting them into my pocket. This occasioned farther talk, and I saw the company was pleased with my behaviour, whereof I soon found the good effects. I was ordered to speak the few words I understood, and while they were at dinner, the master taught me the names for oats, milk, fire, water, and some others: which I could readily pronounce after him, having from my youth a great facility in learning languages.

When dinner was done, the master horse took me aside, and by signs and words made me understand the concern he was in, that I had nothing to eat. Oats in their tongue are called *hlunnh*. This word I pronounced two or three times; for although I had refused them at first, yet upon second thoughts, I considered that I could contrive to make of them a kind of bread, which might be sufficient with milk to keep me alive, till I could make my escape to some other country, and to creatures of my own species. The horse immediately ordered a white mare-servant of his family to bring me a good quantity of oats in a sort of wooden tray. These I heated before the fire as well as I could, and rubbed them till the husks came off, which I made a shift to winnow from the grain; I ground and beat them between two stones, then took water, and made them into a paste or cake, which I toasted at the fire, and eat warm with milk. It was at first a very insipid diet, although common enough in many parts of Europe, but grew tolerable by time; and having been often reduced to hard fare in my life, this was not the first experiment I had made how easily nature is satisfied. And I cannot but observe, that I never had one hour's sickness, while I stayed in this island. It is true, I sometimes made a shift to catch a rabbit, or bird, by springes[8] made of yahoos' hairs, and I often gathered wholesome herbs, which I boiled, or eat as salads with my bread, and now and then, for a rarity, I made a little butter, and drank the whey. I was at first at a great loss for salt; but custom soon reconciled the want of it; and I am confident that the frequent use of salt among us is an effect of luxury,

[8] snares.

and was first introduced only as a provocative to drink; except where it is necessary for preserving of flesh in long voyages, or in places remote from great markets. For we observe no animal to be fond of it but man: and as to myself, when I left this country, it was a great while before I could endure the taste of it in anything that I eat.

This is enough to say upon the subject of my diet, wherewith other travellers fill their books, as if the readers were personally concerned whether we fared well or ill. However, it was necessary to mention this matter, lest the world should think it impossible that I could find sustenance for three years in such a country, and among such inhabitants.

When it grew towards evening, the master horse ordered a place for me to lodge in; it was but six yards from the house, and separated from the stable of the yahoos. Here I got some straw, and covering myself with my own clothes, slept very sound. But I was in a short time better accommodated, as the reader shall know hereafter, when I come to treat more particularly about my way of living.

CHAPTER III

THE AUTHOR STUDIOUS TO LEARN THE LANGUAGE, THE HOUYHNHNM HIS MASTER ASSISTS IN TEACHING HIM. THE LANGUAGE DESCRIBED. SEVERAL HOUYHNHNMS OF QUALITY COME OUT OF CURIOSITY TO SEE THE AUTHOR. HE GIVES HIS MASTER A SHORT ACCOUNT OF HIS VOYAGE.

My principal endeavour was to learn the language, which my master (for so I shall henceforth call him) and his children, and every servant of his house were desirous to teach me. For they looked upon it as a prodigy that a brute animal should discover such marks of a rational creature. I pointed to every thing, and enquired the name of it, which I wrote down in my journal-book when I was alone, and corrected my bad accent, by desiring those of the family to pronounce it often. In this employment, a sorrel nag, one of the under servants, was very ready to assist me.

In speaking, they pronounce through the nose and throat, and their language approaches nearest to the High Dutch or German, of any I know in Europe; but is much more graceful and significant. The Emperor Charles V made almost the same observation, when he said, that if he were to speak to his horse, it should be in High Dutch.[9]

The curiosity and impatience of my master were so great, that he spent

[9] that is, German.

many hours of his leisure to instruct me. He was convinced (as he afterwards told me) that I must be a yahoo, but my teachableness, civility and cleanliness astonished him; which were qualities altogether so opposite to those animals. He was most perplexed about my clothes, reasoning sometimes with himself, whether they were a part of my body; for I never pulled them off till the family were asleep, and got them on before they waked in the morning. My master was eager to learn from whence I came, how I acquired those appearances of reason which I discovered in all my actions, and to know my story from my own mouth, which he hoped he should soon do by the great proficiency I made in learning and pronouncing their words and sentences. To help my memory, I formed all I learned into the English alphabet, and writ the words down with the translations. This last, after some time, I ventured to do in my master's presence. It cost me much trouble to explain to him what I was doing; for the inhabitants have not the least idea of books or literature.

In about ten weeks time I was able to understand most of his questions, and in three months could give him some tolerable answers. He was extremely curious to know from what part of the country I came, and how I was taught to imitate a rational creature, because the yahoos (whom he saw I exactly resembled in my head, hands and face, that were only visible), with some appearance of cunning, and the strongest disposition to mischief, were observed to be the most unteachable of all brutes. I answered, that I came over the sea, from a far place, with many others of my own kind, in a great hollow vessel made of the bodies of trees. That my companions forced me to land on this coast, and then left me to shift for myself. It was with some difficulty, and by the help of many signs, that I brought him to understand me. He replied, that I must needs be mistaken, or that I 'said the thing which was not.' (For they have no words in their languages to express lying or falsehood.) He knew it was impossible that there could be a country beyond the sea, or that a parcel of brutes could move a wooden vessel whither they pleased upon water. He was sure no Houyhnhnm alive could make such a vessel, or would trust yahoos to manage it.

The word *Houyhnhnm*, in their tongue, signifies a *horse*, and in its etymology, *the perfection of nature*. I told my master, that I was at a loss for expression, but would improve as fast as I could; and hoped in a short time I should be able to tell him wonders: he was pleased to direct his own mare, his colt and foal, and the servants of the family to take all opportunities of instructing me, and every day for two or three hours he was at the same pains himself: several horses and mares of quality in the neighbourhood came often to our house upon the report spread of a wonderful yahoo, that could speak like a Houyhnhnm, and seemed in his words and actions to discover some glimmerings of reason. These delighted to converse with me; they put many questions, and received such answers as I was able to return. By all which advantages, I made so great a progress, that in five months from my arrival I understood whatever was spoke, and could express myself tolerably well.

The Houyhnhnms who came to visit my master, out of a design of seeing and talking with me, could hardly believe me to be a right[10] yahoo, because my body had a different covering from others of my kind. They were astonished to observe me without the usual hair or skin except on my head, face, and hands; but I discovered that secret to my master, upon an accident, which happened about a fortnight before.

I have already told the reader, that every night, when the family were gone to bed, it was my custom to strip and cover myself with my clothes: it happened one morning early, that my master sent for me, by the sorrel nag, who was his valet; when he came, I was fast asleep, my clothes fallen off on one side, and my shirt above my waist. I awaked at the noise he made, and observed him to deliver his message in some disorder; after which he went to my master, and in a great fright gave him a very confused account of what he had seen: this I presently discovered; for going, as soon as I was dressed, to pay my attendance upon his Honour, he asked me the meaning of what his servant had reported, that I was not the same thing when I slept as I appeared to be at other times; that his valet assured him, some part of me was white, some yellow, at least not so white, and some brown.

I had hitherto concealed the secret of my dress, in order to distinguish myself as much as possible from that cursed race of yahoos; but now I found it in vain to do so any longer. Besides, I considered that my clothes and shoes would soon wear out, which already were in a declining condition, and must be supplied by some contrivance from the hides of yahoos or other brutes; whereby the whole secret would be known: I therefore told my master, that in the country from whence I came those of my kind always covered their bodies with the hairs of certain animals prepared by art, as well for decency, as to avoid inclemencies of air both hot and cold; of which, as to my own person, I would give him immediate conviction, if he pleased to command me; only desiring his excuse, if I did not expose those parts that nature taught us to conceal. He said my discourse was all very strange, but especially the last part; for he could not understand why nature should teach us to conceal what nature had given. That neither himself nor family were ashamed of any parts of their bodies; but however I might do as I pleased. Whereupon, I first unbuttoned my coat, and pulled it off. I did the same with my waistcoat; I drew off my shoes, stock-

[10] true.

ings, and breeches. I let my shirt down to my waist, and drew up the bottom, fastening it like a girdle about my middle to hide my nakedness.

My master observed the whole performance with great signs of curiosity and admiration. He took up all my clothes in his pastern, one piece after another, and examined them diligently; he then stroked my body very gently and looked round me several times, after which he said, it was plain I must be a perfect yahoo; but that I differed very much from the rest of my species, in the whiteness and smoothness of my skin, my want of hair in several parts of my body, the shape and shortness of my claws behind and before, and my affectation of walking continually on my two hinder feet. He desired to see no more, and gave me leave to put on my clothes again, for I was shuddering with cold.

I expressed my uneasiness at his giving me so often the appellation of *yahoo,* an odious animal, for which I had so utter an hatred and contempt; I begged he would forbear applying that word to me, and take the same order in his family, and among his friends whom he suffered to see me. I requested likewise, that the secret of my having a false covering to my body might be known to none but himself, at least as long as my present clothing should last; for as to what the sorrel nag his valet had observed, his Honour might command him to conceal it.

All this my master very graciously consented to, and thus the secret was kept till my clothes began to wear out, which I was forced to supply by several contrivances, that shall hereafter be mentioned. In the mean time, he desired I would go on with my utmost diligence to learn their language, because he was more astonished at my capacity for speech and reason than at the figure of my body, whether it were covered or no; adding, that he waited with some impatience to hear the wonders which I promised to tell him.

From thenceforward he doubled the pains he had been at to instruct me; he brought me into all company, and made them treat me with civility, because, as he told them privately, this would put me into good humour, and make me more diverting.

Every day when I waited on him, beside the trouble he was at in teaching, he would ask me several questions concerning myself, which I answered as well as I could; and by those means he had already received some general ideas, although very imperfect. It would be tedious to relate the several steps by which I advanced to a more regular conversation: but the first account I gave of myself in any order and length, was to this purpose:

That I came from a very far country, as I already had attempted to tell him, with about fifty more of my own species; that we travelled upon the seas, in a great hollow vessel made of wood, and larger than his Honour's house. I described the ship to him in the best terms I could, and explained by the help of my handkerchief displayed, how it was driven forward by the wind. That upon a quarrel among us, I was set on shore on this coast, where I walked forward without knowing whither, till he delivered me from the persecution of those execrable yahoos. He asked me, who made the ship, and how it was possible that the Houyhnhnms of my country would leave it to the management of brutes? My answer was, that I durst proceed no farther in my relation, unless he would give me his word and honour that he would not be offended, and then I would tell him the wonders I had so often promised. He agreed; and I went on by assuring him, that the ship was made by creatures like myself, who in all the countries I had travelled, as well as in my own, were the only governing, rational animals; and that upon my arrival hither, I was as much astonished to see the Houyhnhnms act like rational beings, as he or his friends could be in finding some marks of reason in a creature he was pleased to call a yahoo, to which I owned my resemblance in every part, but could not account for their degenerate and brutal nature. I said farther, that if good fortune ever restored me to my native country, to relate my travels hither, as I resolved to do, every body would believe that I 'said the thing which was not'; that I invented the story out of my own head; and with all possible respect to himself, his family and friends, and under his promise of not being offended, our countrymen would hardly think it probable, that a Houyhnhnm should be the presiding creature of a nation, and a yahoo the brute.

CHAPTER IV

THE HOUYHNHNMS' NOTION OF TRUTH AND FALSEHOOD. THE AU-
THOR'S DISCOURSE DISAPPROVED BY HIS MASTER. THE AUTHOR GIVES
A MORE PARTICULAR ACCOUNT OF HIMSELF, AND THE ACCIDENTS OF
HIS VOYAGE.

My master heard me with great appearances of uneasiness in his countenance, because *doubting* or *not believing,* are so little known in this country, that the inhabitants cannot tell how to behave themselves under such circumstances. And I remember in frequent discourses with my master concerning the nature of manhood, in other parts of the world, having occasion to talk of *lying* and *false representation,* it was with much difficulty that he comprehended what I meant, although he had otherwise a most acute judgment. For he argued thus; that the use of speech was to make us understand one another, and to receive information of facts; now if any one *said the thing which was not,* these ends were defeated; because I cannot properly be said to understand him, and I am so far from receiving information, that he leaves me worse than in ignorance, for I am led to believe a thing black when it is white, and short when it is long. And these were all the notions he had concerning that faculty of lying, so perfectly well understood, and so universally practised among human creatures.

To return from this digression; when I asserted that the yahoos were the only governing animals in my country, which my master said was altogether past his conception, he desired to know, whether we had Houyhnhnms among us, and what was their employment: I told him, we had great numbers, that in summer they grazed in the fields, and in winter were kept in houses, with hay and oats, where yahoo servants were employed to rub their skins smooth, comb their manes, pick their feet, serve them with food, and make their beds. I understand you well, said my master, it is now very plain, from all you have spoken, that whatever share of reason the yahoos pretend to, the Houyhnhnms are your masters; I heartily wish our yahoos would be so tractable. I begged his Honour would please to excuse me from proceeding any farther, because I was very certain that the account he expected from me would be highly displeasing. But he insisted in commanding me to let him know the best and the worst: I told him, he should be obeyed. I owned, that the Houyhnhnms among us, whom we called horses, were the most generous and comely animal we had, that they excelled in strength and swiftness; and when they belonged to persons of quality, employed in travelling, racing, and drawing chariots, they were treated with much kindness and care, till they fell into diseases, or became foundered in the feet; but then they were sold, and used to all kind of drudgery till they died; after which their skins were stripped and sold for what they were worth, and their bodies left to be devoured by dogs and birds of prey. But the common race of horses had not so good fortune, being kept by farmers and carriers and other mean people, who put them to greater labour, and feed them worse. I described, as well as I could, our way of riding, the shape and use of a bridle, a saddle, a spur, and a whip, of harness and wheels. I added, that we fastened plates of a certain hard substance called 'iron' at the bottom of their feet, to preserve their hoofs from being broken by the stony ways on which we often travelled.

My master, after some expressions of great indignation, wondered how we dared to venture upon a Houyhnhnm's back, for he was sure that the weakest servant in his house would be able to shake off the strongest yahoo, or by lying down, and rolling upon his back, squeeze the brute to death. I answered, that our horses were trained up from three or four years old to the several uses we intended them for; that if any of them proved intolerably vicious, they were employed for carriages; that they were severely beaten while they were young, for any mischievous tricks; that the males, designed for the common use of riding or draught, were generally castrated about two years after their birth, to take down their spirits, and make them more tame and gentle; that they were indeed sensible of rewards and punishments; but his Honour would please to consider, that they had not the least tincture of reason any more than the yahoos in this country.

It put me to the pains of many circumlocutions to give my master a right idea of what I spoke; for their language doth not abound in variety of words, because their wants and passions are fewer than among us. But it is impossible to express his noble resentment at our savage treatment of the Houyhnhnm race, particularly after I had explained the manner and use of castrating horses among us, to hinder them from propagating their kind, and to render them more servile. He said, if it were possible there could be any country where yahoos alone were endued with reason, they certainly must be the governing animal, because reason will in time always prevail against brutal strength. But, considering the frame of our bodies, and especially of mine, he thought no creature of equal bulk was so ill contrived for employing that reason in the common offices of life; whereupon he desired to know whether those among whom I lived resembled me or the yahoos of his country. I assured him, that I was as well shaped as most of my age: but the younger and the females were much more soft and tender, and the skins of the latter generally as white as milk. He said, I differed indeed from other yahoos, being much more cleanly, and not altogether so deformed, but in point of real advantage he thought I differed for the worse. That my nails were of no use either to my fore or hinder feet; as to my forefeet, he could not properly call them by that name, for he never observed me to walk upon them; that they were too soft to bear the ground; that I generally went with them uncovered, neither was the covering I sometimes wore on them of the same shape or so strong as that on my feet behind. That I could not walk with any security, for if either of my hinder feet slipped, I must inevitably fall. He then began to find fault with other parts of my body, the flatness of my face, the prominence of my nose, my eyes placed directly in front, so that I could not look on either side without turning my head: that I was not able to feed myself without lifting one of my forefeet to my mouth: and therefore nature had placed those joints to answer that necessity. He knew not what could be the use of those several clefts and divisions in my feet behind; that these were too soft to bear the hardness and sharpness of stones without a covering made from the skin of some other brute; that my whole body wanted a fence against heat and cold, which I was forced to put on and off every day with tediousness and trouble. And lastly, that he observed every animal in this country naturally to abhor the yahoos, whom the weaker avoided, and the stronger drove from them. So that supposing us to have the gift of reason, he could not see how it were possible to cure that natural antipathy which every creature discovered against us; nor consequently, how we could tame and render them serviceable. However, he would (as he said) debate the matter no farther, because he was more desirous to know my own story, the country where I was born, and the several actions and events of my life before I came hither.

I assured him how extremely desirous I was that he should be satisfied in every point; but I doubted much, whether it would be possible for me to explain myself on several subjects whereof his Honour could have no conception, because I saw nothing in his country to which I could resemble them. That however, I would do my best, and strive to express myself by similitudes, humbly desiring his assistance when I wanted proper words; which he was pleased to promise me.

I said, my birth was of honest parents, in an island called England, which was remote from this country as many days' journey as the strongest of his Honour's servants could travel in the annual course of the sun. That I was bred a surgeon, whose trade is to cure wounds and hurts in the body, got by accident or violence; that my country was governed by a female man, whom we called *queen*. That I left it to get riches, whereby I might maintain myself and family when I should return. That in my last voyage I was commander of the ship, and had about fifty yahoos under me, many of which died at sea, and I was forced to supply them by others picked out from several nations. That our ship was twice in danger of being sunk; the first time by a great storm, and the second, by striking against a rock. Here my master interposed, by asking me, how I could persuade strangers out of different countries to venture with me, after the losses I had sustained, and the hazards I had run. I said, they were fellows of desperate fortunes, forced to fly from the places of their birth, on account of their poverty or their crimes. Some were undone by lawsuits; others spent all they had in drinking, whoring, and gaming; others fled for treason; many for murder, theft, poisoning, robbery, perjury, forgery, coining false money, for committing rapes or sodomy, for flying from their colours, or deserting to the enemy, and most of them had broken prison; none of these durst return to their native countries for fear of being hanged, or of starving in a jail; and therefore were under a necessity of seeking a livelihood in other places.

During this discourse, my master was pleased often to interrupt me; I had made use of many circumlocutions in describing to him the nature of the several crimes, for which most of our crew had been forced to fly their country. This labour took up several days' conversation before he was able to comprehend me. He was wholly at a loss to know what could be the use or necessity of practising those vices. To clear up which I endeavoured to give him some ideas of the desire of power and riches, of the terrible effects of lust, intemperance, malice and envy. All this I was forced to define and describe by putting of cases, and making suppositions. After which, like one whose imagination was struck with something never seen or heard of before, he would lift up his eyes with amazement and indignation. Power, government, war, law, punishment, and a thousand other things had no terms wherein that language could express them, which made the difficulty almost insuperable to give my master any conception of what I meant. But being of an excellent understanding, much improved by contemplation and converse, he at last arrived at a competent knowledge of what human nature in our parts of the world is capable to perform, and desired I would give him some particular account of that land which we call Europe, especially of my own country.

In Chapters V to VII Gulliver describes the laws and institutions of England to his master. The result, although Gulliver admits he has painted the best picture that honesty allowed, is that he (along with the reader) is convinced more than ever of the depravity of mankind.

CHAPTER VIII

THE AUTHOR RELATES SEVERAL PARTICULARS OF THE YAHOOS. THE GREAT VIRTUES OF THE HOUYHNHNMS. THE EDUCATION AND EXERCISE OF THEIR YOUTH. THEIR GENERAL ASSEMBLY.

As I ought to have understood human nature much better than I supposed it possible for my master to do, so it was easy to apply the character he gave of the yahoos to myself and my countrymen, and I believed I could yet make farther discoveries from my own observation. I therefore often begged his Honour to let me go among the herds of yahoos in the neighbourhood, to which he always very graciously consented, being perfectly convinced that the hatred I bore those brutes would never suffer me to be corrupted by them; and his Honour ordered one of his servants, a strong sorrel nag, very honest and good-natured, to be my guard, without whose protection I durst not undertake such adventures. For I have already told the reader how much I was pestered by those odious animals upon my first arrival. And I afterwards failed very narrowly three or four times of falling into their clutches, when I happened to stray at any distance without my hanger. And I have reason to believe they had some imagination that I was of their own species, which I often assisted myself, by stripping up my sleeves, and showing my naked arms and breast in their sight, when my protector was with me. At which times they would approach as near as they durst, and imitate my actions after the manner of monkeys, but ever with great signs of hatred, as a tame jackdaw, with cap and stockings, is always persecuted by the wild ones, when he happens to be got among them.

They are prodigiously nimble from their infancy; however, I once caught a young male of three years old, and endeavoured by all marks of tenderness to make it quiet; but the little imp fell a squalling, and scratching, and biting with such violence, that I was forced to let it go, and it was high time, for a whole troop of old ones came about us at the noise, but finding the cub was safe (for away it ran), and my sorrel nag being by, they durst not venture near us. I observed the young animal's flesh to smell very rank, and the stink was somewhat between a weasel and a fox, but much more disagreeable. I forgot another circumstance (and perhaps I might have the reader's pardon if it were wholly omitted) that while I held the odious vermin in my hands, it voided its filthy excrements of a yellow liquid substance all over my clothes; but by good fortune there was a small brook hard by, where I washed myself as clean as I could, although I durst not come into my master's presence, until I were sufficiently aired.

By what I could discover, the yahoos appear to be the most unteachable of all animals, their capacities never reaching higher than to draw or carry burthens. Yet I am of opinion this defect ariseth chiefly from a perverse, restive disposition. For they are cunning, malicious, treacherous and revengeful. They are strong and hardy, but of a cowardly spirit, and by consequence insolent, abject, and cruel. It is observed, that the redhaired of both sexes are more libidinous and mischievous than the rest, whom yet they much exceed in strength and activity.

The Houyhnhnms keep the yahoos for present use in huts not far from the house; but the rest are sent abroad to certain fields, where they dig up roots, eat several kinds of herbs, and search about for carrion, or sometimes catch weasels and *luhimuhs* (a sort of wild rat), which they greedily devour. Nature hath taught them to dig deep holes with their nails on the side of a rising ground, wherein they lie by themselves, only the kennels of the females are larger, sufficient to hold two or three cubs.

They swim from their infancy like frogs, and are able to continue long under water, where they often take fish, which the females carry home to their young. And upon this occasion, I hope the reader will pardon my relating an odd adventure.

Being one day abroad with my protector the sorrel nag, and the weather exceeding hot, I entreated him to let me bathe in a river that was near. He consented, and I immediately stripped myself stark naked, and went down softly into the stream. It happened that a young female yahoo, standing behind a bank, saw the whole proceeding, and inflamed by desire, as the nag and I conjectured, came running with all speed, and leaped into the water within five yards of the place where I bathed. I was never in my life so terribly frighted; the nag was grazing at some distance, not suspecting any harm. She embraced me after a most fulsome manner; I roared as loud as I could, and the nag came galloping towards me, whereupon she quitted her grasp, with the utmost reluctancy, and leaped upon the opposite bank, where she stood gazing and howling all the time I was putting on my clothes.

This was matter of diversion to my master and his family, as well as of mortification to myself. For now I could no longer deny that I was a real yahoo in every limb and feature, since the females had a natural propensity to me as one of their own species: neither was the hair of this brute of a red colour (which might have been some excuse for an appetite a little irregular) but black as a sloe, and her countenance did not make an appearance altogether so hideous as the rest of the kind; for, I think, she could not be above eleven years old.

Having already lived three years in this country, the reader I suppose will expect that I should, like other travellers, give him some account of the manners and customs of its inhabitants, which it was indeed my principal study to learn.

As these noble Houyhnhnms are endowed by nature with a general disposition to all virtues, and have no conceptions or ideas of what is evil in a rational creature, so their grand maxim is, to cultivate reason, and to be wholly governed by it. Neither is reason among them a point problematical as with us, where men can argue with plausibility on both sides of a question; but strikes you with immediate conviction; as it must needs do where it is not mingled, obscured, or discoloured by passion and interest. I remember it was with extreme difficulty that I could bring my master to understand the meaning of the word *opinion,* or how a point could be disputable; because reason taught us to affirm or deny only where we are certain; and beyond our knowledge we cannot do either. So that controversies, wranglings, disputes, and positiveness in false or dubious propositions are evils unknown among the Houyhnhnms. In the like manner, when I used to explain to him our several systems of natural philosophy, he would laugh that a creature pretending to reason should value itself upon the knowledge of other people's conjectures, and in things where that knowledge, if it were certain, could be of no use. Wherein he agreed entirely with the sentiments of Socrates, as Plato delivers them;[11] which I mention as the highest honour I can do that prince of philosophers. I have often since reflected what destruction such a doctrine would make in the libraries of Europe, and how many paths to fame would be then shut up in the learned world.

Friendship and benevolence are the two principal virtues among the Houyhnhnms, and these not confined to particular objects, but universal to the whole race. For a stranger from the remotest part is equally treated with the nearest neighbour, and wherever he goes, looks upon himself as at home. They preserve decency and civility in the highest degrees, but are

[11] allusion, possibly, to *The Republic* (Bk. V), where *opinion* is distinguished from *real knowledge.*

altogether ignorant of ceremony. They have no fondness[12] for their colts or foals, but the care they take in educating them proceeds entirely from the dictates of reason. And I observed my master to show the same affection to his neighbour's issue that he had for his own. They will have it that nature teaches them to love the whole species, and it is reason only that maketh a distinction of persons, where there is a superior degree of virtue.

When the matron Houyhnhnms have produced one of each sex, they no longer accompany with their consorts, except they lose one of their issue by some casualty, which very seldom happens: but in such a case they meet again, or when the like accident befalls a person whose wife is past bearing, some other couple bestows on him one of their own colts, and then go together a second time till the mother be pregnant. This caution is necessary to prevent the country from being overburthened with numbers. But the race of inferior Houyhnhnms bred up to be servants is not so strictly limited upon this article; these are allowed to produce three of each sex, to be domestics in the noble families.

In their marriages they are exactly careful to choose such colours as will not make any disagreeable mixture in the breed. Strength is chiefly valued in the male, and comeliness in the female, not upon the account of love, but to preserve the race from degenerating; for where a female happens to excel in strength, a consort is chosen with regard to comeliness. Courtship, love, presents, jointures, settlements, have no place in their thoughts, or terms whereby to express them in their language. The young couple meet and are joined, merely because it is the determination of their parents and friends: it is what they see done every day, and they look upon it as one of the necessary actions in a reasonable being. But the violation of marriage, or any other unchastity, was never heard of: and the married pair pass their lives with the same friendship and mutual benevolence that they bear to all others of the same species who come in their way; without jealousy, fondness,[13] quarrelling, or discontent.

In educating the youth of both sexes, their method is admirable, and highly deserves our imitation. These are not suffered to taste a grain of oats, except upon certain days, till eighteen years old; nor milk, but very rarely; and in summer they graze two hours in the morning, and as many in the evening, which their parents likewise observe, but the servants are not allowed above half that time, and a great part of the grass is brought home, which they eat at the most convenient hours, when they can be best spared from work.

Temperance, industry, exercise and cleanliness, are the lessons equally enjoined to the young ones of both sexes: and my master thought it monstrous in us to give the females a different kind of education from the males,

---

[12] foolish sentimental attachment.   [13] foolishness.

except in some articles of domestic management; whereby, as he truly observed, one half of our natives were good for nothing but bringing children into the world: and to trust the care of their children to such useless animals, he said, was yet a greater instance of brutality.

But the Houyhnhnms train up their youth to strength, speed, and hardiness, by exercising them in running races up and down steep hills, or over hard stony grounds, and when they are all in a sweat, they are ordered to leap over head and ears into a pond or a river. Four times a year the youth of certain districts meet to show their proficiency in running and leaping, and other feats of strength or agility, where the victor is rewarded with a song made in his or her praise. On this festival the servants drive a herd of yahoos into the field, laden with hay, and oats, and milk for a repast to the Houyhnhnms; after which these brutes are immediately driven back again, for fear of being noisome to the assembly.

Every fourth year, at the vernal equinox, there is a representative council of the whole nation, which meets in a plain about twenty miles from our house, and continues about five or six days. Here they inquire into the state and condition of the several districts; whether they abound or be deficient in hay or oats, or cows or yahoos. And wherever there is any want (which is but seldom) it is immediately supplied by unanimous consent and contribution. Here likewise the regulation of children is settled: as for instance, if a Houyhnhnm hath two males, he changeth one of them with another who hath two females: and when a child hath been lost by any casualty, where the mother is past breeding, it is determined what family in the district shall breed another to supply the loss.

CHAPTER IX

A GRAND DEBATE AT THE GENERAL ASSEMBLY OF THE HOUYHNHNMS,
AND HOW IT WAS DETERMINED. THE LEARNING OF THE HOUYHNHNMS.
THEIR BUILDINGS. THEIR MANNER OF BURIALS. THE DEFECTIVENESS
OF THEIR LANGUAGE.

One of these grand assemblies was held in my time, about three months before my departure, whither my master went as the representative of our district. In this council was resumed their old debate, and indeed, the only debate that ever happened in their country; whereof my master after his return gave me a very particular account.

The question to be debated was, whether the yahoos should be exterminated from the face of the earth. One of the members for the affirmative offered several arguments of great strength and weight, alleging, that as the yahoos were the most filthy, noisome, and deformed animal which nature ever produced, so they were the most restive and indocible, mischievous and malicious: they would privately suck the teats of the Houyhnhnms' cows, kill and devour their cats, trample down their oats and grass, if they were not continually watched, and commit a thousand other extravagancies. He took notice of a general tradition, that yahoos had not been always in their country: but that many ages ago two of these brutes appeared together upon a mountain, whether produced by the heat of the sun upon corrupted mud and slime, or from the ooze and froth of the sea, was never known. That these yahoos engendered, and their brood in a short time grew so numerous as to overrun and infest the whole nation. That the Houyhnhnms, to get rid of this evil, made a general hunting, and at last enclosed the whole herd; and destroying the older, every Houyhnhnm kept two young ones in a kennel, and brought them to such a degree of tameness, as an animal so savage by nature can be capable of acquiring; using them for draught and carriage. That there seemed to be much truth in this tradition, and that those creatures could not be *ylnhniamshy* (or *aborigines* of the land) because of the violent hatred the Houyhnhnms, as well as all other animals, bore them; which although their evil disposition sufficiently deserved, could never have arrived at so high a degree, if they had been aborigines, or else they would have long since been rooted out. That the inhabitants taking a fancy to use the service of the yahoos, had very imprudently neglected to cultivate the breed of asses, which were a comely animal, easily kept, more tame and orderly, without any offensive smell, strong enough for labour, although they yield to the other in agility of body; and if their braying be no agreeable sound, it is far preferable to the horrible howlings of the yahoos.

Several others declared their sentiments to the same purpose, when my master proposed an expedient to the assembly, whereof he had indeed borrowed the hint from me. He approved of the tradition, mentioned by the 'honourable member' who spoke before, and affirmed, that the two yahoos said to be first seen among them had been driven thither over the sea; that coming to land, and being forsaken by their companions, they retired to the mountains, and degenerating by degrees, became in process of time much more savage than those of their own species in the country from whence these two originals came. The reason of his assertion was, that he had now in his possession a certain wonderful yahoo (meaning myself) which most of them had heard of, and many of them had seen. He then related to them how he first found me; that my body was all covered with an artificial composure of the skins and hairs of other animals: that I spoke in a language of my own, and had thoroughly learned theirs: that I had related to him the accidents which brought me thither: that when he saw me without my covering, I was an exact yahoo in every part, only of a whiter colour, less hairy, and with shorter claws. He added, how I had endeavoured to persuade him, that in my own and other countries the yahoos acted as the governing, rational animal, and held the Houyhnhnms in servitude: that he observed in me all the qualities of a yahoo, only a little more civilized by some tincture of reason, which however was in a degree as far inferior to the Houyhnhnm race as the yahoos of their country were to me: that, among other things, I mentioned a custom we had of castrating Houyhnhnms when they were young, in order to render them tame; that the operation was easy and safe; that it was no shame to learn wisdom from brutes, as industry is taught by the ant, and building by the swallow. (For so I translate the word *lyhannh*, although it be a much larger fowl.) That this invention might be practised upon the younger yahoos here, which, besides rendering them tractable and fitter for use, would in an age put an end to the whole species without destroying life. That in the mean time the Houyhnhnms should be exhorted to cultivate the breed of asses, which, as they are in all respects more valuable brutes, so they have this advantage, to be fit for service at five years old, which the others are not till twelve.

This was all my master thought fit to tell me at that time of what passed in the grand council. But he was pleased to conceal one particular, which related personally to myself, whereof I soon felt the unhappy effect, as the reader will know in its proper place, and from whence I date all the succeeding misfortunes of my life.

The Houyhnhnms have no letters, and consequently their knowledge is all traditional. But there happening few events of any moment among a people so well united, naturally disposed to every virtue, wholly governed by reason, and cut off from all commerce with other nations, the historical part is easily preserved without burthening their memories. I have already observed, that they are subject to no diseases, and therefore can have no need of physicians. However, they have excellent medicines composed of herbs, to cure accidental bruises and cuts in the pastern or frog[14] of the foot by sharp stones, as well as other maims and hurts in the several parts of the body.

They calculate the year by the revolution of the sun and the moon, but use no subdivisions into weeks. They are well enough acquainted with the motions of those two luminaries, and understand the nature of eclipses; and this is the utmost progress of their astronomy.

In poetry they must be allowed to excel all other mortals; wherein the justness of their similes, and the minuteness, as well as exactness of their descriptions, are indeed inimitable. Their verses abound very much in both of these, and usually contain either some exalted notions of friendship and benevolence, or the praises of those who were victors in races and other

[14] horny pad in the middle of the sole of a horse's foot.

bodily exercises. Their buildings, although very rude and simple, are not inconvenient, but well contrived to defend them from all injuries of cold and heat. They have a kind of tree, which at forty years old loosens in the root, and falls with the first storm; it grows very straight, and being pointed like stakes with a sharp stone (for the Houyhnhnms know not the use of iron), they stick them erect in the ground about ten inches asunder, and then weave in oat-straw, or sometimes wattles betwixt them. The roof is made after the same manner, and so are the doors.

The Houyhnhnms use the hollow part between the pastern and the hoof of their forefeet as we do our hands, and this with greater dexterity than I could at first imagine. I have seen a white mare of our family thread a needle (which I lent her on purpose) with that joint. They milk their cows, reap their oats, and do all the work which requires hands, in the same manner. They have a kind of hard flints, which, by grinding against other stones, they form into instruments, that serve instead of wedges, axes, and hammers. With tools made of these flints they likewise cut their hay, and reap their oats, which there groweth naturally in several fields: the yahoos draw home the sheaves in carriages, and the servants tread them in certain covered huts, to get out the grain, which is kept in stores. They make a rude kind of earthen and wooden vessels, and bake the former in the sun.

If they can avoid casualties, they die only of old age, and are buried in the obscurest places that can be found, their friends and relations expressing neither joy nor grief at their departure; nor does the dying person discover the least regret that he is leaving the world, any more than if he were upon returning home from a visit to one of his neighbours; I remember my master having once made an appointment with a friend and his family to come to his house upon some affair of importance; on the day fixed, the mistress and her two children came very late; she made two excuses, first for her husband, who, as she said, happened that very morning to *lhnuwnh*. The word is strongly expressive in their language, but not easily rendered into English; it signifies, 'to retire to his first mother'. Her excuse for not coming sooner was, that her husband dying late in the morning, she was a good while consulting her servants about a convenient place where his body should be laid; and I observed she behaved herself at our house as cheerfully as the rest: she died about three months after.

They live generally to seventy or seventy-five years, very seldom to four-score: some weeks before their death they feel a gradual decay, but without pain. During this time they are much visited by their friends, because they cannot go abroad with their usual ease and satisfaction. However, about ten days before their death, which they seldom fail in computing, they return the visits that have been made them by those who are nearest in the neighbourhood, being carried in a convenient sledge drawn by yahoos, which vehicle they use, not only upon this occasion, but when they grow old, upon long journeys, or when they are lamed by any accident. And therefore when the dying Houyhnhnms return those visits, they take a solemn leave of their friends, as if they were going to some remote part of the country, where they designed to pass the rest of their lives.

I know not whether it may be worth observing, that the Houyhnhnms have no word in their language to express any thing that is evil, except what they borrow from the deformities or ill qualities of the yahoos. Thus they denote the folly of a servant, an omission of a child, a stone that cuts their feet, a continuance of foul or unseasonable weather, and the like, by adding to each the epithet of *yahoo*. For instance, *hhnm yahoo, whnaholm yahoo, ynlhnmawihlma yahoo,* and an ill-contrived house *ynholmhnmrohlnw yahoo.*

I could with great pleasure enlarge farther upon the manners and virtues of this excellent people; but intending in a short time to publish a volume by itself expressly upon that subject, I refer the reader thither. And in the mean time, proceed to relate my own sad catastrophe.

CHAPTER X

THE AUTHOR'S ŒCONOMY AND HAPPY LIFE AMONG THE HOUYHNHNMS. HIS GREAT IMPROVEMENT IN VIRTUE, BY CONVERSING WITH THEM. THEIR CONVERSATIONS. THE AUTHOR HAS NOTICE GIVEN HIM BY HIS MASTER THAT HE MUST DEPART FROM THE COUNTRY. HE FALLS INTO A SWOON FOR GRIEF, BUT SUBMITS. HE CONTRIVES AND FINISHES A CANOE, BY THE HELP OF A FELLOW-SERVANT, AND PUTS TO SEA AT A VENTURE.

I had settled my little œconomy to my own heart's content. My master had ordered a room to be made for me after their manner, about six yards from the house, the sides and floors of which I plastered with clay, and covered with rush mats of my own contriving; I had beaten hemp, which there grows wild, and made of it a sort of ticking: this I filled with the feathers of several birds I had taken with springes made of yahoos' hairs, and were excellent food. I had worked two chairs with my knife, the sorrel nag helping me in the grosser and more laborious part. When my clothes were worn to rags, I made myself others with the skins of rabbits, and of a certain beautiful animal about the same size, called *nnuhnoh*, the skin of which is covered with a fine down. Of these I likewise made very tolerable stockings. I soled my shoes with wood which I cut from a tree, and fitted to the upper leather, and when this was worn out, I supplied it with the skins of yahoos dried in the sun. I often got honey out of hollow trees, which I mingled with water, or eat it with my bread. No man could more verify the truth of these two maxims, *That nature is very easily satisfied;* and *That necessity is the mother of invention.* I enjoyed perfect health of body and tranquillity of mind; I did not feel the treachery or inconstancy of a friend, nor the injuries of a secret or open enemy. I had no occasion of bribing, flattering or pimping to procure the favour of any great man or of his minion. I wanted no fence against fraud or oppression; here was neither physician to destroy my body, nor lawyer to ruin my fortune; no informer to watch my words and actions, or forge accusations against me for hire: here were no gibers, censurers, backbiters, pickpockets, highwaymen, housebreakers, attorneys, bawds, buffoons, gamesters, politicians, wits, splenetics, tedious talkers, controvertists, ravishers, murderers, robbers, virtuosos: no leaders or followers of party and faction: no encouragers to vice, by seducement or examples: no dungeon, axes, gibbets, whipping-posts, or pillories: no cheating shopkeepers or mechanics: no pride, vanity, or affectation: no fops, bullies, drunkards, strolling whores, or poxes: no ranting, lewd, expensive wives: no stupid, proud pedants: no importunate, overbearing, quarrelsome, noisy, roaring, empty, conceited, swearing companions: no scoundrels, raised from the dust upon the merit of their vices, or nobility thrown into it on account of their virtues: no lords, fiddlers, judges or dancing-masters.

I had the favour of being admitted to several Houyhnhnms, who came to visit or dine with my master; where his Honour graciously suffered me to wait in the room, and listen to their discourse. Both he and his company would often descend to ask me questions, and receive my answers. I had also sometimes the honour of attending my master in his visits to others. I never presumed to speak, except in answer to a question, and then I did it with inward regret, because it was a loss of so much time for improving myself: but I was infinitely delighted with the station of an humble auditor in such conversations, where nothing passed but what was useful, expressed in the fewest and most significant words: where (as I have already said) the greatest decency was observed, without the least degree of ceremony; where no person spoke without being pleased himself, and pleasing his companions; where there was no interruptions, tediousness, heat, or difference of sentiments. They have a notion, that when people are met together, a short silence doth much improve conversation: this I found to be true; for during those little intermissions of talk, new ideas would arise in their minds, which very much enlivened the discourse. Their subjects are generally on friendship and benevolence, or order and œconomy, sometimes upon the visible operations of nature, or ancient traditions, upon the bounds and limits of virtue, upon the unerring rules of reason, or upon some determinations to be taken at the next great assembly, and often upon the various excellencies of poetry. I may add without vanity, that my presence often gave them sufficient matter for discourse, because it afforded my master an occasion of letting his friends into the history of me and my country, upon which they were all pleased to descant in a manner not very advantageous to human kind; and for that reason I shall not repeat what they said: only I may be allowed to observe, that his Honour, to my great admiration, appeared to understand the nature of yahoos much better than myself. He went through all our vices and follies, and discovered many which I had never mentioned to him, by only supposing what qualities a yahoo of their country, with a small proportion of reason, might be capable of exerting; and concluded, with too much probability, how vile as well as miserable such a creature must be.

I freely confess, that all the little knowledge I have of any value was acquired by the lectures I received from my master, and from hearing the discourses of him and his friends; to which I should be prouder to listen, than to dictate to the greatest and wisest assembly in Europe. I admired the strength, comeliness, and speed of the inhabitants; and such a constellation of virtues in such amiable persons produced in me the highest veneration. At first, indeed, I did not feel that natural awe which the yahoos and all other animals bear towards them; but it grew upon me by degrees, much sooner than I imagined, and was mingled with a respectful love and gratitude, that they would condescend to distinguish me from the rest of my species.

When I thought of my family, my friends, my countrymen, or human race in general, I considered them as they really were, yahoos in shape and disposition, only a little more civilized, and qualified with the gift of speech, but making no other use of reason than to improve and multiply those vices whereof their brethren in this country had only the share that nature allotted them. When I happened to behold the reflection of my own form in a lake or fountain, I turned away my face in horror and detestation of myself, and could better endure the sight of a common yahoo, than of my own person. By conversing with the Houyhnhnms, and looking upon them with delight, I fell to imitate their gait and gesture, which is now grown into a habit, and my friends often tell me in a blunt way that I 'trot like a horse'; which, however, I take for a great compliment: neither shall I disown, that in speaking I am apt to fall into the voice and manner of the Houyhnhnms, and hear myself ridiculed on that account without the least mortification.

In the midst of all this happiness, when I looked upon myself to be fully settled for life, my master sent for me one morning a little earlier than his usual hour. I observed by his countenance that he was in some perplexity, and at a loss how to begin what he had to speak. After a short silence, he told me, he did not know how I would take what he was going to say; that in the last general assembly, when the affair of the yahoos was entered upon, the representatives had taken offence at his keeping a yahoo (meaning myself) in his family more like a Houyhnhnm than a brute animal. That he was known frequently to converse with me, as if he could receive some advantage or pleasure in my company: that such a practice was not agreeable to reason or nature, or a thing ever heard of before among them. The assembly did therefore exhort him, either to employ me like the rest of my species, or command me to swim back to the place from whence I came. That the first of these expedients was utterly rejected by all the Houyhnhnms who had ever seen me at his house or their own: for they alleged, that because I had some rudiments of reason, added to the natural pravity[15] of those animals, it was to be feared, I might be able to seduce them into the woody and mountainous parts of the country, and bring them in troops by night to destroy the Houyhnhnms' cattle, as being naturally of the ravenous kind, and averse from labour.

My master added, that he was daily pressed by the Houyhnhnms of the neighbourhood to have the assembly's exhortation executed, which he could not put off much longer. He doubted it would be impossible for me to swim to another country, and therefore wished I would contrive some sort of vehicle resembling those I had described to him, that might carry me on the sea, in which work I should have the assistance of his own servants, as well as those of his neighbours. He concluded, that for his own part he could have been content to keep me in his service as long as I lived, because he found I had cured myself of some bad habits and dispositions, by endeavouring, as far as my inferior nature was capable, to imitate the Houyhnhnms.

I should here observe to the reader, that a decree of the general assembly in this country is expressed by the word *hnhloayn*, which signifies an *exhortation*, as near as I can render it: for they have no conception how a rational creature can be compelled, but only advised or exhorted, because no person can disobey reason, without giving up his claim to be a rational creature.

I was struck with the utmost grief and despair at my master's discourse, and being unable to support the agonies I was under, I fell into a swoon at his feet; when I came to myself he told me that he concluded I had been dead. (For these people are subject to no such imbecilities of nature.) I answered, in a faint voice, that death would have been too great an happiness; that although I could not blame the assembly's exhortation, or the urgency of his friends, yet, in my weak and corrupt judgment, I thought it might consist with reason to have been less rigorous. That I could not swim a league, and probably the nearest land to theirs might be distant above an hundred; that many materials, necessary for making a small vessel to carry me off, were wholly wanting in this country, which, however, I would attempt in obedience and gratitude to his Honour, although I concluded the thing to be impossible, and therefore looked on my self as already devoted [16]

---

[15] perversity.   [16] doomed.

to destruction. That the certain prospect of an unnatural death was the least of my evils: for, supposing I should escape with life by some strange adventure, how could I think with temper[17] of passing my days among yahoos, and relapsing into my old corruptions, for want of examples to lead and keep me within the paths of virtue? That I knew too well upon what solid reasons all the determinations of the wise Houyhnhnms were founded, not to be shaken by arguments of mine, a miserable yahoo; and therefore, after presenting him with my humble thanks for the offer of his servants' assistance in making a vessel, and desiring a reasonable time for so difficult a work, I told him I would endeavour to preserve a wretched being; and, if ever I returned to England, was not without hopes of being useful to my own species, by celebrating the praises of the renowned Houyhnhnms, and proposing their virtues to the imitation of mankind.

My master in a few words made me a very gracious reply, allowed me the space of two months to finish my boat; and ordered the sorrel nag, my fellow-servant (for so at this distance I may presume to call him) to follow my instructions, because I told my master, that his help would be sufficient, and I knew he had a tenderness for me.

In his company my first business was to go to that part of the coast where my rebellious crew had ordered me to be set on shore. I got upon a height, and looking on every side into the sea, fancied I saw a small island, towards the northeast: I took out my pocket-glass, and could then clearly distinguish it about five leagues off, as I computed; but it appeared to the sorrel nag to be only a blue cloud: for as he had no conception of any country beside his own, so he could not be as expert in distinguishing remote objects at sea as we who so much converse in that element.

After I had discovered this island, I considered no farther; but resolved it should, if possible, be the first place of my banishment, leaving the consequence to fortune.

I returned home, and consulting with the sorrel nag, we went into a copse at some distance, where I with my knife, and he with a sharp flint fastened very artificially[18] after their manner, to a wooden handle, cut down several oak wattles about the thickness of a walking-staff, and some larger pieces. But I shall not trouble the reader with a particular description of my own mechanics; let it suffice to say that in six weeks' time, with the help of the sorrel nag, who performed the parts that required most labour, I finished a sort of Indian canoe, but much larger, covering it with the skins of yahoos well stitched together, with hempen threads of my own making. My sail was likewise composed of the skins of the same animal; but I made use of the youngest I could get, the older being too tough and thick, and I likewise provided myself with four paddles. I laid in a

---

[17] composure.　　[18] artfully.

stock of boiled flesh, of rabbits and fowls, and took with me two vessels, one filled with milk, and the other with water.

I tried my canoe in a large pond near my master's house, and then corrected in it what was amiss; stopping all the chinks with yahoos' tallow,[19] till I found it staunch, and able to bear me and my freight. And when it was as complete as I could possibly make it, I had it drawn on a carriage very gently by yahoos to the seaside, under the conduct of the sorrel nag and another servant.

When all was ready, and the day came for my departure, I took leave of my master and lady, and the whole family, my eyes flowing with tears, and my heart quite sunk with grief. But his Honour, out of curiosity, and perhaps (if I may speak it without vanity) partly out of kindness, was determined to see me in my canoe, and got several of his neighbouring friends to accompany him. I was forced to wait above an hour for the tide, and then observing the wind very fortunately bearing towards the island, to which I intended to steer my course, I took a second leave of my master: but as I was going to prostrate myself to kiss his hoof, he did me the honour to raise it gently to my mouth. I am not ignorant how much I have been censured for mentioning this last particular. Detractors are pleased to think it improbable, that so illustrious a person should descend to give so great a mark of distinction to a creature so inferior as I. Neither have I forgot how apt some travellers are to boast of extraordinary favours they have received. But if these censurers were better acquainted with the noble and courteous disposition of the Houyhnhnms, they would soon change their opinion.

I paid my respects to the rest of the Houyhnhnms in his Honour's company; then getting into my canoe, I pushed off from shore.

CHAPTER XI

THE AUTHOR'S DANGEROUS VOYAGE. HE ARRIVES AT NEW HOLLAND, HOPING TO SETTLE THERE. IS WOUNDED WITH AN ARROW BY ONE OF THE NATIVES. IS SEIZED AND CARRIED BY FORCE INTO A PORTUGUESE SHIP. THE GREAT CIVILITIES OF THE CAPTAIN. THE AUTHOR ARRIVES AT ENGLAND.

I began this desperate voyage on February 15, 1714–5,[20] at 9 o'clock in the morning. The wind was very favourable; however, I made use at first only of my paddles, but considering I should soon be weary, and that

[19] fat. [20] In Swift's time the New Year began on March 25. According to our calendar the date was 1715.

the wind might probably chop about, I ventured to set up my little sail; and thus with the help of the tide I went at the rate of a league and a half an hour, as near as I could guess. My master and his friends continued on the shore till I was almost out of sight; and I often heard the sorrel nag (who always loved me) crying out, *Hnuy illa nyha maiah yahoo,* Take care of thyself, gentle yahoo.

My design was, if possible, to discover some small island uninhabited, yet sufficient by my labour to furnish me with the necessaries of life, which I would have thought a greater happiness than to be first minister in the politest court of Europe; so horrible was the idea I conceived of returning to live in the society and under the government of yahoos. For in such a solitude as I desired, I could at least enjoy my own thoughts, and reflect with delight on the virtues of those inimitable Houyhnhnms, without any opportunity of degenerating into the vices and corruptions of my own species.

The reader may remember what I related when my crew conspired against me, and confined me to my cabin. How I continued there several weeks, without knowing what course we took, and when I was put ashore in the long-boat, how the sailors told me with oaths, whether true or false, that they knew not in what part of the world we were. However, I did then believe us to be about ten degrees southward of the Cape of Good Hope, or about 45 degrees southern latitude, as I gathered from some general words I over-heard among them, being I supposed to the southeast in their intended voyage to Madagascar. And although this were but little better than conjecture, yet I resolved to steer my course eastward, hoping to reach the southwest coast of New Holland, and perhaps some such island as I desired, lying westward of it. The wind was full west, and by six in the evening I computed I had gone eastward at least eighteen leagues, when I spied a very small island about half a league off, which I soon reached. It was nothing but a rock, with one creek, naturally arched by the force of tempests. Here I put in my canoe, and climbing a part of the rock, I could plainly discover land to the east, extending from south to north. I lay all night in my canoe, and repeating my voyage early in the morning, I arrived in seven hours to the southeast point of New Holland. This confirmed me in the opinion I have long entertained, that the maps and charts place this country at least three degrees more to the east than it really is; which thought I communicated many years ago to my worthy friend Mr. Herman Moll,[21] and gave him my reasons for it, although he hath rather chosen to follow other authors.

I saw no inhabitants in the place where I landed, and being unarmed, I was afraid of venturing far into the country. I found some shellfish on

[21] well-known map-maker.

the shore, and eat them raw, not daring to kindle a fire, for fear of being discovered by the natives. I continued three days feeding on oysters and limpets, to save my own provisions, and I fortunately found a brook of excellent water, which gave me great relief.

On the fourth day, venturing out early a little too far, I saw twenty or thirty natives upon a height, not above five hundred yards from me. They were stark naked, men, women, and children, round a fire, as I could discover by the smoke. One of them spied me, and gave notice to the rest; five of them advanced towards me, leaving the women and children at the fire. I made what haste I could to the shore, and getting into my canoe, shoved off: the savages observing me retreat, ran after me; and before I could get far enough into the sea, discharged an arrow, which wounded me deeply on the inside of my left knee (I shall carry the mark to my grave). I apprehended the arrow might be poisoned, and paddling out of the reach of their darts (being a calm day), I made a shift to suck the wound, and dress it as well as I could.

I was at a loss what to do, for I durst not return to the same landing-place, but stood to the north, and was forced to paddle; for the wind, although very gentle, was against me, blowing northwest. As I was looking about for a secure landing-place, I saw a sail to the north-northeast, which appearing every minute more visible, I was in some doubt, whether I should wait for them or no; but at last my detestation of the yahoo race prevailed, and turning my canoe, I sailed and paddled together to the south, and got into the same creek from whence I set out in the morning, choosing rather to trust myself among these barbarians, than live with European yahoos. I drew up my canoe as close as I could to the shore, and hid myself behind a stone by the little brook, which, as I have already said, was excellent water.

The ship came within a half a league of this creek, and sent out her long-boat with vessels to take in fresh water (for the place it seems was very well known) but I did not observe it until the boat was almost on shore, and it was too late to seek another hiding-place. The seamen at their landing observed my canoe, and rummaging it all over, easily conjectured that the owner could not be far off. Four of them well armed searched every cranny and lurking-hole, till at last they found me flat on my face behind the stone. They gazed a while in admiration at my strange uncouth dress, my coat made of skins, my wooden-soled shoes, and my furred stockings; from whence, however, they concluded I was not a native of the place, who all go naked. One of the seamen in Portuguese bid me rise, and asked who I was. I understood that language very well, and getting upon my feet, said, I was a poor yahoo, banished from the Houyhnhnms, and desired they would please to let me depart. They admired to hear me answer them in their own tongue, and saw by my complexion

I must be an European; but were at loss to know what I meant by yahoos and Houyhnhnms, and at the same time fell a laughing at my strange tone in speaking, which resembled the neighing of a horse. I trembled all the while betwixt fear and hatred: I again desired leave to depart, and was gently moving to my canoe; but they laid hold on me, desiring to know, what country I was of, whence I came, with many other questions. I told them I was born in England, from whence I came about five years ago, and then their country and ours were at peace. I therefore hoped they would not treat me as an enemy, since I meant them no harm, but was a poor yahoo, seeking some desolate place where to pass the remainder of his unfortunate life.

When they began to talk, I thought I never heard or saw any thing so unnatural; for it appeared to me as monstrous as if a dog or a cow should speak in England, or a yahoo in Houyhnhnmland. The honest Portuguese were equally amazed at my strange dress, and the odd manner of delivering my words, which however they understood very well. They spoke to me with great humanity, and said they were sure their captain would carry me *gratis* to Lisbon, from whence I might return to my own country; that two of the seamen would go back to the ship, inform the captain of what they had seen, and receive his orders; in the mean time, unless I would give my solemn oath not to fly, they would secure me by force. I thought it best to comply with their proposal. They were very curious to know my story, but I gave them very little satisfaction; and they all conjectured that my misfortunes had impaired my reason. In two hours the boat, which went loaden with vessels of water, returned with the captain's commands to fetch me on board. I fell on my knees to preserve my liberty; but all was in vain, and the men having tied me with cords, heaved me into the boat, from whence I was taken into the ship, and from thence into the captain's cabin.

His name was Pedro de Mendez; he was a very courteous and generous person; he entreated me to give some account of my self, and desired to know what I would eat or drink; said, I should be used as well as himself, and spoke so many obliging things, that I wondered to find such civilities from a yahoo. However, I remained silent and sullen; I was ready to faint at the very smell of him and his men. At last I desired something to eat out of my own canoe; but he ordered me a chicken and some excellent wine, and then directed that I should be put to bed in a very clean cabin. I would not undress myself, but lay on the bed-clothes, and in half an hour stole out, when I thought the crew was at dinner, and getting to the side of the ship was going to leap into the sea, and swim for my life, rather than continue among yahoos. But one of the seamen prevented me, and having informed the captain, I was chained to my cabin.

After dinner Don Pedro came to me, and desired to know my reason for so desperate an attempt: assured me he only meant to do me all the service he was able, and spoke so very movingly, that at last I descended to treat him like an animal which had some little portion of reason. I gave him a very short relation of my voyage, of the conspiracy against me by my own men, of the country where they set me on shore, and of my three years' residence there. All which he looked upon as if it were a dream or a vision; whereat I took great offence; for I had quite forgot the faculty of lying, so peculiar to yahoos in all countries where they preside, and, consequently, the disposition of suspecting truth in others of their own species. I asked him, whether it were the custom of his country to *say the thing that was not.* I assured him I had almost forgot what he meant by falsehood, and if I had lived a thousand years in Houyhnhnmland, I should never have heard a lie from the meanest servant; that I was altogether indifferent whether he believed me or no; but however, in return for his favours, I would give so much allowance to the corruption of his nature as to answer any objection he would please to make, and he might easily discover the truth.

The captain, a wise man, after many endeavours to catch me tripping in some part of my story, at last began to have a better opinion of my veracity. But he added, that since I professed so inviolable an attachment to truth, I must give him my word of honour to bear him company in this voyage without attempting anything against my life, or else he would continue me a prisoner till we arrived in Lisbon. I gave him the promise he required; but at the same time protested that I would suffer the greatest hardships rather than return to live among yahoos.

Our voyage passed without any considerable accident. In gratitude to the captain I sometimes sat with him at his earnest request, and strove to conceal my antipathy to human kind, although it often broke out, which he suffered to pass without observation. But the greatest part of the day, I confined myself to my cabin, to avoid seeing any of the crew. The captain had often entreated me to strip myself of my savage dress, and offered to lend me the best suit of clothes he had. This I would not be prevailed on to accept, abhorring to cover myself with anything that had been on the back of a yahoo. I only desired he would lend me two clean shirts, which having been washed since he wore them, I believed would not so much defile me. These I changed every second day, and washed them myself.

We arrived at Lisbon, Nov. 5, 1715. At our landing the captain forced me to cover myself with his cloak, to prevent the rabble from crowding about me. I was conveyed to his own house, and, at my earnest request, he led me up to the highest room backwards.[22] I conjured him to conceal from all persons what I had told him of the Houyhnhnms, because the least hint of

---

[22] at the back of the house.

such a story would not only draw numbers of people to see me, but probably put me in danger of being imprisoned, or burnt by the Inquisition. The captain persuaded me to accept a suit of clothes newly made, but I would not suffer the tailor to take my measure; however, Don Pedro being almost of my size, they fitted me well enough. He accoutred me with other necessaries all new, which I aired for twenty-four hours before I would use them.

The captain had no wife, nor above three servants, none of which were suffered to attend at meals, and his whole deportment was so obliging, added to very good *human* understanding, that I really began to tolerate his company. He gained so far upon me, that I ventured to look out of the back window. By degrees I was brought into another room, from whence I peeped into the street, but drew my head back in a fright. In a week's time he seduced me down to the door. I found my terror gradually lessened, but my hatred and contempt seemed to increase. I was at last bold enough to walk the street in his company, but kept my nose well stopped with rue,[23] or sometimes with tobacco.

In ten days Don Pedro, to whom I had given some account of my domestic affairs, put it upon me as a point of honour and conscience, that I ought to return to my native country, and live at home with my wife and children. He told me, there was an English ship in the port just ready to sail, and he would furnish me with all things necessary. It would be tedious to repeat his arguments, and my contradictions. He said it was altogether impossible to find such a solitary island as I had desired to live in; but I might command in my own house, and pass my time in a manner as recluse as I pleased.

I complied at last, finding I could not do better. I left Lisbon the 24th day of November, in an English merchantman, but who was the master I never inquired. Don Pedro accompanied me to the ship, and lent me twenty pounds. He took kind leave of me, and embraced me at parting, which I bore as well as I could. During this last voyage I had no commerce with the master or any of his men, but pretending I was sick kept close in my cabin. On the fifth of December, 1715, we cast anchor in the Downs about nine in the morning, and at three in the afternoon I got safe to my house at Redriff.

My wife and family received me with great surprise and joy, because they concluded me certainly dead; but I must freely confess the sight of them filled me only with hatred, disgust and contempt, and the more by reflecting on the near alliance I had to them. For although, since my unfortunate exile from the Houyhnhnm country, I had compelled myself to tolerate the sight of yahoos, and to converse with Don Pedro de Mendez, yet my memory and imaginations were perpetually filled with the virtues

[23] strong-scented herb.

and ideas of those exalted Houyhnhnms. And when I began to consider, that by copulating with one of the yahoo species I had become a parent of more, it struck me with the utmost shame, confusion, and horror.

As soon as I entered the house, my wife took me in her arms, and kissed me, at which, having not been used to the touch of that odious animal for so many years, I fell in a swoon for almost an hour. At the time I am writing it is five years since my last return to England: during the first year I could not endure my wife or children in my presence, the very smell of them was intolerable, much less could I suffer them to eat in the same room. To this hour they dare not presume to touch my bread, or drink out of the same cup, neither was I ever able to let one of them take me by the hand. The first money I laid out was to buy two young stone-horses,[24] which I keep in a good stable, and next to them the groom is my greatest favourite; for I feel my spirits revived by the smell he contracts in the stable. My horses understand me tolerably well; I converse with them at least four hours every day. They are strangers to bridle or saddle; they live in great amity with me, and friendship to each other.

CHAPTER XII

THE AUTHOR'S VERACITY. HIS DESIGN IN PUBLISHING THIS WORK. HIS
CENSURE OF THOSE TRAVELLERS WHO SWERVE FROM THE TRUTH.
THE AUTHOR CLEARS HIMSELF FROM ANY SINISTER ENDS IN WRITING.
AN OBJECTION ANSWERED. THE METHOD OF PLANTING COLONIES. HIS
NATIVE COUNTRY COMMENDED. THE RIGHT OF THE CROWN TO THOSE
COUNTRIES DESCRIBED BY THE AUTHOR IS JUSTIFIED. THE DIFFICULTY
OF CONQUERING THEM. THE AUTHOR TAKES HIS LAST LEAVE OF THE
READER, PROPOSETH HIS MANNER OF LIVING FOR THE FUTURE, GIVES
GOOD ADVICE, AND CONCLUDES.

Thus, gentle reader, I have given thee a faithful history of my travels for sixteen years, and above seven months, wherein I have not been so studious of ornament as of truth. I could perhaps like others have astonished thee with strange improbable tales; but I rather chose to relate plain matter of fact in the simplest manner and style, because my principal design was to inform, and not to amuse thee.

It is easy for us who travel into remote countries, which are seldom visited by Englishmen or other Europeans, to form descriptions of wonderful animals both at sea and land. Whereas a traveller's chief aim should be to make

[24] stallions.

men wiser and better, and to improve their minds by the bad as well as good example of what they deliver concerning foreign places.

I could heartily wish a law were enacted, that every traveller, before he were permitted to publish his voyages, should be obliged to make oath before the Lord High Chancellor that all he intended to print was absolutely true to the best of his knowledge; for then the world would no longer be deceived as it usually is, while some writers, to make their works pass the better upon the public, impose the grossest falsities on the unwary reader. I have perused several books of travels with great delight in my younger days; but having since gone over most parts of the globe, and been able to contradict many fabulous accounts from my own observation, it hath given me a great disgust against this part of reading, and some indignation to see the credulity of mankind so impudently abused. Therefore since my acquaintance were pleased to think my poor endeavours might not be unacceptable to my country, I imposed on myself as a maxim, never to be swerved from, that I would *strictly adhere to truth;* neither indeed can I be ever under the least temptation to vary from it, while I retain in my mind the lectures and example of my noble master, and the other illustrious Houyhnhnms, of whom I had so long the honour to be an humble hearer.

Nec si miserum Fortuna Sinonem Finxit, vanum etiam mendacemque improba finget.[25]

I know very well how little reputation is to be got by writings which require neither genius nor learning, nor indeed any other talent, except a good memory or an exact journal. I know likewise, that writers of travels, like dictionary-makers, are sunk into oblivion by the weight and bulk of those who come after, and therefore lie uppermost. And it is highly probable, that such travellers who shall hereafter visit the countries described in this work of mine, may, by detecting my errors (if there be any), and adding many new discoveries of their own, jostle me out of vogue, and stand in my place, making the world forget that ever I was an author. This indeed would be too great a mortification if I wrote for fame: but, as my sole intention was the PUBLIC GOOD, I cannot be altogether disappointed. For who can read of the virtues I have mentioned in the glorious Houyhnhnms, without being ashamed of his own vices, when he considers himself as the reasoning, governing animal of his country? I shall say noth-

---

[25] "Although vile Fortune has made Sinon wretched, she has not made him false and a liar" (Virgil, *Aeneid,* II, 79–80). It is curious that Gulliver here would seem to identify himself with Sinon, the treacherous Greek who helped bring about the downfall of Troy by convincing the Trojans to allow the wooden horse, with its secret cargo of Greek warriors, to enter their city.

ing of those remote nations where yahoos preside, amongst which the least corrupted are the Brobdingnagians,[26] whose wise maxims in morality and government it would be our happiness to observe. But I forbear descanting[27] further, and rather leave the judicious reader to his own remarks and applications.[28]

I am not a little pleased that this work of mine can possibly meet with no censurers: for what objections can be made against a writer who relates only plain facts that happened in such distant countries, where we have not the least interest with respect either to trade or negotiations? I have carefully avoided every fault with which common writers of travels are often too justly charged. Besides, I meddle not the least with any *party,* but write without passion, prejudice, or ill-will against any man or number of men whatsoever. I write for the noblest end, to inform and instruct mankind, over whom I may, without breach of modesty, pretend to some superiority from the advantages I received by conversing so long among the most accomplished Houyhnhnms. I write without any view towards profit or praise. I never suffer a word to pass that may look like reflection, or possibly give the least offence even to those who are most ready to take it. So that I hope I may with justice pronounce myself an author perfectly blameless, against whom the tribe of answerers, considerers, observers, reflecters, detecters, remarkers, will never be able to find matter for exercising their talents.

I confess, it was whispered to me that I was bound in duty, as a subject of England, to have given in a memorial to a secretary of state, at my first coming over; because, whatever lands are discovered by a subject belong to the crown. But I doubt whether our conquests in the countries I treat of would be as easy as those of Ferdinando Cortez over the naked Americans. The Lilliputians,[29] I think, are hardly worth the charge of a fleet and army to reduce them, and I question whether it might be prudent or safe to attempt the Brobdingnagians. Or whether an English army would be much at their ease with the Flying Island [30] over their heads. The Houyhnhnms, indeed, appear not to be so well prepared for war, a science to which they are perfect strangers, and especially against missive weapons. However, supposing myself to be a minister of state, I could never give my advice for invading them. Their prudence, unanimity, unacquaintedness with fear, and their love of their country would amply supply all defects in the military art. Imagine twenty thousand of them breaking into the midst of an European army, confounding the ranks, overturning the carriages, battering the warriors' faces into mummy,[31] by terrible yerks from their hinder hoofs. For they would well deserve the character given to

---

[26] giants whose land Gulliver had visited in Book II.   [27] discoursing.   [28] interpretations.   [29] midget beings whose country Gulliver had visited in Book I.   [30] Swift's fantastic embodiment of England in Book III.   [31] pulp.

Augustus; *Recalcitrat undique tutus*.[32] But instead of proposals for conquering that magnanimous nation, I rather wish they were in a capacity or disposition to send a sufficient number of their inhabitants for civilizing Europe, by teaching us the first principles of honour, justice, truth, temperance, public spirit, fortitude, chastity, friendship, benevolence, and fidelity. The names of all which virtues are still retained among us in most languages, and are to be met with in modern as well as ancient authors; which I am able to assert from my own small reading.

But I had another reason which made me less forward to enlarge his Majesty's dominions by my discoveries. To say the truth, I had conceived a few scruples with relation to the distributive justice of princes upon those occasions. For instance, a crew of pirates are driven by a storm they know not whither, at length a boy discovers land from the topmast, they go on shore to rob and plunder, they see an harmless people, are entertained with kindness, they give the country a new name, they take formal possession of it for the king, they set up a rotten plank or a stone for a memorial, they murder two or three dozen of the natives, bring away a couple more by force for a sample, return home, and get their pardon. Here commences a new dominion acquired with a title by *divine right*. Ships are sent with the first opportunity, the natives driven out or destroyed, their princes tortured to discover their gold, a free license given to all acts of inhumanity and lust, the earth reeking with the blood of its inhabitants: and this execrable crew of butchers employed in so pious an expedition, is a modern colony sent to convert and civilize an idolatrous and barbarous people.

But this description, I confess, doth by no means affect the British nation, who may be an example to the whole world for their wisdom, care, and justice in planting colonies; their liberal endowments for the advancement of religion and learning; their choice of devout and able pastors to propagate Christianity; their caution in stocking their provinces with people of sober lives and conversations from this the mother kingdom; their strict regard to the distribution of justice, in supplying the civil administration through all their colonies with officers of the greatest abilities, utter strangers to corruption; and to crown all, by sending the most vigilant and virtuous governors, who have no other views than the happiness of the people over whom they preside, and the honour of the king their master.

But as those countries which I have described do not appear to have any desire of being conquered, and enslaved, murdered or driven out by colonies, nor abound either in gold, silver, sugar or tobacco; I did humbly conceive they were by no means proper objects of our zeal, our valour, or our interest. However, if those whom it may concern think fit to be of another

[32] "He kicks backward, secure on every side" (Horace, *Satires*, II, i, 20).

opinion, I am ready to depose, when I shall be lawfully called, that no European did ever visit these countries before me. I mean, if the inhabitants ought to be believed; unless a dispute may arise about the two yahoos, said to have been seen many ages ago on a mountain in Houyhnhnmland, from whence the opinion is, that the race of those brutes hath descended; and these, for any thing I know, may have been English, which indeed I was apt to suspect from the lineaments of their posterity's countenances, although very much defaced. But, how far that will go to make out a title, I leave to the learned in colony-law.

But as to the formality of taking possession in my sovereign's name, it never came once into my thoughts; and if it had, yet as my affairs then stood, I should perhaps, in point of prudence and self-preservation, have put it off to a better opportunity.

Having thus answered the *only* objection that can ever be raised against me as a traveller, I here take a final leave of my courteous readers, and return to enjoy my own speculations in my little garden at Redriff, to apply those excellent lessons of virtue which I learned among the Houyhnhnms, to instruct the yahoos of my own family as far as I shall find them docible animals, to behold my figure often in a glass, and thus if possible habituate myself by time to tolerate the sight of a human creature; to lament the brutality of Houyhnhnms in my own country, but always treat their persons with respect, for the sake of my noble master, his family, his friends, and the whole Houyhnhnm race, whom these of ours have the honour to resemble in all their lineaments, however their intellectuals came to degenerate.

I began last week to permit my wife to sit at dinner with me, at the farthest end of a long table, and to answer (but with the utmost brevity) the few questions I ask her. Yet the smell of a yahoo continuing very offensive, I always keep my nose well stopped with rue, lavender, or tobacco leaves. And although it be hard for a man late in life to remove old habits, I am not altogether out of hopes in some time to suffer a neighbour yahoo in my company without the apprehensions I am yet under of his teeth or his claws.

My reconcilement to the yahoo-kind in general might not be so difficult if they would be content with those vices and follies only which nature hath entitled them to. I am not in the least provoked at the sight of a lawyer, a pickpocket, a colonel, a fool, a lord, a gamester, a politician, a whoremonger, a physician, an evidence,[33] a suborner, an attorney, a traitor, or the like; this is all according to the due course of things: but when I behold a lump of deformity and diseases both in body and mind, smitten with pride, it immediately breaks all the measures of my patience; neither shall

[33] witness.

I be ever able to comprehend how such an animal and such a vice could tally together. The wise and virtuous Houyhnhnms, who abound in all excellencies that can adorn a rational creature, have no name for this vice in their language, which hath no terms to express any thing that is evil, except those whereby they describe the detestable qualities of their yahoos, among which they were not able to distinguish this of pride, for want of thoroughly understanding human nature, as it showeth itself in other countries, where that animal presides. But I, who had more experience, could plainly observe some rudiments of it among the wild yahoos.

But the Houyhnhnms, who live under the government of reason, are no more proud of the good qualities they possess, than I should be for not wanting a leg or an arm, which no man in his wits would boast of, although he must be miserable without them. I dwell the longer upon this subject from the desire I have to make the society of an English yahoo by any means not insupportable, and therefore I here entreat those who have any tincture of this absurd vice, that they will not presume to appear in my sight.

Voltaire (François-Marie Arouet)

FROM *Candide*

TRANSLATED BY RICHARD ALDINGTON
NOTES BY NORMAN L. TORREY

Voltaire (1694–1778)

THE EIGHTEENTH CENTURY IN EUROPE NOT ONLY INHERITED THE great scientific revolution initiated in the seventeenth century but translated that revolution into a new approach to life. The period of the Enlightenment, or the Age of Reason as it is sometimes called, was distinguished by three new modes of thought. The first of these was deism—the belief that God was only responsible for having set the universe in motion and since then has taken no further role in human affairs. The second was rationalism—the concomitant belief in man's ability to achieve whatever he may choose through his own unaided intellectual powers. The third was liberalism—the desire to see man freed from the harsh exactions of autocratic governments.

Voltaire—a rationalist, a deist, and a liberal—was a champion and at times a formulator of many of the beliefs cherished by the men of the Enlightenment. In place of a completed system of thought, he created and supported an atmosphere of witty criticism of existing systems of government and thought. This atmosphere culminated in the rising desire for social reform, which was one of the important causes of the French Revolution.

Epic poet, dramatist, biographer, and historian, Voltaire rose from middle-class Parisian beginnings to become one of the most famous and widely read men of his time. In our age he is best known for his "philosophical" prose fiction, of which *Candide* (1759) is justly the most famous example. The work reflects Voltaire's growing disillusionment with events, both personal and universal. Perhaps the most important element in Voltaire's discontent, at least as far as *Candide* is concerned, was the great Lisbon earthquake of 1756. It was this tragedy that brought to a head Voltaire's infuriation—a rationalist's disgust with the misuse of reason—with those eighteenth-century philosophers and men of letters who maintained that this is the best of all possible worlds. Such justifications of God's ways to man, as Alexander Pope's "God sends not ill; if rightly understood,/ Or partial ill is universal good," now seemed, in the light of the terrible destruction of a city and its population by a whim of nature, not only indefensible on rational grounds but a positive affront on moral ones. As a result, one of the main features of *Candide* is an unlimited attack on rationalizations that attempt to account for the existence of evil.

Candide

How Candide Was Brought Up
in a Noble Castle
and How He Was Expelled
from the Same

In the castle of Baron Thunder-ten-tronckh in Westphalia[1] there lived a youth, endowed by Nature with the most gentle character. His face was the expression of his soul. His judgment was quite honest and he was extremely simple-minded; and this was the reason, I think, that he was named Candide. Old servants in the house suspected that he was the son of the Baron's sister and a decent honest gentleman of the neighborhood, whom this young lady would never marry because he could only prove seventy-one quarterings,[2] and the rest of his genealogical tree was lost, owing to the injuries of time.

The Baron was one of the most powerful lords in Westphalia, for his castle possessed a door and windows. His Great Hall was even decorated with a piece of tapestry. The dogs in his stable-yards formed a pack of hounds when necessary; his grooms were his huntsmen; the village curate was his Grand Almoner. They all called him "My Lord," and laughed heartily at his stories.

The Baroness weighed about three hundred and fifty pounds, was therefore greatly respected, and did the honors of the house with a dignity which rendered her still more respectable. Her daughter Cunegonde, aged seventeen, was rosy-cheeked, fresh, plump and tempting. The Baron's son appeared in every respect worthy of his father. The tutor Pangloss was the oracle of the house, and little Candide followed his lessons with all the candor of his age and character.

[1] section of Germany just east of Holland. In Voltaire's day, it was a poor agricultural province through which he passed in 1750 on his way to the court of Frederick the Great. [2] These divisions on coats of arms are indications of the number of noble ancestors.

Pangloss taught metaphysico-theologo-cosmolonigology.[3] He proved admirably that there is no effect without a cause and that in this best of all possible worlds, My Lord the Baron's castle was the best of castles and his wife the best of all possible Baronesses.

" 'Tis demonstrated," said he, "that things cannot be otherwise; for, since everything is made for an end, everything is necessarily for the best end. Observe that noses were made to wear spectacles; and so we have spectacles. Legs were visibly instituted to be breeched, and we have breeches.[4] Stones were formed to be quarried and to build castles; and My Lord has a very noble castle; the greatest Baron in the province should have the best house; and as pigs were made to be eaten, we eat pork all the year round; consequently, those who have asserted that all is well talk nonsense; they ought to have said that all is for the best."

Candide listened attentively and believed innocently; for he thought Mademoiselle Cunegonde extremely beautiful, although he was never bold enough to tell her so. He decided that after the happiness of being born Baron of Thunder-ten-tronckh, the second degree of happiness was to be Mademoiselle Cunegonde; the third, to see her every day; and the fourth to listen to Doctor Pangloss, the greatest philosopher of the province and therefore of the whole world.

One day when Cunegonde was walking near the castle, in a little wood which was called The Park, she observed Doctor Pangloss in the bushes, giving a lesson in experimental physics to her mother's waiting maid, a very pretty and docile brunette. Mademoiselle Cunegonde had a great inclination for science and watched breathlessly the reiterated experiments she witnessed; she observed clearly the Doctor's sufficient reason, the effects and the causes, and returned home very much excited, pensive, filled with the desire of learning, reflecting that she might be the sufficient reason of young Candide and that he might be hers.

On her way back to the castle she met Candide and blushed; Candide also blushed. She bade him good-morning in a hesitating voice; Candide replied without knowing what he was saying. Next day, when they left the table after dinner, Cunegonde and Candide found themselves behind a screen; Cunegonde dropped her handkerchief, Candide picked it up; she innocently held his hand; the young man innocently kissed the young lady's hand with remarkable vivacity, tenderness and grace; their lips met, their eyes sparkled, their knees trembled, their hands wandered. Baron Thunder-ten-tronckh passed near the screen, and, observing this cause and effect, expelled Candide

---

[3] The suggestion is that Pangloss ("all-tongue") is the teacher of abstract nonsense. Swift used a similar term for similar effect in *Gulliver's Travels*. [4] Clear but ludicrous examples of what are called in philosophy final causes, that is, ends or purposes which serve as causes of created things.

from the castle by kicking him in the backside frequently and hard. Cune-gonde swooned; when she recovered her senses, the Baroness slapped her in the face; and all was in consternation in the noblest and most agreeable of all possible castles.

CHAPTER II

What Happened to Candide
Among the Bulgarians

Candide, expelled from the earthly paradise, wandered for a long time without knowing where he was going, weeping, turning up his eyes to Heaven, gazing back frequently at the noblest of castles which held the most beautiful of young Baronesses; he lay down to sleep supperless between two furrows in the open fields; it snowed heavily in large flakes. The next morning the shivering Candide, penniless, dying of cold and exhaustion, dragged himself towards the neighboring town, which was called Wald-berghoff-trarbk-dikdorff. He halted sadly at the door of an inn. Two men dressed in blue noticed him.

"Comrade," said one, "there's a well-built young man of the right height." They went up to Candide and very civilly invited him to dinner.

"Gentlemen," said Candide with charming modesty, "you do me a great honor, but I have no money to pay my share."

"Ah, sir," said one of the men in blue, "persons of your figure and merit never pay anything; are you not five feet five tall?"

"Yes, gentlemen," said he, bowing, "that is my height."

"Ah, sir, come to table; we will not only pay your expenses, we will never allow a man like you to be short of money; men were only made to help each other."

"You are in the right," said Candide, "that is what Doctor Pangloss was always telling me, and I see that everything is for the best."

They begged him to accept a few crowns, he took them and wished to give them an I O U; they refused to take it and all sat down to table. "Do you not love tenderly . . ."

"Oh, yes," said he. "I love Mademoiselle Cunegonde tenderly."

"No," said one of the gentlemen. "We were asking if you do not tenderly love the King of the Bulgarians." [5]

[5] Voltaire has his reasons to refer to Frederick the Great, king of Prussia, under this title.

"Not a bit," said he, "for I have never seen him."

"What! He is the most charming of Kings, and you must drink his health."

"Oh, gladly, gentlemen." And he drank.

"That is sufficient," he was told. "You are now the support, the aid, the defender, the hero of the Bulgarians; your fortune is made and your glory assured."

They immediately put irons on his legs and took him to a regiment.[6] He was made to turn to the right and left, raise the ramrod and return the ramrod, to take aim, to fire, to double up,[7] and he was given thirty strokes with a stick; the next day he drilled not quite so badly, and received only twenty strokes; the day after, he only had ten, and was looked on as a prodigy by his comrades.

Candide was completely mystified and could not make out how he was a hero. One fine spring day he thought he would take a walk, going straight ahead, in the belief that to use his legs as he pleased was a privilege of the human species as well as of animals. He had not gone two leagues when four other heroes, each six feet tall, fell upon him, bound him and dragged him back to a cell. He was asked by his judges whether he would rather be thrashed thirty-six times by the whole regiment or receive a dozen lead bullets at once in his brain. Although he protested that men's wills are free and that he wanted neither one nor the other, he had to make a choice; by virtue of that gift of God which is called *liberty*, he determined to run the gauntlet thirty-six times and actually did so twice. There were two thousand men in the regiment. That made four thousand strokes which laid bare the muscles and nerves from his neck to his backside. As they were about to proceed to a third turn, Candide, utterly exhausted, begged as a favor that they would be so kind as to smash his head; he obtained this favor; they bound his eyes and he was made to kneel down. At that moment the King of the Bulgarians came by and inquired the victim's crime; and as this King was possessed of a vast genius, he perceived from what he learned about Candide that he was a young metaphysician very ignorant in worldly matters, and therefore pardoned him with a clemency which will be praised in all newspapers and all ages. An honest surgeon healed Candide in three weeks with the ointments recommended by Dioscorides.[8] He had already regained a little skin and could walk when the King of the Bulgarians went to war with the King of the Abares.[9]

---

[6] It was a common practice in England and on the continent to "press" young men into military service. [7] Double time. [8] Famous Greek doctor. [9] The French-Austrian coalition, which fought against Frederick in the Seven Years' War.

CHAPTER III

How Candide Escaped
From the Bulgarians and
What Became of Him

Nothing could be smarter, more splendid, more brilliant, better drawn up than the two armies. Trumpets, fifes, hautboys, drums, cannons, formed a harmony such as has never been heard even in hell. The cannons first of all laid flat about six thousand men on each side; then the musketry removed from the best of worlds some nine or ten thousand blackguards who infested its surface. The bayonet also was the sufficient reason for the death of some thousands of men. The whole might amount to thirty thousand souls. Candide, who trembled like a philosopher, hid himself as well as he could during this heroic butchery.

At last, while the two Kings each commanded a *Te Deum*[10] in his camp, Candide decided to go elsewhere to reason about effects and causes. He clambered over heaps of dead and dying men and reached a neighboring village, which was in ashes; it was an Abare village which the Bulgarians had burned in accordance with international law. Here, old men dazed with blows watched the dying agonies of their murdered wives who clutched their children to their bleeding breasts; there, disembowelled girls who had been made to satisfy the natural appetites of heroes gasped their last sighs; others, half-burned, begged to be put to death. Brains were scattered on the ground among dismembered arms and legs.

Candide fled to another village as fast as he could; it belonged to the Bulgarians, and Abarian heroes had treated it in the same way. Candide, stumbling over quivering limbs or across ruins, at last escaped from the theatre of war, carrying a little food in his knapsack, and never forgetting Mademoiselle Cunegonde. His provisions were all gone when he reached Holland; but, having heard that everyone in that country was rich and a Christian, he had no doubt at all but that he would be as well treated as he had been in the Baron's castle before he had been expelled on account of Mademoiselle Cunegonde's pretty eyes.

He asked an alms of several grave persons, who all replied that if he continued in that way he would be shut up in a house of correction to teach him how to live. He then addressed himself to a man who had been discoursing on charity in a large assembly for an hour on end. This orator, glancing at him askance, said: "What are you doing here? Are you for the good cause?"

"There is no effect without a cause," said Candide modestly. "Everything

[10] hymn of thanks to God for victory.

is necessarily linked up and arranged for the best. It was necessary that I should be expelled from the company of Mademoiselle Cunegonde, that I ran the gauntlet, and that I beg my bread until I can earn it; all this could not have happened differently."

"My friend," said the orator, "do you believe that the Pope is Anti-Christ?"

"I had never heard so before," said Candide, "but whether he is or isn't, I am starving."

"You don't deserve to eat," said the other. "Hence, rascal; hence, you wretch; and never come near me again."

The orator's wife thrust her head out of the window and seeing a man who did not believe that the Pope was Anti-Christ, she poured on his head a full . . . O Heavens! To what excess religious zeal is carried by ladies!

A man who had not been baptized, an honest Anabaptist[11] named Jacques, saw the cruel and ignominious treatment of one of his brothers, a featherless two-legged creature with a soul; he took him home, cleaned him up, gave him bread and beer, presented him with two florins, and even offered to teach him to work at the manufacture of Persian stuffs which are made in Holland. Candide threw himself at the man's feet, exclaiming: "Doctor Pangloss was right in telling me that all is for the best in this world, for I am vastly more touched by your extreme generosity than by the harshness of the gentleman in the black cloak and his good lady."

The next day when he walked out he met a beggar covered with sores, dull-eyed, with the end of his nose fallen away, his mouth awry, his teeth black, who talked huskily, was tormented with a violent cough and spat out a tooth at every cough.

CHAPTER IV

How Candide Met His Old Master in Philosophy, Doctor Pangloss, and What Happened

Candide, moved even more by compassion than by horror, gave this horrible beggar the two florins he had received from the honest Anabaptist, Jacques. The phantom gazed fixedly at him, shed tears and threw its arms round his neck. Candide recoiled in terror.

"Alas!" said the wretch to the other wretch, "don't you recognise your dear Pangloss?"

"What do I hear? You, my dear master! You, in this horrible state! What misfortune has happened to you? Why are you no longer in the noblest of

[11] member of a Protestant sect which opposed infant baptism.

castles? What has become of Mademoiselle Cunegonde, the pearl of young ladies, the masterpiece of Nature?"

"I am exhausted," said Pangloss. Candide immediately took him to the Anabaptist's stable where he gave him a little bread to eat; and when Pangloss had recovered: "Well!" said he, "Cunegonde?"

"Dead," replied the other.

At this word Candide swooned; his friend restored him to his senses with a little bad vinegar which happened to be in the stable. Candide opened his eyes. "Cunegonde dead! Ah! best of worlds, where are you? But what illness did she die of? Was it because she saw me kicked out of her father's noble castle?"

"No," said Pangloss. "She was disembowelled by Bulgarian soldiers, after having been raped to the limit of possibility; they broke the Baron's head when he tried to defend her; the Baroness was cut to pieces; my poor pupil was treated exactly like his sister; and as to the castle, there is not one stone standing on another, not a barn, not a sheep, not a duck, not a tree; but we were well avenged, for the Abares did exactly the same to a neighboring barony which belonged to a Bulgarian Lord." At this, Candide swooned again; but, having recovered and having said all that he ought to say, he inquired the cause and effect, the sufficient reason which had reduced Pangloss to so piteous a state.

"Alas!" said Pangloss, " 'tis love; love, the consoler of the human race, the preserver of the universe, the soul of all tender creatures, gentle love."

"Alas!" said Candide, "I am acquainted with this love, this sovereign of hearts, this soul of our soul; it has never brought me anything but one kiss and twenty kicks in the backside. How could this beautiful cause produce in you so abominable an effect?"

Pangloss replied as follows: "My dear Candide! You remember Paquette, the maidservant of our august Baroness; in her arms I enjoyed the delights of Paradise which have produced the tortures of Hell by which you see I am devoured; she was infected and perhaps is dead. Paquette received this present from a most learned monk, who had it from the source; for he received it from an old countess who had it from a cavalry captain, who owed it to a marchioness, who derived it from a page, who had received it from a Jesuit, who, when a novice, had it in a direct line from one of the companions of Christopher Columbus. For my part, I shall not give it to anyone, for I am dying."

"O Pangloss!" exclaimed Candide, "this is a strange genealogy! Wasn't the devil at the root of it?"

"Not at all," replied that great man. "It was something indispensable in this best of worlds, a necessary ingredient; for, if Columbus in an island of America had not caught this disease, which poisons the source of generation, and often indeed prevents generation, we should not have chocolate and cochineal;[12] it must also be noticed that hitherto in our continent this disease is peculiar to us, like theological disputes. The Turks, the Indians, the Persians, the Chinese, the Siamese and the Japanese are not yet familiar with it; but there is a sufficient reason why they in their turn should become familiar with it in a few centuries. Meanwhile, it has made marvellous progress among us, and especially in those large armies composed of honest, well-bred stipendiaries who decide the destiny of States; it may be asserted that when thirty thousand men fight a pitched battle against an equal number of troops, there are about twenty thousand with the pox on either side."

"Admirable!" said Candide. "But you must get cured."

"How can I?" said Pangloss. "I haven't a sou, my friend, and in the whole extent of this globe, you cannot be bled or receive an enema without paying or without someone paying for you."

This last speech determined Candide; he went and threw himself at the feet of his charitable Anabaptist, Jacques, and drew so touching a picture of the state to which his friend was reduced that the good easy man did not hesitate to succor Pangloss; he had him cured at his own expense. In this cure Pangloss only lost one eye and one ear. He could write well and knew arithmetic perfectly. The Anabaptist made him his bookkeeper. At the end of two months he was compelled to go to Lisbon on business and took his two philosophers on the boat with him. Pangloss explained to him how everything was for the best. Jacques was not of this opinion.

"Men," said he, "must have corrupted nature a little, for they were not born wolves, and they have become wolves.[13] God did not give them twenty-four-pounder cannons or bayonets, and they have made bayonets and cannons to destroy each other. I might bring bankruptcies into the account and Justice which seizes the goods of bankrupts in order to deprive the creditors of them."

"It was all indispensable," replied the one-eyed doctor, "and private misfortunes make the public good, so that the more private misfortunes there are, the more everything is well." [14]

While he was reasoning, the air grew dark, the winds blew from the four quarters of the globe and the ship was attacked by the most horrible tempest in sight of the port of Lisbon.

---

[12] scarlet dye, prized in Europe, but an absurdly disproportionate advantage. [13] a favorite contention of Jean-Jacques Rousseau, Voltaire's contemporary. [14] a further step in reducing philosophical optimism to absurdity.

CHAPTER V

Storm, Shipwreck, Earthquake, and What Happened to Dr. Pangloss, to Candide and the Anabaptist Jacques

Half the enfeebled passengers, suffering from that inconceivable anguish which the rolling of a ship causes in the nerves and in all the humors of bodies shaken in contrary directions, did not retain strength enough even to trouble about the danger. The other half screamed and prayed; the sails were torn, the masts broken, the vessel leaking. Those worked who could, no one cooperated, no one commanded. The Anabaptist tried to help the crew a little; he was on the main deck: a furious sailor struck him violently and stretched him on the deck; but the blow he delivered gave him so violent a shock that he fell head-first out of the ship. He remained hanging and clinging to part of the broken mast. The good Jacques ran to his aid, helped him to climb back, and from the effort he made was flung into the sea in full view of the sailor, who allowed him to drown without condescending even to look at him. Candide came up, saw his benefactor reappear for a moment and then be engulfed for ever. He tried to throw himself after him into the sea; he was prevented by the philosopher Pangloss, who proved to him that the Lisbon roads[15] had been expressly created for the Anabaptist to be drowned in them. While he was proving this a priori,[16] the vessel sank, and every one perished except Pangloss, Candide and the brutal sailor who had drowned the virtuous Anabaptist; the blackguard swam successfully to the shore and Pangloss and Candide were carried there on a plank.

When they had recovered a little, they walked toward Lisbon; they had a little money by the help of which they hoped to be saved from hunger after having escaped the storm. Weeping the death of their benefactor, they had scarcely set foot in the town when they felt the earth tremble under their feet; the sea rose in foaming masses in the port and smashed the ships which rode at anchor. Whirlwinds of flame and ashes covered the streets and squares; the houses collapsed, the roofs were thrown upon the foundations, and the foundations were scattered; thirty thousand inhabitants of every age and both sexes were crushed under the ruins. Whistling and swearing, the sailor said: "There'll be something to pick up here."

"What can be the sufficient reason for this phenomenon?" said Pangloss.

"It is the last day!"[17] cried Candide.

[15] "Where ships may safely ride at anchor."   [16] the deductive method of argument which proceeds from preestablished principles, rather than from experience.   [17] that is, the Day of Judgment.

The sailor immediately ran among the debris, dared death to find money, found it, seized it, got drunk, and having slept off his wine, purchased the favors of the first woman of good will he met on the ruins of the houses and among the dead and dying. Pangloss, however, pulled him by the sleeve. "My friend," said he, "this is not well, you are disregarding universal reason, you choose the wrong time."

"Blood and 'ounds!" he retorted, "I am a sailor and I was born in Batavia; four times have I stamped on the crucifix during four voyages to Japan;[18] you have found the right man for your universal reason!"

Candide had been hurt by some falling stones; he lay in the street covered with debris. He said to Pangloss: "Alas! Get me a little wine and oil; I am dying."

"This earthquake is not a new thing," replied Pangloss. "The town of Lima felt the same shocks in America last year; similar causes produce similar effects; there must certainly be a train of sulphur underground from Lima to Lisbon."

"Nothing is more probable," replied Candide; "but, for God's sake, a little oil and wine."

"What do you mean, probable?" replied the philosopher; "I maintain that it is proved."

Candide lost consciousness, and Pangloss brought him a little water from a neighboring fountain.

Next day they found a little food as they wandered among the ruins and regained a little strength. Afterwards they worked like others to help the inhabitants who had escaped death. Some citizens they had assisted gave them as good a dinner as could be expected in such a disaster; true, it was a dreary meal; the hosts watered their bread with their tears, but Pangloss consoled them by assuring them that things could not be otherwise. "For," said he, "all this is for the best; for, if there is a volcano at Lisbon, it cannot be anywhere else; for it is impossible that things should not be where they are; for all is well."

A little, dark man, a familiar of the Inquisition,[19] who sat beside him, politely took up the conversation, and said: "Apparently, you do not believe in original sin; for, if everything is for the best, there was neither fall nor punishment." [20]

"I most humbly beg your excellency's pardon," replied Pangloss still more politely, "for the fall of man and the curse necessarily entered into the best of all possible worlds."

---

[18] regulation imposed on merchants in an attempt to prevent commerce with Christians.   [19] officer of the Inquisition, or Holy Office, a tribunal which, from the thirteenth century to the eighteenth, attempted to stamp out heresy.   [20] The fall of man (Gen. 3), with his subsequent redemption, is the orthodox Christian explanation of evil.

"Then you do not believe in free will?" said the familiar.

"Your excellency will pardon me," said Pangloss; "free will can exist with absolute necessity; for it was necessary that we should be free; for in short, limited will . . ."

Pangloss was in the middle of his phrase when the familiar nodded to his armed attendant who was pouring out port or Oporto wine for him.

CHAPTER VI

How a Splendid Auto-da-fé
Was Held to Prevent Earthquakes,
And How Candide Was Flogged

After the earthquake which destroyed three-quarters of Lisbon, the wise men of that country could discover no more efficacious way of preventing a total ruin than by giving the people a splendid *auto-da-fé*.[21] It was decided by the university of Coimbre[22] that the sight of several persons being slowly burned in great ceremony is an infallible secret for preventing earthquakes. Consequently they had arrested a Biscayan convicted of having married his fellow-godmother, and two Portuguese who, when eating a chicken, had thrown away the bacon,[23] after dinner they came and bound Dr. Pangloss and his disciple Candide, one because he had spoken and the other because he had listened with an air of approbation; they were both carried separately to extremely cool apartments,[24] where there was never any discomfort from the sun; a week afterwards each was dressed in a sanbenito[25] and their heads were ornamented with paper mitres; Candide's mitre and sanbenito were painted with flames upside down and with devils who had neither tails nor claws; but Pangloss's devils had claws and tails, and his flames were upright.

Dressed in this manner they marched in procession and listened to a most pathetic sermon, followed by lovely plain song music. Candide was flogged in time to the music, while the singing went on; the Biscayan and the two men who had not wanted to eat the bacon were burned, and Pangloss was hanged, although this is not the custom. The very same day, the earth shook again with a terrible clamor.

Candide, terrified, dumbfounded, bewildered, covered with blood, quivering from head to foot, said to himself: "If this is the best of all possible

[21] act of faith, the ceremony of burning heretics at the stake. [22] Portuguese city north of Lisbon. [23] thus indicating that they were Jews. [24] ironical for "dank cells." [25] ceremonial frocks worn by condemned heretics. Voltaire's description is accurate.

worlds, what are the others? Let it pass that I was flogged, for I was flogged by the Bulgarians, but, O my dear Pangloss! The greatest of philosophers! Must I see you hanged without knowing why! O my dear Anabaptist! The best of men! Was it necessary that you should be drowned in port! O Mademoiselle Cunegonde! The pearl of women! Was it necessary that your belly should be slit!"

He was returning, scarcely able to support himself, preached at, flogged, absolved and blessed, when an old woman accosted him and said: "Courage, my son, follow me."

CHAPTER VII

How an Old Woman Took Care
of Candide and How He Regained That
Which He Loved

Candide did not take courage, but he followed the old woman to a hovel; she gave him a pot of ointment to rub on, and left him food and drink; she pointed out a fairly clean bed; near the bed there was a suit of clothes. "Eat, drink, sleep," said she, "and may our Lady of Atocha, my Lord Saint Anthony of Padua and my Lord Saint James of Compostella take care of you; I shall come back tomorrow."

Candide, still amazed by all he had seen, by all he had suffered, and still more by the old woman's charity, tried to kiss her hand. " 'Tis not my hand you should kiss," said the old woman, "I shall come back tomorrow. Rub on the ointment, eat and sleep."

In spite of all his misfortune, Candide ate and went to sleep. Next day the old woman brought him breakfast, examined his back and smeared him with another ointment; later she brought him dinner, and returned in the evening with supper. The next day she went through the same ceremony.

"Who are you?" Candide kept asking her. "Who has inspired you with so much kindness? How can I thank you?"

The good woman never made any reply; she returned in the evening without any supper. "Come with me," said she, "and do not speak a word."

She took him by the arm and walked into the country with him for about a quarter of a mile; they came to an isolated house, surrounded with gardens and canals. The old woman knocked at a little door. It was opened; she led Candide up a back stairway into a gilded apartment, left him on a brocaded sofa, shut the door and went away. Candide thought he was dreaming, and felt that his whole life was a bad dream and the present moment an agreeable dream. The old woman soon reappeared; she was supporting with some difficulty a trembling woman of majestic stature, glittering with precious stones and covered with a veil.

"Remove the veil," said the old woman to Candide. The young man advanced and lifted the veil with a timid hand. What a moment! What a surprise! He thought he saw Mademoiselle Cunegonde, in fact he was looking at her, it was she herself. His strength failed him, he could not utter a word and fell at her feet. Cunegonde fell on the sofa.[26] The old woman dosed them with distilled waters; they recovered their senses and began to speak: at first they uttered only broken words, questions and answers at cross purposes, sighs, tears, exclamations. The old woman advised them to make less noise and left them alone.

"What! Is it you?" said Candide. "You are alive, and I find you here in Portugal! Then you were not raped? Your belly was not slit, as the philosopher Pangloss assured me?"

"Yes, indeed," said the fair Cunegonde; "but those two accidents are not always fatal."

"But your father and mother were killed?"

" 'Tis only too true," said Cunegonde, weeping.

"And your brother?"

"My brother was killed too."

"And why are you in Portugal? And how did you know I was here? And by what strange adventure have you brought me to this house?"

"I will tell you everything," replied the lady, "but first of all you must tell me everything that has happened to you since the innocent kiss you gave me and the kicks you received."

Candide obeyed with profound respect; and, although he was bewildered, although his voice was weak and trembling, although his back was still a little painful, he related in the most natural manner all he had endured since the moment of their separation. Cunegonde raised her eyes to heaven; she shed tears at the death of the good Anabaptist and Pangloss, after which she spoke as follows to Candide, who did not miss a word and devoured her with his eyes.

[26] ladylike! Voltaire both uses and parodies the recognition scenes so frequent in tall tales of adventure.

CHAPTER VIII

Cunegonde's Story

"I was fast asleep in bed when it pleased Heaven to send the Bulgarians to our noble castle of Thunder-ten-tronckh; they murdered my father and brother and cut my mother to pieces. A large Bulgarian six feet tall, seeing that I had swooned at the spectacle, began to rape me; this brought me to, I recovered my senses, I screamed, I struggled, I bit, I scratched, I tried to tear out the big Bulgarian's eyes, not knowing that what was happening in my father's castle was a matter of custom; the brute stabbed me with a knife in the left side where I still have the scar."

"Alas! I hope I shall see it," said the naïf Candide.

"You shall see it," said Cunegonde, "but let me go on."

"Go on," said Candide.

She took up the thread of her story as follows: "A Bulgarian captain came in, saw me covered with blood, and the soldier did not disturb himself. The captain was angry at the brute's lack of respect to him, and killed him on my body. Afterwards, he had me bandaged and took me to his billet as a prisoner of war. I washed the few shirts he had and did the cooking; I must admit he thought me very pretty; and I will not deny that he was very well built and that his skin was white and soft; otherwise he had little wit and little philosophy; it was plain that he had not been brought up by Dr. Pangloss. At the end of three months he lost all his money and got tired of me; he sold me to a Jew named Don Issachar, who traded in Holland and Portugal and had a passion for women. This Jew devoted himself to my person but he could not triumph over it; I resisted him better than the Bulgarian soldier; a lady of honor may be raped once, but it strengthens her virtue. In order to subdue me, the Jew brought me to this country house. Up till then I believed that there was nothing on earth so splendid as the castle of Thunder-ten-tronckh; I was undeceived.

"One day the Grand Inquisitor noticed me at Mass; he ogled me continually and sent a message that he wished to speak to me on secret affairs. I was taken to his palace; I informed him of my birth; he pointed out how much it was beneath my rank to belong to an Israelite. A proposition was made on his behalf to Don Issachar to give me up to His Lordship. Don Issachar, who is the court banker and a man of influence, would not agree. The Inquisitor threatened him with an *auto-da-fé*. At last the Jew was frightened and made a bargain whereby the house and I belong to both in common. The Jew has Mondays, Wednesdays and the Sabbath day, and the Inquisitor has the other days of the week. This arrangement has lasted for six months. It has not been without quarrels; for it has often been debated whether the night between Saturday and Sunday belonged to the old law or the new. For my part, I have hitherto resisted them both; and I think that is the reason why they still love me.

"At last My Lord the Inquisitor was pleased to arrange an *auto-da-fé* to remove the scourge of earthquakes and to intimidate Don Issachar. He honored me with an invitation. I had an excellent seat; and refreshments were served to the ladies between the Mass and the execution. I was indeed horror stricken when I saw the burning of the two Jews and the honest Biscayan who had married his fellow-godmother; but what was my surprise, my terror, my anguish, when I saw in a sanbenito and under a mitre a face which resembled Pangloss's! I rubbed my eyes, I looked carefully, I saw him hanged; and I fainted. I had scarcely recovered my senses when I saw you stripped naked; that was the height of horror, of consternation, of grief and despair. I will frankly tell you that your skin is even whiter and of a more perfect tint than that of my Bulgarian captain. This spectacle redoubled all the feelings which crushed and devoured me. I exclaimed, I tried to say: 'Stop, Barbarians!' but my voice failed and my cries would have been useless. When you had been well flogged, I said to myself: 'How does it happen that the charming Candide and the wise Pangloss are in Lisbon, the one to receive a hundred lashes, and the other to be hanged, by order of My Lord the Inquisitor, whose darling I am? Pangloss deceived me cruelly when he said that all is for the best in the world.'

"I was agitated, distracted, sometimes beside myself and sometimes ready to die of faintness, and my head was filled with the massacre of my father, of my mother, of my brother, the insolence of my horrid Bulgarian soldier, the gash he gave me, my slavery, my life as a kitchen wench, my Bulgarian captain, my horrid Don Issachar, my abominable Inquisitor, the hanging of Dr. Pangloss, that long plain song *miserere*[27] during which you were flogged, and above all the kiss I gave you behind the screen that day when I saw you for the last time. I praised God for bringing you back to me through so many trials, I ordered my old woman to take care of you and to bring you here as soon as she could. She has carried out my commission very well; I have enjoyed the inexpressible pleasure of seeing you again, of listening to you, and of speaking to you. You must be very hungry; I have a good appetite; let us begin by having supper."

Both sat down to supper; and after supper they returned to the handsome sofa we have already mentioned; they were still there when Signor Don Issachar, one of the masters of the house, arrived. It was the day of the Sabbath. He came to enjoy his rights and to express his tender love.

[27] Latin chant: "Have mercy upon me, O God."

CHAPTER IX

What Happened to Cunegonde, to Candide, to the Grand Inquisitor and to a Jew

This Issachar was the most choleric Hebrew who had been seen in Israel since the Babylonian captivity.[28] "What!" said he. "Bitch of a Galilean, isn't it enough to have the Inquisitor? Must this scoundrel share with me too?"

So saying, he drew a long dagger which he always carried and, thinking that his adversary was unarmed, threw himself upon Candide; but our good Westphalian had received an excellent sword from the old woman along with his suit of clothes. He drew his sword, and although he had a most gentle character, laid the Israelite stone-dead on the floor at the feet of the fair Cunegonde.

"Holy Virgin!" she exclaimed, "what will become of us? A man killed in my house! If the police come we are lost."

"If Pangloss had not been hanged," said Candide, "he would have given us good advice in this extremity, for he was a great philosopher. In default of him, let us consult the old woman."

She was extremely prudent and was beginning to give her advice when another little door opened. It was an hour after midnight, and Sunday was beginning. This day belonged to My Lord the Inquisitor. He came in and saw the flogged Candide sword in hand, a corpse lying on the ground, Cunegonde in terror, and the old woman giving advice. At this moment, here is what happened in Candide's soul and the manner of his reasoning: "If this holy man calls for help, he will infallibly have me burned; he might do as much to Cunegonde; he had me pitilessly lashed; he is my rival; I am in the mood to kill, there is no room for hesitation."

His reasoning was clear and swift; and, without giving the Inquisitor time to recover from his surprise, he pierced him through and through and cast him beside the Jew.

"Here's another," said Cunegonde, "there is no chance of mercy; we are excommunicated, our last hour has come. How does it happen that you, who were born so mild, should kill a Jew and a prelate in two minutes?"

"My dear young lady," replied Candide, "when a man is in love, jealous, and has been flogged by the Inquisition, he is beside himself."

The old woman than spoke up and said: "In the stable are three Andalusian horses, with their saddles and bridles; let the brave Candide prepare

[28] The Jews were held in captivity by the Babylonians in the sixth century, B.C.

them; mademoiselle has moidores[29] and diamonds; let us mount quickly, although I can only sit on one buttock, and go to Cadiz; the weather is beautifully fine, and it is most pleasant to travel in the coolness of the night."

Candide immediately saddled the three horses. Cunegonde, the old woman and he rode thirty miles without stopping. While they were riding away, the Holy Hermandad [30] arrived at the house; My Lord was buried in a splendid church and Issachar was thrown into a sewer. . . .

Chapters X through XVI recount a few adventures and include several extended anecdotes. Candide and his party arrive at Cadiz and decide to flee from Europe. They travel by ship to South America, debarking at Buenos Aires. The governor of Buenos Aires decides to have Cunegonde for his own, and Candide decides he must escape when Cunegonde informs him that the governor plans his death. He is accompanied by Cacambo, a half-breed valet he had taken on in Cadiz. They reach Paraguay, where they are welcomed by the "Reverend Father Commandant" of a Jesuit community. To Candide's surprise, the priest turns out to be Cunegonde's lost brother. The young baron is delighted to see Candide again, but when he discovers that Candide hopes to marry his sister, he falls into a rage at the commoner's impudence and strikes Candide across the face with the flat of his sword. Candide draws his own sword and runs the baron through. He and Cacambo escape, have a brief adventure among a tribe of Indians, and then again find themselves wandering.

CHAPTER XVII

Arrival of Candide and His Valet in the Country of Eldorado [31] and What They Saw There

When they reached the frontiers of the Oreillons, Cacambo said to Candide: "You see this hemisphere is no better than the other; take my advice, let us go back to Europe by the shortest road."

"How can we go back," said Candide, "and where can we go? If I go to

---

[29] Portuguese coin. As a slight concession to local color and realism, Voltaire invariably used the terms for money and food that were proper to the country concerned.   [30] Holy Brotherhood, an association formed in Spain to track down criminals.   [31] fabulous Land of Gold, in which even Sir Walter Raleigh once believed.

my own country, the Bulgarians and the Abares are murdering everybody; if
I return to Portugal I shall be burned; if we stay here, we run the risk of
being spitted at any moment. But how can I make up my mind to leave
that part of the world where Mademoiselle Cunegonde is living?"

"Let us go to Cayenne," [32] said Cacambo, "we shall find Frenchmen there,
for they go all over the world; they might help us. Perhaps God will have
pity on us."

It was not easy to go to Cayenne. They knew roughly the direction to
take, but mountains, rivers, precipices, brigands and savages were everywhere terrible obstacles. Their horses died of fatigue; their provisions were
exhausted; for a whole month they lived on wild fruits and at last found
themselves near a little river fringed with cocoanut-trees which supported
their lives and their hopes.

Cacambo, who always gave advice as prudent as the old woman's, said to
Candide: "We can go no farther, we have walked far enough; I can see an
empty canoe in the bank, let us fill it with cocoanuts, get into the little boat
and drift with the current; a river always leads to some inhabited place. If
we do not find anything pleasant, we shall at least find something new."

"Come on then," said Candide, "and let us trust to Providence."

They drifted for some leagues between banks which were sometimes
flowery, sometimes bare, sometimes flat, sometimes steep. The river continually became wider; finally it disappeared under an arch of frightful
rocks which towered up to the very sky. The two travellers were bold
enough to trust themselves to the current under this arch. The stream,
narrowed between walls, carried them with horrible rapidity and noise.
After twenty-four hours they saw daylight again; but their canoe was
wrecked on reefs; they had to crawl from rock to rock for a whole league
and at last they discovered an immense horizon, bordered by inaccessible
mountains. The country was cultivated for pleasure as well as for necessity;
everywhere the useful was agreeable. The roads were covered or rather
ornamented with carriages of brilliant material and shape, carrying men
and women of singular beauty, who were rapidly drawn along by large red
sheep whose swiftness surpassed that of the finest horses of Andalusia,
Tetuan, and Mequinez.[33]

"This country," said Candide, "is better than Westphalia."

He landed with Cacambo near the first village he came to. Several children
of the village, dressed in torn gold brocade, were playing quoits outside the
village. Our two men from the other world amused themselves by looking
on; their quoits were large round pieces, yellow, red and green which shone
with peculiar lustre. The travellers were curious enough to pick up some of

[32] capital of French Guiana.   [33] Tetuan and Mequinez are Moroccan towns.

them; they were of gold, emeralds and rubies, the least of which would have been the greatest ornament in the Mogul's throne.

"No doubt," said Cacambo, "these children are the sons of the King of this country playing at quoits."

At that moment the village schoolmaster appeared to call them into school.

"This," said Candide, "is the tutor of the Royal Family."

The little beggars immediately left their game, abandoning their quoits and everything with which they had been playing. Candide picked them up, ran to the tutor, and presented them to him humbly, giving him to understand by signs that their Royal Highnesses had forgotten their gold and their precious stones. The village schoolmaster smiled, threw them on the ground, gazed for a moment at Candide's face with much surprise and continued on his way. The travellers did not fail to pick up the gold, the rubies and the emeralds.

"Where are we?" cried Candide. "The children of the King must be well brought up, since they are taught to despise gold and precious stones."

Cacambo was as much surprised as Candide. At last they reached the first house in the village, which was built like a European palace. There were crowds of people round the door and still more inside; very pleasant music could be heard and there was a delicious smell of cooking. Cacambo went up to the door and heard them speaking Peruvian; it was his maternal tongue, for everyone knows that Cacambo was born in a village of Tucuman where nothing else is spoken.

"I will act as your interpreter," he said to Candide, "this is an inn, let us enter."

Immediately two boys and two girls of the inn, dressed in cloth of gold, whose hair was bound up with ribbons, invited them to sit down to the table d'hôte. They served four soups each garnished with two parrots, a boiled condor which weighed two hundred pounds, two roast monkeys of excellent flavor, three hundred colibris in one dish and six hundred hummingbirds in another, exquisite ragouts and delicious pastries, all in dishes of a sort of rock crystal. The boys and girls brought several sorts of drinks made of sugarcane. Most of the guests were merchants and coachmen, all extremely polite, who asked Cacambo a few questions with the most delicate discretion and answered his in a satisfactory manner.

When the meal was over, Cacambo, like Candide, thought he could pay the reckoning by throwing on the table two of the large pieces of gold he had picked up; the host and hostess laughed until they had to hold their sides. At last they recovered themselves.

"Gentlemen," said the host, "we perceive you are strangers; we are not accustomed to seeing them. Forgive us if we began to laugh when you offered us in payment the stones from our highways. No doubt you have none of the money of this country, but you do not need any to dine here. All the hotels established for the utility of commerce are paid for by the government. You have been ill entertained here because this is a poor village; but everywhere else you will be received as you deserve to be."

Cacambo explained to Candide all that the host had said, and Candide listened in the same admiration and disorder with which his friends Cacambo interpreted. "What can this country be," they said to each other, "which is unknown to the rest of the world and where all nature is so different from ours? Probably it is the country where everything is for the best; for there must be one country of that sort. And, in spite of what Dr. Pangloss said, I often noticed that everything went very ill in Westphalia."

CHAPTER XVIII

What They Saw in the Land of Eldorado

Cacambo informed the host of his curiosity, and the host said: "I am a very ignorant man and am all the better for it; but we have here an old man who has retired from the court and who is the most learned and most communicative man in the kingdom." And he at once took Cacambo to the old man. Candide now played only the second part and accompanied his valet. They entered a very simple house, for the door was only of silver and the panelling of the apartments in gold, but so tastefully carved that the richest decorations did not surpass it. The antechamber indeed was only encrusted with rubies and emeralds; but the order with which everything was arranged atoned for this extreme simplicity.

The old man received the two strangers on a sofa padded with colibri feathers, and presented them with drinks in diamond cups; after which he satisfied their curiosity in these words: "I am a hundred and seventy-two years old and I heard from my late father, the King's equerry, the astonishing revolutions of Peru of which he had been an eye-witness. The kingdom where we now are is the ancient country of the Incas, who most imprudently left it to conquer part of the world and were at last destroyed by the Spaniards. The princes of their family who remained in their native country had more wisdom; with the consent of the nation, they ordered that no inhabitants should ever leave our little kingdom, and this it is that has preserved our innocence and our felicity. The Spaniards had some vague knowledge of this country, which they called Eldorado, and about a hundred years ago an Englishman named Raleigh came very near to it; but, since we are surrounded by inaccessible rocks and precipices, we have hitherto been exempt from the rapacity of the nations of Europe who have an inconceivable lust for the pebbles and mud of our land and would kill us to the last man to get possession of them."

The conversation was long; it touched upon the form of the government, manners, women, public spectacles and the arts. Finally Candide, who was always interested in metaphysics, asked through Cacambo whether the country had a religion.

The old man blushed a little. "How can you doubt it?" said he. "Do you think we are ingrates?"

Cacambo humbly asked what was the religion of Eldorado.

The old man blushed again. "Can there be two religions?" said he. "We have, I think, the religion of every one else; we adore God from evening until morning."

"Do you adore only one God?" said Cacambo, who continued to act as the interpreter of Candide's doubts.

"Manifestly," said the old man, "there are not two or three or four. I must confess that the people of your world ask very extraordinary questions."

Candide continued to press the old man with questions; he wished to know how they prayed to God in Eldorado.

"We do not pray," said the good and respectable sage, "we have nothing to ask from him; he has given us everything necessary and we continually give him thanks."

Candide was curious to see the priests; and asked where they were.

The good old man smiled. "My friends," said he, "we are all priests; the King and all the heads of families solemnly sing praises every morning, accompanied by five or six thousand musicians."

"What! Have you no monks to teach, to dispute, to govern, to intrigue and to burn people who do not agree with them?"

"For that, we should have to become fools," said the old man; "here we are all of the same opinion and do not understand what you mean with your monks."

At all this Candide was in an ecstasy and said to himself: "This is very different from Westphalia and the castle of His Lordship the Baron; if our friend Pangloss had seen Eldorado, he would not have said that the castle of Thunder-ten-tronckh was the best of all that exists on the earth; certainly, a man should travel."

After this long conversation the good old man ordered a carriage to be harnessed with six sheep and gave the two travellers twelve of his servants to take them to court. "You will excuse me," he said, "if my age deprives me of the honor of accompanying you. The King will receive you in a manner which will not displease you and doubtless you will pardon the customs of the country if any of them disconcert you."

Candide and Cacambo entered the carriage; the six sheep galloped off and in less than four hours they reached the King's palace, which was situated at one end of the capital. The portal was two hundred and twenty feet high and a hundred feet wide; it is impossible to describe its material. Anyone can see the prodigious superiority it must have over the pebbles and sand we call *gold* and *gems*.

Twenty beautiful maidens of the guard received Candide and Cacambo as they alighted from the carriage, conducted them to the baths and dressed them in robes woven from the down of colibris; after which the principal male and female officers of the Crown led them to his Majesty's apartment through two files of a thousand musicians each, according to the usual custom. As they approached the throneroom, Cacambo asked one of the chief officers how they should behave in his Majesty's presence; whether they should fall on their knees or flat on their faces, whether they should put their hands on their heads or on their backsides; whether they should lick the dust of the throneroom; in a word, what was the ceremony?

"The custom," said the chief officer, "is to embrace the King and to kiss him on either cheek."

Candide and Cacambo threw their arms round his Majesty's neck; he received them with all imaginable favor and politely asked them to supper. Meanwhile they were carried to see the town, the public buildings rising to the very skies, the market-places ornamented with thousands of columns, the fountains of rose-water and of liquors distilled from surgarcane, which played continually in the public squares paved with precious stones which emitted a perfume like that of cloves and cinnamon.

Candide asked to see the law courts; he was told there were none, and that nobody ever went to law. He asked if there were prisons and was told there were none. He was still more surprised and pleased by the palace of sciences, where he saw a gallery two thousand feet long, filled with instruments of mathematics and physics.

After they had explored all the afternoon about a thousandth part of the town, they were taken back to the King. Candide sat down to table with his Majesty, his valet Cacambo and several ladies. Never was better cheer, and never was anyone wittier at supper than his Majesty. Cacambo explained the King's witty remarks to Candide and even when translated they still appeared witty. Among all the things which amazed Candide, this did not amaze him the least.

They enjoyed this hospitality for a month. Candide repeatedly said to Cacambo: "Once again, my friend, it is quite true that the castle where I was born cannot be compared with this country; but then Mademoiselle Cunegonde is not here and you probably have a mistress in Europe. If we remain here, we shall only be like everyone else; but if we return to our own world with only twelve sheep laden with Eldorado pebbles, we shall be richer than all the kings put together; we shall have no more Inquisitors to fear and we can easily regain Mademoiselle Cunegonde."

Cacambo agreed with this; it is so pleasant to be on the move, to show off before friends, to make a parade of the things seen on one's travels, that these two happy men resolved to be so no longer and to ask his Majesty's permission to depart.

"You are doing a very silly thing," said the King. "I know my country is small; but when we are comfortable anywhere we should stay there; I certainly have not the right to detain foreigners, that is a tyranny which does not exist either in our manners or our laws; all men are free, leave when you please, but the way out is very difficult. It is impossible to ascend the rapid river by which you miraculously came here and which flows under arches of rock. The mountains which surround the whole of my kingdom are ten thousand feet high and are perpendicular like walls; they are more than ten leagues broad, and you can only get down from them by way of precipices. However, since you must go, I will give orders to the directors of machinery to make a machine which will carry you comfortably. When you have been taken to the other side of the mountains, nobody can proceed any farther with you; for my subjects have sworn never to pass this boundary and they are too wise to break their oath. Ask anything else of me you wish."

"We ask nothing of your Majesty," said Cacambo, "except a few sheep laden with provisions, pebbles and the mud of this country."

The King laughed. "I cannot understand," said he, "the taste you people of Europe have for our yellow mud; but take as much as you wish, and much good may it do you."

He immediately ordered his engineers to make a machine to hoist these two extraordinary men out of his kingdom. Three thousand learned scientists worked at it; it was ready in a fortnight and only cost about twenty million pounds sterling in the money of that country. Candide and Cacambo were placed on the machine; there were two large red sheep saddled and bridled for them to ride on when they had passed the mountains, twenty sumpter sheep[34] laden with provisions, thirty carrying presents of the most curious productions of the country and fifty laden with gold, precious stones and diamonds. The King embraced the two vagabonds tenderly. Their departure was a splendid sight and so was the ingenious manner in which they and their sheep were hoisted on to the top of the mountains. The scientists took leave of them after having landed them safely, and Candide's only desire and object was to go and present Mademoiselle Cunegonde with his sheep.

"We have sufficient to pay the governor of Buenos Ayres," said he, "if Mademoiselle Cunegonde can be bought. Let us go to Cayenne, and take ship, and then we will see what kingdom we will buy."

---

[34] pack-sheep.

CHAPTER XIX

What Happened to Them at Surinam and How Candide Made The Acquaintance of Martin

Our two travellers' first day was quite pleasant. They were encouraged by the idea of possessing more treasures than all Asia, Europe and Africa could collect. Candide in transport carved the name of Cunegonde on the trees. On the second day two of the sheep stuck in a marsh and were swallowed up with their loads; two other sheep died of fatigue a few days later; then seven or eight died of hunger in a desert; several days afterwards others fell off precipices. Finally, after they had travelled for a hundred days, they had only two sheep left.

Candide said to Cacambo: "My friend, you see how perishable are the riches of this world; nothing is steadfast but virtue and the happiness of seeing Mademoiselle Cunegonde again."

"I admit it," said Cacambo, "but we still have two sheep with more treasures than ever the King of Spain will have, and in the distance I see a town I suspect is Surinam,[35] which belongs to the Dutch. We are at the end of our troubles and the beginning of our happiness."

As they drew near the town they came upon a negro lying on the ground wearing only half his clothes, that is to say, a pair of blue cotton drawers; this poor man had no left leg and no right hand. "Good heavens!" said Candide to him in Dutch, "what are you doing there, my friend, in that horrible state?"

"I am waiting for my master, the famous merchant Monsieur Vanderdendur."

"Was it Monsieur Vanderdendur," said Candide, "who treated you in that way?"

"Yes, sir," said the negro, "it is the custom. We are given a pair of cotton drawers twice a year as clothing. When we work in the sugar mills and the grindstone catches our fingers, they cut off the hand; when we try to run away, they cut off a leg. Both these things happened to me. This is the price paid for the sugar you eat in Europe. But when my mother sold me for ten patagons on the coast of Guinea, she said to me: 'My dear child, give thanks to our fetishes, always worship them, and they will make you happy; you have the honor to be a slave of our lords the white men and thereby you have made the fortune of your father and mother.' Alas! I do not know whether I made their fortune, but they certainly did not make mine. Dogs, monkeys and parrots are a thousand times less miserable than we are; the

[35] in Dutch Guiana.

Dutch fetishes who converted me tell me that we are all of us, whites and blacks, the children of Adam. I am not a genealogist, but if these preachers tell the truth, we are all second cousins. Now, you will admit that no one could treat his relatives in a more horrible way."

"O Pangloss!" cried Candide. "This is an abomination you had not guessed; this is too much, in the end I shall have to renounce optimism."

"What is optimism?" said Cacambo.

"Alas!" said Candide, "it is the mania of maintaining that everything is well when we are wretched." [36] And he shed tears as he looked at his negro; and he entered Surinam weeping.

The first thing they inquired was whether there was any ship in the port which could be sent to Buenos Ayres. The person they addressed happened to be a Spanish captain, who offered to strike an honest bargain with them. He arranged to meet them at an inn. Candide and the faithful Cacambo went and waited for him with their two sheep. Candide, who blurted everything out, told the Spaniard all his adventures and confessed that he wanted to elope with Mademoiselle Cunegonde.

"I shall certainly not take you to Buenos Ayres," said the captain. "I should be hanged and you would, too. The fair Cunegonde is his Lordship's favorite mistress."

Candide was thunderstruck; he sobbed for a long time; then he took Cacambo aside. "My dear friend," said he, "this is what you must do. We have each of us in our pockets five or six millions worth of diamonds; you are more skilful than I am; go to Buenos Ayres and get Mademoiselle Cunegonde. If the governor makes any difficulties give him a million; if he is still obstinate give him two; you have not killed an Inquisitor so they will not suspect you. I will fit out another ship, I will go and wait for you at Venice; it is a free country where there is nothing to fear from Bulgarians, Abares, Jews or Inquisitors."

Cacambo applauded this wise resolution; he was in despair at leaving a good master who had become his intimate friend; but the pleasure of being useful to him overcame the grief of leaving him. They embraced with tears. Candide urged him not to forget the good old woman. Cacambo set off that very same day; he was a very good man, this Cacambo.

Candide remained some time longer at Surinam waiting for another captain to take him to Italy with the two sheep he had left. He engaged servants and bought everything necessary for a long voyage. At last Monsieur Vanderdendur, the owner of a large ship, came to see him.

"How much do you want," he asked this man, "to take me straight to Venice with my servants, my baggage and these two sheep?"

[36] This is Voltaire's main point. Happiness in the abstract has no meaning for the suffering individual.

The captain asked for ten thousand piastres. Candide did not hesitate. "Oh! Ho!" said the prudent Vanderdendur to himself, "this foreigner gives ten thousand piastres immediately! He must be very rich." He returned a moment afterwards and said he could not sail for less than twenty thousand.

"Very well, you shall have them," said Candide.

"Whew!" said the merchant to himself, "this man gives twenty thousand piastres as easily as ten thousand." He came back again, and said he could not take him to Venice for less than thirty thousand piastres.

"Then you shall have thirty thousand," replied Candide.

"Oho!" said the Dutch merchant to himself again, "thirty thousand piastres is nothing to this man; obviously the two sheep are laden with immense treasures; I will not insist any further; first let me make him pay the thirty thousand piastres, and then we will see."

Candide sold two little diamonds, the smaller of which was worth more than all the money the captain asked. He paid him in advance. The two sheep were taken on board. Candide followed in a little boat to join the ship which rode at anchor; the captain watched his time, set his sails and weighed anchor; the wind was favorable. Candide, bewildered and stupefied, soon lost sight of him. "Alas!" he cried, "this is a trick worthy of the old world."

He returned to shore, in grief; for he had lost enough to make the fortunes of twenty kings. He went to the Dutch judge; and, as he was rather disturbed, he knocked loudly at the door; he went in, related what had happened and talked a little louder than he ought to have done. The judge began by fining him ten thousand piastres for the noise he had made; he then listened patiently to him, promised to look into his affair as soon as the merchant returned, and charged him another ten thousand piastres for the expenses of the audience.

This behavior reduced Candide to despair; he had indeed endured misfortunes a thousand times more painful; but the calmness of the judge and of the captain who had robbed him, stirred up his bile and plunged him into a black melancholy. The malevolence of men revealed itself to his mind in all its ugliness; he entertained only gloomy ideas.

At last a French ship was about to leave for Bordeaux and, since he no longer had any sheep laden with diamonds to put on board, he hired a cabin at a reasonable price and announced throughout the town that he would give the passage, food and two thousand piastres to an honest man who would make the journey with him, on condition that this man was the most unfortunate and the most disgusted with his condition in the whole province. Such a crowd of applicants arrived that a fleet would not have contained them. Candide, wishing to choose among the most likely, picked out twenty persons who seemed reasonably sociable and who all claimed to deserve his preference. He collected them in a tavern and gave them supper, on condition that each took an oath to relate truthfully the story of his life, promising that he would choose the man who seemed to him the most deserving of pity and to have the most cause for being discontented with his condition, and that he would give the others a little money. The sitting lasted until four o'clock in the morning. As Candide listened to their adventures he remembered what the old woman had said on the voyage to Buenos Ayres and how she had wagered that there was nobody on the boat who had not experienced very great misfortunes. At each story which was told him, he thought of Pangloss.

"This Pangloss," said he, "would have some difficulty in supporting his system. I wish he were here. Certainly, if everything is well, it is only in Eldorado and not in the rest of the world."

He finally determined in favor of a poor man of letters who had worked ten years for the booksellers at Amsterdam. He judged that there was no occupation in the world which could more disgust a man.[37] This man of letters, who was also a good man, had been robbed by his wife, beaten by his son, and abandoned by his daughter, who had eloped with a Portuguese. He had just been deprived of a small post on which he depended and the preachers of Surinam were persecuting him because they thought he was a Socinian.[38] It must be admitted that the others were at least as unfortunate as he was; but Candide hoped that this learned man would help to pass the time during the voyage. All his other rivals considered that Candide was doing them a great injustice; but he soothed them down by giving each of them a hundred piastres.

CHAPTER XX

What Happened to Candide and Martin at Sea

So the old man, who was called Martin, embarked with Candide for Bordeaux. Both had seen and suffered much; and if the ship had been sailing from Surinam to Japan by way of the Cape of Good Hope they would have been able to discuss moral and physical evil during the whole voyage. However, Candide had one great advantage over Martin, because he still hoped to see Mademoiselle Cunegonde again, and Martin had nothing to hope for; moreover, he possessed gold and diamonds; and, although he had lost a hundred large red sheep laden with the greatest

[37] Voltaire had had unhappy personal dealings with the Dutch publishers. [38] sect resembling the Unitarians.

treasures on earth, although he was still enraged at being robbed by the Dutch captain, yet when he thought of what he still had left in his pockets and when he talked of Cunegonde, especially at the end of a meal, he still inclined towards the system of Pangloss.

"But what do you think of all this, Martin?" said he to the man of letters. "What is your view of moral and physical evil?"

"Sir," replied Martin, "my priests accused me of being a Socinian; but the truth is I am a Manichean." [39]

"You are poking fun at me," said Candide, "there are no Manicheans left in the world."

"I am one," said Martin. "I don't know what to do about it, but I am unable to think in any other fashion."

"You must be possessed by the devil," said Candide.

"He takes so great a share in the affairs of this world," said Martin, "that he might well be in me, as he is everywhere else; but I confess that when I consider this globe, or rather this globule, I think that God has abandoned it to some evil creature—always excepting Eldorado. I have never seen a town which did not desire the ruin of the next town, never a family which did not wish to exterminate some other family. Everywhere the weak loathe the powerful before whom they cower and the powerful treat them like flocks of sheep whose wool and flesh are to be sold. A million drilled assassins go from one end of Europe to the other murdering and robbing with discipline in order to earn their bread, because there is no honester occupation; and in the towns which seem to enjoy peace and where the arts flourish, men are devoured by more envy, troubles and worries than the afflictions of a besieged town. Secret griefs are even more cruel than public miseries. In a word, I have seen so much and endured so much that I have become a Manichean."

"Yet there is some good," replied Candide.

"There may be," said Martin, "but I do not know it."

In the midst of this dispute they heard the sound of cannon. The noise increased every moment. Every one took his telescope. About three miles away they saw two ships engaged in battle; and the wind brought them so near the French ship that they had the pleasure[40] of seeing the fight at their ease. At last one of the two ships fired a broadside so accurately and so low down that the other ship began to sink. Candide and Martin distinctly saw a hundred men on the main deck of the sinking ship; they raised their hands to Heaven and uttered frightful shrieks; in a moment all were engulfed.

"Well!" said Martin, "that is how men treat each other."

[39] believer in the two Principles of Good and Evil which dispute the government of the universe and man's fate. The sect flourished at the time of St. Augustine.
[40] ironical.

"It is certainly true," said Candide, "that there is something diabolical in this affair."

As he was speaking, he saw something of a brilliant red swimming near the ship. They launched a boat to see what it could be; it was one of his sheep. Candide felt more joy at recovering this sheep than grief at losing a hundred all laden with large diamonds from Eldorado.

The French captain soon perceived that the captain of the remaining ship was a Spaniard and that the sunken ship was a Dutch pirate; the captain was the very same who had robbed Candide. The immense wealth this scoundrel had stolen was swallowed up with him in the sea and only a sheep was saved.

"You see," said Candide to Martin, "that crime is sometimes punished; this scoundrel of a Dutch captain has met the fate he deserved."

"Yes," said Martin, "but was it necessary that the other passengers on his ship should perish too? God punished the thief, and the devil punished the others."

Meanwhile the French and Spanish ships continued on their way and Candide continued his conversation with Martin. They argued for a fortnight and at the end of the fortnight they had got no further than at the beginning. But after all, they talked, they exchanged ideas, they consoled each other. Candide stroked his sheep. "Since I have found you again," said he, "I may very likely find Cunegonde."

CHAPTER XXI

Candide and Martin Approach
the Coast of France
and Argue

At last they sighted the coast of France.

"Have you ever been to France, Monsieur Martin?" said Candide.

"Yes," said Martin, "I have traversed several provinces. In some half the inhabitants are crazy, in others they are too artful, in some they are usually quite gentle and stupid, and in others they think they are clever; in all of them the chief occupation is making love, the second scandal-mongering and the third talking nonsense."

"But Monsieur Martin, have you seen Paris?"

"Yes, I have seen Paris; it is a mixture of all the species; it is a chaos, a throng where everybody hunts for pleasure and hardly anybody finds it, at least so far as I could see. I did not stay there long; when I arrived there I was robbed of everything I had by pickpockets at Saint-Germain's fair;

they thought I was a thief and I spent a week in prison; after which I became a printer's reader to earn enough to return to Holland on foot. I met the scribbling rabble, the intriguing rabble and the fanatical rabble. We hear that there are very polite people in the town; I am glad to think so."

"For my part, I have not the least curiosity to see France," said Candide. "You can easily guess that when a man has spent a month in Eldorado he cares to see nothing else in the world but Mademoiselle Cunegonde. I shall go and wait for her at Venice; we will go to Italy by way of France; will you come with me?"

"Willingly," said Martin. "They say that Venice is only for the Venetian nobles but that foreigners are nevertheless well received when they have plenty of money; I have none, you have plenty, I will follow you anywhere."

"Apropos," said Candide, "do you think the earth was orginally a sea, as we are assured by that large book[41] belonging to the captain?"

"I don't believe it in the least," said Martin, "any more than all the other whimsies we have been pestered with recently!"

"But to what end was this world formed?" said Candide.

"To infuriate us," replied Martin.

"Are you not very much surprised," continued Candide, "by the love those two girls of the country of the Oreillons had for those two monkeys, whose adventure I told you?"

"Not in the least," said Martin. "I see nothing strange in their passion; I have seen so many extraordinary things that nothing seems extraordinary to me."

"Do you think," said Candide, "that men have always massacred each other, as they do today? Have they always been liars, cheats, traitors, brigands, weak, flighty, cowardly, envious, gluttonous, drunken, grasping, and vicious, bloody, backbiting, debauched, fanatical, hypocritical and silly?"

"Do you think," said Martin, "that sparrow hawks have always eaten the pigeons they came across?"

"Yes, of course," said Candide.

"Well," said Martin, "if sparrow hawks have always possessed the same nature, why should you expect men to change theirs?"

"Oh!" said Candide, "there is a great difference; free will . . . ." Arguing thus, they arrived at Bordeaux.

[41] The large book might well be the Bible, or *The Theory of the Earth* by Buffon, with whom Voltaire entered into more or less friendly debate. The new geological ideas seemed at first to confirm the Biblical flood.

CHAPTER XXII

What Happened to Candide
and Martin in France

Candide remained in Bordeaux only long enough to sell a few Eldorado pebbles and to provide himself with a two-seated post chaise, for he could no longer get on without his philosopher Martin; but he was very much grieved at having to part with his sheep, which he left with the Academy of Sciences at Bordeaux. The Academy offered as the subject for a prize that year the cause of the redness of the sheep's fleece; and the prize was awarded to a learned man in the North, who proved by A plus B minus c divided by z that the sheep must be red and die of the sheep-pox.

However all the travellers Candide met in taverns on the way said to him: "We are going to Paris." This general eagerness at length made him wish to see that capital; it was not far out of the road to Venice.

He entered by the Faubourg Saint-Marceau[42] and thought he was in the ugliest village of Westphalia. Candide had scarcely reached his inn when he was attacked by a slight illness caused by fatigue. As he wore an enormous diamond on his finger, and a prodigiously heavy strongbox had been observed in his train, he immediately had with him two doctors he had not asked for, several intimate friends who would not leave him and two devotees who kept making him broth.

Said Martin: "I remember that I was ill too when I first came to Paris; I was very poor; so I had no friends, no devotees, no doctors, and I got well."

However, with the aid of medicine and bloodletting,[43] Candide's illness became serious. An inhabitant of the district came and gently asked him for a note payable to bearer in the next world;[44] Candide would have nothing to do with it. The devotees assured him that it was a new fashion; Candide replied that he was not a fashionable man. Martin wanted to throw the inhabitant out the window; the clerk swore that Candide should not be buried; Martin swore that he would bury the clerk if he continued to annoy them. The quarrel became heated; Martin took him by the shoulders and turned him out roughly; this caused a great scandal, and they made an official report on it.

Candide got better; and during his convalescence he had very good company to supper with him. They gambled for high stakes. Candide was

---

[42] in Voltaire's time, a dirty Parisian suburb. Voltaire wrote often in favor of the embellishment of Paris.   [43] almost universal "remedy," from the Middle Ages to the eighteenth century.   [44] As a means of detecting their rivals, the Jansenists, the Jesuits in power required Parisians to carry proof that they had been to confession.

vastly surprised that he never drew an ace; and Martin was not surprised at all.[45]

Among those who did the honors of the town was a little abbé from Périgord, one of those assiduous people who are always alert, always obliging, impudent, fawning, accommodating, always on the lookout for the arrival of foreigners, ready to tell them all the scandals of the town and to procure them pleasures at any price. This abbé took Candide and Martin to the theatre. A new tragedy was being played. Candide was seated near several wits. This did not prevent his weeping at perfectly played scenes. One of the argumentative bores near him said during an interval: "You have no business to weep, this is a very bad actress, the actor playing with her is still worse, the play is still worse than the actors; the author does not know a word of Arabic and yet the scene is in Arabia; moreover, he is a man who does not believe in innate ideas;[46] tomorrow I will bring you twenty articles written against him."

"Sir," said Candide to the abbé, "how many plays have you in France?"

"Five or six thousand," he replied.

"That's a lot," said Candide, "and how many good ones are there?"

"Fifteen or sixteen," replied the other.

"That's a lot," said Martin.

Candide was greatly pleased with an actress who took the part of Queen Elizabeth in a rather dull tragedy which is sometimes played. "This actress," said he to Martin, "pleases me very much; she looks rather like Mademoiselle Cunegonde; I should be very glad to pay her my respects."

The abbé offered to introduce him to her. Candide, brought up in Germany, asked what was the etiquette, and how queens of England were treated in France.

"There is a distinction," said the abbé. "In the provinces we take them to a tavern; in Paris we respect them when they are beautiful and throw them in the public sewer when they are dead." [47]

"Queens in the public sewer!" said Candide.

"Yes, indeed," said Martin, "the abbé is right; I was in Paris when Mademoiselle Monime[48] departed, as they say, this life; she was refused what people here call the *honors of burial*—that is to say, the honor of rotting with all the beggars of the district in a horrible cemetery; she was

[45] Cheating at cards was a common practice, even at the court, as Voltaire knew from sad experience. [46] Descartes' philosophy was based on "innate ideas." Voltaire followed Locke in denying them. [47] Under the Old Regime, actors and actresses were refused burial in holy ground. Voltaire waged a strenuous and finally successful campaign against this discrimination. [48] an actress (Adrienne Lecouvreur) whom Voltaire greatly admired and whom he helped to bury secretly at night.

buried by herself at the corner of the Rue de Bourgogne; which must have given her extreme pain, for her mind was very lofty."

"That was very impolite," said Candide.

"What do you expect?" said Martin. "These people are like that. Imagine all possible contradictions and incompatibilities; you will see them in the government, in the law courts, in the churches and the entertainments of this absurd nation."

"Is it true that people are always laughing in Paris?" said Candide.

"Yes," said the abbé, "but it is with rage in their hearts, for they complain of everything with roars of laughter and they even commit with laughter the most detestable actions."

"Who is that fat pig," said Candide, "who said so much ill of the play I cried at so much and of the actors who gave me so much pleasure?"

"He is a living evil," replied the abbé, "who earns his living by abusing all plays and all books; he hates anyone who succeeds, as eunuchs hate those who enjoy; he is one of the serpents of literature who feed on filth and venom; he is a scribbler."

"What do you mean by a scribbler?" said Candide.

"A scribbler of periodical sheets," said the abbé. "A Fréron." [49]

Candide, Martin and the abbé from Périgord talked in this manner on the stairway as they watched everybody going out after the play.

"Although I am most anxious to see Mademoiselle Cunegonde again," said Candide, "I should like to sup with Mademoiselle Clairon, [50] for I thought her admirable."

The abbé was not the sort of man to know Mademoiselle Clairon, for she saw only good company. "She is engaged this evening," he said, "but I shall have the honor to take you to the house of a lady of quality, and there you will learn as much of Paris as if you had been here for four years."

Candide, who was naturally curious, allowed himself to be taken to the lady's house at the far end of the Faubourg Saint-Honoré; [51] they were playing faro; twelve gloomy punters [52] each held a small hand of cards, the foolish register of their misfortunes. The silence was profound, the punters were pale, the banker was uneasy, and the lady of the house, seated beside this pitiless banker, watched with lynx's eyes every double stake, every seven-and-the-go, with which each player marked his cards; she had them unmarked with severe but polite attention, for fear of losing her customers; the lady called herself Marquise de Parolignac. Her fifteen-year-old daughter was among the punters and winked to her to let her know the tricks of

---

[49] the name of a successful journalist and critic who long and insidiously attacked Voltaire.   [50] a noted actress who was often leading lady in Voltaire's plays.   [51] a wealthy, aristocratic section of Paris.   [52] those who bet against the banker.

the poor people who attempted to repair the cruelties of fate. The abbé from Périgord, Candide and Martin entered; nobody rose, nobody greeted them, nobody looked at them; every one was profoundly occupied with the cards.

"Her Ladyship, the Baroness of Thunder-ten-tronckh was more civil," said Candide.

However the abbé whispered in the ear of the Marquise, who half rose, honored Candide with a gracious smile and Martin with a most noble nod. Candide was given a seat and a hand of cards, and lost fifty thousand francs in two hands; after which they supped very merrily and everyone was surprised that Candide was not more disturbed by his loss. The lackeys said to each other, in the language of lackeys: "He must be an English Milord."

The supper was like most suppers in Paris; first there was a silence and then a noise of indistinguishable words, then jokes, most of which were insipid, false news, false arguments, some politics and a great deal of scandal; there was even some talk of new books.

"Have you seen," said the abbé from Périgord, "the novel by Gauchat,[53] the doctor of theology?"

"Yes," replied one of the guests, "but I could not finish it. We have a crowd of silly writings, but all of them together do not approach the silliness of Gauchat, doctor of theology. I am so weary of this immensity of detestable books which inundates us that I have taken to faro."

"And what do you say about the *Mélanges* by Archdeacon Trublet?" said the abbé. "Ah!" said Madame de Parolignac, "the tiresome creature! How carefully he tells you what everybody knows! How heavily he discusses what is not worth the trouble of being lightly mentioned! How witlessly he appropriates other people's wit! How he spoils what he steals! How he disgusts me! But he will not disgust me any more; it is enough to have read a few pages by the Archdeacon."

There was a man of learning and taste at table who confirmed what the marchioness had said. They then talked of tragedies; the lady asked why there were tragedies which were sometimes played and yet were unreadable. The man of taste explained very clearly how a play might have some interest and hardly any merit; in a few words he proved that it was not sufficient to bring in one or two of the situations which are found in all novels and which always attract the spectators; but that a writer of tragedies must be original without being bizarre, often sublime and always natural, must know the human heart and be able to give it speech, must be a great poet but not let any character in his play appear to be a poet, must know his language perfectly, speak it with purity, with continual harmony and never allow the sense to be split for the sake of the rhyme.

[53] another enemy of Voltaire and the Encyclopedists.

"Anyone," he added, "who does not observe all these rules may produce one or two tragedies applauded in the theatre, but he will never be ranked among good writers; there are very few good tragedies; some are idylls in well-written and well-rhymed dialogue; some are political arguments which send one to sleep, or repulsive amplifications; others are the dreams of an enthusiast, in a barbarous style, with broken dialogue, long apostrophes to the gods (because he does not know how to speak to men), false maxims and turgid commonplaces."

Candide listened attentively to these remarks and conceived a great idea of the speaker; and, as the marchioness had been careful to place him beside her, he leaned over to her ear and took the liberty of asking her who was the man who talked so well.

"He is a man of letters," said the lady, "who does not play cards and is sometimes brought here to supper by the abbé; he has a perfect knowledge of tragedies and books and he has written a tragedy which was hissed and a book of which only one copy has ever been seen outside his bookseller's shop and that was one he gave me."

"The great man!" said Candide. "He is another Pangloss."

Then, turning to him, Candide said: "Sir, no doubt you think that all is for the best in the physical world and in the moral, and that nothing could be otherwise than as it is?"

"Sir," replied the man of letters, "I do not think anything of the sort. I think everything goes awry with us, that nobody knows his rank or his office, nor what he is doing, nor what he ought to do, and that except at supper, which is quite gay and where there appears to be a certain amount of sociability, all the rest of their time is passed in senseless quarrels: Jansenists with Molinists,[54] lawyers with churchmen, men of letters with men of letters, courtiers with courtiers, financiers with the people, wives with husbands, relatives with relatives—'tis an eternal war."

Candide replied: "I have seen worse things; but a wise man, who has since had the misfortune to be hanged, taught me that it is all for the best; these are only the shadows in a fair picture."

"Your wise man who was hanged was poking fun at the world," said Martin; "and your shadows are horrible stains."

"The stains are made by men," said Candide, "and they cannot avoid them."

"Then it is not their fault," said Martin.

Most of the gamblers, who had not the slightest understanding of this kind of talk, were drinking; Martin argued with the man of letters and Candide told the hostess some of his adventures.

---

[54] synonym for Jesuits. Molina, a member of the order, was an authority used against the Jansenist heresy.

After supper the marchioness took Candide into a side room and made him sit down on a sofa.

"Well!" said she, "so you are still madly in love with Mademoiselle Cunegonde of Thunder-ten-tronckh?"

"Yes, madame," replied Candide.

The marchioness replied with a tender smile: "You answer like a young man from Westphalia. A Frenchman would have said: 'It is true that I was in love with Mademoiselle Cunegonde, but when I see you, madame, I fear lest I should cease to love her.' "

"Alas! madame," said Candide, "I will answer as you wish."

"Your passion for her," said the marchioness, "began by picking up her handkerchief; I want you to pick up my garter."

"With all my heart," said Candide; and he picked it up.

"But I want you to put it on again," said the lady; and Candide put it on again.

"You see," said the lady, "you are a foreigner; I sometimes make my lovers in Paris languish for a fortnight, but I give myself to you the very first night, because one must do the honors of one's country to a young man from Westphalia."

The fair lady, having perceived two enormous diamonds on the young foreigner's hands, praised them so sincerely that they passed from Candide's fingers to the fingers of the marchioness. As Candide went home with his abbé from Périgord, he felt some remorse at having been unfaithful to Mademoiselle Cunegonde. The abbé sympathised with his distress; he had only had a small share in the fifty thousand francs Candide had lost at cards and in the value of the two half-given, half-extorted, diamonds. His plan was to profit as much as he could from the advantages which his acquaintance with Candide might procure for him. He talked a lot about Cunegonde and Candide told him that he should ask that fair one's forgiveness for his infidelity when he saw her at Venice. The abbé from Périgord redoubled his politeness and civilities and took a tender interest in all Candide said, in all he did, and in all he wished to do.

"Then, sir," said he, "you are to meet her at Venice?"

"Yes, sir," said Candide, "without fail I must go and meet Mademoiselle Cunegonde there."

Then, carried away by the pleasure of talking about the person he loved, he related, as he was accustomed to do, some of his adventures with that illustrious Westphalian lady.

"I suppose," said the abbé, "that Mademoiselle Cunegonde has a great deal of wit and that she writes charming letters."

"I have never received any from her," said Candide, "for you must know that when I was expelled from the castle because of my love for her, I could not write to her; soon afterwards I heard she was dead, then I found her again and then I lost her, and now I have sent an express messenger to her two thousand five hundred leagues from here and am expecting her reply."

The abbé listened attentively and seemed rather meditative. He soon took leave of the two foreigners, after having embraced them tenderly.

The next morning when Candide woke up he received a letter composed as follows: "Sir, my dearest lover, I have been ill for a week in this town; I have just heard that you are here. I should fly to your arms if I could stir. I heard that you had passed through Bordeaux; I left the faithful Cacambo and the old woman there and they will soon follow me. The governor of Buenos Ayres took everything, but I still have your heart. Come, your presence will restore me to life or will make me die of pleasure."

This charming, this unhoped-for letter, transported Candide with inexpressible joy; and the illness of his dear Cunegonde overwhelmed him with grief. Torn between these two sentiments, he took his gold and his diamonds and drove with Martin to the hotel where Mademoiselle Cunegonde was staying. He entered trembling with emotion, his heart beat, his voice was broken; he wanted to open the bed curtains and to have a light brought.

"Do nothing of the sort," said the waitingmaid. "Light would be the death of her." And she quickly drew the curtains.

"My dear Cunegonde," said Candide, weeping, "how do you feel? If you cannot see me, at least speak to me."

"She cannot speak," said the maidservant.

The lady then extended a plump hand, which Candide watered with his tears and then filled with diamonds, leaving a bag full of gold in the armchair. In the midst of these transports a police officer arrived, followed by the abbé from Périgord and a squad of policemen.

"So these are the two suspicious foreigners?" he said.

He had them arrested immediately and ordered his bravoes to hale them off to prison.

"This is not the way they treat travellers in Eldorado," said Candide.

"I am more of a Manichean than ever," said Martin.

"But, sir, where are you taking us?" said Candide.

"To the deepest dungeon," said the police officer.

Martin, having recovered his coolness, decided that the lady who pretended to be Cunegonde was a cheat, that the abbé from Périgord was a cheat who had abused Candide's innocence with all possible speed, and that the police officer was another cheat of whom they could easily be rid. Rather than expose himself to judicial proceedings, Candide, enlightened by this advice and impatient to see the real Cunegonde again, offered the police officer three little diamonds worth about three thousand pounds each.

"Ah! sir," said the man with the ivory stick, "if you had committed all imaginable crimes you would be the most honest man in the world. Three diamonds! Each worth three thousand pounds each! Sir! I would be killed for your sake, instead of taking you to prison. All strangers are arrested here, but trust to me. I have a brother at Dieppe in Normandy, I will take you there: and if you have any diamonds to give him he will take as much care of you as myself."

"And why are all strangers arrested?" said Candide.

The abbé from Périgord then spoke and said: "It is because a scoundrel from Atrebatum[55] listened to imbecilities; this alone made him commit a parricide, not like that of May 1610, but like that of December 1594,[56] and like several others committed in other years and in other months by other scoundrels who had listened to imbecilities."

The police officer then explained what it was all about.

"Ah! the monsters!" cried Candide. "What! Can such horrors be in a nation which dances and sings! Can I not leave at once this country where monkeys torment tigers? I have seen bears in my own country; Eldorado is the only place where I have seen men. In God's name, sir, take me to Venice, where I am to wait for Mademoiselle Cunegonde."

"I can only take you to Lower Normandy," said the barigel.[57]

Immediately he took off their irons, said there had been a mistake, sent his men away, took Candide and Martin to Dieppe, and left them with his brother. There was a small Dutch vessel in the port. With the help of three other diamonds the Norman became the most obliging of men and embarked Candide and his servants in the ship which was about to sail for Portsmouth in England. It was not the road to Venice; but Candide felt as if he had escaped from Hell, and he had every intention of taking the road to Venice at the first opportunity.

CHAPTER XXIII

Candide and Martin
Reach the Coast of England;
and What They Saw There

"Ah! Pangloss, Pangloss! Ah! Martin, Martin! Ah! my dear Cunegonde! What sort of a world is this?" said Candide on the Dutch ship.

"Something very mad and very abominable," replied Martin.

"You know England; are the people there as mad as they are in France?"

---

[55] Latin name for the region around Arras, the home of Damiens, who attempted to stab Louis XV in 1757.   [56] In 1610, Ravaillac assassinated Henry IV, after Châtel's earlier attempt in 1594 had failed.   [57] police officer.

" 'Tis another sort of madness," said Martin. "You know these two nations are at war for a few acres of snow in Canada, and that they are spending more on this fine war than all Canada is worth.[58] It is beyond my poor capacity to tell you whether there are more madmen in one country than in the other; all I know is that in general the people we are going to visit are extremely melancholic." [59]

Talking thus, they arrived at Portsmouth. There were multitudes of people on the shore, looking attentively at a rather fat man who was kneeling down with his eyes bandaged on the deck of one of the ships in the fleet; four soldiers placed opposite this man each shot three bullets into his brain in the calmest manner imaginable; and the whole assembly returned home with great satisfaction.

"What is all this?" said Candide. "And what Demon exercises his power everywhere?" He asked who was the fat man who had just been killed so ceremoniously.

"An admiral," was the reply.

"And why kill the admiral?"

"Because," he was told, "he did not kill enough people. He fought a battle with a French admiral and it was held that the English admiral was not close enough to him."

"But," said Candide, "the French admiral was just as far from the English admiral!"

"That is indisputable," was the answer, "but in this country it is a good thing to kill an admiral from time to time to encourage the others." [60]

Candide was so bewildered and so shocked by what he saw and heard that he would not even set foot on shore, but bargained with the Dutch captain (even if he had to pay him as much as the Surinam robber) to take him at once to Venice. The captain was ready in two days. They sailed down the coast of France; and passed in sight of Lisbon, at which Candide shuddered. They entered the Straits and the Mediterranean and at last reached Venice. "Praised be God!" said Candide, embracing Martin, "here I shall see the fair Cunegonde again. I trust Cacambo as I would myself. All is well, all goes well, all goes as well as it possibly could."

---

[58] Voltaire favored the French colonies in Louisiana and the West Indies at the expense of Canada, which was more under Jesuit control.   [59] Voltaire believed the cause of this national trait was England's east wind.   [60] Voltaire had tried by every means in his command to secure a reprieve for Admiral Byng, executed in 1757. This ironical shaft conceals his bitterness over his failure to obtain justice.

CHAPTER XXIV

Paquette and Friar Giroflée

As soon as he reached Venice, he inquired for Cacambo in all the taverns, in all the cafés, and of all the ladies of pleasure; and did not find him. Every day he sent out messengers to all ships and boats; but there was no news of Cacambo. "What!" said he to Martin, "I have had time to sail from Surinam to Bordeaux, to go from Bordeaux to Paris, from Paris to Dieppe, from Dieppe to Portsmouth, to sail along the coasts of Portugal and Spain, to cross the Mediterranean, to spend several months at Venice, and the fair Cunegonde has not yet arrived! Instead of her I have not only a jade and an abbé from Párigord! Cunegonde is certainly dead and the only thing left for me is to die too. Ah! It would have been better to stay in the Paradise of Eldorado instead of returning to this accursed Europe. How right you are, my dear Martin! Everything is illusion and calamity!"

He fell into a black melancholy and took no part in the opera à la mode or in the other carnival amusements; not a lady caused him the least temptation.

Martin said: "You are indeed simple-minded to suppose that a half-breed valet with five or six millions in his pocket will go and look for your mistress at the other end of the world and bring her to you at Venice. If he finds her, he will take her for himself; if he does not find her, he will take another. I advise you to forget your valet Cacambo and your mistress Cunegonde."

Martin was not consoling. Candide's melancholy increased, and Martin persisted in proving to him that there was little virtue and small happiness in the world except perhaps in Eldorado where nobody could go.

While arguing about this important subject and waiting for Cunegonde, Candide noticed a young Theatine[61] monk in the Piazza San Marco,[62] with a girl on his arm. The Theatine looked fresh, plump and vigorous; his eyes were bright, his air assured, his countenance firm, and his step lofty. The girl was very pretty and was singing; she gazed amorously at her Theatine and every now and then pinched his fat cheeks.

"At least you will admit," said Candide to Martin, "that those people are happy. Hitherto I have only found unfortunates in the whole habitable earth, except in Eldorado; but I wager that this girl and the Theatine are very happy creatures."

"I wager they are not," said Martin.

"We have only to ask them to dinner," said Candide, "and you will see whether I am wrong."

He immediately accosted them, paid his respects to them, and invited them to come to his hotel to eat macaroni, Lombardy partridges, and caviare,

[61] Catholic order formed in 1524.   [62] the most famous square in Venice.

and to drink Montepulciano, Lacryma Christi, Cyprus and Samos wine. The young lady blushed, the Theatine accepted the invitation, and the girl followed, looking at Candide with surprise and confusion in her eyes which were filled with a few tears. Scarcely had they entered Candide's room when she said: "What! Monsieur Candide does not recognise Paquette!"

At these words Candide, who had not looked at her very closely because he was occupied entirely by Cunegonde, said to her: "Alas! my poor child, so it was you who put Dr. Pangloss into the fine state I saw him in?"

"Alas! sir, it was indeed," said Paquette. "I see you have heard all about it. I have heard of the terrible misfortunes which happened to Her Ladyship the Baroness's whole family and to the fair Cunegonde. I swear to you that my fate has been just as sad. I was very innocent when you knew me. A Franciscan friar who was my confessor easily seduced me. The results were dreadful; I was obliged to leave the castle shortly after His Lordship the Baron expelled you by kicking you hard and frequently in the backside. If a famous doctor had not taken pity on me I should have died. For some time I was the doctor's mistress from gratitude to him. His wife, who was madly jealous, beat me every day relentlessly; she was a fury. The doctor was the ugliest of men, and I was the most unhappy of all living creatures at being continually beaten on account of a man I did not love. You know, sir, how dangerous it is for a shrewish woman to be the wife of a doctor. One day, exasperated by his wife's behavior, he gave her some medicine for a little cold and it was so efficacious that she died two hours afterwards in horrible convulsions. The lady's relatives brought a criminal prosecution against the husband; he fled and I was put in prison. My innocence would not have saved me if I had not been rather pretty. The judge set me free on condition that he took the doctor's place. I was soon supplanted by a rival, expelled without a penny, and obliged to continue the abominable occupation which to you men seems so amusing and which to us is nothing but an abyss of misery. I came to Venice to practise this profession. Ah! sir, if you could imagine what it is to be forced to caress impartially an old tradesman, a lawyer, a monk, a gondolier, an abbé; to be exposed to every insult and outrage; to be reduced often to borrow a petticoat in order to go and find some disgusting man who will lift it; to be robbed by one of what one has earned with another, to be despoiled by the police, and to contemplate for the future nothing but a dreadful old age, a hospital and a dunghill, you would conclude that I am one of the most unfortunate creatures in the world."

Paquette opened her heart in this way to Candide in a side room, in the presence of Martin, who said to Candide: "You see, I have already won half my wager."

Friar Giroflée had remained in the dining room, drinking a glass while he waited for dinner.

"But," said Candide to Paquette, "when I met you, you looked so gay, so happy; you were singing, you were caressing the Theatine so naturally; you seemed to me to be as happy as you are unfortunate."

"Ah! sir," replied Paquette, "that is one more misery of our profession. Yesterday I was robbed and beaten by an officer, and today I must seem to be in a good humor to please a monk."

Candide wanted to hear no more; he admitted that Martin was right. They sat down to table with Paquette and the Theatine. The meal was quite amusing and towards the end they were talking with some confidence.

"Father," said Candide to the monk, "you seem to me to enjoy a fate which everybody should envy; the flower of health shines on your cheek, your face is radiant with happiness; you have a very pretty girl for your recreation and you appear to be very well pleased with your state of life as a Theatine."

"Faith, Sir," said Friar Giroflée, "I wish all the Theatines were at the bottom of the sea. A hundred times I have been tempted to set fire to the monastery and to go and be a Turk. My parents forced me at the age of fifteen to put on this detestable robe,[63] in order that more money might be left to my cursed elder brother, whom God confound! Jealousy, discord, fury, inhabit the monastery. It is true, I have preached a few bad sermons which bring me in a little money, half of which is stolen from me by the prior; the remainder I spend on girls; but when I go back to the monastery in the evening I feel ready to smash my head against the dormitory walls, and all my colleagues are in the same state."

Martin turned to Candide and said with his usual calm: "Well, have I not won the whole wager?"

Candide gave two thousand piastres to Paquette and a thousand to Friar Giroflée. "I warrant," said he, "that they will be happy with that."

"I don't believe it in the very least," said Martin. "Perhaps you will make them still more unhappy with those piastres."

"That may be," said Candide, "but I am consoled by one thing; I see that we often meet people we thought we should never meet again; it may very well be that as I met my red sheep and Paquette, I may also meet Cunegonde again."

"I hope," said Martin, "that she will one day make you happy; but I doubt it very much."

"You are very hard," said Candide.

"That's because I have lived," said Martin.

"But look at these gondoliers," said Candide, "they sing all day long."

"You do not see them at home, with their wives and their brats of chil-

---

[63] Forced vows were common and constituted one of the greatest abuses of the Old Regime.

dren," said Martin. "The Doge has his troubles, the gondoliers have theirs. True, looking at it all round, a gondolier's lot is preferable to a Doge's; but I think the difference so slight that it is not worth examining."

"They talk," said Candide, "about Senator Pococurante[64] who lives in that handsome palace on the Brenta and who is hospitable to foreigners. He is supposed to be a man who has never known a grief."

"I should like to meet so rare a specimen," said Martin.

Candide immediately sent a request to Lord Pococurante for permission to wait upon him next day.

CHAPTER XXV

Visit to the Noble Venetian, Lord Pococurante

Candide and Martin took a gondola and rowed to the noble Pococurante's palace. The gardens were extensive and ornamented with fine marble statues; the architecture of the palace was handsome. The master of this establishment, a very wealthy man of about sixty, received the two visitors very politely but with very little cordiality, which disconcerted Candide but did not displease Martin. Two pretty and neatly dressed girls served them with very frothy chocolate. Candide could not refrain from praising their beauty, their grace and their skill.

"They are quite good creatures," said Senator Pococurante, "and I sometimes make them sleep in my bed, for I am very tired of the ladies of the town, with their coquetries, their jealousies, their quarrels, their humors, their meanness, their pride, their folly, and the sonnets one must write or have written for them; but, after all, I am getting very tired of these two girls."

After this collation, Candide was walking in a long gallery and was surprised by the beauty of the pictures. He asked what master had painted the two first.

"They are by Raphael," said the Senator. "Some years ago I bought them at a very high price out of mere vanity; I am told they are the finest in Italy, but they give me no pleasure; the color has gone very dark, the faces are not sufficiently rounded and do not stand out enough; the draperies have not the least resemblance to material; in short, whatever they may say, I do not consider them a true imitation of nature. I shall only like a picture

---

[64] The name ("caring little," in Italian) suggests the indifference and boredom of its bearer.

when it makes me think it is nature itself; and there are none of that kind. I have a great many pictures, but I never look at them now."

While they waited for dinner, Pococurante gave them a concert. Candide thought the music delicious.

"This noise," said Pococurante, "is amusing for half an hour; but if it lasts any longer, it wearies everybody although nobody dares to say so. Music nowadays is merely the art of executing difficulties and in the end that which is only difficult ceases to please. Perhaps I should like the opera more, if they had not made it a monster which revolts me. Those who please may go to see bad tragedies set to music, where the scenes are only composed to bring in clumsily two or three ridiculous songs which show off an actress's voice; those who will or can, may swoon with pleasure when they see an eunuch humming the part of Cæsar and Cato as he awkwardly treads the boards; for my part, I long ago abandoned such trivialities, which nowadays are the glory of Italy and for which monarchs pay so dearly."

Candide demurred a little, but discreetly. Martin entirely agreed with the Senator.

They sat down to table and after an excellent dinner went into the library. Candide saw a magnificently bound Homer and complimented the Illustrissimo on his good taste. "That is the book," said he, "which so much delighted the great Pangloss, the greatest philosopher of Germany."

"It does not delight me," said Pococurante coldly; "formerly I was made to believe that I took pleasure in reading it; but this continual repetition of battles which are all alike, these gods who are perpetually active and achieve nothing decisive, this Helen who is the cause of the war and yet scarcely an actor in the piece, this Troy which is always besieged and never taken—all bore me extremely. I have sometimes asked learned men if they were as bored as I am by reading it; all who were sincere confessed that the book fell from their hands, but that it must be in every library, as a monument of antiquity, and like those rusty coins which cannot be put into circulation."

"Your Excellency has a different opinion of Virgil?"[65] said Candide.

"I admit," said Pococurante, "that the second, fourth and sixth books of his Æneid are excellent, but as for his pious Æneas and the strong Cloanthes and the faithful Achates and the little Ascanius and the imbecile king Latinus and the middle-class Amata and the insipid Lavinia, I think there could be nothing more frigid and disagreeable. I prefer Tasso and the fantastic tales of Ariosto."[66]

"May I venture to ask you, sir," said Candide, "if you do not take great pleasure in reading Horace?"

[65] placed generally by critics above Homer, until the nineteenth century. [66] Voltaire himself was especially fond of Tasso's *Jerusalem Delivered* and Ariosto's *Roland* (*Orlando furioso*).

"He has some maxims," said Pococurante, "which might be useful to a man of the world, and which, being compressed in energetic verses, are more easily impressed upon the memory; but I care very little for his Journey to Brundisium, and his description of a Bad Dinner, and the street brawlers' quarrel between—what is his name?—Rupilius, whose words, he says, were full of pus, and another person whose words were all vinegar.[67] I was extremely disgusted with his gross verses against old women and witches; and I cannot see there is any merit in his telling his friend Mæcenas that, if he is placed by him among the lyric poets, he will strike the stars with his lofty brow. Fools admire everything in a celebrated author. I only read to please myself, and I only like what suits me."

Candide, who had been taught never to judge anything for himself, was greatly surprised by what he heard; and Martin thought Pococurante's way of thinking quite reasonable.

"Oh! There is a Cicero," said Candide. "I suppose you are never tired of reading that great man?"

"I never read him," replied the Venetian. "What do I care that he pleaded for Rabirius or Cluentius? I have enough cases to judge myself; I could better have endured his philosophical works; but when I saw that he doubted everything, I concluded I knew as much as he and did not need anybody else in order to be ignorant."

"Ah! There are eighty volumes of the Proceedings of an Academy of Sciences," exclaimed Martin, "there might be something good in them."

"There would be," said Pococurante, "if a single one of the authors of all that rubbish had invented even the art of making pins; but in all those books there is nothing but vain systems and not a single useful thing."

"What a lot of plays I see there," said Candide. "Italian, Spanish, and French!"

"Yes," said the Senator, "there are three thousand and not three dozen good ones. As for those collections of sermons, which all together are not worth a page of Seneca, and all those large volumes of theology you may well suppose that they are never opened by me or anybody else."

Martin noticed some shelves filled with English books. "I should think," he said, "that a republican woul denjoy most of those works written with so much freedom."[68]

"Yes," replied Pococurante, "it is good to write as we think; it is the privilege of man. In all Italy, we only write what we do not think; those who inhabit the country of the Cæsars and the Antonines dare not have an idea without the permission of a Dominican monk. I should applaud the

[67] Eighteenth-century taste was finical and could not tolerate such "low" words.
[68] England enjoyed great freedom of thought compared with the strict censorship in France.

liberty which inspires Englishmen of genius if passion and party spirit did
not corrupt everything estimable in that precious liberty."

Candide, in noticing a Milton, asked him if he did not consider that
author to be a very great man.

"Who?" said Pococurante. "That barbarian who wrote a long commentary
on the first chapter of Genesis in ten books of harsh verses? That gross imita-
tor of the Greeks, who disfigures the Creation, and who, while Moses represents the Eternal Being as producing the world by speech, makes the
Messiah take a large compass from the heavenly cupboard in order to trace
out his work? Should I esteem the man who spoiled Tasso's hell and devil;
who disguises Lucifer sometimes as a toad, sometimes as a pigmy; who
makes him repeat the same thing a hundred times; makes him argue about
theology; and imitates seriously Ariosto's comical invention of firearms by
making the devils fire a cannon in Heaven? Neither I nor anyone else in Italy
could enjoy such wretched extravagances. The marriage of Sin and Death
and the snakes which sin brings forth nauseate any man of delicate taste,
and his long description of a hospital would only please a gravedigger. This
obscure, bizarre and disgusting poem was despised at its birth; I treat it
today as it was treated by its contemporaries in its own country. But then I
say what I think, and care very little whether others think as I do."

Candide was distressed by these remarks; he respected Homer and rather
liked Milton.[69]

"Alas!" he whispered to Martin, "I am afraid this man would have a
sovereign contempt for our German poets."

"There wouldn't be much harm in that," said Martin.

"Oh! What a superior man!" said Candide under his breath. "What a
great genius this Pococurante is! Nothing can please him."

After they had thus reviewed all his books they went down into the
garden. Candide praised all its beauties.

"I have never met anything more tasteless," said the owner. "We have
nothing but gewgaws; but tomorrow I shall begin to plant one on a more
noble plan."

When the two visitors had taken farewell of his Excellency, Candide
said to Martin: "Now you will admit that he is the happiest of men, for
he is superior to everything he possesses."

"Do you not see," said Martin, "that he is disgusted with everything he
possesses? Plato said long ago that the best stomachs are not those which
refuse all food."

"But," said Candide, "is there not pleasure in criticising, in finding faults
where other men think they see beauty?"

[69] Voltaire, too, rather liked Milton, in spite of his "flaws."

"That is to say," answered Martin, "that there is pleasure in not being pleased."

"Oh! Well," said Candide, "then there is no one happy except me—when I see Mademoiselle Cunegonde again."

"It is always good to hope," said Martin.

However, the days and weeks went by; Cacambo did not return and Candide was so much plunged in grief that he did not even notice that Paquette and Friar Giroflée had not once come to thank him.

CHAPTER XXVI

How Candide and Martin
Supped With Six Strangers
and Who They Were

One evening when Candide and Martin were going to sit down to table with the strangers who lodged in the same hotel, a man with a face the color of soot came up to him from behind and, taking him by the arm, said: "Get ready to come with us, and do not fail."

He turned round and saw Cacambo. Only the sight of Cunegonde could have surprised and pleased him more. He was almost wild with joy. He embraced his dear friend.

"Cunegonde is here, of course? Where is she? Take me to her, let me die of joy with her."

"Cunegonde is not here," said Cacambo. "She is in Constantinople."

"Heavens! In Constantinople! But, were she in China, I would fly to her; let us start at once."

"We will start after supper," replied Cacambo. "I cannot tell you any more; I am a slave, and my master is waiting for me; I must go and serve him at table! Do not say anything; eat your supper, and be in readiness."

Candide, torn between joy and grief, charmed to see his faithful agent again, amazed to see him a slave, filled with the idea of seeing his mistress again, with turmoil in his heart, agitation in his mind, sat down to table with Martin (who met every strange occurrence with the same calmness), and with six strangers, who had come to spend the Carnival at Venice.

Cacambo, who acted as butler to one of the strangers, bent down to his master's head towards the end of the meal and said: "Sire, your Majesty can leave when you wish, the ship is ready." After saying this, Cacambo withdrew.

The guests looked at each other with surprise without saying a word, when another servant came up to his master and said: "Sire, your Majesty's post chaise is at Padua, and the boat is ready." The master made a sign and the servant departed.

Once more all the guests looked at each other, and the general surprise was increased twofold. A third servant went up to the third stranger and said: "Sire, believe me, your Majesty cannot remain here any longer; I will prepare everything." And he immediately disappeared.

Candide and Martin had no doubt that this was a Carnival masquerade. A fourth servant said to the fourth master: "Your Majesty can leave when you wish." And he went out like the others. The fifth servant spoke similarly to the fifth master. But the sixth servant spoke differently to the sixth stranger who was next to Candide, and said: "Faith, sire, they will not give your Majesty any more credit nor me either, and we may very likely be jailed tonight, both of us; I am going to look to my own affairs, good bye."

When the servants had all gone, the six strangers, Candide and Martin remained in profound silence. At last it was broken by Candide.

"Gentlemen," said he, "this is a curious jest. How is it you are all kings? I confess that neither Martin nor I are kings."

Cacambo's master then gravely spoke and said in Italian: "I am not jesting, my name is Achmet III. For several years I was Sultan; I dethroned my brother; my nephew dethroned me; they cut off the heads of my viziers; I am ending my days in the old seraglio; my nephew, Sultan Mahmoud, sometimes allows me to travel for my health, and I have come to spend the Carnival at Venice."

A young man who sat next to Achmet spoke after him and said: "My name is Ivan; I was Emperor of all the Russias; I was dethroned in my cradle;[70] my father and mother were imprisoned and I was brought up in prison; I sometimes have permission to travel, accompanied by those who guard me, and I have come to spend the Carnival at Venice."

The third said: "I am Charles Edward, King of England;[71] my father gave up his rights to the throne to me and I fought a war to assert them; the hearts of eight hundred of my adherents were torn out and dashed in their faces. I have been in prison; I am going to Rome to visit the King, my father, who is dethroned like my grandfather and me; and I have come to spend the Carnival at Venice."

The fourth then spoke and said: "I am the King of Poland; the chance of war deprived me of my hereditary states; my father endured the same reverse of fortune; I am resigned to Providence like the Sultan Achmet, the Emperor Ivan and King Charles Edward, to whom God grant long life; and I have come to spend the Carnival at Venice."

---

[70] Ivan IV, dethroned in 1741, before he was two years old. All these kings are genuine. [71] the "Young Pretender," son of James Stuart.

The fifth said: "I also am the King of Poland,[72] I have lost my kingdom twice; but Providence has give me another state in which I have been able to do more good than all the kings of the Sarmatians together have been ever able to do on the banks of the Vistula; I also am resigned to Providence and I have come to spend the Carnival at Venice."

It was now for the sixth monarch to speak. "Gentlemen," said he, "I am not so eminent as you; but I have been a king like anyone else. I am Theodore; I was elected King of Corsica; I have been called Your Majesty and now I am barely called Sir. I have coined money and do not own a farthing; I have had two Secretaries of State and now have scarcely a valet; I have occupied a throne and for a long time lay on straw in a London prison. I am much afraid I shall be treated in the same way here, although I have come, like your Majesties, to spend the Carnival at Venice."

The five other kings listened to this speech with a noble compassion. Each of them gave King Theodore twenty sequins[73] to buy clothes and shirts; Candide presented him with a diamond worth two thousand sequins.

"Who is this man," said the five kings, "who is able to give a hundred times as much as any of us, and who gives it?"

As they were leaving the table, there came to the same hotel four serene highnesses who had also lost their states in the chance of war, and who had come to spend the rest of the Carnival at Venice; but Candide did not even notice these newcomers, he could think of nothing but of going to Constantinople to find his dear Cunegonde.

CHAPTER XXVII

Candide's Voyage to Constantinople

The faithful Cacambo had already spoken to the Turkish captain who was to take Sultan Achmet back to Constantinople and had obtained permission for Candide and Martin to come on board. They both entered this ship after having prostrated themselves before his miserable Highness.

On the way, Candide said to Martin: "So we have just supped with six dethroned kings! And among those six kings there was one to whom I gave charity. Perhaps there are many other princes still more unfortunate. Now, I have only lost a hundred sheep and I am hastening to Cunegonde's arms. My dear Martin, once more, Pangloss was right, all is well."

"I hope so," said Martin.

[72] Stanislas Leczinski, father-in-law of the French king, Louis XV. He became Duke of Lorraine and befriended Voltaire. [73] gold coin of Venice.

"But," said Candide, "this is a very singular experience we have just had at Venice. Nobody has ever seen or heard of six dethroned kings supping together in a tavern."

" 'Tis no more extraordinary," said Martin, "than most of the things which have happened to us. It is very common for kings to be dethroned; and as to the honor we have had of supping with them, 'tis a trifle not deserving our attention."

Scarcely had Candide entered the ship when he threw his arms round the neck of his old valet, of his friend Cacambo.

"Well!" said he, "what is Cunegonde doing? Is she still a marvel of beauty? Does she still love me? How is she? Of course you have bought her a palace in Constantinople?"

"My dear master," replied Cacambo, "Cunegonde is washing dishes on the banks of Propontis[74] for a prince who possesses very few dishes; she is a slave in the house of a former sovereign named Ragotsky,[75] who receives in his refuge three crowns a day from the Grand Turk; but what is even more sad is that she has lost her beauty and has become horribly ugly."

"Ah! beautiful or ugly," said Candide, "I am a man of honor and my duty is to love her always. But how can she be reduced to so abject a condition with the five or six millions you carried off?"

"Ah!" said Cacambo, "did I not have to give two millions to Señor Don Fernando d'Ibaraa y Figueora y Mascarenes y Lampourdos y Souza, Governor of Buenos Ayres, for permission to bring away Mademoiselle Cunegonde? And did not a pirate bravely strip us of all the rest? And did not this pirate take us to Cape Matapan, to Milo, to Nicaria, to Samos, to Petra, to the Dardanelles, to Marmora, to Scutari? Cunegonde and the old woman are servants to the prince I mentioned, and I am slave to the dethroned Sultan."

"What a chain of terrible calamities!" said Candide. "But after all, I still have a few diamonds; I shall easily deliver Cunegonde. What a pity she has become so ugly."

Then, turning to Martin, he said: "Who do you think is the most to be pitied, the Sultan Achmet, the Empeor Ivan, King Charles Edward, or me?"

"I do not know at all," said Martin. "I should have to be in your hearts to know."

"Ah!" said Candide, "if Pangloss were here he would know and would tell us."

"I do not know," said Martin, "what scales your Pangloss would use to weigh the misfortunes of men and to estimate their sufferings. All I presume is that there are millions of men on the earth a hundred times more to be

---

[74] now the Sea of Marmora, above the Dardanelles.   [75] formerly, Prince of Transylvania.

pitied than King Charles Edward, the Emperor Ivan and the Sultan Achmet."

"That may very well be," said Candide.

In a few days they reached the Black Sea channel. Candide began by paying a high ransom for Cacambo and, without wasting time, he went on board a galley with his companions bound for the shores of Propontis, in order to find Cunegonde however ugly she might be. Among the galley slaves were two convicts who rowed very badly and from time to time the Levantine captain applied several strokes of a bull's pizzle to their naked shoulders. From a natural feeling of pity Candide watched them more attentively than the other galley slaves and went up to them. Some features of their disfigured faces appeared to him to have some resemblance to Pangloss and the wretched Jesuit, the Baron, Mademoiselle Cunegonde's brother. This idea disturbed and saddened him. He looked at them still more carefully. "Truly," said he to Cacambo, "if I had not seen Dr. Pangloss hanged, and if I had not been so unfortunate as to kill the Baron, I should think they were rowing in this galley."

At the words Baron and Pangloss, the two convicts gave a loud cry, stopped on their seats and dropped their oars. The Levantine captain ran up to them and the lashes with the bull's pizzle were redoubled.

"Stop! Stop, sir!" cried Candide. "I will give you as much money as you want."

"What! Is it Candide?" said one of the convicts.

"What! Is it Candide?" said the other.

"Is it a dream?" said Candide. "Am I awake? Am I in this galley? Is that my Lord the Baron whom I killed? Is that Dr. Pangloss whom I saw hanged?"

"It is, it is," they replied.

"What! Is that the great philosopher?" said Martin.

"Ah! sir," said Candide to the Levantine captain, "how much money do you want for My Lord Thunder ten tronckh, one of the first Barons of the empire, and for Dr. Pangloss, the most profound metaphysician of Germany?"

"Dog of a Christian," replied the Levantine captain, "since these two dogs of Christian convicts are Barons and metaphysicans, which no doubt is a high rank in their country, you shall pay me fifty thousand sequins."

"You shall have them, sir. Row back to Constantinople like lightning and you shall be paid at once. But, no, take me to Mademoiselle Cunegonde."

The captain, at Candide's first offer had already turned the bow towards the town, and rowed there more swiftly than a bird cleaves the air.

Candide embraced the Baron and Pangloss a hundred times. "How was it I did not kill you, my dear Baron? And, my dear Pangloss, how do you happen to be alive after having been hanged? And why are you both in a Turkish galley?"

"Is it really true that my dear sister is in this country?" said the Baron. "Yes," replied Cacambo.

"So once more I see my dear Candide!" cried Pangloss.

Candide introduced Martin and Cacambo. They all embraced and all talked at the same time. The galley flew; already they were in the harbor. They sent for a Jew, and Candide sold him for fifty thousand sequins a diamond worth a hundred thousand, for which he swore by Abraham he could not give any more. The ransom of the Baron and Pangloss was immediately paid. Pangloss threw himself at the feet of his liberator and bathed them with tears; the other thanked him with a nod and promised to repay the money at the first opportunity. "But is it possible that my sister is in Turkey?" said he.

"Nothing is so possible," replied Cacambo, "since she washes up the dishes of a prince of Transylvania."

They immediately sent for two Jews; Candide sold some more diamonds; and they all set out in another galley to rescue Cunegonde.

CHAPTR XXVIII

What Happened to
Candide, to Cunegonde, to Pangloss,
to Martin, Etc.

"Pardon once more," said Candide to the Baron, "pardon me, reverend father, for having thrust my sword through your body."

"Let us say no more about it," said the Baron. "I admit I was a little too sharp; but since you wish to know how it was you saw me in a galley, I must tell you that after my wound was healed by the brother apothecary of the college, I was attacked and carried off by a Spanish raiding party; I was imprisoned in Buenos Ayres at the time when my sister had just left. I asked to return to the Vicar-General in Rome. I was ordered to Constantinople to act as almoner to the Ambassador of France. A week after I had taken up my office I met towards evening a very handsome young page of the Sultan. It was very hot; the young man wished to bathe; I took the opportunity to bathe also. I did not know that it was a most serious crime for a Christian to be found naked with a young Mahometan. A cadi sentenced me to a hundred strokes on the soles of my feet and condemned me to the galley. I do not think a more horrible injustice has ever been committed. But I should very much like to know why my sister is in the kitchen of a Transylvanian sovereign living in exile among the Turks."

"But, my dear Pangloss," said Candide, "how does it happen that I see you once more?"

"It is true," said Pangloss, "that you saw me hanged; and in the natural course of events I should have been burned.[76] But you remember, it poured with rain when they were going to roast me; the storm was so violent that they despaired of lighting the fire; I was hanged because they could do nothing better; a surgeon bought my body, carried me home and dissected me. He first made a crucial incision in me from the navel to the collarbone. Nobody could have been worse hanged than I was. The executioner of the holy Inquisition, who was a sub-deacon, was marvellously skilful in burning people, but he was not accustomed to hang them; the rope was wet and did not slide easily and it was knotted; in short, I still breathed. The crucial incision caused me to utter so loud a scream that the surgeon fell over backwards and, thinking he was dissecting the devil, fled away in terror and fell down the staircase in his flight. His wife ran in from another room at the noise; she saw me stretched out on the table with my crucial incision; she was still more frightened than her husband, fled, and fell on top of him. When they had recovered themselves a little, I heard the surgeon's wife say to the surgeon: 'My dear, what were you thinking of, to dissect a heretic? Don't you know the devil always possesses them? I will go and get a priest at once to exorcise him.'

"At this I shuddered and collected the little strength I had left to shout: 'Have pity on me!' At last the Portuguese barber[77] grew bolder; he sewed up my skin; his wife even took care of me, and at the end of a fortnight I was able to walk again. The barber found me a situation and made me lackey to a Knight of Malta who was going to Venice; but, as my master had no money to pay me wages, I entered the service of a Venetian merchant and followed him to Constantinople.

"One day I took it into my head to enter a mosque; there was nobody there except an old Imam and a very pretty young devotee who was reciting her prayers; her breasts were entirely uncovered; between them she wore a bunch of tulips, roses, anemones, ranunculus, hyacinths and auriculas; she dropped her bunch of flowers; I picked it up and returned it to her with a most respectful alacrity. I was so long putting them back that the Imam grew angry and, seeing I was a Christian, called for help. I was taken to the cadi, who sentenced me to receive a hundred strokes on the soles of my feet and sent me to the galleys. I was chained on the same seat and in the same galley as My Lord the Baron. In this galley there were four young men from Marseilles, five Neapolitan priests and two monks from Corfu, who assured us that similar accidents occurred every day. His Lordship the

[76] but burning would not have served Voltaire's purposes. [77] Like the Barber of Seville, he was also the surgeon.

Baron claimed that he had suffered a greater injustice than I; and I claimed that it was much more permissible to replace a bunch of flowers between a woman's breasts than to be naked with one of the Sultan's pages. We argued continually, and every day received twenty strokes of the bull's pizzle, when the chain of events of this universe led you to our galley and you ransomed us."

"Well! my dear Pangloss," said Candide, "when you were hanged, dissected, stunned with blows and made to row in the galleys, did you always think that everything was for the best in this world?"

"I am still of my first opinion," replied Pangloss, "for after all I am a philosopher; and it would be unbecoming for me to recant, since Leibnitz could not be in the wrong and pre-established harmony is the finest thing imaginable like the plenum and subtle matter." [78]

CHAPTER XXIX

How Candide Found Cunegonde and the Old Woman Again

While Candide, the Baron, Pangloss, Martin and Cacambo were relating their adventures, reasoning upon contingent[79] or non-contingent events of the universe, arguing about effects and causes, moral and physical evil, free will and necessity, and the consolation to be found in the Turkish galleys, they came to the house of the Transylvanian prince on the shores of Propontis.

The first objects which met their sight were Cunegonde and the old woman hanging out towels to dry on the line. At this sight the Baron grew pale. Candide, that tender lover, seeing his fair Cunegonde sunburned, bleareyed, flat-breasted, with wrinkles round her eyes and red, chapped arms, recoiled three paces in horror, and then advanced from mere politeness. She embraced Candide and her brother. They embraced the old woman; Candide bought them both.

In the neighborhood was a little farm; the old woman suggested that Candide should buy it, until some better fate befell the group. Cunegonde did not know that she had become ugly, for nobody had told her so; she reminded Candide of his promises in so peremptory a tone that the good

---

[78] According to Leibnitz, harmony between the spiritual and material worlds was pre-established by God. The plenum and subtle matter form part of the German philosopher's outmoded physics.   [79] A contingent event is a possible but not inevitable eventuality.

Candide dared not refuse her. He therefore informed the Baron that he was about to marry his sister.

"Never," said the Baron, "will I endure such baseness on her part and such insolence on yours; nobody shall ever reproach me with this infamy; my sister's children could never enter the chapters[80] of Germany. No, my sister shall never marry anyone but a Baron of the Empire."

Cunegonde threw herself at his feet and bathed them in tears; but he was inflexible.

"Madman," said Candide, "I rescued you from the galleys, I paid your ransom and your sister's; she was washing dishes here, she is ugly, I am so kind as to make her my wife, and you pretend to oppose me! I should re-kill you if I listened to my anger."

"You may kill me again," said the Baron, "but you shall never marry my sister while I am alive."

CHAPTER XXX

Conclusion

At the bottom of his heart Candide had not the least wish to marry Cunegonde. But the Baron's extreme impertinence determined him to complete the marriage, and Cunegonde urged it so warmly that he could not retract. He consulted Pangloss, Martin and the faithful Cacambo. Pangloss wrote an excellent memorandum by which he proved that the Baron had no rights over his sister and that by all the laws of the empire she could make a left-handed marriage[81] with Candide. Martin advised that the Baron should be thrown into the sea; Cacambo decided that he should be returned to the Levantine captain and sent back to the galleys, after which he would be returned by the first ship to the Vicar-General at Rome. This was thought to be very good advice; the old woman approved it; they said nothing to the sister; the plan was carried out with the aid of a little money and they had the pleasure of duping a Jesuit and punishing the pride of a German Baron.

It would be natural to suppose that when, after so many disasters, Candide was married to his mistress, and living with the philosopher Pangloss, the philosopher Martin, the prudent Cacambo and the old woman, having brought back so many diamonds from the country of the ancient Incas, he would lead the most pleasant life imaginable.[82] But he was so

[80] knightly assemblies. [81] a morganatic marriage, which does not give equality to the party of lower rank. [82] If this were an idle tale of adventure, the couple would have been left here, to "live happily ever afterwards."

cheated by the Jews[83] that he had nothing left but his little farm; his wife, growing uglier every day, became shrewish and unendurable; the old woman was ailing and even more bad tempered than Cunegonde. Cacambo, who worked in the garden and then went to Constantinople to sell vegetables, was overworked and cursed his fate. Pangloss was in despair because he did not shine in some German university.

As for Martin, he was firmly convinced that people are equally uncomfortable everywhere; he accepted things patiently. Candide, Martin and Pangloss sometimes argued about metaphysics and morals. From the windows of the farm they often watched the ships going by, filled with effendis, pashas, and cadis, who were being exiled to Lemnos, to Mitylene and Erzerum. They saw other cadis, other pashas and other effendis coming back to take the place of the exiles and to be exiled in their turn. They saw the neatly impaled heads which were taken to the Sublime Porte.[84] These sights redoubled their discussions; and when they were not arguing, the boredom was so excessive that one day the old woman dared to say to them: "I should like to know which is worse, to be raped a hundred times by negro pirates, to have a buttock cut off, to run the gauntlet among the Bulgarians, to be whipped and flogged in an *auto-da-fé*, to be dissected, to row in a galley, in short, to endure all the miseries through which we have passed, or to remain here doing nothing?"

" 'Tis a great question," said Candide.

These remarks led to new reflections, and Martin especially concluded that man was born to live in the convulsions of distress or in the lethargy of boredom. Candide did not agree, but he asserted nothing. Pangloss confessed that he had always suffered horribly; but having once maintained that everything was for the best, he had continued to maintain it without believing it.

One thing confirmed Martin in his destestable principles, made Candide hesitate more than ever, and embarrassed Pangloss. And it was this. One day there came to their farm Paquette and Friar Giroflée, who were in the most extreme misery; they had soon wasted their three thousand piastres, had left each other, made it up, quarrelled again, been put in prison, escaped, and finally Friar Giroflée had turned Turk. Paquette continued her occupation everywhere and now earned nothing by it.

"I foresaw," said Martin to Candide, "that your gifts would soon be wasted and would only make them the more miserable. You and Cacambo were once bloated with millions of piastres and you are no happier than Friar Giroflée and Paquette."

"Ah! Ha!" said Pangloss to Paquette, "so Heaven brings you back to us,

[83] Voltaire suffered several severe financial losses through the bankruptcies of Jewish bankers. [84] gate of the Turkish Sultan's palace, which was also the Palace of Justice.

my dear child? Do you know that you cost me the end of my nose, an eye and an ear! What a plight you are in! Ah! What a world this is!"

This new occurrence caused them to philosophise more than ever. In the neighborhood there lived a very famous Dervish, who was supposed to be the best philosopher in Turkey; they went to consult him; Pangloss was the spokesman and said: "Master, we have come to beg you to tell us why so strange an animal as man was ever created."

"What has it to do with you?" said the Dervish. "Is it your business?"

"But, reverend father," said Candide, "there is a horrible amount of evil in the world."

"What does it matter," said the Dervish, "whether there is evil or good? When his highness sends a ship to Egypt, does he worry about the comfort or discomfort of the rats in the ship?" [85]

"Then what should we do?" said Pangloss.

"Hold your tongue," said the Dervish.

"I flattered myself," said Pangloss, "that I should discuss with you effects and causes, this best of all possible worlds, the origin of evil, the nature of the soul and pre-established harmony."

At these words the Dervish slammed the door in their faces.

During this conversation the news went round that at Constantinople two viziers and the mufti had been strangled and several of their friends impaled. This catastrophe made a prodigious noise everywhere for several hours. As Pangloss, Candide and Martin were returning to their little farm, they came upon an old man who was taking the air under a bower of orange trees at his door. Pangloss, who was as curious as he was argumentative, asked him what was the name of the mufti who had just been strangled.

"I do not know," replied the old man. "I have never known the name of any mufti or of any vizier. I am entirely ignorant of the occurrence you mention; I presume that in general those who meddle with public affairs sometimes perish miserably and that they deserve it; but I never inquire what is going on in Constantinople; I content myself with sending there for sale the produce of the garden I cultivate."

Having spoken thus, he took the strangers into his house. His two daughters and his two sons presented them with several kinds of sherbet which they made themselves, caymac flavored with candied citron peel, oranges, lemons, limes, pineapples, dates, pistachios and Mocha coffee which had not been mixed with the bad coffee of Batavia and the Isles. After which this good Mussulman's two daughters perfumed the beards of Candide, Pangloss and Martin.

"You must have a vast and magnificent estate?" said Candide to the Turk.

"I have only twenty acres," replied the Turk. "I cultivate them with my

[85] This pessimistic passage seems to limit severely the extent of Divine Providence. Compare the ending of the Book of Job.

children; and work keeps at bay three great evils: boredom, vice and need." [86]

As Candide returned to his farm he reflected deeply on the Turk's remarks. He said to Pangloss and Martin: "That good old man seems to me to have chosen an existence preferable by far to that of the six kings with whom we had the honor to sup."

"Exalted rank," said Pangloss, "is very dangerous, according to the testimony of all philosophers; for Eglon, King of the Moabites, was murdered by Ehud; Absalom was hanged by the hair and pierced by three darts; King Nadab, son of Jeroboam, was killed by Baasha; King Elah by Zimri; Ahaziah by Jehu; Athaliah by Jehoiada; the Kings Jehoiakim, Jeconiah and Zedekiah were made slaves.[87] You know in what manner died Crœsus, Astyages, Darius, Denys of Syracuse, Pyrrhus, Perseus, Hannibal, Jugurtha, Ariovistus, Cæsar, Pompey, Nero, Otho, Vitellius, Domitian, Richard ii of England, Edward ii, Henry vi, Richard iii, Mary Stuart, Charles i, the three Henrys of France, the Emperor Henry iv. You know . . ."

"I also know," said Candide, "that we should cultivate our gardens."

"You are right," said Pangloss, "for, when man was placed in the Garden of Eden, he was placed there *ut operaretur eum,* to dress it and to keep it; which proves that man was not born for idleness."

"Let us work without theorizing," [88] said Martin; " 'tis the only way to make life endurable."

The whole small fraternity entered into this praiseworthy plan, and each started to make use of his talents. The little farm yielded well. Cunegonde was indeed very ugly, but she became an excellent pastry cook; Paquette embroidered; the old woman took care of the linen. Even Friar Giroflée performed some service; he was a very good carpenter and even became a man of honor; and Pangloss sometimes said to Candide: "All events are linked up in this best of all possible worlds; for, if you had not been expelled from the noble castle, by hard kicks in your backside for love of Mademoiselle Cunegonde, if you had not been clapped into the Inquisition, if you had not wandered about America on foot, if you had not stuck your sword in the Baron, if you had not lost all your sheep from the land of Eldorado, you would not be eating candied citrons and pistachios here." [89]

" 'Tis well said," replied Candide, "but we must cultivate our gardens."

---

[86] This is the key to Voltaire's philosophy of life. *Candide* gives abundant examples of all three of these evils.   [87] To explain these Biblical references would be pedantry—which Voltaire is here satirizing.   [88] that is, since men never grasp the ultimate ends of life, let us make the best of it without worrying—an "optimistic" acceptance of life as it is.   [89] The final reduction of Pangloss's philosophy to the absurd.